E. W. KENYON

THE ESSENTIAL WORKS OF E. W. KENYON

SIX CLASSIC BOOKS IN ONE VOLUME

WHITAKER HOUSE

Unless otherwise indicated, all Scripture quotations are taken from the King James Version of the Holy Bible. Scripture quotations marked (ASV) are taken from the American Standard Edition of the Revised Version of the Holy Bible. Scripture quotations marked (MOFF) are taken from *The Bible: James Moffatt Translation*, © 1922, 1924, 1925, 1926, 1935 by HarperCollins San Francisco; © 1950, 1952, 1953, 1954 by James A. R. Moffatt. Scripture quotations marked (YLT) are taken from *Young's Literal Translation* by Robert Young (1898). Scripture quotations marked (JPS) are taken from *The Holy Scriptures According to the Masoretic Text: A New Translation with the Aid of Previous Versions and with Constant Consultation of Jewish Authorities*. Scripture quotations marked (WEY) are taken from *The New Testament in Modern Speech* by R. F. (Richard Francis) Weymouth.

The Essential Works of E. W. Kenyon
Six Classic Books in One Volume

Includes the following books:
The Wonderful Name of Jesus
Jesus the Healer
The New Kind of Love: God's Heart Cry to Broken Humanity
In His Presence: The Secret of Prayer
New Creation Realities: A Revelation of Redemption
The Blood Covenant: The Hidden Truth Revealed at the Lord's Table

Kenyon's Gospel Publishing Society
P.O. Box 973
Lynnwood, WA 98046-0973
www.kenyons.org

ISBN: 979-8-88769-375-0

Printed in the United States of America

Whitaker House
1030 Hunt Valley Circle
New Kensington, PA 15068
www.whitakerhouse.com

Library of Congress Control Number: 2025931251

1 2 3 4 5 6 7 8 9 10 11 WJ 32 31 30 29 28 27 26 25

CONTENTS

THE WONDERFUL NAME OF JESUS

CONTENTS

FIRST WORDS

This message is a struggle to make real to the modern church: the hidden wealth of an almost unknown truth of the Word of God.

The writer has felt for years that the disciples had a power to which we are utterly strangers, and that this power should belong to the church. He has been seeking a solution to this problem and believes that this book will be an unveiling of the hidden spring.

We trust that others will build upon this foundation and that before the return of our Lord, a portion, at least, of the body of believers will be living in the freshness of the power of the early church.

If the book helps you, pass it on.

1

THE WHY OF THE BOOK

Several years ago, I was holding meetings in a city in Tennessee. One afternoon, while giving an address on "The Name of Jesus," a lawyer interrupted me.

"Do you mean to say that Jesus gave us the power of attorney, the legal right to use His name?" he asked.

I said to him, "Brother, you are a lawyer and I am a layman. Tell me—did Jesus give us the power of attorney?"

He said, "If language means anything, then Jesus gave to the church the power of attorney."

Then I asked him, "What is the value of this power of attorney?"

He answered, "It depends upon how much there is behind it, how much authority, how much power, this name represents."

Then I began the search to find how much power and authority Jesus had.

THEN THIS BOOK CAME

The measure of His ability is the measure of the value of that name, and all that is invested in that name belongs to us, for Jesus gave us the unqualified use of His name.

> *Hitherto have ye asked nothing in my name: ask, and ye shall receive, that your joy may be full.* (John 16:24)

Here, Jesus not only gives us the use of His name, but He also declares that the prayer prayed in His name will receive His special attention.

> *Whatsoever ye shall ask the Father in my name, he will give it you.* (John 16:23)

Jesus says, "When you ask of the Father in My name, I will endorse that and the Father will give it to you."

This puts prayer on a purely legal basis for He has given us the legal right to use His name.

As we take our privileges and rights in the new covenant and pray in Jesus's name, it passes out of our hands into the hands of Jesus; He then assumes the responsibility of that prayer, and we know that He said, *"Father, I thank thee that thou hast heard me. And I knew that thou hearest me always"* (John 21:41–42). In other words, we know that the Father always hears Jesus, and when we pray in Jesus's name, it is as though Jesus Himself were doing the praying—He takes our place.

PRAYER IS A BUSINESS PROPOSITION

This places prayer not only on legal grounds, but makes it a business proposition.

When we pray, we take Jesus's place here to carry out His will, and He takes our place before the Father.

He said that it should not only cover our prayer life, but it also can be used in our combat against the unseen forces that surround us.

> *And these signs shall accompany them that believe: in my name shall they cast out demons; they shall speak with new tongues; they shall take up serpents, and if they drink any deadly thing, it shall in no wise hurt them; they shall lay hands on the sick, and they shall recover.*
>
> (Mark 16:17–18 ASV)

"Them that believe" literally means the believing ones, for every child of God is a believing one. And here, Jesus is revealing His part in the Great Commission. In that great document, He says:

> *All authority hath been given unto me in heaven and on earth. Go ye therefore, and make disciples of all the nations....Lo, I am with you always.* (Matthew 28:18–20 ASV)

He is with us in the power and authority of His name. What does the name mean to the Father, to the church, and to Satan?

To the Father, it must mean more than our hearts or minds will ever grasp, but we can suggest a little of the wealth that the Father has stored in that name.

First, He inherited a more excellent name than any of the angels as the first begotten Son. Second, God gave Him a name *"which is above every name: that at the name of Jesus every knee should bow, of things in heaven, and things in earth, and things under the earth"* (Philippians 2:9–10). Third, by His conquest over sin, Satan, disease, death, hell, and the grave, He acquired a name that is above all names.

When Jesus gave us the legal right to use this name, the Father knew all that that name would imply when breathed in prayer by oppressed souls, and it is His joy to recognize that name.

So the possibilities enfolded in the name of Jesus are beyond our understanding. When He says to the church, "Whatsoever you shall ask of the Father in My name," He is giving us a signed check on the resources of heaven and asking us to fill it in.

It would benefit the church to begin an exhaustive study of the resources of Jesus in order to get a measurement of the wealth that name holds for her today.

2

HOW HE OBTAINED HIS NAME

Before we go further in the study of the name of Jesus, it would be well for us to know something of the Man, see His standing in heaven, His achievements in the plan of redemption, and the glory and honor that belong to Him today as He sits at the right hand of the majesty on high.

> *Many were the forms and fashions in which God spoke of old to our fathers by the prophets, but in these days at the end he has spoken to us by a Son — a Son whom he appointed heir of the universe, as it was by him that he created the world. He, reflecting God's bright glory and stamped with God's own character, sustains the universe with his word of power; when he had secured our purification from sins, he sat down at the right hand of the Majesty on high; and thus he is superior to the angels, as he has inherited a Name superior to theirs.* (Hebrews 1:1–4 MOFF)

God spoke through men of old by special illumination of their minds, but in these last days, He speaks to us in the person of His Son.

It is more than through Him; it is more than by Him. It is God manifest in the flesh, carrying out His will, speaking His own inner thoughts in the life and acts of the Son.

Not only did He speak through Jesus, but more especially was God manifest in the Son—it was God in Christ, and from this new throne, the body of His Son, He is speaking to man in a new revelation of Himself.

He appointed this Son heir of all things, being the outshining of His very glory, the very image of His substance, and upholding all things by the Word of His power. When He had made a substitution for sins, when He had satisfied every claim of justice and met every need of man, He sat down at the right hand of the majesty on high—the highest seat in the universe.

When God speaks through man, He must absolutely take possession of the man so the man will not use his reasoning faculties.

But in the case of Jesus, it was not possession—it was the eternal Son Himself.

He could say, "Father, give Me the glory I had with Thee before the worlds were." He remembered His place in the Father's bosom.

He could say, "I came out from the Father. I came into the world." Again, He could say, "I leave the world, and go unto the Father."

Show us the Father, Philip said.

> *Jesus saith unto him, Have I been so long time with you, and yet hast thou not known me, Philip? he that hath seen me hath seen the Father.* (John 14:9)

He was the revelation of the Father. He did not have to imitate God—He was God!

HIS THREEFOLD GREATNESS

Some men are born to a great name as a czar or a king; others make their name great by achievements or have a great name conferred upon them.

Jesus is great because He inherited a great name; His name is great because of achievements; He is great because a great name was conferred upon Him.

He inherited a greater name than any angelic being, and as a Son, He is heir of all things, and through Him, the ages have been brought into being.

He is the effulgence—the very outshining of the Father.

His name comes to Him as an inheritance. What it must have been to have inherited this name from His great Father—God!

> *Wherefore God also hath highly exalted him, and given him a name which is above every name: that at the name of Jesus every knee should bow, of things in heaven, and things in earth, and things under the earth; and that every tongue should confess that Jesus Christ is Lord, to the glory of God the Father.* (Philippians 2:9–11)

If it tells us in Hebrews that He inherited a greater name than the angels, here it declares that God gave unto Him the name that is above every name.

The inference is that there was a name known in heaven, unknown elsewhere, and this name was kept to be conferred upon someone who should merit it. And Jesus, as we know Him—the eternal Son as He is known in the bosom of the Father—was given this name. And at this name, every knee shall bow in the three worlds—heaven, earth, and hell—and every tongue shall confess that He is Lord of the three worlds to the glory of God the Father.

THIS IS THE MAN

It is this Being who has given us the right to use His name. In Ephesians 1:17–19, we find a prayer by Paul—a most unusual prayer. He prays that the Father will open the eyes of our understanding that we may know something of the riches of the Father's inheritance in us, and then, that our eyes may be opened that we may see *"what is the exceeding greatness of his power"* on behalf of those who believe.

He declares it is according to the working of the strength of God's might that was wrought in the dead body of Jesus when He raised Him from among the dead.

> *And set him at his own right hand in the heavenly places, far above all principality, and power, and might, and dominion, and every name that is named, not only in this world* [age], *but also in that which is to come: and hath put all things under his feet, and gave him to be the head over all things to the church, which is his body, the fulness of him that filleth all in all.* (Ephesians 1:20–23)

Jesus not only inherited a more excellent name than any other being in the universe—God not only gave Him a name before which every being in the three worlds shall bow and confess His lordship—but here, God has given to Him a name that is above every name, He has seated Him in the highest place in the universe, and has made Him Head over all things.

FOR WHAT PURPOSE?

God has made this investment for the benefit of the church; He has made this deposit on which the church has a right to draw for her every need.

He has given to Jesus the name that has within it the fullness of the Godhead, the wealth of the eternities, and love of the heart of Father God. And that name is given us. We have the right to use that name against our enemies. We have the right to use it in our petitions. We have the right to use it in our praises and worship. That name has been given unto us.

But this is only the beginning of the wonders and the value of the greatness of that name.

Here, we get a deeper view of His conquest of the satanic forces just before He rose from the dead:

> *Having despoiled the principalities and the powers, he made a show of them openly, triumphing over them in it.* (Colossians 2:15 ASV)

The margin reads, *"Having put off from himself, the principalities and powers."*

The picture here is of Christ in the dark regions of the lost, in awful combat with the hosts of darkness. It gives us a glimpse of the tremendous battle and victory that Jesus won before He rose from the dead.

It is evident that the whole demon host, when they saw Jesus, in their power simply intended to swamp Him and overwhelm Him. They held Him in fearful bondage until the cry came forth from the throne of God that Jesus had met the demands of justice, the sin problem was settled, and man's redemption was a fact.

THE MIGHTY VICTOR

When this cry reached the dark regions, Jesus rose and hurled back the hosts of darkness, and met Satan in awful combat as described in Hebrews 2:14 (MOFF): *"So that by dying he might crush him who wields the power of death (that is to say, the devil)."*

In other words, after Jesus had put off from Himself the demon forces and the awful burden of guilt, sin, and sickness that He carried with Him down there, He grappled with Satan, conquered him, and left him paralyzed, whipped, and defeated. The words that Jesus spoke are fulfilled in Luke 11:21–22 (ASV): *"When the strong man fully armed guardeth his own court, his goods are in peace: but when a stronger than he shall come upon him, and overcome him, he taketh from him his whole armor wherein he trusted, and divideth his spoils."*

So when Christ rose from the dead, He not only had the keys of death and hell but He had the very armor in which Satan trusted.

He has defeated the devil, He has defeated all hell, and He stands before the three worlds—heaven, earth, and hell—as the undisputed victor over man's ancient destroyer. He conquered Satan before his own cohorts, his own servants in the dark regions of the damned, and He stood in that dread place, the absolute victor and Master.

Is it any wonder that fresh from such tremendous victories, He should say to the disciples, *"All power is given unto me in heaven and in earth"* (Matthew 28:18)?

He stands as the master and the ruler of the universe.

His name now is above every name, and at His name, we can understand how every knee shall bow. All this authority and power that Jesus gained by His mighty conquest is in that name—and He has given that name to us.

The authority that He has won is delegated to us in the use of His name. All He was is in that name; all He is today is in that name—and that name is ours.

Jesus was given that name that He might give it to us.

He gave His name to us that we might carry out the will of the Father in this dispensation in which we are living.

We know the early church utilized this authority. The early church acted for Jesus in His stead. They wrought miracles and the miracles opened doors for ministry and service.

AUTHORITY

It gave authority to their credentials, a standing in the communities where they preached. They had the coin of the unseen kingdom.

The omnipotence of God was invested in that name in the early church, and the disciples used it with a fearless abandonment that is absolutely thrilling!

They believed in God! They lived and walked in the realm of the supernatural.

It was the days of God on earth to the people where they ministered.

THE USE OF THE NAME

It might be well for us now to look at the promises Jesus made in regard to the use of His name.

> *And whatsoever ye shall ask in my name, that will I do, that the Father may be glorified in the Son.* (John 14:13)

This is a striking promise when we realize that Jesus is seated at the right hand of the Father—that Jesus holds the highest position in the universe as the Head of the church.

Here is the charter promise: *"Hitherto have ye asked nothing in my name: ask, and ye shall receive, that your joy may be full"* (John 16:24).

Jesus says, "Up until this time, you have never prayed in My name, but now, whatsoever you shall ask of the Father in My name, He will give it you."

This promise is perhaps the most staggering statement that ever fell from the lips of the Man of Galilee—that we are to have the use of His name, that name of omnipotence.

He does not say to use His name if we believe, or if we have faith. This name has been given to us. It is ours! What is mine, I do not need faith to use.

When we are born into the family of God, the right to use the name and the privilege to use it comes with the new birth. All the authority vested in that name is given to us to bring glory to the name of the Father, that the Father may be glorified in the Son.

The name of this Son—who was an outcast on the earth and crucified, hung naked before the world—shall go ringing down through the ages.

Wherever the shame of the crucifixion has gone, the glory, might, power, and honor of that name will go. Wherever men have ridiculed Jesus, that name will go. Wherever men have cursed that Man, that name will go with its omnipotence, might, and power, shedding blessings, healing, and comfort upon the human race, and honor and glory to God the Father.

He now is to be with us in the power of that name—that name is to take His place.

All that He could do locally then can be done locally now by every believer.

In other words, He multiplies Himself as rapidly as He multiplies the church, for the weakest son has a legal right now to all the grace, might, power, blessing, health, healing, and life enwrapped in the person who bore that name.

All that Jesus was, His name is. All that Jesus was, that name will ever be during this dispensation. That name has lost none of the power of the man who bore it.

In these Scriptures, we have seen that the Father has lifted Him to the highest position in the universe. He has conferred upon Him the highest name in the universe.

He has bestowed upon Him honor, glory, and power, and seated Him at His own right hand in the heavenlies, far above every known authority. Now, all this honor, glory, authority, and power is vested in the name of Jesus—and this name is given to us.

NEW LAND AHEAD

Oh, that our eyes were open, that our souls would dare rise into the realm of omnipotence where the name would mean to us all that the Father has invested in it, that we would act up to our high privileges in Christ Jesus.

This is practically an unexplored tableland in Christian experience.

Here and there, some of us have experienced the authority vested in the name of Jesus. We have seen the lame walk, the deaf hear, the blind see, and those on the verge of death brought back instantly to health and vigor. So far, however, none of us have been able to take a permanent place in our privileges and abide where we may enjoy the fullness of this mighty power.

But we have a conviction that before the Lord Jesus returns, there will be a mighty army of believers who will learn the secret of living in the name and reigning in life, living the victorious, transcendent, resurrection life of the Son of God among men.

If our minds could only grasp the fact that Satan is paralyzed, stripped of his armor by the Lord Jesus, and that disease and sickness are servants of this Man, that at His voice, they must depart, it would be easy to live in this resurrection realm.

You remember when the centurion talked with Jesus, he said, *"But speak the word only, and my servant shall be healed. For I am a man under authority, having soldiers under me: and I say to this man, Go, and he goeth; and to another, Come, and he cometh"* (Matthew 8:8–9).

Jesus marveled at the centurion's great faith (verse 10). In effect, the centurion was saying, "You have been set over diseases, as I am set over these hundred men; You are Master over disease and sickness, over demons and the laws of nature. All You have to do is to speak and Your servants obey, as I speak and my servants obey."

In this beautiful illustration, we see that the centurion had risen to a higher plane of spiritual appreciation of Jesus than most believers enjoy today.

3

WHAT IS BEHIND THE NAME?

There has never been a more intense battle over the deity of the Man of Galilee than is being waged today. The great body of the church do not see—as they never have seen—the issue squarely, neither have they realized the result of this struggle.

Unfortunately, we have arrayed against the deity of Christ a body of semi-intellectuals. There are scarcely a half dozen who belong to the first rank, either of scholastic or intellectual strength, who have been engaged on either side.

The debates that have been staged in different parts of the country have savored more of the barnstorming tactics of the modern political demagogue than of cold-blooded intellectual investigation into the merits of the issue.

The deity of the Man of Galilee is the crux of Christianity. If this can be successfully challenged, then Christianity has lost its heart and it will cease to function; it will become a dead religion.

There is no denial that the challenge of His Deity has already begun its reactionary effect upon society.

If Jesus is not Deity, He is not Lord.

If He is not Lord, then He cannot interfere with our moral activities.

If He is not Lord, then the laws that have been founded upon His teachings have lost their force.

The morals that surround marriage, with its lofty ideals, have no basis of fact.

If Jesus of Nazareth is not a revelation from God with divine authority, then He is but a man.

If He is but a man, all that we have built around Him must be destroyed. And we have built around this Man our modern civilization.

He has been the inspiration of young men who have kept themselves clean and pure as they have looked upon His wonder life and sought to win His smile.

Young women in the secret of their chamber have looked upon the face of the Man of Galilee and have pledged to preserve the purity of their womanhood that they might be worthy of the love and confidence of the Man who died two thousand years ago for humanity.

Children have been incited to obedience and purity by the example and teachings of that Man.

Businessmen have been deterred from crooked dealings by the consciousness that one day they would meet that Man and give an account of the deeds done in their office.

Men of all walks of life have felt a strange kinship with this Man who walked the shores of Galilee, solitary among a multitude.

To say He was but a good man is an insult.

To say that He was the highest expression of deity in humanity is to throw the lie into His face.

Jesus is or He is not what He said He was.

We have no record of His sayings nor of His doings outside the four Gospels. If we repudiate them, then we have but a mythical picture of the Man. If we challenge one of them, we have a right to challenge all of them: either He stands or falls on those four biographical sketches.

If He is not the Son of God, who is He?

I want to believe that He is an incarnation.

I want to believe that He dealt with the sin problem.

I want to believe that He died for my sins and that He rose again for my justification.

I want to believe that He is seated at God's right hand today as the Intercessor and Mediator of the human race.

I want to believe that what He said about heaven is true:

> *In my Father's house are many mansions: if it were not so, I would have told you. I go to prepare a place for you. And if I go and prepare a place for you, I will come again, and receive you unto myself.* (John 14:2–3)

Skepticism holds no guarantee for my future.

Civilization has not only been built around this Man, but He has been built into civilization.

If you destroy His character, His standing, and His place, then civilization must disintegrate.

The wave of crime and lawlessness that is sweeping over the land is but a byproduct of the modernists' challenge of His integrity.

4

THE USE OF THE NAME

It might be a helpful study for us to notice the name in the plan of salvation and its relation to the believer in his Christian life.

> *And she shall bring forth a son, and thou shalt call his name* JESUS*: for he shall save his people from their sins. Now all this was done, that it might be fulfilled which was spoken of the Lord by the prophet, saying, Behold, a virgin shall be with child, and shall bring forth a son, and they shall call his name Emmanuel, which being interpreted is, God with us.*
> (Matthew 1:21–23)

The name Jesus is inseparably connected with salvation. The very name is filled with music to a repentant soul. "*And in none other is there salvation: for neither is there any other name under heaven, that is given among men, wherein we must be saved*" (Acts 4:12 ASV).

It is the one name through which the sinner approaches the great Father God; it is the one name that gives him a hearing; it is the one name that unveils to him the mediatorial ministry of Jesus.

> *Baptize them in the name of the Father and the Son and the holy Spirit.*
> (Matthew 28:19 MOFF)

> *Repent ye, and be baptized every one of you in the name of Jesus Christ unto the remission of your sins; and ye shall receive the gift of the Holy Spirit.* (Acts 2:38 ASV)

Not only are we saved by the name, but the believer is baptized into the name. And we find in the same verse that not only are we baptized into the name, but on the ground of the name, we shall receive the gift of the Holy Spirit.

Then Jesus gave us these promises of the use of His name in prayer:

> *Whatsoever ye shall ask in my name, that will I do, that the Father may be glorified in the Son. If ye shall ask any thing in my name, I will do it. If ye love me, keep my commandments.* (John 14:13–15)

> *Hitherto have ye asked nothing in my name: ask, and ye shall receive, that your joy may be full.* (John 16:24)

In the book of Acts, we hear Peter saying, "*Silver and gold have I none; but such as I have give I thee: In the name of Jesus Christ of Nazareth rise up and walk*" (Acts 3:6).

Men are baptized into the name and men pray in the name. In that name, the impotent and helpless are made to walk.

In Acts 16:18, we see the apostle Paul casting a demon out of a possessed girl, setting her free and stirring the city of Philippi to its very foundation. What power that name has for the church today!

> *For where two or three are gathered together in my name, there am I in the midst of them.* (Matthew 18:20)

The assemblies were taught that when they met, they gathered about that name. What a strange hush must have come upon the hearts of the disciples when they realized, as they gathered in their little meetings, that the name of Jesus was the center around which everything revolved!

Their prayers were addressed through that name and in that name, the sick were healed. In that name, the demons were cast out. In that name, the Holy Spirit came upon believers. In that name, they worshipped. In that name, the name of their absent Lord, all of the work of the early church was wrought.

They were washed, sanctified, and justified in that name. (See 1 Corinthians 6:11.)

> *Whatsoever ye do in word or deed, do all in the name of the Lord Jesus.* (Colossians 3:17)

> *Giving thanks always for all things...in the name of our Lord Jesus Christ.* (Ephesians 5:20)

> *Make confession to his name.* (Hebrews 13:15 ASV)

> *Is any sick among you? let him call for the elders of the church; and let them pray over him...in the name of the Lord.* (James 5:14)

> *And this is his commandment, That we should believe on the name of his Son Jesus Christ, and love one another, as he gave us commandment.* (1 John 3:23)

The new commandment was that they love one another and believe in the name.

We can see by this that the name of Jesus touched every phase of the church life in those early days, that it filled a place in their thought, in their prayer, and in their preaching of which we are utterly ignorant today.

May the Lord open the eyes of our hearts that we may know the riches of the glory of God that are hidden in that name.

5

IN MY NAME, YE SHALL CAST OUT DEMONS

Most of the readers of this book know what they are worth financially.

If you are a farmer, you know practically every rod of land that your deed covers.

If you own city property, or if you rent, you know every room in the house.

In this grasping world of ours, we attempt to utilize all our possessions, but in the spiritual world, how few of us really know, possess, or enjoy what our deed covers.

The spiritual life is so little understood by even the wisest of us.

You remember that Jesus said as He left the disciples, "In My name, you will cast out demons." You also remember that a large part of His ministry was filled with combats with the unseen hosts of darkness.

In reading our modern religious literature and listening to the average preacher's sermon, one would naturally think that demons had gone out of existence, or else they had been herded together in the slums of the city and were spending their entire time among the lower strata of humanity.

Years ago, I was led to study this subject. I found that the Scriptures taught a great deal about demons and their habits, influence, and power over men.

When Paul was writing to the Ephesian church, he told them that their combat was *"not against flesh and blood, but against principalities, against powers, against the rulers of the darkness of this world, against spiritual wickedness in high places"* (Ephesians 6:12).

Writing to the Colossians, he said, *"Epaphras, who is one of you, a servant of Christ Jesus, saluteth you, always striving for you in his prayers, that ye may stand perfect and fully assured in all the will of God"* (Colossians 4:12 ASV).

You notice that the word *striving* literally means to wrestle, struggle, or combat. With whom was Epaphras struggling? With whom was this agonizing? Surely not with the Father; the eternal purpose of the Father is to bless men.

We know that prayer cannot change God's purpose, in any ordinary sense of the word. Prayer may accelerate God, stir Him up to come to our rescue, or enlist His cooperation, sympathy, and help in a time of need, but all through the Revelation, there is breathed out here and there the fact of a hidden force that is intelligently warring against the purpose of God.

For years in my own ministry, I found a great deal of trouble, that perhaps every preacher or evangelist finds, with certain types of people who were always trying and never seemed to get settled in God. They were always standing up for prayers, but never seemed to get any farther.

Another class really seemed to get the light, but were held by some unseen powers.

These people naturally caused me a great deal of trouble. I wondered how I could help them. One day, I was strangely led beyond myself to command that unseen power be broken over a person whom it was holding.

I prayed in the name of Jesus. I cried, "In the name of Jesus, I command your power broken over this life."

Instantly, the person was delivered, and I stood amazed at the effect.

A strange fear came over me that I had been able to exercise this marvelous power by this simple command in Jesus's name. Since that time, I have seen many startling results in revival services through using the name of Jesus.

I found that the reason many men did not accept Jesus as their Savior was because they were held by the power of demons. The people are hungry; they want deliverance from sin and they crave eternal life, but many of them are unable to break loose from the bonds that are holding them.

Hundreds of people told me, "I cannot become a Christian. I want to, but something holds me."

I have simply laid my hand on their shoulder and said, "In the name of Jesus of Nazareth, I command the power that holds you be broken. Now, in His mighty name, get on your feet."

With tears of joy, they have obeyed.

I have prayed with men who were held by habits—tobacco, liquor, lusts—and in the same mighty name, I have seen them delivered, usually instantaneously.

I have found Christians who were unable to testify or lead in prayer in public meetings, who felt their mouths closed while their hearts cried for liberty.

I have scarcely met a case for whom I have prayed in the name and over whom I have commanded the power broken, but what they have had immediate deliverance.

In cases of divine healing, I have seen some cases that would move the country, had they known of them. A woman who was almost blind was healed by the power of the name of Jesus, so that today, she can read without glasses. Some have been cured of heart disease and various other infirmities.

Many of those cases found it very difficult to take their healing. I prayed for them several times and found that the difficulty lay in the fact that they were held, bound by the power of demons. They were delivered when I said, "In the name of Jesus, demons leave this body."

I cannot conceive how successful work can be done today, or how believers can be in a place of continual victory, unless they know that the source of their danger lies in demoniacal power, and that the power to conquer it is in the name of Jesus of Nazareth, the Son of God.

The more quickly we recognize that the very air about us is filled with hostile forces who are attempting to destroy our fellowship with the Father and deprive us of our usefulness in the service of our Master, the better it will be for us.

Three things are necessary in order to pray and take deliverance and victory over demons.

First, we must be children of God.

Second, we must not have any unconfessed or unforgiven sin in our hearts, for if we do, the demons will laugh at our prayers.

Third, we must know the power of the name of Jesus and know how to use it. Read the book of Acts carefully and notice how the disciples used the name.

Readers, if your own life has been defeated and hemmed in by the power of the adversary, rise up in that almighty name of Jesus, hurl back the enemy, take your deliverance, go, and set others free.

IN HIS NAME

What does the expression *in His name* mean?

We know that the expression *in Christ*, as used about one hundred and thirty times in the New Testament, shows us the believer's position, his legal standing, and his place in God's family and in the purposes or program of God.

When Jesus gave to the early church the right to use His name, it meant that they were to represent Him; they were acting in His stead and when they prayed in Jesus's name, it was as though Jesus Himself were praying.

We are taking Christ's place and acting as Christ's representatives.

Christ is at the right hand of the Father; we are here as His representatives, not only collectively, but individually.

When we pray in Jesus's name, we are taking the place of the absent Christ; we are using His name, His authority, to carry out His will on the earth.

When we say, "Father, we ask this in Jesus's name," we are praying representatively.

We are saying, "Father, Jesus is up there at Thy right hand and He gave us the power of attorney to carry out Thy will on earth. So here is this great need. We ask Thee in His name to meet it."

That need may be for finances, power in ministry, salvation of souls, or the healing of a sick one, but we take Jesus's place and use Jesus's name just as though Jesus Himself were here.

The only difference is that instead of Jesus doing it, we are doing it for Him; we are doing it at His command.

He has given to us the same authority He had when He was here. The believer's position in Christ gives him the same standing with the Father that Christ had when He was here.

This unlimited use of the name of Jesus reveals to us the implicit confidence that the Father has in the church. This in itself is a challenge.

The simplicity of Peter's use of the name of Jesus in the book of Acts compels us to believe that Peter knew he was acting in Jesus's stead, with the same authority that Jesus had. You will notice he does not stop even to pray for a sick one; all he does is to say, "In Jesus's name, rise and walk."

There is no hint that he attempted to exercise what we call *faith* in any manner; it reduced itself to a simple business proposition with the early church. They remembered what the Master said and what He said was true to them.

He said, "*Whatsoever ye shall ask in my name, that will I do*" (John 14:13).

They did not argue about it, worry about it, or stop to analyze what it meant. All they did was to act on the words of Jesus.

They did not understand all that Paul afterwards revealed to us in his letters to the Romans, Galatians, and Ephesians, but they did know that Jesus had given them a right to use His name and they entered into that right with the simplicity of a child.

It seems to me that this is what we need to do today.

Jesus said, "In My name, you will cast out demons. You will lay hands on the sick and they shall recover." (See Mark 16:17–18.)

This was given to believers—and we are believers. "*Whatsoever ye shall ask the Father in my name, he will give it you*" (John 16:23) is a declaration that is simple enough for anyone to understand.

We have been baptized into that name publicly; spiritually, we have been put into Christ by the new birth so that we now are in the Vine, Jesus Christ, as one of the branches.

We are in Christ and being in Christ, we have a right to use His name, and so in that name, we legally act as representatives.

This glorifies the Father, this magnifies Jesus, and this answers the need of humanity.

Here is supernatural power that is available to every believer.

It is not a question of education or ordination but merely a question of my apprehending my own true position in Christ, and there using the power that has been legally given to me and to every believer.

Oh, the wonder and grace of God!

6

MAN AND MIRACLES

Jesus! The very name has within it miracle-working power, even to this day, though nearly two thousand years have rolled away since He walked with men.

Jesus, the Galilean, was a miracle worker.

Jesus's life was a miracle. His wisdom and teachings were miraculous. He lived and walked in the realm of the miraculous. He made miracles common. His death was a miracle. His resurrection was a miracle. His appearances were miraculous. His ascension was a staggering miracle.

But perhaps the most outstanding miracle of all those wonder days was the event of Pentecost. From the upper room, men and women went forth boldly to testify of Jesus's name, who fifty days before shrank in fear from the very names of the high priest and his associates.

Peter—the trembling, fearful Peter—is now clothed with a power and fearlessness that is inexplicable; he goes out and faces the Sanhedrin, senate, and high priests with a courage that amazes us.

A stream of miracles flowed from the hands of the apostles that upset Judaism and shook the Roman government to its foundation.

The apostles had made a discovery—the name of the Man they had loved, who they had seen nailed to that cross in nakedness, now has power equal to the power that He Himself exercised when He was among them.

The sick were healed, the dead were raised, and demons were cast out by simply breathing that name over the afflicted ones. What a stream of miraculous love, life, hope, and joy showered from the ministry of those humble Galileans.

Those first thirty-three years of early history, as seen in Acts, were sample years of the acts of the church until the return of her Lord and Master.

Man is the offspring of the miracle worker. The miracle-working desire is embedded deep in the consciousness of man. Christianity is based on a series of miracles culminating in Pentecost.

MIRACLES ARE NORMAL

Christianity began in miracles and it is propagated by miracles. Every new birth is a miracle, every answer to prayer is a miracle, and every victory over temptation is a miracle.

When reason takes the place of the miraculous, Christianity loses its virility, fascination, and fruitfulness.

Christianity is not a religion. Christianity is the life of God in man. Christianity was the unveiling of the heart and nature of the great Father God in the Man Jesus.

There could not be a religion that would appeal to humanity that was not founded upon miracles and propagated by miracles.

Man craves a miracle-working God today. Whenever there arises a man or woman whose prayers are heard and answered, the multitudes flock to them. Man wants a living God. Man craves a miracle.

The deep-seated hunger in the human heart for God is the reason for all religions. Men are easily deceived by pseudo miracle workers because of this hunger after the supernatural.

One of America's greatest psychologists—who ridiculed the miraculous for over thirty years in his classroom at one of the leading universities—finally sat at the feet of the high priestess of spiritualism and confessed over his own signature in a popular magazine that at last he had found faith in the supernatural.

What a pitiable picture, turning from the miracle-working Jesus to the miracle-working Satan!

God created man in His own image and in His own likeness, and through Jesus Christ, allows him to become a partaker of His own nature. This lifts man into the realm of God, and in that realm, the Father God can unveil Himself to His child.

The answer to the universal craving of man for the supernatural is found in the new birth, the indwelling presence of the Holy Spirit, and the name of Jesus.

Prayer becomes a miracle-working force in the world.

CHRISTIANITY IS A MIRACLE

God is a miracle worker. Jesus Christ *was* a miracle and *is* a miracle. The Bible is a miracle Book.

If we take the supernatural out of Christianity, we have a religion. Miracles are not out of harmony with the desire of humanity.

A miracle worker, either real or false, will draw a greater congregation than the greatest philosopher or statesman in the world. This love of the miraculous is not a mark of ignorance but rather an outreaching after the unseen God.

Education does not eliminate the desire for the miraculous in man. That desire is intensified, as education unveils man's impotence in the presence of the laws of nature and shows him his utter dependence upon the unseen. It is not a mark of great scholarship, piety, or mental acumen to deny the miraculous.

THE UNIVERSAL MAN BELIEVES IN MIRACLES

The Bible is a record of miracles and divine interventions. It is history of the outbreakings of the supernatural realm into the natural.

Beginning with Abraham, all of the major characters of Old Testament history were miracle workers—or better, God wrought miracles through them. The thing that lifted Joseph from the prison to the office of premier of Egypt was a miracle. Israel's deliverance from Egypt's bondage was by a series of miracles that shook Egypt to its very foundation. The crossing of the Red Sea and the forty years in the wilderness were a series of miracles unparalleled in human history.

The object of these miracles was to separate Israel from the dead gods of Egypt and bind them to the worship of the living God of Abraham.

Judaism was Judaism as long as the miracle-working God was manifest. When miracles ended, Israel lapsed into heathenism and only came back into fellowship with their God after a series of staggering miracles.

Had we space, it would be interesting to study the miracles of the conquest of Canaan, the period of the kings, and the four great miracles recorded in Daniel that sent Israel back from captivity into their own land, free from idolatry, establishing a precedent of a nation of slaves set free and sent to their own country with permission—aye, more—with funds to rebuild their city, their temple, and establish its worship. It has no parallel in human history; it is a distinct and definite miracle.

When Jesus began His public ministry, it was a ministry of miracles.

When the church began her ministry, it was a ministry of miracles.

Every revival since Pentecost that has honored the humble Galilean has been a revival of miracles.

The church has never been rescued from her backslidings by great philosophical teachers but humble laymen who have had a new vision of the Christ, of Him who is *"the same yesterday, and to day, and for ever"* (Hebrews 13:8).

We crave the manifest presence of the Spirit in our religious services. A dry, dead meeting has no drawing power, but a service where men are being richly blessed in the unfolding of Scripture or the saving of souls, the healing of the sick, or the filling with the Spirit has a drawing power.

An outpouring of the Spirit is a challenge to a community any time. All normal men crave the supernatural; they long to see the manifestation of the power of God and feel the thrill of the touch of the unseen.

MAN DEMANDS MIRACLES

Man was created by a miracle-working God, and so that miracle element is in man. Man yearns to perform miracles and live in the atmosphere of the supernatural. This miracle element in man has made him an inventor, discoverer, and investigator.

It has caused him to experiment until he has conquered chemicals, electricity, and the air. It is this element that has given to us the airplane, submarine, radio, wireless, and all of the other devices, inventions, and discoveries that make up our modern civilization.

The miracle realm is man's natural realm; he is by creation the companion of the miracle-working Father God.

Sin dethroned man from the miracle realm, but through grace, he is coming into his own.

It has been a hard struggle for us to grasp the principles of this strange life of faith. Sin has made us workers; grace would make us trusters. In the beginning, man's spirit was the dominant force in the world; when he sinned, his mind became dominant—sin dethroned the spirit and crowned the intellect, but grace is restoring the spirit to its place of dominion. And when man comes to recognize the dominance of the spirit, he will live in the realm of the supernatural without effort.

No longer will faith be a struggle and fight but an unconscious living in the realm of God.

The spiritual realm is man's normal home; it places him where communion with God is a normal experience, where faith in the miraculous, miracle-working God is unconscious, where he will exercise the highest type of faith and yet be as unconscious of having exercised faith as he is when he writes a check.

7

THE PLACE OF FAITH IN THE USE OF THE NAME

The prayerful student of the Word is confronted with the fact that nowhere does Jesus mention faith or belief when He is talking about using His name, except in the future tense.

Here is an illustration:

> *And these signs shall follow them that believe; In my name shall they cast out devils; they shall speak with new tongues; they shall take up serpents; and if they drink any deadly thing, it shall not hurt them; they shall lay hands on the sick, and they shall recover.* (Mark 16:17–18)

A literal rendering of that is *the believing ones* shall do these things in Jesus's name.

It is taken for granted that only believers have a right to the use of the name of Jesus. The right to use His name is a conferred blessing to the church: it is a right that belongs to every child of God.

We have a fourfold right to use the name:

- First, we are born into the family of God and the name belongs to the family.
- Second, we are baptized into the name and being baptized into the name, we are baptized into Christ Himself.
- Third, it was conferred upon us by Jesus, who gave us the power of attorney.
- Fourth, we are commissioned as ambassadors to go and herald this name among the nations.

Then if this authority is conferred upon us, we act as representatives for Christ. We do this first on the ground of our birthright; second on the ground of having been baptized into this name; third that the legal right to use this name has been conferred upon us; and last on the ground that we have been sent out as ambassadors to herald this name among the nations.

I cannot see where we need to have any special faith to use the name of Jesus because it is legally ours. If I had a thousand dollars in the bank, it would not require any conscious act of faith on my part to write a check for one hundred, but if I wanted to draw eleven hundred dollars where I only had one thousand on deposit, that might require faith.

Some of us have had the unhappy experience of having overdrawn our bank account on earth, but the finished work of Jesus Christ has made a deposit for us in heaven's bank, where it cannot be overdrawn. It is ours—blessedly, eternally ours. Thank God!

If you are a child, then you are an heir of God—a joint heir with Christ—and you have a right to the use of the name of Jesus. And if you have this right, it is because of your place in the family.

I believe the hour will come when large companies of believers will live this simple life of faith, live it unconsciously and live it daily. They will live in this upper realm where they will see in the name of Jesus the fullness of the authority and power that was in Christ when He walked on the earth.

We are now in the babyhood stage. We are trying to have faith, we are trying to believe, and we meet together in our services, each one urging the other to do what he does not do himself.

In many cases, it would seem that we are practicing a game of bluff. Are we using scriptural expressions and high-sounding phrases that have no meaning to our inner consciousness?

Thank God, there are some who are coming to see this new light, which will only come by intensive study and actually thinking through on this problem.

Too many of us are listening to preachers, always listening and never digesting or doing any original thinking. Instead, we must be "*doers of the word, and not hearers only*" (James 1:22).

The instant a man or woman thinks through on this problem, in that moment, he or she rises into a new realm of life in Christ and actually begins to reign in the realm of life. Then he is able to meet demons and diseases on their own plane and conquer them, able to enjoy the fruits of the finished work of Christ, and enter into the riches of His inheritance.

JESUS IS IN THAT NAME

Jesus is that name. All He was, all He did, all He is, and all that He ever will be is in that name now.

He wrought the healing for us; He is healing for us now. He satisfied the claims of justice and became our righteousness; He is now our righteousness.

He passed down through death and up into life, and He is our life now.

He gave us life; He is that life He gave.

He is healing, He is health, He is victory, and He is our all and in all.

THAT NAME IS HEALING

And when He gave us the right to use His name to heal the sick, it was simply that we might bring on the scene by the use of that name the fullness of His finished work, and that the afflicted one might know that in the use of that name, the living, healing Christ is present.

It is not trying to believe; it is not trying to take healing. Believing becomes unnecessary in the modern sense of that term. That healing is ours; that name makes it available to us. That name is ours, and in that name is all help, all victory, all power, and all health.

Do not try and do not struggle—just use it.

Use that name with the same freedom that you use your checkbook.

The money is on deposit; you write the check without exercising any special faith. That is, you are not conscious of exercising it, although you do.

And in the use of Jesus's name, you do exercise faith—it is the unconscious faith, the faith that is borne in upon us by evidences that convince us beyond the shadow of a doubt.

Any other kind of faith is abnormal.

At the second coming of Christ, it will not require any act of faith to receive immortality—we shall simply be made immortal. We shall be translated.

That is in the plan, in the eternal program of God. It will not require any special faith to be resurrected. The resurrection is in the program.

HIS PROGRAM

Now, if we understand His program for today, the sick would simply be healed the moment that sickness touched them.

> *If the Spirit of him that raised up Jesus from the dead dwell in you, he that raised up Christ from the dead shall also quicken [or heal] your mortal bodies by his Spirit that dwelleth in you.* (Romans 8:11)

This does not have reference to our resurrection; it refers to our bodies now. Mortal means death—doomed. Our bodies will not be mortal in the grave, neither will the spirit be in them then.

This is a part of the program—the Spirit dwells in us for that purpose. That is not the only purpose, but that is one of the reasons of His indwelling—to heal our physical bodies of the diseases that are continually attaching themselves to us.

When we understand this, we shall not be trying to exercise faith for our healing or for any other need; we shall simply recognize the fact that this healing, this need, is in the program, is a part of it, and we shall accept what belongs to us.

Take this Scripture as an illustration:

> *Who his own self bare our sins in his own body on the tree, that we, being dead to sins, should live unto righteousness: by whose stripes ye were healed.* (1 Peter 2:24)

He bore our sins in His body on the tree and He died because of those sins. If we believe that we died with Him, then we do not have to die again to sin.

WE ARE ALIVE

He was made alive and we were made alive with Him. We died to our sins, we died to our old nature, and we died to our diseases. We rose in the fullness of His life, free from our old sin nature, free from our sins that we had committed, and free from our diseases.

As we come to understand this, we know that our old sin nature hasn't any right, any privilege, to reign over us because it is dead, and we will not accept any imitation of it that Satan may, in our ignorance, impose upon us. Neither will we recognize any condemnation that might come to us through any sins we may have committed in the past, for Christ bore them, and we need never bear them again, neither do we need to suffer any condemnation for them because He was condemned for them and He bore them.

Consequently, we are free. There is therefore now no condemnation to us because we are in Christ Jesus. (See Romans 8:1.)

The same thing is true with our sicknesses. He bore our sicknesses and carried our pains. (See Isaiah 53:4.) He was made sick for us and bore our sicknesses; when He rose, the sickness had been put away and He rose in resurrection life, free from the dominion of sickness.

Now, sickness hasn't any right to impose itself upon us and Satan hasn't any right to impose any diseases upon us. We are free! And when these diseases and sicknesses come, all we need to do is treat them exactly the same as we treat our old sins.

The devil may try to put us under condemnation by reminding us of our past sins, but we say, "Satan, there is therefore now no condemnation upon us, for we are in Christ Jesus. He has dealt with those sins and put them away and you cannot get them. You may bring back a photograph of them, but you cannot get the actual real sin because it has been put away."

MY LEGAL RIGHTS

When he imposes diseases upon me, I have a right to say to him, "Satan, those diseases were borne in the body of Jesus and you have no right to bring their photograph around here and frighten me with them. Those diseases were unconditionally put away and I am free from disease as the body of Jesus was when He rose from the dead. For I am in Christ Jesus and you cannot put those things on me."

And if Satan should attack my body, all I have to do is to call my Father's attention to the fact and the disease must go because I am free!

I know that by His stripes, I am healed. If I am healed, I am healed!

I know that by His resurrection, I am justified and I do not need to be justified again. I am already justified!

I know that by His life, I am made alive, and I am alive!

I know that I died with Him, I know that I rose with Him, and I know that I am in Him.

I know that by His stripes, I am healed, and if I am healed, I am well—thank God! I have no more to do with my healing than I have to do with my resurrection for He is my resurrection! He is my healing!

He said, *"I am the resurrection, and the life"* (John 11:25).

He is my resurrection; He is my life; He is my healing; He is my health; He is my victory; and He is my all and in all.

Now, I simply recognize the fact that He healed me in His substitutionary work and because of that, I am healed.

The hour is coming when this kind of knowledge will be so common that men and women who are in Christ and walking in Him will be healed the moment they are afflicted. They will live in perfect health—in body as well as soul and spirit. They will live like this until their bodies are worn out and they fall asleep in Christ.

There is no more need of our bearing our sicknesses in our bodies than there is of bearing an unforgiven sin in our spiritual nature.

HIS WORD IS TRUE

For the very moment I confess my sins, He is faithful and righteous to forgive me. (See 1 John 1:9.) When He forgives me, I am forgiven.

On the same ground, the moment I confess that Satan has put a disease or infirmity upon me, in just that moment, Jesus is faithful and righteous to heal me—and I am healed! He healed me of my sin; He now heals me of my sickness. They both come from the same source.

It requires no struggle, no long drawn out siege of struggling after faith and trying to believe. There is the written Word and the eternal throne of God is behind it. That Word cannot fail any more than God can fail. When I confess my sins, I am forgiven.

If I refuse this or if I challenge it, I declare by that challenge or that refusal that God is a liar, that His Word is not true, and that all He has said in the Scriptures is a lie. For all unbelief is a challenge of the integrity of God.

Then this new kind of faith in Him becomes the stabilizer of one's whole spiritual nature. It is a faith that grows out of the knowledge of God's faithfulness—of evidences given in the Word, of facts that have become a part of spiritual knowledge so that when the believer is *exercising faith,* he unconsciously acts as he does when writing a check for money he knows is in the bank.

Then the greatest need of the hour is not more faith but more knowledge that will produce an unconscious faith in our great, loving Father God.

THE PLACE CONFESSION HOLDS

The church has never given this vital subject a place in its teaching and yet answered prayer, the use of Jesus's name, and faith are utterly dependent upon it.

> *Wherefore, holy brethren, partakers of the heavenly calling, consider the Apostle and High Priest of our profession, Christ Jesus.* (Hebrews 3:1)

While this verse reads *profession,* in the Greek, it means witnessing a confession of our lips. Christianity is called our confession. It is the same with Hebrews 4:14: *"Let us hold fast our profession."*

You understand then this Scripture from Romans:

> *That if thou shalt confess with thy mouth the Lord Jesus, and shalt believe in thine heart that God hath raised him from the dead, thou shalt be saved. For with the heart man believeth unto righteousness; and with the mouth confession is made unto salvation.* (Romans 10:9–10)

You see the place that confession holds in salvation. It holds the same place in our faith walk. Christianity is our open confession of what we are in Christ and of what Christ is to us.

Our faith is gauged by our confession. We never believe beyond our confession.

It is not a confession of sin; it is the confession of our place in Christ, our legal rights, what the Father has done for us in Christ, what the Spirit has done in us through the Word, and what He is able to do through us.

There is a grave danger of our having two confessions. One would be the integrity of the Word and the other would be of our doubts and fears. Every time we confess weakness and failure, doubt and fear, we go to the level of them.

We may pray very ardently and earnestly and declare our faith in the Word in our prayers...and yet, the next moment, we question whether He heard us or not, for we confess we have not the things for which we prayed. Our last confession destroys our prayer.

One asked me to pray for his healing. I prayed for him and then he said, "I want you to keep on praying for me." I asked then what he wished me to pray for. He said, "Oh, for my healing." I said, "Prayer will be of no value. You have just denied the Word of God."

The Word says those who believe "*shall lay hands on the sick, and they shall recover*" (Mark 16:18) and "*whatsoever ye shall ask in my name, that will I do*" (John 14:13).

I prayed the prayer of faith and he denied it. By his confession, he annulled my prayer and destroyed the effect of my faith.

Your confession must absolutely agree with the Word. If you have prayed in Jesus's name, you are to hold fast your confession. It is easy to destroy the effect of your prayer by a negative confession.

8

THE NAME IN THE GOSPELS

Behold, thou shalt conceive in thy womb, and bring forth a son, and shalt call his name JESUS.
—Luke 1:31

Little did Mary know the meaning of that angelic visit nor of the command that His name shall be called Jesus. That name has grown until today it fills the whole earth. That name means justice, love, righteousness, civilization, invention, discovery, art, literature, music, health, happiness, and home. Yet in our study, we have discovered that the name means even more.

> *Behold, a virgin shall conceive, and bear a son, and shall call his name Immanuel.* (Isaiah 7:14)

Immanuel means *God with us,* or the incarnate one. "*The Word was made flesh, and dwelt among us*" (John 1:14). It is the name of this incarnate one that is engaging our attention now.

> *And ye shall be hated of all men for my name's sake.* (Matthew 10:22)

Jesus knew the place His name would hold among men. Men would love it enough to die for it; others would hate it enough to commit murder on account of it. This name makes sinners tremble and saints rejoice.

"*And in his name shall the Gentiles hope*" (Matthew 12:21 ASV). How true that is! The name of Jesus has been the only name that would stop wars between nations.

That name bears within it love, life, light, liberty, and joy. "*And whoso shall receive one such little child in my name receiveth me*" (Matthew 18:5). For the first time in human history, little children have a friend—little children can be received in His name.

And what a judgment He pronounces upon anyone who injures or hurts one of the little ones who have believed in Him or in His name! It is peculiarly precious the way Jesus links His name with the childhood of humanity.

Verse 20 carries us into the mystery of Christ's oneness with believers when they meet together: *"For where two or three are gathered together in my name, there am I in the midst of them."*

How well Jesus understood what His name would mean to the world!

> *For many shall come in my name, saying, I am Christ; and shall deceive many.* (Matthew 24:5)

He knew that false teachers and imposters would come in His name and He warns the church of the danger that shall confront her down through the ages.

> *Go ye therefore, and make disciples of all the nations, baptizing them into the name of the Father and of the Son and of the Holy Spirit.* (Matthew 28:19 ASV)

This is the Great Commission and the apostolic formula of baptism.

THE NAME IN THE GOSPEL OF MARK

In the Gospel of Mark, there are but four references.

> *John said unto him, Teacher, we saw one casting out demons in thy name; and we forbade him, because he followed not us. But Jesus said, Forbid him not: for there is no man who shall do a mighty work in my name, and be able quickly to speak evil of me.* (Mark 9:38–39 ASV)

You see that the name of Jesus was great even before He died, that men were casting out demons and healing the sick in His name before His death, resurrection, and ascension to the right hand of the Father. This in itself is a very striking fact and worthy of much meditation.

> *And ye shall be hated of all men for my name's sake: but he that shall endure unto the end, the same shall be saved.* (Mark 13:13)

Jesus knew the hatred that His name would engender for His followers in the world and He prepares them by this warning:

> *And these signs shall accompany them that believe: in my name shall they cast out demons; they shall speak with new tongues; they shall take up serpents, and if they drink any deadly thing, it shall in no wise hurt them; they shall lay hands on the sick, and they shall recover.*
>
> (Mark 16:17–18 ASV)

This is the Great Commission that He gave to the disciples. In this Scripture, Jesus specifies some of the things that His name will do.

It almost bewilders us when we think that the God of the universe will give to humanity the right to use His name, will give to men a legal right to use the power and the authority of the Son of God. In that name, a mother can lay her hands upon her baby when he is sick and take healing for him.

The Greek here for "*them that believe*" means *the believing ones* shall lay hands on the sick in that name and they shall recover. That includes every child of God. No special gift and no special faith are required—just *the believing ones.*

Jesus said, "*Lo, I am with you always, even unto the end of the world*" (Matthew 28:20 ASV). The margin rendering has this as "*the consummation of the age.*" This is His method of being present today.

He has given them the use of His name, and in the heathen nations where they go as heralds of His grace, they shall do as Paul did on the island of Melita and many other fields. In that name, they are to cast out demons, heal the sick, and perform other mighty miracles that will arrest the attention of the people and cause them to ask, "Who is this Jesus in whose name you work today?"

God never intended there should ever be any change in the methods or ministry down through the ages; only as nations developed, should these methods be broadened, but the miraculous element enfolded in the name of Jesus should be the means of opening closed doors to the church everywhere; the sick should be healed; the power of Satan broken over men's lives, and captives set free.

All this is to be done in the name of this unseen Savior.

THE NAME IN THE GOSPEL OF LUKE

The Gospel of Luke has seven references; let us briefly scan them.

> *Whosoever shall receive this child in my name receiveth me: and whosoever shall receive me receiveth him that sent me: for he that is least among you all, the same shall be great.* (Luke 9:48)

We have the same thought brought out in Matthew 18:5. It is Jesus honoring the little child and giving to the little child his place in the assembly.

It is not enough that our children are taken into the Sunday school. The child has his place in the church and should receive instructions, not from an unsaved Sunday school teacher, but from a real man or woman of God.

Another striking suggestion is in this verse: "*Whosoever shall receive this child in my name receiveth me.*"

His name then is equivalent to Himself. "*Inasmuch as ye have done it unto one of the least of these my brethren, ye have done it unto me*" (Matthew 25:40).

Jesus teaches us the sacredness of His name.

> *John answered and said, Master, we saw one casting out demons in thy name; and we forbade him, because he followeth not with us. But Jesus said unto him, Forbid him not: for he that is not against you is for you.* (Luke 9:49–50 ASV)

Thank God for anyone who is being helped or blessed, whether they walk with us or not.

> *And the seventy returned with joy, saying, Lord, even the demons are subject unto us in thy name.* (Luke 10:17 ASV)

The disciples had the opportunity of seeing the power of Jesus's name before the day of Pentecost.

> *Take heed that ye be not deceived: for many shall come in my name, saying, I am Christ; and the time draweth near: go ye not therefore after them.* (Luke 21:8)

Jesus knew that false prophets would arise and impersonate Him. He said the disciples would be "*brought before kings and rulers for my name's sake*" (verse 12).

> *And that repentance and remission of sins should be preached in his name among all nations, beginning at Jerusalem.* (Luke 24:47)

This is a part of the Great Commission: that repentance and remission of sins are to be preached in His name. How few of the evangelists and preachers have caught a glimpse of this mighty truth, the place of the name of Jesus in evangelism!

In the eighth chapter of Acts, we read that when they listened to Philip preaching the kingdom of God and the name of Jesus, they were led to accept Christ.

What a small place the name of Jesus has in the modern church!

THE NAME IN THE GOSPEL OF JOHN

> *But as many as received him, to them gave he power to become the sons of God, even to them that believe on his name.* (John 1:12)

Salvation here then comes by believing on the name.

> *Now when he was in Jerusalem at the passover, in the feast day, many believed in his name, when they saw the miracles which he did.* (John 2:23)

Christianity would have a new element in it if we taught the people intelligently what it meant to believe *on* the name as a sinner and then to believe *in* the name as a believer. As a sinner, I believe *on* the name of Jesus; as a believer, I am baptized *into* it and then I walk and live *in* the name and this Man, the Head of the church.

Jesus is the Head: we are the body. We are baptized into the Head. To the Head belongs the name and the Head gives us, the body, the right to live, to walk, and to use the power of that name.

> *He that believeth on him is not condemned: but he that believeth not is condemned already, because he hath not believed in the name of the only begotten Son of God.* (John 3:18)

Judgment is coming to man because he has not believed on the name.

> *Whatsoever ye shall ask in my name, that will I do, that the Father may be glorified in the Son. If ye shall ask any thing in my name, I will do it.*
> (John 14:13–14)

This is the first time that man had ever been taught to pray in the name of a Mediator. Here, Jesus gives to His disciples the unique privilege of praying in His name. Up until that time, they had prayer through the high priest; now, they were to pray through this new High Priest.

Wherever they go, whatever they do, they are to bear with them the name of this One who is seated at the right hand of the Father; and Jesus says the Father is glorified in the Son by our praying and asking in His name.

Jesus says, *"If ye shall ask any thing in my name, I will do it."* Jesus is seated there at the Father's right hand to endorse our petitions when they come up to the Father in His name.

> *That whatsoever ye shall ask of the Father in my name, he may give it you.* (John 15:16)

> *And in that day ye shall ask me nothing. Verily, verily, I say unto you, Whatsoever ye shall ask the Father in my name, he will give it you. Hitherto have ye asked nothing in my name: ask, and ye shall receive, that your joy may be full.* (John 16:23–24)

This is the great charter promise in the name of Christ. In this, we can plainly see the legal foundation for a wonderful prayer life for the church—a legal right to use the name of Jesus without any restrictions.

If we are children of God, all that is in that name belongs to us. It is not a question of our worthiness: it is a question of His standing in heaven. As sons and daughters, we take our place and claim our rights.

9

THE BOOK OF ACTS

Repent, and be baptized every one of you in the name of Jesus Christ.
—Acts 2:38

This first use of the name of Jesus must have struck the Jews with a peculiar force. Fifty days before, they had hung Him stark naked upon a cross; now, three thousand of them cry out, *"Men and brethren, what shall we do?"* (verse 37).

Peter answers, *"Repent, and be baptized every one of you in the name of Jesus Christ for the remission of sins."*

This meant a break with Judaism, although it was not clearly in their minds yet. But to be baptized into that name was to put on that name and bear the stigma of that name among their fellows.

THE FIRST MIRACLE IN THE NAME

In the third chapter, we get the first public use of the name.

Peter and John are going up to the temple to worship—for they had not yet been separated from the temple worship—and as they arrived at the door of the temple that was called Beautiful, they saw a cripple lying in his dirt and helplessness, with outstretched hands beseeching them for an offering. (See Acts 3:1–11.)

Peter and John, fastening their eyes on him, said, *"Look on us."*

And he, expecting to receive something, looked up.

Then said Peter, *"Silver and gold have I none; but such as I have give I thee."*

I can see the disappointed look followed by a mystified expression in the lame man's eyes as he looked upon those two humble fishermen.

Peter continued, *"In the name of Jesus Christ of Nazareth rise up and walk."*

And immediately a thrill passed through his body; Peter reached down, grasped him by the hand, and lifted him to his feet. And those ankles that had been useless from babyhood were filled with the strength of manhood. For the first time in his life, this man could walk, leap, and run.

During all of his youth, he had watched others playing while he himself was unable to take any part in their sport, but now, he throbbed with health and life.

He rushed into the temple, leaping, jumping, and shouting praises to God; finally, he turned and grasped Peter and John by the hands while the multitude gathered about them.

Peter declared:

> *Ye men of Israel, why marvel ye at this? or why look ye so earnestly on us, as though by our own power or holiness we had made this man to walk? The God of Abraham, and of Isaac, and of Jacob, the God of our fathers, hath glorified his Son Jesus; whom ye delivered up, and denied him in the presence of Pilate, when he was determined to let him go. But ye denied the Holy One and the Just, and desired a murderer to be granted unto you; and killed the Prince of life, whom God hath raised from the dead; whereof we are witnesses. And his name through faith in his name hath made this man strong, whom ye see and know: yea, the faith which is by him hath given him this perfect soundness in the presence of you all.*
>
> (Acts 3:12–16)

HOW THE EARLY CHURCH USED THE NAME

This is the first recorded miracle in the name of Jesus. Note how the Scripture reads: *"His name through faith in his name hath made this man strong."*

For the first time, we come in vital contact with this strange power vested in the name of Jesus. This miracle created a sensation; the disciples were arrested and put in jail until the morrow.

Through this miracle, the number of disciples had increased to about five thousand.

> *And it came to pass on the morrow, that their rulers, and elders, and scribes, and Annas the high priest, and Caiaphas, and John, and Alexander, and as many as were of the kindred of the high priest, were gathered together at Jerusalem. And when they had set them in the midst, they asked, By what power, or by what name, have ye done this? Then Peter, filled with the Holy Ghost, said unto them, Ye rulers of the people, and elders of Israel, if we this day be examined of the good deed done to the impotent man, by what means he is made whole; be it known unto you all, and to all the people of Israel, that by the name of Jesus Christ of Nazareth, whom ye crucified, whom God raised from the dead, even by him doth this man stand here before you whole. This is the stone which was set at nought of you builders, which is become the head of the corner. Neither is there salvation in any other: for there is none other name under heaven given among men, whereby we must be saved.* (Acts 4:5–12)

CONSTERNATION IN THE SANHEDRIN

They wanted to know what power or what means they used, or by what name they had done that mighty act. Peter told them it was in the name of Jesus of Nazareth, whom they crucified, whom God had raised from the dead—that in His name did this man stand before them whole.

Then the council acted.

They said, "*What shall we do to these men? for that indeed a notable miracle hath been done by them is manifest to all them that dwell in Jerusalem; and we cannot deny it*" (Acts 4:16).

No matter how much we may wish to deny it, the fact stands before us: a man who had been impotent for years was suddenly healed in the name of Jesus.

No miracle like this had ever happened before in human history; it shook the Sanhedrin to their foundation. Their wisest men were in confusion; the disciples were ordered aside for a moment while the Sanhedrin conferred... and in their fear, they threatened.

> *But that it spread no further among the people, let us straitly threaten them, that they speak henceforth to no man in this name. And they called them, and commanded them not to speak at all nor teach in the name of Jesus.* (Acts 4:17–18)

It does not seem that they objected so much to the teaching of His resurrection but they feared the power of that name, so they charged them not to teach nor preach in that name and sent them out.

Peter and John went back to their own company and told the story. Then we have their remarkable prayer:

> *And now, Lord, behold their threatenings: and grant unto thy servants, that with all boldness they may speak thy word, by stretching forth thine hand to heal; and that signs and wonders may be done by the name of thy holy child Jesus.* (Acts 4:29–30)

The disciples now expected that signs and wonders were to follow the preaching in the name of Jesus. And the place where they had prayed was shaken, they were all filled with the Holy Spirit, and they spoke the Word of God with boldness. (See Acts 4:31.)

> *And by the hands of the apostles were many signs and wonders wrought among the people....There came also a multitude out of the cities round about unto Jerusalem, bringing sick folks, and them which were vexed with unclean spirits: and they were healed every one.* (Acts 5:12, 16)

JAIL DOORS WERE OPENED

The apostles were arrested again and put in a prison, but the angel of the Lord opened the prison doors and told them, "*Go, stand and speak in the temple to the people all the words of this life*" (Acts 5:20). And so they did.

Later, they were brought before the council and the high priest, who told them, "*Did not we straitly command you that ye should not teach in this name? and, behold, ye have filled Jerusalem with your doctrine, and intend to bring this man's blood upon us*" (Acts 5:28).

Then came one of the most dramatic events in the early church. The council was divided and the power of God was so manifest among the people that the Pharisee Gamaliel warned them not to touch the apostles because they might find themselves fighting against God. (See Acts 5:34–39.)

But in the face of this, they beat the apostles and charged them not to speak in the name of Jesus. Then they let them go. (See verse 40.)

They departed from the presence of the council, rejoicing that they were counted worthy to suffer shame for his name. (Acts 5:41)

No student can read this section of the book of Acts without being impressed with the large place the name of Jesus held in the early church.

Following the death of Stephen and the preaching of the Word by Philip in Samaria, we come to this significant statement:

But when they believed Philip preaching the things concerning the kingdom of God, and the name of Jesus Christ, they were baptized, both men and women. (Acts 8:12)

He not only preached the kingdom but he preached the name of Jesus. It seems that the early church devoted the time to instructing the people in regard to the use of the name of Jesus. They must have understood that they had what we would call today a legal right to use the name of Jesus.

THE NAME FOR HEALING

They used it in connection with the sick; it would seem that they did not pray for the sick especially but that they laid their hands upon them in Jesus's name, or as at the Beautiful gate, they said, "In the name of Jesus Christ of Nazareth, rise and walk."

At Paul's conversion, when God was sending Ananias to baptize Paul, He said:

For he is a chosen vessel unto me, to bear my name before the Gentiles, and kings, and the children of Israel: for I will shew him how great things he must suffer for my name's sake. (Acts 9:15–16)

The name of Jesus was the battle-axe in the ministry of Paul. That name in the hands of Paul was like the rod in the hand of Moses.

If the Egyptians could have stolen that rod, they would have stripped Moses of his weapon.

Now, if the gentiles and Jews could stop the church from using the name of Jesus, they would rob the church of its supernatural power. The church would be common men like Sampson was when his hair was cut. The modern church, having lost the power of the name of Jesus, is reduced to the position of the shorn Sampson.

We read how boldly Paul preached in the name of Jesus:

> *But Barnabas took him, and brought him to the apostles, and declared unto them how he had seen the Lord in the way, and that he had spoken to him, and how he had preached boldly at Damascus in the name of Jesus. And he was with them coming in and going out at Jerusalem. And he spake boldly in the name of the Lord Jesus.* (Acts 9:27–29)

That means more than simply preaching the gospel, as we understand it today.

Again, in the council at Jerusalem, James said, *"Simeon hath declared how God at the first did visit the Gentiles, to take out of them a people for his name"* (Acts 15:14).

A PEOPLE GATHERED ABOUT THE NAME

The gentile church is a people taken out of the world unto the name of Jesus, and we are a people who are gathered about the name. When we meet as an assembly or a church, we are gathered about the name of Jesus.

It is a supernatural body, clothed with supernatural power, gathered about a supernatural name.

The Lord have mercy upon us! How we have fallen from our high estate. One can go into the average church or assembly and hear men and women pleading with God for faith, bemoaning their weakness, confessing their inability to meet the crisis of the hour, when if they only knew the truth, they would gather about the name of Jesus—this mighty name that has enwrapped within it the omnipotence of God, the power of Him who bore it, and they know it not!

Oh, if they only knew how to turn on the switch and receive the light, the glory, and the might of omnipotence that is at their disposal.

In Acts 16, we have a striking illustration of the use of the name:

> *And it came to pass, as we went to prayer, a certain damsel possessed with a spirit of divination met us, which brought her masters much gain by soothsaying: the same followed Paul and us, and cried, saying, These men are the servants of the most high God, which shew unto us the way of salvation. And this did she many days. But Paul, being grieved, turned*

and said to the spirit, I command thee in the name of Jesus Christ to come out of her. And he came out the same hour. (Acts 16:16–18)

The girl was delivered, the apostles were arrested, and then came the mighty miracle of the opening of the jail at Philippi. The jailer fell trembling at the feet of Paul and Silas, crying, "*Sirs, what must I do to be saved? And they said, Believe on the Lord Jesus Christ, and thou shalt be saved, and thy house*" (Acts 16:30–31).

This same name that had liberated the girl from the power of the demon in the afternoon now has led this man into sonship privileges in the family of God. The name of Jesus meant more to the early church than it does to us; it had a place in their ministry that we do not give it in these days.

Have we anything to take its place? They tell us that education will take its place, that the church no longer needs the supernatural power of God.

They reason that we have outgrown the teaching of the Holy Spirit and that the wisdom of man is to take the place of the power of the name of Christ. They reason that the name has been stripped of its power because we—through our colleges, universities, and our great intellectual development—have outgrown God, and we can perform mental miracles so that God's physical miracles are unnecessary.

Shame upon us! We have become an apostate church. We are groveling in the dust and are held in bondage to our ignorance.

Israel, when carried into captivity by the Babylonians, is typical of the church that has been carried into a Babylon-like captivity by the world forces. Nothing but a supernatural God will ever deliver us!

How little we realize that our vain preaching and our vain writing are simply the laughing stock of the enemy. One mighty miracle today in the name of Jesus Christ is worth more than a hundred modernistic sermons that are being preached in many churches.

HAS GOD LOST HIS POWER?

Has Jesus gone out of business? Have we any record anywhere that God said the name of Jesus is no longer needed, that colleges, universities, and scholasticism will take its place?

Let us read of another striking event in the book of Acts:

God wrought special miracles by the hands of Paul: so that from his body were brought unto the sick handkerchiefs or aprons, and the diseases departed from them, and the evil spirits went out of them. Then certain of the vagabond Jews, exorcists, took upon them to call over them which had evil spirits the name of the Lord Jesus, saying, We adjure you by Jesus whom Paul preacheth. And there were seven sons of one Sceva, a Jew, and chief of the priests, which did so. And the evil spirit answered and said, Jesus I know, and Paul I know; but who are ye? And the man in whom the evil spirit was leaped on them, and overcame them, and prevailed against them, so that they fled out of that house naked and wounded. And this was known to all the Jews and Greeks also dwelling at Ephesus; and fear fell on them all, and the name of the Lord Jesus was magnified.

(Acts 19:11–17)

Paul's ministry in the name of Jesus was so outstanding, the miracles so pronounced, that even wicked sorcerers attempted to use it. And that name, through the mighty things that were wrought, was glorified in Ephesus.

Would that the name of Jesus could be so glorified today in the churches and assemblies! It would be if the believers knew their legal rights and knew how to enjoy them.

Speaking in his defense before King Agrippa in Acts 26, Paul explains how he once punished the Jews before meeting Jesus on the road to Damascus:

I verily thought with myself, that I ought to do many things contrary to the name of Jesus of Nazareth. (Acts 26:9)

Notice the place that Paul gives the name in this Scripture—that he thought he "*ought to do many things contrary to the name*"!

If we were to draw a conclusion from the use and place of the name in the book of Acts, what would we say?

The name of Jesus actually took the place of the ascended Lord; wherever Jesus would have been glorified by His personal presence, that name took His place.

May the Lord open our blinded eyes! That name has lost none of its authority, none of its power, and the effort to rob us of some of the major portions of Scripture by a false dispensational division of Scripture fails utterly. For in Paul's ministry with the gentiles and his epistles to them, he gives the name of Jesus a place that absolutely refutes the entire teaching of those who would put the power of the name of Jesus over into the kingdom period.

No! The name of Jesus belongs to us *now*. It is our legal right; that name belongs to us.

How rich would be the church today in power, experience, and grace, if she knew her privileges and arose in that name and dared take them!

10

THE NAME IN THE EPISTLES

The use of the name in the Epistles is very illuminating. Paul writes:

> *Unto the church of God which is at Corinth, even them that are sanctified in Christ Jesus, called to be saints, with all that call upon the name of our Lord Jesus Christ in every place, their Lord and ours.*
> (1 Corinthians 1:2 ASV)

"With all that call upon the name." In those early days, the believers knew the value, place, and authority of that name. They appreciated it. They walked and lived in the conscious freshness of the power of the name of Jesus.

When they made an appeal to the brethren, they used language like this:

> *Now I beseech you, brethren, by the name of our Lord Jesus Christ, that ye all speak the same thing, and that there be no divisions among you.*
> (1 Corinthians 1:10)

Their appeal was in the name of Jesus.

In 1 Corinthians 5:4, we read, *"In the name of our Lord Jesus Christ, when ye are gathered together."*

Here, the church is facing an internal trouble—one of the young men has committed a very grave misdemeanor. And Paul tells them that when they have gathered together in the name of the Lord Jesus Christ, they are *"to deliver such an one unto Satan for the destruction of the flesh, that the spirit may be saved in the day of the Lord Jesus"* (verse 5).

That name had the power of life and of death in those days.

> *But ye are washed, but ye are sanctified, but ye are justified in the name of the Lord Jesus, and by the Spirit of our God.* (1 Corinthians 6:11)

Here, they are washed, sanctified, and justified in that name. The farther you go in the Epistles, the more deeply you are impressed with the power, dignity, and grace of God vested in that name.

> *Giving thanks always for all things unto God and the Father in the name of our Lord Jesus Christ.* (Ephesians 5:20)

Even our praises and our worship cannot go directly to God; they must come in the name of our Lord Jesus Christ. That does not hinder us from worshipping and praising Jesus Himself, but when we praise the Father, it must be done in the name of our Lord Jesus Christ.

> *Wherefore God also hath highly exalted him, and given him a name which is above every name: that at the name of Jesus every knee should bow, of things in heaven, and things in earth, and things under the earth; and that every tongue should confess that Jesus Christ is Lord, to the glory of God the Father.* (Philippians 2:9–11)

God has highly exalted the name of Jesus in the three worlds—and every knee bows. All of the angelic beings bow before the name of this wonder Man, Jesus. No name is so great and no name has so many glories attached to it as the name of Jesus.

On earth, the name of Jesus has steadily grown from the day when He lay as an infant in the manger and Mary, looking upon Him, remembered what the angels had said: "And His name shall be called Jesus, for it is He who shall save His people from their sins."

From the cradle with its prophecy to the cross with its tragedy, and sweeping down through the ages, that name has steadily grown until today, when the Jew, the gentile, and the heathen of all lands are compelled to recognize that name.

No man writes a deed in Christian lands who does not honor the name of Jesus. The date on that document, showing the year of our Lord AD, must be written. The Lord has so arranged it that everyone, regardless of his belief, must acknowledge the birth of Christ every time he dates a letter.

Wherever that name has become known, honored, and venerated, habitations have changed to homes; the mother's position from that of a slave to that of the honored queen, girlhood from being despised to being honored and loved.

Wherever that name is honored, educational institutions spring up, and inventions, scientific investigation, and discoveries are fostered.

This name that men have ignored and trampled upon during this dispensation will be the name that will fill the hearts of wicked men with fear.

DO ALL THINGS IN THE NAME

And whatsoever ye do in word or deed, do all in the name of the Lord Jesus, giving thanks to God and the Father by him. (Colossians 3:17)

In Ephesians, He told us that when we worshipped the Father, it must be through the name. But now, *"whatsoever ye do in word or deed, do all in the name of the Lord Jesus."*

This ends the controversy in regard to praying to Jesus. This gives Jesus His position; this exalts the name in our daily life. Whatsoever we do in word or in deed must be done in that name and in that name only.

In Paul's second letter to the Thessalonians, we have another view of this:

We pray always for you, that our God would count you worthy of this calling, and fulfil all the good pleasure of his goodness, and the work of faith with power: that the name of our Lord Jesus Christ may be glorified in you, and ye in him. (2 Thessalonians 1:11–12)

This sets forth more clearly perhaps, than any other Scripture we have used, the place of the name in our daily life and ministry, that this name may be glorified in our lives and glorified through our ministry.

How could it be glorified more than by using it as the early church used it?

Now we command you, brethren, in the name of our Lord Jesus Christ, that ye withdraw yourselves from every brother that walketh disorderly, and not after the tradition which he received of us. (2 Thessalonians 3:6)

Here, Paul commands the church, in the name of the Lord Jesus, to withdraw from every brother who walks in a disorderly manner. How mighty that name must have been in the mind of the early church!

Through him then let us offer up a sacrifice of praise to God continually, that is, the fruit of lips which make confession to his name.

(Hebrews 13:15 ASV)

Their public testimony was a confession of that name.

I can understand now what it means in Acts 8, where it speaks of Philip preaching the kingdom of God and the name of Jesus. They preached the name; they heralded the power, might, and wonder of that name. They appreciated what the promise of Jesus meant when He said, *"Hitherto have ye have asked nothing in my name"* (John 16:24).

They went out and suffered for the name.

I understand more clearly how the Jews felt when they forbade the disciples preaching any more in that name. Afterward, when the disciples were arrested, the Jews said, "Did we not straightway forbid you preaching in this name? And yet you have filled Jerusalem with it." (See Acts 4:18.)

The disciples knew its value and they lived in the freshness of its power. Those Jews knew its power too.

In James 2:7 (ASV), we read, *"Do not they blaspheme the honorable name by which ye are called?"*

Yes, that *"honorable name"* that had wrought such mighty deeds throughout all the country was looked up to with honor, respect, and love.

> *Is any sick among you? let him call for the elders of the church; and let them pray over him, anointing him with oil in the name of the Lord.*
> (James 5:14)

The sick were anointed in that name for their healing.

> *If ye are reproached for the name of Christ, blessed are ye.*
> (1 Peter 4:14)

They gladly bore the reproach of that name.

You can see very clearly that the name of Jesus held a position in the front rank of their teaching. Whenever they entered a heathen village or city, they preached to them that name as Philip preached it in Samaria. They let the people know that the name of Jesus had power to heal the sick, cast out demons, and perform miracles and prodigies—that their God was represented in that name.

> *I write unto you, little children, because your sins are forgiven you for his name's sake.* (1 John 2:12)

Here, the name is used in another sense, but with what a wealth of suggestiveness. Sins are forgiven for His name's sake, for the sake of that name.

> *And this is his commandment, That we should believe on the name of his Son Jesus Christ, and love one another.* (1 John 3:23)

The command that we should believe in the name is literally that we should believe the name; the preposition *in* is not the Greek. That we should believe the name—believe it for what it stands, believe it for all that it means in the heart of the Father. We must believe the name!

Reader, ask your heart this question, "Do I believe the name of Jesus? What does it mean to my life?"

> *These things have I written unto you that believe on the name of the Son of God; that ye may know that ye have eternal life, and that ye may believe on the name of the Son of God.* (1 John 5:13)

Here is a contrast between *in* and *on*. We believe *on* the name for salvation; we believe *in* the name for power in service. Our position as believers in Christ gives us a legal right to pray in the name of Jesus and take out of that name the wealth of love, riches, grace, salvation, and redemption that belongs to us.

We see by the teachings in the Epistles what Jesus meant when He gave the great promise of the use of His name. The name of Jesus became the center around which everything was built in their missionary activities. They lived, wrought, and praised in that name.

That name meant food and raiment; it meant deliverance from the hand of their enemies. It meant power over demons and diseases; it meant worship, praise, and access to God.

Enwrapped in that mighty name is the invisible power and miracle-working might of the church of Jesus Christ today.

11

THE NAME IN DAILY CONFLICT

In this name lies the very essence of Christianity. It is the one thing which differentiates it from all other religions. It is the one name that challenges an adjective to qualify it.

While here in the flesh, Jesus was the all-powerful One; God always heard His prayers and permitted Him to use omnipotence as He willed.

Before He went away, He promised that this same right to use the omnipotence of God should be left on earth, available to man.

He told the disciples not to leave Jerusalem until they were endued or clothed with power from on high. The Holy Spirit was to come into them and enable them to use His name in the will of God, so that it would be as though Christ were again in the flesh exercising this divine power, only in a larger sense, because there would be so many using His name.

Filled with the Spirit, they preached in this name with mighty power. The sick were healed, demons were cast out, and the dead were raised. In this name, a serpent's bite became the means of the inhabitants of a whole island receiving Jesus Christ as their Savior. (See Acts 28:1–9.)

In this name came the gift of tongues, which enabled all nations on the day of Pentecost to hear the glad tidings of remission of sins.

HE WILLED US HIS NAME

All this was in fulfillment of the words spoken by Jesus Christ before His ascension.

> *In my name shall they cast out demons; they shall speak with new tongues; they shall take up serpents, and if they drink any deadly thing, it shall*

in no wise hurt them; they shall lay hands on the sick, and they shall recover. (Mark 16:17–18 ASV)

This power was not in the Holy Spirit, but in the Spirit's enabling the disciples to use the name of the Lord Jesus Christ, the Son of God. All power is in the name of the risen Man, Christ Jesus, who is seated at the Father's right hand in the heavens.

The power is not in fasting or consecration, not in long prayers, but it is in the simple name of Jesus of Nazareth, the Son of God. Men are seeking power—they call it Pentecostal power—and they seek it in all directions but the right one. It is in the name—seek it there.

If you learn to use the name according to the Word, in the power of the Spirit, you have the secret that shook the world through the apostles.

HOW TO USE HIS NAME

You must be a scriptural believer, a child of God, obedient to the Word. You must come to God the Father through Christ.

Don't pray to Jesus and don't pray to the Holy Spirit. Never ask for the *sake* of Jesus—always pray in His name. Be definite; don't insult the Father by indefinite ramblings, but ask for what you want.

Approach the Father as a son, not as a slave or servant. You are His child and He is your loving Father. He loves you, you love Him, and are free and happy in His presence.

Your chief desire is that He may receive glory so talk plainly with Him, open your heart, lay your desire before His eyes, and make your case clear. Let Him see that it is for His glory and the good of others.

Then clinch it by making your worthy claim in the name of His Son who sits at His right hand, reminding Him of His promise: "*Whatsoever ye shall ask the Father in my name, he will give it you*" (John 16:23).

THE DIVINE ADVOCATE

Now, you have a clear case and the Lord Jesus is there to present your claim. By asking in His name, you have made Christ your Advocate and now the case belongs to Him.

Your humble, simple prayer, made in this scriptural way, becomes Christ's prayer at God's right hand. You drop out of the question and the mighty Advocate takes your case.

This shows us what power we have up there and down here. Be fearless after this; challenge your mountain in that all-sufficient name. It must move. Sin, sickness, circumstances, Satan—all must yield to that name.

Use this name although you tremble when you do it—it is not you, but the power behind the name. You do not need to feel its power—you know it—and everything must flee at this all-conquering name.

> *Hitherto have ye asked nothing in my name: ask, and ye shall receive, that your joy may be full.* (John 16:24)

THE SIMPLICITY OF PRAYER

This is one of the startling statements of the Gospels:

> *Whatsoever ye shall ask in my name, that will I do, that the Father may be glorified in the Son.* (John 14:13)

Notice Jesus said, "You ask and I will do it." This is a most wonderful thing—prayer simplified.

"You do the asking," Jesus says, "and I will do the doing."

Jesus says all authority has been given to Him in heaven and on earth. Jesus's power is unlimited and now He challenges you to do unlimited asking. He is big enough to do anything you ask Him to do. His authority is great enough to see that any request from you is honored.

For that unsaved friend, He says, "You ask for his salvation and I will do it."

It may be your church is cold and your pastor as bound as Lazarus in the grave clothes of convention, yet you ask Jesus to warm your church, and He says, "I will do it."

You ask for a revival and Jesus will do it.

Jesus sits at the right hand of the Father and whatsoever you ask of the Father in His almighty name, He says, "I will do it."

Ask for healing for that loved one who is sick and as surely as God is on His throne, so surely must He do it.

You ask for the finances for that undertaking for the Lord. Your business is to ask; His business is to see that it is done. Behind everything stand these words of Christ, "I will do it."

There is no reason for our weakness; there is no reason for our sickness. There is no reason for a fruitless church or ministry. There is no reason for powerless lives.

You resolve your life into the service of asking, challenging the omnipotence of the living, reigning Christ, and He will take care of His end of the deal.

You are a partner with Him now. This is not a *limited partnership* because His company is not limited. He is able to meet the demands; He is able to finance any undertaking.

The great and mighty Christ is willing for you to ask that He may give.

Weakness is a crime now, poverty of spirit is a sin. All you need to do is ask and He will act.

HOW TO PRAY

Jesus told us how to pray: *"When ye pray, say, Our Father"* (Luke 11:2).

We are not to pray to Jesus. That does not exclude the privilege of joy, fellowship, and communion with Him, nor the praise and worship of Him. But when we have a special petition, our prayer is to be addressed to the Father in the name of Jesus.

Not *for Jesus's sake* for that would mean to do it for His sake rather than for the sake of the one who needs it.

The prayer should be addressed simply to our Father, in Jesus's name. This guarantees the Father's answer and Jesus's endorsement and intercession.

I know that the habit of praying to Jesus is very widespread, but if we want the truth and we desire to pray in such a manner that we can be sure of our answer, then we must obey the Scriptures and pray as they teach us.

You see, Jesus's name was to take the place of Jesus. What the rod was in the hands of Moses, the name of Jesus is in the hands of the weakest child of

God. It was not that Moses was great but that the rod was great. It is not that the believer is great but that the name of Jesus is great.

The use of that name is promised to every believer and every believer has a right to lay hands on the sick in that name. The believer has a right to use it in every condition of life where the Father's presence and help are necessary.

The fact is that the name of Jesus in the hands of every believer should be the same as though Jesus Himself were present and operating.

Jesus has given us a legal right to use His name. He has given to us His power of attorney, and the power of attorney in the legal and business world is identical with the presence of the person who gave it. It is just as though Jesus said, "When you pray in My name, that gives Me an opportunity to begin to work and in that way, I may glorify My Father. If you don't pray in My name, you don't give Me an opportunity to manifest My power."

In this way, both the Father and the Son become vitally interested in the petition that we make. You are praying to the Father and you are praying in the name of His Son.

12

CONTRAST OF SENSE KNOWLEDGE FAITH AND REVELATION FAITH

Sense knowledge faith is based upon physical evidence. One believes in what they can see, hear, or feel. We know that we have the Holy Spirit because we have had physical evidences to prove it.

Multitudes have taken this attitude and have been unhappily deceived. Had they based their confidence upon the Word of God regardless of all sense knowledge evidence, life would have been another thing for them.

Others, when they have prayed for finances, have not believed the Word until they could see the evidence. As one said, "When I see the money, then I will believe the Word."

You see, that is not believing at all, because one needs not believe what they can see.

Faith is giving substance to things you cannot see, feel, or hear.

One says, "I know that I am healed because the pain is gone." He did not say, "I know I am healed because the Word says by His stripes, I am healed." His faith was not in what God had said, but in what he could see, feel, or hear.

These people give the Word a second place in their lives. They give the first place to their body, the home of the senses.

One says, "I know that I am saved because I have repented of my sins. I have given up all of my bad habits."

Every one of these things that he claims for his salvation are things that he did himself. He has given no scriptural evidence of his salvation. He has depended upon physical evidence rather than the Word of God. After a while, he makes the discovery that the evidence of the senses cannot satisfy the craving of the spirit.

Sense knowledge philosophy has gained control of the church, but it cannot answer the cry of the human spirit, which seeks God as the flower seeks the sun.

Basing our faith upon what we have done and counting more on experiences than upon the Word eventually leads us into darkness and doubt. Acting on reason instead of the Word means to trust in man instead of God's Word.

> *Thus saith the* Lord; *Cursed be the man that trusteth in man, and maketh flesh his arm.* (Jeremiah 17:5)

Trusting in the faith of some other person is dangerous. We should trust in the Word of God ourselves.

Most people who are untaught in the Word are seeking for someone who can pray the prayer of faith for them. The prayer of faith may deliver them temporarily, but unbelief will annul the effect of their prayer eventually.

It is having faith, believing in your own faith, and trusting in the Word of God for yourself that will put you over. It is not talking about faith or the need of faith, but it is resting implicitly in the living Word.

The prayer for faith will necessarily be a prayer of unbelief. Consequently, there can be no answer for it. Then your praying for faith is simply unbelief attempting to get what the Word alone can give.

You understand that simple confidence in the Word is never sensible to the man who lives in the realm of the senses, for he only believes what he can see, hear, or understand.

Faith is giving substance to things that sense knowledge cannot understand or see. It lifts one out of the realm of the senses into the realm of the recreated human spirit.

Faith is always limited, as it was with Martha and Thomas. Martha said of her dead brother Lazarus, *"By this time the body decayeth"* (John 11:39 asv). Thomas said, *"Except I shall see in his hands the print of the nails, and put my finger into the print of the nails, and thrust my hand into his side, I will not believe"* (John 20:25).

This kind of faith is commended by our modern religious leaders...but this is not the faith mentioned by Jesus or the writers of the New Testament.

We have been trained to believe in the skill of men. We have more confidence in the surgeon than we have in the Word. Because of that, we see little manifestations of real faith in the living Word, for the skill of man and what we call science has taken the place of the Word in the hearts of the people. Their faith is in man and they honor man with their lips.

Their confession is not that the Word of God is true, but that man and his words are true. You see, they honor God with their lips, but they trust in the arm of flesh with their hearts.

MENTAL ASSENT

This assenting to the fact that God cannot fail to help us at a crisis period and yet, at the same time, turning to the world for assistance is a dangerous symptom.

Mental assent is one of the most dangerous enemies of a life of faith. It looks and sounds so religious. It will go so far as to say, "I believe in the verbal inspiration of the Bible. I am contending for the faith once delivered to the saints." Yet, they dare not act on the Word; they do not give it its place; they merely talk about its integrity.

The mental assenter is in the gravest danger. He is where God cannot reach him, but where Satan can enter into his inner counsel. He therefore loses his rights and privileges in Christ.

ACTING ON THE WORD

The greatest battle that any child of God will ever fight is the battle of faith.

We often wonder why it is so hard to believe God. The reason is that we are surrounded by an antagonistic atmosphere that is presided over by the enemy of all righteousness. We live in his unreal world and we are surrounded by currents of unbelief so subtle that one almost does not realize them and so resistless that only a few ever rise above them.

To believe in God for finances is a continual struggle against the materialistic currents that buffet us.

To believe in Christ for victory over sin is a battle with the spiritual hosts of darkness during every hour of consciousness.

To believe in God for the physical body when one is ill is to put up a battle against the centuries of trust in medicine.

So it is not at all strange that so many break down in their faith life. We should not be harsh or censorious against those who fail.

FAITH AND BELIEVING

Faith is a noun; believe is a verb. An analysis of these two words may help you in trusting the Lord.

Believing, being a verb, is an action word. It really means *taking.* To believe in a biblical sense means to *take,* to *grasp.* To believe Jesus means to take Jesus for all that the Scriptures declare Him to be. To believe on Christ as a Savior means to take Christ as a Savior; to believe in Christ as a healer means to take Him as your healer and recognize Him as your healer.

Believing is an act of the will. When I believe, I have acted—and having acted, I have reached what is called faith.

Faith is a noun. I take a step—and having taken the step, I have arrived. Arriving is faith.

To believe, then, is to act on the Word of God. Faith is action. Doubting is refusing to act on the Word.

There are two kinds of unbelief. First, a refusing to act on the knowledge of the Word that we have. This can be called unpersuadableness—we refuse to be persuaded to act on what we know to be true. We refuse to act in the light of knowledge.

The other kind of unbelief arises from lack of knowledge of the Word. We do not know; hence, we cannot act. We do not understand; hence, we are afraid to act. We would act, but we do not know how to act.

The cure for this unbelief is knowledge of the Word; the cure for the other is obedience.

13

THE NAME IN BAPTISM

When a believer is baptized into the name of the Lord Jesus, He puts on Christ, as Paul tells us:

> *For as many of you as have been baptized into Christ have put on Christ.* (Galatians 3:27)

Baptism, in this sense, is equivalent to marriage.

When the wife puts on marriage, she takes her husband's name and enters into her husband's possessions and has legal rights in his home.

So when the believer is baptized into the name of the Lord Jesus, he puts on the name of the Lord Jesus and takes his legal rights and privileges in Christ.

When we are baptized into the name of the Father, it gives us the place of a child and all the privileges of a child, all the inheritance and wealth of the child.

We are baptized into the protection, care, and fellowship of the God of the universe as our Father. We take on all that union means. We have the standing of a son, the privilege of a son, and the responsibilities of a son.

We have become, by that baptism, a joint heir with Jesus and an heir of God. We have entered into the wealth of an inheritance from the God of the universe.

When we are baptized into the name of the Holy Spirit, we are baptized into the name, wealth, power, wisdom, and glory of God's representative on the earth. We are baptized into all that the Spirit has. We have become a fellowshipper of His grace, His tenderness, His wisdom, His ability, His power, and His life.

So when we are baptized into the name of the Lord Jesus, all that His name stands for in heaven is ours; all the mighty victories that Jesus won in His death and resurrection are ours.

What does it mean to be baptized into the name? Take this Scripture:

> *Baptizing them into the name of the Father and of the Son and of the Holy Spirit.* (Matthew 28:19 ASV)

Spiritually, it means this if it means anything: that we are baptized into all that name means in the plan of redemption—we are baptized into the finished work of Christ.

CHRIST OUR FULLNESS

Of His fullness, we have received, and in Him, we are full or complete. All of the grace that was manifest in Christ enwraps us, enfolds us—we are in it. All the perfections and beauties in the character and life of Jesus are ours.

Paul says, "*Ye are complete in him*" (Colossians 2:10).

It means in the mind of Paul that the completeness, the fullness, and the perfection of Christ was all reckoned unto us.

Paul said, "*As many of you as have been baptized into Christ have put on Christ*" (Galatians 3:27).

Think of the responsibilities attached to it! Think of the glories enwrapped in it! Think of the blessings that accrue from it! To be baptized into the name of Christ, the putting on of Christ, and bearing the name of Christ is the greatest honor that heaven can confer upon a human.

What mighty works can be wrought through the holy child Jesus! The Lord lifts us up and enables us, by His grace, to enter into our inheritance and assume our responsibilities in His wonderful family!

He won no victory and He won no triumph in His substitutionary work that was not for the benefit of the church.

OUR INHERITANCE

All that name stands for, the believer stands for in the presence of the Father.

You are baptized into the legal right to use the name. You are baptized into the legal privilege of that name. You are baptized into all the responsibilities of a son, vested with prerogatives of that mighty name.

God help us by the power of the Spirit to enter into the riches of our inheritance in Him.

When He said, "All authority is given unto me in heaven and on earth; I send you out as heralds"—then that authority He had is ours; we stand as His representatives.

His righteousness is ours, His love is ours, and all the graces that adorned His beautiful life are ours. When we put on Christ in baptism, we are by His grace able to enjoy all the graces.

As believers, all these riches and all these graces are ours. It requires no special act on the part of God and no special act or preparation on our part. By faith, we accept Christ as our Savior and Lord and when we do, all the wealth and riches in Christ Jesus become ours automatically.

We stand clothed in the rights, privileges, and powers of the Son of God.

A THREEFOLD MEANING

> *We are buried with him by baptism into death: that like as Christ was raised up from the dead by the glory of the Father, even so we also should walk in newness of life.* (Romans 6:4)

Baptism has a threefold significance. First, it is the death and burial of the past. Second, it is a resurrection into a new relationship. Third, it is a union with the One in whose name we have been baptized.

We are baptized into the name of the Father. This means sonship, with all the privileges that come with a relationship of such a person as the Father God.

It means that we have died to all our previous relationships. From now on, our life is dependent upon Him.

To be baptized into the Holy Spirit means that I have died to my past—my old relationships are severed and I am raised in Him, to live and walk in fellowship with Him.

His wisdom is to take the place of my ignorance; His strength is to take the place of my weakness; His goodness is to take the place of my failures. In other words, I am so fully identified and so completely at one with Him that it can no longer be I that live but He who lives His life in me.

Baptizing into the name of the Lord Jesus Christ is even richer and fuller than either of these for it comprehends all that is in them with additions. When I am baptized into Christ, I put on Christ. I am now legally a Christian before the world and before heaven.

Baptism in this sense is equivalent to marriage. When the wife puts on marriage, she takes her husband's name, enters into her husband's possessions, and has legal rights in her husband's home.

When the believer is baptized into the name of Christ, he puts on all that is in Christ. He not only puts on the name, but takes his legal rights and privileges in Christ.

When a wife is married into the name of the husband, she is married into his wealth, honor, and glory and becomes identified with him in all that he was or ever will be.

So when we are baptized into the name of the Lord Jesus, we are baptized into all that name stands for—all its wealth, all its honor, all its power, and all its past, present, and future glory. All that His name stands for in heaven is ours; all the mighty victories He won in His death, suffering, and conquest in hell and His resurrection are ours.

ALL IS OURS

He won no victory nor triumph in His substitutionary work that was not for the benefit of those united to Him in baptism.

All that name stands for before the Father belongs to the believer.

We are baptized into the legal right to use the name, the legal privileges of that name, and all the responsibility of a son, vested with the prerogatives of that mighty name.

When He said, *"All authority hath been given unto me in heaven and on earth"* (Matthew 28:18 ASV) and *"Behold, I send you forth"* (Matthew 10:16), then that authority He had is ours. We stand as His representatives as we go out into this world bearing His name.

Thus instead of our bearing the name, the name actually bears and succors us.

We are baptized into His righteousness, into His resurrection, power, and glory. Now, His righteousness is ours, His grace is ours, His love is ours, His power is ours, and yes, He Himself is ours. How rich we are!

Now to use this name does not require any special or unusual faith... because it is ours. As believers, all the riches and graces are ours—there is no special act on the part of God and no special preparation is necessary on our part when some great crisis arises. That name is ours, given to us legally to use against the host of God's enemies, and we stand clothed in the rights, privileges, and powers of the sons of God.

We do not have to exercise any conscious faith; all we have to do is to use the name.

The heart can hardly take it in, that when we were baptized into that name, we were baptized into the fullness, the completeness, and the perfections of Jesus Christ.

Of his fulness have all we received, and grace for grace. (John 1:16)

14

IDENTIFICATION WITH CHRIST

The glorious fact of our identification with Christ is one of the richest facts in the whole plan of redemption.

We were crucified with Christ—we were nailed to the cross with Him, in the mind of God.

As He was stripped naked and hung there in His shame and disgrace, so we also were stripped naked and hung there, for He took our place on the cross. We died with Christ, as He died. As He died to sin, so we died to sin.

As He died to Satan's rule, so we died to it. As He died to sickness and disease, we died.

We were buried together with Him as He went down into the place of suffering and paid the penalty of our sins and union with Satan. As He put off from Himself the forces of darkness and sin, the sickness and diseases of man, so we put them off in Him—and we left them there.

We were raised together with Christ. He was raised up by the glory of the Father when He had satisfied the claims of justice, met our great enemy Satan and His army in the dark regions of hell, and conquered them.

He then was made alive in spirit and justified in spirit. Then, He arose and we rose with Him. He was raised up because God justified Him and He could not be held any longer by death and hell.

When He was justified, we were justified in Him. When He was healed of death, we were healed in Him.

When He conquered sickness and disease, so also did we, in Him. To all who are in Christ, disease is a conquered foe.

We are seated with Christ at the right hand of God, in the highest place of power in the universe. We are identified with Him in suffering and shame, and in glory.

LAW OF IDENTIFICATION

Christ has conquered death, hell, and the grave. He has risen as a Victor from the conquest of our enemies. We were identified with Him in that conquest.

We died with Him and we suffered with Him. When He put off from Himself the principalities and powers and conquered Satan, paralyzing his death-dealing power, we were identified with Him. When He rose from among the dead and stood triumphant over death, hell, Satan, disease, and the grave, we stood with Him.

Now, He gives to us the use of the name that was conferred upon Him when He had accomplished this mighty work in satisfying the claims of justice, defeating Satan, and meeting the needs of humanity.

He gives to us the name that is above every name—the name to which every knee shall bow and every tongue confess in heaven, on earth, and under the earth. (See Philippians 2:9–10.)

In His great grace, He gave us the use of that name; He gave us a legal right to use it.

He died as our representative; now we live as His representatives.

That name represents all that He was or is and all that He ever did or will do.

When we have been ushered into this faith realm by a thorough understanding of this and we use that name intelligently, all that name means in heaven, it will mean to us.

He has put absolutely no limitation upon our use of that name. The only question is, "Do I understand what God means in giving me the use of that name?"

We are not to use it as the heathen use their fetishes, but we are to use it in a business sense, the legal sense of power of attorney. We use His name as His representatives.

The sick and afflicted come to us and healing virtue that is in Christ—that is in His finished work—is available to the sick one in that name. Then, it is not healing through Christ; that name becomes Christ, the healer.

A LIVING FACT

When Jesus was crucified, He took my place as a sinner. He bore my sins in His body on the tree. He bore my shame that came through my union with Satan. He bore my diseases that Satan had put upon me. He bore my judgment, which was mine because of my union with God's enemy.

When He died, He carried all of this off into the land of forgetfulness and He rose because He had put it all away. He not only put away my sin, my shame, and my diseases, but He put away the old me, the sinner. He put my sin nature away.

He put my infirmities away, along with my sin, sicknesses, and diseases, so now I stand with Him and in Him as free from them as He was free when He rose.

A NEW CREATION

His justification is my justification; His righteousness is my righteousness; His health is my health; His freedom from Satan's dominion is my freedom; His freedom from condemnation is my freedom from condemnation; and His freedom from infirmities is my freedom from infirmities. For in Him, I enjoy all that He did and all that He now is. All that He did, He did for me.

JESUS, MY SUBSTITUTE

Let me state it again: if He bore my sins, I do not need to bear them; if He bore my sin nature, I do not need to bear it; if He bore my infirmities, I do not need to carry them. If I *do* bear any of these, then He died for naught.

So when I accepted Him as my Savior, confessed Him as my Lord, and was baptized into His name, I was baptized into His standing before the Father.

I was baptized into His righteousness that He wrought; I was baptized into His justification; I was baptized into His health for the body, soul, and spirit; I was baptized into the victory that He had won over Satan; and I was baptized into all He means to the Father, for He died representatively for me and now, He reigns up there, representatively for me.

As He is my representative up there now, I am His representative here in the earth. He has put me, mine, and all the sin that was in me away, and He has given me all that was His: all that He did, all that He was, so that as He is now, so am I in this world.

THE STRUGGLE IS OVER

It does not require any faith on my part to enjoy this because He gave it to me. It is mine and what is mine I do not have to have faith to obtain, for I have already obtained it; I am in possession of it. All I need to do is praise Him for it. When I praise Him and thank Him for it, then the thing becomes operative in my life.

So now, I stand before God and the angels—yes, and before Satan—clothed in Christ, hidden in Christ, enwrapped in Christ. Think what it means! His name is the name of the conqueror, and I am baptized into this name and bear this name; I bear the name of the conqueror.

> *For as many of you as have been baptized into Christ have put on Christ.* (Galatians 3:27)

I have put on Christ; Christ tabernacles Himself over me. It is no longer I then who lives but Christ who lives in me. (See Galatians 2:20.)

> *Therefore if any man be in Christ, he is a new creature: old things are passed away; behold, all things are become new.* (2 Corinthians 5:17)

Then, I am a new creature and that new creature is seated with Christ. The old things of weakness, failure, impotence, and unbelief are passed away while the new things of faith, life, and health for body, soul, and spirit are mine. I live in the new realm where the new things are a reality.

> *The life which I now live in the flesh I live by the faith of the Son of God, who loved me, and gave himself for me.* (Galatians 2:20)

I do not have to *take* this position; I am *in* this position.

I do not have to struggle for it, believe for it, or die daily for it, for I am in it—it is mine. It is mine because when I was born again and baptized into the name of the Lord Jesus, I was born into it, I was baptized into it, and I am in it. Hallelujah!

This gives me the undisputed right to the use of His name and all that name stands for in earth, heaven, and hell.

PRAYER BATTLE

If planning to use the name of Jesus in prayer battles, one needs to know the power invested in that name that God esteems above every name. That name stands for us as Jesus stands for us.

When one really prays in that name intelligently, scripturally, and in the will of God, it is as though Christ Himself prayed. There is no force, might, or authority in earth, air, or hell that can prevent its answer: it simply must come to pass.

In your own integrity, in your rights, privileges, and authority, you approach your mountain and you command it in that name, "Up, hurl yourself into the sea." The mountain cannot help it. You cannot help it. All hell cannot help it. It simply must go.

Behind your command lies God's integrity, His omnipotence, and Christ's unlimited power, all at your disposal.

STAND IN THE NAME

The hosts of hell may assault you, but you meet them in the name that once spread consternation through hell, when He put *"to nought him that had the power of death, that is, the devil"* (Hebrews 2:14 ASV).

Satan dares not face the warrior who is clothed in Christ's righteousness and who knows the power of that mighty name.

> *Whosoever shall say unto this mountain, Be thou removed, and be thou cast into the sea; and shall not doubt in his heart, but shall believe that those things which he saith shall come to pass; he shall have whatsoever he saith.* (Mark 11:23)

You think your mountain is large, the sea is a great distance away, and your own faith is small. Well, all of this may be true, but you have confidence in that name even if you have not in your own faith. So, in that great name, command the mountain to go—not in your faith, but in that name. It will go. It must go!

It is not the quantity of faith, but the place where it is centered.

If you ask in that name, you are a victor from this hour; whether it concerns money, health, or souls, you cannot fail. The mighty name that heads up all the power of the universe says so, and it must be so.

GOD'S WILL

An unswerving, unconquerable will knows no defeat. You come to your mountain, you know its power and its greatness; you have compassed it more than seven days; you have faced it perhaps for a long period, but the battle must be fought today.

You know you are in His will. So now you will this mountain to go; your will becomes His will; your command becomes His command.

You say, "In the name of Jesus, I command you to go." That makes Jesus say it…and when He says it, that makes the Father say it.

Standing behind you are the union of the Trinity and the power of the universe. Your will and God's will are allied against the enemy. They are now identical.

Through you, God is able to fight His enemies. Through you, He can act. Through you, He can use His power as He wills to use it.

You hurl that matchless name of His Son against the hosts of hell, and they will fly in confusion.

You walk among men as a man of God. God has put Himself in your hands and says, "Use my will, name, Word, and power," and your mountain becomes a plain.

Your opponents have to fight God. The battle is His. It is His honor now that is assailed. He fights; men tremble and fall to rise no more.

GIRD YOURSELF WITH THE NAME

As the hosts of evil come against you, you gather up your entire moral, mental, and spiritual energy, and in the name of Christ, you throw yourself against them. You are a part of that name as you are a part of God, so your victory must be complete.

You are identified in Christ in all He is, was, or will be.

Your enemy may be stubborn and resist you, but your will is set; you are going to win. You literally charge on the enemy in that all-conquering name.

The enemy may stand for a time, but he must yield; it takes a strong will to hold us quiet in some places, but God can make our wills strong enough to do it.

PERSISTENCE

You know and have set your will to do the will of God. Now push your way up through every obstacle the enemy may place in your way.

Gather up all there is in you and drive your shrinking, halting flesh into the briars. It must go—shout your command and stand to it until you are obeyed.

> *Now the just shall live by faith: but if any man draw back, my soul shall have no pleasure in him.* (Hebrews 10:38)

This Scripture has spurred me over many a rough place and held me true in some awful hours. If you have taken hold of the plow, hold on until the field is finished.

These weak-kneed men and women are a sad army. Look up to that mountain; it is yours!

> *Every place that the sole of your foot shall tread upon, to you have I given it.* (Joshua 1:3 ASV)

This blessed, inspiring promise greeted Israel as they faced the promised land. Footprints meant possession, but it must be their own footprints.

Our Joshua, Jesus, gives us the same incentive for conquest. Every promise in the New Testament that we put our feet upon is ours. The rich plain of healing is yours if you will simply put your foot there.

The upland of spiritual power is yours, though Anak may live there; it is yours if you will but go against him and drive him out of his strongholds in the might of the name.

All the blessed promises of the old Book are yours. Why are you so slack to go up and possess your land?

Between you and your possessions that huge mountain looms up. Gather your forces and in that all-sufficient name, go against it. Don't give up until the last enemy is conquered and is paying tribute to you.

The size of your inheritance depends upon how much land you have trodden under foot, really stood on, or walked over. You can claim as many promises—and hold them as your property—as you have tested and found true. So march up to this mountain and make it yours.

Every lust and passion can be captured and made a soldier of the cross if you persevere with a will that will not be beaten or driven from the field.

Persistence is greater than genius.

Satan knows that you realize that your interests and God's are identified, and that God cannot see you fail without seeing Himself fail. And this He will not allow.

Then with a knowledge of your privileges as a son of God and a will to have them for yourself and others, coupled with a persistent spirit that will not admit defeat, you can cast into the sea any mountain that stands before you.

Go in this thy might. God will get glory and you the victory.

15

MAN'S THREEFOLD NATURE

Man is a threefold being—body, soul, and spirit.

Man's education should cover his whole being. To train only the physical is to make a prize fighter. To train only the mental is to make an intellectual anarchist. To train only the spiritual is to make a fanatic.

But God planned to develop the whole man.

Man's spiritual nature is capable of culture that will enable him to know God and commune intelligently with Him.

It was God's dream that man should be His companion, so his spiritual faculties were originally attuned to the pitch of this dream.

Through the fall, man was alienated from God and his spiritual faculties were greatly impaired. Yet through Christ, this lost fellowship is restored.

The spiritual faculty in man is capable of marvelous development, yet our educational institutions fail to recognize its possibilities.

OUR REALM

The supernatural realm is really the realm of the believer. No one knows how much the mind and spirit can be developed. If the body is kept in fine fettle, there is almost no limitation to man's mental and spiritual development.

We have been slow to come to a realization that man is spirit and that his spirit nature is his basic nature. We have sought to educate him along intellectual lines, utterly ignoring the spiritual, so man is a self-seeking and self-centered being. Thus man has lost his sense of relationship and responsibility toward God and man.

This makes him lawless—an anarchist.

We cannot ignore the spiritual side of man without magnifying the intellectual and physical; to do this without the restraint of the spirit is to unleash sex passions and give them dominance over the whole man.

Man must have fellowship for his spiritual nature. There must be a culture and development of the spiritual nature to the point where it can enjoy fellowship with the Father God.

The heart or spirit of man craves the touch of the supernatural. The love for the miraculous is in man.

The spirit of man cannot be analyzed or classified by the mind; it is above mind, as God is above the physical nature.

Man's intellect is ever conscious of supernatural forces about him that he cannot understand or interpret; perhaps that is the reason why man longs to perform miracles.

THE SOUL CRY FOR MIRACLES

The curiosity for the miraculous is deep-seated in man. Man was brought into being by a miracle-working God and man will ever yearn to work miracles. The supernatural realm is really man's realm.

Sin has blinded us and has kept us from finding the secret door that will lead us back to our lost estate. But the hunger is there, and the miracle is the way to bring man to God.

Is there a miracle element in Christianity today? Did miracles end with the death of the disciples? Are the so-called miracles that men claim to perform today fraudulent or purely psychic?

These are questions that we cannot ignore.

There has come a falling away on the part of the churches. Modernism dominates the great religious forces of Christendom; its denial of the supernatural element in Christianity makes it simply an ethical religion.

On the other hand, we have those who are contending for an original, miraculous element in Christianity, but declaring that miracles ceased with the death of the apostles, that Christianity does not need the miraculous today to convince men of the deity of Jesus.

Then we have a third group who claim miracles are still being performed, that the sick are healed, prayers are answered, and God is a living reality in the daily life of the believer.

We cannot ignore the amazing growth of Christian Science, unity, new thought, and Spiritism. The people who are flocking to them are not the ignorant masses, but the most cultured and wealthy of the land. Their strongest appeal is the supernatural element of their so-called religions; the testimonies of healings by their followers are their strongest asset.

We cannot close our eyes to the fact that in many of our cities on the Pacific Coast, Mary Baker Eddy has a stronger following today and a larger attendance at her churches than have the old line denominations. The largest percentage of her followers have at one time been worshippers in the denominations; they have left them because they believe they are receiving more help from Mrs. Eddy's teaching than from the preachers. They will tell you how they were healed and how they were helped in their spiritual life by this strange cult.

This is a libel upon the modern church—it is not only a libel but a challenge.

WHAT WE NEED

We have lost the supernatural element out of Christianity and we are clinging with trembling hands to a historical Christ that has no power to heal the sick and no ability to meet our daily needs.

The spirit of real evangelism is almost a thing of the past. We have driven the miracle-working Christ out of the church and now we are driving those who believe in miracles out of the church.

We cannot blame the missions and nonconformist cults that are rising everywhere. It is a protest of the people against the modern theological thought that dominates the church.

Christian Science could not have grown to the place where it is dominating many of our large cities unless there had been a demand in the heart of the people for a supernatural religion.

The Pentecostal movement could not have risen with the power that it has had not the heart of the people been craving a new, fresh vision of Christ.

A dead orthodoxy has no resurrection power within it, no miracle-working force behind it.

The people are putting up with extravagances and fanaticism in order that they may get a little touch of the supernatural God. Cultured men and women will listen to uneducated preachers because the uneducated preacher in the dingy mission has faith in a living God.

When men tell us that we do not need miracles today, that education will take their place, they have not thought through on this subject. No man can actually live and walk with the Man of Galilee without living in the realm of the miraculous. Jesus is as much a miracle now as ever. Man needs His miraculous touch now more than ever.

Nothing but a return to this God of miracles will save our land and nation.

IS THIS TRUE?

> *And these signs shall follow them that believe; In my name...they shall lay hands on the sick, and they shall recover.* (Mark 16:17–18)

> *Is any sick among you? let him call for the elders of the church; and let them pray over him, anointing him with oil in the name of the Lord: and the prayer of faith shall save the sick.* (James 5:14–15)

If a preacher has the reputation of acting on these Scriptures, he is disqualified for most of the denominational pulpits. The church is no longer in the grip of God, but under the sway of scholastic intolerance.

Our slogan should be, "Back to the living, miracle-working Christ."

People want Him, so they crowd the building where He is allowed to act. Jesus attracted the multitude by miracles. Jesus will attract them today. "*Jesus Christ the same yesterday, and to day, and for ever*" (Hebrews 13:8).

We have three classes today:

- First, those in whom the physical dominate. These are governed by their passions, appetites, and physical desires.
- Second, those in whom the mind dominates. In this class, we have the great financial, educational, social, and political leaders. A purely intellectual development makes man a dangerous asset to society; it develops his ego, his selfishness, and self-consciousness.
- Third, those in whom the spirit dominates. These are the great spiritual leaders of the church today—men who are seeking to restore man to his original spiritual realm.

THREEFOLD DEVELOPMENT

There must be a threefold education in order to make society sane and safe.

A purely intellectual attainment lacks balance, lacks the governing and discipline that the spiritual only can give.

This explains the crime wave that is sweeping over the land. For two generations, we have been developing the physical and mental at the expense of the spiritual. Where children have no spiritual training in the home or in the school and are not brought in contact with it in the church, they unconsciously develop an abnormal individualism.

This is the basis of anarchy. Every man becomes a law unto himself. The result is the gratification of his desires, the carrying out of his own plans, and the utter ignoring of personal responsibility toward his brother.

All normal men crave the supernatural. The supernatural realm was man's original realm; here, he reigned as king. Sin came and he was dethroned. Yet all through human history, we see man reaching out for the miraculous.

Satan has offered man many substitutes but all have been disappointing.

THE SPIRIT SHOULD RULE

When God created man, He planned that man's spirit should be the dominant reigning force. Sin dethroned the spirit and made the body or mind dominant.

Humanity is divided between those whose minds rule the body and spirit, and those whose bodies rule the mind and spirit. Among the great leaders in the educational, financial, and social world, the mind is dominant. Among another large portion in our land, the physical is dominant.

A generation ago, we taught the boy and girl that they must keep the body under or it would destroy them. Today in our high schools, the physical has gained the ascendancy.

Christianity would restore the spirit to the place of dominance, if it had the opportunity.

Man must have food for his spiritual nature. It must be exercised, developed, and cultured until it gains the ascendancy over the intellectual and physical. When this becomes a reality, man shrinks from lawlessness.

This awakening of man's spiritual nature gives us our moral consciousness; it develops in us a responsibility toward our fellow man.

For a man to be educated mentally is to be one-third educated. To be educated physically and mentally is to be two-thirds educated. But to be educated mentally, physically, and spiritually is a well-rounded education.

THE WHY OF BOLSHEVISM

To leave out the spiritual and magnify the mental makes man an anarchist—an unbalanced, ungoverned, and dangerous force in the world.

Take the supernatural out of Christianity and its flavor is gone; the element that makes it attractive to youth is eliminated. Christianity must have a living God in it—One who rules and demands a certain sacrifice, for religion without self-denial will fail.

Through all the ages, it has been a battle of the supernatural versus the intellectual. The God of miracles is the God of the human. When you eliminate the miraculous, you take away the attractive element of Christianity.

16

FELLOWSHIP AND RELATIONSHIP

God is faithful, by whom ye were called unto the fellowship of his Son Jesus Christ our Lord.
—1 Corinthians 1:9

The entire plan of redemption heads up in this wonderful word, *fellowship*. For what would redemption and a new creation mean if He had no fellowship with His children?

The secrets of the Lord are with those who are in fellowship with Him.

The reason why *believers* are unable to get into the Word and enjoy the fruit and privileges in Christ is because their fellowship is either broken or they have a very low type of fellowship.

The happiness of the home is in the fellowship between the members of that household. The real fruit of life is fellowship.

There would never be a divorce if fellowship had not been broken by the husband and wife. When they are in fellowship, they desire children. When they are out of fellowship, they shrink from the very thought of it. When fellowship is broken, they simply live together and endure each other.

The desire for fellowship is the reason for marriage, and the joy of fellowship is the fruitage of marriage.

When one is born again and becomes a new creation, the highest joy that the spirit has ever known comes from his fellowship with the Father, with Jesus, and with the Word.

The thing that breaks fellowship in the home is the thoughtless act and unkind word or look. It wounds the heart; it bruises the spiritual nature.

Fellowship is not a mental thing; it is spiritual. The mind comes into harmony with the spirit and enriches the fellowship.

When fellowship is broken with the Lord, the Bible becomes a closed Book that only condemns and hurts. That is the reason why people who are out of fellowship have no appetite for the Word. They have no desire for prayer. They cannot use the name of Jesus with any degree of felicity or joy. Their spirit nature is benumbed just like a paralyzed hand.

The Spirit says:

> *That which we have seen and heard declare we unto you, that ye also may have fellowship with us: and truly our fellowship is with the Father, and with his Son Jesus Christ. And these things write we unto you, that your joy may be full.* (1 John 1:3–4)

Do you understand the difference between *happiness* and *joy*? Happiness comes from right association. Joy comes from fellowship with the Father through the Word.

It is a strange, sweet experience, having prayer answered, knowing that in the name of Jesus, you can cast out demons and can set men free. You can bring joy to the heart of the Father and joy to your own heart.

> *If we say that we have fellowship with him, and walk in darkness, we lie, and do not the truth: but if we walk in the light, as he is in the light, we have fellowship one with another, and the blood of Jesus Christ his Son cleanseth us from all sin.* (1 John 1:6–7)

Our fellowship is threefold: with the Father, with the Word, and with one another—and, I might add, with our own selves. When your fellowship is broken, you know that you have lost something and you quarrel with your own mind and accuse yourself of having done something to break your fellowship and forfeit your joy.

If we are so unwise to say that we have not sinned or done anything to break our fellowship, we are telling an untruth for the Father never withdraws His fellowship from anyone who is walking in the light.

> *He that saith he is in the light, and hateth his brother, is in darkness even until now. He that loveth his brother abideth in the light, and there is none occasion of stumbling in him. But he that hateth his brother is in darkness, and walketh in darkness, and knoweth not whither he goeth, because that darkness hath blinded his eyes.* (1 John 2:9–11)

> *If we confess our sins, he is faithful and just to forgive us our sins, and to cleanse us from all unrighteousness.* (1 John 1:9)

> *These things write I unto you, that ye sin not. And if any man sin, we have an advocate with the Father, Jesus Christ the righteous.*
> (1 John 2:1)

The moment that you break fellowship, you should say, "Father, in Jesus's name, forgive." And your Advocate or lawyer, seated at the right hand of the Father, takes up your case and restores your broken fellowship.

It is not safe to be out of fellowship for a moment, for when you are out of fellowship, you are in Satan's fellowship, without protection. You see that you are in the darkness and you cannot make wise decisions, you cannot get the Lord's will. You will never be led into false teaching as long as you are in fellowship with Him.

When you break your fellowship, it does not mean that you have broken your relationship; you are still His son. He alone can break your relationship. You alone can break your fellowship.

It is of vital importance that you know this lesson and walk in the light of it, for you never know when you will need the ability to approach the Father without fear for yourself or for some loved one, so walk in the light as He is in the light.

No one can use Jesus's name while out of fellowship, so it is vitally important that one keep in the fullest fellowship every moment.

17

OUR SPIRITUAL INITIATIVE IN PRAYER

The hindrance to our spiritual initiative in prayer comes from the neglect of reading and feeding on the Word. It is evidence of a low type of spiritual fellowship.

When we lose our spiritual initiative, we lose something that would drive us through to victory in hard places. It is time then that we should give ourselves to the study of the Word. It is the personal study of the Word that counts.

Whenever your faith loses its aggressiveness, the senses have gained the ascendancy.

Whenever spiritual things take second place, it is evidence that the realities of the divine things are losing out, that sense knowledge is slowly but surely gaining the mastery. It dominates at the crossroads where it is necessary that we have keen spiritual discernment. We cannot take a negative attitude toward the Word.

We assent to the Word instead of acting upon it. That holy fearlessness is lost. The heart will not be saying, "I can do all things in Him today."

When the spiritual initiative is low, you will never hear one say, "Greater is He that is in me than the forces that surround me."

When the great things of Scripture are held as doctrines rather than a reality, the opinions of men are put above the Word of God. Out of this will grow an inferiority complex in the spiritual realm.

Whenever your heart loses its boldness towards the Lord and its fearlessness in acting on the Word, you are in danger. The prayer life has lost its reality and things of the senses have taken its place.

You see that is a real spiritual disease. Now the body becomes helpless. The mind—where disease and fear grow and mature—is under the dominion of an outside power. You are in a dangerous condition.

The cure is going to the Word again and giving yourself over to it, resolutely taking your place. Refuse to give up your confession.

YOUR RESPONSIBILITY

We have seen the marvelous possibilities that belong to the believer who knows the authority and power that is invested in the name of Jesus. This knowledge carries with it a responsibility that cannot be ignored. You can never be the same kind of a Christian that you have been in the past.

You have caught a glimpse of what you might do if you dared to use the authority that is now your own because the moment that you are recreated, that name became yours. It gives you an opportunity to help those about you.

Most of us have been brought up to court our weaknesses and failings and to think of our lack of ability. But there are sick and needy ones who could be helped through the wonderful name of Jesus. There are those bound by habits and ruled by Satan with a merciless hand who could be set free if you would take your place.

I want you to notice the distinction between these two Scriptures:

> *Whatsoever ye shall ask in my name, that will I do, that the Father may be glorified in the Son. If ye shall ask any thing in my name, I will do it.*
> (John 14:13–14)

> *Whatsoever ye shall ask the Father in my name, he will give it you.*
> (John 16:23)

With this go these verses from the last chapter of Mark:

> *He that believeth and is baptized shall be saved; but he that disbelieveth shall be condemned. And these signs shall accompany them that believe: in my name shall they cast out demons; they shall speak with new tongues; they shall take up serpents, and if they drink any deadly thing, it shall in no wise hurt them; they shall lay hands on the sick, and they shall recover....And they went forth, and preached everywhere, the Lord*

working with them, and confirming the word by the signs that followed.
(Mark 16:16–18, 20 ASV)

Notice carefully that this Scripture differs from this one in which Jesus says, *"And in that day ye shall ask me nothing. Verily, verily, I say unto you, Whatsoever ye shall ask the Father in my name, he will give it you....Ask, and ye shall receive, that your joy may be full"* (John 16:23–24). Here, you are praying to the Father in Jesus's name. In your praises and petitions, you come to the Father in Jesus's name.

In the other Scripture, you are not praying, but you are using the authority of the name to heal the sick, cast out demons, and set men and women free.

Acts 3:1–10 illustrates this. Peter did not pray when he said to the lame man, *"In the name of Jesus Christ of Nazareth rise up and walk"* (verse 6).

There is no record of their praying for the sick in the book of Acts. They simply laid hands on them and commanded the adversary to leave and for the sick to arise and walk.

From Mark 16, you can see that the moment a man is born again, he is expected to begin to use Jesus's name. You lay your hands on the sick and say, "Disease, leave this body."

Another staggering fact was that the name was used largely in healing men and women who were not Christians. It evidently was God's method of advertising the ministry. So you can lay hands on the unsaved.

When you realize that this authority has been given to the individual members of the body of Christ and not to the ministry alone, it puts the responsibility squarely upon every believer. You are not only a member of the body, but you have become a responsible member of that body.

Another significant fact is that the words *faith* and *believe* do not occur in these Scriptures from the Gospel of John. It is evident that the believer had a legal right to the use of the name and it was not a problem of faith, but obedience to use the ability that God had given.

LAST WORDS

You have read this remarkable book. Many think it one of the most outstanding messages that has been given to the church in the last fifty years. What is your responsibility after having read it? Should you not help us to give this message to the men and women who need it so desperately?

This book has changed the prayer life and the thinking of hundreds of thousands of people. The first ten thousand copies are said to have changed the prayer life of the whole Pacific Coast wherever this truth has gone.

The book has been translated into Chinese and has had a mighty ministry there.

Would it not be possible for you to invite some of your friends into your home and start a Bible class, going through this book and reading it carefully with your Bible in your hands? You should also read it along with my other books, which will fit you to teach the Word in such a way that you may become a blessing to the world.

If one understands what is written in this book, he need never live a life of defeat.

JESUS THE HEALER

CONTENTS

FIRST WORDS

This little book with its mighty message comes from the very heart of the Master to you. If you have been defeated in life's fight, if you have failed to get into the program of success, this little book will show you how to win.

If you are sick, there is healing for you.

If you are weak, it will give you strength.

If you are discouraged, it will put the spirit of a conqueror into you.

Be honest with it. Don't read it with your mind full of preconceived notions.

Go to it fairly, honestly, and let it put you over the mountain that stands between you and victory.

1

THE TWO KINDS OF KNOWLEDGE

One of the recent discoveries in our spiritual laboratory has been that there are two kinds of knowledge.

The knowledge that our schools, colleges, and universities teach has come to us through the five senses.

It is safe to say that there is no knowledge of chemistry, biology, metallurgy, or mechanics, or any other field of research, but that which has come to us through the five senses—seeing, tasting, hearing, smelling, and feeling.

Our bodies have really been the laboratory in which the research work has steadily gone on through the ages.

That knowledge is limited. It cannot find the human spirit.

It cannot discover how the mind functions in the physical brain.

It cannot find God, nor discover the origin of matter, of life, of force, or of creation.

All that it can discover are things it can see, hear, taste, smell, or feel.

We call it "sense knowledge."

Then there is another kind of knowledge that has come to us through the revelation called the Bible.

This is revelation knowledge.

It brings us in contact with the Creator.

It explains the "why" of creation, the reason for man, the nature of man, and the ultimate goal of man.

It deals with things that the senses cannot discover or know without assistance from this revelation knowledge.

The unhappy fact is that sense knowledge has gained the supremacy in the church.

The church is a spiritual organization, a spiritual body, to be governed through the spirit instead of through the senses.

When sense knowledge gained the ascendancy in the church and the fountain of the church, the theological school, the church ceased to be a spiritual body and simply became a body of men governed by sense knowledge.

You can see why sense knowledge, which cannot understand spiritual things, will deny miracles, will deny answers to prayer, and will deny the deity of Jesus, discrediting His resurrection and miracles.

It is to be expected that sense knowledge will deny the miraculous because it cannot explain it or understand it.

The chief quest of sense knowledge has been for reality. Man's spirit craves it.

Reality cannot be found by the senses. It is only discovered by the spirit.

Sense knowledge has sent forth men called philosophers, searchers after reality.

It is a profound fact, worthy of every man's consideration, that the man who really knows Jesus Christ, who has received eternal life, never turns to philosophy.

If he has been a philosopher, he gives it up because he has arrived at reality in Christ.

Jesus said, "I am the way, the reality, and the life." (See John 14:6.) Jesus, then, is the answer to all true philosophy.

2

GOD IS A FAITH GOD

I never knew the "why" of faith until I read Hebrews 11:3: "*Through faith we understand that the worlds were framed* [or created] *by the word of God, so that things which are seen were not made of things which do appear.*" In a flash, I grasped the secret of Genesis 1:1: "*In the beginning God created.*"

How did He create? By the Word of faith.

He said, "*Let there be.*" He created with words.

Jesus knew the secret of words. He healed the sick with words. He raised the dead with words. He stilled the sea with, "*Peace, be still*" (Mark 4:39).

Peter healed the sick by using the name of Jesus. Paul cast out demons by saying, "In the name of Jesus Christ, come out." (See Acts 16:18.)

They used words that were born of faith. They were faith's words. We become the sons of God, partakers of His very nature, by acting on words.

We become faith men and women, we use faith words, and we produce faith results.

"FAITH IN MY FAITH"

The first time those words came to me, they startled me. I began to examine myself and ask the question, "Why is it that people haven't faith in their own faith?" They have faith in *my* faith.

I receive letters from many far-away countries asking for prayer.

Why? Because the people who ask for prayer haven't confidence in their own faith.

For some reason they do not believe in themselves. They do not believe in what Christ has wrought for them, or what they are in Christ.

The reason for their unbelief is that they do not know what they are in Christ. They have a feeling that they are not good enough, that their faith is not strong enough.

They are acquainted with all of their own failings and weaknesses. They accept every condemnation from the pulpit. They are willing always to believe anything against themselves, their unworthiness, their unfitness, their weakness, their lack of faith.

SOME FACTS

The Father has no favorites. Every person born into His family has the same redemption.

He has been redeemed out of the hand of his enemy. Satan was conquered for him personally.

He can say, "He was delivered up on the account of my trespasses and He was raised for my justification."

He can confidently say, "Who delivered me out of the authority of darkness, and translated me into the kingdom of the Son of His love. In whom I have my redemption, the remission of my trespasses."

It is a personal, an absolute redemption from the dominion of the adversary.

CHRIST WAS YOUR SUBSTITUTE

When Jesus put Satan to naught and stripped him of his authority, it was you, in Christ, who did that work. Christ acted in your stead; He did it for you.

You can say, "In Christ, I conquered Satan. I stripped him of his authority, and when Jesus arose from the dead, I arose with Him." You can confidently say, "But God being rich in mercy with His great love wherewith He loved me, even when I was dead through my trespasses and sins, made me alive together with Christ (by grace have I been saved, or healed) and raised me up with Him, and made me to sit with Him in the heavenlies in Christ."

It is when you take your place and begin to assume your rights and privileges that God begins to respond to you.

You have the same eternal life that Jesus had.

"He that hath the Son hath the life" (1 John 5:12). You have the Son; you have the life.

Now you may say, "I have taken Jesus Christ as my Savior. I have confessed Him as my Lord. God has given to me eternal life, His own nature. I am now a new creation, created in Christ Jesus, and I have God's ability to perform the good works that were afore prepared that I should walk in them.

"I have God's ability because I have God's nature. I have the same great, mighty Spirit who raised Jesus from the dead dwelling in me.

"Greater is he that is in me, than he that is in the world." (See 1 John 4:4.)

YOU ARE HIS RIGHTEOUSNESS

You have the same righteousness as Jesus. "Him who knew no sin, God made to be sin on your behalf, that you might become the righteousness of God in Him." (See 2 Corinthians 5:21.)

You can say, "I have become the righteousness of God in Him. There is therefore now no condemnation to me, because I am in Christ Jesus."

That righteousness gives you the privilege of standing in the Father's presence as though you had never committed sin.

You have His nature. You are His very own child. He is your Father.

You can say, "He has declared me righteous. He has made me righteous. I am the righteousness of God in Christ."

As a son, you have the legal right to use the name of Jesus.

No one has a better right to the use of the name of Jesus than you.

ALL AUTHORITY IS IN THAT NAME

Now you say with me, "Jesus declares that whatever I ask in His name, He will give it to me; fearlessly I take my place. I lay my hands upon that loved one who is sick and say, 'In the name of Jesus, disease, leave this body; demon, leave this body and go off into the abyss where you belong. Don't you ever touch this loved one again.'

"Christ said to me that they who believe should lay hands on the sick, and they should recover. 'In my name they shall cast out demons.' He said this to me. I accept it at its face value and I act upon it because He said it to me."

3

THE FATHER HAS NO FAVORITES

It was a great comfort to my heart when I realized that the Father has no favorites, that all the children have their own place in His heart.

He loves each one of them even as He loves the Lord Jesus.

Jesus said, "*That the world may know that thou … hast loved them, as thou hast loved me*" (John 17:23).

We all have the same redemption.

The work that He wrought in Christ absolutely destroyed the power of the enemy and now redeems every person who will accept Christ as Savior and confess Him as Lord.

That redemption is from the works of the adversary and from his dominion over our lives.

Everyone has the same righteousness. No one has a better righteousness or more righteousness.

Righteousness comes through the new creation. When we are born again, we receive the life and nature of God, the Father.

His nature makes us righteous. No one has more of it than another.

All who receive His nature have come into the family and are recognized as the sons and daughters of the great Father God.

Everyone has the same rights in the family.

Each one may have a different gift, but the gift does not make him any dearer to the heart of the Father.

Everyone has the same love nature, the same great Holy Spirit who raised Jesus from the dead.

Each one has a right to the same kind of fellowship with the Father.

Each one has a right to the use of the name of Jesus.

Each one has a right to the authority invested in that name to deliver people from the dominion of Satan, to heal the sick, and to cast out demons.

The Father has no favorites.

The closer your fellowship is with the Father, the sweeter and richer your life will be.

4

THE LIVING WORD

The problem of healing is a problem of the integrity of the Word. Many have never recognized it, but the Word is the healer today.

God, in Christ, wrought a perfect redemption. In that redemption, there is perfect healing for every believer, but because of lack of knowledge of the Word, Christians everywhere are sick.

Psalm 107:20 (JPS) perfectly illustrates this: "*He sent His word, and healed them.*"

> *In the beginning was the Word, and the Word was with God, and the Word was God.* (John 1:1)

A few verses later, we read, "*And the Word was made flesh, and dwelt among us, (and we beheld his glory, the glory as of the only begotten of the Father,) full of grace and truth*" (John 1:14).

That is the Word He sent. He had sent His spoken Word through the prophets. The living Word was made flesh.

Now He unveils the life-giving Word in the Gospels and the Epistles.

> *The words that I speak unto you, they are spirit, and they are life.* (John 6:63)

> *For the Logos of God is a living thing, active and more cutting than any sword with double edge, penetrating to the very division of soul and spirit, joints and marrow — scrutinizing the very thoughts and conceptions of the heart.* (Hebrews 4:12 MOFF)

The Word becomes a living thing only as we act upon it.

The Word is God speaking. It is always a present-tense fact. You might say that the Word is always now, just as God is always now. The Word is a part of God Himself. God and His Word are one, just as you and your word are one.

The Word is the will of the Father, just as Jesus, the Word made flesh, was the will of the Father during His earthly ministry.

What God says, is; what God says, will become. Had He not wanted it to be, He would not have said it.

You can depend upon His Word utterly. You have depended upon institutions and men.

Institutions may fail, individuals may die, nations may disintegrate, but God cannot deny Himself.

Behind the Word is the integrity of God. Not only is His integrity behind the Word, but His very throne is involved in His Word.

Hebrews 7:22 (ASV) declares that Jesus is the surety of the new covenant: *"By so much also hath Jesus become the surety of a better covenant."*

He is behind every word from Matthew to Revelation. Every word was God-breathed.

The throne upon which Jesus is seated is behind every Word.

FAITH, HOPE, AND MENTAL ASSENT

There must be a clear distinction in your mind between believing and mental assent.

Believing the Word is acting on the Word.

Mental assent is acknowledging the truthfulness of the Word and the integrity of the Word but never acting upon it.

Mental assent is standing outside the bakery and coveting the cake in the window. It is not possessing.

Hope is not faith. It is not believing. Hope is always living in the future.

Faith is always now. It is not passivity. Passivity lies quietly without action, without choice, inert.

Believing is acting on the Word.

Believing the Word is not only recognizing its utter truthfulness, but it is taking it to be your very own now.

To act on His Word is to do His will and to act in His will. He is honored by our acting on the Word.

He is dishonored by our mentally assenting to its truthfulness, by our hoping that it will become true sometime, and by our passivity that lies quietly rejoicing in the Word but has no part in it.

"He that believeth hath" (John 6:47 ASV). If you believe, you have!

His name is glorified by our acting on the Word. The Father is glorified by our acting on the Word.

Remember that His throne is behind His Word. His integrity is involved in it.

> *If ye abide in me, and my words abide in you, ye shall ask what ye will, and it shall be done unto you. Herein is my Father glorified, that ye bear much fruit; so shall ye be my disciples.* (John 15:7–8)

That is the fruit of the indwelling Word, which has prompted prayers that are answered.

THE CASE STATED

There are two views of healing.

The most common view is that healing is not in the redemptive work of Christ but belongs to us if we have faith enough to claim it.

This belief holds that faith is the gift of God. If God gives you faith for your healing, you will be healed. If He does not give you faith, there is no need to struggle for your healing. Your only hope is the arm of flesh.

This view is superficial. It is the result of sense knowledge.

Sense knowledge is the knowledge of natural man that is gained through the senses. It is the kind of knowledge taught in all our technical schools and universities.

The other kind of knowledge is revelation knowledge. It teaches that miracles are for today.

Sense knowledge repudiates it in a very large measure because it is above the knowledge of the senses.

The second view of healing is that it is a part of the plan of redemption, that disease came with the fall, and that sickness is a work of the adversary.

Because disease came with the fall, God is the natural, logical Healer.

Man cannot deal with the sin problem. He cannot make himself righteous. He cannot rid himself of sin-consciousness.

These can only come through the finished work of Christ. God planned that when we were recreated—the recreation that comes through our receiving the nature and life of God—we would be righteous and partake of His righteousness, which is His very nature. This would give us the position of sons.

The new creation is more than being baptized or confirmed. It is receiving the life and nature of the Father. Our spirits are recreated by receiving eternal life.

Isaiah 53 holds the key of redemption. Jesus was made sin with our sins. Not only was He made sin with our sins, but He was made sick with our sicknesses.

Natural man is called sin.

> *Be not unequally yoked with unbelievers: for what fellowship have righteousness and iniquity? or what communion hath light with darkness?*
>
> (2 Corinthians 6:14 ASV)

The believer is called righteousness; the unbeliever is called iniquity.

He has not only committed sin, but he is sin.

The believer is called light and the unbeliever is called darkness.

Just as the sinner is "sin," the sick man is not only sick, but he is "sickness." Sin deals with the spirit; sickness is a spiritual thing revealed in the body.

"And what concord hath Christ with Belial?" (2 Corinthians 6:15). The believer is called Christ, because Christ is a part of the body. The branch is a part of the vine. It is as much a part of the vine as the vine itself.

> *For as the body is one, and hath many members, and all the members of that one body, being many, are one body: so also is Christ.*
>
> (1 Corinthians 12:12)

The man outside of Christ is called Belial. That perfectly agrees with 1 John 3:10: *"In this the children of God are manifest, and the children of the devil."*

When God laid our sin on Jesus, He laid us on Jesus. He laid the whole man on Jesus. He laid his sins, his weaknesses, his infirmities and diseases, his union with the adversary, on Jesus. Jesus became sin with our sin, became sick with our sickness.

"Yet it pleased the Lord *to bruise him; he hath put him to grief"* (Isaiah 53:10). Another translation reads, *"Jehovah hath delighted to bruise him, He hath made Him sick"* (YLT).

> *All we like sheep have gone astray; we have turned every one to his own way; and the* Lord *hath laid on him the iniquity of us all.* (Isaiah 53:6)

AFFLICTED IN SPIRIT

Jesus was made sick with our sicknesses. He was made sin with our sin. This was God's method of dealing with the sin problem.

He settled the sin problem.

There is no sin problem. Christ put sin away and satisfied the claims of justice for man.

The real problem is the "sinner problem."

There is no sickness problem. There is simply a problem of the believer's coming to know his inheritance in Christ.

When John the Baptist said, in John 1:29, *"Behold the Lamb of God, which taketh away the sin of the world,"* he was giving public notice that this Man whom he had baptized was the Sin-Substitute, the Sickness-Substitute for the human race.

Sin and sickness come from the same source.

Satan is the author of both. I am sure that it is God's order that the believer should be as free from sickness as he is from sin. He should be as free from the fear of disease as he is from the condemnation of sin.

God cannot see sin in the new creation. Neither can He see sickness in the new creation.

James 5:14 asks, *"Is any sick among you?"*

There should not be any sick among you, but if there is anyone sick, this tells what he should do.

It was the plan of the Father that every believer should know what Peter tells us in 1 Peter 2:24: Christ *"who his own self bare our sins in his own body on the tree, that we, being dead to sins, should live unto righteousness: by whose stripes ye were healed."*

He wants us to know that when He laid our sins and sicknesses on Jesus and Jesus bore them away, it was to the end that sin and disease should no longer have dominion over us.

He wants us to know, in the second place, that sickness and disease do not belong in the family of God.

If there should be any sickness among us, it is because of a low state of knowledge of our rights and privileges in our redemption. It is due to a lack of knowledge of the fact that God, by laying our diseases on Christ, has settled the disease problem in redemption.

We should be as free from the fear of sickness as we are free from the condemnation of sin. Both are of the adversary.

At the new birth, sins are all remitted. The sin nature is displaced by the nature of God.

Disease leaves with the sins.

So the Father can see no sickness in the new creation. He put it all on Christ.

When we recognize the fact that our sickness was laid on Christ, and that He bore our diseases in His body on the tree, and that by His stripes we are healed, it will be the end of the dominion of disease in our lives.

But this knowledge is of no value until your heart says, "Surely He bore my diseases and my pains, and by His stripes, I am healed" just as though you were the only sick person in the world.

The Word is like God—eternal. It cannot be destroyed. He watches over it to make it good.

His Word brought man into being. Now He is building Himself into man through the Word.

The Word is part of Himself, and it is this Self that is changing the conduct of believers and bringing them into harmony with Himself

He shares Himself with us; He gives us His nature in the new creation. He makes Himself one with us.

We are united with Him in the new birth.

We are to take advantage of this union. His nature gives us new ability, new wisdom, and we must take advantage of it.

His strength is ours. His life is ours. His health is ours; His ability is ours. Disease is Satan's work. When you tell anyone of it, you glorify him. You ignore the fact that God laid that disease upon Jesus and He put it away.

The Word says that you are healed. Get used to acting on the Word.

5

THE VALUE OF CONFESSION

It is necessary that there be a continual confession of our redemption from Satan's dominion and that he no longer rules us with condemnation nor fear of disease.

We hold fast to this confession, as our confession is Satan's defeat.

We believers do not ask to be healed, because we *have* been healed. We do not ask to be made righteous, because we *have* been made righteous.

We do not ask to be redeemed, for our redemption is an absolute fact.

In the mind of the Father, we are perfectly healed and perfectly free from sin, because He laid our diseases and our sins upon His Son.

His Son was made sin with our sins. He was made sick with our diseases.

In the mind of Christ, we are perfectly healed because He can remember when He was made sin with our sins, when He was made sick with our diseases. He remembers when He put our sin and our diseases away.

In the mind of the Holy Spirit, we are absolutely free from both, for He remembers when Christ was made sin and when He was made sick. He remembers when He raised Jesus from the dead.

Christ was free from our sin and our sickness. Both had been put away before His resurrection.

The Word declares, "By His stripes we were healed." (See Isaiah 53:5; 1 Peter 2:24.)

The whole problem is our recognition of the absolute truthfulness of that Word.

It is not good taste to ask Him to heal us, for He has already done it.

This truth came with a shock when I first saw it. He declared that we are healed; therefore we are.

The only problem now is to get in perfect harmony with His Word.

If He declares we are healed, then our part is to thank Him for the work He has already accomplished.

RENEWING OF THE MIND

I feel I should introduce another subject for a moment. That is the renewing of our minds. It is only the renewed mind that can grasp these truths.

Your spirit has been recreated, but not your mind. Heretofore, it has received all of its knowledge through the senses, so it must be renewed.

> *And be not conformed to this world: but be ye transformed by the renewing of your mind, that ye may prove what is that good, and acceptable, and perfect, will of God.* (Romans 12:2)

The same truth is brought out in these verses:

> *Not by works of righteousness which we have done, but according to his mercy he saved us, by the washing of regeneration, and renewing of the Holy Ghost.* (Titus 3:5)

> *And be renewed in the spirit of your mind; and that ye put on the new man, which after God is created in righteousness and true holiness.* (Ephesians 4:23–24)

> *And have put on the new man, which is renewed in knowledge after the image of him that created him.* (Colossians 3:10)

This renewing of the mind comes through meditation and action on the Word.

As soon as one is born again, he should ask the Holy Spirit to come in and make His home in his body.

Luke 11:13 shows the Father's attitude in regard to this: "*How much more shall your heavenly Father give the Holy Spirit to them that ask him?*"

As surely as we ask Him, so surely will the Spirit make His home in our bodies.

The renewed mind sees that all there is to be done for its healing is to praise the Father for it. It says, "My diseases were laid on Christ and He put them away. I am healed. I thank the Father that it is done."

The pain may be there. The soreness may be in evidence. These are only the testimony of the senses.

We refuse to listen to the witness of our senses. We accept the Word of God and act upon it. As surely as God sits on the throne, He will make that Word good in us.

We do not ask for power, for He who is the power is in us.

We do not ask for wisdom, for Christ was made wisdom unto us. We do not ask for redemption, for He is our redemption.

We do not ask for sanctification, for He is made unto us sanctification.

We do not ask for righteousness, because He is made unto us righteousness.

This faith life is the most beautiful thing in the world. We step out of the old sense realm where we have lived.

We have always lived with Thomas. He said, in John 20:25, *"Except I shall see in his hands the print of the nails, and put my finger into the print of the nails, and thrust my hand into his side, I will not believe."*

Jesus met him and said, *"Reach hither thy finger, and behold my hands; and reach hither thy hand, and thrust it into my side: and be not faithless, but believing"* (verse 27).

Then Thomas cried, *"My Lord and my God."*

But Jesus said to him, *"Because thou hast seen me, thou hast believed: blessed are they that have not seen, and yet have believed"* (John 20:29). We should not need the evidence of the senses. Let us rest on the Word.

> *Blessed be the God and Father of our Lord Jesus Christ, who hath blessed us with all spiritual blessings in heavenly places in Christ.*
>
> (Ephesians 1:3)

You are in the family. Everything that the Father has belongs to the children. You are one of them. You have been blessed.

HEALING FOR THE WORLD

God meets man where he is.

Most of the healings that were performed by the apostles and the early church were among men and women who had not yet become Christians. They were heathens or they were Jews.

Healing was God's method of advertising, God's method of revealing Himself to the natural mind.

Jesus was an intrusion into the sense realm. The church, the new creation, was an invasion into the sense realm.

But today, the sense knowledge men have invaded the church and taken it captive.

The sense realm is the realm of the natural man, that is, the man who believes only what he can hear, taste, smell, feel, or see.

God's intrusion into that realm in the person of His Son as head of the church was a miraculous invasion.

Mark 16:16–17 (ASV) gives us evidence for this: *"He that believeth and is baptized shall be saved; but he that disbelieveth shall be condemned. And these signs shall accompany them that believe."*

Confession imprisons us or sets us free.

A strong confession coupled with a corresponding action on the Word brings God on the scene.

Holding fast to one's confession when the senses contradict shows that one has become established in the Word.

A Satan-inspired confession is always dangerous. Remember that he brought that disease and put it upon you.

Your acknowledgement of the disease is like signing for a package that the express company has left you. Satan then has the receipt for your disease. You have accepted it.

> *That the word spoken by the prophet Isaiah might be fulfilled, he took away our sicknesses and he removed our diseases.* (Matthew 8:17 MOFF)

This is God's receipt for our perfect healing.

A positive confession dominates circumstances, while a vacillating confession permits circumstances to govern one.

Your confession is what God says about your disease. A negative confession will make the disease stronger. Then your confession heals or keeps you sick.

The confession of your lips should have your heart's full agreement.

6

"THESE SIGNS"

As soon as a man believed, these signs were to accompany him: *"In my name shall they cast out demons; they shall speak with new tongues; they shall take up serpents, and if they drink any deadly thing, it shall in no wise hurt them; they shall lay hands on the sick, and they shall recover"* (Mark 16:17–18 ASV). The word "believer" means "a believing one."

As soon as a man was born again, God planned that he should advertise the new creation by healing sick folk in the presence of the unsaved world.

Jesus's entire ministry was a combat with the demonical forces.

The same thing is true of the church. All disease, all sickness, all pain, all trouble, all sin, is a result of the Satanic hatred of the human race.

"In my name shall they cast out demons." They were to take Jesus's place. They were going out into the world and acting for Him.

First John 3:8 tells us that Jesus came to destroy the works of the devil. We are to act for Him today.

In John 14:12–14, Jesus says, *"Greater works than these shall* [ye] *do; because I go unto my Father. And whatsoever ye shall ask in my name, that will I do, that the Father may be glorified in the Son. If ye shall ask any thing in my name, I will do it."*

He is not talking about prayer. He is talking about casting out demons, about healing the sick, and miracles.

"Whatsoever ye shall ask in my name...." That word *ask* means *demand.* You are demanding as Peter did at the beautiful gate that morning when he said to the lame man, *"In the name of Jesus Christ of Nazareth rise up and walk"* (Acts 3:6).

The man was instantly healed. He was not a Christian. He had not accepted Christ. It is likely that the great multitudes who were healed, recorded in Acts 5, were made up of unsaved people.

The majority of the healings in the book of Acts were healings of sick people who had not yet become believers.

Read carefully Acts 5:12–16. Practically all these people were unsaved Jews.

In Acts 8:8–10, the power of God is again unveiled. All of these miracles performed in Jesus's name were upon the unsaved world. The church has missed its greatest method of advertising. God's method of advertising was through miracles.

Divine healing has a large ministry with the unsaved today.

Christ was a miracle.

Christianity is Christ living in men today.

The incarnation and the new birth are both of God. Both are miracles.

Answered prayer is a miracle. When prayer does not produce miracles, it is but empty words.

A miracle is God moving into the sense realm.

Don't condemn yourself for your doubts. Cure them by getting acquainted with your Father.

Confession always goes ahead of healing.

Don't watch symptoms; watch the Word and be sure that your confession is bold and vigorous.

Don't listen to people. Act on the Word. Be a doer of the Word.

It is God speaking.

You are healed. The Word says you are.

Don't listen to the senses. Give the Word its place. God cannot lie.

7

GOD'S METHOD OF HEALING BABES IN CHRIST

Is any among you sick? There should be no sick among you because "by His stripes you are healed."

Because there has been no spiritual development or growth, and you are still babes in Christ, you are sick.

HEALING FOR THE CARNALLY MINDED MAN

Carnal means sense-ruled.

The carnally minded man is a Christian who has not yet come to the place where the Word rules him and governs his thinking.

He is called "a babe in Christ," carnally minded, fleshly.

He is ruled by the flesh, by what he sees with his eyes, what he feels, hears, tastes, and smells.

He is a body-ruled, sense-governed child of God. He is a babe in Christ.

First Corinthians 3:1: *"And I, brethren, could not speak unto you as unto spiritual"*—that is, men whose spirits have gained the ascendancy over their thinking. Their spirit is recreated, but the unrenewed mind rules their spirit.

Paul was saying, "I cannot speak to you as men whose minds are subordinate to the Word of God." Their minds were not renewed. They were still babes.

> *Of whom we have many things to say, and hard of interpretation, seeing ye are become dull of hearing.* (Hebrews 5:11 ASV)

How many believers fall under this admonition? They cannot understand the Word.

> *For every one that partaketh of milk is without experience of the word of righteousness; for he is a babe.* (Hebrews 5:13 ASV)

This *"word of righteousness"* is very little understood. They have never had an experience in living righteousness.

What do we mean by that?

Righteousness means the ability to stand in the presence of the Father, or of demons, or of sickness and disease, without the sense of inferiority, condemnation, or of sin-consciousness.

Those who live righteousness, or who know by the Word that they are the righteousness of God in Christ, are absolute masters over circumstances, demons, and disease.

> *Him who knew no sin he made to be sin on our behalf; that we might become the righteousness of God in him.* (2 Corinthians 5:21 ASV)

You are having experience in the Word of righteousness. You are finding that it is the Word that heals.

This ministry of the Word of God is the Word of righteousness. It is the Word of righteousness that sets men free, leads them out of Satan's dominion into the liberty and freedom of the sons of God.

How fearless they become. How mightily they speak.

> *But solid food is for fullgrown men, even those who by reason of use have their senses exercised to discern good and evil.* (Hebrews 5:14 ASV)

The believer described above has grown up into a spiritual life in Christ.

He has fed on the Word until the Word has transfigured him.

James 5:14–16 is God's method of healing the carnally minded, or the babes in Christ. God, in great grace, says: *"Is any sick among you? let him call for the elders of the church; and let them pray over him, anointing him with oil in the name of the Lord: and the prayer of faith shall save the sick, and the Lord shall raise him up; and if he have committed sins, they shall be forgiven him. Confess your faults one to another, and pray one for another, that ye may be healed. The effectual fervent prayer of a righteous man availeth much."*

Notice very carefully these facts. He cannot see that his disease was laid on Christ, but he can see the elders, hear their prayers, and feel the anointing oil upon his forehead. He can feel their hands upon his head.

He is living in the realm of the senses. Grace comes down and meets him in this realm.

If he had taken advantage of his privileges, he would have acted on 1 John 1:9: *"If we confess our sins, he is faithful and just to forgive us our sins, and to cleanse us from all unrighteousness."*

This Scripture is to the Christian. Had that believer, that babe in Christ, taken advantage of his rights and privileges, he would have looked up and said, "Father, forgive me for the thing I have done which caused my sickness."

The Father would have forgiven him and healed him then.

But he has to see and feel before he can believe. He belongs to Thomas's class, "When I see, I will believe."

Practically all the faith that men had in Jesus before His death and resurrection was sense knowledge faith.

They believed in things they saw and heard. They could not believe in a resurrection. They had never seen a resurrection.

They had seen Lazarus raised from the dead. He was simply raised, brought back to life again. He was not resurrected; he died again.

Oh, the grace of our Lord Jesus Christ that comes down to our level and meets us where we cannot apparently act on the Word because we are governed by the senses.

8

HEALING IN REDEMPTION

We have seen healing for the world in the name of Jesus. We have seen healing for the carnally minded believer through the elders.

Now let us see healing for the man who enjoys the fullness of his privileges in Christ.

Isaiah 53 is a preview of Jesus's public ministry and His substitutionary sacrifice.

It is a veiled prophecy, but it is revealed now through the Pauline revelation as belonging to us.

LOVE'S GOOD PLEASURE

> *He was despised, and forsaken of men, a man of pains, and acquainted with disease.* (Isaiah 53:3 JPS)

He was a root out of dry ground. But He was precious to the Father, though condemned by the world.

> *As one from whom men hide their face: he was despised, and we esteemed him not. Surely our diseases did he bear, and our pains he carried; whereas we did esteem him stricken, smitten of God, and afflicted.*
> (Isaiah 53:3–4 JPS)

> *As many were astonied at thee; his visage was so marred more than any man, and his form more than the sons of men.* (Isaiah 52:14)

The margin of *The Cross-Reference Bible* reads, "[Men] were dumbfounded at Him, for deformed was His appearance so as not to be a man, and His figure so as not to be human.... So shall many be amazed over Him. His visage was so marred, unlike to a man, and His form unlike to the sons of men. [His visage was] so as not to be a man, and His figure no more resembled man."

He was made sin with our sin. He was under the dominion of Satan.

This is a description of Jesus's spirit, not His body.

He was made sick with our diseases and when those diseases came upon His precious spirit, He no longer resembled a man.

The heart cannot take it in. Reason stands dumb in the presence of statements like these.

He was *"stricken, smitten of God, and afflicted."*

It was God who laid our diseases upon Him. It was justice that demanded a recompense for our offenses.

> *He was wounded for our transgressions, he was bruised for our iniquities: the chastisement of our peace was upon him; and with his stripes we are healed.* (Isaiah 53:5)

SICKNESS IS SPIRITUAL

Now you can see this fact, that sickness was healed spiritually. God did not deal with sickness physically.

Disease today is spiritual. I have found that when I can prove, through the Word, that our diseases were laid on Jesus, and the sick man accepts that fact, he is instantly healed.

As long as we think that disease is purely physical, we will not get our deliverance.

But when we know it is spiritual, and it must be healed by the Word of God—for you remember He said, *"He sent His word, and healed them"* (Psalm 107:20 JPS)—then healing becomes a reality.

"He was wounded for our transgressions." This was spiritual. *"He was bruised for our iniquities."* It was a spiritual bruising.

The wounds that the soldiers made did not take away sin, for if they had, sin would be a physical thing, a sense knowledge thing.

Human justice deals only with sense evidences—not what a man thinks, but what he says or does.

He endured sufferings that the senses cannot understand. They stand mute and helpless in the presence of this great spiritual tragedy that took place on Calvary.

"The chastisement of our peace was upon him; and with his stripes we are healed."

It was not the physical wounds made by the lictor. It was the stripes that justice laid upon His spirit.

> *All we like sheep have gone astray; we have turned every one to his own way; and the LORD hath laid on him the iniquity of us all.* (Isaiah 53:6)

And the tenth verse: *"Yet it pleased the LORD to bruise him; he hath put him to grief."* The Jewish Bible puts it this way: *"Yet it pleased the LORD to crush him by disease"* (Isaiah 53:10 JPS). Love could see humanity redeemed. Faith could see a new creation.

He made Him sick with our sickness. We need not be sick. Only ignorance of our rights, or refusal to act upon the Word, can keep us ill.

He made Him sin with our sin. We need not remain in sin. He became sin that we might become righteous. He went to hell that we might go to heaven.

He was made weak so that we might be made strong. He took our place, met every need, satisfied every claim of justice, and set us free.

If this be the case, sickness on the part of the believer is wrong, just as weakness and every other thing that Satan brought upon man is wrong, because He suffered to put it away.

SOME FACTS ABOUT THE SUPERNATURAL LIFE

In the mind of the Father, we are supermen. We are conquerors; we are overcomers.

> *For whatsoever is born of God overcometh the world: and this is the victory that overcometh the world, even our faith. Who is he that overcometh the world, but he that believeth that Jesus is the Son of God?*
> (1 John 5:4–5)

It was our faith that brought us into the family of conquerors.

We believe that Jesus is the Son of God, that He died for our sins according to Scripture and that He arose again for our justification.

We believe that the moment we take Him to be our Savior and confess Him as our Lord, God takes us to be His children and gives us eternal life.

This places us in the realm of conquerors. We are supermen and superwomen.

BELIEVERS ARE WINNERS

Healing and victory are ours. They are ours without asking. All we need to do is to simply know it and praise Him for it.

> *As we have a great high priest, then, who has passed through the heavens, Jesus the Son of God, let us hold fast to our confession.*
>
> (Hebrews 4:14 MOFF)

Some Bible translations say "profession."

We are to *"hold fast to our confession."* What is our confession? It is that we are new creations, that sin has been put away, and that we are the righteousness of God in Him.

We confess that surely He has borne our sicknesses and carried our diseases.

Our confession is that He was stricken, smitten of God with our infirmities and weaknesses, and now by His stripes we are absolutely healed.

Sin and disease have been put away, and in the name of Jesus, we have dominion over Satan and the work of his hands.

In Jesus's name, we cast out demons. In His name, we lay hands on the sick and they do recover.

If we can cast out demons, we can also command the demon disease to leave our bodies, for disease was brought there by a demon and is being developed by a demon.

We say, "In Jesus's name, demon, leave this body." That demon is under obligation to the name of Jesus to obey.

When Jesus arose from the dead, He arose because we with Him had conquered Satan.

> *Having despoiled the principalities and the powers, he made a show of them openly, triumphing over them in it.* (Colossians 2:15 ASV)

Jesus's triumph is our triumph. Jesus's victory is our victory. He did nothing for Himself. It was all for us. Today we are more than conquerors through Him who loved us.

We should never talk about our diseases. When we tell our troubles to people, it is always to get their sympathy.

That trouble came from the adversary. When we tell our troubles, we are giving our testimony of Satan's ability to get us into difficulty.

When we talk about our diseases, we are glorifying the adversary who had the ability to put that disease upon us.

When we confess our lack of strength or ability, we confess that Satan has so blinded us that we cannot enjoy our rights and privileges.

> *The LORD is my light and my salvation; whom shall I fear? the LORD is the strength of my life; of whom shall I be afraid?* (Psalm 27:1)

God has made Him to be wisdom unto us. He has made Him to be redemption unto us.

If this is true, then Satan has no right to reign over us with sickness, disease, weakness, or failure.

Every time we talk of our troubles, we glorify the being who put the troubles upon us.

Our confession should be that God is today our strength, our wisdom, our complete and perfect redemption, our sanctification, and our righteousness.

We are the righteousness of God in Him. We can do all things in Him who strengthens us.

Today the name of Jesus on our lips can conquer disease and sickness. That name can bring courage and victory to the defeated and whipped.

A prayer of unbelief never gives faith.

When you pray for faith, you confess your unbelief.

This increases your doubts, for the prayer is never heard. The doubter often prays for things already his own.

God has blessed him with every spiritual blessing that governs every spiritual need.

Redemption has never been seen as a reality. It is a theory, a creed, a doctrine.

Few expect experimental evidence of it.

Satan has taken advantage of our ignorance of redemption and put disease upon us, holding us in bondage.

The defeated one holds his master in bondage. The believer is Satan's master.

9

METHODS OF HEALING

There are five ways by which healings are obtained through the Word. It will be interesting to notice them. In a previous chapter, I have called your attention to the fact that the early church used healing as a means of advertising the gospel as well as blessing the people.

FIRST METHOD

John 14:13–14 can be used in this connection:

And whatsoever ye shall ask [or demand] in my name, that will I do, that the Father may be glorified in the Son. If ye shall ask any thing in my name, I will do it.

If a pain comes, you say, "In the name of Jesus Christ, leave my body." The pain must go. You are the master of your own body. You rule it.

You have a right to freedom from pain or sickness. In that name, you command it to leave. You are not demanding it of the Father, because the Father has given you authority over these demoniacal forces.

You can use Jesus's name to break the power of the adversary over the unsaved and make it easy for them to accept Christ. In that name, "They that believe shall lay hands on the sick and they shall recover."

Every believer should understand clearly that he has a right to perfect deliverance from the hand of his enemy in that name.

SECOND METHOD

A second method is found in Mark 16:17–18: *"In my name … they shall lay hands on the sick, and they shall recover."*

The believer has the nature of God in him. He has the life of God in him. The Spirit dwells in him. It is that power within him that goes out through his hands in the name of Jesus and heals the sick.

Sometimes it is accompanied by manifestations. The person feels the life of God go pouring through his body.

Other times, there is no manifestation.

It makes no difference whether or not there is any sense witness. They that believe *"shall lay hands on the sick, and they shall recover."*

The same power that is in him can be exercised in the name of Jesus for a sick one in a distant place. The moment he prays in that name, God's healing power reaches out to that one and he is healed.

THIRD METHOD

A third method is for the carnal believer—that is, the believer who is governed by the senses and not by the Word.

First Corinthians 3:1–3 calls him a babe in Christ.

> *Is any sick among you? let him call for the elders of the church; and let them pray over him, anointing him with oil in the name of the Lord: and the prayer of faith shall save the sick, and the Lord shall raise him up; and if he have committed sins, they shall be forgiven him.* (James 5:14–15)

This Scripture is not for full-grown believers, but for those who have never developed their spiritual life so as to take their places in Christ. It is for those who must depend on others to pray for them.

FOURTH METHOD

A fourth method of healing is found in John 16:23–24:

> *And in that day ye shall ask me nothing. Verily, verily, I say unto you, Whatsoever ye shall ask the Father in my name, he will give it you. Hitherto have ye asked nothing in my name: ask, and ye shall receive, that your joy may be full.*

Every believer has a right to ask the Father for healing or any other blessing and if he asks in the name of Jesus, he has the absolute guarantee that the Father will hear and answer his petition.

FIFTH METHOD

A fifth method of healing is found in Matthew 18:19–20:

> *If two of you shall agree on earth as touching any thing that they shall ask, it shall be done for them of my Father [who] is in heaven. For where two or three are gathered together in my name, there am I in the midst of them.*

Where two are united and are demanding the healing of loved ones in Jesus's name, prayer is bound to be answered. God watches over His Word to make it good.

HEALING IN REDEMPTION

There is another method of healing which I believe to be the best.

> *Surely our diseases did he bear, and our pains he carried; whereas we did esteem him stricken, smitten of God, and afflicted.* (Isaiah 53:4 JPS)

He was smitten with our diseases.

> *He was wounded for our transgressions, he was bruised for our iniquities: the chastisement of our peace was upon him; and with his stripes we are healed.* (Isaiah 53:5)

Here is the absolute statement of fact that by His stripes, we are healed.

> *Who his own self bare our sins in his own body on the tree, that we, being dead to sins, should live unto righteousness: by whose stripes ye were healed.* (1 Peter 2:24)

> *That it might be fulfilled which was spoken through Isaiah the prophet, saying, Himself took our infirmities, and bare our diseases.* (Matthew 8:17 ASV)

These Scriptures prove that healing is ours. We simply know that by His stripes, we are healed. We thank the Father for our perfect deliverance. It is not necessary that we pray or ask the Father to heal us.

We know that He said, "By His stripes you were healed." The afflictions in our bodies were laid upon Jesus. He bore them. We do not need to bear them.

All we need to do is to recognize and accept that fact. We refuse to allow disease in our bodies. We are healed.

Every believer should thoroughly understand that his healing was consummated in Christ.

It would mean the end of chronic troubles in the body of the believer.

10

JESUS THE HEALER

"If it were not for this thing you call sin-consciousness, I would have faith. If I had faith, I would have my healing. But the Word does not seem real to me. I read it and I say, 'By His stripes I am healed' and yet in my mind, I hear another voice saying, 'But the pain is still there.'

"I find I am giving two testimonies continually, one with my lips and another with my intellect."

We should fully understand this: no matter what one's standing is in heaven, if he has no faith in it, it does him no good.

No matter what a man's privileges are, if the hand of faith is paralyzed, he cannot take hold of them.

As long as he is ruled by sin-consciousness, he has no sense of redemption. He is under condemnation. Satan rules him.

As long as Satan rules, faith will be shriveled and undeveloped. All through the Pauline revelation, from Romans through Hebrews, a complete redemption is taught.

There is a perfect redemption. Satan is conquered.

> *As the children are partakers of flesh and blood, he also himself likewise took part of the same; that through death he might destroy him that had the power of death, that is, the devil.* (Hebrews 2:14)

The devil is stripped of his authority.

In Revelation 1:18 (ASV), Jesus triumphantly says, *"I was dead, and behold, I am alive for evermore, and I have the keys of death and of Hades."*

Satan was put to nought; his ability was paralyzed.

> *Having despoiled the principalities and the powers, he made a show of them openly, triumphing over them in it.* (Colossians 2:15 ASV)

Satan, then, has no dominion over us.

> *Sin shall not have dominion over you.* (Romans 6:14)

If redemption does not deliver us from sin-consciousness, it is no better than Judaism. If it cannot free us now from condemnation, God and Christ have failed; Satan has become the master.

If sin-consciousness rules, acting on the Word is impossible. Faith is a withered flower where sin-consciousness rules.

The problem of faith, then, is to get rid of sin-consciousness. The Word is the only cure. It declares that we are redeemed.

> *In whom we have our redemption through his blood, the forgiveness of our trespasses.* (Ephesians 1:7 ASV)

If we have been redeemed, Satan's dominion is broken, and we are free. Not only has a perfect redemption been accomplished, but provision for a perfect recreation has been made.

> *Therefore if any man be in Christ, he is a new creature: old things are passed away; behold, all things are become new. And all things are of God, who hath reconciled us to himself by Jesus Christ, and hath given to us the ministry of reconciliation.* (2 Corinthians 5:17–18)

There is a complete recreation and a complete reconciliation.

If God has recreated us, we are not under bondage to the things of the old creation.

If a man has been recreated, it is God's own work. He did it through the Holy Spirit and His own Word.

That new creation is effected by the impartation of God's own nature.

Second Peter 1:4 says we become partakers of the divine nature. We are actually born from above. The old sin nature has gone, and a new nature, which is free from condemnation, has taken its place.

> *There is therefore now no condemnation to them which are in Christ Jesus.* (Romans 8:1)

We have been made free from the law of sin and of death.

> *Who shall lay any thing to the charge of God's elect?... Who is he that condemneth?* (Romans 8:33–34)

God has justified or declared us righteous.

The word *justify* means "to make righteous." Righteousness is the ability to stand in the Father's presence without the sense of guilt, sin, or inferiority.

We stand there as though sin had never been.

If redemption does not mean that, if the new creation does not give that, God has failed.

The new creation must be as free from sin as Adam was before he committed sin, or God has failed in His redemptive work.

Someone says, "What about 1 John 1:8—'*If we say that we have no sin, we deceive ourselves, and the truth is not in us*'?"

John is speaking of broken fellowship. If a man says he has fellowship with the Father when he is living under condemnation, he is telling a lie.

> *If we say that we have fellowship with him, and walk in the darkness, we lie, and do not the truth.* (1 John 1:6)

Every man who is living in broken fellowship is walking in darkness.

> *If we confess our sins, he is faithful and just to forgive us our sins, and to cleanse us from all unrighteousness.* (1 John 1:9)

If we say that we have not sinned when we are living out of fellowship, we are telling an untruth. But if we do sin, we have an Advocate with the Father, Jesus Christ the righteous.

> *We are his workmanship.* (Ephesians 2:10)

He not only made us new creations, but He made us righteous.

> *For the shewing forth of His righteousness in the present time, for His being righteous, and declaring him righteous who [is] of the faith of Jesus.* (Romans 3:26 YLT)

This declares that He has become the righteousness of the man who has faith in Jesus as Savior.

If God has become our righteousness, we have a legal standing in His presence.

First Corinthians 1:30 tells us that He was made unto us righteousness: *"But of him are ye in Christ Jesus, who of God is made unto us wisdom, and righteousness, and sanctification, and redemption."*

Then we have God as our righteousness and Jesus as our righteousness.

> *Who was delivered up because of our offences, and was raised up because of our being declared righteous.* (Romans 4:25 YLT)

> *Therefore being justified* [declared righteous] *by faith, we have peace with God through our Lord Jesus Christ.* (Romans 5:1)

> *He hath made him to be sin for us, who knew no sin; that we might be made the righteousness of God in him.* (2 Corinthians 5:21)

He not only becomes our righteousness, but now He also makes us His righteousness by a new birth, a recreation.

We stand before Him reconciled, without condemnation, in fellowship with Him.

If the Scripture means anything, it means exactly what it says.

The believer has a legal right to stand in the Father's presence without condemnation. If he can do that, then acting on the Word is possible. If acting on the Word is possible, everything that belongs to us in Christ becomes available at once.

When Jesus arose from the dead, He left an eternally defeated Satan behind Him.

Always think of Satan as the eternally defeated one.

11

THE DISEASE PROBLEM

This is Jesus's spiritual ministry. It began on the cross.

> *He was despised, and forsaken of men, a man of pains, and acquainted with disease, and as one from whom men hide their face: he was despised, and we esteemed him not. Surely our diseases did he bear, and our pains he carried; whereas we did esteem him stricken, smitten of God, and afflicted. But he was wounded because of our transgressions, he was crushed because of our iniquities: the chastisement of our welfare was upon him, and with his stripes we were healed.* (Isaiah 53:3–5 JPS)

The disciples could not see it when they looked upon the thorncrowned Man of Galilee.

He was then bearing our sicknesses and diseases.

Verse 10 (JPS) reads: *"Yet it pleased the LORD to crush him by disease."*

He made Him sin with our sins, sick with our sicknesses.

> *So marred was his visage unlike that of a man.* (Isaiah 52:14 JPS)

It was so marred that He no longer looked like a man. That was not His physical body.

God could not look on His soul. God made His soul an offering for sin. He was stricken, smitten of God, and afflicted.

It was God who laid our diseases on Him. He was smitten by justice because He was our substitute.

He was bruised for our iniquities. The chastisement of our peace was upon Him and with His stripes, we are healed.

It was not the physical stripes upon His back made by the Roman lictor, but the stripes that God put upon Him with our diseases when He was judged and cast out in our stead.

> *That it might be fulfilled that was spoken through Isaiah the prophet, saying, "Himself took our infirmities, and the sicknesses he did bear."*
>
> (Matthew 8:17 YLT)

Our infirmities are our little mental quirks, the things that make us disagreeable and unpleasant to people. These are largely infirmities of the mind.

He bore them all. What He bore, we do not need to bear. What He took upon Himself, we need not suffer.

We have come to believe that it is just as wrong for a believer to bear his sickness when Jesus bore it, as it is for him to bear his sins when Christ bore them.

We have no right to live in sin and bear those hateful habits that make life a curse, because Christ bore them.

It was wrong for Him to bear them if we are going to bear them too.

It is wrong for us to have sickness and disease in our bodies when God laid those diseases on Jesus.

He became sick with our diseases, that we might be healed.

He knew no sickness until He was made sick with our diseases.

The object of His sin-bearing was to make righteous the ones who believe in Him.

The object of disease-bearing was to make well the ones who believe in Him as the disease-bearer.

His sin-bearing made righteousness sure to the new creation. His disease-bearing makes healing sure to the new creation.

He took our sins and made us righteous. He took our diseases and made us well. He took our infirmities and gave us His strength. He exchanged His strength for our weakness, His success for our failings.

DISEASE IS NOT THE WILL OF THE FATHER

We understand that disease is broken ease, broken fellowship with heaven. Disease is pain, weakness, loss of ability to bless and help.

It makes slaves of the people who care for the sick. The loved ones who are up night and day working over the sick ones are robbed of joy and rest.

Sickness is not of love, and God is love. Disease is a robber. It steals health; it steals happiness. It steals money we need for other things. Disease is an enemy.

Look at what it has stolen from that tuberculosis patient. It came upon him in the midst of young manhood and has made him a burden to his family, filled him with anxiety and doubt, fear and pain. It has robbed him of his faith.

See what disease has done to that woman; it has robbed her of her beauty and her joy and love. She is no longer able to fill the place of a mother or wife. All this is of the devil.

Jesus said that disease was of Satan.

> *And, behold, there was a woman which had a spirit of infirmity eighteen years, and was bowed together, and could in no wise lift up herself. ... And ought not this woman, being a daughter of Abraham, whom Satan hath bound, lo, these eighteen years, be loosed from this bond?* (Luke 13:11, 16)

She was Satan-bound.

Acts 10:38 tells us that Jesus "*went about doing good, and healing all that were oppressed of the devil.*"

From the beginning to the end of Jesus's public ministry, He was combating Satan.

His battle was not with men, but entirely with demons who indwelt men.

It was the devil who used the high priesthood to stir up the strife that finally nailed Jesus to the cross.

Don't tell anyone that disease is the will of love. It is the will of hate; it is the will of Satan.

If disease becomes the will of love, love has turned to hatred.

If disease is the will of God, heaven will be filled with disease and sickness.

Jesus was the express will of the Father; He went about healing the sick.

Disease and sickness are never the will of the Father. To believe that they are is to be disillusioned by the adversary.

If healing had not been in the plan of redemption, it would not have been in the substitutionary chapter of Isaiah 53.

If healing had not been in redemption, the Father would not have taught it in His Word.

Jesus healed all who came to Him, Jews and gentiles alike. He was carrying out the will of the Father. He was the will of the Father.

12

MADE WELL IN CHRIST

No matter from what angle you look at Christianity, it is a miracle. The most amazing miracle is the new creation. We have never been able to get at the heart of it. We have stood outside as spectators and looked at it from its various angles.

A man becomes a new creation by receiving the very life and nature of God.

Take these Scriptures as illustrations.

> *And you, being dead through your trespasses and the uncircumcision of the flesh, you, I say, did he make alive together with him, having forgiven us all our trespasses.* (Colossians 2:13 ASV)

We have been made alive together with Him.

Verse 12 (ASV) reads: *"Wherein ye were also raised with him through faith in the working of God, who raised him from the dead."*

This is the legal aspect of the new creation and everything that is legally ours can become a vital reality.

In the mind of the Father, we were made alive with Christ. When He was made alive in spirit, we were made alive in spirit. This becomes a reality to us when we personally accept Christ as Savior and confess Him as Lord. The life of God comes into our spirits and recreates us.

> *And you did he make alive, when ye were dead through your trespasses and sins.* (Ephesians 2:1 ASV)

This can be called the miracle of Christianity, an actual new creation.

There would be more pleasure in old age than in youth if we did not fear it.

We dread it because of the haunting fear of pain and disease and the struggle with death.

LIFE AND DEATH

A few facts about life and death may be helpful to us.

Spiritual death is the parent of physical death. There was no physical death until Adam died spiritually.

There was no death in the original blueprints of creation. We know that at the end of this age, death will be swallowed up of immortality.

> *The last enemy that shall be destroyed is death.* (1 Corinthians 15:26)

There is going to be a deathless eternity. Why can't there be a sickless present? I believe it is the will of the Father that the church be as free from sickness as it is from sin.

Death is an enemy. Weakness and disease are enemies. Death is not only the enemy of man, but it is also the enemy of God.

Second Timothy 1:10 (ASV) tells us that in the resurrection of the Lord Jesus, death lost its dominion: *"But hath now been manifested by the appearing of our Savior Christ Jesus, who abolished death, and brought life and immortality to light through the gospel."*

He did two things: He brought life and immortality to us, and He abolished the dominion of death.

When He arose from the dead, He had conquered death personally.

He conquered death in Lazarus. He conquered death in the widow's son. He was the Lord of life.

> *And death and hell were cast into the lake of fire.* (Revelation 20:14)

> *And God shall wipe away all tears from their eyes; and there shall be no more death, neither sorrow, nor crying, neither shall there be any more pain.* (Revelation 21:4)

It will be the end of death. This promise of the final destruction of death has in it a suggestion that there is in the plan of redemption, something to give us assurance of a sickless life, until our bodies wear out and mortality wins without a struggle.

> *He was despised, and forsaken of men, a man of pains, and acquainted with disease. And as one from whom men hide their face: he was despised, and we esteemed him not. Surely our diseases he did bear, and our pains he carried; whereas we did esteem him stricken, smitten of God, and afflicted. But he was wounded because of our transgressions, he was crushed because of our iniquities: the chastisement of our welfare* [or peace] *was upon him, and with his stripes we were healed.*
>
> (Isaiah 53:3–5 JPS)

Then the tenth verse, *"And Jehovah hath delighted to bruise him, he hath made him sick"* (YLT) or *"put him to grief"* (ASV).

> *He hath poured out his soul unto death: and he was numbered with the transgressors; and he bare the sin of many, and made intercession for the transgressors.* (Isaiah 53:12)

That is His high priestly ministry now at the right hand of the Father.

We can see in this whole program that heads up in these words, "With His stripes, we are healed." The sin and disease problems have been settled.

As surely as Jesus was our sin substitute as described in 2 Corinthians 5:21, so surely have we become the righteousness of God in Him.

The object of His being made sick with our diseases was that we might be perfectly healed with His life.

There is no escaping the fact that as surely as He dealt with the sin problem, He dealt with the disease problem.

> *But now once at the end of the ages hath he been manifested to put away sin by the sacrifice of himself.* (Hebrews 9:26 ASV)

> *But this man, after he had offered one sacrifice for sins for ever, sat down on the right hand of God.* (Hebrews 10:12)

Jesus put sin away that we might be born again, become new creations, that the sin nature which had held us in bondage to the adversary should be eradicated and that the nature of God should take its place.

It is the new nature that settles the sin problem for us individually. The problem of sins is settled. The things we did before we accepted Christ are wiped out as though they had never been.

Now we are in God's family. We are the righteousness of God in Him.

> *But my righteous one shall live by faith: and if he shrink back, my soul hath no pleasure in him.* (Hebrews 10:38 ASV)

The new creation is called the righteousness of God. He is the righteousness of God.

His standing with the Father is just like Jesus's standing. But if he sins, he has an Advocate with the Father, Jesus Christ the righteous.

He loses the sense of righteousness when he sins, but Jesus, the righteous one, intercedes for him and restores his lost fellowship and sense of righteousness.

FELLOWSHIP AND HEALING

> *If we confess our sins, he is faithful and just to forgive us our sins, and to cleanse us from all unrighteousness.* (1 John 1:9)

This restores his fellowship, brings him back into full communion with the Father.

Now by the same token, after one has been healed—because by His stripes, we are healed—in the mind of God, he is just as much healed of disease as he is healed of sin.

If, after he has been healed of disease, the adversary puts upon him some other disease or infirmity, all he needs to do is to follow the procedure that he followed when he broke fellowship with the Father spiritually.

Sickness is breaking fellowship with the Father physically. As he can get restoration of fellowship and a restoration of his sense of righteousness by confessing his sins and by the advocacy of Jesus Christ, he can get his physical healing.

Disease of the spirit is the thing that keeps one from his healing. Diseases of the spirit are doubts, fears, sin-consciousness, a sense of inferiority, fear of unworthiness, and a sense of unfitness to stand in God's presence.

The blood of Jesus Christ, God's Son, cleanses from all this, the moment he acknowledges his sin.

Forgiveness means the absolute wiping out of everything he has confessed, as though he had never committed the act.

> *For we that are in this tabernacle do groan, being burdened: not for that we would be unclothed, but clothed upon, that mortality might be swallowed up of life. Now he that hath wrought us for the selfsame thing is God, who also hath given unto us the earnest of the Spirit.*
>
> (2 Corinthians 5:4–5)

The Greek word here for "life" is *zoe*. It means eternal life, resurrection life.

In other words, it means that the life of the Son of God, eternal life, can absolutely dominate, rule, swallow up, and control our physical lives.

If this is true, then sickness is absolutely defeated, physical weakness is eliminated, and Psalm 27:1 is a reality: "*The Lord is my light and my salvation; whom shall I fear? the Lord is the strength of my life; of whom shall I be afraid?*"

Light is knowledge. Jesus is the light of the world. He who walks in that light will not stumble as one who walks in darkness, because he will have the light of life.

In John 8:12, Jesus says: "*I am the light of the world: he that followeth me shall not walk in the darkness, but shall have the light of life.*"

The Word will be his lamp, his light, his salvation. That is true deliverance; that is redemption.

Psalm 119:105 says, "*Thy word is a lamp unto my feet, and light unto my path.*" It is deliverance from the things that are not in the Father's will.

You cannot for a moment believe that mortality is in the will of the Father.

Mortality means weakness, sickness, death. You cannot conceive of disease and sickness being the will of the Father.

"*The Lord is my light and my salvation*" (Psalm 27:1). This means salvation from sickness, disease, and weakness of the physical body.

Fear will no longer dominate your life.

If a man could be delivered from fear of weakness, death, or pain, he would be a conqueror.

Redemption planned that very thing, that these bodies of ours should never be subject to disease after we are born again.

Someone says, "What about Paul's '*thorn in the flesh*'?" (See 2 Corinthians 12:7.)

That was not sickness. It was a demon interfering with Paul's public ministry in his speech, making him stammer. It had nothing to do with disease.

All that foolish talk about Luke being Paul's physician is not true. Physicians were sorcerers. They belonged to the spiritualistic group.

The Greek word *pharmacia* from which we get "pharmacist" is the word for sorcerer.

In 2 Corinthians 4:10–11, Paul says, *"Always bearing about in the body the dying of the Lord Jesus, that the life also of Jesus might be made manifest in our body. For we which live are always delivered unto death for Jesus' sake."*

Why? They lived in the constant fear of stoning, of being thrown to the lions, or being burned at the stake.

"That the life also of Jesus may be made manifest in our mortal flesh" (2 Corinthians 4:11) is a startling statement; God's life reigning in our physical bodies.

> *The LORD is the strength of my life; of whom shall I be afraid?*
> (Psalm 27:1)

These mortal bodies, these death-doomed bodies of ours, now have the strength of God, the life of God.

Jesus's life is imparted to our physical bodies. That is not healing. That is preservation from sickness. That is protection. That is the strength, power, and the ability of God in our physical bodies.

Don't try to get your healing. God has given it to you.

Don't try to believe. You are a believer and all things are yours. Don't talk doubt. It breeds more doubt.

13

DESTROYING THE WORKS OF THE DEVIL

One of the strongest Scriptures in connection with healing is this:

> *But if the Spirit of him that raised up Jesus from the dead dwelleth in you, he that raised up Christ Jesus from the dead shall give life also to your mortal bodies through his Spirit that dwelleth in you.* (Romans 8:11 ASV)

This is physical healing. This is the Holy Spirit, taking the life of God and making it efficacious in our physical bodies, making it health, strength, and life to us.

This same Holy Spirit who raised the dead body of Jesus is now working in our death-doomed bodies, making them perfect—sickless and sinless.

> *He that committeth sin is of the devil; for the devil sinneth from the beginning. For this purpose the Son of God was manifested, that he might destroy the works of the devil.* (1 John 3:8)

Jesus did His part of destroying the works of the devil. After He left the earth, He sent the Holy Spirit and gave us the use of His own name and this wonderful revelation, the New Testament, that we, His representatives here on the earth, might go on destroying the works of the devil.

The sin, the sickness, and the diseases that are in the church today are there because of our not taking our places in Christ.

They are prevalent in the church today because we have never been exercised to do the work that Jesus said we were to do.

Do you think He would have given us John 14:12–14 if we were not to use it? *"Verily, verily, I say unto you, He that believeth on me, the works that I do shall he do also; and greater works than these shall he do; because I go unto my Father"* (verse 12).

Jesus meant that we should do greater works than He did, because there are a greater number of us.

Our work is that of destroying the works of the adversary. The weapon we are to use is found in the thirteenth and fourteenth verses: *"And whatsoever ye shall ask in my name, that will I do, that the Father may be glorified in the Son. If ye shall ask any thing in my name, I will do it"* (John 14:13–14).

That word *"ask"* means "demand."

His name is to be used in the sense that we see it used in Acts 3 by Peter, who spoke to the lame man at the gate of the temple saying, *"In the name of Jesus Christ of Nazareth rise up and walk"* (Acts 3:6).

This is not prayer. This is casting out demons in that name. There is healing for the sick in that name.

There is power to break disease and sickness in the hearts and lives of men in that name.

Can that name of Jesus keep us from sickness? Can it keep us from want? Can it keep us from poverty, fear, and the dread of hunger and cold?

Can that name be used just as Jesus suggested in Mark 16?

> *And these signs shall accompany them that believe: in my name shall they cast out demons; they shall speak with new tongues; they shall take up serpents, and if they drink any deadly thing, it shall in no wise hurt them; they shall lay hands on the sick, and they shall recover.*
>
> (Mark 16:17–18 ASV)

The early church was utterly independent of circumstances. I don't mean the whole church. I mean the apostles who understood fully the use of the name of Jesus.

Men could be sick then by breaking fellowship and because of lack of knowledge, just as they can be today.

The gentile portion of the early church had never had any revelation from God.

It was utterly raw material.

The Jews were in worse condition. They were covenant breakers, as the modern church is.

The most difficult to deal with today are the most religious. If there was sickness in the early church, it was to be expected, because they had no precedent, no examples ahead of them.

Jesus came to destroy the works of the devil. We are His instruments to do His work.

We are to destroy sickness in the church. Our new slogan is: "No more sickness in the body of Christ."

His Word is to become a reality in the lives of men.

The fact that He bore our sins and put sin away by the sacrifice of Himself, and that He made provision for the remission of all we have ever done or said, proves that we should not be sick or in bondage to sin.

He made the sacrifice for sins, the things we had done as a result of the sin nature.

The new birth wipes out everything we have ever done.

> *Therefore if any man be in Christ, he is a new creature: old things are passed away; behold, all things are become new.* (2 Corinthians 5:17)

Romans 8:1 becomes a reality: "*There is therefore now no condemnation to them which are in Christ Jesus.*"

The people who are in Christ Jesus are sin free, disease free, and condemnation free.

Let us then arise, take our place, and go out and carry this message of deliverance and victory to others.

It is very important that we grasp clearly 1 John 5:13: "*These things have I written unto you that believe on the name of the Son of God; that ye may know that ye have eternal life.*"

We have God's nature, which gives us a perfect fellowship with the Father, a perfect right to use His name, a perfect deliverance and freedom from Satan's dominion.

> *Whereby are given unto us exceeding great and precious promises: that by these ye might be partakers of the divine nature.* (2 Peter 1:4)

If ye shall ask any thing in my name, I will do it. (John 14:14)

For sin shall not have dominion over you. (Romans 6:14)

If sin cannot lord it over you, disease cannot lord it over you, because they come from the same source.

The nature and life of God that has come into you will give you life and health.

With long life will I satisfy him, and show him my salvation.
(Psalm 91:16 ASV)

We all admit that the ninety-first Psalm belongs to the church. It could not apply to the Jew, but it does apply to us.

He shall cover thee with his feathers, and under his wings shalt thou trust: his truth [or Word] shall be thy shield and buckler. Thou shalt not be afraid for the terror by night; nor for the arrow that flieth by day; nor for the pestilence that walketh in darkness; nor for the destruction that wasteth at noonday. A thousand shall fall at thy side, and ten thousand at thy right hand; but it shall not come nigh thee. (Psalm 91:4–7)

There is protection from earthquakes, from cyclones, pestilence, from sickness, from war.

This thing puts us into the realm of the supernatural. We are linked up with Christ so that He said, "*I am the vine, ye are the branches*" (John 15:5).

The life in the vine is in the branch. As soon as the branch is wounded, the vine pours life into the wounded branch so it can go on bearing fruit.

So the life of God pours into the body of Christ and heals the members of sickness, disease, and want, so they can go on bearing fruit to the glory of God.

Worry and fear poison the bloodstream. Faith in the Lord Jesus purifies it.

Disease is defeated by your confession of the Word.

Disease gains the ascendency when you confess the testimony of your senses.

Satan is whipped with words. You are healed with words.

Make your lips do their duty. Fill them with His Word.

14

THE ABUNDANT LIFE

Christianity is a living reality.

> *I am come that they might have life, and that they might have it more abundantly.* (John 10:10)

It is the abundance of life that gives healing, strength, and energy.

> *Casting all your anxiety upon him, because he careth for you.* (1 Peter 5:7 ASV)

This means that in the mind of the Father, there has come an end to worry, fear, and doubt.

The work of the adversary has been destroyed.

Exodus 23:25–26 was given to the Jews under the first covenant, but it may become a living, sweet reality to us:

> *And ye shall serve the Lord your God, and he shall bless thy bread, and thy water; and I will take sickness away from the midst of thee. There shall nothing cast their young, nor be barren, in thy land: the number of thy days I will fulfil.*

Is our covenant as good as that?

> *My God shall supply every need of yours according to his riches in glory [unveiled] in Christ Jesus.* (Philippians 4:19 ASV)

> *I can do all things through Christ which strengtheneth me.* (Philippians 4:13)

> *Not that I speak in respect of want: for I have learned, in whatsoever state I am, therewith to be content.* (Philippians 4:11)

We rise into the realm of the supernatural, absolute overcomers, perfect victors in Christ.

Is it any wonder that Paul declares, "*Nay, in all these things we are more than conquerors*" (Romans 8:37)?

There is nothing that can separate us from the love of God as unveiled in Christ Jesus, our Lord.

> *He that spared not his own Son, but delivered him up for us all, how shall he not with him also freely give us all things?* (Romans 8:32)

We stand upon the mount of victory. Now we can say, "There is no more sickness in the body of Christ."

His Word is a reality in the lives of the sons of God. We are going out today to destroy the works of the enemy in the bodies, minds, and spirits of men.

There are several methods of healing, but the one that stands first in the mind of the Spirit is found in Isaiah 53.

> *Surely our diseases he did bear, and our pains he carried; whereas we did esteem him stricken, smitten of God, and afflicted.* (Isaiah 53:4 JPS)

He was stricken and smitten with our diseases.

> *But he was wounded for our transgressions, he was bruised for our iniquities: the chastisement of our peace was upon him; and with his stripes we are healed.* (Isaiah 53:5)

Sin and sickness are one in the mind of the Father. Anything that touches the man and injures the man, God is against. Disease touches the man, and God laid it upon Jesus. Sin touches the man, and God laid it upon Jesus.

> *All we like sheep have gone astray; we have turned every one to his own way; and the LORD hath laid on him the iniquity of us all.* (Isaiah 53:6)

> *And Jehovah hath delighted to bruise him, He hath made him sick.* (Isaiah 53:10 YLT)

When He declares that by His stripes we are healed, that means our freedom from sickness.

That is our receipt in full for a sickless and sinless life, for sin and disease shall not have dominion over us.

We take what belongs to us as sons and daughters of God.

We know that sin shall not have dominion over us. (See Romans 6:14.) We know that the blood of Jesus Christ cleanses from sin.

> *But if we walk in the light, as he is in the light, we have fellowship one with another, and the blood of Jesus Christ his Son cleanseth us from all sin.*
> (1 John 1:7)

If we have committed sin, we have an Advocate with the Father.

> *My little children, these things write I unto you, that ye sin not. And if any man sin, we have an advocate with the Father, Jesus Christ the righteous.*
> (1 John 2:1)

We know that if we confess our sins, He will forgive us and cleanse us.

> *If we confess our sins, he is faithful and just to forgive us our sins, and to cleanse us from all unrighteousness.* (1 John 1:9)

We come to Him with all our diseases knowing that all those diseases were laid on Jesus.

Then it is not right that we should bear them. The adversary has no right to put diseases on us, because they were laid on Christ.

I can say to the Father, "Do you see what the adversary has done in my body? In the name of Jesus, I take deliverance from this thing with which Satan has afflicted me."

I whisper to my heart, "By His stripes, I am healed." The pain must go. Multitudes are being healed like that today through our ministry.

We can be just as free from diseases as we are free from bad habits, and after all, the habit of sickness is like any other unclean habit.

There is provision made for a perfect healing. None of us need suffer from the hand of the enemy. Your deliverance is in the redemptive work of Christ.

15

THE ORIGIN OF SICKNESS

THE CRUELTY OF NATURE

It is hard for us to understand that the laws that are governing the earth very largely came into being with the fall of man and with the curse upon the earth.

It is because of this that many accuse God of the accidents that take place, of the sickness and death of loved ones, of storms and catastrophes, of earthquakes and floods that continually occur.

All these natural laws, as we understand them, were set aside by Jesus whenever it was necessary to bless humanity.

They came with the fall. Their author is Satan, and when Satan is finally eliminated from human contact, or rather, from the earth, these laws will stop functioning.

THE ORIGIN OF SICKNESS

Jesus's description of the Father and His declaration that "*he that hath seen me hath seen the Father*" (John 14:9) makes it impossible for us for a moment to accept the teaching that disease and sickness are of God.

The Father's very nature refutes the argument that He would use sickness to discipline us or to deepen our piety.

Jesus plainly taught us in Luke 13, in speaking of the woman with the infirmity, that disease is of the adversary.

> *And ought not this woman, being a daughter of Abraham, whom Satan hath bound, lo, these eighteen years, be loosed from this bond on the sabbath day?* (Luke 13:16)

If you will read the four gospels carefully, you will notice that Jesus was continually casting demons out of sick people, breaking Satan's dominion over the lives of men and women.

In Acts 10:38, Peter tells us, "*God anointed Jesus of Nazareth with the Holy Ghost and with power: who went about doing good, and healing all that were oppressed of the devil; for God was with him.*"

In the Great Commission, Jesus said:

> *And these signs shall accompany them that believe: in my name shall they cast out demons; they shall speak with new tongues; they shall take up serpents, and if they drink any deadly thing, it shall in no wise hurt them; they shall lay hands on the sick, and they shall recover.*
>
> (Mark 16:17–18 ASV)

There is no such thing as the separation of disease and sickness from Satan. Disease came with the fall of man.

You cannot conceive of sickness in the garden of Eden before Adam sinned. The fall was of the adversary. Sickness and sin have the same origin.

Jesus's attitude toward sickness was an uncompromising warfare with Satan. He healed all who were sick. No one ever came to Him who did not receive immediate deliverance.

Jesus's attitude toward sin and His attitude toward sickness were identical. He dealt with sickness as He dealt with demons.

We have been driven to the conclusion that if disease and sickness are of the devil, and we have found that they are, then there is only one attitude that the believer can take in regard to them: we must follow in Jesus's footsteps and deal with disease as Jesus dealt with it.

HOW GOD DEALT WITH DISEASE UNDER THE FIRST COVENANT

When Israel came out of Egypt, she was God's own covenant people. As soon as that nation had crossed the Red Sea and started toward its homeland, the angel of the covenant said to Moses:

> *If thou wilt diligently hearken to the voice of the* Lord *thy God, and wilt do that which is right in his sight, and wilt give ear to his commandments, and keep all his statutes, I will put [permit] none of these diseases upon thee, which I have brought [permitted] upon the Egyptians: for I am the* Lord *that healeth thee.* (Exodus 15:26)

The student of Hebrew will recognize that I have taken liberty to translate literally that expression, *"I will put none of these diseases upon thee."* I believe it to be a correct translation.

God did not put the diseases upon Israel. Neither did He put the diseases upon the Egyptians. It is Satan, the god of this world, who has made men sick.

Here, God declares that He is to be Israel's healer:

> *And ye shall serve the Lord your God, and he shall bless thy bread, and thy water; and I will take sickness away from the midst of thee. There shall nothing cast their young, nor be barren, in thy land: the number of thy days I will fulfil.* (Exodus 23:25–26)

He says He will take sickness from the midst of them. It is a remarkable fact that as long as Israel walked in the covenant, there was no sickness among them.

There is no record of any babies or young people ever having died as long as they kept the covenant.

"There shall nothing cast their young" means there were to be no miscarriages nor abnormal abortions.

There were to be no barren wives in the land. Every home was to have children.

"The number of thy days I will fulfil" indicates there were to be no premature deaths. Every person was to grow to full age before he laid down his work.

This is remarkable. God took over that nation. He became their healer, protector, and supplier of every need.

HE WAS EVERYTHING THEY NEEDED

> *And he will love thee, and bless thee, and multiply thee: he will also bless the fruit of thy womb, and the fruit of thy land, thy corn, and thy wine, and thine oil, the increase of thy kine, and the flocks of thy sheep, in the*

> *land which he sware unto thy fathers to give thee. Thou shalt be blessed above all people: there shall not be male or female barren among you, or among your cattle. And the* Lord *will take away from thee all sickness.*
> (Deuteronomy 7:13–15)

The Lord was to meet every need, supply every demand of that nation.

He was to be intimately in contact with every member of the family.

Everything connected with them was to bear the stamp of prosperity and success. Disease and sickness were not to be tolerated among them.

> *And, behold, the acts of Asa, first and last, lo, they are written in the book of the kings of Judah and Israel. And Asa in the thirty and ninth year of his reign was diseased in his feet, until his disease was exceeding great: yet in his disease he sought not to the* Lord*, but to the physicians. And Asa slept with his fathers.* (2 Chronicles 16:11–13)

One can see clearly here that God was displeased with Asa for seeking the help of man when God had promised to be his healer.

Read the Psalms carefully and you will find that God was Israel's healer. It is continually mentioned.

> *Bless the* Lord *... who forgiveth all thine iniquities; who healeth all thy diseases; who redeemeth thy life from destruction; who crowneth thee with lovingkindness and tender mercies; who satisfieth thy mouth [desire] with good things; so that thy youth is renewed like the eagle's.*
> (Psalm 103:2–5)

The fact that disease came through disobedience to the Law is evident. Forgiveness for the disobedience meant the healing of their bodies.

We share with Him in His resurrection life.

We reign as kings in the realm of this resurrection life.

You are what He says you are whether you recognize it or not. You share in all He is or did.

As He was in His earth walk, you are today.

As He is seated at the Father's right hand, you are there legally.

16

PROPHECIES IN REGARD TO THE COMING HEALER

After God had told Israel that the reason for disease and sickness was that they had rebelled against the Word of God and condemned the counsel of the Most High, He declared, *"Fools because of their transgression, and because of their iniquities, are afflicted"* (Psalm 107:17).

They took themselves out of the protection of the covenant.

I believe it is in the plan of the Father that no believer should ever be sick, that he should live his full length of time and actually wear out and fall asleep.

It is not the Father's will that we should suffer with cancer and the other dread diseases that bring pain and anguish.

> *Their soul abhorreth all manner of meat [food]; and they draw near unto the gates of death. Then they cry unto the LORD in their trouble, and he saveth them out of their distresses. He sent his word, and healed them, and delivered them from their destructions.* (Psalm 107:18–20)

Men were sick because of broken laws, of sinning against the Word of God. I am speaking now of the Jews.

As they kept the covenant laws, no illness was among them. But when they sinned, their bodies were filled with diseases. They had a right to turn to the Lord and find their healing.

Practically all the outstanding prophets had the ability to heal the sick under the first covenant.

Isaiah 53 gives us a picture of the coming Messiah. It is a very graphic description.

> *He was despised, and forsaken of men, a man of pains, and acquainted with disease, and as one from whom men hide their face: he was despised, and we esteemed him not. Surely our diseases did he bear, and our pains he carried; whereas we did esteem him stricken, smitten of God, and afflicted.* (Isaiah 53:3–4 JPS)

This Scripture has to do with the disease problem that confronts the church and the world today, as well as the sin problem. He has borne our sicknesses and our diseases. He was stricken, smitten of God and afflicted with our diseases. It was God who laid our diseases on Jesus.

> *Yet it pleased the* Lord *to crush him by disease; to see if his soul would offer itself in restitution, that he might see his seed, prolong his days, and that the purpose of the* Lord *might prosper by his hand.*
> (Isaiah 53:10 JPS)

God made Him sick with our sickness. He was afflicted with our diseases.

As to our sins, *"He was wounded for our transgressions, he was bruised for our iniquities: the chastisement of our peace was upon him; and with his stripes we are healed"* (Isaiah 53:5).

He dealt with man's body, his soul, and his spirit. He laid our iniquities and our diseases upon Jesus. He was stricken, smitten, and afflicted with our diseases and our sins.

> *He hath made him to be sin for us, who knew no sin; that we might be made the righteousness of God in him.* (2 Corinthians 5:21)

He has already healed you.

In the mind of the Father, you are healed. Jesus knows that He bore your diseases.

How it must hurt Him to hear you talk about bearing them yourself.

Learn to say, "I am healed because He did that work and satisfied the supreme court of the universe."

That makes you free.

Sin shall not lord it over you because you are a new creation.

When were you healed? When Jesus defeated Satan, stripped him of his authority, and arose, you were healed.

17

JESUS'S MINISTRY

Following the temptation, as recorded in Matthew 4, Jesus went down out of the mountain and the multitudes thronged Him.

> *And the report of him went forth into all Syria: and they brought unto him all that were sick, holden with divers diseases and torments, possessed with demons, and epileptic, and palsied; and he healed them.*
>
> (Matthew 4:24 ASV)

In every contact of Jesus with the people, He healed their sick.

He did not turn any away. Everyone was healed.

Some would have us believe that there are some cases that are not the will of the Father to heal.

Yet, those same people will take medicine and send for a physician when they declare it is not the will of God to heal them.

The fact is, there aren't any cases that are not the will of the Father to heal. It is not the Father's will that any die of disease.

Sickness does not belong to the body of Christ. It is not normal or natural.

When Jesus said, *"I am the vine, ye are the branches"* (John 15:5), He meant we are united with Him as closely and vitally as the branch is connected to the vine.

You can understand how Jesus could not have cancer, tuberculosis, pneumonia, or any of those other deadly diseases. He is the vine. We, as branches, should have none of these things either.

It is abnormal for believers to be in bondage to poverty so that they have to go to the world for help. Also it is abnormal for them to go to physicians for healing.

The believer is of God. He has been redeemed out of the hand of the enemy. He has the very nature and life of God in him.

He is the righteousness of God in Christ. He is not only redeemed out of the hand of Satan and made a new creation, but he stands in the Father's presence without the sense of guilt or condemnation.

He has the same liberty and freedom with the Father now that he will have after death when he goes to heaven.

He stands before the Father now as Jesus stood before him. The Father's love nature has taken the place of the nature of Satan in his life. He is no longer afraid of disease or adverse circumstances.

He is not filled with fear and bondage. The Son has made him free.

Perfect love has cast out fear. He is filled with the nature and life of God, and God's nature is love.

There is no ground for disease and sickness in the body of Christ. These new creations are the sons of God, heirs of God, joint heirs with Jesus Christ.

They have God dwelling in them. They have the life and nature of God, and God Himself, in the person of the Holy Spirit who raised Jesus from the dead, has made His home in their bodies.

> *But if the Spirit of him that raised up Jesus from the dead dwelleth in you, he that raised up Christ Jesus from the dead shall give life also to your mortal bodies through his Spirit that dwelleth in you.* (Romans 8:11 ASV)

In the ministry of Jesus, there was a perfect coordination between Himself and the Father.

Jesus's attitude toward disease and sin was the Father's attitude.

He lived among the Jews, God's covenant people, and healed their diseases, breaking Satan's dominion over them individually.

When He went to the cross, He became their substitute, their sin-bearer, their disease-bearer.

When He was nailed to that cross, Isaiah 53:4 became a reality.

> *Surely our sicknesses he hath borne, and our pains—he hath carried them, and we—we have esteemed him plagued, smitten of God, and afflicted.* (Isaiah 53:4 YLT)

Fulfilling the words of the prophet, Jesus *"took our infirmities, and the sicknesses he did bear"* (Matthew 8:17 YLT).

It was the hand of justice that fell on Him as our substitute as He bore away our diseases.

18

THE GREAT COMMISSION

This is of the most vital importance to every believer.

When Jesus was bidding goodbye to the disciples, as recorded in Matthew 28, He said:

> *All authority hath been given unto me in heaven and on earth. Go ye therefore, and make disciples of all the nations, baptizing them into the name of the Father and of the Son and of the Holy Spirit: teaching them to observe all things whatsoever I commanded you: and lo, I am with you always, even unto the end of the world.* (Matthew 28:18–20 ASV)

All authority had been given unto Jesus in heaven and on earth. He did not need authority. He had always had it. Why was it given to Him now that He was leaving the earth? It was given to Him because He was the head of the church, the firstborn from among the dead.

He was the Lord of the church. The church was to be His body. He was to use that authority through the church. All the authority that had been given to Him was for the benefit of the church.

If there is no way for the church to use it, then it is ability like our unused capital.

We have, for instance, billions of dollars' worth of gold buried in the ground by the government. Some folk think this is a mark of poor judgment, when it could be in circulation bringing blessing to the people.

The church has done the same thing with the *"all authority"* that God gave to Jesus. It has buried it in its theology and creeds.

No one seems to have been able to reach it. It is doing no one any good.

The church does not know that before Jesus went away, He gave to it the power of attorney to use His name.

This power of attorney gives to the believer access to that *"all authority."*

> *Whatsoever ye shall ask [or demand] in my name, that will I do, that the Father may be glorified in the Son. If ye shall ask any thing in my name, I will do it.* (John 14:13–14)

This is not prayer. It is the use of the name of Jesus to draw on this *"all authority."*

The book of Acts gives case after case where men tapped that authority. Men were blessed by it.

That *"all authority"* is still available to those who use the name of Jesus. That authority has never been withdrawn.

If one part of that Great Commission has been abrogated, then all of it has been set aside.

If one miracle has been set aside, then all miracles have been set aside, and the name of Jesus has no authority. But we know that His name was given to us for miracle work.

Jesus said, *"In my name shall they cast out demons; they shall speak with new tongues; they shall take up serpents, and if they drink any deadly thing, it shall in no wise hurt them; they shall lay hands on the sick, and they shall recover"* (Mark 16:17–18 ASV).

Every one of these five things are things that the adversary brings upon the church of God and the unsaved world.

Five miraculous manifestations are to take place.

Satan holds men in bondage, fills them with fear of poison.

Satan has robbed them of their testimony so they no longer speak in new tongues of deliverance and victory.

They have been robbed of the ability to lay hands on the sick and see their loved ones recover.

Why? Because sense knowledge has gained the mastery over the ministry.

Jesus said that as soon as men believed on Him, at once these signs should accompany them. At once they begin to cast out demons. At once they begin to speak with tongues of power. At once they master disease. Serpents are typical of disease and demons.

> *So then after the Lord had spoken unto them, he was received up into heaven, and sat on the right hand of God. And they went forth, and preached every where, the Lord working with them, and confirming the word with signs following.* (Mark 16:19–20)

The Word that He had spoken and the Word they dared to confess was confirmed by signs that followed.

God's attitude toward sin and disease has never changed.

"Jesus Christ the same yesterday, and to day, and for ever" (Hebrews 13:8). He was opposed to disease then; He is opposed to disease now.

He suffered on account of sin, and His attitude toward sin now is as it was then.

The seated Christ is a receipt in full for your healing. The seated Christ proves that He finished His work.

Always think of Satan as the defeated one, as the one over whom you, in Jesus's name, have dominion.

In that name, the new creation is the master of demons and disease and every circumstance that would hold you in bondage.

We have a perfect redemption, a perfect new creation, and perfect union with Christ.

He said, *"I am the vine, ye are the branches"* (John 15:5).

We have a message that brings success, health, happiness, and victory to every man.

Every man is a failure outside of Christ.

We hold God's solution to the human problem.

The living Word on your lips makes you a victor, makes disease and poverty your servants.

The living Word on your lips brings God on the scene, brings victory and joy and success to the defeated.

19

GOD'S REVELATION OF JESUS CHRIST GIVEN TO THE APOSTLE PAUL

In this revelation, we see the supernatural element of Christianity in a light that the modern church has never seen.

Paul's revelation begins with Jesus being made sin. It deals with what He did and what was done to Him during the three days and three nights until finally He arose from the dead, carried His blood into the heavenly holy of holies, and sat down at the right hand of the Father.

That period covers the forty days from His crucifixion to His seating at the right hand of the Majesty on High.

It deals with three major facts: what God did for us in Christ in the great substitution; what the Holy Spirit, through the Word, can do in us in the new creation; and what Jesus is doing for us now at the right hand of the Father.

We can deal with only two phases of this work of Christ.

WHAT HE DID FOR US

It is deeply important that the reader fully grasps these basic facts.

Christ did not arise from the dead until He had broken Satan's dominion. It was imperative that Satan's authority over man be broken.

Christ did not arise from the dead until He had conquered the adversary.

> *Who delivered us out of the power of darkness, and translated us into the kingdom of the Son of his love; in whom we have our redemption, the forgiveness of our sins.* (Colossians 1:13–14 ASV)

He delivered us out of Satan's authority. The word translated "*power*" here means "authority."

He translated us into the kingdom of the Son of His love. That is the new birth. That is recreation. We have our redemption.

Every believer has been delivered out of Satan's authority and has been translated into the family of God and has his redemption in Christ. He is redeemed. Satan has no more dominion over him.

> *For sin over you shall not have lordship.* (Romans 6:14 YLT)

Sin is Satan. Satan shall not lord it over you. Satan has no more dominion over the believer than Pharaoh had over the children of Israel after they had crossed the Red Sea.

Satan has no dominion over you. Satan cannot put diseases upon you without your consent. It may be a consent of ignorance, but it is a consent.

Satan is defeated, conquered, as far as you are concerned. Satan is not only conquered, but God has made you a new creation over whom Satan has no dominion whatsoever.

> *Therefore if any man be in Christ, he is a new creature: old things are passed away; behold, all things are become new. And all things are of God, who hath reconciled us to himself by Jesus Christ, and hath given to us the ministry of reconciliation.* (2 Corinthians 5:17–18)

Those old things are the things of defeat, failure, weakness, poverty, sin, and spiritual death.

We are new creations. Jesus is the head of this new creation. He is the Lord of this new creation. He has taken Satan's place.

Satan no longer has dominion over you. You need have no fear of him, for he has been conquered.

In Romans 8:31–37, the Spirit, through the apostle Paul, gives us the position of the church. He climaxes it in the last verse: "*Nay, in all these things we are more than conquerors.*" We have a complete and perfect redemption.

This new creation has not only been declared righteous and been made righteous, but both God and Jesus declare that they are his righteousness.

Righteousness means the ability to stand in the Father's presence without a sense of guilt, with the same freedom and liberty that Jesus has.

Why? Because Romans 3:26 (YLT) declares, *"For His being righteous, and declaring him righteous who [is] of the faith of Jesus."*

God has become your righteousness in Christ Jesus.

First Corinthians 1:30 tells us that God has made Jesus to be righteousness unto you. This is a most amazing fact.

He does not stop there.

> *He hath made him to be sin for us, who knew no sin; that we might be made the righteousness of God in him.* (2 Corinthians 5:21)

If language means anything, then every believer stands complete in Christ.

> *And in him ye are made full* [complete], *who is the head of all principality and power.* (Colossians 2:10 ASV)

> *Of his fulness have all we received, and grace for grace.* (John 1:16)

The believer is not a cringing suppliant, begging for favors. He is a son of God, an heir of God, a prince of God.

He stands in the Father's presence, unabashed, unafraid, made righteous with God's own righteousness, made free with God's own freedom.

The Son has made you free. You are free in reality. Disease and sickness have no dominion over you.

Had we the space, we could show you that you are not only redeemed, a new creation, and the righteousness of God, but you are a son of God, in His family.

More than that, the Spirit who raised Jesus from the dead actually makes His home in your body.

You may never have given Him His place, or you may never have been conscious that God made His home in you, or that you had the ability of God in you.

You may have never taken advantage of the fact that your mind might be renewed to the extent that you might know the will of God in reality.

Not only do you have God in you, but you have the name of Jesus with the authority that God gave to Jesus in it.

In that name, you can lay hands on yourself if pain comes and receive your deliverance. In that name, you can break the power of the adversary over your finances, over your home, over your loved ones' bodies.

Limitless power and authority are given to the individual member of the body of Christ.

SOME OF THE HINDRANCES TO HEALING

Perhaps the most subtle and dangerous weapons of the devil are the sense of unworthiness and the sense of lack of faith.

Your worthiness is Jesus Christ, the righteous. You are the righteousness of God in Him.

The sense of unworthiness is a denial of the substitutionary sacrifice of Christ and of your standing in Christ, and of Christ's righteousness before the Father that has been granted to you.

A second hindrance is that you have accepted hope and mental assent instead of faith.

You never hope for a thing that you possess. You hope for the unpossessed.

When you hope for your healing, it means that you have no faith in it, but you expect to get it sometime.

Hope is a beautiful delusion. Mental assent is a kindred of hope. Mental assent is the substitute that the adversary has given to the church today for faith.

Many declare that the whole Bible is true from Genesis to Revelation, but they do not accept miracles except in isolated cases.

They assent to the truth of the Word, but they do not believe it. They say, "Yes, I believe the Bible is true" and never act on it.

Believing is acting on the Word of God. There is no faith without action.

James says our actions must correspond with our faith. *"My brothers, what is the use of anyone declaring he has faith, if he has no deeds to show?"* (James 2:14 MOFF).

There can be no faith without action on the Word. I can assent to it and remain as I am. I can admire it, but it is not mine.

The thing that the Scripture declares belongs to me. As soon as I found out the difference between mental assent and faith, I became a blessing to multitudes.

Many have been healed over the radio when they stopped mentally assenting and acted on the Word.

Another enemy of faith is sense knowledge evidence. A man believes what he can see. He is like Thomas who said, "I will not believe unless I can put my hand into His side." (See John 20:25.)

Several days later, Jesus appeared and told Thomas, "*Reach hither thy hand, and thrust it into my side: and be not faithless, but believing*" (John 20:27).

Faith is giving substance to things you have hoped for. It is a conviction of the reality of things that are not seen. Faith is changing hope into reality. (See Hebrews 11:1.)

Faith is acting in the face of contrary evidence. The senses declare, "It cannot be," but faith shouts above the turmoil, "It is!"

Faith counts the thing done before God has acted. That compels God's action. God is a faith God.

> *It is by faith we understand that the world was fashioned by the word of God, and thus the visible was made out of the invisible.*
>
> (Hebrews 11:3 MOFF)

All God did at the beginning was to say, "*Let there be,*" and there was.

All that faith has to say is, "Let there be perfect quietness in this man's body and spirit," and disease must go.

Faith says, "Let there be plenty where poverty has reigned. Let there be freedom where bondage has held sway." These things must come to pass.

20

HEALING BELONGS TO US

"I have prayed and prayed and have received no benefit. I have had others pray for me and my disease grows worse and worse. Can you do anything for me?"

"Yes, I believe I can. Did you ever realize that healing belongs to you, that you need not pray for it?"

"I never heard anything like that!"

"It is true. Let me prove it to you. Isaiah 53:4, 'Surely he hath borne our sicknesses and carried our diseases; yet we did esteem him stricken, smitten of God, and afflicted.' What does He say He did with our diseases?"

"I don't know as I understand it."

"'Surely he (that is Christ) hath borne our sicknesses and carried our diseases; yet we did esteem him stricken, smitten of God and afflicted.' You understand that don't you?"

"Yes."

"Do you understand that it pleased Jehovah to bruise Him? He made Him sick with our diseases."

"What does that mean to me?"

"It means that these pains and afflictions you are suffering were laid on Jesus. Jesus actually bore them just as He bore your sins. He was wounded for your transgressions, he was bruised for your iniquities; the chastisement of your peace was upon him; and with his stripes you are healed.

"God actually laid your iniquities upon Jesus. Then you do not have to bear them."

"I never saw it like that before. You mean God actually laid my sickness upon Him, and made Him sick with my diseases?"

"Yes, that is what the Word declares.

"He made Him sin with your sins that you might be the righteousness of God in Christ; 2 Corinthians 5:21. He made Him sick with your diseases that you might be perfectly well in Christ.

"It is a gift. Healing is yours now, as you thank Him for it.

"God put your diseases on Him. He bore them. He was stricken, smitten of God and afflicted with your diseases. Satan has no right to put on you what God put on Jesus.

"When your heart comes to know this as you know other facts of life, you are through with sickness.

"You cannot be sick when you come to know this fact, know it as you know that God laid upon Him 'the iniquity of us all.'

"Romans 6:14, 'For sin shall not lord it over you' is yours today. I like that translation.

"Sickness and pain are things of the past for 'whom the Son sets free is free in reality.'

"If He has set you free from sin, sin has no dominion over you. If He has set you free from disease, it must not lord it over you. If He has set you free from Satan, Satan has no dominion over you. If He has set you free from circumstances, circumstances cannot lord it over you any longer.

"How they have held sway over us in the past! Now we belong to a new order of things.

"We are the masters of circumstances, of demons, of diseases. Sin and demons have no dominion over us. The Son has set us free.

"In God's sight we are free. In Jesus's sight we are free. According to the Word, we are free.

"Stand fast in the liberty wherewith Christ has made you free. Hold fast to this confession. Make it your very own.

"Take your place. Act the part. Refuse to allow Satan to have anything to do with this body in which you live.

"Know ye not that your body is the temple, the home, the house of God? First Corinthians 6:15–20.

"It is God's place. You are the overseer living in it. You are to see that Satan does not trespass on God's property."

"How am I to keep him from it?"

"Jesus said, 'In my name ye shall cast out demons.'

"Jesus has given you the right to use His name. That name can break the power of disease, the power of the adversary. That name can stop disease and failure from reigning over you.

"There is no disease that has ever come to man which this name cannot destroy."

Our confession is our faith speaking.

JESUS AND HIS NAME ARE ONE

That name and Jesus are one, just as your name is one with you.

You do not have to make this liberty yours. All you have to do is to enjoy it and walk in the light of the Word.

Make these facts your confession. You are to tell the world that by His stripes you are healed, that disease has lost its dominion, that it can no longer lord it over you.

If we speak words of faith instead of words of doubt, we will be speaking God's language. Doubt words come from another source.

You cannot talk sickness and disease and walk in health.

You cannot tell folk about your disease and about your pains, and moan over your troubles to get sympathy, without losing your fellowship with Him.

When we tell our troubles to people, we lose our faith and sweet fellowship with the Father.

We tell people our troubles to get their sympathy. We should cast our anxiety and troubles upon Him for He cares for us.

When we talk about our weakness and failure and disease, we glorify the devil who gave them to us. We glorify doctors and lawyers by taking our troubles to them. They get paid for listening to people's troubles. That is the secret of their success—being good trouble listeners.

Telling our troubles that are caused by Satan is a confession that Satan is the master and that he has gained the supremacy.

It makes the troubles bigger; it makes the disease worse; it makes us feel worse.

The real confession in our lives should be of God's ability, His faithfulness, and that our troubles are being borne by Jesus just as He bore our diseases and sins.

Hold fast to your confession of what God is to you and what you are in Christ.

Give up your confession of Satan's supremacy. You know that disease comes from the adversary, that lack of ability comes from the adversary. All our troubles are demon-made.

If you are using demon-inspired words, don't expect to have the sweetest fellowship with heaven.

It is the Word of faith which we speak. Our lips are filled with the Word of faith.

Our hearts are singing the song of faith.

> *Verily, verily, I say unto you, He that believeth hath eternal life.*
> (John 6:47 ASV)

It is the believer who possesses. I believe; I have. Then I rejoice in my possession. I enjoy my possession. Health is my possession. Success is my possession.

I have plenty because He is my supply. He meets every need of mine according to His riches in glory in Christ Jesus. (See Philippians 4:19.)

I am not moaning and groaning. I am praising and rejoicing.

Faith possesses. Faith's possessions are real, just as real as sense possessions.

Spiritual things are as real as material things.

"For we walk by faith, not by sight" (2 Corinthians 5:7). We walk in the realm of God. We not only walk by faith, but we talk by faith. We have left the realm of the senses.

When you learn to talk by faith, the dominion of disease is broken over you. But just as long as you walk by reason and you follow the suggestions of the senses—feeling, seeing, tasting—you are going to live and walk in the realm where disease will hold sway over your life, and pain will hold carnival in your body.

If you will learn to talk faith talk, you will be a victor.

First John 5:4–5 should be known by every believer. It should be a part of your conscious knowledge that you can use day by day.

> *For whatsoever is born of God overcometh the world: and this is the victory that overcometh the world, even our faith.* (1 John 5:4)

SOME THINGS THAT ARE BEGOTTEN OF GOD

The new creation is begotten of God. Righteousness is begotten of God. Love is begotten of God. Faith is begotten of God. These are the overcomers of the world.

> *Who is he that overcometh the world, but he that believeth that Jesus is the Son of God?* (1 John 5:5)

You believe that. That means you are a victor.

The believers are winners.

Leave the lowlands of doubt and fear. Come out onto the highlands and walk in fellowship with Him.

Healing and victory are yours. Leave failure to the failures.

We are walking with the power of God, fighting with the weapons of righteousness both for attack and for defense.

"Nay, in all our fight we are more than conquerors." Why? Because we are raised together with Christ.

When Jesus arose from the dead, it was our victory over the enemy. In *The Epistles of Paul,* W. J. Conybeare's translation of Colossians 2:15 tells us: *"And*

He disarmed the Principalities and the Powers [which fought against Him], and put them to open shame, leading them captive in the triumph of Christ."

You remember that we were crucified with Him, died with Him, were buried with Him, suffered with Him, were justified with Him, and were made alive with Him.

Then we met the enemy, and we conquered him in Christ.

So Paul can say to us: "Wherein also ye are made partakers of His righteousness through your faith in God who raised Him from the dead."

And God raised Christ so that we might share in His life.

We were made partakers in Christ's resurrection victory, Christ's resurrection life, and Christ's resurrection new creation.

Of His fullness have all we received.

For we are His workmanship created in Christ Jesus.

21

WHAT GOD HATH DECLARED

Here is the foundation for faith, the living Word of God. What God says, is. What man says, may be.

What God says is never "may be"; it is always made good. God's Word is a part of Himself, just as your word is a part of you. What you say reveals the real "you."

People come to trust in the "you" in your voice. Your voice and your words are "you."

Jesus was God's voice. What Jesus said, the Father said. Jesus was the Logos, the Word of God. When you read what Jesus said, or you hear it read, you are hearing God, you are hearing the living Word.

God is behind what He has spoken. The throne of God is behind what He has spoken.

God's character and Jesus's character are involved in what the Father or Jesus has spoken.

So when He says, "Surely He hath borne our sicknesses and carried our diseases, yet we did esteem Him stricken, smitten of God and afflicted," we know that our diseases were laid on Him.

When He climaxes that statement with, "By His stripes we are healed," we know that we are healed.

It is a problem of the integrity of the Word.

> *But he was wounded for our transgressions, he was bruised for our iniquities: the chastisement of our peace was upon him; and with his stripes we are healed. All we like sheep have gone astray; we have turned every one*

to his own way; and the Lord hath laid on him the iniquity of us all.
(Isaiah 53:5–6)

This solves the sin problem.

But now once at the end of the ages hath he been manifested to put away sin by the sacrifice of himself. (Hebrews 9:26 ASV)

The sin problem is a settled problem because God said it was settled. Disease and sickness problems are settled because God said He had settled them.

He bore the diseases.

God said, "By His stripes, you were healed" so that ends the discussion.

He said the issue was closed. The diseases have been put away, so sickness and disease shall not lord it over you.

He said, "*There is a new creation whenever a man comes to be in Christ; what is old is gone, the new has come*" (2 Corinthians 5:17 MOFF).

Disease has no standing with the new creation. That is His declaration. That statement is a part of Himself.

He says you are a new creation. He says you are His son, born from above.

"That which is born of the spirit is spirit." This is a statement of fact.

Sin and disease are one. They cannot dominate the new creation.

You are not only His son, but you are a joint heir with Jesus. You are a joint fellowshipper in all that Christ did and is.

This shows how near you are to Him; "*I am the vine, ye are the branches*" (John 15:5).

God is a part of what He said. In Christ, you are what He says you are.

You are a new creation created in Christ. "*There is therefore now no condemnation to them which are in Christ Jesus*" (Romans 8:1)—that is, to the new creation.

What God says, is. If you are a new creation, then there is no condemnation for you.

If there is no condemnation, disease cannot lord it over you. If you have committed sins and you confess them, "He is faithful and righteous to forgive you and cleanse you from all unrighteousness." (See 1 John 1:9.)

You are forgiven. What God says, is. You do not need to make this yours. It was written for you. Just act on it. It is like God. It is a part of God.

If He says He has forgiven you, He has forgiven you. What He has forgiven, He forgets. It is as though it had never been.

There is no memory of it. You stand as free as Jesus is in the Father's presence.

Our faulty vision, caused by sense knowledge, has made us see as through a glass darkly. The Word has been obscured.

We have not been able to catch God's dream of the reality of it.

The reality of it has never dawned upon the church. They have never realized that they were free from the dominion of Satan.

> *Who delivered us out of the power of darkness, and translated us into the kingdom of the Son of his love; in whom we have our redemption, the forgiveness of our sins.* (Colossians 1:13–14 ASV)

We are delivered out of the authority of Satan. We are translated into the kingdom of the Son of His love.

We are in the kingdom. We are members of it. We are heirs of God and joint heirs with Jesus Christ.

Satan's dominion is ended. We are free, absolutely delivered. What God says, is. We are redeemed.

Not only do we have a perfect redemption, but we have a perfect remission of our sins.

Remission has to do with what we did before we were born again. Forgiveness has to do with what we do after we are born again. Remission is the wiping out of everything connected with our old life. There are no hangovers in the divine life. You are absolutely a new creation. There are no sin scars upon you.

You are a new creation created in Christ Jesus. You are the righteousness of God, created in Christ Jesus.

You are complete in Him. What God has made righteous is righteous. What God has declared righteous is righteous.

What Jesus made righteous in His substitutionary sacrifice is just what God says it is, a completed, perfect thing in His sight.

When the believer, in the quietness of his own spirit, recognizes the utter integrity of the Word of God, disease, sickness, and failure are the things of the past.

> *Ye are of God, little children, and have overcome them: because greater is he that is in you, than he that is in the world.* (1 John 4:4)

The power and ability of God is in you right now. You stand a victor in every combat.

You have no apologies to make for weakness. God is the strength of your life.

What God says, is. There is no supposition about it. It is an absolute present-tense reality.

If He says you are more than a conqueror, you are, no matter how mighty the force against you may be.

It makes no difference what sense knowledge has told you. You "cast down reasonings" and give the Word of God its place. (See 2 Corinthians 10:5.)

You act as though there were not an enemy in the world. When He says, "*My God shall supply every need of yours*" (Philippians 4:19 ASV), you are not afraid to do anything He tells you to do.

The money will be there to meet every obligation. God cannot lie. His Word is a part of Himself.

He and His Word are one. He watches over His Word to perform it. He is utterly jealous over His Word. He watches over it with the utmost care.

All you need to do is to call His attention to what He has promised, and He will make the promise good.

God's Word has the ability in it to make good anything He has promised. The Logos of God is a living thing. It produces in the heart of man the very thing He promises He would do.

We preach it and teach it because it is the living Word today. God says, "*Whosoever believeth on him shall not be put to shame*" (Romans 10:11 ASV).

THE LIVING WORD

The Word is lifeless until faith is breathed into it on our own lips. Then it becomes a supernatural force.

You may have entire chapters of the Word committed to memory, but they lie dead in your life.

As you act on the Word, it becomes a living thing. Then as you witness, make your confession of that Word, it becomes a dominating force on your lips.

Jesus's Word was the Father's, but He spoke it, He lived it, He acted it. That made it a living thing.

He said, "The words that I speak are not mine, but my Father's words."

He said, "The words that I have spoken unto you are spirit and are life."

We take Jesus's words and we act upon them. That makes them live.

22

WHY I LOST MY HEALING

"I felt perfectly well for several days after you prayed for me. Then all the symptoms came back and I have been in hell ever since. Can you tell me what is the difficulty?"

"Yes. It is very simple. You received your healing through another's faith. The adversary took advantage of your lack of faith and brought back the symptoms, camouflaged the entire thing, and you were filled with fear instead of faith.

"Instead of rising resolutely and meeting the adversary with the Word and commanding his power broken in Jesus's name, you yielded.

"Why did you yield? Because you had no foundation in your life. You were like the man who built his house upon the sand. The storm came and destroyed it. The thing for you to do is to get to know the Lord yourself through the Word.

"When you know that 'By His stripes you are healed,' and you know it as you know that two and two are four, the adversary will have no power over you.

"When you know the power and authority of the name of Jesus and that you have a legal right to use it, and the adversary lays siege to you, you will not be filled with fear. You will simply laugh at him and say, 'Satan, did you know you were whipped? Leave my body.' He will leave.

"No one can maintain his healing which has come as a result of another's faith unless his faith is developed through the Word, so he can maintain his own rights in the redemption of Christ."

23

GOD'S METHOD OF HEALING IS SPIRITUAL

You must have seen as you have studied this book that healing is spiritual.

It is not mental as Christian Science and Unity and other metaphysical teachers claim. Neither is it physical as the medical world teaches. When God heals, He heals through the spirit. When man heals, he must either do it through the mind that is governed by the physical senses, or he does it through the physical body.

You understand that man is a spirit being, and that life's greatest forces are spiritual.

We have witnessed a great nation, after months of fearful warfare, conquer one of the smallest nations in the world. They conquered them physically. They are not conquered mentally yet. That will take brutal force. They are not conquered spiritually. They never will be.

We can understand that the great forces in life are spiritual forces. Love and hate, fear and faith, joy and grief, are all of the spirit.

It is a remarkable thing that when Jesus comes on the scene as a healer, He demands faith. He declares, "Thy faith hath made thee whole" and "All things are possible to him that believeth."

We might multiply these statements. All of them prove one thing: that all of Jesus's healings were spiritual. He demanded faith, and faith is born of the spirit.

In our own ministry where we have seen multitudes of people healed of many kinds of incurable diseases, they have been healed invariably by the Word of God.

He sent His word, and healed them. (Psalm 107:20 JPS)

Sin had brought the disease upon them, but the Word delivered them. The Word is the healer today. Man gets his healing by acting upon the Word.

That action is called faith. We have found that healing belongs to the believer.

24

RIGHT AND WRONG CONFESSIONS

For a long time, I was confused over the fact that in my own life and the lives of others, there was a continual sense of defeat and failure.

I prayed for the sick. I knew that the Bible was true, and I searched diligently to find the leakage.

One day, I saw in Hebrews 4:14 (MOFF) that we are to *"hold fast to our confession."* Some Bible translations say "profession."

In the third chapter of Hebrews, I discovered that Christianity is called "the great confession."

I asked myself, "What confession am I to hold fast?"

I am to hold fast to my confession of the absolute integrity of the Bible.

I am to hold fast to the confession of the redemptive work of Christ.

I am to hold fast to my confession of the new creation, of receiving the life and nature of God.

I am to hold fast to the confession that God is the strength of my life.

I am to hold fast to the confession that "surely He hath borne my sicknesses and carried my diseases, and that by His stripes I am healed."

I found it very difficult to hold fast to the confession of perfect healing when I had pain in my body.

I made the discovery that I had been making two confessions. I had been confessing the absolute truthfulness of the Word of God, and at the same time, I was making a confession that I was not healed.

If you had said, "Do you believe that by His stripes you are healed," I would have said, "Yes, sir, I do."

But in the next breath, I would have said, "But the pain is still there." The second confession nullified the first.

In reality, I had two confessions: first, a confession of my perfect healing and redemption in Christ; and a second, that the redemption and healing was not a fact.

Then came the great battle to gain the mastery over my confession, until I learned to have but one confession.

If I confess, "My God shall supply every need of mine," I must not nullify that confession by saying, "Yes, God supplies my needs, but I cannot pay my rent. I cannot pay the telephone bill."

Faith holds fast to the confession of the Word.

Sense knowledge holds fast to the confession of physical evidences.

If I accept physical evidence over against the Word of God, I nullify the Word as far as I am concerned.

But I hold fast to my confession that God's Word is true, that by His stripes I am healed, that my God does supply my needs.

I hold fast to that confession in the face of apparent contradictions, and He is bound to make good.

Many believers have failed when things became difficult because they lost their confession.

While the sun was shining brightly, their confessions were vigorous, strong, and clear.

But when the storms came, the testings came, and the adversary was taking advantage of them, they gave up their testimony.

Every time that you confess disease and weakness and failure, you magnify the adversary above the Father, and you destroy your own confidence in the Word.

You are to hold fast to your confession in the face of apparent defeat.

You are to study the Word until you know what your rights are, and then hold fast to them.

Some make confessions without any foundations. Then the adversary whips and beats them badly.

You are to find out what your rights are. For instance, you know that He says, "Surely He hath borne our sicknesses and carried our diseases." Now you can make your confession.

"Nay, in all these things we are more than conquerors." There you can make your confession.

"Greater is He that is in me, than he that is in the world." You can make your confession here.

Stand by your confession through thick and thin, through good report and evil. You know that your confession is according to the Word.

> *And they overcame him by the blood of the Lamb, and by the word of their testimony.* (Revelation 12:11)

25

THE HIGH PRIESTHOOD OF JESUS

Jesus's ministry at the right hand of the Father is one of the rarest features of the Pauline revelation.

The problem of the authorship of Hebrews is settled. Hebrews is a part of that revelation.

No one else could have given it as Paul has given it to us. It is a revelation of what Jesus did from the time He was made sin on the cross until He sat down on the right hand of the Father.

That entire work is given to us in this wonderful unveiling.

Not only did he make us know what Christ did for us in His substitution, but he has made us know what the Holy Spirit, through the Word on the ground of the substitutionary work of Christ, does in the individual life.

There are really four phases of this revelation. First, what Christ did for us.

Second, what the Holy Spirit, through the Word, does in us.

Third, what Jesus is doing now at the right hand of the Father for us.

Fourth, what His love does through us in ministry.

We spend much time studying what Christ has done for us, but very little time has been given to what He does in us and less has been given to what He is now doing in His great high priestly office at the right hand of the Father.

His entire ministries for us would have been a total failure had He not carried on a ministry now at the right hand of the Father on our behalf.

Jesus died as the Lamb. He arose as the Lord High Priest. His first ministry, after He arose from the dead, is illustrated in John 20:15–18.

Jesus met Mary after His resurrection. She fell down at His feet, and no wonder.

He said to her, *"Touch me not; for I am not yet ascended to my Father: but go to my brethren, and say unto them, I ascend unto my Father, and your Father; and to my God, and your God"* (verse 17).

What did He mean? He died as the substitute Lamb. He arose as the Lord High Priest.

> *Wherefore in all things it behoved him to be made like unto his brethren, that he might be a merciful and faithful high priest in things pertaining to God, to make reconciliation for the sins of the people.* (Hebrews 2:17)

He is a merciful and faithful High Priest, not in things pertaining to man, but in things pertaining to God.

The claims of justice had to be satisfied as well as the needs of man met.

It was necessary that as a High Priest, He should make propitiation for the sins of the people.

This is recorded in Hebrews 9:11–12 (ASV): *"But Christ having come a high priest of the good things to come, through the greater and more perfect tabernacle, not made with hands, that is to say, not of this creation, nor yet through the blood of goats and calves, but through his own blood, entered in once for all into the holy place, having obtained eternal redemption."*

"Christ having come"—from whence did He come? Out of the place where He had gone as a substitute, when He had met the claims of justice, where He had satisfied the claims of the supreme court of the universe against rebellious humanity.

He had to carry His blood into the heavenly holy of holies and seal the document of our redemption with it.

His blood is the guarantor now of the integrity of our redemption.

Just as the high priest under the first covenant carried the blood into the holy of holies once a year and made a yearly atonement, Jesus carried His own blood in and made an eternal redemption once for all.

Atonement simply meant to cover the sin of Israel while the sins were borne away by the scapegoat.

The sin nature in man that had caused him to break the law—not the act, but the cause of the act—was antagonistic against God and had to be covered.

Now Jesus came and put that nature away by the sacrifice of Himself.

> *But now once at the end of the ages hath he been manifested to put away sin by the sacrifice of himself.* (Hebrews 9:26 ASV)

It was not the sins that man had committed; it was man's sin nature that had to be put away. That sin nature was spiritual death, the nature of Satan.

His sins were small things that could be wiped out. But that sin nature required God's own beloved Son to become sin, that we might become the righteousness of God in Him.

He took our sin that we might become righteous. He took our spiritual death that we might have eternal life.

He took our ostracism, our outlawed nature, that we might take the place of sons with the Father.

Oh, the unmeasured grace of God unveiled in the sacrifice of Jesus. He carried His own blood into the heavenly holy of holies and instead of making the yearly atonement, He gave us an eternal redemption.

> *Wherefore in all things it behoved him to be made like unto his brethren, that he might be a merciful and faithful high priest in things pertaining to God.* (Hebrews 2:17)

He is a merciful and faithful High Priest.

God had to be satisfied. The claims of justice had to be met.

He was made sin, was under condemnation, and for three days and three nights, He was in hell, locked up in the prison house of death.

The supreme court was able to absolutely justify Him as our substitute and declare Him utterly righteous.

He met the demands of justice and was liberated. God said of Him, "*This day have I begotten thee*" (Psalm 2:7).

What day was it He was begotten? It was the third day down in the prison house of death that He was born again of the Spirit.

That was His new birth.

That was when we were recreated, for we are His workmanship created in Christ Jesus.

He was there justified in spirit.

Not only was He declared righteous, but He was made righteous with the very nature of God.

Now having been made righteous, having conquered Satan and stripped him of his authority, He arose from the dead and the supreme court of the universe absolutely puts the stamp of approval on His work for us.

Then He was able to go into the heavenly holy of holies and sit down at the right hand of the Majesty on High.

He has made propitiation for our sins. That word *propitiation* means "substitution."

He has made substitution for the sins of the people.

Having Himself suffered being tempted, He is able to succor those who are tempted.

> *Wherefore, holy brethren, partakers of a heavenly calling, consider the Apostle and High Priest of our confession.* (Hebrews 3:1 ASV)

Christianity is called a *confession*. The finished work of Jesus Christ is called a confession.

Now you can understand Romans 10:9: *"If thou shalt confess with thy mouth the Lord Jesus, and shalt believe in thine heart that God hath raised him from the dead, thou shalt be saved."*

Christianity is a confession.

It is a confession of the finished work of Jesus.

It is a confession that He is seated at the right hand of the Father having perfectly redeemed us.

It is a confession of our sonship, of our place in Christ, of our rights and privileges.

It is a confession of our supremacy over disease and weakness, over Satan in the name of Jesus.

What a confession that is!

Hebrews 4:14–16 (ASV) carries us a step farther in the development of this high priestly ministry of Jesus:

> *Having then a great high priest, who hath passed through the heavens, Jesus the Son of God, let us hold fast our confession. For we have not a high priest that cannot be touched with the feeling of our infirmities; but one that hath been in all points tempted like as we are, yet without sin. Let us therefore draw near with boldness unto the throne of grace, that we may receive mercy, and may find grace to help us in time of need.*

The entire ministry of Jesus swings about this high priestly office. As a High Priest, He carried His blood into the holy of holies. As a High Priest, He sat down at the right hand of the Majesty on High.

He is the mediatorial High Priest between God and man. No man can reach the Father but through Him.

Jesus said, "I am the way, the reality, and the life. No man can get to the Father but by Me." (See John 14:6.)

Peter said, "*Neither is there salvation in any other: for there is none other name under heaven given among men, whereby we must be saved*" (Acts 4:12).

Jesus is the only way into the Father's presence without condemnation.

Is it any wonder that the early church was called *the Way*?

> *And asked of him letters to Damascus unto the synagogues, that if he found any that were of the Way, whether men or women, he might bring them bound to Jerusalem.* (Acts 9:2 ASV)

> *But when some were hardened and disobedient, speaking evil of the Way before the multitude, he departed from them, and separated the disciples, reasoning daily in the school of Tyrannus.* (Acts 19:9 ASV)

> *And about that time there arose no small stir concerning the Way.*
> (Acts 19:23 ASV)

(See also Isaiah 30:21; Isaiah 35:8; Acts 16:17; Acts 24:14, 22.)

He is not only the Lord High Priest and the Mediator, but the moment a man accepts Christ, He becomes his High Priestly Intercessor.

He ever lives to make intercession for the believer. (See Isaiah 53:12; Romans 8:34; Hebrews 7:25.) He is set forth as the Intercessor for the believer.

He ever lives to make intercession. What a ministry, what a service.

He does not have a chance to take a vacation. He has no opportunity to step aside for a moment.

No one else can act as High Priest, as Mediator, as Intercessor. He has another important ministry. He is the Advocate.

When the believer is tempted and Satan gains the mastery over him, and he cries out in agony for mercy, we hear Him whisper, *"If we confess our sins, he is faithful and just to forgive us our sins, and to cleanse us from all unrighteousness"* (1 John 1:9).

Then He climaxes it by saying, *"My little children, these things write I unto you, that ye sin not. And if any man sin, we have an advocate with the Father, Jesus Christ the righteous"* (1 John 2:1).

He is righteous so that He can go into the Father's presence when we lose the sense of righteousness by our wrongdoings.

As our Advocate, He restores to us our lost sense of righteousness.

He is the Lord and Head of the church.

David prophesied of Him in Psalm 23:1, *"The Lord is my shepherd; I shall not want."*

He is the caretaker, the lover, the bridegroom of the body.

He is the firstborn from the dead, the head of all principalities and powers.

He is my risen Lord seated at the Father's right hand.

Follow me through the entire epistle of Hebrews and you will find a continual unveiling of these different phases of His high priestly ministry.

This Scripture carries us a step farther in the development of this high priestly ministry of Jesus:

> *Having then a great high priest, who hath passed through the heavens, Jesus the Son of God, let us hold fast our confession.*
>
> (Hebrews 4:14 ASV)

This is the High Priestly Son.

"Let us hold fast our confession." What is our confession? It is our redemption, our recreation, our union with the Father in Christ, our victory over circumstances and demons and diseases, our independence in Christ, of natural law.

This High Priest, knowing that man has received an inferiority complex on account of spiritual death says we are to *"draw near with boldness unto the throne of grace, that we may receive mercy, and may find grace to help us in time of need"* (Hebrews 4:16 ASV).

That word *boldness* means "freedom of speech."

In the Pshitto, there is a marginal reference that reads "barefacedness." We are coming without any sense of guilt or sin, as a child would come to an earthly parent.

> *For we have not a high priest that cannot be touched with the feeling of our infirmities; but one that hath been in all points tempted like as we are, yet without sin.* (Hebrews 4:15 ASV)

"For every high priest taken from among men" has infirmities. (See Hebrews 5:1–2.) Jesus had no infirmities.

He had nothing but what He took on from us. He did not come from the seed of Levi. He was not in the priesthood by birth.

He is a priest after an order on the part of God.

> *(The Lord sware and will not repent himself, thou art a priest for ever); by so much also hath Jesus become the surety of a better covenant.* (Hebrews 7:21–22)

He is a High Priest; He is the surety of this new covenant. The new covenant heads up in Him.

He was the sacrifice of the covenant. His blood was the blood of the covenant. His life was the life of the covenant.

Now He is the surety of it.

Every Scripture from Matthew to Revelation is backed up by the Lord Jesus Himself.

His very throne is behind every Word.

Just as God became the surety of the Abrahamic covenant, Jesus now becomes the surety of this new covenant.

He can be because *"he abideth for ever"* (Hebrews 7:24 ASV). He has His unchangeable priesthood.

> *Wherefore he is able also to save them to the uttermost that come unto God by him, seeing he ever liveth to make intercession for them. For such an high priest became us.* (Hebrews 7:25–26)

"For such an high priest became us." I think there is no sweeter expression in the entire revelation than this.

Consider Him in all His grace and beauty and His overflowing love.

It is such a High Priest becomes us.

We are new creations. We are in the beloved.

We are the sweetest, most beautiful things that the Father has. We are members of His own body.

This Christ says in the twenty-seventh verse, *"First for his own sins, and then for the people's: for this he did once, when he offered up himself."*

He was made sin for us.

He made one sacrifice for sins forever, then He sat down at the right hand of the Majesty on High.

Do you realize what it means when it says He sat down?

It means your redemption is a completed thing. You are healed.

You are as well as Jesus, in the mind of the Father. You are an absolute overcomer.

Poverty, want, and need are things of the past.

> *That we may obtain mercy, and find grace to help in time of need.* (Hebrews 4:16)

> *My God shall supply every need of yours.* (Philippians 4:19 ASV)

> *Your heavenly Father knoweth that ye have need of all these things.* (Matthew 6:32)

Jesus demonstrated this in His earth walk.

He fed the multitudes.

He gave the disciples that great draft of fish. He turned water into wine.

He healed the sick and met every need of man. That is my Lord.

He is the Mediator of this new covenant.

He stands between humanity and the Father with the pierced hands and the wounded side and the thorn-scarred brow.

He is the Mediator. Do you think He will turn anyone away who comes to the Father?

Never!

Every unsaved man has a legal right to eternal life.

Jesus takes his part and vouches for him the moment he says, "God, I will take your Son as my Savior and confess Him as my Lord."

Jesus's high priestly ministry meets every need of the believer from the moment he is born again until he is ushered into the presence of the Father at the end of life.

CONCLUSION

You have read the book.

It will do you no good unless you have made up your mind that you are going to act upon the Scriptures quoted.

The promises that cover your case are of no value until you act upon them.

Believing is acting on the Word. Faith is the result of action.

But there can be no healing, no deliverance, no victory until you act on the Word.

You may get others to act for you. They will give you temporary relief. What you need is to learn to act for yourself

It would pay for you to send for our Bible study course *The Bible in the Light of Our Redemption* and begin to know the Word. Several people have requested that we include in this book testimonies of the miraculous healings we have seen in our ministry, but we do not consider this wise.

Our purpose in printing this book was that people might see their deliverance in Christ from oppression and sickness, that they might see their complete redemption already purchased for them. We feel that if they were to read of the physical manifestations in others' lives, they would unconsciously look to the other person's healing and not see their own deliverance already accomplished.

For this reason, we are leaving this message in the book to be just a statement from the Word of God on our rights and privileges in Christ.

We want you to look to the Word for your healing.

THE NEW KIND OF LOVE

CONTENTS

THE AUTHOR'S REASON

We are passing through the most critical period of human history. All that has been built through the centuries is in danger of being destroyed.

Is there a remedy that can be applied at this dark hour that will save the situation?

Our home life is disintegrating. The whole moral structure of family life is endangered.

There is something lacking. Natural human love has failed. Again and again, we have asked the question, "Why has it failed?"

It is because it is based upon selfishness. It has been unable to stand the tremendous test of selfishness that has been developed by modern education.

There is a combat that is touching every life. It is the war between natural human love and selfishness, and love is losing the fight. You see it in the divorce court, in the struggle between capital and labor, between the classes.

Has God a solution for this problem? We believe He has.

It is *The New Kind of Love* that has been overlooked by the church but has recently been rediscovered. This book is an attempt to bring this new kind of love into the modern life.

HOW IT CAME

For years, I had the conviction that I did not understand love. I knew Jesus majored it, and it was majored in the Pauline revelation. I gave much time to the study of it, but I always had the sense of not having arrived.

One day, I saw an article by Canon Frederic W. Farrar in which he called attention to the fact that there were two Greek words translated as "love" or "charity" in the New Testament: *agape* and *phileo*. He said that agape was evidently born in the realm of divine revelation, for that word did not occur in the classical Greek before the time of Christ.

Like a flash, I saw the truth. Jesus had brought a new kind of love to the world.

I saw that these two words are never used interchangeably. I had the secret.

John tells us that God is agape.

We partake of God's nature, eternal life, and this makes us sons of love.

1

LOVE, GREATEST THING IN THE WORLD

Love has never given birth to a pain. Love has never wantonly crushed or broken the tender flower of faith that grows in the heart of trust.

Love is God unveiled. "*God is love*" (1 John 4:8).

This love life is God actually living Himself in us as He lived in Jesus.

There was a ruggedness about the Master and yet a gentle tenderness that caused children to climb up into His arms and put their hands on His face. They longed to touch Him, to hold His hand, to be near Him.

The love that was in the Man of Galilee is the love that is to rule the church, rule the home, and rule this heart of mine.

Love is to the human heart what flowers are to the hillside. Flowers cover the naked, ragged places in the soil. They grow around the rocks. They grow among the roots. They cover up the wounds in the earth's surface. They cover the clay and bleak soil with a garment of glory, royalty, and lustrous beauty. So love covers the ragged rough spots in the human.

Love is the reason for the flower garden, just as love was the reason for the flowers being.

Love gathers the flowers and arranges them to please the eye and make glad the heart.

Love makes the home beautiful. Love comes and lives in the home to keep it a place of happiness.

Love is the most beautiful thing. It may be the most fragile thing, yet it has the most enduring strength of anything that we know.

When man is love ruled, love owned, and love motivated, he does not shrink from any sacrifice. Christ did not shrink from bearing the sin, pain, and anguish of the world.

LOVE AND THE CROSS

Love made that ugly cross beautiful. Love made that tomb beautiful—that darksome, dreaded place where death held sway. Love stripped death of its terror. Love made the naked, thorn-crowned Man of Galilee the King of lonely hearts.

My heart calls Him the naked King of the storm-tossed, broken human. Love made me crown Him, not with thorns, but with my heart and its devotion.

Love drives that delicate tender spirit into the darkest heathenism of Africa to endure every privation, to be shut alone with heathen minds that have no sense of appreciation, no touch of love, just cold indifference and selfish greed. And yet that love spirit lives, thrives, and pours itself out until that dark place blossoms with all the tender fragrance of the new creation.

Such is love, the mightiest thing among the mighty, and the most beautiful thing among the beautiful. It is this God nature gaining the ascendancy in the heart of man.

"EVEN AS"

There are two little words in the new law of the new covenant that challenged me. They reached out their tender hands and gripped me. I saw the dainty tendril of a climbing vine lay its soft, fragile hand upon the coarse, hard rock, and after a bit, it had fastened itself to the rock.

Those two little words seem like the delicate fingers of that beautiful climbing vine.

You ask me what the words are? *"Even as."*

> *This is my commandment, that ye love one another, **even as** I have loved you.* (John 15:12 ASV)

At first, I tried to get away from them, but they followed me, followed as only love can follow. I could hear them in the chambers of my soul, like the memory of a long-forgotten hymn that comes back and raps at the door of the heart.

I kept saying, "Even as." Then I turned and listened. I asked, "Even as what?"

"As I have loved you."

I said, "I can't do it, Master. I can't love like that. If I loved like that, I would be obliged to give away everything I own."

Then He asked so gently, "What is it that you would need to give away?"

I took an inventory of the things that I felt I would have to give away if I loved *"even as"* He loved me.

After the inventory, I said, "But what would I get in place of these rich treasures of mine?"

Then He showed me wealth that I had never seen before. If I loved *"even as"* He loved, I would have His companionship. I would have His strength. I would have His gentleness and His forbearance. I would give away the toys of the senses to get the wealth of the Spirit.

LOVE'S METHOD

I would give away things that perish after much use to receive something that increased when used. I saw then a joy I had never known.

I had been seeking happiness. I did not realize that happiness came from things, people, and circumstances, that I could lose happiness as I once lost my knife. I saw what an illusion it had been.

I felt that I was willing to forego some of the things that make men happy, if I could have this joy.

This new life gives a joy that springs from love. Happiness springs from sensuous things around me. I found that joy was as far superior to happiness as the diamond is to glass, as gold is to common dirt.

Then I knew what love meant. I am to love even as He loved. I am to take His place.

He is seated yonder upon the throne, ministering to me, enabling me to take His place down here. I am to speak His words and to do the kind deeds that He would do.

I will feel the same kind of passion for the lost and broken that He felt.

I am to love in His place.

Oh, the joy, the unspeakable joy that comes. I have joy even as He had joy because I am loving even as He loved.

2

THE PLACE OF LOVE IN LIFE

It is hard to speak of love without becoming lyrical, without the spirit of poetry gaining the mastery.

We find ourselves in love's own realm of melody. We feel the pulsation of another world where hatred has never been. We feel the lift of a strange power that almost makes us float above the turmoil of bitterness, greed, and hatred.

Love is the reason for man's being. Man would not have not been created had love not been hungry ages on ages ago. Love brought men into being.

When man was created, the earth was full of music and laughter. Flowers abounded everywhere. Their perfume filled the air, and all creation sang its anthem of welcome.

Man had come! Love had conquered. Love had won.

LOVE TO BE THE LAW OF HIS BEING

Love is the healing for every wound. It is God's love poured upon the sore of human failure.

Love is the creative force in creation. It is the creative law.

Love is the reason for parenthood in every realm of life. Love brings fatherhood and motherhood into the holy union of expectation. Love waits for its offspring.

Love alone can give and nurture babyhood. Giving birth to a baby born outside of love is a crime against the child. Every child has a right to be love-born!

There is no crime among all the crimes in the realm of wrong like the murder of love. Love has given us all that is beautiful. When love is slain, all that is beautiful lies dead.

Love is the heart force of life. It is the homemaking force. If we go where there is no love, we will find no home. We may find a house and we may find furniture, but as soon as we enter the building, we are conscious of something lacking. We feel as though there has been a funeral or there is going to be one. It is dead love. It is unburied love. There may be wealth, but it is not a home.

Love and love alone has given us the sacred place called "home."

They do not have it in heathen lands where plural marriages are practiced. They have no home. It is just a habitation. Eternal life destroys polygamy.

A home is a thing born out of the Jesus kind of love. Love is the mating law of life. There isn't anything as utterly beautiful as the mating time. All creation celebrates it.

I saw a couple of doves celebrating the mating season. I saw the sparrows making love to each other. I saw the bees carrying the pollen from flower to flower. All creation mates, and all creation loves.

LOVE GIVES

I saw the blossom loving and giving itself to the fruit that was soon to take its place. I smelled the fragrance on the air as the rose gave its best to make others glad. I saw its beautiful petals turn brown and seared. I watched them as they dropped upon the ground. I saw the rosebush stand, dry and dead.

Why? It was love pouring out itself for others.

Love is the reason for life. When love is gone, life has lost its reason.

Love is the reason for all that goes to make civilization. When love dies, all worthwhile in life fades.

When love grows cold, the sun ceases to shine. The clouds gather, dark and ominous. The storm threatens. And we hide away in the darkness under the doom of lost love.

No wonder that broken fellowship has the deepest sorrow, the keenest anguish known to the human heart! No wonder that love flows at flood-tide when fellowship is the richest!

The heart is the life of man. Love is the life of the heart.

Love makes a romance out of the commonplace. It makes the ugly, lovely. It has a light of its own. It sheds a radiance over life that no sorrow can slay or destroy.

Love will redeem a wasted life and transform it into beauty and usefulness.

Love is a spiritual thing. It is above reason. It is not in the reason realm. It is God, invading the realm of the human.

RELATION OF LOVE TO ANSWERED PRAYER

The love walk is the love way. The love life is the way of the new covenant. When we step out of love, we step out of the will of the Master. Whenever we act out of love, we act contrary to the will of our Lord.

When our prayers are not answered, we invariably ask this question, "Have I stepped out of love?"

First John shows why prayer is often unanswered:

> *Hereby know we love, because he laid down his life for us: and we ought to lay down our lives for the brethren. But whoso hath the world's goods, and beholdeth his brother in need, and shutteth up his compassion from him, how doth the love of God abide in him?... Hereby shall we know that we are of the truth, and shall assure our heart before him: because if our heart condemn us, God is greater than our heart, and knoweth all things.*
>
> (1 John 3:16–17, 19–20 ASV)

He knew when we turned our brother down and refused to help him that our hearts were not in sympathy with him. The Father knows when we close up our hearts of compassion.

He says, "*If our heart condemn us not, then have we confidence toward God. And whatsoever we ask, we receive of him, because we keep his commandments, and do those things that are pleasing in his sight. And this is his commandment, that we should believe on the name of his Son Jesus Christ, and love one another*" (1 John 3:21–23).

Our refusal to help our brother was not pleasing in His sight.

The name of Jesus gives us access to the Father. But if we step out of love, the name is of no value to us. We can only use the name of Jesus as we walk in love. When we step out of love, it breaks our fellowship with the Father, weakens our faith, and makes the Bible almost a closed book to our hearts.

Love is the greatest thing in the world. It is the nature of the Father revealed to us.

The new law of the new family is that we love one another even as He loved us. (See John 13:34.)

If we are sick and do not get our healing, we should find out if we are walking in love.

Most people when they are sick become very selfish. This is not true in all cases, but it is in many cases. They have the whole family looking after them, ministering to them. Their selfishness takes them out of the love realm where prayer is answered.

If someone can pray for us and get our healing, we will not maintain it unless we walk in love.

We cannot love with words only. We must love in reality. That means bearing each other's burdens.

3

WHAT JESUS SAID

Jesus came to fulfill the first covenant with its priesthood, atonement, sacrifices, and law, and at the same time to establish a new covenant based upon a perfect redemption instead of atonement, giving to a new creation a new priesthood with new sacrifices and a new law. He says:

> *A new commandment I give unto you, That ye love one another; as I have loved you, that ye also love one another. By this shall all men know that ye are my disciples, if ye have love one to another.* (John 13:34–35)

He gives us in this Scripture the new word *agape*, which is translated as either "love" or "charity."

Not only that, but based upon His finished work, He is introducing a new creation that is going to live under the dominion of this new law.

Stephen, in his defense in Acts 7:8, calls the first covenant "*the covenant of circumcision*" given to Abraham.

But the one Jesus is establishing is the covenant of the new creation. It is a circumcision of the heart prophesied by Ezekiel.

> *A new heart also will I give you, and a new spirit will I put within you; and I will take away the stony heart out of your flesh, and I will give you a heart of flesh. And I will put my Spirit within you, and cause you to walk in my statutes, and ye shall keep mine ordinances, and do them.*
> (Ezekiel 36:26–27 ASV)

This is a prophecy of the new creation of a recreated human spirit. "*A new spirit will I put within you; and I will take away the stony heart out of your flesh.*" That is the heart of selfishness of the natural man.

"I will put my Spirit within you." The new creation is going to have the Holy Spirit.

Ezekiel 11:19 develops the thought a little further: *"And I will give them one heart, and I will put a new spirit within you; and I will take the stony heart out of their flesh, and will give them a heart of flesh."*

With one heart, they are all ruled by love. With a new spirit, the old human spirit, the real man, is to be recreated with the nature and life of God.

Again he says, *"And I will take the stony heart out of their flesh, and will give them a heart of flesh."* This is the new covenant man.

The Jew entered the old covenant by circumcision. We enter the new covenant by the new birth. The old covenant made them servants. The new covenant makes them sons.

> *In whom ye were also circumcised with a circumcision not made with hands, in the putting off of the body of the flesh.* (Colossians 2:11 ASV)

The Spirit's argument is easy to understand. Our circumcision is not physical but spiritual. It is God taking away not a portion of the physical body but putting off the body of the senses or flesh. That means He is taking away the dominion of the physical body over the human spirit.

When man was created, his spirit dominated him, but when he sinned, the physical body gained the ascendency, and his spirit was dominated by the body.

Here, Paul calls it *"putting off of the body of the flesh."*

He tells us in Romans 6:6: *"Knowing this, that our old man is crucified with him, that the body of sin might be destroyed, that henceforth we should not serve sin."*

Here the Spirit is trying to make clear in the language of the senses the fact that when a man is recreated, the physical body loses its dominion.

If we should put it in another way, in Adam, the physical body gained the ascendency in the fall. In the new creation, through Christ, the spirit wins back the ascendency over the physical body or the senses.

The reason why men could not love God and love one another under the first covenant was because the heart was selfish, dominated by spiritual death. The only love that he had was *phileo*, a love based upon selfishness.

Now we are prepared to understand what Jesus meant when He said, "*A new commandment I give unto you, That ye love one another; as I have loved you, that ye also love one another*" (John 13:34).

The natural man cannot do this, only the new creation man. You can see the absurdity of telling the world folk that they must love. They cannot do so until they receive the nature of love in the new birth.

> *As the Father hath loved me, so have I loved you: continue ye in my love. If ye keep my commandments, ye shall abide in my love; even as I have kept my Father's commandments, and abide in his love.* (John 15:9–10)

The word *abide* here comes from the Greek word *meno*. It means "to settle down" or "to remain."

Jesus said, "I want you to settle down in My love just as I have settled down in My Father's love. I have remained in My Father's love. I want you to remain in My love."

In other words, this new kind of love has created a new realm, a new kingdom. We are to settle down in that kingdom as permanent inhabitants, never to move out of the realm of love.

One ceases to be dangerous to others when he moves into the realm of love. Every migration out of the realm of love is into a land of danger.

Love becomes beautiful and very attractive as we continue to abide in love and let love abide in us.

This Scripture helps us to grasp it more fully:

> *And we know and have believed the love which God hath in us. God is love; and he that abideth in love abideth in God, and God abideth in him.* (1 John 4:16 ASV)

I wish we knew what that meant in reality, in daily life, to have faith in love, greater faith than we have in any other law of life, for us to consciously know that we are living in the love realm, that we are acting as citizens should act who live in that realm, that we are taking our place as sons of love in the realm of love.

I am convinced that we would have to learn the love language, the love etiquette, and the laws that govern that wonder kingdom.

4

JESUS CONTRASTS THE TWO KINDS OF LOVE

JOHN 21

We all remember that beautiful scene in John 21 that took place after the resurrection of the Master. It was a cold morning. The disciples had been fishing all night and had caught nothing.

Cold and hungry, they started to row to the shore. As they drew near, they saw a man cooking over a fire.

He asked them, *"Children, have ye aught to eat?"* (John 21:5 ASV). "No," they answered.

> *And he said unto them, Cast the net on the right side of the ship, and ye shall find. They cast therefore, and now they were not able to draw it for the multitude of fishes.* (John 21:6)

John whispered, "It is the Lord."

When Peter heard that it was the Lord, he put his coat about him, cast himself into the sea, and waded to the shore. The disciples saw fish cooking on a fire and some bread.

Of all the pictures that we have of the Master, there is nothing as intriguing as this.

Jesus—who governed the universe with His Word, had just gone through the awful suffering of His substitutionary work, and was about to take His place at the right hand of the Majesty on High—steps aside for a moment and cooks breakfast for those cold, hungry disciples.

That is not the reason for His appearing, however. He wanted to give us this vivid contrast of the two words translated "love" or "charity."

"So when they had dined, Jesus saith to Simon Peter... lovest thou me more than these?" (John 21:15). Jesus used the word *agape.*

Peter answered, *"Yea, Lord; thou knowest that I love thee."* Peter used the word *phileo.*

A second time, Jesus asked, using the word *agape,* and again, Peter replied that he loves Jesus using the word *phileo.*

Then He asked Peter a third time, *"Lovest thou me?"* (verse 17). This time, the Lord came down to Peter's level by using the word *phileo,* the same word Peter used.

Peter was grieved. *"Lord, thou knowest all things; thou knowest that I love thee."*

Twice the Lord had used that new word *agape.* It is evident that the disciples knew about this word that Jesus evidently had coined because there was no question asked about it.

The Master unveiled to us the contrast of natural human love and the new kind of love that was to displace it after the day of Pentecost.

For years, I was confused about this love fact. One day, I discovered it in one of Canon Frederic W. Farrar's books. He said there are two Greek words translated "love" or "charity," and one of them is *agape.* It is not found in classical Greek before the time of Jesus.

Farrar says it is evident that the word *agape* was coined in the realm of divine revelation. That would mean that Jesus coined the word.

True, it is used several times in the *Septuagint* translation of the Hebrew into Greek, which was translated two hundred and eighty years before Christ. The only copies that we have today are those that were copied three to five hundred years after Christ. The word *agape* had then become current in religious literature.

5

THIS JESUS KIND OF LOVE

The measure of our love is the measure of our worth to society. Perhaps we have never thought of it in these terms.

Men are valued according to their financial or political standing in a community. It is a problem of how much money they have or how much political influence they can swing. Yet, in the final analysis, the men who love are the men who help the community.

Man was created by love to answer the heart cry of the Father God. Man outside of love is a failure.

Selfishness is the blighting curse of the human. Love stops the rust of selfishness, preserves the home and church life from decay. The lover is like rust-free steel. We know that the largest part of steel is destroyed by rust. We know that the largest portion of home life in America is destroyed by selfishness.

Marriage is wrecked by selfishness. The home life disintegrates because the husband is selfish, and the wife seeks her own. The children are born and grow up in that atmosphere. They go out into life handicapped.

It is a well-known fact that children who grow up in godly homes have a better chance in life than those who grow up in homes where there is quarreling and bitterness.

More than seventy-five percent of the boys and girls who are delinquent have come out of broken homes. It is almost impossible to find in any of our penal institutions a young man or woman whose father and mother were both walking in the new kind of love when the child was born and while it was growing up.

Love is God's adhesive power that binds us together.

LOVE MAKES THE HOME

I wonder if you have ever realized that the word *home* does not occur in any primitive language.

In the Bible, the word we have translated *home* comes from the Hebrew meaning "house," "tent," or "a dwelling place." It may be a place where a man lives with one or two or three wives. It is not a home.

The same thing is true of the Greek word that we have translated "home" in the New Testament.

"Home" in a Christian sense is the place where a man and a woman who have received eternal life, the nature of God, live in harmony. Men and women who have received eternal life never seek a divorce. You cannot find in the United States or Canada a case where a couple who have received eternal life and walked in love ever went to the divorce court.

Isn't that a staggering fact? Doesn't it show that there is a solution for the home problem and for marriage?

Selfishness separates, but *agape* binds together.

The new kind of love that Jesus brought to the world, which was manifested in His life first and then unveiled in the new church that came into being on the day of Pentecost, was God's solution of the home problem.

LOVE IS THE FRUIT OF THE RECREATED HUMAN SPIRIT

It took me a long time to make the discovery that love does not spring from our reasoning faculties. They never give birth to a love life. Love is born of the spirit.

> *The love of God hath been shed abroad in our hearts through the Holy Spirit.* (Romans 5:5 ASV)

The word *heart* is another term for *spirit*. These words are used synonymously.

After we are born again, we breathe into our spirits His love life just as we breathe air into our lungs.

There is no limit to the Jesus kind of love. It is of God. It is having God's nature within us. As we learn to give love freedom to develop, it will unveil to us the ability of God to help men.

We can train ourselves so that at the first dawn of consciousness in the morning, we will say, "I have God inside of me today. It is going to be easy to do my work because He is going to move through me today, act through me, love through me, and speak through me. I will not be left alone to meet any crisis. He will be there to make me a success."

Just as the vine drives its life into the branches, so does God pour Himself into us as we open our spirits to Him.

Knowledge has its limitations, but love knows none. How that thrills the heart! When we realize this fact, life becomes such a big, real, rich romance.

So every morning as you awaken, you may say, "Today, I am walking in love. Today, I am fearless. I have God's ability. I have God's nature. I have His love life."

Love is God in action. There is no love without action. God so loved that He gave. God so loved that He acted. Jesus so loved that He acted.

It would be a great day in your life if you would let love loose in you. It will mean letting God loose in you. His grace then would be without limitation.

Grace is love in manifestation.

> *We are bound to give thanks to God always for you, brethren, even as it is meet, for that your faith groweth exceedingly, and the love of each one of you all toward one another aboundeth.* (2 Thessalonians 1:3 ASV)

Think of abounding love among the brethren and love gaining the mastery in a church.

6

WHAT IT WILL DO

A man sat listening to our broadcast on love one morning and said to his wife, "I don't know what would happen in our office if I should practice this love of which he is speaking."

His wife said, "Why don't you try it, dear?"

He said, "I believe I am a coward."

She quickly quoted 1 John 4:18: "Perfect love casts out fear."

"Yes," he said, "I know that. You pray for me that I will have courage to begin to live this thing, because it is the biggest thing in the world."

A few days later, the wife said to her husband, "Dear, have you been practicing this Jesus kind of love?"

He said, "Do you know, it amazed me today. One of the men said to me, 'What has come over you? You are so different.'"

The Jesus kind of love had been manifested in this man. Love will transform your office and your home. It will make life different.

How sweet life becomes when we let love loose in us, when our hearts remember that Jesus loves us, even as the Father loves Him, and the Father loves us even as He loves the Master.

> *That the world may know that thou didst send me, and lovedst them, even as thou lovedst me.* (John 17:23 ASV)

If the Father loves us as He loves Christ, He will never leave us. He will watch over us as a mother watches over her baby, but with infinitely more wisdom.

Let us say now, "Father, I thank You for Your love for me. I am going out and love even as Jesus and You have loved me."

THE LOVE SLAVE

In Romans 1:1, there is a startling Scripture when we understand it: *"Paul, a servant of Jesus Christ, called to be an apostle, separated unto the gospel of God."*

The Greek word that is translated "servant" is *doulos*. No translator apparently has been satisfied with the translation "a servant" or "a household slave." The reason is that the Holy Spirit has given it another meaning. It reads like this: "The little love slave of Jesus Christ."

The name "Paul" means "the little one," so "a love slave" is Paul's most endearing title. He has become a slave to this new kind of love.

Sons and servants cannot always be trusted, but a love slave can be trusted to the very limit. The challenge comes to us to become love slaves of Jesus Christ.

This new kind of love has captured us and enslaved us, until we cry out, "Oh, Master, accept me, enroll me as a slave of this new kind of love. There is no sacrifice too great, no place too hard. Love impels me and is driving me to be one with You in this ministry for a lost world."

CONSTRAINING LOVE

There is a master thought in 2 Corinthians 5:14: *"For the love of Christ constraineth us."* Weymouth translates it, *"For the love of Christ overmasters us"* (WEY).

Someone had accused Paul of being beside himself. He explains it on the ground that this new kind of love has overwhelmed him and gained the ascendency in his life.

Moffatt's translation puts it this way:

> *For I am controlled by the love of Christ, convinced that as One has died for all, then all have died, and that he died for all in order to have the living live no longer for themselves but for him who died and rose for them.*
>
> (2 Corinthians 5:14–15 MOFF)

When we learn the secret of this strange, new kind of love, it will gain the mastery over us as it did with Paul. It will make us lovers like God. There will no longer be any fear of man, for this love will cast out all that demoniacal fear. On the one hand, it will make us as gentle as Jesus; on the other hand, it will make us conquerors.

We understand what it means to have love abounding in all its fullness through us. It will illumine the knowledge we have gained from our study of the Word.

> *And this I pray, that your love may abound yet more and more in knowledge and all discernment.* (Philippians 1:9 ASV)

> *Above all things being fervent in your love among yourselves.* (1 Peter 4:8 ASV)

The word *fervent* means "white-heated" or "heated to the welding point." When love becomes white-heated, the whole congregation will blend into one.

The blacksmith heats the metal until it is white-heated. Then he puts the two pieces together, and they became welded together as one. Welded together in love! Wouldn't that make a beautiful church, fitly framed and welded together, made after the design of the Father Himself?

You remember the Father gave Moses the design of the tabernacle and the holy of holies. Now He has designed the church, and He is going to weld it together into one, so that we may be one even as He and the Father are one. (See John 17:21.)

The church can only be welded together with this Jesus kind of love.

> *That their hearts might be comforted, being knit together in love, and unto all riches of the full assurance of understanding, to the acknowledgement of the mystery of God, and of the Father, and of Christ.* (Colossians 2:2)

Do you see the wealth wrapped up in this? Hearts knit together in love. As love touches the mind and illuminates the spirit, the fullness of assurance fills your very being.

How we have prayed for faith and power, but this eliminates all that useless struggling. We have the fullness and ability of God; the very sufficiency of God is in us.

BEING ESTABLISHED IN LOVE

Now may our God and Father himself, and our Lord Jesus, direct our way unto you: and the Lord make you to increase and abound in love one toward another, and toward all men, even as we also do toward you; to the end he may establish your hearts unblamable in holiness before our God and Father, at the coming of our Lord Jesus with all his saints.

(1 Thessalonians 3:11–13 ASV)

Can you conceive of anything more beautiful than these words? The evangel must be set on fire with love. A loveless church is no evangel. The Father wants us to love one another and to love all men, that being the objective to the end that we may be established in our hearts at the coming of the Lord Jesus.

Increasing in love is like increasing in physical strength or knowledge. This would imply that our ability to absorb, reveal, and give love is unlimited.

Love is the one thing in the human that never grows old, never wears out. It is something as imperishable as the human spirit, something so much a part of the Father that when we and the Father become united and utterly one, we pass out of the failure realm into the realm of the resurrected Christ.

To sense knowledge, the cross appeared to be a failure, but in reality, it was leading to the resurrection, where victory crowned the Christ, not with thorns but with a diadem of love.

They crowned the weak and helpless Christ with thorns. God crowned the resurrected Christ with a crown of glory. That crown is made up of the love of the multitudes whom He has redeemed.

Love will make you what your heart has craved. If you follow the law of love, you cannot fail!

7

GOD-INSIDE MINDED

And we know and have believed the love which God hath in us.
God is love; and he that abideth in love abideth in God,
and God abideth in him.
—1 John 4:16 (ASV)

We have come to know the love way is best. We have come to believe in love. We believe it is better than force, better than argument, better than money, and better than going to court.

The hardest thing for some of us to learn is that the love way is best, that we cannot fail if we walk in love.

It has been hard for us to believe in God's love for us when difficulties came into our lives, but we know now that all of these abnormal things are not the product of love. They come from the adversary, who is seeking to dethrone love in our hearts.

For us to become God-inside minded is for us to become victors. As soon as we become conscious of God inside us, we will begin to depend upon the God inside. We will know that *"greater is he that is in you, than he that is in the world"* (1 John 4:4).

There will be a holy boldness in us, a Jesus-like fearlessness. No matter what happens to us, He is inside, and He will take us over. We have His ability, His courage, and His strength. It takes us out of the failure realm and puts us over into the realm of success.

For if, through the transgression of the one individual, Death made use of the one individual to seize the sovereignty, all the more shall those who

> *receive God's overflowing grace and gift of righteousness reign as kings in Life through the one individual, Jesus Christ.* (Romans 5:17 WEY)

We have received the gift of righteousness. We have received the abundance of grace. We reign as kings in the realm of life and love. God never intended that we should be servants or have a servile spirit. Love takes us out of the servant realm up into the Son realm.

Love takes the sense of inferiority away from us and gives us the sense of our oneness with Christ. The old inferiority complex that comes from sin consciousness has been destroyed. Love consciousness and Son consciousness have taken its place.

One cannot have a servile spirit and enjoy the reality of sonship. We are masters, we are conquerors, and we are overcomers because we are one with Him. We have His ability, His wisdom, His strength, and His love.

Spiritually, we are free men. We abide in God, and God abides in us.

LOVE AND WISDOM

Wisdom is the ability to use knowledge. It matters not how much knowledge we have; if we haven't wisdom to use it, we will be failures. That is the reason why a large percentage of the men and women who graduate from our colleges and universities make a failure of life. They have knowledge, but they lack wisdom.

First Corinthians 1:30 tells us, "*But of him are ye in Christ Jesus, who of God is made unto us wisdom.*" God is love. If we walk in love, we will walk in wisdom.

When love governs our life, we will say nothing that injures anyone.

You remember that statement in Proverbs 6:2: "*Thou art snared with the words of thy mouth.*"

We would never have signed that paper had love governed us. We would never have entered into that contract if love had governed us. We might not have married as we did if love had been our master. If we had yielded to love and let it have dominion over us, the mistakes that have marred our lives would never have taken place.

Love, in the final analysis, is wisdom. It has caused us to create, invent, and search until we have discovered things that will make others happy.

Love will make us thoughtful, gentle, and tender. When we speak, there will be something in our voices that will win people to us. We will not only be in earnest, but we will speak wisdom in love.

When we love people, it is easy to work for them.

If you are a preacher and want to be a success, love will be the key that opens the door to success. People will want you because you are a lover. They will come to hear you because everyone wishes to hear a lover. They will linger to talk with you because they want to be loved.

So the Master tells us, *"abide ye in my love"* (John 15:9 ASV).

LOVE HUNGER

Everything that has life longs for love. In my ministry, I found that the whole world was love hungry. They put up with their old, selfish, human love for the want of something better. But oh, how they respond to the Jesus kind of love!

Boys and girls are love hungry. They go to the arms of love with utmost freedom. If you want to reach them, love them. Never scold. Don't criticize. Don't tell them how bad they are; tell them how good they may be. Never preach sin; preach its cure.

Tell men and women that God so loved them that He gave His Son for them. Tell them the story of love's unveiling, and you will win their hearts.

When they ask for bread, don't give them a stone. Give them the Bread of Life.

Don't give them your philosophy about love. Unveil Jesus to them.

8

SEEING MEN THROUGH LOVE'S EYES

We have been seeing men through sense-dominated eyes. Now we see them as the Father sees them. I am sure He saw them through the eyes of faith. It was love, seeing men through the eyes of faith.

He believes they will respond to the sacrifice made in Christ. He believes they will want eternal life that will give them joy where sorrow has reigned, victory when failure has held carnival.

He believes men will respond to His love and will come over into the love way. He can see the sinner as a recreated man. He sees the believer as a victor. He sees him walking in love.

We must close our natural sense-ruled eyes and see others as the Father sees them, through the eyes of our heart. He sees the poor made rich, the naked clothed, and selfishness turned into love.

Our faith must arise to meet His faith. Then we can help others. But as long as we see them through sense-governed eyes, we will never be able to take Jesus's place and do the love acts that Jesus did.

The new creation must become love conscious. It is love that is going to lead us out of the labyrinth of selfishness in which we have been walking and struggling all these years. It is love that will put us over and make us winners in life's fight.

We have been need conscious. And as long as we are weakness conscious and sickness conscious, faith will have no place in our lives. But when we yield ourselves to the lordship of love and cut every shore line that binds us to selfishness, love will put us over and make us conscious of what we are.

You remember that striking sentence in Ephesians 2:10, *"We are his workmanship, created in Christ Jesus."* That means we are God's workmanship, just as creation was His workmanship.

This new creation is His workmanship, and just as the first creation was perfect, we believe this new creation is perfect. The first creation pleased Him, and we know this one does.

He is the Lover. He created us in love. He has built love into us. He has taken the things of Jesus, the things of love, and built them into us. As we act on the Word, it becomes built into us and forms a part of us.

He did not make us to be slaves of circumstances or demons. He did not create us in Christ Jesus to be servants of world influences, but He created us in His Son that we might reign with Him now as victors in the realm of life.

He planned that we should walk in love and act in His stead. We actually take His place.

It is beautiful that we can be so united with Him, so utterly one with Him, that His life absorbs and takes us over—He living in us and loving through us both in word and in deed.

The word translated *"power"* in Acts 1:8 is *dunamis,* which in a true translation should read "ability." Jesus said He wanted the disciples to tarry in Jerusalem until they received power from on high. That power was love. Only love could conquer the Roman Empire and the Jewish Sanhedrin that had crucified Jesus.

When you receive love, you are receiving the ability of God. You are clothed from on high with God's ability.

Something new has come to man. Failure and the sense of inferiority that had become a part of the consciousness of man has been overthrown.

> *Now unto him that is able to do exceeding abundantly above all that we ask or think, according to the power that worketh in us.* (Ephesians 3:20)

Love is able to do exceeding abundantly above all that we could ask or even think. It is according to the ability of love that is functioning in us. We are going to surrender our weakness to that love. We are going to let love's ability make us a success.

The old curse of inferiority complex that has held men in bondage since Adam sinned in Eden at last has found its master.

Love in us is greater than anything that can oppose us. Love has made us conquerors today.

Love has led us out of the wilderness of doubts and fears into the rose-strewn fields of God's grace and omnipotence.

At last, we have won! At last, we are conquerors!

9

TAKING OUR PLACE IN LOVE

A home could never be destroyed if every member could be taught to take his place in love.

The wife would never remember the past mistakes of her husband, nor the husband ever remind the wife of any unpleasant happenings. All the mistakes and failures of the past would be wiped out.

What homes we would have! There would be no more quarreling over finances and no more bitter words. Each one would be walking in love.

Love never takes advantage of anyone. Love always bears the burdens of the weak. Love says, "It is all my fault, dear. Had I done differently, or spoken differently, or lived in love, it would never have happened."

There never has been a divorce in a home where the husband and wife both walked in love. This is the solution of the divorce problem.

When men and women receive eternal life, the nature of the Father God, and let that nature dominate them, they grow in this new kind of love until eventually it absorbs them, takes them over, and renews their minds until their thinking is in the realm of love. All suspicion and jealousy die out because there is no soil for them to take root.

The men and women who walk in this new kind of love never injure anyone, never take advantage of anyone. They simply walk and live in God.

No matter what evil the adversary may bring into a life, love will change that evil so that it will bring forth good fruit.

You remember that Jesus said, *"All things are possible to him that believeth"* (Mark 9:23). That means "a believing one" or "a child of God."

You can understand it now. The believing one is linked up with God. He is a branch of the vine. The branch is the fruit-bearing portion of the vine.

He has a legal right to the Father's love and Jesus's ability. He has a legal right to use Jesus's name, which has all authority behind it. He really has the power of attorney to use that name.

The real lover is taking Jesus's place in life. He is a reproduction of Jesus. He is carrying out the dreams and will of the Father as Jesus did.

You remember He said, *"I came down from heaven, not to do mine own will, but the will of him that sent me"* (John 6:38). Jesus was the first man who ever walked in love.

When selfishness is eliminated in us and love gains the ascendency, we will not seek our own any longer. We will live as the Master lived in His earth walk. We will seek only the Father's will, which will be for the best interests of all the Father's children.

If we walk in love, we will be walking as Jesus walked. We will give ourselves for the redemption of the world, just as Jesus gave Himself. We cannot die for their sins, but we can live the love life for their salvation. We will slowly but surely develop into real lovers like our Lord.

Faith will no longer be a struggle or a thing to be desired.

LOVE'S CHALLENGE

Love is challenging the lovers to come into a richer, more beautiful Christian experience, to leave the lowlands of doubt and fear and enter into their inheritance.

> *Giving thanks to the Father who did make us meet* [able] *for the participation of the inheritance of the saints in the light.* (Colossians 1:12 YLT)

God is our ability. He is able to make your life a success.

There isn't a thing in the new covenant or in the finished work of Christ that does not belong to you. He is able to make you all that His great heart desires you to be.

He delivered you out of the hand of the enemy. He gave you His own nature. He made you a new creation. You are *"his workmanship, created in Christ Jesus"* (Ephesians 2:10).

He is in you now, living and working His own good pleasure. You are to yield to His Word and His sway and let Him have the right of way in you.

You have written yourself up as a failure for the last time. From today, you step into the new ranks of the conquerors, the overcomers, and the people who put things over. You can do all things in Him, who is your strength, your wisdom, and your ability.

Let the world hear you confess what God's ability is in you. They have heard your confession of weakness and failure. Now change your song and sing the song of a victor.

Every time you confess weakness, you become weaker. Every time you tell people about your sickness, you grow worse. Every time you tell people about your lack, you have more lack.

Begin to confess your fullness and the ability of God to make good. Tell the world that you are more than a conqueror and that you have no other testimony to give.

It thrilled me through and through the first time I ever said the words, "Christ now lives in me."

I had expected Him to be with me, but I was not quite sure but that I would leave Him sometime. I was afraid that sometimes He would forget to go along. Then it came into my spirit consciousness that He was in me, and greater was He that was in me than he that was in the world. (See 1 John 4:4.)

Christ was in me! What couldn't I do? I could get an education. I could develop latent abilities. I could become a blessing to the world. Why? Because He was in me. His enabling ability was there.

Feverishly, I scanned the pages of Paul's epistles to get the proof of this mighty fact that I had God in me, that God was at work within me, willing and working for "*his good pleasure*" (Philippians 2:13).

I knew that I was no longer in the failure ranks. I knew I had moved into the success realm. I knew God and I were united. He was not on the outside any longer. He was not only with me, but He was in me.

Oh, the wonder of it, the thrill of it, the amazing grace of it—God in me! And the biggest asset of the whole thing was that He loved me!

"*The Son of God, who loved me, and gave himself up for me*" (Galatians 2:20 ASV). He had identified Himself with me in my earth walk. There could never be any separation from now on. I would not give Him up, and He would not give me up.

I have His life. He has mine. He gives me His ability.

We labor together, my Lord and me.

10

A MOTHER'S CONFESSION

The mother said, "It is no use, I can't do anything with my girls. Two of them are in high school, and one is in grade school. I have lost control over them. I have scolded, threatened, done everything, but it is of no avail."

I said, "Mother, have you tried love?"

"You know I love them," she said.

"I am not speaking of that kind of love. You came to seek help from me. You wanted advice for your family, and I am going to give it to you. Let me ask you some questions. Do you know anything about the Jesus kind of love?"

Her face was blank as she looked at me. "I don't know what you mean."

I made as clear as possible the fact of the two kinds of love.

"I think I see the reason for my failure," she said. "I have never had anything but mother love. I want this Jesus kind of love."

I explained to her how simple it was to receive it, that it would come to her when she received eternal life.

"How may I receive eternal life?" she asked.

"Do you know that Jesus died for your sins?"

"Yes. I believe He did."

Then I shared Romans 10:9–11 with her:

> *That if thou shalt confess with thy mouth the Lord Jesus, and shalt believe in thine heart that God hath raised him from the dead, thou shalt be saved. For with the heart man believeth unto righteousness; and with the mouth confession is made unto salvation. For the scripture saith, Whosoever believeth on him shall not be ashamed.*

Then I asked her if she knew that God raised Jesus from the dead for her justification.

"Yes. I do know that."

"Do you confess Him as your Lord?"

"I do."

"Then according to God's Word, what are you?"

"I am saved."

I explained to her that she had received eternal life, the nature of the Father God, that the Father is love, and she had received into her heart this new kind of love. I urged her to yield to that love, study the Word, and begin to practice love in her home.

Days went by, and she finally came to see me. Her face was aglow.

She said, "One of my girls asked me what had happened to me. I told her I had accepted this Jesus kind of love, and she wanted to know how she might receive it. I told her to read your little tract on 'How to Become a Christian.' She did, and together with her sister, she was born again. They both have found this Jesus kind of love."

WALKING IN LOVE

This is the walk of the recreated spirit, the walk of one who has received the love nature of the Father. To walk in love is actually to live in God.

> *If ye abide in me, and my words abide in you, ye shall ask what ye will, and it shall be done unto you.* (John 15:7)

In other words, if you live in love and love lives in you, ask and you will receive.

It is the realm where the Word dominates, where faith functions. Faith grows in the atmosphere of love. Faith becomes a dominating and creative force when love really rules.

It is the realm of fellowship with the Father, with the Word, and with one another. The sweetest thing about this love life is fellowship. We come together without suspicion, in utter unselfishness, to give our best. We come to give.

The person who comes to get is impoverished by getting. How many Christian workers have lost the beauty and fragrance of life by always dreaming of getting rather than giving?

As we live in this realm of love, the Holy Spirit is able to guide us into all truth, all reality. (See John 16:13.)

As we walk in love, the Word opens and becomes responsive to us. God is in His Word, and as we read it, our hearts are filled with joy and gladness.

I question if anyone can ever understand the Psalm 23 until they abide in this realm of love.

Repeat the first verse softly: *"The Lord is my shepherd; I shall not want."* The Hebrew word for "Lord" is *Jehovah*, which is a word of three tenses—past, present, and future. He is the Jehovah of yesterday and the God of now, and He will be the same tomorrow.

He is our Shepherd, so we do not want. He is leading us into the rich pastures of fellowship, into the marvelous fields of love that we find in the Word.

The Spirit's unveiling of the Word is love's unveiling. He is letting us see Himself in the Word. We see Him as the Father, the Lover, the Comforter, and the Overcoming One.

Walking in love means vast possibilities of growth, development, and entering into our rights and privileges in Christ.

We come to understand the reality of His indwelling. We remember that the greater One is in us, and His ability is at our disposal.

We remember that His Word on our lips has dominating authority. We rule diseases and circumstances as we walk in love. We take Jesus's place, speak Jesus's words, and do Jesus's work.

It leads us into the reality of His ability in the living Word. Some of us have never grasped this, but God's ability to heal the sick is in the Word. It becomes mighty on our lips in prayer.

When we love someone, we act on their word unconsciously.

We love Him, and we act on His Word unconsciously.

It is no effort to believe. Love never tries to believe, never tries to have faith. The very word *love* suggests faith. Love makes our faith become limitless.

Now we can understand, as never before, our utter oneness with Him. This blessed oneness suggests our usefulness and our ability to help men.

WE ARE IN GOD'S CLASS

God is a spirit. We are spirits. God has imparted His nature to us. His nature is love. It is the most normal thing for us to live, talk, and act love. Our greatest difficulty has been that we forget what we are in Christ. We remember what we have been. We remember what we were in the old life. We remember our failures, our weaknesses, and our lack, but we forget that the new creation is the end of failure because God has imparted Himself to us.

We remember that Paul said, *"I can do all things through Christ which strengtheneth me"* (Philippians 4:13). There is no lack, no weakness, and no problem that He cannot solve. There is no difficulty that He cannot surmount, no disease that He cannot heal.

He is in us. His ability is ours. His grace is ours. His love is ours. We have become one with Him.

11

SELFISHNESS IS ABSORBED IN LOVE

Love is God's crucible, God's melting pot, where He melts us all into one.

We become one with Him. That union is love. It is the solution to all the problems that confront us.

If there were a chair in our universities where a thorough course could be taught on the two kinds of love, it would revolutionize them. It is the most vital thing and the most important thing in the world. Yet we know so little about it.

Natural, human love has become the goddess of the divorce court, the football of lawyers. What fortunes they salvage from the wreckage of human love! If this Jesus kind of love gained the supremacy in our country, it would put a large percentage of lawyers out of business.

The major portion of diseases that put men and women under a doctor's care come from the irritations and nervousness of thwarted, natural human love. When a person becomes jealous, that jealousy poisons the blood in his system and brings on stomach trouble or some other eruption in his body.

The awful plague that followed World War I was caused by hatred that had been developed by the Old World. That hatred had poisoned the system, the bloodstream of the human race, and after a while, it turned into that deadly plague.

It is almost impossible for a man or woman to be healed whose mind and heart are filled with hatred.

> *Beloved, let us love one another: for love is of God; and every one that loveth is born of God, and knoweth God.* (1 John 4:7)

Only lovers know each other. We may live with a man or woman for forty years and not truly know that person. Only love opens the heart and reveals the depth of our nature.

Everyone who loves is born of God. It is God's test that we may know the reality of the Jesus love in us.

Unless we are born of God, we will not love. We may feign love, or we may try to imitate love, but we will not be successful. Love is reality.

Romans 8:9 tells us, *"If any man have not the Spirit of Christ, he is none of his."* That does not mean the Holy Spirit. That means the spirit that dominated Jesus's life, just as our spirits dominate us. The Christlike spirit is a love spirit. Jesus was a lover. Jesus loved Zacchaeus, He loved Judas, and He loved Pontius Pilate.

The reason He healed the sick was not to prove that He was God. He could not help it. He loved them, and human suffering challenged Him. He died on the cross because He loved us. He loved us, *"and gave himself up for us"* (Ephesians 5:2 ASV).

"Let love be without hypocrisy" (Romans 12:9 ASV). In other words, let love be without selfishness because selfishness always breeds hypocrisy.

Selfishness is the outlaw in the realm of love. It breaks into that realm and seeks to dethrone love and take its crown. Selfishness is a bold, wicked robber. It makes men dissemble. It breaks friendships. It wrecks homes. It ruins churches. It destroys the fruit of love.

There is only one force able to conquer selfishness and destroy its effectiveness in the lives of men. That force is the new kind of love.

The natural man loves a woman because she satisfies the desires of his heart. He doesn't think of making her happy. He only desires pleasure for himself. If he cannot have her affections, he would rather destroy her than have another man win her. Love murderers are a part of human history. Through neglect, natural human love turns to hatred, jealousy, and murder.

Only a few months ago, a man standing in the courtroom in one of our coast cities said to the judge, "I loved her so I could not help it. I killed her."

Agape, the Jesus kind of love, never turns to jealousy, bitterness, hatred, or murder. It is the solution to the human problem. There is not a phase of life that it does not meet the issue.

Because of it, the laboring man will do more than he is hired to do, and the employer will pay more than the laborer asks. There will be no quarreling between them. Each will seek to give more than the other gives.

Can't you see what it would mean to the commercial world? There would no longer be this deadly competition of the strong destroying the weak.

When God's nature comes into a man, and he gives that nature sway, he cannot do differently than Jesus would in his place.

In Ephesians 5:2, the Spirit tells us to *"walk in love."* Here, "walk" means *conduct*. It means the businessman's attitude toward his competitor or his customer. We are going to treat men as God treats them.

Sense knowledge has kept us in slavery.

Do you understand what I mean by sense knowledge? All the knowledge that man possesses, which is taught in our grade schools, colleges, and technical schools, has come to us through the five senses: seeing, hearing, tasting, smelling, and feeling. Our body has been the laboratory, and all our knowledge has come to us through experimentation.

Sense knowledge cannot understand spiritual things nor spiritual values. Consequently, love has never been given its place. We have used it as a toy, as a means to an end.

Now the hour has come when love must have its place.

Society is going to break under the strain. Anarchy is going to reign.

Do you know what anarchy is? It is selfishness without restraint. It is the absence of God. It is man attempting to solve life's problems and leaving God out of his reckoning. That makes him an anarchist.

12

THE LOVE OF CHRIST CONSTRAINETH

Someone asked, "Why did you go to Africa?"

The answer was given, "Because love drew me, and love drove me there. I could not help it."

The love of Christ becomes the mightiest force in the world to the man who is yielded to it. It constrains us or holds us back from saying or doing what we should not. It may cause us to do or give.

When this Jesus kind of love gains control over a man's spirit and takes possession of his thinking, he unconsciously becomes a Jesus man. He will think in terms of love; he will find that he can no longer do things as he has done them in the past.

If he is a businessman, love will get into every phase of his life. If he is working for a firm, he will find that he must work as Jesus would in his place. He does not take advantage of the company because he is working from the heart. He always gives more than he gets. He keeps the company in debt to him.

If he employs help, he takes the place of the Master and seeks to give instead of get. This new kind of love changes *getting* into *giving*. It destroys the soil out of which selfishness finds its strength.

You see love is revolutionary; it is not commonplace. It changes the crude base metals of the human into the most priceless. It takes a common man and makes him uncommon.

I know a man who has no education, no training, and has always lived in semi-poverty—and yet he is much wanted. How quietly they listen when he speaks! What is it that he offers? It is love. He actually lives the Jesus life.

"IF A MAN LOVES ME"

Jesus never said a more searching thing than this:

> *If a man love me, he will keep my words: and my Father will love him, and we will come unto him, and make our abode with him.* (John 14:23)

He says, "If love rules in you, I will come in and live with you. If love governs your home life, I will feel at home with you."

Can you see what that would mean to us? How it would sanctify the home! How safe that home would be if Jesus and the Father lived in it! What it would mean to the children, growing up in the atmosphere and presence of Jesus and the Father!

The problems of rent, taxes, and bills would be solved. If Jesus lived in the house, He would meet the bills.

We remember when Jesus sat in Peter's boat to talk to the multitudes. Afterward, the Lord told the disciple to put out into the deep and let down his nets for a catch. Peter said, *"Master, we have toiled all the night, and have taken nothing: nevertheless at thy word I will let down the net"* (Luke 5:5). And they caught so many fish, it took two boats to hold them all.

Jesus paid for the use of Peter's boat. If He lives with you, He will pay your bills. Not only that, but see what it would mean to have the Father God and Jesus with you. How safe the home would be!

> *He that hath my commandments, and keepeth them, he it is that loveth me: and he that loveth me shall be loved of my Father, and I will love him, and will manifest myself to him.* (John 14:21)

His commandment was that we should love one another, even as He loved us.

He will unveil Himself in the Word. You will come to know Him as intimately through the Word as you know the dearest friend or loved one. He will unveil Himself to you if you love Him. He never unveils Himself to those who do not love Him. He was silent when they stripped Him naked and crowned Him with thorns.

He reveals Himself to the lover.

> *As the Father hath loved me, so have I loved you: continue ye in my love. If ye keep my commandments, ye shall abide in my love; even as I have kept my Father's commandments, and abide in his love.* (John 15:9–10)

Can you imagine what it would mean to live in love? It would mean the end of strife, the end of quarreling and bitterness, and living in His love. A husband and wife who live in love would live in a heaven-like atmosphere, wouldn't they?

A LITTLE CHILD SHALL LEAD THEM

Children who grow up in that atmosphere would never know what quarreling and bitterness meant.

A little boy who had grown up in this kind of atmosphere, had never heard his father or mother quarrel, and never had heard a bitter word spoken in their home, went to live for a week with his aunt and uncle while the father and mother took a trip to a distant city.

For the first time in his young life, the boy heard a man swear at his wife. The child listened in amazement and began to cry. His uncle took him in his arms and said, "Danny, what is the matter, dear?"

Between sobs, the little boy said, "Uncle, I thought you loved Auntie."

The uncle said, "I do."

"Oh, no you don't; you don't love like Daddy does, or like Mamma loves. They never say bad words."

The man looked at the child and turned to his wife. "Dear, I guess we have missed a great deal in life, haven't we?" he said.

You see, the man who misses love misses the most beautiful thing that life has to offer.

One day, a little boy whose parents had been listening in to our broadcast said, "Mamma, if we had that Jesus kind of love in our home, we would be happier, wouldn't we?"

The mother told it to the husband that night when he came home. The man said, "You know, I have been thinking about it ever since that address that Sunday morning on 'the Jesus kind of love,' and if you are willing, I am. We will invite the Master to come and live with us. I want that kind of love."

He then told the little boy. The child clapped his hands and said, "Won't we be happy, Daddy?"

You see, children want love. No parent has a right to deny his children this Jesus kind of love. It should be preached from the pulpit until every member of the congregation becomes love conscious, until it would be impossible for them to quarrel or say unkind things to one another.

13

LOVE PERFECTED IN US

Herein is our love made perfect, that we may have boldness in the day of judgment: because as he is, so are we in this world. There is no fear in love; but perfect love casteth out fear.
—1 John 4:17–18

That is masterful. As He is now at the right hand of the Father, so are we in our earth walk. Why? Because His nature is in us. The great, mighty Holy Spirit who raised Jesus from the dead is in us. We are united with Him in life, and life is love.

We can understand how love can be perfected in one's life. We may never be perfect in wisdom, may never be perfect in knowledge, but we may have love perfected in us.

What a thrilling fact! Love so fills us that fear has no place in our life. We have the use of the name of Jesus that has all authority over demons, disease, circumstances, and the laws of nature, so the source of fear is vanquished.

Love lifts one out of the commonplace into the supernatural. This revelation of love is given to enable us to face the problems that are bound to confront us in these last days as victors.

The book of Revelation shows us how love finally conquers, how the armies of men and demons are overcome by the Lamb. The Lamb is love. Over twenty times in the book of Revelation, Jesus is called *"the Lamb"*—literally "the baby Lamb" or "the helpless Lamb."

We see how helpless love is, and yet love conquers. Love finally dominates, for *"God is love"* (1 John 4:8).

PERFECT LOVE

The Master said, *"A new commandment I give unto you, That ye love one another; as I have loved you, that ye also love one another"* (John 13:34). If we love like this, we will never injure anyone, we will never take advantage of anyone, and we will never say anything we ought not to say or do anything we should not do.

He commanded them to love one another under the old law, but they had no ability to do so.

Now He has given us the love nature, and it is easy for us to do the things He commands us to do. It is easy for a child to love its parents because that is natural. This new kind of love has made us natural lovers. We love because He first loved us, and to obey the love law is easy.

The old law was called the law of death (see Romans 8:2) because it had a penalty attached to each of the commandments.

There is no penalty attached to this new covenant law. The only penalty is that we suffer when we step out of the love life. Every step out of love is a step into trouble. If you will think back over your life, you will find that every mistake you have ever made has been when you stepped out of love or acted out of love.

The bitter words you spoke that separated you from someone you loved was a step out of love. Every time we bruise or hurt someone, we step out of love.

THE LOVE LAW

Under the first covenant, there were many rules and regulations. Many laws given to regulate the lives of the old covenant men, but there was no inward ability to do or obey.

In this new covenant, there is only one law and one word: love. That law is to govern man in every phase of his life. We have God's nature in us to enable us to do it.

> *Love worketh no ill to his neighbor: love therefore is the fulfilment of the law.* (Romans 13:10 ASV)

Jesus emphasizes this new law:

As the Father hath loved me, so have I loved you: continue ye in my love. If ye keep my commandments, ye shall abide in my love; even as I have kept my Father's commandments, and abide in his love. These things have I spoken unto you, that my joy might remain in you, and that your joy might be full. (John 15:9–11)

Living in love, practicing love in everyday life, will lead one into the joy of the Master, and Jesus's joy will be fulfilled in him. We are to love one another even as He has loved us. When one does this, there is no wrongdoing. No one sins who walks in love. Every step out of love will be a step out of fellowship and joy.

It has taken some of us a long time to believe in love, to believe that love is the solution to every human problem, and that every difficulty could be solved by love.

BELIEVING IN LOVE

And we know and have believed the love which God hath in us. God is love; and he that abideth in love abideth in God, and God abideth in him. (1 John 4:16 ASV)

We do believe in love. We believe in the love that God has in our case. We believe that to walk in love is to walk in the highest spiritual realm. As long as one walks in love, he will never transgress against anyone. We are to walk as sons of God. We are to let God live in us as He lived in Christ.

The person who lives in love lives in God, in God's realm. He is living as God would live in his place. He is letting God unveil Himself in him.

John's first letter sheds more light on this:

Ye are of God, little children, and have overcome them: because greater is he that is in you, than he that is in the world. (1 John 4:4)

We are born of love. This love of God has come into us, and love in us is greater than any opposition or any enemy that can come against us.

As long as one walks in the realm of love, one has constant fellowship with the Father.

LOVE PREVENTS A MULTITUDE OF SINS

First Peter 4:8 (ASV) says, *"Above all things being fervent in your love among yourselves; for love covereth a multitude of sins,"* but a better rendering might be, "For love prevents a multitude of sins."

Love not only shields the sinning one from your criticism and your harshness, but it also prevents the quarreling and bitterness that would naturally follow if you had *spoken your mind* as we sometimes do.

I'm sure you have heard the expression, "I gave him what was coming to him. He can't run over me and get away with it." That is not love talking. Love would have suffered in silence. Love would never answer a word.

When they had Jesus on trial, it is said that He *"gave* [Pilate] *no answer, not even to one word"* (Matthew 27:14 ASV). That was the Jesus way. That was the love way. They accused Jesus of many things, but He was silent. Love won in the resurrection, didn't it?

Love will win in your case.

THE LOVE OF MANY SHALL WAX COLD

And because iniquity shall abound, the love of many shall wax cold.
(Matthew 24:12)

This is the only time that the word *agape* is used in the book of Matthew. It is speaking of the apostasy that is coming upon the church; it is going to be an apostasy from love.

Men are going to leave the love realm and go down into the sense realm. They are going to say, "It is no use. We can never walk in love under these conditions. Every man has to fight for himself."

The moment the church leaves the love realm, Satan gains the ascendency. Satan gains the mastery over a man the moment he steps out of love.

NOT SEEKING OUR OWN

Here is the solution of labor and capital. Instead of legislating new laws, we need a revival. Men need to receive this new life. Then they will repeat the words of Paul:

Even as I please all men in all things, not seeking mine own profit, but the profit of many, that they may be saved. (1 Corinthians 10:33)

This is the law that should govern us in our economics. It solves every problem. It straightens out all the rough places in the home life and in church work; each man seeking *"the profit of many, that they may be saved."*

Paul's ambition was to bring man in contact with Jesus. When he did, and they received the Jesus life and the Jesus love, then they began to walk the Jesus way.

Selfishness is like a great mogul engine drawing the long train of human agony and suffering down through the ages. The unhappy terminal will be the judgment. Let's get off the train. Let's get out of that kind of fellowship. Let's live the love life, live the love way.

It is not preaching; it is loving. It is not criticizing; it is loving. It is not new laws to stop sin and wrongdoing, it is a new kind of life that destroys sin by destroying selfishness.

LOVE'S WAY

We then that are strong ought to bear the infirmities of the weak, and not to please ourselves. (Romans 15:1)

Christ did not please Himself; He gave Himself. So we who are strong give not only our money but we give ourselves. We seek to improve that self and make it a better self.

If we have a voice to sing, we will train it and make it a better voice. Whatever gift has been allotted to us, we hold it as a treasure and develop it and train it to make it a better gift.

His very strength that He has given to us has been to bear the burdens of the weaker ones. His ability that has been given to us is for the benefit of those who lack ability.

There will always be the weak and inefficient. They will be ever learning but never coming to the realities of redemption. Because of this, we must gird ourselves with love to go out and serve the unworthy and selfish, give ourselves as He gave Himself for us.

He did not die for the righteous. He died for the unrighteous. He died for the ungodly. He died for the men and women who have gone wrong, who have nothing to give Him but a shattered life. He takes them over and gives them Himself.

How rich is love in its ministry!

One said of another, "I don't see what she can do for anyone. She has no money. She has no training, no education."

But the other answered, "She has love. Do you know when she laid her hands on that fevered brow, a strange quietness came over the patient. The fever left. The patient looked up with a gentle smile and said, 'I thought it was Jesus touching me.' And the one by her said, 'You are not mistaken.'"

The branch was bearing fruit.

14

WALKING IN LOVE

Walking means daily conduct.

As children of God, walk in love, even as Christ also walked in love toward you. (See Ephesians 5:1–2.) How beautiful life becomes when we walk in love.

Love is God's flower garden of the soul, filled with music and laughter. Kindly deeds, loving looks, little gifts—all of these are a part of the love walk.

When the mother awakens in the morning, she remembers how she loves. She goes about the house, picking up little toys and playthings here and there. She waits for the loved ones who come one by one to gather about the table. She is the queen. Her husband, their father, is the king. The children are the loving subjects of their kingdom.

What a realm! What a place! Never an unkind word is spoken. There are no selfish acts. Each one is living to make the other glad.

The husband carries that atmosphere down to the office. The children carry it to school. The mother lives in it joyously, working and singing the whole day through. The neighbors come in for a little chat. It is hard for them to leave a house of love. They think of their own desolate, loveless homes, and they linger in this sylvan retreat where Jesus lives.

Jesus said, *"If a man love me, he will keep my words: and my Father will love him, and we will come unto him, and make our abode with him"* (John 14:23).

That will be a love home. What a place for babies to be born! What a place for them to play, romp, learn to walk and talk, and take their place in life's great game, in a home where love reigns.

All this is possible. This is not poetry. This is not philosophy. This is the everyday life of the everyday man who walks in love.

Love is the reason for creation's being. Man came on the scene because love wanted him. Love gave him birth. This is a strangely beautiful thing.

Ephesians 3:17 says we are to be *"rooted and grounded in love."* That is so the storms of life will not overcome us.

I saw one going through the deepest sorrow. His home had been torn into shreds spiritually. No cyclone ever left a home in more desperate shape physically than this cyclone left it spiritually.

I watched the wife. She was quiet and calm. No bitter words left her lips. There was no bitterness in her heart. When she spoke to the one who had destroyed all that was beautiful, she told him how she loved him and how sorry she was about it.

I could see that love was waiting for this man who had killed love with wantonness and slain that holy thing. Love was waiting back there, believing in a resurrection. All it required was his footstep to make it arise from the grave.

Love is the only reason for being. Love is the only thing that makes life rich and worthwhile.

But, oh, how ruthlessly love is slain, how unkindly love is starved, how thoughtlessly love is neglected and forgotten.

We thought we would always remember to say the kind words and do the kind deeds on which love feeds. But in the multitude of our activities in life's great fight, we have forgotten so many times.

How we tax love to forgive our forgetfulness, to overlook the thoughtless hurt.

We are to be *"rooted and grounded"* in the very heart of the Master, drawing strength from the very heart of God, enabling us to remember.

> *That ye may be in strength to comprehend, with all the saints, what [is] the breadth, and length, and depth, and height, to know also the love of the Christ that is exceeding the knowledge, that ye may be filled — to all the fulness of God.* (Ephesians 3:18–19 YLT)

Then He tells us so gently about *"forbearing one another in love; giving diligence to keep the unity of the Spirit"* (Ephesians 4:2–3 ASV).

Someone has aptly said, "There are two bears in every home—bear and forbear." I bear for the other, and the other bears for me.

We watch over our words so that we will not do or say anything that would break the tranquility of the atmosphere of love. We speak the truth in love, tenderly, gently.

The words fall from the Jesus man's lips, the Jesus woman's lips. They may be words of correction but they drip with love.

We think in love terms. Out of the heart where love reigns, tender words spring into being. They fill the air around us with the very fragrance and aroma of heaven.

We become tenderhearted and gentle with each other, even as God also in Christ has been gentle and tender toward us.

We live in love. We think in terms of love, and we bless the world.

15

LOVE MINDED

We Christians have a love background. We have a love parentage. We are born of God, and God is love.

We are partakers of His nature, and His nature is love. The new creation is a love creation. It was designed and wrought by love. If love is your nature, selfishness is dethroned.

But we are surrounded by selfishness. Everything connected with the natural life is tinged and colored by selfishness. You see it in the animal creation. You see it in natural man everywhere. Our labor and capital war is the war of selfishness.

The thing that the world needs is the love nature of God, eternal life. We must give this love nature full sway and yield to it absolutely. If you followed the recreated spirit's impulses, you would live just as the Master lived, in love.

But we quench the recreated spirit. We say that we are not able to do it, and that we cannot afford to do it. We are afraid to walk the way of love. We are afraid to depend upon the Word. We are afraid to give love a free course.

We have not taken into consideration that He is with us. He has said, "*Fear thou not; for I am with thee*" (Isaiah 41:10).

Hear Him saying, "Be not dismayed at the great demands that come to you. Give, and I will give back to you. For I am your God, and I am love. Let Me love through you, and I will bless humanity." That is the language of the Holy Spirit to your spirit.

THE FEAR OF MAN SNARES US

We have been afraid, so we have quenched love until it has lost its initiative. It no longer dares to suggest action.

Husbands and wives, do you know there would never be a quarrel in your home if you were big enough to say, "Dear, forgive me. I should not have said that. I should not have done that."

After you have confessed your lack of love and have given love its place, you will stop doing the things that break fellowship and spoil the harmony of your home.

Remember, wife, you are taking Jesus's place in that home. Husband, you are taking the Master's place. Let loose, this love life in you will solve your domestic problems.

I believe that 1 John 4:16 (ASV) has wrapped up in it the answer to every heart cry and the solution to every problem: *"And we know and have believed the love which God hath in us."* We have believed in love. We have believed that love could not fail.

Everything else has failed. Our human wisdom and our human abilities have failed. We have made life bankrupt because we did not dare to give love its place and let love have the right-of-way.

God is love, and he who loves abides in God, and God abides in him. Now if God is abiding in you, then you have in you the solution to the problem that confronts you if you give Him the right-of-way to solve it.

REASON'S FAILURE

But if you do as Martha did at the grave of Lazarus, you will hinder Him. She said, "Don't roll the stone away. His body is decaying for he has been dead for four days. Had You come earlier, You could have raised him." (See John 11:17–44.)

Human wisdom, born of sense knowledge, gets in the way and mars the plan. It hinders the work of the recreated spirit.

Christ wants to bring deliverance to you, but He wants to bring it in love's way. You want to bring deliverance in reason's way. You cannot do it. You have failed. Your old human love has failed.

Your education and your training have been unable to make you a success. If you will give love its place, things will adjust themselves. You must dare to go the way of love. It will be necessary for you to think of yourself as a lover—to see yourself in your home, in the shop, in the school, or wherever you spend your time in contact with people, as a lover.

Galatians 6:2 says, *"Bear ye one another's burdens, and so fulfil the law of Christ."* You see yourself bearing men and women's burdens. You see yourself acting exactly as Jesus would do in your place.

With love comes the ability to love and do the thing that love would prompt you to do. This love will carry you into the supernatural realm, where you will do the Jesus things. You had been doing mankind's things, which are so dependent upon money, people, influence, and pull. But now, you have changed it all; you have taken the Jesus way.

Sometimes you may feel as though it could not be put over. But you give love the right-of-way and see what happens to you.

Some people say, "If I had money, I would help the poor." That is beautiful, but if you will not help the poor now with what little you have, you would not help them if you were rich. If you cannot share with them now, you would not share with them then. Love shares the half loaf. Love shares the little.

It is seeing yourself now with your limited means, sharing with those who are not as well off as you are. You see yourself ruled by love, giving as Jesus gave.

It is hard to love hypocrites. But Jesus did it, and you can do it too. He loved Judas when he sat at the table, and He knew that Judas had already planned to sell Him for thirty pieces of silver.

He loved the man who drove the nails in His hands.

What Jesus did, you can do, because you have His nature and ability.

16

MAKING LOVE ATTRACTIVE

We should make our gifts beautiful. We should make giving an art and cultivate it until it outshines the arts of those about us.

We should lift it out of duty, out of philanthropy, into the Jesus way and the Jesus reason for giving. We must learn Jesus's technique of giving.

Some people give in such a crude, unlovely way that their gift is repellent. Others have learned the secret of love. They have a beautiful technique. Love puts a fragrance into giving and doing that fills the heart of the receiver with joy.

HOW LOVE GIVES

When love gives, it never pauperizes. Philanthropy pauperizes. Governmental giving is a curse.

The man of the world does not always make the highest order of giver. It is better than not giving, but why can't we, as believers, make giving a beautiful and refined art?

Love will enable us to do it if we meditate on love. We must meditate on love until our words and actions are filled with love, until our looks are in harmony with our words and our deeds.

You can give, but your eyes will condemn. You can speak loving words when the tone in your voice is so sharp and ragged that it tears and wounds.

I have known husbands and wives to give in such a way that they cursed in their giving. They throw it at the person as they would throw a bone to a mangy, ugly dog. They say, "There, take it." Many a child has been cursed in the receiving from its parents.

Some people's giving is like soggy, heavy bread. You must eat it, but you do not enjoy it. There is no need of giving like that. You can give as Jesus gave. But you must put real thought into it. Give it as much thought as you do to your business to put it over.

I know a businessman who had worked night and day to put his business over. Then after success had come, he had to work night and day to keep the thing running. But in those years, he had forgotten to love. He loved the woman he married, but he paid no attention to her. He did not have time. At first, she pitied him, but as years went by, she grew lonely and heart hungry.

Their children were neglected by their father. He gave them plenty of money, scolded them properly, and found fault with them, but he had never put any love into the home end of his business. After he had become a millionaire, this man confessed that his money did not satisfy him because he had no home. He had a magnificent house, sons, and daughters, but he had no love.

There is a home end to your business. Unless you put love there, it will fail and break down.

17

THE MESSAGE OF THE CROSS

The cross was love's method of war on sin.

The cross was love unleashed, let loose, and set free from every anchorage. It was love becoming weak and accepting defeat.

Sin slew the Son, the Son of love, and nailed Him to the cross. That cross was the symbol of Satan's victory, triumphing over God and over love.

Satan had seen Jesus made sin; he had seen God turn His back upon Him. He had witnessed the tragedy of eternity. He had seen the dead Son of love nailed to a cross.

The cross was love's way to the throne. When Jesus said, *"I am the way"* (John 14:6), no one dreamed that the way was the way of a cross. No one can understand it from the Father's point of view.

The Son was made sin. It was the Lamb on a cross. Then the cross was love's way of conquering sin, conquering Satan, and setting man free.

The Lamb of Revelation is the same Lamb who hung on the cross. He conquered sin by love; He conquered the world led by Satan through love.

No one dreamed of the empty tomb and Satan's defeat when they saw Him hanging there on the tree. That cross was the symbol of the defeat and failure of every dream of the men who had walked with Jesus. It was the climax of misery, the very crown of agony. That crown of thorns placed upon the brow of the Master seemed a fitting climax to the tragedy of the ages.

The Man who hung on the cross is yet to be crowned King of the ages. The people who take up their cross—an untrimmed, thorn-covered cross, a brutally heavy cross—may be climbing up their Golgotha because they love Him, because they would rather suffer than run; they would rather endure than fail.

The cross folk are a strange folk; they are the Lamb's folk. They are the folk who will join in His coronation. They can use no carnal weapons; they cannot use reason's method.

Satan always seems to be the victor. We often seem defeated—and yet we are winning all the time. The senses can see only our defeat. Our hearts know we are conquering.

This cross message is a message to us. Jesus said, "If a man loves Me, he will take up his cross and follow Me daily." (See Matthew 16:24.) That is discipleship.

The cross may be heavy and the burden beyond our ability to carry, and yet somehow or other, there is an unseen strength pouring into us.

We bear our cross daily. Our cross does not save us. It is Christ who saves us. We do not bear the cross to make us good; we have the goodness, and that is the reason we bear the cross.

Bearing your cross will lead you into a deeper trust in Him, a finer steadfastness. Your cross may be a person who makes life hell for you, and yet you bear the cross for Jesus's sake.

Your cross may be circumstances that imprison you, and yet in the prison, you crown Him Lord, and you rejoice that you are able to bear the cross within the prison of circumstances.

Your cross may be an unhealed sore in your heart, an old sore, an aggravating grievous sore that memory keeps raw. You bear it. Daily you drink of His grace; daily you feed on the bread of the Mighty One and are strong.

Your cross may be a dead love that you cannot bury. God help you. A dead love that cannot be buried becomes an unseen, unknown cross. It is a hard cross. But there is grace to bear it, and every cross bearer is a winner.

Your cross may be a cherished dream denied. You saw what you could have been, but you stayed by the stuff and let others go. You turned your dream into prayers for others, but you will win.

Just remember that following the cross leads to the empty tomb and the triumphant, resurrected life. Following from the cross and the empty tomb, you go to the coronation. If you have had your cross, you will have your resurrection out of the agony of the cross into the risen life with Jesus Christ.

18

SOME LOVE FACTS

You will need love more as you grow old. Store it up and hoard love so that when the hour of need comes, you will be able to draw on it. Then you will have it.

Real love will destroy all that is unreal. Shame cannot abide in the light of love. Selfishness is destroyed in the heart when love takes over the life.

Self-preservation is the first law of selfishness. The preservation of others is the first law of love.

Only love made it necessary for God to give His Son. Love drove Him to give Jesus. Love drove Jesus to give Himself.

Love is the propelling power that makes us care for the needy and the weak. The strong, according to the love law, must bear the infirmities of the weak and not please themselves.

Selfishness is the mother of practically all of our miseries. Most of our tears are born of selfishness.

Love makes one lighthearted, companionable, and helpful. The Jesus kind of love is God's cure for every ill. Love lifts one out of the realm of the senses into the realm of the spirit.

GOD'S SUPERMEN

The reason love has made supermen of common men is that God is love. When God's nature gains the mastery, one begins to act like God.

It is impossible for the man who has never been recreated to love with this new kind of love. This new love is bound to make the most mediocre person unusual when it becomes the lord of his heart.

Human love is the most beautiful flower that humanity has naturally, but it is a poison flower. It has caused the heartaches, the divorces, the broken homes, and the wrecked families that disgrace our civilization.

The Jesus kind of love has never broken a home. It has never wrecked a life. It has never made a criminal out of a single child. This in itself should awaken thinking men and women.

The moment that one becomes love minded, he becomes broad minded, God minded, and humanity minded. He sees the need. His ears become attuned to catch the sigh and feel the sob of the broken hearts around him.

When we become love minded, we actually take Jesus's place.

The teaching of love in the Gospel of John cannot be understood until one has received the nature of the Father. Jesus said, *"As the Father hath loved me, so have I loved you: continue ye in my love"* (John 15:9).

He wants us to live in His love just as you have lived in the love of that man or that woman. He is living in the Father's love, and He wishes us to live in His love.

If we live in love, we begin to bear the fruits of love. The fruit of love will be in the actions, conduct, and words that are born of love. The days of hatred, jealousy, bitterness, and revenge are past.

A NEW ORDER HAS COME

A new day has dawned. It is the love day.

A woman said, "I cannot make you understand the transformation that has come into our home. There was always irritation and friction. This brought out sharp words, sometimes much bitter thought. But since we received eternal life, there has come a tenderness, a beauty of life, and a sweetness of expression that has affected the children as well as my husband and myself. We are living in a love realm.

"The other night, after he had been home a little while from the office, my husband said, 'How beautiful our home has become because each one is making a contribution of love. The children are more thoughtful. They feel the new sweet atmosphere of love, and they respond to it.' Mother is different, daddy is different."

A little boy once said, "Daddy, I wish you would love like Mr. Kenyon told us to over the air this morning. That would make mama and me so happy."

This Jesus kind of love is the answer to the heart cry of childhood, youth, manhood, and old age. It will take the bitterness out of the heart and soften the lines of the face. It will make the husband and wife more than content with their own home.

This love is a home builder and a home preserver. This is God's method of protecting marriage. This is God's method of protecting childhood and motherhood.

When the Jesus kind of love gains the ascendency in the hearts of husband and wife, no other law is necessary to preserve the home.

19

BLOSSOM LIKE THE ROSE

The wilderness and the dry land shall be glad; and the desert shall rejoice, and blossom as the rose. It shall blossom abundantly, and rejoice even with joy and singing.
—Isaiah 35:1–2 (ASV)

I never knew what this verse meant until recently. It is messianic. It belongs to Christianity.

What is there in Christianity that will make the wilderness and a dry land be glad, and the desert to blossom as a rose? It is the new kind of love that the Master brought to the world. It is the miracle of Christianity.

It is the most amazing feature of the Christ life. It has been the most outstanding challenge to sense knowledge.

The thing about Jesus's life that awakens thought is not His miracles. It is something else. For the want of a better word, we have called it love. But it is not love that can be measured by human love. It was distinctly different.

"God is love" (1 John 4:8), and Jesus was God manifested in the flesh. Jesus manifested this love that has gripped the heart of the world. Jesus's attitude toward men and His death on the cross illustrate this new thing.

Every revival of Christianity has been characterized by an outflowing of this love.

The old human love is based upon selfishness. It can easily turn to hatred, jealousy, bitterness, and murder.

But the very provocations that would make the old love turn to bitterness make the new kind of love more beautiful. It *"seeketh not its own"* (1 Corinthians 13:5 ASV). It bears with all kinds of persecutions and bitterness; it never sinks to the level of its provocateur.

In these hard days through which the nations are passing, this new kind of love shines out as a beacon, inviting to a higher and better civilization. It lifts us out of the sordid life around us. It keeps us above the strife and bitterness of contending selfishness.

The war among nations is but selfishness coming into full bloom. The war between labor and capital is selfishness gaining the control of the hearts of men, selfishness becoming the master passion that rules the hearts of men.

The Jesus kind of love would eliminate war and destroy selfishness, greed, and the bitterness of classes and the masses. It would solve every economic problem. Where this Jesus kind of love reigns, there would never be a strike.

Where the Jesus kind of love reigns, there would be no more lawsuits. The halls of justice would be turned into meetings of praise and fellowship. Where the Jesus kind of love dominates, divorce never comes.

Jesus brought a new kind of love to the world, fresh from the Father's heart. It cannot be imitated. It beggars a definition by words. Its best definition is Jesus Christ Himself. This new kind of love comes into a barren life and makes it blossom as a rose. It takes away the hardness and bitterness of life.

One day, I was riding through the Mojave Desert with a friend and I said, "How desolate and barren it is." He said, "Yes, but after the first rain, it becomes a paradise of beauty. Those barren hills will be covered with gorgeous flowers."

Then I saw how this love life is. After our first contact with the Master, it makes our desert lives to blossom as a rose. This love can fill the life. There will be no empty lives, no barren lives. Every life may become a garden of delight. God has made it possible.

All that is needed is that Jesus become the Master, the Lord of the life. Then the heart will sing, *"The LORD is my shepherd; I shall not want"* (Psalm 23:1). Love will fill your heart, and there will be songs on your lips. This love will make your barren life a garden of beauty, a thing of joy forever.

20

"GOD IS LOVE"

This chapter title does not mean much unless we know that He is our Father. You say, "God loves me" and note the reaction in your soul. Then you whisper, "The Father Himself loves me," or you say, "My Father loves me now."

You get no sense of nearness from the word *God* but you cannot say the word *Father* without the sense of relationship intruding, pushing itself into your consciousness. So I linger over this precious fact that the Father Himself loves me.

My heart asks, "How much does He love me?" Jesus told us in one of His prayers to the Father *"that the world may know that thou didst send me, and lovedst them, even as thou lovedst me"* (John 17:23 ASV). Then the Father loves me *"even as"* He loved Jesus.

I cannot understand it. I cannot reason it out. I take it to my heart and thank Him for it. How utterly beautiful it is, how utterly beyond reason, how out of harmony with everything that I have ever known. It just seems as though we were lifted into a new realm, when He whispers that the Father loves me *"even as"* He loves Jesus.

I feel like a prince, as though I reign in the realm of love, it is so utterly new and wonderful. This Father God is love, and He gives this love nature to us, but we are love's children, children of love.

I cannot take it in. It is too wonderful and yet I hold it to my breast. I shed tears of joy. He loves me. I cannot understand the Father and why He should love me so, but He does.

We reach our best and we do our best in a love atmosphere. Children grow up best in homes of love. Husbands do their best work when love waits for them at home. Wives do their best work when they are expecting love to come home and command it.

Now I can see why every thought, every motive, and every act outside of love dwarfs us, binds us, holds us in bondage, and keeps us from our best. Every love act enriches us. Every love thought makes us better. We think love, then we act love. What a plan it was that planned love for the human!

Love promotes health. God is love; God is my healer. Love is the healer. Now I can understand why bitter thoughts upset the stomach and disturb the circulation of the blood.

I can understand why when a mother is nursing a babe and is filled with anger and bitterness that the milk poisons the child. God never intended that the mother should have anything but thoughts of love while she nurses her child. She should love her husband and everyone around her until her milk is made sweet with her love.

I can understand why every step outside of love is a challenge to disease and failure, unhappiness and weakness. I can understand now that there is only one sin for the believer and that is to step outside of love. All other sins are the children of the mother sin of sins.

If I walk in love, I will never sin. Isn't that wonderful? That solves the problem of human conduct. To live in love's realm and learn love's language, love's methods, and love's way brings about a just education. Now we will whisper again, "God is love, and this love God is my Father; I am His child. I am in love's family.

Jesus is love. Jesus is the way of love where we walk the Jesus way, where we walk the love way. Jesus was love in action, love in manifestation. I will be the same. I will love Him. I will walk with Him. I will introduce Him to the world in my daily life for God, my Father, is love.

LET LOVE WORDS REIGN

Learn to think in terms of love, learn to give in love so that the background of your life, the mother of your actions, is love, this Jesus kind of love. Get love's language; learn it. Let it displace the language of the world.

Sense knowledge has ruled us; now the Jesus kind of love language is to displace it. We are going to learn the little love ways, the gentle, tender beautiful love ways, and how to look love, so our eyes will be love-filled, so men can see Jesus in us. There will never be any more of those little hate acts, selfish acts, or bitter acts or words. All will be tender and beautiful.

We are going to take our words, all of these sense knowledge words, and put them to soak in love. Then when they come forth and leap from our lips, they will have the fragrance of love; they will have the beauty of love, the gentle tenderness of love. There will be something exquisitely beautiful about them.

Wouldn't it be a wonderful thing to have all our words love filled? So many words are hate filled. But we will have just love-filled words.

We will send them out on the air. My voice has been heard over the radio sometimes a thousand or two thousand miles away. One day, a person picked up my voice way over in the state of Maine. It came in as clear as a bell nearly four thousand miles away.

Oh, how important it was that morning that those words should be love filled. They traveled so far through the cold bleak icy weather in the northern part of Maine—warm words, tender words, Jesus-filled words. In order to do this, you must be a Jesus kind of lover who *"seeketh not its own"* (1 Corinthians 13:5 ASV) and does not try to rob anyone. Just a lover.

Wouldn't it be beautiful if we could get the love habit, if our conversations could be born out of love, had all the dainty beautiful little tricks of love, the delicate intonation, the sweet, beautiful love words blended with love thoughts? Jesus would be manifested in us, wouldn't He?

In our daily walk in our contacts with men and women, it would be love in action. We are Jesus folks. We must live the Jesus life. We must let this love life live in us as it lived in Jesus.

Jesus represented the Father; now we will represent Jesus. We will let love reign as a queen in our homes. How beautiful it will make them.

We are going to let the Jesus kind of love reign as queen in our hearts until every thought that is born there will be born of love, and every thought that is transformed into words will be love thoughts going out through the medium of love words to bless, cheer, comfort, and help.

We are going to let love reign over our reason. We are going to make reason become the servant of love. This may be hard because reason is so self-assertive and so hard to yield, but it must yield to love.

We are going to let Love reign in our businesses until men can feel it in the office. Office help will work better in an atmosphere of love than they do in an atmosphere of hate.

You will get more done in an atmosphere of love. So today, we are going to let love rule us in every way. All we think and do and say will be born of love.

21

WE ARE THE SONS OF LOVE

Christianity is a divine-human love affair. We are born of love. We have received the love nature of God.

This makes Christianity utterly different from every other religion in the world. It is not a religion. It is a love nature imparted to man. It is man rising to the height of this love nature. It is lifting man out of the normal realm in which the human race has been since the fall into the realm of God. It makes us as different from the world as was the Man Jesus.

This has never been clearly taught by the church, yet it is the heart of everything.

Jesus is the head of the new creation. The love law that He gave was to rule it.

> *By this shall all men know that ye are my disciples, if ye have love one to another.* (John 13:35)

This is the new love commandment, the new love law by which we are to be governed. Jesus is the love Lord. He is the Lord of this new creation.

> *A new commandment I give unto you, That ye love one another; as I have loved you, that ye also love one another. By this shall all men know that ye are my disciples, if ye have love one to another.* (John 13:34–35)

This is the badge by which the new creation is known. It is a badge of conduct. It is not like a gold badge worn upon the lapel of a coat, but it is a life. It is acting like Jesus. This is not dogma or creed. This is Jesus in daily life.

> *Do all things without murmurings and questionings: that ye may become blameless and harmless, children of God without blemish in the midst of a*

> *crooked and perverse generation, among whom ye are seen as lights in the world.* (Philippians 2:14–15 ASV)

We are blameless and harmless, sons of God. We are lovers, different from other men, because of love at work in our daily lives.

God is love, and God is light.

> *This is the message which we have heard from* [Jesus] *and announce unto you, that God is light, and in him is no darkness at all.* (1 John 1:5 ASV)

If we walk in the fullness of love, we are walking in the light. We have fellowship with the Father. We live in sweetest communion with each other.

I never understood what this Scripture meant:

> *Ye are of God, little children, and have overcome them: because greater is he that is in you, than he that is in the world.* (1 John 4:4)

This Scripture challenges us. "*Ye are of God.*" You are of love. You have overcome them by love. Greater is the love God in you than the hate god outside.

LOVE'S DOMINION

This strange new relationship with God in us as a lover makes us as gentle and thoughtful as Jesus. Jesus was the gentle love miracle. We have the gentle love miracle in us, loving through us, living in us, reproducing Himself in us.

This life is heaven's light. It is letting Jesus loose in us. It is translating the Jesus life into daily life. It is Jesus set free in us.

It is not a theory, not a creed, not a religion. It is the real Jesus thinking through us, acting through us. It is the love Lord in us unveiling Himself.

Jesus, the lover of old Galilee

Loving and living His life in me,

Meeting men's needs with Jesus deeds.

Yes, Jesus is loving through me.

The great lover is in us now. He is living in us now. "*It is no longer I that live, but Christ liveth in me*" (Galatians 2:20 ASV). Jesus is the lover unveiled in a believer.

Greater is the lover in you than any force from without that can touch your life. We can trustfully say, "I am of God." This greater One is He who burst the bars of death asunder and broke Satan's dominion. He is greater than the confusion in your heart or home. He is the absolute monarch of the heart of man.

He is love's dictator, ruling in love in us.

LOVE'S PEACE

"Peace I leave with you, my peace I give unto you: not as the world giveth, give I unto you" (John 14:27). His presence in you is your peace and gentle quietness. *"For he is our peace"* (Ephesians 2:14).

How little we have appreciated this. How we have wanted peace and cried for peace, not knowing that peace was in us.

How we have craved for love, not knowing that love was in us.

How we have longed for faith, not knowing that Jesus Christ, who is faith itself, was living in us.

God's peace is greater than the restlessness of the world, the restlessness of your heart and mind. The God of rest is in your heart. He is the God of all quietness.

> *Beloved, let us love one another: for love is of God; and every one that loveth is born of God, and knoweth God. He that loveth not knoweth not God; for God is love.* (1 John 4:7–8)

He is the lover, and the lover is in you. He loved in the throes of death upon the cross. He loved when He arose from the dead. He loves now.

"And my God shall supply every need of yours" (Philippians 4:19 ASV). Love is greater than your needs. He is the greater One, the Lord of finances, and the Lord of grace. We can rise above home influence, business influence, or any other hindrance because the enabling One is in us.

No matter how unkind men may be, you love them. He loved. You love. He died for them. You live for them. He is in you, the lover of men, loving through you.

THE WINNING POWER OF LOVE

It is giving love its place in life. Love must be first. The believer moves in love. It is the center of his being.

> *Above all things being fervent in your love among yourselves; for love covereth a multitude of sins.* (1 Peter 4:8 ASV)

It is not passive love. It is a white-heated love. It is not love governed by sense knowledge but love without restraint.

It is love that prevents a multitude of sins. It lifts a man into a realm where he does not quarrel, is not bitter, and does not answer back. It is a white-heated love like the love of the Master.

Love has all the earmarks of Jesus. It is a love that covers up the failings and weaknesses of those about it. It never talks unkindly, never bears a tale. It is the unfeigned love that loves from the heart fervently—a love that lifts us out of the commonplace into its own realm.

This new kind of love is the miracle of the ages. It is love that works within us.

> *For God it is who is working in you both to will and to work for His good pleasure.* (Philippians 2:13 YLT)

22

THE LOVE LAW INTERPRETED

The book of Leviticus is the interpretation of the Ten Commandments.

This love chapter is the interpretation of the new commandment of the new creation.

> *A new commandment I give unto you, That ye love one another; as I have loved you, that ye also love one another. By this shall all men know that ye are my disciples, if ye have love one to another.* (John 13:34–35)

> *If I speak with the tongues of men and of angels, but have not love, I am become sounding brass, or a clanging cymbal. And if I have the gift of prophecy, and know all mysteries and all knowledge; and if I have all faith, so as to remove mountains, but have not love, I am nothing.*
> (1 Corinthians 13:1–2 ASV)

The ability to master many languages has been a coveted achievement in the scholastic world, but the Spirit shows us here that one might speak in all the languages of men and angels, yet if he does not have this new kind of love, he is but sounding brass and a clanging cymbal.

Again he says, *"If I have the gift of prophecy, and know all mysteries and all knowledge; and if I have all faith, so as to remove mountains, but have not love, I am nothing."*

If I have the gift of prophecy so that I could foretell the events of a century, or understand all mysteries and have all knowledge, but have not love, I am nothing.

We all know the struggle of our chemists and metallurgists to unravel the mysteries of the chemicals, metals, and oils of the earth. One may know all these things and beside that, have faith so as to remove mountains, faith like the Master had in His earth walk; he may have all this, but if he does not have the Jesus kind of love, he is nothing.

He takes another step: *"And if I bestow all my goods to feed the poor, and if I give my body to be burned, but have not love, it profiteth me nothing"* (1 Corinthians 13:3 ASV).

I may be able to give as Rockefeller or Carnegie, or go into the jungles of Africa and pour my life out in the service of humanity, but if I do not have this Jesus kind of love, my philanthropy means nothing.

> *Love suffereth long, and is kind; love envieth not; love vaunteth not itself, is not puffed up, doth not behave itself unseemly, seeketh not its own, is not provoked, taketh not account of evil; rejoiceth not in unrighteousness, but rejoiceth with the truth; beareth all things, believeth all things, hopeth all things, endureth all things. Love never faileth.*
>
> (1 Corinthians 13:4–8 ASV)

We cannot refrain from comparing it with *phileo*—natural, human love. *Phileo* may suffer long but while it suffers, it is bitter, unhappy under the stress. Natural, human love is born of selfishness, and when that selfishness is thwarted, it becomes miserable.

"Love envieth not." The entire economic and social upheaval that is manifested throughout the whole world is caused by the poor envying the rich, and the failures envying the successful. Sense knowledge makes the poor restless but gives no formula to relieve their condition.

"Love vaunteth not itself, is not puffed up." Natural love does vaunt itself and parade itself; it is ever boasting of its achievements. The Jesus kind of love is the very opposite.

"Doth not behave itself unseemly." Go to the divorce court and note the behavior of natural love. Husband and wife are uncovering the secrets of their past love. Now filled with bitterness, selfishness, and hatred, they war against each other.

Go into the modern home and witness the unhappy condition, how the husband and wife quarrel before the children. How unseemly natural love acts under provocation.

"Seeketh not its own." Selfishness is eliminated. Bible scholar Benjamin Wilson put it this way: "Seeks not what belongs to another." That is striking.

This new kind of love does not seek its own in the divorce court or in the court of law.

What a heavenly thing this new kind of love really is!

"Is not provoked, taketh not account of evil." That would end the reign of scandal. It would eliminate the unhappy suspicion that separates lovers and wrecks homes.

"Rejoiceth not in unrighteousness, but rejoiceth with the truth." It finds no pleasure in sin, no pleasure in wrong, no pleasure in the thing that injures another. Its joy is in the truth.

"Beareth all things." It never repeats scandal. It never remembers the unkindness of the past. Natural, human love remembers the old sins and has the scars on exhibition.

What God forgives, He forgets. This new kind of love is of God. What it forgives, it forgets. It has no memory of old sins.

"Believeth all things." This is a new unveiling of faith. We believe in the person we love. It is hard for us to doubt where love has found a nesting place. Here is the secret of faith. If you want the kind of faith that Jesus had, this new kind of love alone will give birth to it.

"Hopeth all things." This means that under the most adverse circumstances, hope, which is the kindred of joy, holds forth and brings the sense of victory in the presence of defeat.

"Endureth all things." This is perhaps one of the most amazing features of this new kind of love. Through years of suffering and privation, it remains steadfast, immovable, and always abounding in good works. It endures years of self-denial without complaint. This lifts man into the realm of God. This is an unveiling of what God can do in common men.

The next step is the most suggestive perhaps of the entire chapter: *"Love never faileth."*

Knowledge will break down. Everything else will fail. We have tried force. We have tried law. We have tried willpower. But they have all failed.

The mother has scolded and prayed. She has gone through a miniature hell and has failed. Now she sees a vision. She understands what the Spirit meant in 1 John 4:16 (ASV): *"And we know and have believed the love which*

God hath in us. God is love; and he that abideth in love abideth in God, and God abideth in him."

It will be a victorious hour when we learn to believe in love. It is something that lifts us into a realm above the senses where we trust in an unseen force.

"He that abideth in love abideth in God, and God abideth in him."

If you trust in love, you trust in God. You can say, "Greater is love in me than this problem that confronts me, this difficulty that has held me in bondage." Love lifts us into the realm of God.

We can understand now why love cannot fail.

FOLLOW AFTER LOVE

We have followed after money, after pleasure, and after the things of the senses.

In 1 Corinthians 14:1 (ASV), the Spirit says to us, at the close of that marvelous exposition of *agape* in chapter 13, that we are to *"follow after love."*

God is love. So then it is following after God. We will go where love leads. We will do what love suggests. That is the way Jesus lived. He followed after love.

That was the way Paul walked. He followed after love. Many another voices called, and many another roads beckoned, but his path was love.

Jesus's path lead Him to Calvary. Your path may have a Calvary conclusion too.

We set aside the things that we once craved for love's sake, for we are going down the path of love. It may be thorn-filled, or it may be strewn with roses, but we will follow after love.

If it is service in a foreign field, we will follow after love. If love beckons us to go to the slums of our city, we will follow after love.

We know no other path. We know no other way than the love way, the Jesus way.

We can hear Him whisper, "You who are strong ought to bear the infirmities of the weak and not to please yourselves." (See Romans 15:1.)

Christ pleased not Himself. He is your life pattern.

CONCLUSION

There is a love that can stand the test of modern life.

There is a love that will enable us to love the unlovely, the disagreeable, and the hateful.

There is a love that will lift us up into God's class, where we love the ungodly and the unworthy.

There is a love that will make us just like the Master so that we would not only live for men but also die for them.

There is a love that will enable us to love them when they are doing all they can to injure us.

There is a love that will whisper, *"Forgive them; for they know not what they do"* (Luke 23:34).

Yes, there is a love. If you are a new creation, you have found this new kind of love.

HOW IT WORKS

Yes, this new kind of love works. It can be trusted to do the thing we declare it will do.

It is God's nature gaining the mastery in our lives, and wherever it gains the mastery, it works.

It makes hard, bitter men gentle as Jesus. It will take a man like Saul of Tarsus and make him like Paul. It will take men out of the lowest depths of the slums and lead them into the pulpits, where they will lead multitudes to Christ.

It is the miracle of modern days.

HEED THE CALL

You have read. You have been thrilled. You have been convicted. He, the Unseen One, has been talking to your heart. What are you going to do about it?

You must not ignore the call. This is your great moment. You must respond to the tug of your spirit. Your spirit is craving this deep, rich, wonderful life.

Do not follow sense knowledge. Give your spirit the right of way. Let this love exercise its lordship from this hour. It will make life big to you. It will make you a blessing to the world.

The broken lives and the crushed hearts beating to the rhythm of misery are a challenge. We are attempting to answer that challenge.

We believe we have the message for this crisis hour of human suffering.

God has been speaking to your heart. You have seen the failure of natural human love.

You see what this new kind of love can do for men and women. You know of many homes where they need this message. It would save the home. It would save the children.

Here is the challenge to you: will you stir yourself to send for a few copies to mail to your friends with a letter telling them what this message has meant to you?

Will you see that every clergyman in your city has a copy?

You may do another thing: call in your friends and read the book together with them.

Watch the reactions. You will be filled with joy at this ministry in which you are able to have a share.

It is in your hands now. Don't let the impulse of the Spirit die without action.

IN HIS PRESENCE

CONTENTS

FIRST WORDS

This book is not written about what others were and did, but about what we are and can do! It is a revelation of what we are in Christ, an unveiling of what He can do through us.

It is a lifting of the curtain and a revealing of the holy of holies and our ability to enter it and stand in the presence of the Father.

It is a revelation of our ability to stand in His presence on the behalf of others.

It is a discovery of God's ability available to anyone in Christ—an introduction to ourselves in Christ.

Much of it will be new and a challenge to earnest spirits to climb the heights and to sound the depths of these tremendous spiritual realities.

It will enable us to know Him and the power and the ability that was revealed in His resurrection, and the amazing fact that that ability is ours!

It will show us our legal rights in Christ: that we do not stand upon His sufferance or His pity, but upon our legal rights, claiming them for our very own.

It will remove the mist that has surrounded the prayer life and lead us out of spiritual mysticism into the light of life.

It will show us the authority of the name of Jesus, and how to use it.

It will show us the ability of the Indwelling One in us.

It will reveal our place in the Family and show us how to take that place.

This is not a book of philosophy or of theories, but it is a book of reality.

It shows us what belongs to us and our ability to enjoy all these rights in Christ.

The call to prayer is the Father's invitation to visit with Him. This is more than the consciousness of a great need that often drives us to intercession. It is the call of Love to come and fellowship. It is really visiting with the Father.

Few of us have realized the fact that the Father's heart is hungry for the companionship of His children. His heart hunger is the reason for man and the reason for redemption, *"For God so loved the world, that He gave His only begotten Son"* (John 3:16).

That love impels Him to call us to prayer.

That call is the proof of our ability to stand in His presence. It is the proof of His making us righteous enough to stand in His presence without reproof or condemnation.

It means that we are ever welcome to the throne room.

How few of us have ever realized this?

It is sons visiting their Father.

It is children coming joyously into the presence of a Loving Parent.

He does not demand faith of His children. He doesn't say, "Now if you believe," or "If you have faith," or "If you love me." He said that to the Jews, His servants, the men of the broken covenant. But He says to us, *"Come unto me, all ye that labour and are heavy laden, and I will give you rest"* (Matthew 11:28). It is the Father's invitation to the throne room of Love.

1

WHAT PRAYER IS

Prayer is our need crying out for help. Prayer is the voice of faith to the Father. Prayer is born then of the sense of need, and the assurance that the need will be met.

Unbelief cannot pray; it can only utter words.

Prayer is the living Word on lips of faith.

It is holding His Word up to Him in prayer like a mirror.

He sees Himself in His Word.

He said it. You are asking Him to do it.

He promised. You hold that promise up to Him in prayer.

You see, God and His Word are One, just as He and Jesus are One.

He honored His Word by calling His Son, "the Word."

His Son, then, and the Word are One.

He was with the Son, and in the Son; so He is in the Word and with the Word today.

When we quote the Word, we quote Him. When we rest on the Word, we rest on Him.

His Word is my contact with Him.

His Word on the lips of faith is He Himself speaking.

Then we are speaking His Word back to Him.

We hold His Word as a bank holds our note. Just as we have collateral to make the note good, God has ability to make His Word good.

Prayer then is facing God with man's needs, with His promise to meet those needs.

He taught us to pray. He taught us to trust His Word.

Prayer is a part of God's program for us.

He encourages us to act on His Word. He is one with us in this prayer life.

It is His way of saving, healing, and blessing men.

Jesus said in Luke 18:1, *"Men ought always to pray, and not to faint."* You see, prayer means vital contact with the Father. We are near enough to Him to breathe in His very presence.

Prayer means that we have come boldly into the throne room and are standing in His presence.

It is more than bringing Him on the scene. It is going into the presence of the Father and Jesus in an executive meeting, laying our needs before them and making our requisitions for ability, grace, healing for someone, victory for someone, or financial needs. Whatever that need may be, we are making a demand upon Him.

One day when the crowd was pressing around the Master, Jesus asked, *"Who touched me?"* (Luke 8:45 MOFF). Peter and the other disciples said, *"Master, the crowds are all round you pressing hard!"* But Jesus answered, *"Somebody did touch me, for I felt power had passed from me"* (verse 46 MOFF).

That is a beautiful translation, and it is so suggestive. There cannot be any touching of the Master without the Master knowing it. When need touches Him, it makes a demand upon His ability to meet that need; and prayer is the way in which we touch Him.

Prayer keeps man in close contact with the Father and with the Word.

It is a constant communion with the Father and it enriches one spiritually.

It illumines the Word, and illumines the mind; and it freshens and heals the body.

A strange feature about this prayer life is that it reaches to the uttermost parts of the earth. When I pray for a man in London or in Africa, my spirit can send to him, through the Father, the blessing that he needs today. It is the original wireless method.

It is the original radio means of communication.

I speak here, and they are instantly blessed there.

What a ministry!

PRAYER IS A SPIRITUAL EXERCISE

Your spirit is contacting the Father.

Your spirit is reaching other human spirits through the Father.

Paul said, "My spirit and the Lord Jesus will be with you in your deliberations." It doesn't seem credible.

Sense knowledge can't grasp this. It is in the realm of the recreated spirit.

We become so utterly one with Him.

We become so utterly ruled and governed by the Word and by the Holy Spirit that we become masters of demons and of their work.

We cast out demons with the Word.

We pray for sick folks and the diseases leave them.

Weakness is destroyed by the strength of God.

The very life of God flows out through our lips.

Do you remember John 7:38 (ASV), where Jesus says, *"He that believeth on me, as the scripture hath said, from within him shall flow rivers of living water"*?

Jesus is speaking of the Holy Spirit's indwelling presence and how, from our inner life of prayer, there gushes forth a torrent of the very life of God that speeds on its way to that one who is in need. No one knows about the fullness of this. We are in the very infancy of this prayer life.

Electricity has made the wireless and the radio realities.

Electricity is God's life in the mechanical world.

Will that life in the mechanical world be stronger, more efficacious than His nature in our spirits? I can't believe it.

I know that our prayers bring the very presence of God upon men in any part of the world.

You see, this is cooperating with Him. God through you is ruling the demons and evil forces all over the world. You become His voice in the name of Jesus.

The Word really becomes the sword of the spirit, and it is waging a war against demoniacal forces who rule men.

His Word through your lips dominates these world forces. They don't know it, but they feel cramped, bound, hindered, and conquered.

Jesus said, *"In my name shall* [you] *cast out demons"* (Mark 16:17 ASV). That means rule them, govern them.

God through you, then, can sway the nations.

Now you can understand 2 Corinthians 6:1 (ASV): *"Working together with him."*

How? Through this marvelous prayer life.

You have entered the holy priesthood in your prayer life. You can be God's voice, His spokesman, His ambassador, His under-ruler in Jesus's name through the Word on your lips.

You become God's will toward a Satan-ruled world.

You are taking Jesus's place. You are acting in His stead.

Once more God is set free among men.

You remember that God gave to Adam dominion over all the universe. That dominion was restored to us through Jesus, but it is of no value to us unless we, the Jesus men, use that authority in His name.

That authority was given to an individual, Adam. Now the authority is given to us as believers in His name.

Jesus exercised that dominion. He ruled the sea. He ruled the fish. He ruled the human body. He made legs grow where they had been amputated. He fed the multitudes.

Jesus did not exercise any authority or ability that is not latent in His Name today.

Someday there is going to rise a people who will take Jesus's place and bless humanity as Jesus blessed them in dear old Galilee.

Did not Jesus say in Matthew 28:18–20:

> *All power is given unto me in heaven and in earth. Go ye therefore, and teach all nations, baptizing them in the name of the Father, and of the Son, and of the Holy Ghost: teaching them to observe all things whatsoever I*

have commanded you: and, lo, I am with you always, even unto the end of the world.

Notice, Jesus wanted students of the Word.

He is with us in the Word, that living Word.

He is with us in His name.

He is with us in the presence of the Holy Spirit.

We join forces with Him in this prayer life.

That *"all power"* was given to Him as the head of the church, and it is for the church to use.

The authority that is in His name is on your lips. You let that authority loose. You give it liberty and it blesses men.

He has made us sons.

He has given us the name.

He has given us the Holy Spirit.

He has restored all that Adam lost and more.

We are Satan's rulers.

We are masters of demons and laws that sin brought into being.

Why did He redeem us? Why make us new creations? Why make us righteous? Why dwell in us? Why give us the name? Why say that in Jesus's name, we could cast out demons?

What did He expect us to do after making us all this? Just to be good, neutral sons who never face the enemy, who simply read the Word but never act on it, who do not take our redemption and new creation seriously?

Is He mocking us? Is His Word like dry clouds in a drought?

Is Satan invincible? Must we yield to Satan's dominion and Satan-ruled circumstances?

Must we say that tanks, planes, and bombs are to rule the world?

Or is God still living, and are we tied up with Him?

I can feel God's question there. He is saying to me, "Have you taken these facts as seriously as your nation has taken the draft laws? Is my redemption and new creation as real as the taxes? Does it mean anything?"

We must face this issue.

We are surrounded by demoniacal forces that are dominating the human on earth, and if the church hasn't authority over these, then no one has.

But the church has! And prayer is our method and mode of dominating these diabolical forces that are wrecking civilization.

TAKING OUR PLACE

Every one of us has a place in the prayer life.

God has no unused members.

There isn't a useless member in the physical body; neither is there in the spiritual body of Christ.

God has planned, with divine wisdom, the body of Christ and the moment that you are born into that body you have your place in which to function.

If anyone thinks that because of lack of training or for lack of this or that, he hasn't a place, he is deluded by the enemy.

You have a place.

With that place comes responsibility, and with responsibility comes a reward or demerit.

If you do not take your place in the family of God, in the church, and begin to function, the body of Christ is weakened because of it.

Some have the idea that their special vocation is to criticize others because they are not doing more.

The Holy Spirit is the only One who has this position.

You have no right to set yourself up as a critic.

Your business is to find your place and fill it.

Until you do, you will pay the price.

I want you to know, my brother, my sister, that the price you pay for staying out of the will of God is expensive.

You may pay it in sickness, in loss of money or in unhappiness with your loved ones, for you can't be the protected one, the cared-for one, as long as you are standing outside of the Lord's will for you.

Take your place!

Give yourself to meditation, prayer, and study of the Word.

Don't allow anything to stand in the way of your finding your place.

Life will not mean much to you outside of His will.

The big thing of life is to be in the Will of the Father.

You say that you were never called to give your life in prayer?

No. You may not have been set apart by the Spirit for that special ministry, but I think it would be wise for you to spend enough time in prayer to get acquainted with the Father. (See Luke 18:1.)

There are only two ways of getting acquainted: through the Word and by prayer.

If you don't take time to pray, you are losing out.

You can't say that you have no responsibility in the prayer life, for you have.

To see a need is to have a call to prayer.

There are people who will be utterly lost unless you take your place.

Unless you do your part, men will cry against you through eternity.

You can't plead that you have too much work to do; you can pray while you work.

You can't put up the plea that you do not know how; you can learn if you wish.

For you to disobey the prayer call is for you to disobey the call of your Father.

The prayer responsibility today is the most important thing of our lives.

Did you ever realize that there are men and women who are defeated and are breaking down in their business, home and spiritual life because we haven't prayed?

Let me change it: because *you* haven't prayed?

You have been occupied with your pleasures and your dreams; and men and women, staggering under the burdens you should have carried, are breaking down.

Oh, God, have mercy upon us!

As you read this, do not read it simply to awaken you for the moment, but let prayer become like your eating, or your business, or your home.

If you are a mother or a wife, and live at home, there are certain duties which you perform every day for your family.

The greatest duty that you will ever perform for your family will be the prayer duty.

It may be that it is no longer a privilege.

You have thrown the privilege away.

You have ignored it.

It has now become a stern duty.

You must go back to your prayer closet and begin anew your fellowship with Him.

Do it for the sake of your family, the boys and girls, and for the sake of your home and church, and God will honor you.

Children are growing up in Christian homes without the restraining power of God over their lives.

The reason is apparent! Mothers and fathers have failed in their responsibilities in the prayer life.

I call on you, men and women, who yourselves are to blame for the crime and the lawlessness of the youth of this generation, to go and ask His forgiveness, and to take up your responsibilities, *now*!

IN HIS PRESENCE

Way back yonder in the garden the first man lived in the presence of the Creator, Jehovah God.

He had no sense of unfitness or need of fitness.

He was like a child who climbs up into his father's arms. The child has no sense of fear, no sense of need, for he belongs, and because he belongs, he takes his place; he takes liberties.

But when the great blunder was made, and Adam in a foolish moment sold out his vast privileges and rights to an enemy, he was driven away from God's presence, and a flaming sword was at the gateway to keep him out.

That garden of desire with its tree of life was known to all the people, for thousands of years, until the flood came, and yet no one could get into the presence of God.

Then Jehovah separated Abraham and cut the covenant with him, giving a promise of the Messiah to come through him; his descendants were also given a law and a priesthood, and they cut the covenant with Jehovah through the priest.

God dwelt in their midst in the holy of holies.

No one could approach Him unless he was covered by a cloud of incense and had in his hand a basin of blood to sprinkle on the mercy seat; and that was only to be done once a year by the appointed priest.

Israel was a servant.

The unapproachable presence was in the holy of holies.

The heart of man was just as hungry after God as it had been on the day that Adam was driven out of the garden.

The heart-hunger of man has given us all the religions of the old world, all the religions of the East.

It has also given us all our modern philosophical and metaphysical religions.

Man's heart-hunger is one of his most outstanding features, a very badge of the human.

But you mustn't think for a moment that the hunger is all on one side.

God's child-hungry and love-hungry heart created a universe, put in the center of it a world to be a home for His man, and He created man after His own image and likeness, an eternal being, and you know how that man failed Him.

All down through human history is the trail of man's hunger and of God's outreaching toward that spirit-hungry man, until the Man, Jesus, came.

The incarnation of Jesus is the master stroke of love.

It was God's intrusion into the sense realm where man began to live when driven from the garden.

God unveiled Himself to the senses of the Jewish nation. They had no spiritual appreciation because they were spiritually dead.

Jesus in His earth walk revealed to the men of the senses who surrounded Him a strange, phenomenal thing: He talked with God Almighty, the God of the Jews, with a sense of intimacy that they couldn't understand, and finally He called their God His Father.

To them, that was blasphemy, and they stoned Him for it; they hounded Him until finally they took Him before Pontius Pilate and accused Him, saying, "He makes God His Father; that's blasphemy and He ought to die."

Jesus paid the price of confessing God as His Father.

But before He did that, He said, as recorded in John 14:6: *"I am the way, the truth, and the life: no man cometh unto the Father, but by me."*

I remembered that Acts 9:2 is the story of Paul's being sent to Damascus with authority to arrest any who he found of "the Way."

"But when some were hardened and disobedient, speaking evil of the Way before the multitude, he departed from them" (Acts 19:9 ASV).

Acts 19:23 (ASV) says, *"And about that time there arose no small stir concerning the Way."*

Acts 18:26 tells the story of how Priscilla and Aquila heard Apollos, a disciple of John the Baptist, who had not yet heard of Jesus, and they *"expounded unto him the way of God."*

The same thought is brought out again in Acts 22:4: *"And I persecuted this way unto the death."* Paul here is standing before the people of Jerusalem, telling how he had persecuted "the Way."

Paul is again defending himself in Acts 24:14: *"But this I confess unto thee, that after the way which they call heresy, so worship I the God of my fathers."*

These Scriptures were puzzling.

Why was it called "the Way?"

> *By this the holy Spirit means that the way into the Holiest Presence was not disclosed so long as the first tent...was still standing.*
>
> (Hebrews 9:8–9 MOFF)

This began to throw light on it as "the Way" into the holy of holies.

But Hebrews 10:19–20 clears it up: *"Having therefore, brethren, boldness to enter into the holiest by the blood of Jesus, by a new and living way, which he hath consecrated for us, through the veil, that is to say, his flesh."*

Now we can understand it.

The way that Paul preached was the way into God's presence.

Way back yonder, Adam lost "the Way."

Jesus came to point it out.

He said, "I am the Way, I am the reality, and I am the new kind of life."

Now in Hebrews 4:16, He tells us to come boldly to the throne of grace; that means to come boldly into the holy of holies, to come with freedom into the very presence of God.

Now our hearts can understand Mark 15:38: *"And the veil of the temple was rent in* [two] *from the top to the bottom."*

Josephus tells us that wonderful veil was four inches thick and fifteen feet square, made of the finest dyed linen, inwrought with threads of gold.

It shielded the holy of holies so that no one could enter but the high priest, and he but once a year in a cloud of incense with a bowl of blood to make the yearly atonement for the nation.

Now an angel has come and that curtain is rent, not from the bottom, but from the top, showing that God has been there and ripped that curtain apart, throwing the holy of holies open, not to the high priest only, but to everyone whom the blood of Jesus Christ has cleansed.

In other words, God the Father is no longer shut in alone.

He can be approached.

He can be met.

But that isn't all. Try to imagine yourself a Jew back yonder under that first covenant, and you know that no Jew could approach God and live.

Nadab and Abihu were struck dead upon the portals when they attempted to go into God's presence uninvited. It was upon that great festival day when the priesthood had just been set apart by Moses. Aaron's two beautiful sons lay dead. (See Leviticus 10:1–3.)

From that day on, no man ever attempted to enter the holy of holies except a king. He was struck with leprosy as he entered the holy place attempting to go into the holy of holies, and he lived in a leper house the rest of his life. (See 2 Chronicles 26:18–21.)

For anyone to touch the ark of the covenant meant death, as it did to David's friend who dared put his hand up to steady it when the oxen had jarred the vehicle that bore it. (See 2 Samuel 6:6–7.)

Now, Jesus said, "I am going to be the Way into the presence of the Father. Men are going to be able to enter into His presence."

Can't you see what that would mean to the prayer life?

Here is the secret of prayer.

We have utterly failed to grasp the significance of the heart hunger of the Father. He longs for our companionship.

John 14:23 gives us an illustration: "*Jesus answered and said unto him, If a man love me, he will keep my words: and my Father will love him, and we will come unto him, and make our abode with him.*"

Does your heart grasp it?

Jesus said: "The Father and I will come and make our home with you."

He is no longer in the holy of holies.

The sin problem has been settled.

Man has received eternal life, has become His very child.

Now His great heart of love says, "I want to come and make My home with you."

Can you see what lies behind this?

There has been a restored righteousness.

Man has become righteous.

He can stand in the Father's presence without the sense of guilt, condemnation or inferiority, and on the basis of this righteousness, man has fellowship.

This is the object, the heart-reason for the entire redemptive program.

What would relationship mean without fellowship?

God could make man His son, but if that son didn't have fellowship with the Father, then there is no joy for the heart of either.

Fellowship really means "drinking out of the same cup."

It was like our old-fashioned communion table, where the pastor or elders passed a cup and each one of us took a sip of the wine.

That was a type of communion.

Now the Father has called us into communion with His Son.

We drink together.

Can't you hear Him say, "Behold, I stand at the door and knock: if any man hear my voice and open the door, I will come in to him, and will drink with him?" (See Revelation 3:20.)

Now what does it mean to us?

It means that the last barrier between the Father and the children has been put away.

We may come into His presence now with the same freedom that Jesus had.

Now we can see what prayer can mean.

It isn't the old idea of getting on our knees and crying and begging.

It is a son coming into the Father's presence for one of our brethren who has been injured, or for one who for some reason cannot come and make his appeal personally. We come on his behalf and ask for a blessing.

Or it may be that we are taking up the need of the great unsaved world.

We stand there in fullness of fellowship and fullness of joy to get a portion for another.

This is entering by the new and living way.

This is coming boldly to the throne of grace.

This is fellowshipping the Father.

This is visiting with Him.

It is not coming into His presence as the Jews came into the presence of Jehovah, or as a sinner would approach, but we are coming as sons and daughters.

We are taking our place.

1 Peter 2:3–5 (ASV) gives us a picture of our holy priesthood:

> *If ye have tasted that the Lord is gracious: unto whom coming, a living stone, rejected indeed of men, but with God elect, precious, ye also, as living stones, are built up a spiritual house, to be a holy priesthood, to offer up spiritual sacrifices, acceptable to God through Jesus Christ.*

It is our holy priesthood to offer up spiritual sacrifices acceptable to the Father through Jesus Christ.

That is our daily worship, our daily fellowship with Him.

We always come to our Father in the name of His beloved Son.

We come with thanksgiving; we come with worship; we come with love.

We bring the fruit of lips.

Would that our hearts could understand what this means.

Our words are the fruit of the vine. Jesus said, "*I am the vine, ye are the branches*" (John 15:5).

And here is lip fruit: our words from which the wine of life can be made.

How it does touch our hearts to think that He drinks of the fruit of our lips.

Jesus said, "I am that living water." Now we can understand that.

Hebrews 13:15 (ASV) makes us know, as we never did, the holy privilege of speech: "*Through him then let us offer up a sacrifice of praise to God continually, that is, the fruit of lips which make confession to his name.*"

Now we can understand what it means to come into His presence.

You come with your petitions.

You come with your heartaches.

You come with your burden, and He partakes of the fruit of your lips.

Oh, how priceless are your words to Him!

The rent veil, the tender heart invitation to come boldly to the throne of grace, all mean something to us now.

We are coming in through the living way that Jesus opened by His great sacrifice; by His victory over the adversary that made our new birth possible and our standing as sons a reality.

Ours is a twofold priesthood. We are not only a holy priesthood, but we are a royal priesthood.

This is pictured in 1 Peter 2:9–10:

> *But ye are a chosen generation, a royal priesthood, an holy nation, a peculiar people; that ye should [show] forth the praises of him who hath called you out of darkness into his marvellous light; which in time past were not a people, but are now the people of God: which had not obtained mercy, but now have obtained mercy.*

This is our public ministry.

Whether it be as a layman or a preacher, we are showing forth in our daily walk, in our conversation, the fruits of this royal priesthood.

You see, we belong to the throne.

We belong to royalty, and we are showing forth His excellencies.

We are advertising His love, His grace, His longsuffering.

We are advertising eternal life, His very nature.

We belong to royalty.

Is it any wonder that we have access to the throne?

Is it any wonder that we can come boldly to the throne of grace?

We are walking up the new and living way!

2

THE PRAYER HABIT

The names that are familiar to us in God's Westminster Abbey of the church are the names of those who pray, men and women who have climbed the mountains of usefulness in the struggle with circumstances through prayer.

There is no denying that the lack of prayer is the bane of the individual member of the body of Christ.

Jesus was a man of prayer.

He taught prayer, not as a slavish duty, but as a glorious privilege.

I used to wonder why He needed to pray.

He took His human place, and lived the human life.

I have a conviction that He didn't draw upon the secret resources that belonged to Him, more than it is possible for us who live and walk in His name.

Jesus's ministry in healing illustrated what our prayer life may do for us.

He didn't exercise His divine prerogatives during His three years' ministry any more than any child of God may exercise them.

He had a human body.

He had the limitations that go with the incarnation.

The believer is a new creation, created in Christ Jesus. He is brought into the family of God. He is an heir of God and a joint-heir with Jesus Christ.

He is a child of God.

The Spirit that raised Jesus from the dead dwells in his body. Plus this, Jesus has given him the power of attorney to use His name.

The more that I study the life of Jesus, I am convinced that He did not exercise divine power in excess of what every intelligent child of God possesses today.

The difference is that Jesus knew what belonged to Him and Jesus used His rights. We do not know what belongs to us. Not knowing what is ours, we cannot use our rights. When Jesus cast out demons, He used authority that He has delegated to the church. He said, "In my name, you shall cast out demons." (See Mark 16:17.) The forces of hell could not touch Him or injure Him; He was simply using the divine ability that is delegated to us.

Jesus said, "You shall take up serpents and they shall not injure you." (See Mark 16:18.)

The poison of vipers has no power over the Christian's body, who knows his place in Christ.

The apostle Paul loosened the deadly fangs of a viper that had fastened itself into his hand, and shook the thing off without injury.

Paul simply illustrated what Jesus had promised.

Let me state it again: I am convinced that intelligent children of the Lord could walk in the same life and power and divine liberty as Jesus walked, if they understood their privileges.

He said, "If you drink any deadly thing, it shall not harm you."

Poison could not be administered to the Lord Jesus and take effect.

It cannot be administered to the body of Christ and take effect if the members of that body walk in the knowledge and liberty of the sons of God.

This is not extreme.

It is simply walking in the realm of life.

We have been translated out of the realm of darkness; that is, the kingdom of weakness, darkness and ignorance.

We have been translated into the kingdom of the Son of His love, which is the realm of wealth, of life, of light, joy, of peace, and of faith.

Let me state it again: Jesus in His earth walk, as the incarnate Son of God, beginning with His baptism, lived exactly as every child of God should live today.

God wasn't any more His Father than He is ours.

He said, "The Father loves you even as He loves me."

He was the Son of God.

You are a son of God.

He was the Deity.

You are a partaker of the divine nature, that is the Deity.

He had the Holy Spirit dwelling in Him.

You have the Holy Spirit dwelling in you.

The difference is that Jesus gave the Holy Spirit right of way in a sense of which we have never yet learned.

He took advantage of the God-life within Him in a way that we have never yet been able to take advantage of the God-life within us.

But, you say, Jesus was not mortal as we are.

That is true.

But by faith, the body is dead because of sin, but the spirit is life because of righteousness.

Our bodies shall not have dominion over us as we walk in the realm of God.

Again, Paul says that our bodies are dead, have lost their mortal effectiveness in reigning over our spirits.

I believe that God planned that we should walk in the fullness of the divine life; that we should dare to take our positions as sons and daughters of God; and that the hour is coming before the Lord's return in which a remnant of the body will rise and walk before God the Father in the fullness of the new creation life.

Disease will not be able to lay hold upon us.

Ignorance and fear will be banished, because the wisdom that comes from above that is in Jesus, will lead us into the full dream, ambitions and purposes of our Father.

Now, I want you to notice that God has made Jesus to be our redemption.

Paul said in Ephesians 1:7, *"In whom we have redemption."*

He declares in 1 Corinthians 1:30, *"Of him are ye in Christ Jesus, who of God is made unto us wisdom, and righteousness, and sanctification, and redemption."*

You dare to measure that!

You dare to set limits on that!

The limits of that redemption are the limits of Jesus.

He was made unto us wisdom from God.

The limits of that wisdom are the limits of the eternal Son of God.

He is made unto us sanctification.

The limits of that sanctification are the limits of Jesus.

He is our life, and the limits of that life are the limits of the life of the Son of God.

You see, our feeble reasoning has pushed faith out of the arena.

The devil can combat successfully against our reason.

But if faith gets reason's place, Satan is whipped.

The great body of the most advanced Bible teachers today are held in the bondage of sense knowledge.

Their interpretations are often evasions.

Because of the opinions of men, they dare not take their real place.

Consequently, the Word of God has little effect.

Let us humbly and fearlessly take our place, in the name of the Lord Jesus Christ.

If we are new creations created in Christ Jesus, let us ask the Father to set the limits of that new creation instead of allowing theologians to do it.

Faith will lead you where reason cannot walk.

Reason has never been a mountain climber.

Faith, like a mountain sheep, can scale the loftiest mountain peaks without fear.

I offer this as a subject for meditation, not controversy.

I offer this as a contribution after years of heart-searching, of out-reaching after the bigger, fuller life in Christ.

I know it is not in the realm of reason, but I know it is where faith walks; and God is challenging us in these last days to get the light and the knowledge that will fit us for the closing of this dispensation.

The message that John Wesley brought was truth, but it was only part of the truth.

John Calvin had only a little of the light.

There have been revelations continually from the Word during these hundreds of years.

Don't you think it is time that we passed out of the swaddling clothes period into the stature of the perfect man in Christ Jesus?

So, let us dare to climb the heights of God.

Let us say without fear, "I am what He says I am. He is in me what He says He is. I can do, with His ability in me, what He says I can."

This makes life big and rich.

This makes us worthwhile to Him!

This will make us partners with Him.

We will be in that prized inner-circle with Him, one of the trusted ones.

When He has a difficult mission, He will call on us.

You see, He will find it easy to reach us as we constantly visit Him.

Take your place!

Enjoy your rights!

ALL KINDS OF PRAYER

Ephesians 6:13–18 (ASV) says:

> *Take up the whole armor of God, that ye may be able to withstand in the evil day, and, having done all, to stand. Stand therefore, having girded your loins with truth, and having put on the breastplate of righteousness, and having shod your feet with the preparation of the gospel of peace; withal taking up the shield of faith, wherewith ye shall be able to quench all the fiery darts of the evil one. And take the helmet of salvation, and the sword of the Spirit, which is the word of God: with all prayer and*

supplication praying at all seasons in the Spirit, and watching thereunto in all perseverance and supplication for all the saints.

You will notice by this translation that the object of the Christian soldier's coat of mail or armor is that he may enter the prayer fight. Preaching and personal work are God-honored and blessed vocations or ministries, but prayer is the foundation of it all.

A man might preach with the eloquence of Henry Ward Beecher and be the most skilled of diplomats as a soul winner, but he will fall short of his ministry in both fields if he isn't backed up by the prayer life.

The failure of all Christian enterprises is a prayer failure.

Prayer alone gives success.

There are many different kinds of prayer.

There is simple petition, lifting its sentences in Jesus's name to the heart of Love.

There is persistent, tenacious prayer that will not yield until the answer comes.

There is prevailing prayer that overcomes every obstacle, and finally lands the answer in the harbor of peace.

There is battle prayer, with its tears and agony, its intense yearning.

There is the quiet prayer of faith whose voice is never lifted above a whisper, but whose persistent faith shakes the very throne of heaven.

There is prayer without ceasing that seems to perfume every act of the one who prays persistently.

Then, there is the unconscious prayer attitude.

Paul says, *"Praying at all times in the Spirit with all manner of prayer"* (Ephesians 6:18 MOFF).

How desperately the nation needs it.

How desperately the church needs it.

Nothing can take the place of prayer.

Every believer should go into the school of prayer with Christ and actually learn the secret of prayer, the precious ministry of intercession.

The prayer of intercession is the prayer for another, not for self. It is the prayer that passes out from your domain, your realm, into the realm of another.

Jesus ever lives to make intercession at the right hand of the Father.

The Holy Spirit in us oft-times makes intercession that cannot be uttered in words.

Oft-times we are depressed; we cannot understand it or see any reason for it; it is the Holy Spirit in agony reaching through us to the Father.

If our spirits were only fruitful, perhaps we could understand the language and the agony of the Spirit in His mighty outreaching toward the throne of grace.

If our lives were only more perfectly under His sway, He might be able to breathe His passion through our conscious faculties, in His mighty agony for lost men and women.

Oft-times our spirits are dull, and He cannot communicate His passion and yearning through them to our minds.

So, it becomes unintelligible agony, *"groanings which cannot be uttered"* (Romans 8:26).

I suppose this is the reason why certain men and women are led to become the prayer channels for a whole congregation.

So few of us, in our busy lives, take time to pray, that the Spirit searches through the congregation for the willing hearts that will deny themselves some of the common pleasures and will be first in the line of prayer instead of last.

On these willing hearts rolls the burden of the entire church.

Thank God, that in our church are found those who are willing to set aside whole nights of prayer; who will leave the joy of visiting with loved ones, and hide away alone with Him to take my burden and yours that we have in some way failed to roll on the Lord.

They encompass our Jericho with their persistent intercession.

It is a pity that more of us do not force ourselves into a life of prayer.

We have the time.

We use it in useless talk, or careless reading.

While the Spirit is searching for an outlet, He must pass us by because we are not ready.

Oh, I beseech you, reader, not to talk about it anymore, or plan when you will do it, but begin it now.

Force yourself into the prayer life. Regardless of how you feel, drive yourself to prayer.

You will be amazed how halting and stumbling will be your first attempts.

You have been rated, perhaps, as an unusual Christian worker in the church.

Men look upon you as an outstanding Christian, but if they knew that in behind your public profession, there was an empty closet, or an unused prayer room, they would be amazed.

If you live with the Lord in secret, you will be able to pray with great freedom in public.

Unconsciously we call upon the people to pray who are on praying terms with the Lord.

Seldom will a spiritual mind reach out to an unspiritual life for help.

It is only when we are clutching at straws that we do it.

You see, prayer has several elements.

It brings you into personal fellowship and touch with the Father, and with the Holy Spirit, and with Jesus.

All three of the Godhead are brought into the prayer life.

You are praying to the Father.

You are praying in the name of Jesus.

You are praying through the Holy Spirit.

Your prayer is based upon the Word.

It brings this earth heart of ours into contact with the heavenly center of all divine power and activity.

You can't spend any length of time in prayer without being affected by it.

The quietness, the unshaken faith, the deep, unsounded peace that pervades the Godhead, will overflow into the life of one who prays.

Said an anxious and nervous mother: "You will have to forgive me, children, but I forgot to visit the Master this morning, and so I lack His quietness and His strength."

Many of us can make the confession that our irritability, weakness, and lack of spiritual insight comes from not sitting in the presence of the Master.

One cannot spend an hour in conscious communion with the Father, the Son, the Spirit, and the Word without carrying away from that trysting place the fragrance that fills the atmosphere.

There is a heavenly fragrance about Jesus that lingers with those who pray.

They are slow to speak.

They are slow to judge.

They are quick to love and quick to help.

There is a holy calmness about their lives that challenges the restless ones; they crave that quietness of spirit.

Again, we cannot spend time with them without partaking of their stability and their unshakableness.

One who is easily disturbed, and who in the jolts of life is unseated, will find a new strength and steadiness that will make him a blessing to the world, by spending just a little time with the Rock of our strength.

You see, a few moments with Him tunes us up, fills the battery, adjusts the carburetor, and makes it easy for us to face life's uneven conditions.

It gives us poise and holy dignity in our contacts.

Faith makes us an intelligent victor.

Faith makes mountains and difficulties take their true position.

You can't sit with the God of all faith and all love, for one half hour each day, without unconsciously breathing in the faith of God. What would it mean to you, if Jesus should come into your home as He came into the home of Mary and Martha?

You would take time to visit with Him!

> *Jesus answered and said unto him, If a man love me, he will keep my words: and my Father will love him, and we will come unto him, and make our abode with him.* (John 14:23)

You love Him, invite Him into your home, and then get acquainted with Him.

Learn to talk things over with Him.

He is there; visit with Him!

Remember, He loves you and is interested in all your problems.

He will make His Word answer every question; He will make Himself real in your life and home.

PRAYER ON A WINNING BASIS

God made prayer a winning business proposition.

We didn't ask Him to do it.

We didn't send our representative and say, "Now, Father, we want you to give us certain promises and certain abilities."

No. He did it all. He planned it all for us.

He based a prayer life upon His own Word.

It was a daring thing for Him to do, but He believed that we would believe.

He dared to give His Son.

He dared to give man eternal life.

He dared to make us new creations.

Why? Because He believed that man would respond to His love and that man, when challenged by such grace, would meet it with a glad response.

And so we are fellowshipping Him in His faith fight for a lost race.

We are helping the men for whom His Son died and has redeemed.

Our combat is warring against God's enemy.

It is saving the men for whom Christ died.

It is making strong the weak.

It is giving God's children a chance for winning in life's fight.

We are the instruments. We are the forerunners. We are the pioneers in this marvelous life of faith.

We are joining the men of all the ages who have dared to walk where paths have never been.

We are opening channels for His grace to reach the human race.

We are God's under-engineers.

We are building roads for others to walk upon.

Our faith life has joined with God's faith life and we have become His "tilled land," His "fellow workers."

We are the branches that are bearing the real fruit from the real vine.

We are opening channels through which He can pour Himself out on man.

Our ministry is not a failure. We are winning.

We are making out of these failure-men, successes.

Our union with Him is beckoning other men to dare come into the union too.

They see failures transfigured into successes.

They see men who have been held for years, absolute slaves to narcotics and drink, set free to walk in the fullness of their liberty in Christ.

And those in bondage reach their hands out for help, and our Father grasps them and lifts them up onto the solid rock.

Come on, you who pray, join this mighty group of intercessors who are making the desert places blossom like the rose.

Come on, you men and women who have never made prayer a business. Make your investment of time. Learn the art, yes, the secret of this the greatest business of the age.

Throw yourself open. Let Him pour Himself through you until your home and your business and your associates will feel the throb of His mighty life and the lift of His love.

Let me state it with all the simplicity possible: you can't have prayers answered without having miracles performed.

PRAYER AND MIRACLES

If you deny that miracles are for this age, you deny the need, the privileges, and the benefits of prayer.

The twofold value of prayer lies first in sitting in His presence, or in direct fellowship with the Father.

The second benefit is the answer that comes to us.

John says, *"If we ask any thing according to his will, he heareth us: and if we know that he hear us, whatsoever we ask, we know that we have the petitions that we desired of him"* (1 John 5:14–15).

For God the Father to hear my prayer is equivalent to His answering it.

Now, for God to hear me is a miracle.

For God to answer my prayer, regardless of its nature, is a miracle.

Whether my petition is for a postage stamp or for a million dollars, it is a miracle.

Any divine intervention, any arrest of the laws of nature that comes in answer to faith, is a miracle.

If prayer brings an answer, that answer is a miracle. It is then that faith has its true place.

The instant that you say there are no miracles in this dispensation, you deny that our walk is a walk by faith, and you declare that our walk is a walk by reason.

I challenge you to find one place where God tells us as believers to walk by reason.

God is a faith God.

We are a Faith family.

We are all born by faith.

We live by faith.

By faith we live, breathe, and have our being in Christ.

If there are no miracles, then there is no reason for faith.

If there are no miracles, God can't answer prayer, because He can't answer prayer of any character that is not a miracle.

You men and women who tell me that you believe the Bible to be the Word of God, that it is God-breathed and without error in the original, and then, in the same breath, tell me that the day of miracles is past, you are the most illogical thinkers, the most inconsistent believers that the devil ever deluded.

I believe profoundly that the devil is the deceiver of the whole inhabited earth and of that type of Christian in particular.

So, let us reverently come back to God.

Let us take our place.

If we pray at all, we expect prayer to be answered.

If that prayer is answered, God has done it; and if God has answered prayer, He has performed something outside of the realm of reason.

We will have to give up our prayer life utterly, or we will have to believe in miracles.

I believe in miracles.

I believe in divine intervention.

I believe that the prayer of faith reaches God our Father, and when it reaches Him, He acts in response to that faith.

When He acts in response to our faith, His action is above our reason. It is in the realm of miracles.

For me to deny the privilege and benefits of prayer would raise a storm of protest among those who deny miracles today.

I want you to see, my brother, as you read this today, that your position is untenable.

Faith causes a man to act like God.

Love makes him like God.

THE SUPERNATURAL

Prayer is an excursion into the supernatural realm.

You are in the throne room in the presence of God, of All Ability. He has promised to hear your petition and to give you your request. You have come on the ground of His Word.

Jesus said, "Whatsoever you ask the Father in My name, He will give it you."

You understand that the words that Jesus spoke were His Father's words; so you come now with the Father's words on your lips, and you are making your appeal on the ground of His own Word.

TAKING A SON'S PLACE

You are not a servant.

You are not a slave.

You are a son. You are taking Jesus's place, acting in His stead, doing the Father's will.

You may know that you are the Father's will, just as Jesus was the Father's will, because of His own will, He begot you.

You are the fruit of His own Word. You came into being by His own power and ability. You have received eternal life, His very nature.

You recognize your place in Christ. You are acting the part of a Son.

The great unsaved world must know what He has done for them in Christ; and so you are taking His ability, doing your part in the saving of men as Jesus did His part.

You belong to a supernatural order of being, whether you recognize it or not, whether you have taken your place or not. You have the ability of the indwelling presence.

You have the wisdom that Jesus had in His earth walk because Jesus has been made unto you wisdom.

You can think of yourself as linked up with ability, linked with omnipotence.

You remember He said, *"And nothing shall be impossible unto you"* (Matthew 17:20).

I know that sense knowledge reasoning shrinks from this, but here is where the challenge of grace leads you.

We dare to take our place, dare confess what we are, dare confess that He made us what we are, that we can do what He says we can do because He is at work within us.

We have His Word that He is in us. The latent ability and energy within us is His who gave it to us.

This makes the prayer life a master thing.

You are not asking for the possible. You are always praying for the impossible. You are asking for things that can't be done by any human method.

3

HOW FAITH IS BUILT

Word. The Word is the source of all faith. The faith must be a quiet assurance, an unconscious faith, something that you do not even think about.

You can't conceive of Jesus saying to Himself, "If I only had faith."

Men and women who have really wrought mighty things have been those who never thought about their faith life.

The Word was a reality.

What He said solved the problem.

This Word is revelation knowledge.

It is God deigning to speak with man.

THE REALITY OF THE INCARNATION

First there must be a reality of the incarnation.

> *And the Word was made flesh, and dwelt among us, (and we beheld his glory, the glory as of the only begotten of the Father,) full of grace and truth.* (John 1:14)

The incarnation cannot be a doctrine or a theory or a metaphysical concept.

It must be as real as your birth is to you.

Not something to argue about, but an absolute fact that God has broken into the human realm and has given to the senses a testimony of His reality.

I can never forget when I knew that God had been and was manifest in the flesh.

I had an unconscious background of doubt that disappeared, and another background of absolute certainty took its place.

THE REALITY OF HIS RESURRECTION

Many of us have reveled in His earth walk, following Him step by step in His miraculous career.

We were thrilled at the demonstrations of divine ability that characterized Him in every crisis.

He faced a dead Lazarus as simply as you and I would face any ordinary event in life.

He was perfectly quiet in the midst of the storm on the Sea of Galilee.

He walked on the waves that night amid the tumult of a raging storm as quietly as you walk up and down on the sidewalk in front of your home.

There was a royalty about His faith; a divine dignity that thrills us.

But was He raised from the dead?

He raised others. Was He raised?

I fought this for years. It was an unknown battle to those about me.

I used to say, "If He was actually raised from the dead, then His deity and His substitutionary work are realities."

One day as I was reading John 20:1–10, I saw the miracle.

The problem of the resurrection of Jesus centers first around the question, "Was He dead?" As one skeptic declares, "He had swooned."

> *When Jesus therefore had received the vinegar, he said, It is finished: and he bowed his head, and gave up his spirit. The Jews therefore, because it was the Preparation, that the bodies should not remain on the cross upon the sabbath (for the day of that sabbath was a high day), asked of Pilate that their legs might be broken, and that they might be taken away. The soldiers therefore came, and [broke] the legs of the first, and of the other that was crucified with him: but when they came to Jesus, and saw that he was dead already, they [broke] not his legs: howbeit one of the soldiers with a spear pierced his side, and straightway there came out blood and water.*
>
> (John 19:30–34 ASV)

That Roman spearhead was four or five inches wide, and when he stood there underneath the Master and thrust the spear up into the side of Jesus, it must have penetrated the sack that holds the heart.

What had happened?

Jesus had died!

The body had grown cold.

His heart had been ruptured when He uttered that cry, "It is finished."

And out through the rupture in the heart flowed the blood into the sack until it was filled.

The body rapidly grows cold. As it does, the blood separates. The white serum settles to the bottom, and the red corpuscles rise to the top; and as the body grows colder, the red corpuscles coagulate.

When the spear pierced the sack that held the blood, the white serum or water flowed out. Then the red corpuscles slowly oozed out and rolled down the side of His body onto the ground.

Jesus was dead.

As soon as the Master was dead, loving hearts began to prepare for His burial.

> *And after this Joseph of Arimathaea, being a disciple of Jesus, but secretly for fear of the Jews, besought Pilate that he might take away the body of Jesus: and Pilate gave him leave. He came therefore, and took the body of Jesus.* (John 19:38)

You understand that, in every family among the wealthy Jews, there was a slave who understood embalming, for that class always embalmed their loved ones.

> *And there came also Nicodemus, which at the first came to Jesus by night, and brought a mixture of myrrh and aloes, about an hundred pound weight. Then took they the body of Jesus, and wound it in linen clothes with the spices, as the manner of the Jews is to bury.* (John 19:39–40)

The body was first washed, and then the cloth was torn up into narrow strips and smeared with a sticky substance. Each finger and toe and hand and foot was wrapped with these strips until the legs and arms and body were completely encased in this sticky substance. The head and neck were completely covered except the face.

When it was finished, over the chest and torso, there was an inch to an inch and a half of this cloth covered with that sticky substance.

The body was then put into Joseph's tomb.

The climate was about the same as they have in Southern California. In a few hours, the embalming garment would become a solid mass, and Jesus's body would be completely imprisoned in the grave clothes.

If He were not dead, this would cause Him to die.

The face was yet to be embalmed. Loved ones laid a napkin upon His face, heavily saturated with something to preserve it until the third day, when loving hands would finish the embalming.

Jesus was dead.

The Roman government had pronounced Him dead.

The soldiers had pronounced Him dead.

The Jews knew He was dead.

> *Now on the first day of the week cometh Mary Magdalene early, while it was yet dark, unto the tomb, and seeth the stone taken away from the tomb. She runneth therefore, and cometh to Simon Peter, and to the other disciple whom Jesus loved, and saith unto them, They have taken away the Lord out of the tomb, and we know not where they have laid him. Peter therefore went forth, and the other disciple, and they went toward the tomb. And they ran both together: and the other disciple outran Peter, and came first to the tomb; and stooping and looking in, he seeth the linen cloths lying; yet entered he not in. Simon Peter therefore also cometh, following him, and entered into the tomb; and he beholdeth the linen cloths lying, and the napkin, that was upon his head, not lying with the linen cloths, but rolled up in a place by itself. Then entered in therefore the other disciple also, who came first to the tomb, and he saw, and believed. For as yet they knew not the scripture, that he must rise again from the dead. So the disciples went away again unto their own home.* (John 20:1–10 ASV)

You notice carefully the last two verses. They knew not that Jesus must arise again from the dead. None of them believed in His resurrection, so you can understand their surprise when Mary came to the house where Peter and John were staying and cried, *"They have taken away the Lord out of the tomb, and we know not where they have laid him."*

Nothing was more sacred to the Jews than the dead. Mary had been filled with anger and sorrow that someone had dared to desecrate the tomb.

Peter and John ran together. John is younger, lighter of foot. He outruns his heavier partner and arrives at the tomb first. It was a sepulcher cut out of a solid ledge. John stops and reverently looks into the darkened tomb. Peter comes, just bows his head, and enters the tomb. John follows. The grave clothes are lying there on the floor. Peter sees the napkin that was upon Jesus's face, rolled up and lying on a niche in the tomb.

> *Then entered in therefore the other disciple also, who came first to the tomb, and he saw, and believed.* (John 20:8 ASV)

What did John see?

He saw the empty cocoon lying there upon the floor. It had become so hard and stiff that it would almost support one's knee as you pressed upon it. But it was empty.

The body of Jesus had come out of that little narrow aperture at the face.

If John had seen that someone with a knife had ripped that cocoon open and taken the body of Jesus, he would never have believed; the empty cocoon convinced John that Jesus was risen from the dead.

In my imagination, I had been with Peter and John when Mary came with her anger and distress, crying, "They have taken away the body."

I had gone with them to the tomb. I had stood there in my imagination, looking into the tomb.

I entered into the tomb with John, and I saw what John saw, and for the first time in my life, I knew that Jesus Christ had risen from the dead.

It has never been a theological dogma since that hour.

Jesus was raised from the dead.

But what does that resurrection mean?

That the sin problem was settled.

That Satan was conquered.

Humanity was redeemed.

That God can now, on legal grounds, impart His nature, eternal life, to man and make him a new creation.

At last, man can become God's actual child, a very son.

There can be perfect fellowship between them.

When God imparted His nature to man, He imparted His righteousness. So, man is a partaker of the divine nature and the righteousness of God.

Man can stand in the Father's presence as did Jesus in His earth walk.

Now God can give the Holy Spirit to live permanently in the body of this new creation, and He can build into that new creation through the Word, the very character and nature of the incarnate One, so that we can say softly, "It is no longer I who live, but Christ lives in me." (See Galatians 2:20.)

Now I know that Romans 4:25 is a reality: "*Who was delivered up for our trespasses, and was raised for our justification*" (ASV).

THE REALITY OF HIS REDEMPTION

The church has had a theological conception of our redemption. It has never been a part of our daily walk.

> *Giving thanks unto the Father...who hath delivered us from the power of darkness, and hath translated us into the kingdom of his dear Son: in whom we have redemption.* (Colossians 1:12–14)

And Ephesians 1:7 says that redemption is according to the riches of His grace.

In the mind of the Father, that redemption is a reality.

It would have been a total failure otherwise.

That redemption meant that Satan had been utterly defeated, stripped of his authority and dominion so that any man, no matter what his condition has been or how deeply he has been enmeshed in sin, can, by whispering the name of Jesus and by confessing His Lordship, step out of bondage into perfect liberty.

Romans 6:14: "*For sin shall not have dominion over you.*" Put another way, "Satan shall not lord it over you."

It has made the new man, the new creation, a master of sin.

In the name of Jesus, the weakest child of God is an absolute master of Satan and demons.

That redemption is a reality.

You who have received eternal life, as you read this, can whisper, "I am free. The Son has made me free, and I am free in reality." (See John 8:36.)

That redemption is a reality to the man who knows his place in Christ.

You cannot be in Christ and not be free from the dominion of the devil.

THE REALITY OF THE NEW CREATION

What substitutions we have had for the new creation!

We have called it "forgiveness of sins," "being converted," "getting religion," "joining the church," and many others.

It is just one thing: a new creation, a child of God, a partaker of the divine nature. These all represent the one fact that you have passed out of death, satanic nature, into life, the realm of God.

That is not just forgiveness of sins, but it is the impartation of a new nature.

The old self, the old man, was crucified with Christ.

A new man was resurrected and when you accepted Jesus Christ as Savior and confessed Him as Lord, God imparted His own nature, eternal life, to you and you became "a new species," a new man over which Satan has no dominion.

THE REALITY IN JESUS'S NAME

How little we have appreciated this. It is one of the greatest gifts the church has ever had given to her.

Before Jesus left us, He gave to the church a legal right to the use of His name, "*That whatsoever ye shall ask of the Father in my name, he may give it you*" (John 15:16).

> *And in that day ye shall ask me nothing. Verily, verily, I say unto you, Whatsoever ye shall ask the Father in my name, he will give it you.*

> *Hitherto have ye asked nothing in my name: ask, and ye shall receive, that your joy may be full.* (John 16:23–24)

Here He gives us the power of attorney to go to the Father and make our requests.

When you pray in that name, it is as though Jesus prayed.

There can be no denial.

You remember Jesus said at the tomb of Lazarus, *"Father, I thank thee that thou hast heard me"* (John 11:41). That is the ground for your assurance.

In John 14:13–14, He gives us the use of His name: *"And whatsoever ye shall ask in my name, that will I do, that the Father may be glorified in the Son. If ye shall ask any thing in my name, I will do it."*

This is not prayer. This is described in Acts 3:6, where Peter and John heal a man at the Beautiful Gate by saying, *"In the name of Jesus Christ of Nazareth rise up and walk."*

It is as Paul used it in Acts 16:18, where he spoke to the demon in the girl and said, *"I command thee in the name of Jesus Christ to come out of her."*

Or as the name was used on the day of Pentecost when they baptized those people in the name of Jesus.

When we pray, we say, "Our Father, in Jesus's name..."

That is our approach.

That gives us the assurance of a hearing.

Jesus said, speaking of the Holy Spirit, *"He dwelleth with you, and shall be in you"* (John 14:17).

THE REALITY OF INDWELLING

On the day of Pentecost, we see four things take place in that upper room.

> *Suddenly there came a sound from heaven as of a rushing mighty wind, and it filled all the house where they were sitting.* (Acts 2:2)

The disciples were immersed in the Holy Spirit. And when they were immersed, they received eternal life, were made new creations.

They were the first people, aside from Jesus, who were ever born again. Jesus, you know, is *"the firstborn."* (See Colossians 1:15; Revelation 1:5.)

The second thing that happened is that tongues of fire sat upon the brow of each one, indicating the method of propagating this gospel of the grace of God. It is going to be with tongues of fire.

For example, Steven's tongue couldn't be withstood, so they had to kill him to get rid of his tongue of fire.

And the third thing is that they were all filled with the Holy Spirit. He couldn't come in until they were recreated.

And the fourth thing is that they all spoke with other tongues.

But note that the great thing was they had not only received eternal life, but they had the One who had raised Jesus from the dead now living in them.

We have made a great deal of receiving the Holy Spirit.

It has been given great importance and we have ignored the fact of His being in us.

First John 4:4 says, *"Ye are of God, little children, and have overcome them: because greater is he that is in you, than he that is in the world."*

According to Philippians 2:13 (ASV), *"For it is God who worketh in you both to will and to work, for his good pleasure."*

Not only are we born again, having become the very sons and daughters of God, but He comes and makes His home in us.

THE REALITY OF RIGHTEOUSNESS

The ministry has kept the church in the bondage of sin-consciousness ever since the Reformation.

None of us have ever been able to get away from it.

Most of our hymns are about sin.

Almost every sermon is about sin.

The church has never known of her absolute freedom from sin-consciousness.

Hebrews 10:1–14 should be studied very carefully. We haven't space to quote it all.

First it tells how the blood of bulls and goats couldn't take away sin, for if it could, the worshippers, having been once cleansed, would have no more consciousness of sins. *"But in those sacrifices there is a remembrance again made of sins every year"* (verse 3).

That makes us think of the altar service where we ask the believer to keep coming Sunday after Sunday to be cleansed from sin.

The blood of Jesus Christ hasn't meant more to some of us than the blood of bulls and goats meant to the Jew.

For it was impossible that the blood of bulls and goats should take away sin.

> *And every priest standeth daily ministering and offering oftentimes the same sacrifices, which can never take away sins: but this man* [Jesus], *after he had offered one sacrifice for sins for ever, sat down on the right hand of God; from henceforth expecting till his enemies be made his footstool. For by one offering he hath perfected for ever them that are sanctified.* (Hebrews 10:11–14)

Jesus dealt with the sin problem for us perfectly when we were recreated and received the nature and life of God.

At that time, He not only put our sin away, but He remitted all that we had ever committed; and at the same time, He imparted His own nature of righteousness to us. *"Him who knew no sin he made to be sin on our behalf; that we might become the righteousness of God in him"* (2 Corinthians 5:21 ASV). By that new creation, we have become the righteousness of God.

So, Romans 3:22 has become a reality: *"It is a righteousness of God which comes by believing in Jesus Christ. And it is meant for all who have faith"* (MOFF).

Here, God declares that He becomes the righteousness of the man who accepts His Son as a Savior.

First Corinthians 1:30 declares that Jesus has been made to be our righteousness.

God is our righteousness, Jesus is our righteousness, and by the new creation, we have become the righteousness of God in Him.

But you ask, "What is the righteousness of God?"

It is the ability to stand in the Father's presence without a sense of guilt, condemnation or inferiority.

It is the ability to stand there as the very sons and daughters of God Almighty so that you can go boldly unto the throne of grace and make your petitions just as Jesus would if He were here.

SOME FAITH FACTS

Faith in the Father is not built upon the word of man but upon His own Word.

Man's testimony to the truth of the Word has its place, but it cannot take the place of the Word itself.

The Word is the Father speaking.

It is as though the Master were here now in person; that Word is taking His place.

That Word has given us life and made us new creations.

That Word has sustained us and upheld us.

It is the Word of faith that proceeds from the very heart of the Father of faith.

The Word is a part of the Father Himself.

I feed on it.

I breathe it into my spirit.

It is being built into my spirit-consciousness.

Its absolute integrity, its life-giving quality, has impregnated my very being.

Man's word, like grass, withers.

God's Word, like Himself, can never die, can never lose its freshness, its power, its ability to recreate, to strengthen and give courage.

You see, the Word on the lips of faith becomes just like the Word on Jesus's lips.

The Word on lips of doubt and fear is a dead thing, but on the lips of faith, it becomes life-giving, dominant.

Through it, the sick are healed; Satan's captives are set free.

This living Word on the lips of faith is God's answer to the heart cry of man.

Man's word may fascinate and satisfy reason for a time, but the heart demands the Word of God.

This Word illumined by the Holy Spirit is God's light on life's pathway.

The Word is a part of Himself.

You can lean on the Word as you would lean on Him.

You can rest in the Word as you would rest in Him.

You can act on the Word as you would act if He had just spoken to you.

The Word is always *now*.

Our modern psychological religions are children of the senses; they use the Bible and quote from it, but it is only man's literature to them. Their writings can't feed the hungry spirit of man; they simply entertain and thrill the people of the senses.

These eternal spirits of ours crave the bread of God. Jesus is the Bread of Life; they that feed on Him have no appetite for the theories of men.

Don't waste time with the philosophies of men. There is no life in them.

In Him is life, and that life is our light.

His Word alone can answer the heart cry of man.

Their words may answer the cry of lost reason-ruled souls groping in the sense realm for light, but never the cry of the heart.

Jesus's bold and continual confession is our example. We are what He made us to be.

Jesus confessed what He was. Sense knowledge could not understand it.

We are to confess what we are in Christ. Men of the senses will not understand us.

To confess that you are redeemed, that your redemption is an actual reality, that you are delivered out of Satan's dominion and authority, would be a daring confession to make.

To confess that you are an actual new creation created in Christ Jesus, that you are a partaker of the very nature and life of the Deity, would amaze your friends.

It isn't confessing it once, but daily affirming your relationship to Him, confessing your righteousness, your ability to stand in His presence without the sense of guilt or inferiority.

Dare to stand in the presence of sense knowledge facts and declare that you are what God says you are!

For instance, sense knowledge declares that I am sick with an incurable illness. I confess that God laid that disease on Jesus and that Satan has no right to put it on me, that "by His stripes, I am healed." (See Isaiah 53:5.) I am to hold fast to my confession in the face of apparent sense knowledge contradiction.

Sense knowledge says that it is not true, that I am confessing an untruth, but I am confessing what God says.

You see, there are two kinds of truth: sense knowledge truth and revelation truth. They are usually opposed to each other.

I live in the new realm above the senses, so I hold fast to my confession that I am what the Word says I am.

Suppose my senses have revealed the fact that I am in great need financially. The Word declares, *"My God shall supply every need of yours"* (Philippians 4:19 ASV).

I call His attention to what the senses have intimated, and He knows that my expectations are from Him. I refuse to be intimidated by sense evidences. I refuse to have my life governed by them. I know that greater is He that is in me than the forces that surround me.

The forces that oppose me are in the senses.

The power that is in me is the Holy Spirit, and I know that spiritual forces are greater than the forces in the sense realm.

I maintain my confession of spiritual values, of spiritual realities, in the face of sense contradictions.

4

THE TWO CONFESSIONS

After having prayed for one the other morning, she was satisfied that she was perfectly healed, but now the symptoms have returned, and her heart is disturbed. She wonders where the difficulty lies.

I asked this party, "Did you tell your husband when you met him at night that you were healed?"

"No, you see, I wasn't sure yet. I didn't want to say anything until I was positive."

"But you had no pain? Was there any soreness?" I asked.

"Oh, that all left; but you see, I have to be careful. My husband is skeptical, and I didn't want to tell him I was healed until I was sure."

I can see where her difficulty lay. She did not believe the Word. Had she made her confession to her husband, the thing would never have come back. But she played into the hands of the enemy, and he restored the same symptoms that she had had, and brought back the pain and soreness. This happened because she invited him to do it.

Had she dared to stand her ground on the Word and hold fast to her confession that she was healed, he would have no ground of approach.

Our faith or unbelief is determined by our confession.

Few of us realize the effect of our spoken word on our own heart or on our adversary.

He hears us make our confession of failure, of sickness, of lack, and, apparently, he doesn't forget, and we unconsciously go down to the level of our confession.

No one ever rises above it.

If you confess sickness, it develops sickness in your system.

If you confess doubt, the doubts become stronger.

If you confess lack of finances, it stops the money from coming in.

You say, "I can't understand this."

No. Because most of us live in the sense realm and spiritual things are very indistinct.

Hebrews 4:14 must become a constant reality: *"Having then a great high priest, who hath passed through the heavens, Jesus the Son of God, let us hold fast our confession"* (ASV).

Our confession is that the Word cannot be broken, that what the Father says is true.

When we doubt the Father, we are doubting His Word.

When we doubt His Word, it is because we believe something else that is contrary to that Word.

Our confidence may be in the arm of flesh; it may be in medicine; it may be in institutions; but whatever our confidence is in, if it contradicts the Word, it destroys our faith life.

It destroys our prayers.

It brings us again into bondage.

Every person who walks by faith will have testings.

They do not come from the Father; they come from the adversary.

He is refusing to allow you to escape him.

You become dangerous to the adversary when you become strong enough to resist him—when you have learned to trust in the ability of the Father to meet your every need.

When that becomes a reality in your consciousness, the adversary is defeated.

But as long as he can confuse the issue and keep you in a state of flux, you are at a disadvantage.

This book is written for one purpose: to strengthen your confidence in the Word, to make you know that *"no Word from God shall be void of power"* (Luke 1:37 ASV) or can go by default.

There isn't power in all the universe to void one statement of fact in this Word.

He said, *"I watch over my word to perform it"* (Jeremiah 1:12 ASV).

And again, *"Whosoever believeth on him shall not be put to shame"* (Romans 10:11 ASV).

Your confidence is in that unbroken, living Word, and you hold fast to your confession in the face of every assault of the enemy.

Note William J. Conybeare's translation of Philippians 1:28: *"And nowise terrified by its enemies; for their enmity is to them an evidence of perdition, but to you of salvation, and that from God."*

Here is James Moffatt's translation of this verse: *"Never be scared for a second by your opponents; your fearlessness is a clear omen of ruin for them and of your own salvation—at the hands of God."*

> *Wherever I go, thank God, he makes my life a constant pageant of triumph in Christ, diffusing the perfume of his knowledge everywhere by me. I live for God as the fragrance of Christ breathed alike on those who are being saved and on those who are perishing.* (2 Corinthians 2:14–15 MOFF)

You take your position in Christ that you are more than a conqueror, that no matter what the testing may be, God cannot let you fail.

You are not standing on sense evidence.

You are not standing on the faith of other people.

You are standing squarely upon His own Word.

Your confidence is not in the prayers of others, but in this unchanging, unbreakable Word, and you refuse to allow your lips to destroy the effectiveness of that Word in your case.

You hold fast to your confession though it would appear as though the prayer was never answered.

It is your quiet assurance in His Word that gives you the supremacy over your adversaries.

You know that all authority is in the name of Jesus, that every demon and every disease and every circumstance must bow to that name.

Philippians 2:9–11 says, "*Wherefore God also hath highly exalted him, and given him a name which is above every name: that at the name of Jesus every knee should bow, of things in heaven, and things in earth, and things under the earth; and that every tongue should confess that Jesus Christ is Lord, to the glory of God the Father.*"

You see that the name of Jesus has all authority, and you have a legal right to use that name in every extremity.

You are His son, His own very child.

You have come to Him in the name of Jesus for this need, and He is under obligation to see that you are not put to shame.

He is under obligation to make His Word good.

One said to me this morning, "God has tied Himself up by His Word. He cannot fail us. He cannot ignore us."

So, let us hold fast to our confession and never cower for a moment, no matter how sense knowledge may produce evidence to the contrary.

You are not standing on sense evidence.

Feelings and appearances have no place here.

This is God's field and God's alone.

REALIZATION FOLLOWS CONFESSIONS

We walk in the light of our testimony—our faith never goes beyond our confession.

The Word becomes real only as we confess its reality. The reason for this is, "*We walk by faith, not by sight*" (2 Corinthians 5:7).

Sense knowledge would confess only what it had seen, heard, or felt.

The people who are seeking experiences always walk by the senses.

Our testimony of the reality of the Word is feared by Satan.

"*That if thou shalt confess with thy mouth*" (Romans 10:9). This reacts on our heart just as doubt spoken by the lips reacts on our heart.

You talk of your doubts and your fears, and you destroy your faith.

You talk of the ability of the Father that is yours and fill your lips with praise for answers to prayers that you have asked. Its reaction upon the heart is tremendous: faith grows by leaps and bounds.

You talk about your trials and your difficulties, of your lack of faith, of your lack of money, and faith shrivels, loses its virility.

Your whole spirit life shrinks.

You study about what you are in Christ and then confess it boldly.

You dare to act on the Word in the face of sense knowledge opposition.

Regardless of appearance, you take your stand; make your confession and hold fast to it in the face of apparent impossibilities.

You see, faith doesn't ask for possible things. Faith is demanding the impossible.

Prayer is never for the possible, but always for the thing that is out of reason.

It is God who is at work with us, in us, and for us.

"How shall he not with him also freely give us all things" (Romans 8:32).

You see, you are launching out into the realm of the impossible just as Abraham did when he asked for a son.

You're not asking for something you can do for yourself, but for something that is beyond reason.

Then you refuse to take counsel with fear or to entertain a doubt.

The hardest battles I have ever fought have been along this line.

The greatest battles I have ever won have been those that seemed the most impossible, where there was the greatest opposition, where reason discredited my faith.

I held fast to my confession and the Word was made good.

Confess your dominion over disease in Jesus's name.

Never be frightened by any condition no matter how forbidding, how impossible the case may be.

It may be cancer, tuberculosis, or an accident in which death seems to be the master of the situation. You never give in.

You know you and God are masters of the situation.

You never for a moment lose your confession of your supremacy over the works of the adversary.

This disease, this calamity, is not of God. It has but one source, Satan.

And in Jesus's name, you are master. You have taken Jesus's place; you are acting in His stead.

You fearlessly take your position; confess your ability in Christ to meet any emergency.

Always remember that Jesus met defeat and conquered it. You are facing defeat everywhere as a master.

Don't let down. Keep your solid front.

Arthur Sanders Way translated Philippians 1:27–28 thus:

> *Let your life as members of one communion be worthy of the glad tidings of the Messiah so that, whether I do come and see you, or whether I must still be afar and only hear news of you, I may know that you are standing firm, animated by one spirit; may know that with united soul you are working strenuously shoulder to shoulder for the faith of the glad tidings; may know that you are not cowed one whit by your adversaries. Their failure to daunt you is clear evidence—an actual sign from God—for them that their destruction is imminent; but for you, that salvation is yours.*

That solid front is spoken of in Colossians 2:5 (MOFF): "*Although I am absent in body I am with you in spirit, and it is a joy to note your steadiness and the solid front of your faith in Christ.*" This is the solid front presented to your enemy.

You can't be conquered.

Your spirit is whispering, "Nay, in all these things, I am more than a conqueror." (See Romans 8:37.)

Every disease is of the adversary.

All kinds of sin are of the adversary.

All opposition to the glad tidings is of the adversary.

God and I are victors.

Greater is He that is in me than this opposition or this disease. There is no need that is greater than my Lord.

There is no lack that He cannot meet.

This indomitable will that God has wrought in you cannot be overwhelmed or conquered.

You remember what you are—you are a new creation.

You are a branch of the vine.

You are an heir of God.

You are united with Him. You and He are one, and He is the greater part of that one.

There is no such thing as conquering God when His instrument refuses to admit that the enemy can overwhelm him.

You are that instrument.

"I have learned, in whatsoever state I am, therein to be content" (Philippians 4:11 ASV).

DEFEATED WITH YOUR OWN LIPS

You said that you could not, and the moment that you said it, you were whipped.

You said you did not have faith, and doubt arose like a giant and bound you.

You are imprisoned with your own words.

You talked failure and failure held you in bondage.

"Thou art snared with the words of thy mouth, thou art taken [captive] *with the words of thy mouth"* (Proverbs 6:2).

Few of us realize that our words dominate us.

A young man said, "I was never whipped until I confessed I was whipped."

Another said, "The moment I began to make a bold, confident confession, a new courage that I had never known took possession of me."

A young woman said, "My lips have been a constant curse. I have never been able to get the mastery of my lips."

Another woman said the other day, "I always speak my mind." She has few friends. Only pity causes people to go see her. Her lips have been her curse.

It isn't so bad speaking your mind if you have the mind of Christ, but as long as you have a mind dominated by the devil, few people care to hear your mind.

Never talk failure.

Never talk defeat.

Never for a moment acknowledge that God's ability can't put you over.

Become "God-inside minded," remembering that greater is He that is in you than any force that can come against you, remembering that God created a universe with words, that words are more mighty than tanks or bombs, more mighty than the Army or Navy.

Learn to use words so they will work for you and be your servants.

Learn that your lips can make you a millionaire or a pauper, wanted or despised, a victor or a captive.

Your words can be filled with faith that will stir heaven and make men want you.

Remember that you can fill your words with love so they will melt the coldest heart, and warm and heal the broken and discouraged.

In other words, your words can become what you wish them to be.

You can make them rhyme. You can fill them with rhythm.

You can fill them with hatred, with poison; or you can make them breathe the very fragrance of heaven.

Now you can see vividly what your confession can mean to your own heart.

Your faith will never register above the words of your lips.

It isn't so bad to think a thing as it is to say it.

Thoughts may come and persist in staying, but you refuse to put them into words and they die unborn.

Cultivate the habit of thinking big things, and then learn to use words that will react upon your own spirit and make you a conqueror.

Jesus's confessions proved to be realities.

Faith's confessions create realities.

Jesus confessed that He was the light of the world. He was it. The rejection of Him has plunged the world into a new darkness.

He said He was the bread from heaven, and it is true. The people who have fed upon His words have never suffered want.

His words build faith as we act on them, let them live in us.

His words were filled with Himself; as we act on them, they fill us with Christ.

His words feed faith and cause it to grow in power in us.

The believer's words should be born of love and filled with love.

Our lips are taking the place of His.

Our words should never bruise or hurt, but should bless and heal.

Jesus was the Way, the reality, and the life.

We are taking His place, showing the Way, confessing the reality, enjoying the life.

You will never enjoy what you are in Christ until His love rules your lips.

5

FAITH IN YOUR OWN RIGHTS

The new creation is based upon legal grounds. You have come into the Father's family because you responded to His call. You could never have gotten in there by your own efforts.

You had to be born of the Holy Spirit. You had to be recreated through the agency of the Word; for He says, *"It was his own will that we should be born by the Word of the truth"* (James 1:18 ASV).

It is the Father's will. It is through the Father's Word. It is by the energy of the Holy Spirit that eternal life has been given to us, and we have become new creations.

Of His own will, He brought us forth.

It is not of man. It is not of the will of the flesh; it is of the will of our own Father. (See John 1:13.)

Romans 3:21–26 gives us the legal background of our redemption:

> *But now the righteousness of God without the law is manifested, being witnessed by the law and the prophets; even the righteousness of God which is by faith of Jesus Christ unto all and upon all them that believe: for there is no difference: for all have sinned, and come short of the glory of God; being justified freely by his grace through the redemption that is in Christ Jesus: whom God hath set forth to be a propitiation through faith in his blood, to declare his righteousness for the remission of sins that are past, through the forbearance of God; to declare, I say, at this time his righteousness: that he might be just, and the justifier of him which believeth in Jesus.*

It is a redemption that gives us the righteousness of God on the ground of faith in Jesus Christ.

It is a redemption that gives us perfect justification freely by His grace, through the redemption that is in Christ Jesus.

Grace is the love of God in action, in manifestation.

It is love doing things for us.

It was love that caused the incarnation.

Love caused this incarnate One we call Jesus, to go on the cross and become sin with our sin; become absolutely identified with us, not only as a man (which He did in the incarnation and in His earth walk), but He became identified with our sin nature on the cross.

God laid upon Him our iniquity.

"For our sakes He made him to be sin who himself knew nothing of sin" (2 Corinthians 5:21 MOFF). That is a serious thing. The heart can hardly take it in. We were sinners, but He was made sin.

He was so identified with the devil that God said He was sin.

He actually went the limit for man. Being sin, He was judged as sin. He was condemned as sin. He was sent to the place of suffering where sin should go.

There, He suffered until the claims of justice against us were fully met. Then He was *"justified in the Spirit"* (1 Timothy 3:16), He was *"made alive in the spirit"* (1 Peter 3:18 ASV). He was actually made as righteous as He was before He was made sin.

He was made so righteous that He who had cried, *"My God, my God, why hast thou forsaken me?"* after His resurrection entered into the presence of the Father with His own blood and sealed our redemption. (See Matthew 27:46.)

> *Neither by the blood of goats and calves, but by his own blood he entered in once into the holy place, having obtained eternal redemption for us.*
>
> (Hebrews 9:12)

He was so righteous that He could sit down in the Father's presence as though He had never been sin. On the ground of His finished work, when you accept it, you are made a new creation.

You become the righteousness of God in Him.

You stand in the Father's presence as though sin had never been. We have never been able to accept this even mentally, but it is coming slowly to the consciousness of the church as they listen to the Word.

Romans 3:26 (ASV) says, "*For the showing, I say, of his righteousness at this present season: that he might himself be just, and the justifier of him that hath faith in Jesus.*"

God actually becomes our righteousness the moment that we accept Christ as Savior and confess Him as our Lord.

Men don't appreciate this, but the moment that a man becomes a new creation, he can stand in the presence of the Father as Jesus did in His earth walk.

He is only a babe, but he has a perfect righteousness and a perfect redemption. That redemption is God-wrought. That righteousness is God Himself.

God paid man's penalty on legal grounds and met the demands of justice absolutely.

It is not a problem of pity. It is not a problem of a mother's love that overlooks a son's disobedience and rebellion, but it is the supreme court of the universe dealing with our rebellion and our sin, dealing with it so effectually that it can never become an issue again.

Another great fact is that the new creation is based upon absolutely legal grounds.

In Ephesians 2:1–3 (ASV), He has shown the condition of natural man:

> *And you did he make alive, when ye were dead through your trespasses and sins, wherein ye once walked according to the course of this world, according to the prince of the powers of the air, of the spirit that now worketh in the sons of disobedience; among whom we also all once lived in the lusts of our flesh, doing the desires of the flesh and of the mind, and were by nature children of wrath, even as the rest.*

Natural man is spiritually dead. He is subject to the prince of the powers of the air. He is a child of disobedience. He is by nature a child of wrath.

Ephesians 2:12 says, without Christ, natural man was "*devoid of hope and God within the world*" (MOFF). He had no covenant claims on God. He was a stranger to the covenant of promise. He was hopeless, godless, spiritually dead, a child of the devil. That is the condition of lost man.

I know they do not like to have that told to them, but if they are not told, then they will never see the need of eternal life.

Ephesians 2:4–5 (MOFF) says, "*Dead in trespasses as we were, God was so rich in mercy that for his great love to us he made us live together with Christ (it is by grace you have been saved).*"

In the plan of redemption, God recreated us by faith.

> *For we are his workmanship, created in Christ Jesus unto good works, which God hath before ordained that we should walk in them.*
>
> (Ephesians 2:10)

By faith, God recreated us in the recreation of Christ when Jesus was made alive, after He had been made sin. In that recreation was our recreation.

All we have to do is accept it. The moment we accept it, it becomes a reality to us in the mind of the Father.

Now you can understand what it means when He says that He "*hath raised us up together*" with Christ (Ephesians 2:6).

When He was raised from the dead by God's faith, we were raised together with Him.

The rest of the sixth verse says, "*And made us sit together in heavenly places in Christ Jesus.*"

We are seated now by God's faith at the right hand of the majesty on high. Do you see what mighty faith the Father had?

He believed that humanity would respond to the tug of His grace. Thank God, we have done it!

In this, He shows "*the exceeding riches of his grace in his kindness toward us through Christ Jesus. For by grace are ye saved through faith; and that not of yourselves: it is the gift of God: not of works, lest any man should boast. For we are his workmanship, created in Christ Jesus unto good works*" (Ephesians 2:7–10).

By faith, He did all the work that is necessary for the recreation of the whole body of Christ.

By the Father's faith, we were new creations in the resurrection of Jesus.

When He said that He made us to sit down with Him at the right hand of the majesty on high, do you realize what that meant? That back yonder, the

Father's faith saw us perfect conquerors, perfect victors, enthroned by the side of His own Son at His own right hand.

I tell you, that was faith!

I have faith in my Father's faith, that this is made good in me. Now, you can understand 2 Corinthians 5:17–18:

"Therefore if any man be in Christ, he is a new creature." The moment you accept Christ, you are in the new creation. *"Old things are passed away."* This is the experimental part of it. *"Behold, all things are become new. And all things are of God, who hath reconciled us to himself by Jesus Christ, and hath given to us the ministry of reconciliation."* This is the ministry of reconciliation for this world that was redeemed from the hand of the enemy, but does not know it.

The redemption is of no value to them as long as they are ignorant of it.

They cannot enter into those riches until we tell them.

Today God is not reckoning unto the world their trespasses. He has committed unto us the Word that is to reconcile them to the fact that they have been recreated in Christ Jesus in His substitutionary work.

All they have to do is accept Him as their Savior and confess Him as their Lord, and they enter into this new thing called the new creation.

We are ambassadors with this new marvelous message of grace.

We are saying to men, "Be reconciled to God—all you need to do is come to Him. He is waiting for you."

Eternal life is yours. Fellowship with Him and relationship all await you. Hear what He says to achieve it.

"For our sakes He made him to be sin who himself knew nothing of sin" (2 Corinthians 5:21 MOFF). Doesn't that break your heart? Doesn't that cause your heart to respond to a love like that? He was made sin to the end that you might become the righteousness of God in Him.

This is masterful. You are led out of failure and weakness and sin and satanic relationship, into the new creation, where you have become partakers of the divine nature, actual sons of God.

God has made you righteous so you can stand in His presence just as though you had never been a sinner, just as though sin has never soiled you.

You stand there complete in Christ.

This belongs to you. This is your legal right, and you can receive it yourself. If you believe in the finished work of Christ in you, and you believe in all God has done for you, it is yours, but it is not yours experimentally until you accept Him as your Savior and confess Him as your Lord.

You believe in your own rights in Christ. Then you are a conqueror.

Romans 8:14 gives us an insight into sonship rights and privileges: *"For as many as are led by the Spirit of God, they are the sons of God."*

You have become a son. You have received not the spirit of bondage again unto fear. You have been delivered out of that. You have received the spirit of adoption. You are crying now, "Father, my dear Father."

The Holy Spirit Himself is bearing witness with your spirit through the Word that you are a child of God.

If you are a child, then you are an heir of God, and a joint-heir with Jesus Christ.

You see, you are taking your place now. You are responding to His challenge.

Romans 8:31 is the climax of this mighty truth: *"What shall we then say to these things? If God be for us, who can be against us?"*

God is for us. He is our Father now. *"He that spared not his own Son, but delivered him up for us all, how shall he not with him also freely give us all things"* (verse 32).

How shall He not give to us, as a Father, all that belongs to us as a son's inheritance, a son's rights in Christ?

Who shall lay anything to our charge now? We are God's elect. It is God who has declared us righteous.

It is God who has made us righteous. It is God who declared He is our righteousness in Christ.

Now to climax it, Jesus is seated at the Father's right hand as our great Intercessor, Advocate, and Lord in the highest seat of the universe, the head of the body, the new creation.

The new creation is seated there with Him. No one can bring a charge against us. No one can conquer us.

Then He gives us a category of all the things that Satan can do against a man:

> *What shall we then say to these things? If God be for us, who can be against us? He that spared not his own Son, but delivered him up for us all, how shall he not with him also freely give us all things? Who shall lay any thing to the charge of God's elect? It is God that justifieth. Who is he that condemneth? It is Christ that died, yea rather, that is risen again, who is even at the right hand of God, who also maketh intercession for us. Who shall separate us from the love of Christ? shall tribulation, or distress, or persecution, or famine, or nakedness, or peril, or sword? As it is written, For thy sake we are killed all the day long; we are accounted as sheep for the slaughter.* (Romans 8:31–36)

Then he shouts this: "*Nay, in all these things we are more than conquerors through him that loved us*" (verse 37).

We stand complete in His completeness. We are victors in His own victory.

NOT WHAT WE SHOULD BE—BUT WHAT WE ARE NOW IN CHRIST!

The modern Christian does not object to my telling what they need, or my telling what they should do or be, but they can't understand me when I tell them what they are in Christ. They think I am bringing a new philosophy, a beautiful error, that will lead them astray.

I remember when I first saw this, I said, "If this were only true;" and then I said, "If I knew how to make it mine."

I didn't know that it was mine.

I didn't know that "He had blessed me with every spiritual blessing in Christ" (see Ephesians 1:3), and when I read it, it didn't register.

I remember 1 Corinthians 3:21 where He declares that all things are mine; whether the revelation was given to Paul, or Cephas, or Apollos, it was mine.

That everything that the Father wrought in Christ in His great substitution belongs to the individual believer.

It makes no difference whether the believer is educated or uneducated, whether he is rich or poor. The boundless grace unveiled in Christ, belongs to every one of us.

Philippians 4:13 is absolutely ours: *"I can do all things through Christ which strengtheneth me."*

That is mine.

I can do anything that is necessary to be done because of His ability that has been imparted to me.

Psalm 27:1 (ASV) says, *"Jehovah is my light and my salvation; whom shall I fear? Jehovah is the strength of my life; of whom shall I be afraid?"*

Note that carefully: *"Jehovah is my light."* That is wisdom. That is ability.

He is my ability to use the knowledge of what belongs to me.

Now I am able to take advantage of what the Epistles tell me belongs to me.

He is not only my ability, but my salvation, my deliverance, my redemption.

I am as free from Satan's dominion in the mind of the Father as Jesus was when He arose from the dead, because His resurrection has freed me.

I have become a partaker of His resurrection the moment I become a new creation. Colossians 3:1 says, *"If ye then be risen with Christ."*

The ability of God that was exercised in the resurrection of Jesus belongs to the believer today.

Notice Ephesians 1:19–20. Let me give you a somewhat freer translation: "I want to show you the exceeding greatness of the ability of God on our behalf who believe. It is according to the working of the strength of His might which He wrought in the Christ when He raised Him from the dead and made Him sit at His right hand."

We have never grasped the significance of this.

The Father has given to us the ability that He exercised in the resurrection of Jesus.

Then we who have received eternal life have in our possession today the resurrection power or ability of God.

I am convinced that, before the Master returns, there will be groups of men and women who will recognize this and take their place and begin to show to the world a type of supernatural ability that will startle a sense-knowledge ruled world.

It is no idle thing to have God in you.

One day it seemed as though He were questioning me. He said, "Have I been so diminished, have I become so small and so weak and ineffectual, that you can ignore Me?"

He said, "The God who raised Jesus from the dead is dwelling in you and He has lost none of His ability or power."

When He enters your life to dwell there, He doesn't lay aside His glory and majesty and might.

When God's Son took upon Him the garment of flesh, He laid aside some of His glory.

But when the Holy Spirit comes into you, He comes full-fledged. He is the same mighty Holy Spirit that raised Jesus from the dead.

Romans 8:11 (ASV) says, *"If the Spirit of him that raised up Jesus from the dead dwelleth in you, he that raised up Christ Jesus from the dead shall give life also to your mortal bodies."*

I like that translation. It is vivid. It is true.

Then I want you to begin to reckon on Him. I want you to say in the morning, "That mighty One is in me. He can put me over today. I can face any emergency. I can do all things in Him because He is my strength."

I can hear Him whisper, in Isaiah 41:10, *"Fear thou not; for I am with thee* [I am in thee]: *be not dismayed; for I am thy* [Father] *God: I will strengthen thee; yea, I will help thee; yea, I will uphold thee."* He is whispering, "I am today all that you need: your helper, your wisdom, your strength, your ability."

You see, it is not what I should be. It is not what I can be.

It is what I am in Christ.

We are not trying to be righteous; we are.

We are not trying to be strong, for God is the strength of our life.

We are not trying to be wise, because Jesus has been made wisdom unto us.

We are what He says we are, so we can do what He says we can do.

GOD'S SUPERMAN

Jesus uttered some prophetic facts about believers.

Matthew 19:26 says, *"With God all things are possible."*

Jesus is uttering a fact, and here is its complement: *"And nothing shall be impossible unto you"* (Matthew 17:20).

Take this with Mark 11:24: *"Therefore I say unto you, What things soever ye desire, when ye pray, believe that ye receive them, and ye shall have them."*

Or, take Mark 9:23: *"All things are possible to him that believeth."*

The word "believeth" means "a believing one." There were no "believing ones" in the time while Christ was preaching. They were Jews under law.

The "believing ones" came into being at Pentecost.

It meant a believer, a new creation man.

The new creation man is a partaker of God's nature.

He is really an incarnation. He has received the nature and life of God.

Then he invites the Spirit who raised Jesus from the dead, who came on the day of Pentecost, to make His home in his body.

This man not only has God's nature, but has God actually living in him.

If this doesn't constitute a superman, then I don't know what a superman is.

But I am going to carry you one step farther.

This man with God's nature, and God dwelling in him, is given a legal right to the use of the name of Jesus with the power of attorney.

The question is: what is that name worth? What authority is there behind it?

In Matthew 28:18–20 (ASV), Jesus said, *"All authority hath been given unto me in heaven and on earth. Go ye therefore, and make disciples of all the nations, baptizing them into the name of the Father and of the Son and of the Holy Spirit: teaching them to observe all things whatsoever I commanded you: and lo, I am with you always, even unto the end of the world."*

You see what we have now?

We have the power of attorney to use the name of Jesus, and all authority in heaven and on earth is invested in that name.

Go over it just once more.

The believer is a new creation. The old things of weakness and failure have passed away and behold: the old man has become a new man and all these things are of God. (See 2 Corinthians 5:17–18.)

This man is a partaker of the divine nature, eternal life.

"He that hath the Son hath the life" (1 John 5:12).

He has the Son—he has the life.

Now he has the Holy Spirit indwelling him. *"Greater is he that is in you, than he that is in the world"* (1 John 4:4).

This believer, this new creation, is a child of the Deity.

He stands before the world as a very branch of the vine.

He is taking Jesus's place in the world.

And if this isn't a superman, then I don't know the meaning of the term.

The church has kept this "Samson" imprisoned by false teachings and by creeds and doctrines. They have not only held him a prisoner to their philosophies and dogmas, but they have actually put out his eyes.

But the Father is going to restore sight to him and break the bonds that hold him.

The bonds of false teaching are going to be broken, and this child of God, this superman, is going to come into his own.

He has two formidable enemies. The worst one is sense knowledge.

Entrenched in all our universities, colleges, and technical schools, backed up by the press and religious periodicals, the great mass of the ministry are the devotees of the achievements of the senses in the realm called science.

And this superman in Christ has been held in bondage by them. They are the jailers.

The Father is calling for His sons and daughters to come out of the foxholes of fear and doubt and meet their enemies in open combat.

Satan can no more conquer this body of Christ, when it knows its rights, than he could conquer Jesus on the day of the resurrection.

We are partakers, sharers in His resurrection.

"If ye then be risen with Christ, seek those things which are above" (Colossians 3:1).

You see, we were raised together with Him in the mind of justice.

We possess resurrection ability.

You doubt it? Read Acts 1:8 (MOFF): *"You will receive power when the holy Spirit comes upon you."*

The word "power" comes from the Greek word *dunamis*.

Robert Young translates it as "ability"—*"Ye shall receive ability when the Holy Spirit has recreated you."*

Ephesians 3:20 says, *"Now unto him that is able to do exceeding abundantly above all that we ask or think, according to the power* [or ability] *that worketh in us."*

If that doesn't make supermen out of common men, then the English language cannot convey God's thought.

The problem is this: How long are we going to be held in bondage by sense knowledge?

How long are we going to refuse to take our place as the sons of God?

How long are we going to be intimidated by the fears and doctrines of men, while the Word of God is ignored?

To them, it is a root out of dry ground. To most of the people, it has been a useless vine, something they could hang their doctrines and creeds upon.

It is coming to be to us what it really is in the mind of the Father.

Here is the Spirit's challenge: that you who read this, take your rights in prayer!

Begin to act like sons of God.

You have all heaven behind you.

You have the very angelic forces to do your bidding.

God is your strength and ability.

All things are possible to you because you are daring to act on the Word of God.

You are daring to live as Jesus dared to live in His earth walk.

You are the righteousness of God—that makes you a master of Satan; that gives you access to the throne; that permits you to take your place as a victor, as a spirit-warrior, as a conqueror.

You can have the consciousness that you are taking Jesus's place.

2 Corinthians 2:14 is becoming a reality in your own life: "*Wherever I go, thank God, he makes my life a constant pageant of triumph in Christ, diffusing the perfume* [or incense] *of his knowledge everywhere by me*" (MOFF). And you can shout, "Yes, I am Messiah's incense wafted up to God in the sight of all!"

I am a master in His name, with His ability.

I can do what He planned the church should do, for I am what He says I am.

GOD'S REAL MAN

Spiritual things are as real as material things.

Spiritual forces are stronger than mental.

Spiritual forces govern disease.

Spiritual forces govern natural laws.

Satan caused the wind on the Sea of Galilee. Jesus caused it to be still.

The believer, in his contact with material, spiritual, and mental forces, is as Jesus was in His earth walk—he is a master.

The believer is a new creation, created by God Himself.

He has God's nature, eternal life.

Jesus is made unto him wisdom.

God is his strength.

The Holy Spirit is his ability.

He has the love nature of God so that he does not and cannot act like common men.

Love makes him like Jesus.

He has the mind of Christ and the ability that Christ had in His earth walk.

This makes him a superman.

God gave to him a legal right to the use of Jesus's name, which has all authority in heaven and on earth, and which has authority over all the laws of nature, over every demon and his work, over all spiritual forces as well as material.

That authority and that ability belongs to the believer.

The recreated man is supernatural.

He is a superman.

Then why live in the senses—seeing, hearing, feeling, tasting, and smelling?!

All the knowledge natural man has came through these channels to his brain.

We have revelation knowledge.

What men of faith this truth will make!

What men of prayer will arise and take their place in Christ!

Here is the foundation on which to build a prayer life.

6

THE INTEGRITY OF THE WORD

The integrity of the Word is the basis of faith. The reason for unbelief and a faltering faith is a lack of assurance of the integrity of the promises in the Word. In Romans 10:8, it is called *"the word of faith."*

God's Word gives birth to faith; it is God's faith expressed.

> *By faith we understand that the worlds have been framed by the word of God, so that what is seen hath not been made out of things which appear.* (Hebrews 11:3 ASV)

In other words, this universe of ours came into being fresh from the womb of our Creator.

All God did to create was to say, *"Let there be"* and there leaped into being the things that are!

You see, God and His Word are one.

He named Jesus *"the Word."*

> *In the beginning was the Word, and the Word was with God, and the Word was God. The same was in the beginning with God. All things were made by him; and without him was not any thing made that was made.*
> (John 1:1–3)

God linked Himself with His Word.

He made Himself a part of it.

He is not only in His Word, but He is behind His Word.

You cannot separate Him from His Word.

> *By myself have I sworn…that in blessing I will bless thee, and multiplying I will multiply thy seed as the stars of the heaven, and the sand which is upon the sea shore.* (Genesis 22:16–17)

This was God's promise that backed the Abrahamic covenant.

No wonder that man had confidence, and that we have this description in Romans 4:17 (ASV): "*(As it is written, A father of many nations have I made thee) before him whom he believed, even God, who giveth life to the dead, and calleth the things that are not, as though they were.*"

He not only called the things that are not, and they leaped into being, but He watches over His Word to see that not one word fails.

In Romans 4:18 (ASV), speaking of Abraham, He says, "*Who in hope believed against hope, to the end that he might become a father of many nations, according to that which had been spoken. So shall thy seed be.*"

Now notice the next verses:

> *And without being weakened in faith he considered his own body now as good as dead (he being about a hundred years old), and the deadness of Sarah's womb; yet, looking unto the promise of God, he wavered not through unbelief, but waxed strong through faith, giving glory to God, and being fully assured that what he had promised, he was able also to perform.* (Romans 4:19–21 ASV)

You can understand that when that angel spoke to Abraham, it solved the problem.

Abraham never tried to believe; he simply acted on the word of that heavenly visitor.

Hebrews 7:22 is one of the unknown Scriptures that every believer should understand: "*By so much also hath Jesus become the surety of a better covenant*" (ASV).

God, who was the surety of the old covenant said, "By Myself have I sworn," and He tells us in Hebrews 6:17–18 (ASV) that He "*interposed with an oath; that by two immutable things, in which it is impossible for God to lie, we may have strong encouragement, who have fled for refuge to lay hold of the hope set before us.*"

Abraham rested on the angel's word.

Now we rest on this living Word given to the apostle Paul through the Holy Spirit.

Jesus is the guarantor for every word from Matthew 1:1 to Revelation 22:21.

All heaven is behind the Word; the very throne of God is behind the Word; and Jesus and the Father are behind the throne. They are all a part of this Word.

John 1:14 says, *"And the Word was made flesh, and dwelt among us."*

This was the eternal "logos," the very Son of God.

Jesus said in John 16:28, *"I came forth from the Father, and am come into the world: again, I leave the world, and go to the Father."* That was the Word who was made flesh.

Then, in the new covenant, the four Gospels, and the Epistles, God puts Himself into man's words.

Man had learned to communicate. Evidently, God had given him His language. Now God is pulling Himself into this word.

And if you remember 1 Thessalonians 2:13:

> *For this cause also thank we God without ceasing, because, when ye received the word of God which ye heard of us, ye received it not as the word of men, but as it is in truth, the word of God, which effectually worketh also in you that believe.*

You understand that 1 Thessalonians was the first book written in what we call the New Testament. All they had had up until that time was "the spoken word." When Paul preached, his message was as authoritative as when he wrote; so he says, "you accepted this Word that I preached, not as though it were the word of a man, but as it really was, the very Word of God, and that Word that I preached to you worked in you; the Spirit built it into your life so that it became a part of you."

Here are some facts about the Word.

The Word is always now.

It has been, it is, and it will be, the voice of God.

It is never old. It is always fresh and new.

To the heart that is in fellowship with the Father, the Word is a present-tense, living voice from heaven.

The Word is like its author: eternal, unchanging, and living.

Jesus was a root out of dry ground to His enemies. His revelation is a root out of dry ground to the skeptics of this day.

But it is a revelation of love to His friends and to those who love Him.

Hebrews 4:12 (MOFF) says, "*The Logos of God is a living thing, active and more cutting than any sword with double edge, penetrating to the very division of soul and spirit, joints and marrow—scrutinizing the very thoughts and conceptions of the heart.*"

And now notice this next sentence: "*And no created thing is hidden from him; all things lie open and exposed before the eyes of him with whom we have to reckon*" (Hebrews 4:13 MOFF).

Of what is He speaking? Of the living "logos" that I hold in my hand; and He says that there is no creative thing hidden from the eyes of this living Word, but all things lie open before Him.

This is a staggering thing to see that this Word is taking Jesus's place. It has all the elements in it that were in Jesus.

Reason will take the Word's place if we allow it to. Acting upon the Word doesn't appeal to the senses. The senses call acting on the Word "fanaticism."

The senses war against the recreated spirit, holding it in bondage, refusing to act on the Word. Until the mind is renewed, the Word will never have its place in the believer's life.

Reason must give place to the Word.

Reason often robs the Word of its authority.

When I know that His Word is as authoritative today as it was when it fell from His lips, then it will be a living thing on my lips.

The Father's Word on Jesus's lips accomplished things. It hushed the sea. It quieted the wind. It raised the dead. It fed the multitudes.

His living Word on lips of faith will do the same today.

When you know that the Word is God speaking, you will speak the Word with authority.

You remember that faith in God is faith in His Word.

You want to build your faith? Feed on the Word; act upon it.

You remember Matthew 4:4: *"Man shall not live by bread alone, but by every word that proceedeth out of the mouth of God."* You can't build faith and feed on any other kind of food.

Unbelief in the Word is unbelief in Him, the Author of it.

Our attitude toward the Word settles everything. You remember that man's word gives faith in man. God's Word, when unveiled, gives faith in God.

The word of a man is what man is. The Word of God is what He is.

"No word from God shall be void of power" (Luke 1:37 ASV). That is what the angel said to Mary about the birth of Jesus, and Mary answered back, *"Be it unto me according to thy word"* (Luke 1:38).

If I could help believers to say that to the Master today, *"Be it unto me according to thy word,"* they would shake this modern age to its foundations.

Here is another translation of Luke 1:37 that I like: *"Nothing is impossible to the Word of God."* The Word on your lips can be as mighty as the Word on the Master's lips.

You remember that Jesus said again and again, "The words that I speak are not My words."

> *For I have not spoken of myself; but the Father which sent me, he gave me a commandment, what I should say, and what I should speak.*
> (John 12:49)

You have in this New Testament the words of the Father.

You understand that the four Gospels give a picture of what Jesus thought of His Father.

Jesus is introducing the Father.

He is trying to make the God of the Jews, the God of Abraham, and of Isaac and Jacob, known to the Jewish heart as a Father God.

John 19:7 shows us that Jesus was crucified because He called God His Father. They had stoned Him for it. They had persecuted Him for it. Now they kill Him for it.

The Pauline revelation is the Father introducing Jesus in reality.

He is introducing to us His substitutionary sacrifice that He wrought in His Son.

Not only that, but He is introducing the new creation. It is a revelation of His sons and daughters here in a crooked and perverse world.

The Word on Jesus's lips was a living fact. What Jesus said was, is, and ever will be.

When we come to know that the Word was Jesus, the Word is Jesus speaking, then we will dare to speak it with confidence.

Then, He had just died and risen from the dead, but it is as fresh today as it was then. Jesus is of the "now" as though He died last month and Pentecost was last week.

He is all this, *now*. His Word is this living message to us, *now*.

What He said was a part of Himself. The reality of it is throbbing in us, flows through us; our lives are governed by it. The Word was real; the Word is real. This is the foundation for Faith, and faith gives substance to prayer and makes prayer a living reality.

Now soak in the Word. Let the Word work in you. John 15:7 (MOFF) says, *"If you remain in me and my words remain in you, then ask whatever you like and you shall have it."*

The living Word on our lips will be like the spoken Word on Paul's lips.

The Father's Word on lips ruled by faith will be like His Word on Jesus's lips.

It is His Word that does things!

His creative ability is in His Word today.

His Word awaits the lips of faith.

This will make a prayer life like Paul's; it will give boldness to enter the holy place.

IS HE SPEAKING TO ME?

A miner lay dying in his shack in the hills of California. A Christian woman read John 3:16 to him. He opened his eyes and looked at her. "Is that in the Bible?"

And she said, "Yes."

"Does it mean me?" He lay quietly for a bit and then said, "Has He said anything else?"

And she read John 1:12 (ASV): *"As many as received him, to them gave he the right to become children of God."*

Then she answered softly, "Yes, He is speaking to you."

And the man opened his eyes and whispered again, "I accept Him. I am satisfied." Then he passed on.

A Christian said, "I wish I knew whether He meant me when He gave us Isaiah 41:10: *'Fear thou not; for I am with thee: be not dismayed; for I am thy God: I will strengthen thee; yea, I will help thee; yea, I will uphold thee with the right hand of my righteousness.'* Did He mean me?"

Jeremiah 33:3 says, *"Call unto me, and I will answer thee, and show thee great and mighty things, which thou knowest not."*

Is He speaking to me? Is He asking me to call unto Him?

Isaiah 45:11 says, *"Ask me of the things to come concerning my sons, and concerning the work of my hands command ye me."*

Is He speaking to me? Can I claim that as mine?

John 15:5 says, *"I am the vine, ye are the branches."* And here's the seventh verse: *"If ye abide in me, and my words abide in you, ye shall ask what ye will, and it shall be done unto you."* Another translation says, *"And you shall have it"* (MOFF). Was that written for me? Does it mean that I can call unto Him anytime, anywhere, and He will hear me?

> *And this is the confidence that we have in him, that, if we ask any thing according to his will, he heareth us: and if we know that he hear us, whatsoever we ask, we know that we have the petitions that we desired of him.*
> (1 John 5:14–15)

Does this mean me, today?

Yes, these are all yours.

It is as though you were the only person in the world, and He was writing it for your special benefit.

> *Hitherto have ye asked nothing in my name: ask, and ye shall receive, that your joy may be full.* (John 16:24)

That is yours. There is no question about its belonging to you. It is as much yours as that check that was made out to you and signed by that businessman. That is your check. You can cash it down at the bank.

But that check is no more yours than are these promises in this wonderful Book.

So, take your place. Begin a real prayer life; you can do it; He is your helper.

Romans 8:26 says, "*The Spirit also helpeth our infirmities: for we know not what we should pray for as we ought: but the Spirit itself maketh intercession for us with groanings which cannot be uttered.*"

Let Him lead you into this prayer life.

He is always there to teach you.

He can open the Word and reveal your rights in Christ.

So act today!

The Word is the Father speaking to you.

It is not an old book that has a record of His message to men of ancient times; but the Bible, like its Author, is always *now.*

And looking down through the ages, He saw you, and this is written for your special benefit.

When He said, "*I watch over my word to perform it*" (Jeremiah 1:12 ASV), He was talking to you so that you would never question His Book again.

When He said, "*If ye abide in me, and my words abide in you, ye shall ask what ye will, and it shall be done unto you*" (John 15:5), that is His present-tense message to your heart.

You can take it as though you heard it over your radio, fresh from His lips, as though He were speaking through a microphone up yonder at the right hand of the Father, and that message came into your room and your name was called.

You knew it was for you.

Well, it would be no more yours than this Scripture I have just given you.

When He said, "*Whatsoever ye shall ask the Father in my name, he will give it you*" (John 16:23), He meant it for you in your daily walk, in your prayer life.

While you are reading this now, it is the Father speaking to you.

It is as though He stood in the room and said, "Whatsoever you ask in my Son's name, I will give it you."

Or, if He said, "In my Son's name, you may cast the demon out of that person, or you can lay hands on that person and they will be healed."

That name is yours to be used any time, any place.

Remember this is not a religion; this is your personal contact with the Father. Your ability to pray and get results can't be questioned.

It is as real as though you were the only person for whom Christ died.

And when He says, *"He hath made him to be sin for us, who knew no sin; that we might be made the righteousness of God in him"* (2 Corinthians 5:21), that means you.

When you accepted Him and received eternal life, you received His righteousness, and you became, that very moment, a new creation.

You became, at the same time, the righteousness of God in Him.

He doesn't have to do anything else—it is all done.

The work is finished.

The new creation is a fact.

All you need to do now is to act as though you knew it to be true, just as you act on any other fact of life.

We will assume that you are working in a factory and you are notified by the management that your pay has been raised. You at once plan what you will do with that new income.

As you sit here reading this, you remember that the great, mighty Holy Spirit who raised Jesus from the dead is in your body.

He is there to cooperate with you.

You are to cooperate with Him.

That greater One is in you with His resurrection power and ability.

You act on it.

You don't try to have faith. Faith is unnecessary now because He is in you, and this all belongs to you.

You have to have faith for things that do not belong to you.

The thing that is yours, is yours, so now, you will act on the Word without fear or questioning!

THE FATHER'S WORD ON YOUR LIPS

Jesus said, *"For I have not spoken of myself; but the Father which sent me, he gave me a commandment, what I should say, and what I should speak"* (John 12:49).

This is a marvelous statement from the lips of the Master.

The next verse says, *"Whatsoever I speak therefore, even as the Father said unto me, so I speak."*

Jesus declared that He came down out of heaven not to do His own will but the will of Him who sent Him.

The works that Jesus did, He declared were His Father's works.

He said, *"The Son can do nothing of his own accord, nothing but what he sees the Father doing; for whatever he does, the Son also does the same"* (John 5:19 MOFF).

The miracles that Jesus performed were the Father's miracles.

The marvelous words that He spoke were the Father's words.

Now you can see the power of the Father's words on Jesus's lips. Jesus knew who He was. He knew He was the Son of God. He knew God was His own Father. He knew that He came out from the Father. He knew He was going back to the Father. He knew His place and His work.

He was never vacillating in His actions or in His speech. There was a positive element in His messages that thrilled the heart.

There was a quiet assurance in every step. He took His place and acted the part of a Son.

He continually confessed His Sonship and His mission in the world.

As I face this fact, I ask myself this question: "Can we have the same assurance today, the same positiveness that Jesus had?"

Yes, a thousand times, yes!

We are redeemed from the hand of the enemy.

Colossians 1:13–14 says, "*Who hath delivered us from the power of darkness, and hath translated us into the kingdom of his dear Son: in whom we have redemption through his blood, even the forgiveness of sins.*"

That is a declarative statement in regard to our place, our standing and liberty in Christ.

We have been delivered out of darkness. We have been translated into the kingdom of the Son of His love.

We are redeemed; our sins have been wiped out. Then we haven't anything to do with bondage nor with our past life, for when we were recreated, as Paul tells us in 2 Corinthians 5:17–18 (MOFF):

> *There is a new creation whenever a man comes to be in Christ; what is old is gone, the new has come. It is all the doing of the God who has reconciled me to himself through Christ and has permitted me to be a minister of his reconciliation.*

We know that we are recreated, and that Satan has no dominion over the new creation.

We know that we are reconciled to the Father. That means a perfect fellowship.

We know that if we are reconciled, we can come into His presence without condemnation.

We know that with that reconciliation has come righteousness, the ability to stand in the Father's presence without condemnation or inferiority.

Jesus had no more than that.

Jesus had no sin-consciousness. We have no sense of sin.

Jesus had no sense of unrighteousness. We have no sense of unrighteousness, because we have been declared righteous with His own righteousness by the very living Word of God.

Jesus had no better righteousness than we have because God is our righteousness.

Jesus had no better fellowship than we have, because our fellowship has been wrought by God Himself.

Jesus had no better right in prayer or any more power in dealing with demons than we have.

All authority was given to Jesus, and He gave us a legal right to the use of His name.

If the Word means what it says, we have a standing with the Father, we have rights and privileges which we have never taken advantage of.

There is no sense of reality, no sense of God, in the modern church.

John 7:29 says, *"I know him: for I am from him, and he hath sent me."*

John 8:54–55 (MOFF) is Jesus's positive confession about His relationship with the Father:

> *It is my Father who glorifies me; you say "He is our God," but you do not understand him. I know him. Were I to say, "I do not know him," I would be a liar like yourselves; but I do know him and I hold to his word.*

We can know the Father. We can know our sonship rights.

He is my Father; I am His child; I am in His family.

Jesus said He came down here to do the Father's will. When we confess the lordship of Jesus, we confess our purpose—to do the Father's will.

He said, "Be not ignorant but understand what the will of the Father is." (See Ephesians 5:17.)

Let us form the habit of thinking that His will for us has more joy in it than anything which is contrary to His will.

Let us educate ourselves in the consciousness that His will is best, that His will has permanent joy and gladness in it, and that His will has success in it.

Outside of His will is confusion, unhappiness, and misery.

Jesus walked in love.

"Greater is he that is in you, than he that is in the world" (1 John 4:4). The One who is in you is love.

"God is love" (1 John 4:16).

For it is God who is at work within you. (See Philippians 2:13.) You have love in you. You have God's nature in you. You have God Himself in you.

We are dealing with realities. Most of our preaching is theory, speculation, telling us what we ought to do and be.

The only difficulty is that we have never confessed what we are in Him!

Jesus continually confessed what He was. Modern teaching has made it almost a crime to acknowledge what we are in Christ.

All that Jesus was to His Father in His earth walk, we may be to the Father in our earth walk.

We have the same Holy Spirit that Jesus had. We have the same words that Jesus uttered, which were the Father's words.

On our lips today, we can have the very message that Jesus had.

The Pauline revelation is the Word of the Father. We can fill our mouth with this revelation of Paul's. We will be speaking the Father's words.

We will be taking Jesus's place in the earth, saying the Father's words just as Jesus did when He walked the earth.

What a prayer life awaits us!

Jesus knew who He was. He knew why He came.

We may know who we are in Christ. We are new creations created in Christ Jesus. We have His nature.

There need not be anything mysterious about our walk. We may know exactly who we are. We may know why we are as Jesus did.

Jesus knew His Father. He said, "I came out from the Father; I came into the world. Again, I leave the world and go unto My Father." (See John 16:28.)

We may know our Father. We are born of God, and God is our Father.

We may know Him as truly as the Master knew Him.

If you start the day with Him, you will fellowship with Him. When you awaken in the morning, you whisper softly, "Good morning, Father. Here is another day to live and walk with Thee."

Whatever problem confronts you, you consult Him in your heart.

If it is wisdom that you need, you thank Him for it. If it is love to meet a disagreeable situation, He is there in you to take you over and live His own life through you.

He can make your words just like Jesus's words, full of love, full of sympathy, full of courage.

It would be good for you once in a while to stop and say to your Father, "Thank you for ability, for giving me wisdom to meet this problem."

Jesus in you is authority over demoniacal forces and over the laws of nature.

We may know our ability. We may know that we have authority over all the demoniacal forces.

"In My name, you shall cast out demons." (See Mark 16:17.)

"Greater is he that is in you, than he that is in the world" (1 John 4:4).

These are facts. We know them. We are not afraid to face life with the consciousness of victors.

In the morning, you take stock. You say, "He and I are going together. I have access to His ability, His wisdom, His love, His grace, and His strength to meet every issue that confronts me. I shall have physical strength for every need today. I shall have wisdom to meet every issue. I shall have love no matter what the provocation may be."

You see, when you walk like this, your prayer life becomes a realistic thing.

Jesus had no sense of need. There was always a sureness in all He did.

Well, if He is in me and for me, and I have His Word, there should be a sureness about my walk. I should not walk as a blind man, feeling my way along. I should walk erect. I should keep pace with the momentum of life around me. There should be an absolute certainty about my decisions.

When I remember that He is my sufficiency, it makes no difference what the problem may be; He is there. I have His guidance. I am assured of His presence, and He will not let me fail.

He was never discouraged, and He whispers to me, *"Fear thou not; for I am with thee: be not dismayed; for I am thy God: I will strengthen thee; yea, I will help thee; yea, I will uphold thee with the right hand of my righteousness"* (Isaiah 41:10).

That is mine. I fearlessly take up the task before me. Unconsciously, I am living *in His presence*. I am walking in His presence. His eye of love is upon me all the time. He and I are carrying out His will.

Why, prayer just becomes a means of communication between Him and me. It is not a slavish duty. It is not a difficult task. It is not hard work.

He and I are working together.

7

RELATIONSHIP AND FELLOWSHIP

There are two great objectives in redemption. The first is relationship. God is working to the end that man may legally become His child, a partaker of His very nature, so that he will be a genuine heir and joint heir with Jesus.

The second objective is to restore to man his lost fellowship. This can only come as righteousness is restored to him. Job 33:26 (ASV) says, *"He restoreth unto man his righteousness."*

There can be no fellowship unless man can stand in the presence of God the Father without the consciousness of guilt, of sin, or of inferiority.

There can be no fellowship of the type that the Father craves unless man is utterly free from sin consciousness and free from the fear of Satan's dominion.

So, the whole redemptive processes have been to the end that He might have children, and that these children should live in the closest fellowship of love and freedom with Himself.

Sonship, then, must be based upon legal grounds. There must be no question as to man's legal standing in the family of God.

The sin problem must be settled on legal grounds so that God will have a perfect right to impart to man His own nature, thereby making this man an absolute new creation.

The sin in his nature must be driven out by the nature of God coming in.

His spirit must be in perfect harmony with the Father. Man is a spirit. The part of man that had to be recreated was the spirit of man.

His mind is renewed, and his body brought into subjection to the Word.

That constitutes the first phase of a perfect redemption.

Man must become an actual child of God, as truly as was Jesus in His earth walk. This can only come by a rebirth of his spirit, a real new creation of which Jesus speaks:

> *Verily, verily, I say unto thee, Except a man be born again, he cannot see the kingdom of God.... Except a man be born of water and of the Spirit, he cannot enter into the kingdom of God. That which is born of the flesh is flesh; and that which is born of the Spirit is spirit. Marvel not that I said unto thee, Ye must be born again.* (John 3:3–7)

James 1:18 tells us that we are begotten of the will of the Father: *"Of his own will begat he us with the word of truth, that we should be a kind of firstfruits of his creatures."*

Two facts are shown here: we are born of His will and we are born of His Word. It is all of God.

Ephesians 2:10 says, *"For we are his workmanship, created in Christ Jesus unto good works, which God hath before ordained that we should walk in them."*

That new creation is all of God, wrought through the Word and of the Holy Spirit.

It is a God-planned and a God-executed relationship.

That new creation is all of God. Man is actually a child of God, as that boy is a child of that man and woman.

As soon as he is recreated, the Father begins the beautiful process of renewing his mind.

> *And be not fashioned according to this world: but be ye transformed by the renewing of your mind, that ye may prove what is the good and acceptable and perfect will of God.* (Romans 12:2 ASV)

That word "transformed" comes from the same Greek word from which the word "transfigured" comes in speaking of Jesus's transfiguration on the Mount.

The renewing of the mind will be a transfiguration of our minds.

No one can overestimate this wonderful fact.

These minds of ours have been dominated by the senses, so that all the knowledge that we have has been sense knowledge.

This mind is going to be renewed by the Spirit, and by our meditation in the Word and practicing of the Word, until our mind is in perfect fellowship with our recreated spirit and with the Word.

Few believers have a renewed mind.

Consequently, only a few of them ever get into the deep things of God, and their prayer life seldom becomes a reality.

Only a few of them know the riches of His grace.

First Corinthians 2:10–13 tells how the Spirit searches all things, even the deep things of God, so that we may know the things that were freely given to us of God. These things we also speak, not in words that man's wisdom teaches but which the Spirit alone can give.

The renewed mind, coming into this deep, rich fellowship with the Father through the Word, is able to appreciate and understand the wealth of the redemptive work that was wrought in Christ.

Ephesians 1:3 says, *"Blessed be the God and Father of our Lord Jesus Christ, who hath blessed us with all spiritual blessings in heavenly places in Christ."*

That falls dead upon the ears of the average believer, and yet that average believer is a possessor of all the things that Christ wrought in his redemption.

He has been blessed with every spiritual blessing in Christ.

Christianity is the life of God imparted to a man, plus the wealth of the riches of God's nature that is imparted to us, and the Spirit's unveiling of the wealth of God that was revealed in Christ in His redemptive work.

It was a faith-provoking thing, a love-stimulating thing.

It revolutionizes the intellect; it thrills the spirit.

It lifts a man out of the natural into the supernatural.

When his mind is renewed on the basis of his sonship rights, he can take his place as a son.

He can enjoy a son's rights and privileges. He can assume a son's responsibility and step into all the riches of the grace of God.

This comes when man loses his sin consciousness, his sense of inferiority.

He never does this until he knows about righteousness.

The church is so woefully ignorant of righteousness today. She thinks righteousness only means doing right deeds.

But in the revelation He gave to Paul, righteousness means the ability to stand in the Father's presence without a sense of guilt, inferiority, or sin, just as free in the Father's presence as was Jesus.

The church thinks we will have to wait until we die before this is possible.

It is ours now, in this present, evil world.

Right here, right now, we may have as sweet a fellowship and communion with the Father as Jesus had in His earth walk.

Speaking of the gifts and sacrifices under the first covenant, Hebrews 9:9 (ASV) says, "*That cannot, as touching the conscience, make the worshipper perfect.*"

The blood of bulls and goats could only cover sin, and the scapegoat could only bear sins away typically.

But when the fullness of time came, and Jesus put sin away by the sacrifice of Himself, then Hebrews 9:14 became a reality: "*How much more shall the blood of Christ, who through the eternal Spirit offered himself without spot to God, purge your conscience from dead works to serve the living God?*"

Hebrews 10:1–3, speaking of the first covenant, says:

> *The law having a shadow of good things to come, and not the very image of the things, can never with those sacrifices which they offered year by year continually make the comers thereunto perfect. For then would they not have ceased to be offered? because that the worshippers once purged should have had no more conscience of sins. But in those sacrifices there is a remembrance again made of sins every year.*

There was nothing perfect about the old covenant.

When He came, He made one sacrifice for sins forever. (See Hebrews 9:26.) Then, He sat down on the right hand of the Majesty on high.

He had put away sin by the sacrifice of Himself. He had made the new creation possible.

He made remission of sins possible. All the sins we committed were remitted, wiped out as though they never were.

That new creation is to be free from sin consciousness so that the believer is no longer held in bondage to Satan's condemnation.

Romans 8:1 becomes a reality: "*There is therefore now no condemnation to them which are in Christ Jesus.*"

Romans 8:33 says, "*Who shall lay any thing to the charge of God's elect?*" It is God who has declared them righteous.

God Himself has done it.

"Him who knew no sin he made to be sin on our behalf; that we might become the righteousness of God in him" (2 Corinthians 5:21 ASV).

We not only have righteousness reckoned to us, and righteousness imputed to us, but we have had righteousness imparted to us in the new creation.

Ephesians 4:24 (ASV) says, *"Put on the new man, that after God hath been created in righteousness and holiness of truth."* We have been created out of righteousness and holiness of truth.

That thrills the heart.

The very fact of a new creation and of sonship demands a perfect righteousness.

Could you think of a son who could not stand in his Father's presence? Sonship would have no meaning, no significance whatever.

We have now a perfect relationship. God is our very Father; we are his very sons and daughters.

Our relationship cannot be challenged because it is based upon the finished work of Christ.

God has wrought it Himself.

When we accepted Christ as our Savior and confessed Him as our Lord, then God Himself, through the Word, by the Holy Spirit's energy, recreated us, imparting to us His own nature, eternal life.

"He that believeth on me hath everlasting life" (John 6:47).

> *These things have I written unto you that believe on the name of the Son of God; that ye may know that ye have eternal life, and that ye may believe on the name of the Son of God.* (1 John 5:13)

> *He that heareth my word, and believeth on him that sent me, hath everlasting life, and shall not come into condemnation; but is passed from death unto life.* (John 5:24)

The death out of which he has passed is spiritual death, union with Satan.

He has passed out of that, by being born out of it.

Now he is in the realm of supernatural life.

Romans 5:17 (MOFF) says, *"For if the trespass of one man allowed death to reign through that one man, much more shall those who receive the overflowing grace and free gift of righteousness reign in life through One, through Jesus Christ."*

Here we get the whole picture: through the abundance of grace and the gift of righteousness, we reign as kings in the realm of life—as conquerors, as overcomers.

That is a triumphant strain right from the heart of the Father, not to become a fact only in heaven, but right here and now.

FELLOWSHIP

Fellowship is based upon righteousness. Fellowship means *sharing together.*

Marriage is a good illustration. It is partnership. It is getting under the burden as one.

It is an equal exchange, both giving of their best. Another word that it suggests is *communion.*

That means the two are pouring into the same cup, and they become perfectly one in the blending, just as God says a man and his wife *"shall be one flesh"* (Genesis 2:24).

That is fellowship. Jesus said, *"I am the vine, ye are the branches"* (John 15:5).

Our fellowship with the Father is based upon relationship.

Fellowship between husband and wife is based upon relationship.

Fellowship is the one thing that makes married life beautiful.

The law that binds the man or woman together does not make fellowship. It is not the fact that the woman is a good cook and housekeeper, or that the man is a splendid provider and a gentleman at all times.

It is when that man and woman are blended together into one, spiritually, physically, and mentally.

That is communion. That is real fellowship.

We often have in our home life a limited fellowship. In the church, we have a limited fellowship with the brethren; that means we also have limited fellowship with the Father.

It is unlimited fellowship that brings happiness into the home. It is unlimited fellowship with the Father and with one another that brings the richest, deepest joy into the believer's life.

> *God is faithful, by whom ye were called unto the fellowship of his Son Jesus Christ our Lord.* (1 Corinthians 1:9)

We were called into fellowship with His Son.

This is a heavenly calling.

We are to bear the burdens of Jesus, in bringing a lost world to the knowledge of the truth.

We are fellowshipping Jesus when we go to Africa, India, or China as a missionary.

We are fellowshipping Jesus when we fellowship the missionary who goes with our money and prayers.

Fellowshipping means giving.

I fellowship the missionary by sending him my offerings.

I have been called into this fellowship of Jesus, and now I am fellowshipping the Master and carrying out His will in the world.

The new birth and righteousness are to one end: that we may enjoy the sweetest fellowship with the Father and with the Son.

Fellowship is the parent of real faith. If you find someone whose faith is weak, you may know that his fellowship has been broken, or it is of a low type.

Fellowship between a husband and wife can be easily broken. The marriage is not broken. It takes the court that married them to do that.

This broken fellowship does not break your relationship, but it mars it and robs that relationship of its richest blessings and benefits.

All low-grade faith comes from a low grade of fellowship.

Most Christians have lost their fellowship and are putting duty in the place of it.

They are like a husband and wife whose fellowship has been broken.

The husband brings home presents that only bring tears to the eyes of his wife.

She does not want the presents. She wants fellowship restored.

Broken fellowship is one of the saddest facts of human experience.

Here is a couple who have lived in absolute heaven. Then an unkind word or a thoughtless act has marred their lives.

They are both too proud to acknowledge the fault, and the gulf between them becomes almost impassable because they are unwilling to ask each other's forgiveness.

The Holy Spirit has given us the way to restore broken fellowship in the first epistle of John.

This short epistle was written to tell us how to maintain our fellowship and how to restore it when it is broken.

> *That which we have seen and heard declare we unto you, that ye also may have fellowship with us: and truly our fellowship is with the Father, and with his Son Jesus Christ. And these things write we unto you, that your joy may be full.* (1 John 1:3–4)

Joy cannot be made full without full fellowship.

> *This then is the message which we have heard of him, and declare unto you, that God is light, and in him is no darkness at all. If we say that we have fellowship with him, and walk in darkness, we lie, and do not the truth.* (1 John 1:5–6)

God is light, and as long as you are in fellowship with Him, you are in the light.

But the instant your fellowship is broken, you go into the dark.

Hatred is darkness. That hatred has blinded our eyes.

> *But he that hateth his brother is in darkness, and walketh in darkness, and knoweth not whither he goeth, because that darkness hath blinded his eyes.* (1 John 2:11)

This man is out of fellowship. He is walking in darkness. He does not know where he is going.

How many Christians are like that! They refuse to walk in the light of the Word.

That means walking in love. Every step out of love is a step into the dark.

> *If we walk in the light, as he is in the light, we have fellowship one with another, and the blood of Jesus Christ his Son cleanseth us from all sin.*
> (1 John 1:7)

As long as we walk in the light, the blood of Jesus Christ cleanses all the blunders and mistakes that we make.

If we say that we have no sin, we deceive ourselves, and the truth is not in us. If we confess our sins, he is faithful and just to forgive us our sins, and to cleanse us from all unrighteousness.

But "*if we say that we have no sin*"—when we have broken fellowship, and are walking in the darkness—"*we deceive ourselves, and the truth is not in us. If we confess our sins, he is faithful and just* [righteous] *to forgive us our sins, and to cleanse us from all unrighteousness*" (1 John 1:8–9).

This Scripture is not written to the world. It is written to the church, the family of God.

It has to do with broken fellowship.

The instant that you confess your sins, in that instant, He is faithful and righteous to forgive you.

Now you are to forgive yourself and forget your sins and go on in love with Him.

For you to continually remind yourself of your past errors and sins is to deny the efficacy of His forgiveness and the value of His Word.

> *My little children, these things write I unto you, that ye sin not. And if any man sin, we have an advocate with the Father, Jesus Christ the righteous.*
> (1 John 2:1)

Jesus is the righteous advocate. He can go into the Father's presence when we are under condemnation and shrink from meeting Him.

He is always righteous. He can always plead our case.

The instant we ask the Father's forgiveness, Jesus takes up our case before the Father and our fellowship is restored.

There is no need of walking in broken fellowship a minute after you have committed sin.

The devil is the author of that sin.

Then to walk on in broken fellowship, grieving over your blunder, is only adding joy and glory to the devil.

The instant you have done wrong and your fellowship is impaired, ask the Father's forgiveness and go on in fellowship with Him. (See 1 John 1:9; 2:1–2.)

Restoring fellowship is restoring joy, restoring power with God.

The richer the fellowship, the deeper one gets into the Word.

Deep, rich fellowship means that we go far below the surface in this mine of wealth.

You cannot walk in love without fellowship.

To walk in love is to walk in fellowship.

To live the love life is to live the fellowship life.

It is bringing joy to the heart of the Father.

It is the sweetest, biggest, richest thing the world ever knew, this fellowship life with Him.

The church knows very little about it. Almost no one ever preaches about it, yet it is the heart of the whole thing.

There can be no growth in faith, or growth in grace, or growth in knowledge, or growth in joy, with broken fellowship.

Every person who has lost power with God has lost it through loss of fellowship.

If their faith has been impaired so their prayer life is but a form, it is because fellowship has been broken.

If their joy has all seeped out, it is because the vessel that held it has been cracked; their usefulness and testimony have lost their grip and power. It is mere empty words because fellowship has been broken.

If you want your testimony rich and full, then you must have fellowship that is rich and full.

There are three things that characterize fellowship.

You are taking advantage of your righteousness. You are bearing the fruits of righteousness. What are those fruits? You are now able to pray with the sick, cast out demons, open the Scriptures, and lead lost men to Christ with unspeakable freedom.

There is joy in this life in Christ. When you are walking in righteousness, you are walking as Jesus walked when He was on earth. There is fullness of joy. It is the joy of Christianity that makes Christianity the most attractive thing in the world. When joy goes, the Word loses its power, its freshness, and its richness. It is only when fellowship is at flood tide, and we are walking in the fullness of righteousness, that God is honored and souls are saved.

A third thing is that there will be no development of faith. There is the Word: it is just as rich and full today as it ever was, but somehow or other, the lips seem paralyzed.

There is no longer light on the Word. The sick cry for help, but find no release because fellowship is broken and faith is slowly ebbing away.

Fellowship in its fullness is the joy life with the throttle wide open on a down grade.

Fellowship in its fullness is the soil out of which living faith grows to fruition.

Faith dies on a low type of fellowship.

It shrivels up.

It is like a desert plant.

By taking your place in righteousness, you will find joy in the Word, freedom to use the name of Jesus, and conquering faith that will master every circumstance that confronts you.

Then the maintaining of a rich, full fellowship is vastly important.

"Let the word of Christ dwell in you richly" (Colossians 3:16).

That is the key. It is the Word dwelling in us in all its fullness, its variety, its beauty, and its graciousness that produces a rich type of fellowship.

It will give place to love. It will produce all the fruits of righteousness. Faith cannot grow rich on any other soil.

A rich prayer life depends on your fellowship.

You must be in fellowship, or you can't enjoy the throne of grace.

If your fellowship is broken, you know what to do to have it restored.

You can't afford to stay in the dark; too many issues are at stake.

8

HE PUT ALL THINGS IN SUBJECTION UNDER HIS FEET

In the first three chapters of the epistle to the Ephesians, we have the consummation of Christ's substitutionary work in regard to Satan and demons. Paul prays that:

> *Having the eyes of your heart enlightened, that ye may know what is the hope of his calling, what the riches of the glory of his inheritance in the saints, and what the exceeding greatness of his power to us-ward who believe.* (Ephesians 1:18–19 ASV)

He fairly shouts that it is "*according to that working of the strength of his might which he wrought in Christ, when he raised him from the dead*" (verses 19 and 20).

He declares the same ability that wrought in the dead body of Jesus when He was raised to immortality is at work within us.

The heart can hardly take it in that the same might, the same resurrection power, that wrought in the dead body of Jesus is ours today.

> *If the Spirit of him that raised up Jesus from the dead dwell in you, he that raised up Christ from the dead shall also quicken [or heal or strengthen] your mortal bodies.* (Romans 8:11)

God the Father set Jesus "*at his own right hand in the heavenly places, far above all principality, and power, and might, and dominion, and every name that is named, not only in this world, but also in that which is to come*" (Ephesians 1:20–21).

You must always keep in mind that we were raised together with Him, and He made us to sit with Him in the heavenlies; so representatively, we are seated on the throne with Christ.

He is the head of the body.

We are members of that body.

So if the head is exalted, the body is exalted with it.

If He has been given all authority, that authority belongs to the church, His body. It is for the benefit of the church.

If He conquered all the forces of darkness and left them paralyzed and broken before He arose from the dead, it is as though we had accomplished that mighty work.

It is all reckoned to us, set to our credit.

When will our hearts take it in, and our minds become fruitful with this mighty unveiling of what we are in Christ today?

Notice carefully the next two verses:

> *He has put everything under his feet and set him as head over everything for the church, the church which is his Body.* (Ephesians 1:22–23 MOFF)

We are His body—then all these malign and wicked influences are beneath our feet.

We are masters of them all.

He did not defeat them for Himself. He defeated them for us.

He did not fight that battle for His glory, but for our good.

Adam had sold us out in his sin of high treason.

Jesus redeemed us, defeated our enemy, and put him beneath our feet.

When will the heart take it in?

That knowledge should become as common to us, and as usable, as the multiplication table. Someone must pioneer it, begin to teach it.

God the Father gave Jesus *"to be the head over all things to the church, which is his body, the fulness of him that filleth all in all"* (Ephesians 1:22–23).

We are the fullness of Him.

John 1:16 says, *"Of his fulness have all we received."*

The same thing is brought out in Colossians 2:9–10: *"For in him dwelleth all the fulness of the Godhead bodily. And ye are complete in him, which is the head of all principality and power."*

He is not only our fullness, but we are His fullness.

The word "fullness" comes from a Greek word that is almost untranslatable: *pleroma,* which means *completeness,* perfection, or any other synonym that suggests fullness.

We have received of that fullness. That fullness has filled us. Can't you see what masters we are of demoniacal forces? They are beneath our feet.

"Thanks be unto God, which always causeth us to triumph in Christ" (2 Corinthians 2:14).

That is the hallelujah chorus of the new creation, and it never becomes real until we begin to confess it, begin to tell to the world what we are in Christ.

Hebrews 9:12 tells us that this is an eternal redemption. It is not just a redemption for the hour in which it was done, but that Satan is as much defeated now as he was when Christ arose from the dead, that he is as much a subject to the name of Jesus as he was when Jesus conquered him.

> *We do discuss "wisdom" with those who are mature; only it is not the wisdom of this world or of the dethroned Powers who rule this world.*
> (1 Corinthians 2:6 MOFF)

This wisdom for the mature, the full-grown, is something that we need to know about.

The great body of the church are in their infancy; they are mere babes in Christ.

Many of our leaders have never passed beyond that. They are still dominated by the senses. They are big men in the sense realm!

Sense knowledge has taken the church captive, bound our leaders and holds them captive.

Very little is known of spiritual wisdom and revelation in the knowledge of Him.

Colossians 1:9 is almost utterly unknown: "*That ye may be filled with the knowledge of his will in all wisdom and spiritual understanding.*"

Let's have that. That belongs to us.

There will never be a struggle after faith again.

Your prayer life will be like the Master's.

The sense of unworthiness that comes from sin-consciousness would be destroyed in that full knowledge, that *exact and perfect knowledge* of our redemption and righteousness in Christ.

He says we need this in order "*to walk worthily of the Lord unto all pleasing, bearing fruit in every good work, and increasing in the knowledge of God; strengthened with all power, according to the might of his glory, unto all patience and longsuffering with joy*" (Colossians 1:10–11 ASV)

What mighty men of God that would make!

Notice the twelfth verse: "*Giving thanks unto the Father, who made us meet* [fit] *to be partakers of the inheritance of the saints in light.*"

We have passed out of the babyhood state, out of the adolescent period, into full manhood and womanhood in Christ.

What prayer bands it would make, when we know the reality of the next two verses:

> *Who delivered us out of the power of darkness, and translated us into the kingdom of the Son of his love; in whom we have our redemption, the forgiveness of our sins.* (Colossians 1:13–14 ASV)

Notice what that means. If you are conscious of a perfect redemption from Satan's dominion, you will walk with a sureness that Jesus had in His earth walk.

That sureness comes from knowing that everything you had ever done, and all that you ever were, stopped being at the new creation.

All of your past has stopped being. You start anew.

Then if you make mistakes, you have the intercession of Jesus.

All you have to do is acknowledge your mistake and it is wiped out instantly, and your fellowship is restored.

You have been delivered out of the authority of Satan. Satan has no authority or legal right to reign over you.

You are the absolute master of satanic forces in the name of Jesus.

You are now in the kingdom of the Son of the Father's love.

We are masters there.

We are conquerors.

I want you to see that you hold exactly the same position that Paul held, and you have a right to do as is recorded in Colossians 1:28 (ASV): "*Admonishing every man and teaching every man in all wisdom, that we may present every man perfect in Christ.*" He is speaking here of the new creation man.

Now notice the next verse: "*Whereunto I labor also, striving according to his working, which worketh in me mightily.*"

For it is God who is at work within you, willing and working His own good pleasure.

You see this combat is not ours. It is His combat. He did it for us.

He is doing a mighty work in us, and a mighty work through us in helping others.

In Ephesians 1:3–5 (MOFF) is a picture of a God-planned and a God-executed redemption and new creation. It is a God-sized work.

> *Blessed be the God and Father of our Lord Jesus Christ who in Christ has blessed us with every spiritual blessing in the heavenly sphere! He chose us in him ere the world was founded, to be consecrated and unblemished in his sight, destining us in love to be his sons through Jesus Christ.*

Go over that again.

Let it soak into your very being that way back yonder, before the foundation of the world, God planned to have us. We are the products of that plan.

And when the fullness of time came, He said to the great heathen world, "Whosoever will may come and become a member of my foreplanned family."

It is "whosoever will," and you have answered that call; you are a member of that holy body that can stand in His presence without the sense of guilt or condemnation.

You have been blessed with every spiritual blessing, purchased in the redemptive work of His Son.

It is all yours.

These riches require no faith to enjoy.

They belong to us as much as the money that was given to us by some loved one.

He tells us in the sixth verse that it was freely bestowed upon us in the Beloved.

Not grudgingly, not scantily, but it was according to the riches of His grace.

Notice this verse: *"In whom we have redemption through his blood, the forgiveness of sins, according to the riches of his grace"* (Ephesians 1:7).

How can you be a weakling?

How can you act like the ignorant and untaught?

Can't you see your place now?

You must glorify Him by taking your place in Christ.

Never think of faith again. This all belongs to you.

Never think of your worthiness, for He is your righteousness.

Don't think of your ability, because *He* is your ability.

Swing free then.

Come out into all the fullness of His marvelous grace.

Enjoy your rights and take your place and fill His heart with joy.

God *"hath raised us up together, and made us sit together in heavenly places in Christ Jesus"* (Ephesians 2:6).

Think of yourself as seated with Him.

We do as Paul did when he cast the demon out of the insane girl, saying, *"I command thee in the name of Jesus Christ to come out of her"* (Acts 16:18).

How we should praise Him for this ability!

We are masters.

We are overcomers.

We reign with Him.

Can't you see what a background this is for a prayer life that will shake the very throne of darkness?

Think of your enemies as beneath your feet, conquered and defeated.

Stop your trying.

This is grace. All is yours.

Take your place.

Circumstances drive us to God in prayer.

The Word gives us faith to come boldly to Him.

His name assures us that He hears our prayer.

Your enemies are filled with malignity and hatred, and will seek to make it unpleasant for you, but you are master of them.

You don't have to fight them.

Your fight is a faith fight, described in Ephesians 6:12: *"We wrestle not against flesh and blood, but against principalities, against powers, against the rulers of the darkness of this world, against spiritual wickedness in high places."*

We are their masters, and we conquer them with words.

Jesus cast out demons with words.

He healed the sick with words.

He hushed the sea with words.

And He gave us the ability to use words, His words, His own name, which has all authority.

Thus we do as Peter did at the temple's Beautiful gate; we say, *"In the name of Jesus Christ of Nazareth rise up and walk"* (Acts 3:6).

FORGETTING WHAT MANNER OF MAN HE IS

> *If any be a hearer of the word, and not a doer, he is like unto a man beholding his natural face in a glass: for he beholdeth himself, and goeth his way, and straightway forgetteth what manner of man he was.*
>
> (James 1:23–24)

The new creation man, unless he has made a careful study of what he is in Christ, in the time of stress or a crisis will forget what "manner of man" he is.

We have lived so long in the realm of the senses that it is difficult for us to realize what we are in Christ.

We unconsciously lapse into the old life, seeing ourselves as we *were*, and not as we *are*.

Ephesians 1:7–9 is not a workable reality for many:

> *In whom we have redemption through his blood, the forgiveness of sins, according to the riches of his grace; wherein he hath abounded toward us in all wisdom and prudence; having made known unto us the mystery of his will, according to his good pleasure which he hath purposed in himself.*

This Scripture is almost an unknown quantity.

Note the first sentence: *"In whom"*—that is, in Christ—*"we have redemption."* It is redemption from Satan's dominion, from Satan's authority, for He has *"translated us into the kingdom of the Son of his love"* (Colossians 1:13 ASV). Jesus has become our new Lord, our love Master; He is our caretaker, the guarantor of our ability to reign over the forces that once dominated us.

We have (a present-tense fact) our redemption from fear and the cause of fear, and we are now not only delivered, but we have become masters where once we were held in bondage.

There has been a remission of all our past trespasses, and that remission has been according to the riches of His grace.

That is an unfathomable expression of love.

Who knows what *the riches of His grace* means to us! And He made this abound toward us in all wisdom, for Christ has been made wisdom unto us.

That is a strange expression. We have the wisdom to face life's problems with prudence, and this wisdom and prudence and ability of God is His will toward us.

At first, I couldn't take it in. Then I saw it.

I am His son. I must act the part of a son. I must take the place of a son. I must do the work of a son.

Then I'll need prudence. I'll need wisdom. I'll need His ability to face every contingency.

This is something I possess. I need no faith to obtain it. Prayer is not necessary, for it is mine.

How often since this possession came to me I have forgotten what manner of man I was.

For the moment I have acted like a "mere man," a very babe.

Sense knowledge throws her dark mantle over my spirit, and I forget Him and His ability.

I forget the name and its authority.

I forget that "greater is He that is in me than he that is in the world." (See 1 John 4:4.)

And I question for a moment.

Then He brings back to me what I am in Christ, and I joyously take my place.

Ofttimes, we forget our righteousness. He has made us to be His righteousness in Christ. (See 2 Corinthians 5:21.)

The adversary would make us forget this, and sense knowledge would cause us to doubt our worthiness and our ability to stand in His presence.

It would make us say, "Oh, if I only had faith," when faith is not needed, for He *"hath blessed us with every spiritual blessing in the heavenly places in Christ"* (Ephesians 1:3 ASV).

We are rich with His riches.

We are strong with His strength in the inward man.

We should make it a business to affirm constantly what we are in Christ. Every believer should make out a list on a little card or in a notebook of what he is in Christ. Then read it over and over.

Start with the fact that in Him, I have my redemption.

In Him, I am a new creation, and Satan has no dominion over me.

Jesus alone is my Lord.

I am the righteousness of God in Christ.

I have as much a right in Jesus's presence, or as much a right in the Father's presence, as Jesus has in His Father's presence.

And I have a standing invitation to the throne room to come boldly and take my place as a son. I need to remember this so that I will never disgrace Him by acting like a "mere man" or by forgetting what manner of man I am.

I should remind myself that I have fellowship with Him; that I am a sharer in the burdens He has, as He is a sharer in mine.

I should remind myself that I am a member of the fruit-bearing body of Christ.

I should never allow myself to forget what manner of man He made me.

I should remember that it is God who is at work within me, willing and working His own good pleasure.

That takes me out of the old life. I may be in the old surroundings. There may be everything about me as it was before, but this inward man of the heart has been recreated.

The real man has been made in the image of my Father God; and I have the use of the name of Jesus; and I have my Father's ability to meet life's problems as they are.

9

PRAYER AND THE CHURCH

Every church should have a prayer program. There should be a prayer organization, as well as the young people's or the Sunday school organization. The prayer life of the church should be so interwoven with every feature of it that God could be seen in every department.

The finances are called the sinews of the church, but this is not true.

Prayer forms the real sinews of the church.

You remember that the prayer life brings those who pray into vital contact with the Father, the Son, and the Holy Spirit, as well as continually in touch with the Word.

It isn't just saying prayers, but meeting Him for a while, getting His mind for the day, His strength, His quietness, and His love.

This vital contact has certain spiritual reactions that are of inestimable value to the life of the church.

We all know what it will mean when a great number of the people in the church enlist in a prayer program and come in vital contact with the Lord daily.

Every man and woman in connection with our church who is not spending time in prayer will be a neutralizing force in the church.

They may be in the choir, they may be in the Sunday school, they may have charge of the finances, or they may act as deacons or elders, but whatever their place, they carry a certain coldness; they are an inert body.

They have a tendency to lower the spiritual temperature of everyone in close contact with them.

So it is vitally important that the largest possible number of the membership should be led into the prayer program of the church.

This isn't any place for theory.

This is the place for positive facts.

A church can't be built up spiritually without prayer.

Numbers can be drawn through personal work or by eloquence, but to build up a real spiritual body is only possible through prayer.

This will need much wise teaching on the part of the pastor, and the teachers of adult classes.

Give prayer a large place in your church program. Don't only teach about prayer, but practice it.

Have prayer services with a real program. Give subjects for definite intercession.

While one intercedes, train the rest to make that prayer theirs, not by shouting loud amens, but silently making that intercession their very own.

The whole group will be crowding into the throne room, making that request as their own.

You can educate the people so that their prayers will prevail.

Make them prayer masters, mighty in intercession.

THE PRAYER PROBLEM

The prayer problem is a problem of faith; and faith is a problem of the integrity of the Word, of the ability of God to stand behind His promises or the statements of fact in the Word.

There is another side of the problem: the ability of the believer to stand in the Father's presence without the sense of guilt, condemnation, or inferiority.

After we know that the Word cannot be broken and that God keeps it to the very letter, the real question is, "Have I a right to stand in the Father's presence and make my petitions known to Him without condemnation?"

Here are a few things that every believer should know.

First, that we are actually new creations, created in Christ Jesus.

> *Therefore if any man be in Christ, he is a new creature [or creation]: old things are passed away; behold, all things are become new. And all things are of God, who hath reconciled us to himself by Jesus Christ.*
> (2 Corinthians 5:17–18)

Notice these facts, that *"if any man be in Christ."* One is in Christ once for all. He doesn't enter Christ and then leave Him. If he leaves Him, it is final.

The second fact: he is a new creation, a new species.

He has received into his spirit the life and nature of God.

"Old things are passed away." These old things are spiritual death, his union with Satan, and his old sins—the sins committed while he was spiritually in union with the adversary. These are remitted.

A new self is given to him.

The old self, or the old man, stops being; for the old self, or the old man as it is called, cannot live in Christ.

Notice again, if any man is in Christ, he is a new creature, a new creation, and the old things are passed away.

That new creation is the product of God.

It is created in Christ Jesus.

It is born from above.

It is born of the Holy Spirit, through the Word.

And that new creation stands uncondemned and reconciled before the Father.

Second Corinthians 5:21 (ASV) states it clearly: *"Him who knew no sin he* [God] *made to be sin on our behalf; that we might become the righteousness of God in him."*

The moment that we become new creations, we become the righteousness of God.

The righteousness of God means the ability to stand in the Father's presence without the sense of guilt, condemnation, or inferiority.

We are, in that moment, sons and daughters of God.

It would be an abnormal thing if He should recreate us, impart to us His own nature, and leave us under the blighting curse of condemnation, unable to stand in His presence without the sense of guilt and inferiority.

Then we know we have the ability to stand in God's presence free from all sense of unworthiness.

We know the second fact that we have a legal right in the Father's presence because we are legally born into His family, and He has legally adopted us and accepted us as sons. *"The Spirit himself beareth witness with our spirit, that we are children of God"* (Romans 8:16 ASV).

We know another fact: that we have a legal right to the use of Jesus's name and whatsoever we ask of the Father in that name, He'll grant us.

This has cleared up every issue in regard to our ability to stand before Him in the throne room without condemnation.

Sin has been preached to us so long and we have been told so often that we are unworthy and unfit, that it has kept us with a sense of inferiority, which has been destructive to a faith life.

No man can walk with God as long as he is under condemnation.

You can see now that prayer is based on legal grounds; not based on promises only but on statements of fact.

It isn't a problem then of faith with the believer, for all things belong to him. *"Blessed be the God and Father of our Lord Jesus Christ, who hath blessed us with all spiritual blessings in heavenly places in Christ"* (Ephesians 1:3).

You cannot grasp this too clearly, that it is not a problem of faith with us as sons and daughters of God.

It is merely a problem of our taking our place, enjoying our rights.

God has blessed us with every spiritual blessing.

Then everything that was wrought in the finished work of Christ belongs to us. It is our own property this moment.

All our struggling to get faith has been the result of ignorance of what belonged to us.

Now we must simply take our place, use our rights.

But someone says, "What about the struggle with the adversary?"

Yes, we have war with a defeated enemy.

Satan was defeated before Jesus arose from the dead.

We were crucified with Christ, died with Christ, buried with Christ, suffered with Christ, justified with Christ, made alive with Christ, and conquered the adversary with Christ. Then we were raised together with Him, and now we are seated together with Him.

That shows us our utter oneness and union with Christ.

It shows what our combat with the adversary was when we conquered Satan with Christ before He arose from the dead.

Everything that Jesus did is accredited to us.

The entire substitutionary work of Christ was for us.

He didn't conquer Satan for Himself.

He didn't put sin away for Himself.

He didn't suffer the judgment that would have fallen upon the sinner for Himself.

But He suffered it on our behalf, and we have entered into His victory; it is accredited to us. So Satan now is a defeated enemy.

We war not with flesh and blood, not with humans, but with demons who know that we are, in Jesus's name, their masters.

Every demon knows that you, the recreated one, are his master.

They rule us by subterfuge, by bluff, by deception.

They put diseases upon us and hold us in bondage through our ignorance of what we are in Christ and what belongs to us.

HAVE YOUR OWN FAITH

One should never trust the great issues of his life to another's faith. He should have faith of his own, faith that can meet any crisis that may come.

Your case is vital to you. It may not be vital to this other party to whose faith you look. He may have troubles that are unsolved, inward struggles that have never been settled. His faith may be at a low ebb when you appeal to him for aid.

It is vitally important to you that you have your own faith to fall back on in these hard places.

Everyone should build his own faith life.

I find that the majority of people float on carelessly until they come to a dangerous place. They are sick, or some loved one is sick, or some financial or heart problem confronts them that may affect their entire future. Then they frantically hunt for someone who can cry and sob and quote Scriptures in what they call their "prayer" and it is of no avail because there is no faith behind it.

If there was faith there, there would be no crying and no sobbing. There would be a rejoicing because they would know that whatever they ask of the Father in Jesus's name, He will do it.

Here are some facts that will help you to begin to build your own faith life.

The Word is yours. It is as though there was no other person in the world but you, and this revelation had been given especially to you; you can say, "It is mine. No one has a better right to it than I have. Every promise is mine. Every statement of fact is mine."

When He said, "*Whatsoever ye shall ask the Father in my name, he will give it to you*" (John 16:23), you can say, "He was talking to me."

You can say, "He is my Father; I am His child. This is His message to me to help me in my earth walk. John 15:7–8 was given by the Master from the Father to me, for He said, 'The words that I speak are not mine, but the Father is speaking through me.'

"Consequently, it is the Father who said, "If ye abide in Christ, and His words abide in you, ask whatsoever ye will, and it shall be done unto you. Herein am I glorified, that ye bear much fruit.' This is prayer fruit. It is going to be borne by one of the branches, and I am that branch."

When your heart can speak like this, then you know that when you approach the throne of grace, there is a willing ear, listening to you, that whatever you ask, you will receive because the Word is living in you.

Do you understand what that means? A lover has written you a letter. It is not written to anyone else. It is too sacred for any other eyes to see. That is your letter. That is your lover writing to you.

God is love and He has written to you the book called the Bible. Jesus came to unveil love, and the revelation of love is given to us in the Word.

Jesus now has spoken a love message to you. He says, *"If ye abide in me."* If you are a new creation, you certainly do abide in Him. His words abide in you just as that lover's words would abide in your heart.

You go over that lover's words again and again. He has asked you to become his companion for life. How sacred is that letter. It is love's own message to your heart. Love has spoken to you.

Love says, "If ye abide in me, and my words have found their place in you, you can ask what you will, and I will see that you get it."

THE HOLY SPIRIT IS YOURS

The Holy Spirit belongs to you.

Luke 11:13 says, *"How much more shall your heavenly Father give the Holy Spirit to them that ask him?"* Only sons and daughters will ever ask Him.

You are His child. You have received His very nature. You are as really His child as was Jesus when He walked in Galilee.

Then you have a right to the Spirit. You can ask Him to come in and make His home in your body; as surely as you ask Him, so surely will He come in, because *"no word from God shall be void of power"* (Luke 1:37 ASV). The Word of God is very sacred to Him.

Jeremiah 1:12 (ASV) says, *"I watch over my word to perform it."*

This is His message to you. It is the lover again speaking to His beloved and saying, "Do you wish the Holy Spirit to make His home in your body? If you do, just invite Him in, for He is standing at the door awaiting your invitation. If you ask Him in, He will enter, then guide you into all the reality of the finished work wrought by Jesus."

More than that, you can confidently say, "His righteousness is mine for He was made unto me righteousness. I have become, through the new birth, the very righteousness of God in Christ. My righteousness is just as good as Jesus's righteousness because it is Jesus's righteousness. It is just as good as Paul, or Peter, or John had. No one has a better righteousness than I."

When I realize that, faith is no longer a problem.

The Word is mine. The Holy Spirit is mine. Jesus is mine. God is my own Father. Their righteousness is my righteousness. I stand complete in their completeness.

I am a new creation, created in Christ Jesus. All the rights and privileges of a child are mine. I did not have to ask for them. They were conferred upon me. When I became His child, these things were a part of the new creation so I enter into my rights.

SATAN'S DEFEAT

One of the greatest blessings, one of the most wonderful facts, is that Satan was defeated for me.

Jesus's victory over him is my victory.

When I was redeemed in Christ, that redemption was out of the hand of the enemy.

I have been translated out of the kingdom of Satan, into the kingdom of the Son of the Father's love, in whom I have my redemption, complete and perfect.

Then I do not have to war to conquer Satan, because Satan is already conquered.

Satan was conquered for me. He knows that he was conquered for me, so I take my deliverance from him and my victory over him in Jesus's name, with thankfulness.

I know that Satan is the author of disease and confusion and heart suffering. I know that Jesus said, "In My name, you shall cast out demons." (See Mark 16:17.) When Jesus said that, He was saying it to me. He was talking to me personally.

He said, "In My name, you shall cast out demons. Do you understand what that means to you?"

I asked for Him to tell me. He said, "It means that you, personally, rule Satan, and his works—that demons are subject to you. Just as demons are subject to Me, and disease and physical needs, and financial needs are all subject to Me, they are subject to you.

"Remember how I paid Peter's poll tax? Remember how I fed the multitudes? Do you remember how I walked upon the sea? Do you remember how

I turned water into wine? Now I am turning over to you this authority over the adversary.

"Not only that, but I am turning over to you the ability to use this authority, for this ability has been given unto Me in heaven and on earth. Now I want you to use this ability. I am turning it over to you. That ability will teach you how to use this authority that has been delegated to you to use My name. In this ability is My wisdom, My ability.

"The Holy Spirit is to bring that ability into you through My Word. You go now and use this delegated authority with My own ability, for I am your sufficiency to meet every need and every crisis of your life."

It is just as though Jesus stood in the room and said this to you. Not only this—and it seems as though this were enough—but He has given you a legal right to the use of the name of Jesus.

You can say, "I have the power of attorney to use the name of Jesus. Jesus declared that all authority in heaven and on earth were His. That authority then is enwrapped in His name. It is a part of His name, and He has given me a legal right to use it— the power of attorney.

"Now I can destroy the works of the adversary. I can set men free. Now I can break the power and dominion of disease and demons over the bodies, hearts, and minds of men.

"Now I can actually take Jesus's place and do His works. I can understand what He meant now when He said, 'Greater works than these shall ye do because I go unto the Father.' (See John 14:12.) I have His own Word for it.

"I have the same Spirit who raised Jesus from the dead within me.

"I have the same righteousness that Jesus had, because He is that righteousness.

"I rejoice in the fact of Satan's defeat on my behalf.

"I have the name of Jesus. God is my own Father. What more could I ask? But that is not all. I am His own child. I do not have to try to be His child. I am. I am born of His Spirit. I am a partaker of His nature, eternal life.

"His Word has given me absolute assurance of my relationship with Him; so fearlessly I make my confession to the world. I am a child of God. I am a new creation. I am an heir of God, and a joint-heir with Jesus Christ.

"He loves me even as He loved Jesus. His home is my home. When I finish my work here, if Jesus tarries, I will go to my Father's home for it is my home.

"These great soul-thrilling facts have given birth to a real faith in my own heart.

"I have my own faith now. I have confidence in my faith. I know that whatever I ask of the Father in Jesus's name, He will give it to me. I know I have authority over all the authority of the enemy in Jesus's name."

10

A STUDY IN FAITH

The reason faith is so difficult is that sense knowledge has gained the ascendancy in our educational and religious life. Sense knowledge has all come through our physical contact with the world.

We have learned to trust so utterly in our eyes and our ears, and the senses of touch, smell, and taste, that spiritual things are hard to understand.

It is easy to believe in things you see.

The crowd said about Jesus, "We see the miracles; now we believe in thee." (See John 6:14.)

Thomas fell down at His feet when he saw the wounded side and the holes in His hands and feet. He said, "Lord, I believe." Jesus said, "Blessed are they who have not seen, yet believe." (See John 20:28–29.) The Master touched the heart of things there.

Faith is independent of sense knowledge.

The antagonism of the scholastic world to the revelation called the Bible is that the Bible demands faith in things the senses cannot apprehend.

Hebrews 11:3 tells us that the worlds have been framed by faith through the Word of God. "*Through faith we understand that the worlds were framed by the word of God, so that things which are seen were not made of things which do appear.*"

That explains the first verse, "*Now faith is the substance of things hoped for, the evidence of things not seen*" (Hebrews 11:1), or, "Faith is giving substance to things hoped for."

Hope is not faith.

Faith is always now.

Hope is always future.

God said, *"Let there be,"* and the sun, moon, and stars came into being. (See Genesis 1.)

He said, "Let there be an earth," and the earth came into being.

He said, *"Let there be light"* (Genesis 1:3), and there was light. It was a warm light that encircled the whole earth and made it a subtropical garden, out of which have come our coal fields, oil, chemicals, and minerals.

Then He said, *"Let the earth bring forth"* (Genesis 1:11), and the earth brought forth.

He said, "Let the animals come," and the animals came.

Faith is the mightiest force in the universe.

It is the creative ability of God.

It is the creative ability of man.

Animals act by instinct, not faith.

Man acts by faith.

Man was created in the image and likeness of the faith of God.

He is created in the image of love. He is created in the image of faith.

Whether you recognize it or not, man's entire life, from the time he becomes conscious as a babe, until he steps off into the unknown, is a faith life; one has faith in his senses, the other in God.

When man loses faith, life has lost its objective.

Great financiers are faith men.

Frank W. Woolworth had faith in five- and ten-cent pieces.

Henry Ford had faith in an automobile.

Thomas Edison had faith in electricity.

Faith is the thing that brings success.

Doubt is the thing that brings failure.

The educational institution that teaches doubt becomes the unconscious enemy of civilization.

The modern trend of sense knowledge has been toward agnosticism.

The agnostic possesses the proud confession of "I do not know."

Atheism says that God does not exist.

The two of them are twin enemies of success and mental spiritual progress of the age.

The agnostic makes no contribution but confusion.

God is love. He works by faith. It is faith that works by love.

He is the faith God.

Man is the crowning work of faith.

Being created in the image of love, he must live by faith.

Man is a faith creation.

When reason usurps the seat of faith, man becomes a failure.

Let us now consider what faith in the spiritual realm can mean.

SOME REALITIES

The bolder the faith, the greater is the success.

Faith wins.

When faith dies, success folds its wings.

We can take this as our slogan of life: *"But with God all things are possible"* (Matthew 19:26).

Unite this with these Scriptures: *"All things are possible to him that believeth"* (Mark 9:23), and *"Greater is he that is in you, than he that is in the world"* (1 John 4:4).

Who is in you? It is God!

Then to the God who is within you, all things are possible.

If you give that God within you liberty, let Him loose in you, you become limitless in your realm.

"All things are possible to him that believeth." The Greek word here for "believe" means "a believing one."

That is a child of God, a believing one.

You and God are linked together. You become invincible.

You see a glimpse of this in Martin Luther's ministry.

We saw it in John Alexander Dowie.

We have seen it in individuals here and there, God and man linked together, doing the impossible.

We know that every step out of love means sin.

We know that every step out of faith means weakness and failure.

The word *believing* is a verb. The word *faith* is a noun.

Believing is acting on the Word.

Faith is the result of this action.

Jesus acted on the Word of His Father. He said, "The words that I speak to you are not mine but my Father's." (See John 14:10.)

All His works were a result of His words.

Matthew 8:5–13 gives us a record of the centurion. He said to Jesus, "*Speak the word only, and my servant shall be healed*" (verse 8).

Jesus spoke the Word.

The healing of the lepers, the healing of the woman with the issue of blood, and the healing of the paralyzed man are miracles performed by His word.

Matthew 14:23–33 is the story of Peter's walking on the waves.

Peter said, "*If it be thou, bid me come*" (verse 28). Jesus simply said one word, "Come." When He did, the waters sustained the weight of Peter.

Again we see Jesus quieting the sea with His Word. He simply said, "*Peace, be still*" (Mark 4:39).

Jesus's faith was in His Word.

Acts 3:1–11 gives us a picture of Peter's faith in the name of Jesus on his lips. "*Then Peter said, Silver and gold have I none; but such as I have give I thee: In the name of Jesus Christ of Nazareth rise up and walk*" (verse 6). The lifelong cripple became well and strong.

Acts 20:9–12 is the story of a young man falling out of the third-floor window and "*taken up dead. And Paul went down, and fell on him, and embracing him said, Trouble not yourselves; for his life is in him. When he therefore was come up again, and had broken bread, and eaten, and talked a long while, even till break of day, so he departed. And they brought the young man alive, and were not a little comforted."*

It was the name of Christ on the lips of Paul that raised the lad from the dead.

Faith, then, is acting and speaking the Word of God.

Sense knowledge speaks the word of man, and faith speaks the Word of God.

Sense knowledge man acts upon sense knowledge.

The faith man acts upon the Word of God.

Faith is giving substance to the thing that you had long hoped would become real.

One translation of Hebrews 11:1 calls faith "the title deed."

Hope never gave a title deed, but faith is the title deed.

When you believe the Word, anxiety and fear leave you.

As long as you hope, you will be filled with anxiety and worry.

"Jesus answered them, 'Have faith in God!'" (Mark 11:22 MOFF), or "Have the faith of God."

It is Jesus's challenge for us to have the God kind of faith. He had it.

> *Verily I say unto you, Whosoever shall say unto this mountain, Be thou taken up and cast into the sea; and shall not doubt in his heart, but shall believe that what he saith cometh to pass; he shall have it.*
>
> (Mark 11:23 ASV)

There are two things to notice: He believes in His heart, and He believes in His words.

You believe in your heart, and then you believe in the words on your lips.

That gives you power over demons and disease and circumstances.

> *All things whatsoever ye pray and ask for, believe that ye receive them, and ye shall have them.* (Mark 11:24 ASV)

They have not been in your possession, but it is just as real as though they were.

Faith counts the things that are not as though they were.

In Romans 4:17, faith counted the things that were not as though they were and they became.

Abraham counted that Sarah was able to give birth to a child when she was ninety years of age, and she became the mother of Isaac.

Abraham believed that his body would be rejuvenated, and it was.

Romans 4:19–21 (ASV) is God's commentary on this:

> *And without being weakened in faith he considered his own body now as good as dead (he being about a hundred years old), and the deadness of Sarah's womb; yet, looking unto the promise of God, he wavered not through unbelief, but waxed strong through faith, giving glory to God, and being fully assured that what he had promised, he was able also to perform.*

You can see the resistlessness, the absolute ability of faith.

Faith in you will conquer as faith in Jesus conquered.

Faith in your own words will drive disease out of sick men's bodies.

When you say, "In the name of Jesus, disease depart from this body," you have confidence in Jesus's words on your lips as Jesus had confidence in His Father's words on His lips, and the healing takes place.

Faith comes by daring to act upon the Word.

Your fear to act upon the Word is unbelief gaining the ascendency.

> *Verily I say unto you, Whatsoever ye shall bind on earth shall be bound in heaven: and whatsoever ye shall loose on earth shall be loosed in heaven.*
> (Matthew 18:18)

Here is God's challenge to united faith.

Every one of you should hunt for a partner who can believe with you, who can unite his faith with yours.

You become a resistless power the moment you do.

You may be mighty in faith alone, but you can be mightier in faith united with another.

> *He that believeth on me, the works that I do shall he do also; and greater works than these shall he do; because I go unto my Father. And whatsoever ye shall ask in my name, that will I do, that the Father may be glorified in the Son.* (John 14:12–13)

The word *ask* here in the Greek means "to demand."

You are not demanding it of Jesus, but you are demanding it as Peter demanded the man at the beautiful gate to rise and walk.

You are demanding sickness and pain to leave bodies in the name of Jesus.

He said, "*That the Father may be glorified in the Son.*"

> *If ye abide in me, and my words abide in you, ye shall ask what ye will, and it shall be done unto you.* (John 15:7)

Satan has taken advantage of you. Disease and sickness have made an invalid out of you.

Circumstances have gained the mastery and made a slave instead of a master of you.

Now you abide in Him, and let His Word abide in you.

Let that Word abide on your lips and contend with your sickness and you will become the master again.

You simply insist that that thing is not for you.

You will not stand for defeat any longer.

You can look the adversary in the face and say, with quiet assurance, "Satan, you are defeated. In Jesus's name, I demand my rights."

> *Hitherto have ye asked nothing in my name: ask, and ye shall receive, that your joy may be full.* (John 16:24)

Your joy cannot be made full while loved ones are sick, while men and women are captives of the adversary.

Your joy cannot be made full unless you can see the will of the Father wrought in the lives of men and women around you.

Go, then, and take what belongs to you in that name.

11

THE FAILURE OF THE HOPER

This is one of the most beautiful types of spiritual failures that is known. So many have mistaken hope for faith. They had a confused idea that if they hoped strongly enough, they could bring the desired thing to them. They didn't know that hope was future.

There are two Scriptures in Romans that will assist us.

> *(As it is written, I have made thee a father of many nations,) before him whom he believed, even God, who quickeneth* [gives life to] *the dead, and calleth those things which be not as though they were. Who against hope believed in hope, that he might become the father of many nations, according to that which was spoken.* (Romans 4:17–18)

Here was a strange combat: faith warring with hope.

Hope wins in most cases, but hope lost here.

Abraham counted the thing for which he had hoped to be his own, and he resolutely put hope aside and claimed the son that God had promised.

But the eighth chapter of Romans throws more light upon it:

> *For we are saved by hope: but hope that is seen is not hope: for what a man seeth, why doth he yet hope for? But if we hope for that we see not, then do we with patience wait for it.* (Romans 8:24–25)

Again, Hebrews 11:1, "*Now faith is the substance of things hoped for, the evidence of things not seen.*" The *Centenary Translation of the New Testament* by Helen Barrett Montgomery gives this translation: "*Faith is the title deed of things hoped for; the putting to the proof of things not seen.*"

Believing is action. Faith is the cause of the action.

You can see that in this: "Faith is giving substance to things hoped for."

It is bringing into the present tense things that were in the future for us—so we can see that hope is never *now*.

If I hope for my healing and only have a hope, the undertaker will have a job.

Now a man's investments are all in the future. He bought stocks hoping for a rise. He bought a piece of land hoping that he might sell it in the future to advantage.

Hope has no present-tense blessing. The hoper lives on hopes. The Word is loved, admired, but not acted upon.

The hoper is merely an assenter to the Word. He admires it, knows it is true, will suffer for his convictions of the utter truthfulness of this revelation, but he does not act upon it.

We have many able Bible teachers who are mere hopers or assenters of the Word. Good people, but they have never enjoyed the realities of the things that belong to them. Many of them will act on their creed, but they will not act on the Word.

Often, they are assenters to the verbal inspiration. They think all the time that they are believers.

You understand that the believer is a possessor. *"He that believeth hath eternal life"* (John 6:47 ASV). He who hopes has not yet arrived.

He who hopes may possess sometime, but not now.

The hoper is a present-tense failure as far as the realities of the Word are concerned. He may be a beautiful failure, but he is a failure.

He fails in the midst of rosy hopes. The fragrance of dead hopes fills the air. He fails because he only hopes.

Abraham believed in spite of hope, and brushing hope aside, grasped the thing that God had promised.

Many people are in bondage to faith's most dangerous enemy.

Faith is giving substance to that for which we vainly hoped.

Hope has no substance. It is an empty cloud.

Hope deludes the lost; it deludes the sick and the defeated.

There is no hope for the hoper if he remains a hoper.

Prayer that is based on hope is sure to fail.

Salvation that is based on hope never comes to maturity.

The sick person who hopes for healing remains sick.

Let us change hope into faith as Abraham did. Then life will be a success.

Jesus was God speaking. How solemn is that statement. It is pregnant with a challenge from the very throne of God.

He was not only the Word, He was the living Word. He was the miracle-performing Word. He was the death-destroying Word. He was the life-giving Word.

He said, "I am come that you might have life." (See John 10:10.) That life was the nature of God, and that nature of God was in His Word.

When He said in Matthew 24:35, *"My words shall not pass away,"* it was simply a statement of fact, just as in 1 Peter 1:23 (MOFF), *"the living, lasting word of God."* It lives, and it lives in me, this living *logos*, the life-giving Word of God.

And hear Him whisper, "I watch over this Word to see that it is performed."

Can't you see how safe it is to trust this living Word?

God speaks, then sets a watch over it to see that it is made good as we trust it or act upon it.

Colossians 3:16 says, *"Let the word of Christ dwell in you."*

It dwells in you in the measure that you practice it. You may have it committed to memory, but if you do not practice it, it doesn't dwell in you.

Revelation 12:11 says, *"And they overcame him by the blood of the Lamb, and by the word* [logos] *of their testimony."* That Greek word *logos* is Jesus; and they overcame the devil with Jesus on their lips.

"My God shall supply all your need according to his riches in glory by Christ Jesus" (Philippians 4:19). That is the *logos* of God on my lips. I stand by it. That is my confession and I maintain it. That is His statement of fact and He stands by it. He meets the need!

First Peter 2:24 says, *"Who his own self bare our sins in his body upon the tree, that we, being dead to sins, should live unto righteousness: by whose stripes ye were healed."* That is a little blind to us. Read it like this: "That we having died unto sins might live in the power of His righteousness that has been imparted to us." Then I can act on the Word, *"by whose stripes ye were healed."*

I know that the Word is true. I do not ask Him to heal me, because I am healed. I simply stand by my confession that I am what He says I am.

Stand by your prayers when you have used His Word on your lips. Don't go back on the spoken word from your own lips. You spoke His Word; that was as though He had spoken it.

You said to the Father, "In Jesus's name, I take this, I take the salvation of this loved one."

He has given you a legal right to the use of His name. You hand that name back to Him with your request.

THE DANGER OF SEEKING EXPERIENCES

She said, "I know it is true for I experienced it."

It isn't a problem of whether the Word declared it or not. It isn't what the Word says, but what our experience says.

Faith in our experiences is not always faith in the Word. Faith in what I have seen or heard is not always faith in the Word.

Practically all religious experiences are products of the physical senses. It is something felt or heard or seen.

Sense experience always leaves one empty when the experience grows old.

Seeking experiences is always dangerous for it is trusting in the arm of the flesh rather than in the Word, because experiences are always connected with the senses.

Sense experiences are fascinating to a soul-hungry man.

They attract the curious.

They are always in the realm where most folks live.

One of the unfortunate things about seeking experiences is that those who are seeking are in the realm that is governed by evil spirits, for Satan rules most people's bodies, the home of practically all of our experiences.

That is the reason that so many have lost their minds; for when people seek experiences for a long time, demons often take advantage and become their helpers.

They are not wrestling with God. It is not with the Word. They struggle with themselves to get their senses to function.

Sense experiences are always based on sense knowledge faith.

We should remember that sense knowledge always fails us in a crisis, and you will notice that the people who are depending on experiences are ever seeking to have the experience repeated.

They believe in experiences because they live in the realm of the senses.

They never believe the Word. They assent to it, or they hope in it.

Experience-seekers are always unstable in their faith.

The Word of God does not carry as much authority as the word of the person who has the experience.

These people are ever seeking faith.

They have continual war with doubts and fears and discouragements.

They will tell you that they are having a hard battle with the adversary.

Most of these people have rented a place at the altar.

They are perpetual seekers who long for experiences and power.

They are seeking their healing, not knowing that the Father laid their diseases on Jesus.

They are honest, but they are walking in the realm of the senses.

Their teachers are sense knowledge taught people.

They believe much about the Word, but they do not believe the Word itself.

They act on the word of man and it breaks under them.

They read much about the Bible and about experiences, but they do not study the Word systematically. Consequently, they are unstable and double-minded.

They are like people who take drugs or liquor. They are drunken with the senses.

If they could only know the sure Word, the unbroken Word, the living Word, the life-giving Word, the all-satisfying Word, they would give up their quest for experiences and let the Word satisfy them.

SEEKING MANIFESTATIONS

What kind of manifestations are they seeking? Something connected with their physical body.

They wish to speak in tongues.

They desire to go under the power.

They wish to have their body vibrate and shake.

They wish to see some physical demonstration of the Spirit's power. The Holy Spirit never gratifies them.

The only spirit that will gratify them is dangerous to play with.

But you ask, "Do you not believe in speaking in tongues?"

Yes, when the Holy Spirit speaks through you, it is beautiful.

But no one needs to wait and tarry for Him to do it, for the tarrying gives the adversary an opportunity to deceive them, and the people who are seeking this are not spiritually minded.

They will not know a demon from the Holy Spirit.

But you say, "Didn't the disciples tarry ten days?"

Yes, they waited until the fullness of time came for the Holy Spirit to come. From that day to this, there has been no need to tarry.

The Holy Spirit is here, and He will enter the body of any man or woman who invites Him in.

Luke 11:13 says, *"How much more shall your heavenly Father give the Holy Spirit to them that ask him?"*

You don't receive eternal life by tarrying and struggling for it. You receive eternal life by acting on the Word.

The same thing is true in regard to the Holy Spirit, and every other blessing that is promised in the Word.

Tarrying means that the Word isn't true, and you have to do something to add to its truthfulness, to its veracity.

Waiting before the Lord for power and for some special blessing that you have heard about is unnecessary because you have in you, if you have received the Holy Spirit, the fountain of all experiences.

You have invited the Holy Spirit to make His home in your body; and He said if you did, He would come in and occupy it.

Well, you have only one thing to do: that is to accept that statement of His as absolutely true, and thank Him—feeling or no feeling—that He has come into your body to make His home.

Now you allow Him to take over your life.

You are not passive, but you are insistent that He take you over; that He illumine your heart and your mind; that He will now guide you into all the reality of the redemptive work of Christ that belongs to you; and that He prove Himself to be greater in you than the forces of darkness that are around you.

He is the power of God, the mind of God, the ability of God, and He is in you.

But give Him place, honor Him, and treat Him with the utmost courtesy.

Become accustomed to talking with Him; He is your continual companion.

He is to guide you daily.

After a while, you will be able to say, "Is it right to do this?" and you will get a "yes" or a "no" in your spirit.

When you have a few minutes to study the Word, remember He is there. He will illumine it.

As you meditate, He will unveil to you the deeper, hidden meanings in the Word that are necessary in your spiritual life, or to those to whom you are ministering.

Act as though He were there.

Plan your work with a consciousness that greater is He that is in you than he that is in the world.

He is the one who can make Jesus wisdom unto you through the Word.

He can make the Word a living thing on your lips.

He gives you the ability to use Jesus's name so that all the authority that is in that name can be exercised by you.

Experiences are not spiritual realities always, but the Holy Spirit's presence in you, unveiling the Word, brings into your spirit consciousness realities of the highest value.

WE MUST NOT FAIL HIM

He has committed unto us the Word of grace.

He has committed unto us the Word of wisdom.

He has committed unto us His ability.

Have you ever taken notice of what you are in Christ? Of what you have, and of what you can do? Why, you are the very sons and daughters of God Almighty. You have His life and nature in you. You have the great mighty Holy Spirit who raised Jesus from the dead. What can you do? Measure it by the ability of God that is at work within you. Measure it by His own wonderful Word.

He knew what needs would face us when He was planning our redemption and when he was planning the new creation. I can hear Him say: "I'll identify Myself with them; I'll be in them; I'll work through them. My ability shall become their ability, My wisdom their wisdom. I won't let them fail. Through the Word, I will build Myself into them."

12

UNDERESTIMATING JESUS

One cannot conceive of anything that will cripple faith and put the believer in bondage more quickly and surely than underestimating what He is, and what we are in Him. Along with that will come an underestimation of the Word.

We will say right out, "Oh, I believe the Bible is the Word of God," and yet we turn to the arm of flesh for help.

And when we pray, we do not come with that quiet assurance that we would if some banker had given us his word in regard to our financial standing at the bank.

This is an unconscious underestimation of the Word, and it is an unconscious underestimation of the integrity of the Master Himself, who is the Author of this Word.

This leads to weakness, to doubt and fear.

It makes a vacillating type of faith.

We become what James calls "*a double minded man*" who is "*unstable in all his ways*" (James 1:8).

What will change it?

When we realize what He has done for us in His great substitution and in the new creation.

We should meditate on the fact that we are partakers of the divine nature. "*These things have I written unto you that believe on the name of the Son of God; that ye may know that ye have eternal life*" (1 John 5:13).

If we say over and over again to our hearts, "I am a partaker of God's very nature. I have in me His faith nature. This makes me a child of faith. I have been begotten of the living Word through the Holy Spirit. The real me was recreated in Christ. I have the very nature of the Father and the Father is love, so I have in me the love nature of the Father," and we meditate on this, we will no longer be "double-minded men."

Repeat it over and over again.

Hold it as a constant affirmation before your mind that you are what He says you are, that you are a partaker of His very nature as He has declared.

And you remember that *"greater is he that is in you, than he that is in the world"* (1 John 4:4). That greater One is the Holy Spirit.

The Holy Spirit is the one who, in creation, gave the color, the beauty, and fragrance to the flowers, to vegetation, to the trees. He is the one who takes of the nature of the Father, and through the Word, builds it into us.

He builds the beauty of Christ into our conduct.

He touches our reasoning faculties until the things that He has made in the floral world assume a new interest, and their beauty is enhanced and their fragrance enjoyed as never before.

I can remember the night that I received eternal life. It seemed as though I hardly touched the sidewalk on my way home. It was a cold winter night in January, but, oh, how beautiful the snow and the frost. Yes, the trees, stripped of their foliage, assumed a beauty I had never noted before.

The Holy Spirit had taken possession and was unveiling the wonders of His grace to me.

An underestimation of the Holy Spirit, of the Word, of Jesus, will keep us in a state of flux, in a realm of uncertainty.

Fear will dominate us; doubt will bind us and hold us in the realm of weakness.

But when we come to know Jesus as our Lord, as the mighty One at the right hand of the Father who ever lives to make intercession for us, our great lawyer who looks after every legal need of ours in Christ, we will no longer be dominated by fear and doubt.

We should come to know the reality of the Holy Spirit's reality, which is all unveiled to us in the Pauline revelation.

I urge you to go back and read Romans, and First and Second Corinthians again. Then abide a while in Ephesians, in those first three chapters especially, until you are lifted out of the realm of the senses into the realm of the new man in Christ Jesus.

WHAT HE MADE US

The fear of seeing what we are in Christ, and of acting as though we knew what we were, has kept us in bondage and robbed us of the reality of His finished work. How slow we have been to act what we are in Him. The Spirit, through the Word, has declared what we are in Christ, *"In whom we have redemption through his blood, the forgiveness of sins, according to the riches of his grace"* (Ephesians 1:7).

That is not a theological redemption. This is not Paul's philosophy. This is the Father's description of what we are in His Son, and He says, *"In whom we have redemption."*

From whom and what are we redeemed?

Satan is the god of darkness. We have been delivered out of Satan's dominion, out of the realm and authority of darkness. We have been delivered out of the dominion of sin, for Romans 6:14 says, *"Sin shall not have dominion over you."* We are delivered out of the authority of disease, for Romans 8:11 says, *"If the Spirit of him that raised up Jesus from the dead dwell in you, he that raised up Christ from the dead shall also quicken* [give life to] *your mortal bodies by his Spirit that dwelleth in you."*

Not only have we a redemption that is literal and absolute, but we are a new creation, and Satan has no dominion over us.

Jesus is the head and Lord of this new creation.

We have been taught so long and so persistently about our weaknesses, our lack of ability, and our unworthiness that we hardly dare say that we are what He says we are. We are afraid that people will misunderstand us and think that we have become fanatical.

But He says, *"There is a new creation whenever a man comes to be in Christ; what is old is gone, the new has come"* (2 Corinthians 5:17 MOFF), and we are reconciled to Him.

We are a part of His very dream.

Satan has no dominion over this new creation.

Ephesians 2:10 says we are created in Christ Jesus, that when Jesus arose from the dead, the work of the new creation was consummated in Christ. It became a reality in us when we took Him as our Savior and confessed Him as our Lord.

The Father in His Word has declared what we are in His Son. That declaration is the truth.

I may not have grown up to it, may not have appreciated it, but it stands there with an open door inviting me to enjoy all the fullness that is mine in Him.

He declares what we may do in the name of His Son. We haven't appreciated it perhaps, but He gave to us the power of attorney to use His Son's name.

Jesus said, *"Hitherto have ye asked nothing in my name: ask, and ye shall receive, that your joy may be full"* (John 16:24).

Seven times Jesus repeats this, giving us the legal right to the use of His name.

Philippians 2:9–11 tells us that God gave him *"a name which is above every name: that at the name of Jesus every knee should bow, of things in heaven, and things in earth, and things under the earth; and that every tongue should confess that Jesus Christ is Lord, to the glory of God the Father."*

Not only that, but Jesus said, after He arose from the dead, *"All authority hath been given unto me in heaven and on earth. Go ye therefore, and make disciples of all the nations"* (Matthew 28:18–19 ASV).

Disciple means a student, a learner. He never said, "Go and make converts." He never said, "Go and make churches." Jesus said, "Go and make disciples."

There will be schools of Christ. Every believer will be a student of this living Word. What masters they will be!

Not only do we have that power to use the name of Jesus to cast out demons, or to heal the sick, but that name gives us access to the Father, and is the absolute guarantee of answered prayer.

You see, this prayer life is based upon absolute knowledge.

It is not based upon emotion, nor feelings, nor the theories of men, but upon the living Word of God, this Word that *"liveth and abideth for ever"* (1 Peter 1:23).

When you know in your heart that you are what He says you are, then you act it in the face of all, confessing what He has done in you, confessing what He has made you. This glorifies Him and His Work.

To deny what we are, to tell what Satan is doing in our bodies and minds, is denying what we are in Christ.

When Jesus said, *"All things are possible to him that believeth"* (Mark 9:23), He meant that all things are possible to the believer. All the believer needs to do is to get to know what he is in Christ, then rise up and take his place.

What masters He has made us to be! How invincible we are!

Can't you see what it would mean for one in the face of all this to be talking about his weakness or his lack, making his confession of his inability?

"For of his fulness we all received" (John 1:16 ASV), and it is grace and the ability of God for us to enjoy to the very limit all that we are in Him.

JESUS

The Man at the right hand of God, who loved me and died for me, now ever lives for me!

He was God's answer to the universal cry of humanity.

He was God manifest to our senses.

He was an intrusion into the sense realm.

He talked like God. He acted like God. He lived like God, and, on the cross, He died like God.

He was not a philosopher searching for the truth. He was the truth.

He was not a mystic. He was reality.

He was not an experimenter searching for reality.

He was not a reformer. He was the recreator.

He was not a visionary. He was the Light of the world.

He never reflected.

He never reasoned.

He knew. He never learned.

He never asked prayers for Himself.

He never sought the help of man.

He was never in a hurry.

He was never afraid.

He never showed weakness.

He never hesitated.

He was always ready.

He was sure. There was a sureness in all He did or said.

He had no sense of sin or need of forgiveness.

He never sought or needed advice.

He knew why He came.

He knew from whence He came.

He knew who He was.

He knew the Father.

He knew about heaven.

He knew where He was going.

He knew man.

He knew Satan.

He had no sense of lack.

He had no sense of limitations.

FROM THE ARREST TO THE CROSS

He had no sense of fear.

He had no anger, no sense of disappointment, no sense of being defeated or being forsaken.

He had no sense of need of human sympathy.

He didn't shrink from pain or brutal treatment.

He was Master when they arrested Him.

He was the Master at the trial.

He ruled the seen and the unseen while He was on the cross.

He was Almighty, yet a man.

He died as God.

AFTER THE RESURRECTION

He had no sense of revenge. He was love.

He was a revelation of a new kind of love.

There were no dramatics. He said, "Go tell Peter, the weakest one."

He died a Lamb. He arose as Lord.

He acted like God.

He spoke like God.

His resurrection had all the simplicity of God.

He was God.

HIS WORD IS SPIRIT AND LIFE

Jesus knew the value and authority of His own words, and He dared to say, *"The words that I speak unto you, they are spirit, and they are life"* (John 6:63).

He knew that His words were living things.

He knew that His words would give life and death.

You remember how He spoke to the barren fig tree and it died from the root up.

You know that He spoke to the widow's son, and he became alive instantly. When the Holy Spirit speaks through Paul in Hebrews 4:12 (ASV), stating, *"The word of God is living,"* the Spirit is simply repeating in different words what Jesus said: *"The words that I speak unto you, they are spirit, and they are life"* (John 6:63).

James 1:18 says we are begotten by the Word, the Word that recreates men and gives them life.

First Peter 1:23 holds a peculiar place in the heart of deeply spiritual men: *"Being born again, not of corruptible seed, but of incorruptible, by the word of God, which liveth and abideth for ever."*

Our birth into the spiritual realm, the thing that gave us eternal life and made us a branch of the vine, was the incorruptible Word of God.

Psalm 107:20 says, *"He sent his word, and healed them."*

That word was His Son.

That word we know by the name of Jesus: *"In the beginning was the Word, and the Word was with God, and the Word was God"* (John 1:1).

That is the Word that brought eternal life to us.

Paul, saying goodbye to the Ephesian brethren, says in Acts 20:32, *"Now, brethren, I commend you to God, and to the word of his grace, which is able to build you up, and to give you an inheritance among all them which are sanctified."*

This Word is the faith-building Word, the grace-revealing Word, the Word of assurance.

THIS WORD IS OUR TESTIMONY

"The word of faith, which we preach" (Romans 10:8).

"If ye continue in my word, then are ye my disciples indeed; and ye shall know the truth, and the truth shall make you free" (John 8:31–32).

We abide in the Word.

We live in it.

Our home is in the Word.

But John 15:7 (MOFF) takes this a step beyond: *"If you remain in me and my words remain in you, then ask whatever you like and you shall have it."*

The thought of the Greek is like something born, "coming into being," and so He says the thing that you desire, if His words abide in you, will be given birth by God.

It is a staggering thing, isn't it?

There is absolutely no limit to the ability of God that is unveiled to us in His Word.

THE WORD OF GOD

The Word is of God—outbreathings of God, the mind of God, the will of God.

It is God speaking.

It is a part of God Himself. It is a living thing.

It abides forever.

"I watch over my word to perform it" (Jeremiah 1:12 ASV).

"No word from God shall be void of power" (Luke 1:37 ASV).

God and His Word are One.

This Word can live in my heart.

I will obey it—I will do it—I will enjoy it!

FAITH IN THE WRITTEN WORD

All the mighty achievements wrought by men of God have been accomplished by faith in the written Word.

It was the Word made flesh. Jesus spoke the Word. He was the Word.

Now it is my faith in the living Word, the written Word.

It is that Word on my lips that heals the sick, that breaks the power of demons over men.

I hold it in my hand.

I have it in my heart.

I have it on my lips.

I live it.

It lives in me.

The Word is my healing, my strength.

It is the Bread of Life to me.

It is the strength, the very ability of God to me.

The Word is my confession.

The Word is my light and my salvation.

The Word is my rest, my pillow.

The Word gives me quietness in the midst of confusion and gives me victory in the midst of defeat.

It gives me joy where desolation reigned.

The Word on my lips becomes the living, lifesaving, soul-inspiring voice of God.

I KNOW WHAT GOD'S WORD ON MY LIPS WILL DO

First, it is the Word in your heart; then it is the Word on your lips.

Jesus knew what His Father's Word would do on His lips.

Peter and John knew what the Word would do on their lips.

It is the Word that goes forth out of my mouth, that cannot return to Him void.

The creative Word on the lips of Jesus is the creative Word on your lips.

Faith is daring to speak His Word to the sick, to the demon-possessed and setting them free.

Real prayer is taking His Word into the throne room and letting His Word speak through your lips to Him on the throne, calling His attention to His own promises.

The written Word is God's testimony about Himself, about His Son and about His family.

It is also a testimony about His old enemy that has sought to destroy the object of His affection, man.

SOME WORD FACTS

The Gospel of John is largely Jesus's testimony about Himself and about His Father.

It is a remarkable fact that Exodus, Leviticus, Numbers, and Deuteronomy are the testimony of Jehovah. About 2,500 times, He says, *"I am Jehovah."*

We have never given place in our thinking to the importance of the right confession.

The Word is God speaking to me.

It is a revelation to me.

So many of us wish to demonstrate our faith; that is, to prove, to our own heart's satisfaction, our own confidence in the Word.

Here is the relation of confession to demonstration:

> *If thou shalt confess with thy mouth the Lord Jesus, and shalt believe in thine heart that God hath raised him from the dead, thou shalt be saved. For with the heart man believeth unto righteousness; and with the mouth confession is made unto salvation.* (Romans 10:9–10)

Notice that confession precedes possession.

You do not have eternal life until you confess the lordship of Jesus and your confidence in His substitutionary sacrifice.

John 6:47 (ASV) says, *"He that believeth hath eternal life."*

There is no possession without action. Believing is acting on the Word.

Acting on the Word is your confession.

Let it be a fixed fact in your mind that confession is proof of faith.

There is no believing that does not climax in confession.

It is faith expressing itself.

So, believing and confessing are practically one.

Your confession locates you. I know where you are. I know what you are.

Mental assent dares not confess.

It wishes to be sure of results first, so it always stands on the negative side of the issue.

It never wins.

It is never a success.

Mental assent is the voice of the senses, the mind of the senses, or the mind of the flesh.

Faith is from the mind of the spirit—your recreated spirit, dominating your reason faculties.

The mind of the senses is a spiritually dead mind.

> *Now the natural* [physical] *man receiveth not the things of the Spirit of God: for they are foolishness unto him.* (1 Corinthians 2:14 ASV)

There is only one attitude to take toward the spiritually dead or the mentally blinded one. They cannot enjoy the riches that belong to them until they act intelligently upon the Word.

Let me state it from another angle: the natural man cannot understand or appreciate the things of God, however hungry he may be for them, but he may recognize the need of them, so God has placed these riches within his reach.

All he needs to do is act upon the Word, and they become his.

TREATING THE WORD AS IF IT WERE A COMMON BOOK

One of the most dangerous habits that Christians have is treating the Word as though it were a common book.

In one breath, we will declare that we believe it to be a revelation from God, and yet we turn to the arm of flesh for help when the Word has promised perfect deliverance.

We treat the fact of redemption as though it were a beautiful fiction.

We read articles about the Word.

We sing hymns confessing it.

And yet we live under the dominion of the adversary, continually confessing sickness, want, fear, weakness, and doubts in the face of this revelation from God of our redemption, of the substitutionary sacrifice of Christ, and the fact that He is seated now at the right hand of God, having finished a work that perfectly satisfies the demands of justice and meets the needs of humanity.

We read about it. We talk about it.

And then we act as though it were but a fable!

This is the reason why the church has more sickness and disease than any other organized body of people, why faith is weak, and why the average believer is ruled by the adversary.

All of this could be changed if we would give the Word the same place we would give Christ if He were here physically in our presence.

OUR WORDS

We are in our words.

They are born in us.

They are part of us.

We live in them.

They live in others.

We know each other by our words.

Our words are ourselves.

Words are given to express ourselves.

The Bible is born of God. He gave birth to it. He gave life to His own Word.

He is in it.

It is a part of Him.

We know God by His Word.

He has expressed Himself in it.

God lives in His Word on our lips.

This sets Jesus free to heal, save, and bless.

Jesus is the Word—He lives in the Word.

The Word lives in us.

The Word's lordship is over us.

We know the Father through the Word.

We know Jesus by His words.

13

SOME ENEMIES OF PRAYER

Some of these enemies are very dear friends. We have associated with them for many years, and it will be hard for us to give them up. One of them is a desire to read about the Bible and about prayer rather than to study the Word and fit ourselves for this, the highest and holiest of all vocations.

More than a vocation, it is a privilege, the rarest of all privileges that have been given to us in grace.

I am convinced that the most outstanding enemy is a lack of knowledge of what we are in Christ, what He is in us, what He did for us, and our standing and legal rights before the throne.

To many, this language is strange, but I want you to come to know what actually belongs to you in Christ.

Until you do, you will never have a prayer life beyond the baby experience.

In another chapter, we are taking up what we are in Christ, what our privileges and abilities are, but now, I want you to think of these enemies that stand in the way of our really assuming our responsibilities.

Another enemy is ignorance of what *believing* is.

You remember that the word "believe" is a verb. It is an action word—it means to act upon the Word.

Then believing the Word is simply acting on it, as we act upon the word of our government in regard to taxes, or of our banker in regard to our overdrawn account.

When Jesus says, *"If ye abide in me, and my words abide in you, ye shall ask what ye will, and it shall be done unto you"* (John 15:7), you simply act on that Word.

There is no believing without acting, and believing means having possession.

I possess what the Word has promised me.

For instance, here is a statement of fact:

> *Surely he hath borne our griefs* [sicknesses], *and carried our sorrows; yet we did esteem him stricken, smitten of God, and afflicted.... With his stripes we are healed.* (Isaiah 53:4–5 ASV)

I don't try to believe this—I merely act upon it.

I say, "Did God say that He laid my diseases on Jesus and that God afflicted Him with them? Well, then if He did, by His stripes, I am healed."

I don't try to *believe* it—because it is true. God said it, and what God says is!

What do I do? I look up and say, "Father, I thank you that at last, I have found the truth—I am healed. I am so happy that at last, this great fact has been unveiled to me in your Word."

Don't try to believe. Don't condemn yourself because you do not believe, but learn to act on His Word as you act on the word of anyone else.

If you went to a doctor and he prescribed medication for you, you would take the prescription to the druggist and act on it, wouldn't you? Do the same thing with His Word.

WRONG CONFESSION

Another desperate enemy, and a persistent one, is wrong confession.

What do I mean by wrong confession?

You know that Christianity is really the great confession:

> *If thou shalt confess with thy mouth the Lord Jesus, and shalt believe in thine heart that God hath raised him from the dead, thou shalt be saved.* (Romans 10:9)

You notice it is a confession here with your lips.

(Whenever the word "confession" is used, we unconsciously think of sin. It is not confession of sin. It is a confession of our knowing that God's Son died for our sins according to the Scriptures, and that on the third day, He was raised again.)

Now, with my mouth, I make confession of the lordship of that raised One. I not only do that, but with my heart, I have accepted His righteousness and I make confession of my salvation.

You see, there is no such thing as salvation without confession.

So, Hebrews 3:1 (ASV) becomes clear: "*Wherefore, holy brethren, partakers of a heavenly calling, consider the Apostle and High Priest of our confession, even Jesus.*"

You see, Christianity is our confession.

Hebrews 4:14 (ASV) says, "*Let us hold fast our confession.*"

What is our confession? Why, it is that God is our Father, we are His children, we are in His family. It is a confession that our Father knows what our needs are and has made provision to meet every one of them. It is a confession of the finished work of Christ, of what I am in Him, and what He is in me.

It is a confession that "greater is He that is in me than he that is in the world."

Now he has the Holy Spirit indwelling him. "*Greater is he that is in you, than he that is in the world*" (1 John 4:4).

It is my confession that my God does supply every need of mine according to His riches in glory.

It is my confession that when I pray, the Father hears my prayer and answers me.

This is a manifold confession.

If I were sick, I would maintain my confession that "by His stripes, I am healed." (See Isaiah 53:5.)

If I were weak, I would insist upon this confession that God is now "the strength of my life," and I can do all things in Him who is enabling me with His own ability.

If it is a problem of wisdom, I confess that Jesus has been made unto me wisdom from God.

HOPE

Another enemy is hope.

Hope is always future. Faith is always now.

Someone comes to me and asks me to pray for them, and I say, "Was the prayer answered?" And they answer, "I hope it was."

Then I know it will not be answered, and I frankly tell them. "No, the hoper's prayers are seldom answered."

Hope is a beautiful thing when it is about heaven, or the coming back of the Master, and everything that belongs to the future. But for present-tense practices and present-tense life, hope is a dangerous enemy.

It is beautiful, but it is dangerous!

The hoper is always a failure. It is the believer who is a success—and believing, you remember, is acting on the Word.

MENTAL ASSENT

Another enemy is mental assent.

You ask, "What is that?" It is mentally accepting the Word as true, but not acting upon it.

It is admiring the Word.

You may have been called a fundamentalist, and you may have confessed that you believe the Word from Genesis to Revelation, but when it comes to acting on it, you have never done it.

You are like one who knows all the ingredients that are in a certain dish that you have for dinner. You are able to diagnose every feature about it. But you don't eat it. It does you no good.

The mental assenter is a failure—a beautiful failure, but a failure.

I say, "Is that Word true?" And you declare, "It is true. I believe every word from Genesis to Revelation." You are self-deceived.

The believer is a "doer of the Word and not a hearer only." (See James 1:22.)

Jesus described him in that last illustration of the Sermon on the Mount. (See Matthew 7:24–27.) The doer was the one who dug deep, went down into the rock and built his house on it. The mental assenter built his house on the sand.

PRAYING FOR FAITH

Another enemy is praying for faith.

How many times we have gone to the altar and to the prayer room to pray for more faith. What a delusion it was.

You never heard of anyone getting more faith or having their faith increased by praying for it.

Why? Because the prayer for faith is a prayer based on unbelief.

If unbelief were not your master, you wouldn't need faith; praying for faith is an absolute proof that you will not get it, and that you are insulting the Father by doing it.

Why, if a child should say to his mother, "Mama, I want you to increase my faith in you. I've been trying all morning to believe that what you said about that trip this Saturday was true." The child is insulting the integrity of his mother.

So, when you pray for faith, you are insulting the author of the Word. You don't intend to, but you are doing that.

DEPENDING ON ANOTHER'S FAITH

Another enemy of prayer is our dependence on other people's faith.

We become, unconsciously, spiritual hitchhikers.

To every man, God has given a measure of faith; that faith came with the new creation. It came when you received the Father's nature. That nature is a faith nature.

As soon as it came into you and you became His child, you began to develop that faith.

Just as you develop your mental strength by certain mental exercises, and develop your physical strength by certain physical exercises, now you are developing your faith by feeding on the Word. (See John 15:7.)

You begin to live in the Word.

You are acting on the Word.

You are taking advantage of your privileges in Christ.

HERE ARE SOME DON'TS

Don't try to believe; just act on the Word.

Don't have a double confession, so that one moment you confess, "Yes, He heard my prayer. I am healed," or "I will get the money," and then begin to question how it is going to come and what you ought to do to get it.

Your latter confession destroys the first.

A wrong confession destroys prayer and destroys faith.

Don't trust in other people's faith—have your own.

Do your own believing. Have your own faith as you have your own clothes. Act on the Word for yourself.

Don't talk doubt or unbelief.

Never admit that you are a "doubting Thomas." That is an insult to your Father.

Don't talk about sickness and disease.

Never talk about failure. Talk about the Word, its absolute integrity, your utter confidence in it, and your ability to act on it. Hold fast to your confession of its truthfulness.

Luke 6:46 says, *"Why call ye me Lord, Lord?"* Jesus is describing the man who talks very religiously, but does not do the Word.

You cannot build faith without practicing the Word.

You cannot develop a prayer life that is anything but words unless the Word actually has a part in your life.

You live the Word; you do the Word.

One may be a teacher of the Bible. He may know the Book from Genesis to Revelation, but if he does not walk by faith, he lives in the realm of the senses.

James describes him very minutely: *"But be ye doers of the word, and not hearers only, deceiving your own selves"* (James 1:22).

There is a vast army of self-deluders today. They teach the Word, they talk the Word, and they preach the Word, but they do not practice it.

The measure that I live the Word is the measure of my faith.

My prayer life is valuable only in the measure that the Word on my lips is a living thing. It lives only as I practice it.

> *For if any one is a hearer of the word and not a doer, he is like unto a man beholding his natural face in a mirror: for he beholdeth himself, and goeth away, and straightway forgetteth what manner of man he was.*
>
> (James 1:23–24 ASV)

What manner of man is he?

Why, he is the new man in Christ.

He is the new creation man.

He is a member of the body of Christ.

He is a son with a legal standing and the ability of God, and yet he lives like a common man.

He has a standing invitation to visit in the throne room any time that he wishes.

He has the righteousness of God, which enables him to stand in the Father's presence with the same freedom that Jesus possessed.

But he lives like a common man, and when a crisis comes, he is hunting for someone to believe for him.

True, he can pray. He is quite adept at that. But his prayers are but empty words when he might have them filled with faith, born of a real fellowship with the Father.

He is a hearer who forgets, a believer who is not a doer, a professor without living and walking in the Word.

It is a wonderful thing to be a doer of Jesus's words. This is the real secret of a prayer life.

I don't know whether it has ever been a reality in your life or not that you are a love creation and, therefore, a lover by nature because you are a possessor of the Father's nature.

You should do identically as Jesus did.

He did the Father's will.

He lived the Father's will.

He spoke the Father's words.

He was a doer as well as a hearer, and because He was that, the believer has a right to call Jesus "Lord" and expect that Jesus will fulfill a Lord's part to him in his daily walk.

Now I can quietly say, "*The* Lord *is my shepherd; I shall not want*" (Psalm 23:1), for He and I walk together.

CONFUSING THE PRAYER PROBLEM

Those who have depended upon prayer as a means of carrying on their religious activities have ofttimes been driven to extremes because the money didn't come, or some other problem that confronted them could not seem to be solved, and so they have resorted to using methods and means suggested by others.

The lives of many men of prayer have been a strong incentive to a life of faith on the part of many, and their method of prayer has influenced these earnest hearts greatly.

In my early days, after I had given up my income and started to live what we call a "life of faith," these problems confronted me.

I heard about "battle prayer" and we tried it. We stormed the throne. We cried aloud. But somehow or other, it didn't bring the results, and I wondered why.

Then we heard about *praying through*, and we tried that.

We prayed through our problems.

After a while, I discovered that it was all works on my part and the part of those whose footsteps I had followed, that *holding onto God* until the answer came or *praying hard* were expressions that came from the realm of the senses.

It was sense knowledge trying to solve a faith problem, a spiritual problem.

Then suddenly it occurred to me that we hadn't been acting on the Word.

Instead, we had read the Word, and then tried to force God to do something.

We had forgotten that "*No word from God* [is] *void of power*" (Luke 1:37 ASV), and "*I watch over my word to perform it*" (Jeremiah 1:12 ASV).

We had forgotten John 15:7: *"If ye abide in me, and my words abide in you, ye shall ask what ye will, and it shall be done unto you."*

The name of Jesus had not yet functioned; we didn't know, *"Whatever you ask the Father, he will give you in my name"* (John 16:23 MOFF).

I had never fathomed the secret of the Master's teaching about His name.

Now it began to dawn on me. We had prayed to Jesus. We had prayed to the Holy Spirit. We had prayed to God.

Now we came to the place where we saw we should pray to the Father in Jesus's name.

We saw that we are to take the Master's place, and the Master had given us the power of attorney to use His name.

That dawned on our spirit.

It changed our whole attitude about prayer.

> *In that day ye shall ask in my name: and I say not unto you, that I will pray the Father for you; for the Father himself loveth you, because ye have loved me, and have believed that I came forth from the Father.*
> (John 16:26–27 ASV)

This brings us into intimate contact with the Father in Jesus's name.

The earlier verses are now clear.

> *In that day ye shall ask me nothing. Verily, verily, I say unto you, Whatsoever ye shall ask the Father in my name, he will give it you. Hitherto have ye asked nothing in my name: ask, and ye shall receive, that your joy may be full.* (John 16:23–24)

Then prayer is based upon the simple ground of coming to the Father in Jesus's name.

His love outreaching toward us caused Him to go a step beyond that, and in Hebrews 4:16, He invites us to come boldly to the throne of grace.

The Greek word *grace* means "love gifts."

Then the throne room is a room where love gifts are given lavishly to those who love Him.

So, I am invited to come boldly, fearlessly, as a son in the Father's presence, or as a slave of love of Jesus, into His presence.

You see, there is no *battle prayer* there. There is no *praying through.*

I am there in His presence to make my needs known.

PRAYING ACCORDING TO HIS WILL

In praying, the problem came up about prayer being according to the will of the Father.

I made this sweet discovery: that I had taken Jesus's place here on the earth, and that I was carrying out the plan of redemption in bringing lost men to the saving knowledge of Christ, building up the babes in Christ, setting the captives free, healing the sick, and doing the same kind of work that the Master did in His earth walk.

Then He comforted me greatly by giving me this Scripture:

> *And this is the confidence that we have in him, that, if we ask any thing according to his will, he heareth us: and if we know that he hear us, whatsoever we ask, we know that we have the petitions that we desired of him.*
> (1 John 5:14–15)

We know that Jesus was the will of the Father manifest, for He said, "*I came down from heaven, not to do mine own will, but the will of him that sent me*" (John 6:38).

Referring to the Father, Jesus said, "*I always do what pleases him*" (John 8:29 MOFF).

Then if we do the same things that Jesus did, plus the things that He has taught us to do that He could not do, we may be sure that we are in the Father's will.

And if we are in His will, then we are certain that our prayers are answered.

We don't try to force Him to answer them.

We don't tease Him like some children do their parents until they wear their parents out.

No, we come as intelligent men and women, grown up in Christ, and take our place, bearing His burdens, fellowshipping His purposes in saving the world.

We come into the throne room, that room of love gifts, into the very presence of the Father, and we talk things over with Him.

But you say, "Don't you think sometimes it is necessary to pray all night? Jesus did."

If we knew the nature of Jesus's prayers during those night sessions, that might help us.

If you have needs enough that it would take a whole night to cover them, then you should take the night.

But you ask, "Don't you think that we should keep on praying until our prayer is answered?"

No, I don't. I think instead we might remind Him and thank Him for it.

Unbelief becomes insistent, thinking that by works of some kind, it can force God to answer.

We are going to act on His Word just as we act on the word of any firm or company. We are going to act on His Word simply as intelligent men and women act on the word of a bank or any other institution that has a record of honesty.

Remember, God cannot lie. He watches over His Word to make it good.

The man who trusts Him is absolutely as safe as Jesus was when He trusted His Father.

A LITTLE STUDY ABOUT THE DEFEATED ONE

When Jesus began His public ministry, He came in contact instantly with demonic forces.

They had wrought unhindered through all the ages. They had held men in bondage. They reigned as kings in the realm of spiritual death.

No one had authority to dispossess them or rule over them.

> *And they went into Capernaum; and straightway on the sabbath day he entered into the synagogue, and taught. And they were astonished at his doctrine: for he taught them as one that had authority, and not as the scribes. And there was in their synagogue a man with an unclean spirit; and he cried out, saying, Let us alone; what have we to do with thee, thou Jesus of Nazareth? art thou come to destroy us? I know thee who thou art, the Holy One of God.* (Mark 1:21–24)

That demon knew Jesus, knew who He was.

He not only knew Jesus, but he knew His authority and His attitude toward him.

Demons feared Him.

Luke 4:1–13 is the story of the temptation of Jesus. Jesus proved Himself to be the master of Satan, and the demons must have known of Satan's defeat. They recognized their master.

> *Forasmuch then as the children are partakers of flesh and blood, he also himself likewise took part of the same; that through death he might destroy him that had the power of death, that is, the devil.* (Hebrews 2:14)

> *And when I saw him, I fell at his feet as dead. And he laid his right hand upon me, saying unto me, Fear not; I am the first and the last: I am he that liveth, and was dead; and, behold, I am alive for evermore, Amen; and have the keys of hell and of death.* (Revelation 1:17–18)

Jesus conquered Satan, as we are shown in Colossians 2:15: "*Having spoiled principalities and powers, he made a shew of them openly, triumphing over them in it.*" This is Satan's eternal defeat.

You can understand Hebrews 9:12: "*Neither by the blood of goats and calves, but by his own blood he entered in once into the holy place, having obtained eternal redemption for us.*"

During Jesus's earth walk, He defeated Satan at every point of contact, from the day of His temptation until He surrendered Himself on the cross.

> *We speak wisdom, however, among them that are fullgrown: yet a wisdom not of this world, nor of the rulers of this world, who are coming to nought.* (1 Corinthians 2:6 ASV)

Satan and the demonic forces are dethroned.

In Colossians 2:15, I showed you that they were disarmed and stripped of their authority; in Hebrews 2:14, Jesus destroyed the authority of the lord of death.

> *For if the trespass of one man allowed death to reign through that one man, much more shall those who receive the overflowing grace and free gift of righteousness reign in life through One, through Jesus Christ.* (Romans 5:17 MOFF)

The new creation, who was the defeated one, the conquered one, now reigns as a king in the realm of life here among men, where he had served as a slave of spiritual death.

Ephesians 1:22–23 (MOFF) says, *"He has put everything under his feet and set him as head over everything for the church, the church which is his Body, filled by him who fills the universe entirely."*

Second Corinthians 2:14 is the Spirit's paean of praise of victory over satanic forces. Let me give you the translation from William J. Conybeare: *"But thanks be to God, who leads me on from place to place in the train of his triumph, to celebrate his victory over the enemies of Christ; and by me sends forth the knowledge of Him, a steam of fragrant incense, throughout the world."*

Now in the face of these facts, what should be our attitude toward the adversary and his works?

You remember in 1 John 3:8: *"For this purpose the Son of God was manifested, that he might destroy the works of the devil."*

We are taking Jesus's place.

We are acting for Him.

He was a destroyer of the works of the adversary. We should follow in His steps.

Paul, although a prisoner in Rome, wrote, *"I Paul, the prisoner of Jesus Christ"* (Ephesians 3:1).

He was not a prisoner of circumstances, nor of men, nor of government. They might hold him in captivity, but he knew that if it was the Father's will for him to be set free, he would be set free as he was in Philippi.

He was not the prisoner of Rome. He was the prisoner of Jesus Christ.

The revelation that God gave to Paul finally destroyed the Roman Empire. It destroys everything that opposes the will and mind of the Father where it is unveiled, where men understand it. Where believers enter into its fullness, they become masters.

What should be our attitude today?

Should we cowardly yield to the forces of darkness?

Should we submit to satanic domination?

Or should we, in the name of Jesus, arise and take our place as sons and daughters of God Almighty?

Colossians 1:12 (ASV) says, "Giving thanks *unto the Father, who made us meet* [fit] *to be partakers of the inheritance of the saints in light.*"

He has given us the ability to enjoy our part.

> *Who delivered us out of the power of darkness, and translated us into the kingdom of the Son of his love; in whom we have our redemption, the forgiveness of our sins.* (Colossians 1:13–14 ASV)

We have within us the ability of God.

We have the wisdom of God.

God is the strength of our life.

What more can we ask?

Can't you see what this means as a background for a prayer life?

Can't you hear the Spirit whispering, "Nay, in all these things, you are more than conquerors?"

Real prayer is inspired of the Spirit, backed up by the living Word. Then it should be a real sharing with Him.

Colossians 3:1 (MOFF) says, "*Since then you have been raised with Christ, aim at what is above, where Christ is, seated at the right hand of God.*"

We have become not only partakers, but also sharers in the resurrection ability of God.

Now He is asking us to share with Him in giving the world the message that will deliver those in bondage from the captivity of Satan.

He is calling on us to become intercessors, prayers, burden-bearers in this world of darkness and fear.

HIS WILL

I saw that if I could get into the will of the Father, I would be stepping into the channel, into the current of His dream for the age.

That current would carry me on into a realm of victory and usefulness that I had never known before.

One day, one of the workers said, "If we only knew where He was working, we would tie up with Him."

Another one said as he was praying, "Lord, lift us out of this little millpond where we are swimming around, out into the current of Your will for us now."

I saw it. His will was unveiled in Jesus. Jesus was His will.

Four times in the Gospel of John, Jesus said, "I came to do the Father's will; I came not to do My own will, but the will of Him who sent Me."

Can we know the Father's will?

We may know it if we know the Master.

Writing to the Ephesian church, Paul said, "Do not be ignorant about the will of the Lord." (See Ephesians 5:17.)

We are not to be ignorant of it.

This Word is His will written for us.

Everything that helps men toward knowing Jesus better is in the will of the Father.

Romans 12:1–2 shows the threefold will of the Father:

> *I beseech you therefore, brethren, by the mercies of God, that ye present your bodies a living sacrifice, holy, acceptable unto God, which is your reasonable service. And be not conformed to this world: but be ye transformed by the renewing of your mind, that ye may prove what is that good, and acceptable, and perfect, will of God.*

It is the renewed mind that gets to know the will of the Father.

When we are recreated, He gives us His nature. Then He renews our minds; they walk in harmony with our recreated spirit. As we fellowship the Word, live in it, and let the Word abide in us, we get to know the good will of the Father.

We get to know the acceptable will of the Father. Then as we go on, we will get to know His perfect will. We will swing into it with an abandonment that will thrill heaven.

You say, "Mr. Kenyon, when Jesus prayed in the garden He said, not my will, but thine be done." I know. That is in the heart of every true follower of the Master.

We do not want our own will. We only want His will. We know that saving lost men is His will. We know that carrying the gospel to the world is His will. We know that teaching and building up the believer is His will.

We know one hundred things that are His will. It is His will that our bills should be paid, that we should be strong and vigorous in our walk, that we should have a testimony that would make people strong to trust in Him.

The man who lives and walks in Him will never pray outside of His will.

I love to think that Jesus did the Father's will, that He taught the Father's will, and then He suffered His Father's will in His substitutionary work.

In the Pauline revelation, He reveals the Father's will to us. Jesus, you see, was His will revealed. As you study Jesus, you will know the Father's will. Jesus's death and substitutionary sacrifice were the will of the Father. Jesus was the will of God unveiled.

WE ARE THE FATHER'S WILL

When that first came to me, how it thrilled me. Jesus came to do the Father's will. Jesus was the Father's will. *"Of his own will he brought us forth by the word of truth"* (James 1:18 ASV). If His own will brought us forth, we are born of His will, aren't we? We are born of God. We are born from above. We are His will.

Say it out loud, "I am the Father's will." Say it until your ears become accustomed to it, until your spirit absorbs it.

"I am my Father's will. It is easy for me to do His will, for I am born of it. I have His nature in me. I have the impulses of His own love heart throbbing through me.

"He is love; I am born of love. I have His nature in me. That nature rules me. His love is shed abroad by the Holy Spirit in my heart. It dominates me. I love because He first loved me. I have come to believe in His love in my case. I believe that His love way is the best way."

When Jesus said that He was the way, the reality, and the life (see John 14:6), that was the love way, and love was the reality of that way.

That was the Father's life. That life has been imparted to us.

We are born of the Father's will, born of His love nature.

We are partakers of the divine nature.

We have the Father's Word now as it fell from the lips of Jesus. We can live in the Father's Word.

The Father's Word is His will, so we may live in His will.

"How can I do this?" you ask. Begin now to say that you are doing it. After a bit, it will become a reality to you.

You never rise above your confession. If you always confess your failings, your weakness, or your lack of ability, your weakness and your lack of ability will rule you.

If you say, "I can do all things in Him who strengthens me," you will rise to the level of it.

You never enjoy anything beyond your confession. Your faith is never stronger than your confession.

If you are afraid to confess that you are the righteousness of God in Christ, there will be an uncertainty about your actions.

You will hesitate.

If you dare say, "I am a branch of the vine, and the same life and love that flows in the vine flows in me," you will rise to the level of your confession.

If you say over and over again, "I know whatever I ask of the Father in Jesus's name, He will give it to me," after a while, that truth will permeate your consciousness until it becomes a literal, absolute fact in you.

Men and women will come to you for prayer. They have not learned the secret. They haven't any faith of their own. But they have faith in *your* faith because you have learned the secret of confessing to be what God says you are.

That is all there is of it.

When you dare join hands with God, when you dare to sing the song with Him, that song will be the harmony of heaven.

In other words, when you dare to say that you are what He says you are, then the two of you have agreed and you become a messenger of heaven, and you will be doing the works that Jesus said you should do in His name.

14

THE THOMAS KIND OF FAITH

I never realized how many people had this kind of faith. You remember the story from the Gospel of John:

> *But Thomas, one of the twelve, called Didymus, was not with them when Jesus came. The other disciples therefore said unto him, We have seen the Lord. But he said unto them, Except I shall see in his hands the print of the nails, and put my finger into the print of the nails, and thrust my hand into his side, I will not believe. And after eight days again his disciples were within, and Thomas with them: then came Jesus, the doors being shut, and stood in the midst, and said, Peace be unto you. Then saith he to Thomas, Reach hither thy finger, and behold my hands; and reach hither thy hand, and thrust it into my side: and be not faithless, but believing. And Thomas answered and said unto him, My Lord and my God. Jesus saith unto him, Thomas, because thou hast seen me, thou hast believed: blessed are they that have not seen, and yet have believed.*
>
> (John 20:24–29)

This is the Thomas type of faith.

It is sense knowledge faith.

We can believe in miracles if we can see them.

In many healing meetings, multitudes have sat in amazement when they have seen the sick instantly healed.

It has given them faith to dare ask for their own healing.

This was not faith in the Word. It is faith in what they see and hear or feel.

We see it again manifest in an instance like this: a sick person comes to me. They are in great pain. When I pray for them, the pain leaves them instantly, and they say, "Thank God I am healed."

I ask, "How do you know you are?"

And they reply, "The pain is gone."

They have no faith in the Word. It is meaningless to them. I read Isaiah 53:4–5 to them.

I ask, "Do you believe that?"

"Oh, yes; I have believed that for years."

I read it again:

> *Surely he hath borne our griefs, and carried our sorrows: yet we did esteem him stricken, smitten of God, and afflicted. But he was wounded for our transgressions, he was bruised for our iniquities: the chastisement of our peace was upon him; and with his stripes we are healed.* (Isaiah 53:4–5)

You see, this person is healed by my faith, or his faith in my faith.

They are like the one in James 5:14 who calls for the elders to come and pray over him and anoint him with oil, and the prayer of the elders heals him.

The only faith he had was in the elders.

That is sense knowledge faith.

He can see the elders. He can hear them pray, can feel their hands upon his head.

The Word actually means nothing to him.

Had he believed the Word instead of sending for the elders or asking anyone to pray for him, he would have looked up and said, "Father, you laid this disease on Jesus, and it is unseemly for me to bear it. I dishonor Thee in bearing it. So, in the name of Jesus, I command it to leave me, and I command Satan to take it with him. I have no use for it, and I refuse to have it."

In Jesus's name, he gets his personal deliverance.

He honors the Word, and the name.

He honors the Father and Jesus.

He has learned to take his place in Christ.

Jesus met only sense knowledge faith among the Jews.

In Matthew 8:5–13 is recorded the story of the centurion who came to Jesus beseeching Him to come and heal his servant, who was sick with palsy.

And Jesus said, "*I will come and heal him*" (verse 7).

The centurion answered, "*Lord, I am not worthy that thou shouldest come under my roof: but speak the word only, and my servant shall be healed*" (verse 8).

He illustrates his confidence in Jesus by saying, "*I am a man under authority, having soldiers under me: and I say to this man, Go, and he goeth; and to another, Come, and he cometh; and to my servant, Do this, and he doeth it*" (Matthew 8:9).

When Jesus heard this, He marveled at the centurion's faith and said, "*I have not found so great faith, no, not in Israel*" (verse 10).

This gentile had faith in the Master's Word that no Israelite had manifested.

In the Gospel of John, you catch a glimpse of the Jews' faith in Jesus. It was exactly like Thomas's faith.

> *"Well then," they said, "what is the Sign you perform, that we may see it and believe you? What work have you to show?"* (John 6:30 MOFF)

When they saw the miracles, they believed.

I question if a single one of the disciples who walked with the Master had anything but sense knowledge until after the day of Pentecost.

Luke 24:11 gives a picture of the disciples after Mary Magdalene, Joanna, Mary the mother of James, and the other women with them told the disciples that Jesus had risen: "*And their words seemed to them as idle tales, and they believed them not.*"

They couldn't believe beyond their senses.

John 6:14 gives us another illustration: "*Those men, when they had seen the miracle that Jesus did, said, This is of a truth that prophet that should come into the world.*"

His words filled them with wonder or with anger, but not with faith.

They had to have some physical evidence to prove His deity.

First John 1:1–3 also illustrates this perfectly:

> *That which was from the beginning, which we have heard, which we have seen with our eyes, which we have looked upon, and our hands have handled, of the Word of life; (for the life was manifested, and we have seen it,*

and bear witness, and shew unto you that eternal life, which was with the Father, and was manifested unto us;) that which we have seen and heard declare we unto you, that ye also may have fellowship with us.

That which we have seen with our eyes, handled with our hands—that is in the realm of the senses.

God sent His Son down here into the realm of sense knowledge, and those sense knowledge folks saw Him, ate with Him, and witnessed His miracles, but not one of them actually believed He was going to rise from the dead, although He had told them so.

They didn't believe that He was going to die for their sins.

They only believed what they could see and hear.

None of the disciples believed in His resurrection until they had some physical evidence of it.

You remember the dramatic scene of Peter and John coming to the tomb, finding the stone rolled away, and the empty grave clothes. John then said that he believed. (See John 20:1–10.)

One of the gravest dangers that we face as believers is sense knowledge faith.

The thing that He demands of us is that we accept His Word as it is, the very Word of God, and that we act upon it, independent of any feeling or any evidence that the eyes can see or the ears can hear.

Notice carefully what the Lord tells us in Paul's letter to the Romans:

But what saith it? The word is nigh thee, even in thy mouth, and in thy heart: that is, the word of faith, which we preach; that if thou shalt confess with thy mouth the Lord Jesus, and shalt believe in thine heart that God hath raised him from the dead, thou shalt be saved. For with the heart man believeth unto righteousness; and with the mouth confession is made unto salvation. For the scripture saith, Whosoever believeth on him shall not be ashamed. (Romans 10:8–11)

You note He is challenging us to accept the Word that we may have heard so many times that we know it from memory.

So, He says, "*The word is nigh thee, even in thy mouth, and in thy heart: that is, the word of faith.*"

Then He demands that I confess my faith in the resurrection of Jesus with my lips; He demands that I confess my salvation and that I have become His righteousness in Christ.

I must confess this before I receive eternal life, before I am recreated, before I become the righteousness of God in Him.

And He says that if I do it, I shall not be put to shame.

This is acting on the Word independent of any sense knowledge whatsoever.

That is faith.

For me to act when I have evidence is not faith.

I require no faith when I have physical evidence.

You see, faith is giving substance to a thing that is not.

I am giving thanks to the Father for the money to pay the bills before the money has arrived.

> *Your heavenly Father knoweth that ye have need of all these things. But seek ye first the kingdom of God, and his righteousness; and all these things shall be added unto you.* (Matthew 6:32–33)

> *My God shall supply all your need.* (Philippians 4:19)

That is all I have. That is all I ask.

And that Word has given me the assurance that I will get the thing that I asked Him for.

Jesus said, "*Whatsoever ye shall ask the Father in my name, he will give it you*" (John 16:23).

I have asked the Father in Jesus's name and now I am thanking Him that His Word cannot fail.

> *In nothing be anxious; but in everything by prayer and supplication with thanksgiving let your requests be made known unto God. And the peace of God, which passeth all understanding, shall guard your hearts and your thoughts in Christ Jesus.* (Philippians 4:6–7 ASV)

"*In nothing be anxious.*"

Why should I be anxious?

Isn't He my Father?

Don't I know Him?

Didn't He say that He would look after my needs, and whatsoever I ask in Jesus's name, He will give to me?

Didn't He say:

> *He that spared not his own Son, but delivered him up for us all, how shall he not with him also freely give us all things?* (Romans 8:32)

How can I be otherwise than perfectly quiet?

The thing hasn't disturbed me.

For instance, suppose my child is very ill. Doctors have given up, but that doesn't disturb me. I have His Word and I know Him. He can't fail me.

Didn't He say, "They who believe shall lay hands on the sick, and they shall recover?" (See Mark 16:18.)

Supposing I can't get to the child, then I have this Scripture: "*Whatsoever ye shall ask the Father in my name, he will give it you*" (John 16:23).

Do I need anything more?

Why, He says, "*I watch over my word to perform it*" (Jeremiah 1:12 ASV).

"*No Word from God shall be void of power*" (Luke 1:37 ASV).

Now you can understand the rest of this: "*In everything by prayer and supplication with thanksgiving let your requests be made known unto God*" (Philippians 4:6 ASV).

Did you notice "*with thanksgiving*"?

I can't help but be thankful.

I can't help but praise Him.

Why, this sickness or this impossible financial obligation simply gives Him an opportunity to reveal Himself as my Father, and Jesus as my Lord and provider.

If I didn't have that need, I would never know the riches of His grace; so, I thank Him for every added burden that comes, for it gives Him an opportunity to reveal Himself to my heart.

Did you notice the next verse?

When I begin to thank Him and praise Him, "*The peace of God, which passeth all understanding, shall guard your hearts and your thoughts in Christ Jesus*" (Philippians 4:7 ASV). The peace of God throws a garrison of faith's soldiers around my heart, guarding it, and guarding my thoughts so that no doubt can come.

Why, I am just as quiet as God is, because God's peace has garrisoned my heart.

Did Jesus ever get disturbed?

Was He anxious when He saw the waves dashing over the little vessel in which He and the disciples were riding?

Not a bit; He simply said, "Peace, be still."

He knew that every Word He spoke was the Father's Word; and it was the Father saying through His lips, "Peace, be still," and the waves became quiet.

When the demonic, fierce, dangerous man came out and intercepted them in the Gadarenes, the Father said through Jesus's lips, "Be still; come out of him." (See Mark 5:1–20.)

And the demon said, "May we go into that herd of swine?"

Jesus answered, "Go."

Jesus was speaking the Father's words; He wasn't excited or anxious.

He knew that what the Father said through His lips would master that legion of demons, or quiet that raging sea.

And that same peace of God comes into your heart that was in the heart of Jesus.

THE BITTER FAILURE OF SENSE KNOWLEDGE FAITH

"I think I am losing faith in God.

"I have had such strong faith. Why, I have been healed so many times. Every time that I have been sick and have asked prayer from my friends, I have been instantly healed; but now, I have had ever so many pray for me and I get no relief.

"I tell you; I am beginning to lose faith."

I asked him, "What are you losing faith in?"

He answered, "Faith in God, to be sure."

And I said to him, "Why, you've never had any special faith in Him to lose. You've had many healings, but have you ever gone to Him for your own healing?"

"No, I've always had you people pray for me."

"Then all you have had is sense knowledge faith. You have trusted in other people's faith.

"You have been a spiritual hitchhiker ever since we first became acquainted. You have never trusted the Word for yourself. You have been a leaner rather than a burden-bearer.

"You have leaned on other people. You have never taken your place in Christ, and the hour has come when their faith can't carry you any longer. You must take your place yourself.

"Are you a son?"

"Oh, yes, I know I was born again years ago."

"But you have never grown any. You are but a babe yet. You live in the realm where you were when I first found you. You have never come out of the sense realm.

"Don't you think now that you had better begin to study the Word?

"Take our correspondence course. Get to know what you are in Christ; what belongs to you.

"Get to know your authority over sickness and disease through the name of Jesus."

He said, "I thank you for speaking so plainly to me. I can see where my difficulty lies, but you see, I have been so busy with my business and I have been struggling so hard to make good, I guess I have failed to get the best out of life."

"No, you have just awakened, and now you will get it. It is a short road. It is only a few blocks up, and you will be rejoicing with the rest of them having your own faith, having your own place in Christ.

"You will be praying with sick folks. Men will be coming to you and saying, 'Won't you pray for me?' or, 'I wish you would pray for my child,' and, oh, the joy that will be yours."

Sense knowledge holds one a prisoner. One is always looking for physical evidence, and as long as one does that, faith doesn't have an opportunity to exercise itself.

You pray for something. Then you must act as though you had it. You must talk as though you had it.

You are never to go back on your prayer, never to allow your lips for one moment to say that you are not certain that you have it, that you are not sure of your answer.

You remember Mark 11:24: "*What things soever ye desire, when ye pray, believe that ye receive them, and ye shall have them.*"

Then there is only one thing to do. We must begin to praise Him for it.

I remember that years ago, I was praying for money to meet our rent bill. I had prayed. Then I went out on the street and I began to wonder how I could get it.

Before I realized it, I had destroyed my prayer. I had nullified the Word.

I came to myself, asked for forgiveness, and then began to thank Him for it. I held myself steady and kept my heart singing songs of victory. That was the beginning of my life of prayer.

Then I remember how I grew out of that and came to the place where, when I had asked Him for something, I forgot it; I left it; I walked away from it.

If it came back to my mind, I thanked Him; I praised Him for it.

Then I learned that when someone brought the subject up, to tell him that it was settled. "I have it."

Once, a man said, "If you have it, then there is no need of my helping you."

I smiled and said, "I have it according to the Word, for no word from my Father is void of fulfillment; so I praise Him as though I had it now."

One day while walking down Halsey Street in Chicago, I was facing a great need. I asked Him for it in Jesus's name, and began to praise Him for it.

It seemed as though I could feel it in my pocket. I wouldn't put my hand in to verify it, but I walked down the street hardly touching the sidewalk. My heart was full of laughter.

When I reached the house where I was called upon to pray for a sick woman, the money was handed to me. It was more than I had asked for.

"In nothing be anxious" (Philippians 4:6 ASV). Is He not for you? Is He not working for those who trust Him?

There is no ground for anxiety or fear if you know His Word.

"Whosoever believeth…shall not be put to shame" (Romans 10:11 ASV).

I know this to be an absolute fact.

You see, your heart will learn to welcome the impossible, the "beyond reason" task; for the greater One is in you, with you, and for you.

15

NEVER URGE PEOPLE TO BELIEVE

Give them something to act upon and they will do it. Open the Bible to them until Acts 20:32 becomes a present tense reality:

> *And now, brethren, I commend you to God, and to the word of his grace, which is able to build you up, and to give you an inheritance among all them which are sanctified.*

Paul is leaving the church at Ephesus. He may never see them again and he commends them to the Father. He turns them over into the hands of love.

And he said, "I not only do this, but I commend you to the word of His grace." These Epistles of Paul's are the words of His grace.

The four Gospels are the words of His grace, and so the whole New Testament makes up the book of the words of the Father's grace.

If he were here, he would say, "I want you to study it. I want you to prove yourself capable of doing the Word."

There will be ability in the Word as you study it to put you over and make you a conqueror.

To merely know the Word has no real value unless it becomes a part of your life.

It does not become a part of your life until you begin to practice it.

As you begin to live the Word, then the Word becomes a part of your very being, enters into your blood, into your very system. The very strength and ability of God becomes a part of you.

First Corinthians 2:12 has a beautiful suggestion here: *"That we might know the things that are freely given to us of God."*

These things that were given to us were in the finished work of Christ. We have access to all the riches of His grace unveiled in Christ's finished work. (See Colossians 2:2–3.)

Notice some of them.

Satan was conquered, defeated by Jesus before He arose from the dead, and that defeat of Satan is set to our credit so you can safely and joyously say, "I conquered Satan in Christ."

As Jesus was Master of the devil, so I am in His name.

I was raised together with Christ.

I have in me His resurrection ability, His resurrection life. I am a master. (See Ephesians 1:17–23)

And that great, mighty Holy Spirit who has come to make His home in my body is guiding me into all the reality of the wealth that has been given to me in Christ.

He is making me know what the resurrection means to me: that if I were raised together with Christ, I am a master of the forces that operated in slaying Jesus, that I am now taking Jesus's place in this earth walk.

I have a legal right to the use of His name, which has all authority.

I have a legal right to the ability of the Holy Spirit and I know it is God who is at work within me, willing and working His own good pleasure. I am not left to my own resources.

> *And God is able to make all grace abound toward you; that ye, always having all sufficiency in all things, may abound to every good work.*
> (2 Corinthians 9:8)

God is making His grace to come leaping toward you in all its fullness, and that grace has within it His all sufficiency for every emergency.

What a master you are!

How ashamed we ought to be that we have ever talked about our weakness and our lack when the ability of God, the measureless ability of God, is ours.

Why, in the tenth verse, He says:

> *And he that supplieth seed to the sower and bread for food, shall supply and multiply your seed for sowing, and increase the fruits of your righteousness.* (2 Corinthians 9:10 ASV)

How little we have appreciated this, that His very sufficiency and ability are all at our disposal.

You understand what He means by "*increase the fruits of your righteousness.*" All the gracious words that Jesus said and all the mighty acts that He performed were the fruits of His righteousness.

I wonder if we have ever thought of it.

Jesus was fearless in the presence of the enemy in every place.

He had no fear of a storm at sea.

He had no fear of lack.

He wasn't afraid of death. He raised Lazarus who had been dead four days.

He wasn't afraid of a mob.

Those were some of the fruits of His righteousness.

When these fruits abound in us, they will make us like Jesus, and these fruits can abound in us.

Righteousness was given to us with that intent.

> *And such confidence have we through Christ to God-ward: not that we are sufficient of ourselves, to account anything as from ourselves; but our sufficiency is from God; who also made us sufficient as ministers of a new covenant.* (2 Corinthians 3:4–6 ASV)

Now notice this carefully. He is not only our ability, but He is our sufficiency.

There is no lack in us—in our service, in our finances, or in anything connected with our earth walk.

You see, when He took us over and came into us and began to build His Word into us, He was building His sufficiency and His ability into us.

That Word of His created this universe, created this earth with all its flowers and fruits, its wealth of minerals, chemicals, and oils. His efficiency in that living Word created these things.

Now He is building into us that living Word with its supernatural efficiency.

A prayer life backed with this knowledge becomes invincible.

We haven't said anything but what is true in regard to the new creation.

All we need to do now is to take our place and act our part, for it is God who is at work within us.

Not only is He building Himself into us, but He is there to work through us.

Now just take this thing home to your heart and read Ephesians 1:3: "*Who hath blessed us with all spiritual blessings in heavenly places in Christ.*"

You are blessed with everything that you need.

His very fullness is yours.

His ability is yours.

His love is yours.

Yes, He Himself is yours!

CONTRAST OF PAUL AND JESUS ON FAITH

Christ tells us what the Jew can be.

Paul tells the believers what they are in Christ.

Christ tells the Jew what he could do if he had faith.

Paul tells us what we are because we have believed on Christ.

Paul reveals to us that we are in the realm with Christ now.

Jesus tells them, "If they believe."

Paul shows us that we are believers and that we possess all things in Christ.

Paul's revelation is what we can do, because we are what Jesus wished the Jews to be.

Jesus is talking to a nation of natural men.

Paul is speaking of the new creation, the sons of God, members of the body of Christ.

Jesus is speaking to the first covenant people who have lost their faith in God.

Paul is speaking to those who are in Christ, sons of God.

Jesus is challenging the unbelieving Jew by revealing what faith will do on the lips of a man.

Paul thanks God for leading him in triumph in Christ.

Jesus said to the disciples before Pentecost, "Greater things than these shall you do because I go to the Father." (See John 14:12.)

All that Jesus had done for Israel was in the sense realm.

He had healed the sick.

He had fed the multitudes.

He had opened blind eyes.

He had raised the dead and stilled the sea.

But the disciples, after they were recreated, were to perform miracles upon men's spirits.

They were to do spiritual things as well as things in the sense realm.

The "greater things" were to lead men into the new creation and unveil spiritual realities for them to enjoy.

Jesus was surrounded by unbelief, and He was seeking to inspire faith in natural man.

It would be well for us to recognize this fact: that natural man cannot have faith in the revelation realm.

He has sense knowledge faith.

He believes what he can see, hear, and feel.

All God asks him to do is to act on the Word.

He demands that he confess Jesus as Lord and act upon the Word that declares Christ died for his sins and was raised for his justification.

For years, I tried to get natural men to believe. I can see them now struggling, crying, weeping, and confessing their sins. It was so hard for them to grasp it.

But now I can see how simple it is.

All I ask them to do is act upon what God has spoken, and He counts that as faith.

The man who acts on that enters into the family, becomes a member of the body of Christ.

He becomes a partaker of the divine nature, so that all things that God wrought in Christ in the substitution belong to him.

Now he can act intelligently on the Word, either for himself or for another.

Believing is acting on the Word.

Faith is the result of acting.

Under the first covenant, the word "faith" does not occur in connection with Moses or Israel until Paul unveils it in the eleventh chapter of Hebrews.

Moses obeyed and did what the angel told him to do.

God never left it as a problem of faith; it was a problem of obedience.

The word "faith" does not occur.

They were servants acting under orders from God, which came through angels.

Malachi 1:6 unveils it to us: *"A son honoureth his father, and a servant his master: if then I be a father, where is mine honour? and if I be a master, where is my fear? saith the Lord of hosts."*

Malachi 3:16 says, *"Then they that feared the Lord spake often one to another: and the Lord hearkened, and heard it, and a book of remembrance was written before him for them that feared the Lord, and that thought upon his name."*

And Malachi 4:2 says, *"But unto you that fear my name shall the Sun of righteousness arise with healing in his wings."*

You will notice that all through the old covenant, especially in the Psalms and in the prophetic books, Israel feared Jehovah.

Fear and love don't blend.

They were natural men who lived under an iron law called the law of death.

We are the new creation folks.

Fear has been taken out of us, and we love because He has imparted His love nature to us.

All of Israel's mighty men were mighty because God revealed Himself to them.

They learned to do what He told them to do.

Elijah said, *"O Jehovah, the God of Abraham, of Isaac, and of Israel, let it be known this day that thou art God in Israel, and that I am thy servant, and that I have done all these things at thy word"* (1 Kings 18:36 ASV).

Then the fire fell upon the altar and consumed the offering and the altar.

Elijah was simply doing what God had told him to do, not through anything that he had read, but an angel always communicated with him, or God gave him a dream or a vision.

Today, we are to act upon the written Word.

During the first century of the early church, only a very few people had the written Word.

Wherever Paul went, it was the spoken Word.

Where Peter and John went, it was the spoken Word.

We have the written Word, but faith makes of it a living Word, a life-giving Word, a healing Word, and a comforting Word.

To the unbelieving, it is just ink on paper, just words that may bring condemnation, or, if the heart is responsive, bring life and healing.

LEGAL AND VITAL SIDE OF THE PLAN OF REDEMPTION

It helped me greatly when I found that prayer was based on legal grounds; that it didn't depend upon struggle and long hours of agonizing before the Lord.

It wasn't based upon pity, but upon a legal foundation.

You remember that the Bible is made up of two covenants, two contracts: the old one and the new one.

The first contract was made with Abraham—sealed with blood.

The second contract was between Jesus and the Father—sealed with the Son's blood.

Israel were the beneficiaries of that first covenant.

We are the beneficiaries of the second.

Our redemption is based on legal grounds.

Our new birth is legal.

Every child of God is legally in His family.

The book of Romans that gives to us the plan of redemption is the greatest legal document in existence.

The New Testament or new covenant is the greatest document on jurisprudence ever given to man.

Hebrews 7:22 (ASV) says, *"By so much also hath Jesus become the surety of a better covenant."*

God said to Abraham, *"By myself have I sworn"* (Genesis 22:16). He becomes the surety of the old covenant.

You see, the throne is behind the covenant. Jesus and the Father are behind the new covenant and prayer is based upon this covenant; consequently, it is based upon legal grounds.

Mrs. Montgomery translates Hebrews 11:1 as, *"Faith is the title deed of things hoped for; the putting to the proof of things not seen."*

Practically all the basic terminology of English law comes from the Bible.

Then if prayer is based on legal grounds, we should learn what they are.

In the first place, we are legally justified or made righteous, legally born again, and have a legal right to eternal life and a son's place in the Father's family.

And He is legally responsible for us because He brought us into being. There are two phases of our redemption: one is the legal and the other is the vital.

The legal is what God has done for us in the past, like the substitutionary sacrifice of Christ.

The vital is what the Holy Spirit through the Word is doing in us.

Romans 4:25 is a good illustration of the legal: *"Who was delivered for our offences, and was raised again for our justification."*

The vital is illustrated in Philippians 2:13: *"For it is God which worketh in you both to will and to do of his good pleasure."* (See also 2 Corinthians 5:17.)

> *That he would grant you, according to the riches of his glory, to be strengthened with might by his Spirit in the inner man; that Christ may dwell in your hearts by faith; that ye, being rooted and grounded in love, may be able to comprehend with all saints what is the breadth, and length, and depth, and height; and to know the love of Christ, which passeth knowledge, that ye might be filled with all the fulness of God.*
>
> (Ephesians 3:16–19)

This is vital.

Notice the next verse: "*Now unto him that is able to do exceeding abundantly above all that we ask or think, according to the power that worketh in us.*"

Redemption is legal. It is in the past. It is a finished work.

The new birth is vital. It is now.

When you know that prayer is based on legal grounds and you know that God has legally tied Himself, has bound Himself, to do certain things, then you will learn to take your place and act accordingly.

His Son, the living Word, is the guarantor, and gives you your rights and privileges in redemption.

God gave us this Word of His own free will.

He has led us into the prayer life.

He has led us to trust Him and now He will not fail us.

So we can confidently turn to Isaiah 41:10 and hear Him whisper:

> *Fear thou not; for I am with thee: be not dismayed; for I am thy* [Father] *God: I will strengthen thee; yea, I will help thee; yea, I will uphold thee with the right hand of my righteousness.*

That "*right hand*" is Jesus and He is upholding us by the Word of His power, by the Word of His grace.

16

CASTING DOWN REASONINGS

The battle of faith is with sense knowledge reasonings. Man's word has been at war with God's Word ever since the beginning in the garden. The real struggle today that every believer must wage is with the sense knowledge that governs the human race.

> *Lead the life of the Spirit; then you will never satisfy the passions of the flesh. For the passion of the flesh is against the Spirit, and the passion of the Spirit against the flesh — the two are at issue, so that you are not free to do as you please.* (Galatians 5:16–17 MOFF)

We may talk about faith in man, faith in ourselves, or faith in the works of man without opposition, but when we talk about having faith in the Bible, in the Word of God, we often find rebellion.

You will find that sense knowledge is faith's worst enemy.

It will never give the Word first place. It admires the Word, but does not obey it.

It often confesses it as God's Word, but obeys man's words.

As I look over the books that fashioned my early Christian life, I note that almost every one of them was written to prove that the Bible agreed with the latest dictum of science, that man's word had more authority than the Word of God.

Having been mentally trained in sense knowledge, I found it difficult to give sense knowledge a second place, and the Word of God its real place.

> *Fight the good fight of faith, lay hold on eternal life, whereunto thou art also called, and hast professed a good profession before many witnesses.*
> (1 Timothy 6:12)

In the fight of faith, there is but one weapon, the sword of the Spirit.

The combat is with reason, which is governed by the adversary, through the senses.

The adversary is like the political boss in our great cities. His name is seldom ever mentioned. He is a hidden force. He puts up puppets to do his will.

Satan uses the same tactics. He has given us a fetish, called science.

How fearful I was of science in my early days. I did not want to appear unscientific.

What is science? It is the knowledge that has been gathered through years of hard study by sense knowledge ruled men.

Through science has come most of our knowledge. It has been gained by experimentation and by observation. How men have worked and sacrificed to get this knowledge. We honor them for their achievements.

Sense knowledge comes from the five senses. The body is the laboratory. The contacts it makes with material things are carried to the brain by the sensory nerves, which divides and classifies it.

It has no other means of knowledge.

Sense knowledge cannot go beyond things it has seen, felt, heard, tasted, or smelled. Whenever it leaves these avenues, it goes into the realm of speculation, of theory, trusting that the theories may become realities in the next step of the experiment.

Charles Darwin had nothing but theories and guesses when it came to the question of creation.

As long as he could see or handle things, he was working on quite sure ground. But when he was asked the reason for creation, the reason for man, the source of life and gravitation, he had but a guess.

We may clothe that guess in the most beautiful language, but it is only a hypothesis at best.

Faith deals with facts. The Word of God has no speculations, no theories, just declarations of fact.

Ephesians 6:11–18 gives a picture of our spiritual warfare. We are to put on the whole armor of God.

> *Stand therefore, having your loins girt about with truth, and having on the breastplate of righteousness; and your feet shod with the preparation of the gospel of peace.* (verses 14–15)

Our shield is faith; our sword is the Word of God.

Every part of this armor is put on by faith. The whole armor in which we are garmented is a faith armor.

You cannot see truth, you cannot see righteousness, you cannot see peace, and you cannot see faith.

You cannot feel or hear any of them. Their substance is all in the spirit.

When we come to recognize that spiritual things are as real as physical things, then we will be able to understand the background of the faith life.

Hebrews 4:14 (ASV) says, *"Let us hold fast our confession."* Our confession has not one physical thing in it. It hasn't anything that can be seen, or felt, or heard, outside of the Word of God.

Faith is not based upon reason, nor upon things that men can see, unless the thing they see is the Word of God.

> *That your faith should not stand in the wisdom of men, but in the power of God.* (1 Corinthians 2:5)

The wisdom of which He is speaking is sense knowledge wisdom.

> *We do discuss "wisdom" with those who are mature; only it is not the wisdom of this world or of the dethroned Powers who rule this world, it is the mysterious Wisdom of God that we discuss.*
> (1 Corinthians 2:6–7 MOFF)

This is God's wisdom.

Jesus dethroned the powers that govern sense knowledge.

Nowhere does Paul make it as clear as he does in 2 Corinthians 10:3–5: *"For though we walk in the flesh, we do not war after the flesh"* or senses (verse 3).

Though we live in the realm of the senses, we do not war with the weapons of the senses.

> *For the weapons of our warfare are not carnal* [senses], *but mighty through God to the pulling down of strong holds.* (2 Corinthians 10:4)

What are the strongholds?

> *Casting down imaginations, and every high thing that exalteth itself against the knowledge [or Word] of God, and bringing into captivity every thought to the obedience of Christ.* (Verse 5)

We cast down reasonings, for men have deified reasonings. The great reasoners of the world and the great philosophers of the world have gained the ascendancy over the human mind.

The philosopher is the apologist for the failure of the sense knowledge man.

No man turns philosopher until he has the sense of utter failure, and he is writing an excuse for that failure.

Philosophy has never given anything of any value to the church.

What we called our Christian philosophers are often men who denied the miraculous and the supernatural.

They denied that God could hear prayer and would heal men today.

Philosophy is the swan song of human failure; it is born of the senses.

We are to cast down imaginations or reasonings, everything that sense knowledge has exalted against the Word of God, and we are to bring into captivity our thinking so we will think God's thoughts instead of man's thoughts, so we will be inspired by the Word of God rather than by the word of man.

God is a faith God. It took many years to find this out. I could think of Him as a love God, a holy God, and an omnipotent God, but to think of Him as a faith God was revolutionary.

There are two Scriptures that we should notice.

Hebrews 11:1 says, "*Now faith is the substance of things hoped for, the evidence of things not seen.*" Mrs. Montgomery calls faith "*the title deed.*"

You never expect anything *now* for which you hope. Hope is always in the future.

There is nothing firm or solid or tangible about hope. But faith gives reality to this thing you have hoped for, that you never would have had otherwise.

Romans 4:17 says, "*Before him whom he believed, even God, who quickeneth* [gives life to] *the dead, and calleth those things which be not as though they were.*" God calls the things that are not, as though they were, and they become.

Speaking of Abraham, He said, "*Who against hope believed in hope, that he might become the father of many nations, according to that which was spoken*" (Romans 4:18).

This is a striking Scripture. Abraham had a battle with hope. Finally, he arrived. He believed against hope. He counted God's word to be absolute.

> *Without being weakened in faith he considered his own body now as good as dead (he being about a hundred years old), and the deadness of Sarah's womb; yet, looking unto the promise of God, he wavered not through unbelief, but waxed strong through faith, giving glory to God, and being fully assured that what he had promised, he was able also to perform.*
>
> (Romans 4:19–21 ASV)

Abraham looked at his body and saw it exactly as it was, an impotent, worn-out thing. He looked at Sarah, another broken vessel. Yet looking unto the promise of God, he waxed strong. He counted that God could make good what He had promised.

Abraham moved into God's class. He counted the things that were not as though they were, and they became.

He counted his body to be as good as it was at the age of thirty-five years. He considered Sarah to be as young, and capable of bearing children.

He counted the thing that was not as though it was, and it became.

Reason would have conquered had he yielded to it. Reason said, "Tradition shows that no man has ever had his youth renewed, that no woman past ninety years of age has ever had a child."

Yet this man believed against all the evidences of sense knowledge, and counted that God was able to make good what He had promised.

> *By faith we understand that the worlds have been framed by the word of God, so that what is seen hath not been made out of things which appear.*
>
> (Hebrews 11:3 ASV)

God had said before, "Let there be an earth," and the earth came into being.

He said, "Let there be light." It was not the light of the sun or moon. It was a light that gave us the subtropical heat during the first four days of creation, that gave us our vast fields of coal and oil. There was no rotation of the earth, thus the whole of it was subtropical.

All that God did to create the universe was to say, "Let there be light in the firmament of heaven to give light upon the earth," and the sun, moon, and stars came into being.

The sun and moon did not function until the beginning of the fifth or sixth day. It would take ages on ages for the light to come to the earth from the distant stars.

God's only machinery for creation was His Word. In that Word was the faith of God expressed.

It is a strange thing that we have not been taught that our words can be filled with either faith or unbelief or cold speculation; we have not realized their effect on the hearer!

It is our words that build up great organizations and institutions.

It is our words that destroy or build. It is words that are filled with faith or unbelief.

Faith words are constructive. The man who inspires faith is a builder. He is constructive.

The man who inspires unbelief is an enemy of progress. Faith giving substance to the Word of God.

It is giving substance to things we have hoped for.

Faith makes man God-like, just as love makes him God-like.

God is a faith God, and when man links up with God, he becomes a faith man.

He and God work together, and walk together.

Second Corinthians 5:7 says, "*We walk by faith, not by sight.*"

The believer is a faith person. He does not walk by reason. He does not walk by sense knowledge.

He lives and walks in the realm of faith.

> *For by grace are ye saved through faith; and that not of yourselves: it is the gift of God: not of works, lest any man should boast. For we are his workmanship, created in Christ Jesus unto good works, which God hath before ordained that we should walk in them.* (Ephesians 2:8–10)

It is by grace we are saved. It is through faith. It is not of man's works. It is the gift of God. It is not of works lest any man should boast.

The new creation comes into being purely on the ground of faith.

God first believed it into being. Now we believe that Creator being, the Holy Spirit, into us. Our whole struggle in the faith life is to take the Word of God instead of the word of man, to rest in God's Word rather than in man's word.

MY RESOURCES

It staggered me when I said out loud, "God is the fount of my resources because He is the strength of my life; He is my ability; He is the Author and substance of my faith."

I am a partaker of the divine nature. "*These things have I written unto you... that ye may know that ye have eternal life, and that ye may believe on the name of the Son of God*" (1 John 5:13).

His life is His nature.

His nature is love.

If I have His nature, I have a measure of His ability. I have a measure of His love.

His wisdom is given to me in Christ without measure, so I can safely say that He is my ability.

You remember that Jesus said to the disciples, "*Tarry ye in the city of Jerusalem, until ye be endued with power from on high*" (Luke 24:49).

The word "power" comes from the Greek word *dunamis*. Robert Young translates this as "ability," and it is a better word. They were to tarry in Jerusalem until they received the ability of God.

You not only received the nature of God, but when the Spirit came into your life, you had in you the ability of God, the very resources of heaven.

No one yet knows the limit of that ability. It must be exhaustless.

Colossians 2:9–10 gives us a suggestion: "*For in him dwelleth all the fulness of the Godhead bodily. And ye are complete in him, which is the head of all principality and power.*"

Take with that Galatians 2:20 (ASV): "*I have been crucified with Christ; and it is no longer I that live, but Christ liveth in me.*"

He has come into me in all His fullness.

He has come into me with all His completeness.

Now we can understand John 1:16: *"Of his fulness have all we received, and grace for grace."*

The limitless One has come into me to take me over.

He gave to me His ability, His completeness.

Now I can understand Colossians 1:9 (MOFF) and Paul's prayer: *"We have never ceased to pray for you, asking God to fill you with the knowledge of his will in all spiritual wisdom and insight."*

The Greek word translated "knowledge" is *epiginosis*, which means "complete, perfect, or exact knowledge."

It means the very fullness of His ability.

First Corinthians 1:30 says God has made Jesus to be wisdom unto us.

Wisdom is the ability to use knowledge to my advantage.

I have the knowledge of the complete and perfect substitutionary work of Jesus.

Now I have the ability to incorporate that knowledge in my daily life.

I have spiritual wisdom and understanding so that I may *"walk worthy of the Lord unto all pleasing, being fruitful in every good work,"* and continually increasing in this exact, perfect knowledge of God. (See Colossians 1:9–12.)

I am made powerful with His ability, according to the might of His glory.

I now have steadfastness and longsuffering because of what I am in Christ.

I do not chide or condemn myself.

I throw myself open to this new life, this new unveiling of what I am in Christ.

I am longsuffering with those who can't see it, who seem to be unable to take it in, as I once was.

In the meantime, with great joy, I am giving thanks unto the Father, who has given me this ability to enjoy my share of the inheritance of the saints in light. For I have been delivered from the power of darkness and translated into the kingdom of the Son of His love, in whom I have my redemption from Satan's thralldom. (See Colossians 1:13–14.)

This new light has given me a new responsibility in the prayer life.

I can understand now why He said, "*Come boldly unto the throne of grace*" (Hebrews 4:16), into the throne room where He and the Father are seated together.

I am not to come as a servant or a slave, but I am to come as a lover, a son.

But prayer is not going to be what it was before I knew who I was, and what my privileges were.

Now I am going in to sit with Him in the council room. I am going to call His attention to the needs of the brethren who are sitting in the darkness of sense knowledge while they pray for faith and seek for power.

I am going to find out how they can be helped to see the light of life, for I remember the Master said:

> *I am the light of the world: he that followeth me shall not walk in darkness, but shall have the light of life.* (John 8:12)

I have found that light of life.

I am no longer walking in the darkness of sense knowledge.

I am no longer crippled by my inferiority complex or my sense of unworthiness.

I know that I am a beloved son; that I have my place in the Father's presence.

When we come to understand love's intimacy, love's privileges, and love's right to the Father's ear, we may rush into His presence at any time without an apology and lay our needs before Him—not only our personal needs, but the needs of those about us.

We can enjoy the ability and wisdom of our Father, and we will go out with that strange, sweet fragrance that is found only in the throne room, a fragrance that will cling to our garments.

Yes, our very words will have in them love's own sweet fragrance.

Men will know that we have been with Jesus, have been in fellowship with Him.

17

FELLOWSHIPPING THE FATHER

If God be for [you], *who can be against* [you]?
He that spared not his own Son, but delivered him up for us all,
how shall he not with him also freely give us all things?
—Romans 8:31–32

God and you are working together in carrying out His dream for the redemption of the world.

He can't get along without you, any more than you can get along without Him.

Jesus's illustration of the vine and the branches perfectly illustrates this. The vine can't bear fruit without the branches and the branches can't live without the vine.

Now you can understand the next two verses: "*Who shall lay any thing to the charge of God's elect? It is God that justifieth. Who is he that condemneth?*"

Not the Master, and He is the only One who has the legal right to do it.

This is a part of the conclusion of the first eight chapters of Romans. It shows the absolute oneness of the Father and His children and of their perfect fellowship and cooperation with the Father. It also shows their mastery over the forces of darkness and circumstances.

He climaxes it with, "*Nay, in all these things we are more than conquerors*" (Romans 8:37).

This is the background for a prayer life.

We have little groups of people who are making prayer a business. They are intercessors.

One group takes the requests for prayers that come in through the mail from our correspondence course and our books.

They have become experts in prayer.

They are getting the things that are being requested.

You see, God is active on your part.

He is standing up for you.

He is fighting for you.

He is supplying your needs.

Out of the treasury of His grace, He is giving you His wisdom and ability.

Second Corinthians 3:4–6 (ASV) likely has become very precious to you:

> *And such confidence have we through Christ to God-ward: not that we are sufficient of ourselves, to account anything as from ourselves; but our sufficiency is from God; who also made us sufficient as ministers of a new covenant.*

You see, we aren't common folks.

We are tied up with omnipotence.

We are united with God Himself.

We are carrying out His will here on the earth.

We are the channels through which He is pouring Himself upon the world.

So, it is perfectly normal that He should become our sufficiency, and that His ability should become our ability.

LIMITLESSNESS OF PRAYER

Now we can understand this Scripture: "*Working together with him*" (2 Corinthians 6:1 ASV).

This is fellowship with the Father. He is supplying strength, grace, and ability to the intercessor.

It is working with all wisdom and ability.

Now you can understand, *"For this cause we also, since the day we heard it, do not cease to pray for you, and to desire that ye might be filled with the knowledge of his will in all wisdom and spiritual understanding"* (Colossians 1:9).

The Greek word translated as "knowledge," you may remember, is *epiginosis*. This is something that He is supplying to you who are entering the prayer life.

It is a perfect knowledge of His will.

You can't make a success of the prayer life unless you know His will; unless you have His own wisdom and understanding, you are going to fail.

No matter how much you pray, your prayers will not be effective until you know His will.

> *And this is the confidence that we have in him, that, if we ask any thing according to his will, he heareth us: and if we know that he hear us, whatsoever we ask, we know that we have the petitions that we desired of him.*
> (1 John 5:14–15)

That settles the issue.

If we are in His will, our prayers are heard and answered and we get the thing for which we are praying.

So it is necessary that we have this perfect knowledge of His will for our prayer ministry, in order to *"walk worthy of the Lord unto all pleasing, being fruitful in every good work, and increasing in the knowledge of God"* (Colossians 1:10).

We are thinking of a prayer fruit now.

Jesus illustrated that, saying, *"If ye abide in me, and my words abide in you, ye shall ask what ye will, and it shall be done unto you. Herein is my Father glorified, that ye bear much fruit; so shall ye be my disciples"* (John 15:7–8).

This is very precious to me. He lets me see my legal standing and rights; now I can go to the Father and get the thing that my neighbor or brother needs.

When they send a handkerchief to us to pray over, we know that our prayer is going to bear fruit, and that the request is granted when I pray.

You see, this is not walking in darkness.

This is having an exact knowledge of His will in all spiritual understanding.

This is moving up into the realm of the recreated spirit, where you fellowship with Him who raised Jesus from the dead.

You learn to pray for the thing that He wishes accomplished.

You are in the groove, the current of His will.

You become His mic. He speaks through you.

You are His transmitter, His willing instrument through which His will can be done.

What He wishes done is done. You see that His will is carried out.

He can cast out demons through your lips now.

He can heal the sick through your lips. Your lips become His transmitter.

The Word on your lips is a living thing.

Jesus's name on your lips becomes omnipotence.

You take His place and do His work.

You have His "all authority" that was given to Him after He arose from the dead.

It thrills you, doesn't it?

You have His ability; that is love's ability.

You will love even as He loved.

His nature, that love nature, fills you.

His name is like a checkbook with a limitless account in the bank.

His Word—who can describe it?

The heart melts as it contemplates it.

His Word!

It is the Master speaking: "*Ye shall ask what ye will, and it shall be done unto you*" (John 15:7).

His Word is the sword of the spirit, one moment slaying unbelief, doubts, and fears, and the next moment, it is the sweet force of love to heal the broken-hearted, to give courage and strength to the weak.

His Word on your lips is like the Father's Word on Jesus's lips.

It defeats the forces of darkness.

It strengthens those whom Satan has made weak.

I hardly dare give you the next sentence: His Word on your lips makes you a superman.

You have all authority over the power of the enemy.

It is love that has been delegated to you.

It is love pouring itself through your lips.

You can enter the throne room at will. You are always welcome.

You are master of the laws of nature that would hurt and hinder.

You stand quietly in the presence of humanity's needs, knowing that you have authority to open the floodgates of grace, life, and love, and let them pour over the wounded broken-hearted men and women struggling in life's uneven fight.

SHARING WITH HIM

The highest order of prayer is a love affair: two lovers meeting, sharing with each other.

Not slaves and the master, neither servants and an overlord, but a Father and His children.

We come together as suggested in Matthew 18:19–20: *"If two of you shall agree on earth as touching any thing that they shall ask, it shall be done for them of my Father which is in heaven. For where two or three are gathered together in my name, there am I in the midst of them."*

This is not talking at Him. Much praying is merely talking at the Father.

This is a meeting together. Jesus said, *"There am I in the midst of them."*

It is a business meeting. It is a meeting in loving council.

You speak, telling your needs, and then wait, listening for Him to bring to you the Word of assurance.

The highest order of prayer is a dialogue: you and He conversing about His work.

You are there to talk things over with Him.

You are a son taking a son's place.

You are not conscious of your standing or righteousness.

You are intent upon doing His will, carrying out His will.

You and He are working together.

You see, He has made you not only a new creation and a son, but He has made you a partner in this work.

You are the fruit-bearing part of the company.

You are the hands and feet and the voice of the company.

Ofttimes, you are asking for another. One of His children is in distress, and you are asking His cooperation and His ability to meet that distress. One of His children has been injured in an accident and you are coming to Him for healing for the injured one, and for strength and courage for the loved ones.

You know your place in Christ and you are taking it now boldly.

You have gone beyond the period when you think of faith or your ability to stand in His presence. That is all of the past.

You know what you are in Christ, and you are assuming the responsibilities that belong to you.

YOU ARE MAKING A BUSINESS OF THIS PRAYER LIFE

You and He have gone into business together. He has furnished the capital and the wisdom; you furnish your ability, time, and talents, with His blessing upon them.

You recognize the gravity of it. It is an eternal thing; you are dealing with eternal issues and eternal spirits.

You are doing business with Him to carry out His will in the redemptive work that was wrought through Christ.

You realize that He cannot work without human aid. Angels can't do the work, nor any other heavenly being.

It devolves upon us, and you are taking your place as a junior member of the firm.

You are His contact man.

It may be that you are in the ministry, or a layman, or an official in some organization. You are taking your place now, representing Him.

You are bringing to Him the needs of your friends.

He is bringing to you the assurance that He will meet the needs.

THE SEATED CHRIST

Jesus did not sit down at the right hand of the majesty on high until He had finished the work of redemption.

Some of the outstanding features of this redemption are His absolute mastery over Satan. He dethroned the adversary. He stripped him of his authority and power.

And you understand that in that substitutionary work of Christ, we were identified with Him.

The Spirit makes it clear in Galatians 2:20 (ASV): *"I have been crucified with Christ."*

Colossians 2:12 says, *"Buried with him in baptism, wherein also ye are risen with him through the faith of the operation of God, who hath raised him from the dead."*

Not only were we crucified with Him, but we died with Him.

We were buried with Him.

We suffered with Him.

We were justified with Him.

We were made alive with Him.

We conquered Satan and stripped him of his authority, with Him.

And then, Ephesians 2:5–6 (ASV) says God *"even when we were dead through our trespasses, made us alive together with Christ (by grace have ye been saved), and raised us up with him, and made us to sit with him in the heavenly places."*

Not only were we made alive and raised, but in the mind of justice, we are seated with Him today.

What does that mean?

It means absolute dominion over our enemies.

It means utter oneness with Christ. As the branch and vine are one, so are the individual and Christ one.

His victory was our victory.

His mastery over the forces of darkness was our mastery.

And so when He sat down, He entered into His rest, for His work was finished.

When we understand, we enter into His rest with Him.

Then we have entered into our rest. Our days of want, fear, and anxiety are over. We have cast all our anxiety upon Him, for He cares for us. (See 1 Peter 5:7.)

So, if Jesus is seated, His work is finished.

All we do when we accept Him as our Savior is enter into the benefits of the work that He has done for us.

We are healed the moment we say, "He has borne our pains and carried our sicknesses, and with His stripes, we are healed." (See Isaiah 53:4–5.) Our anxiety ends and our healing becomes real.

"My God shall supply every need of yours" (Philippians 4:19 ASV). The fear of want ends.

We have entered into our rest with Him.

OF HIS FULLNESS

"Of his fulness have all we received, and grace for grace" (John 1:16).

"For in him dwelleth all the fulness of the Godhead bodily. And ye are complete in him, which is the head of all principality and power" (Colossians 2:9–10).

Another wonderful Scripture is Ephesians 1:22–23: *"And hath put all things under his feet, and gave him to be the head over all things to the church, which is his body, the fulness of him that filleth all in all."*

Again, Ephesians 3:19 says, *"And to know the love of Christ, which passeth knowledge, that ye might be filled with all the fulness of God."*

What is this fullness?

Colossians 2:2–3 may help us. Here is Paul's prayer for the Colossian believers:

> *That their hearts might be comforted, being knit together in love, and unto all riches of the full assurance of understanding, to the acknowledgement*

> *of the mystery of God, and of the Father, and of Christ; in whom are hid all the treasures of wisdom and knowledge.*

All the fullness and riches that belong to the believer, which were purchased for us in Christ's great substitutionary sacrifice, are in Christ.

"Of his fulness have all we received." Every believer has received a portion of that fullness, that completeness.

Among the great treasures of this is His love nature. Every one of us has received eternal life, the nature of the Father, and that nature is love.

"God is love" (1 John 4:16).

We have never majored this fact that we were a love product, that we are begotten of love, or that we have received the love nature, and we have never realized that we have in us the greatest thing in the world.

> *Now abideth faith, hope, love, these three; and the greatest of these is love.* (1 Corinthians 13:13 ASV)

Love is the greatest because it is the nature of God.

One stands mute in the presence of a fact like this, that we have in us God's nature.

The thing that hurts is that we have never given that nature sway. We have held His nature in bondage. God has been a prisoner in us.

Paul was no more a prisoner in Rome than the Holy Spirit has been a prisoner in us.

The second greatest thing that comes to us in the new birth is joy.

This is something that makes trouble lose its grip upon us, makes poverty lose its terror.

It is the joy of the Lord.

And you remember that He said, *"The joy of the LORD is your strength"* (Nehemiah 8:10). That was a prophecy.

Now Jesus said, *"These things have I spoken unto you, that my joy might remain in you, and that your joy might be full"* (John 15:11).

You understand the difference between joy and happiness. Happiness depends on the things that we have, or own, like property or loved ones. But joy is a thing of the spirit. It is the one quality that has made Christianity attractive to the world.

Joy is an artesian well in the spirit that bubbles up and overflows. It is the thing that Jesus said the Holy Spirit would give us.

> *He that believeth on me, as the scripture hath said, out of his belly shall flow rivers of living water.* (John 7:38)

This is joy unhindered, pouring out from us with a joyous spontaneity that attracts at once and captivates.

A person is speaking on the street, holding a meeting, and his voice is filled with a joy that grips the hearts of careless hearers. They draw near and listen. Out from his inner life is gushing torrents of living water full of divine laughter. It is joy unspeakable and full of glory.

Speaking to the early church regarding Jesus, Peter says, "*Whom having not seen, ye love; in whom, though now ye see him not, yet believing, ye rejoice with joy unspeakable and full of glory*" (1 Peter 1:8). This is the attractive feature of the divine life.

Another one of the fruits of His fullness is "*the peace of God, which passeth all understanding*" (Philippians 4:7).

It moves up out of the realm of the senses into the realm of the spirit.

No matter what the persecutions may be, peace like a river flows through the spirit.

No matter what turmoil is around you, the peace of God rules.

Jesus said, "*My peace I give unto you*" (John 14:27). That is one of the most outstanding features of the divine life.

Speaking of a martyr who had been bound to the stake, someone said, "Her face shone with a heavenly joy and her spirit seemed to be held captive by a peace that passed understanding." She had joy in the midst of death, and peace in the midst of agony.

This fullness not only has love, joy, and peace, but all the fruits of the recreated spirit seen in Galatians 5:22–23.

"*Of his fulness have all we received*" (John 1:16). It doesn't belong to just a few, but it belongs to every believer.

18

WHAT HE IS TO US

We know what He was to Israel under Moses in the four books of the law. We know what He was to Israel under the leadership of Joshua. We know what He was to Israel during all the years of their walking under the covenant.

No enemies could stand before them.

We know that under David, Israel conquered the entire inhabited world, and in all their wars, there never was a soldier slain unless Israel had broken the covenant.

If He was that to Israel and they were but servants, what could He be to us, His sons and daughters?

> *Mine hand also hath laid the foundation of the earth, and my right hand hath spanned the heavens: when I call unto them, they stand up together.* (Isaiah 48:13)

Notice that expression: "*When I call unto them, they stand up together.*"

God's voice controls the universe.

And remember that when the Man of Galilee spoke to the sea in the midst of the storm, it became calm and quiet in a moment.

Every law of nature was obedient to that Man.

We stand in the presence of creative faith, God's creative ability.

You can hear Him say, "When I call, they come into being."

Things that were not, become.

In Romans 4:17, speaking of Abraham, Paul said, "*Before him whom he believed, even God, who quickeneth* [gives life to] *the dead, and calleth those things which be not as though they were.*" And they become.

It thrills the heart when we realize what our omnipotent God of love and Father is. Another translation says God *"makes the dead live and calls into being what does not exist"* (MOFF).

That is dominating faith; that is creative faith.

In Matthew 14:15–21 is the story of Jesus feeding the multitude. He took in His hands five loaves of bread and two fish and He blessed them. He broke the bread and fed five thousand men, as well as an unknown number of women and children. After the meal was over, they gathered up twelve baskets full of food.

In this story, we are given two facts. First, Jesus ruled the law of supply and demand by ruling the very laws of nature.

Second, the twelve baskets they collected showed that He not only met their need, but went over and above. It was beyond all that they could ask or think.

That is our Christ. How proud we should be of Him. How we should brag about Him before men. He is our Lord.

If we had a son or father or relative who could do such miracles, we would brag about him.

He is our Lord. He is our Savior.

We are partakers of His nature. Don't you remember John 15:5: *"I am the vine, ye are the branches?"*

How utterly one we are with Him! How we should rejoice in the fact that we have such oneness.

We read in John 5:25–29:

> *The hour is coming, and now is, when the dead shall hear the voice of the Son of God: and they that hear shall live. For as the Father hath life in himself; so hath he given to the Son to have life in himself; and hath given him authority to execute judgment also, because he is the Son of man. Marvel not at this: for the hour is coming, in the which all that are in the graves shall hear his voice, and shall come forth.*

That is our Master, our Lord.

That is dominating, creative faith.

Scripture gives us a picture of Abraham's creative faith. Read this story over carefully until your spirit catches fire.

> *And without being weakened in faith he considered his own body now as good as dead (he being about a hundred years old), and the deadness of Sarah's womb; yet, looking unto the promise of God, he wavered not through unbelief, but waxed strong through faith, giving glory to God, and being fully assured that what he had promised, he was able also to perform.* (Romans 4:19–21 ASV)

Abraham was a blood covenant friend of Jehovah. That blood covenant was sealed with the blood of an animal and the blood of Abraham mingled.

Our covenant is sealed with the blood of Jesus Christ. Deity and humanity united in the incarnation.

How much better is the blood of Jesus Christ than the blood of an animal!

How much better is the life of the Son of God than the life of a mere man like Abraham!

We are bound to Him by an indissoluble covenant. He is bound to us as Jehovah was bound to Abraham in that covenant.

If Abraham, a friend of God, could accept an angel's testimony and act upon it, what can we as sons of God do? You know what happened to Abraham. His youth was renewed. Sarah's youth and beauty were renewed so that a king fell in love with her and wished to marry her, not knowing that she was Abraham's wife. She was past ninety years of age, and the following year, she gave birth to Isaac.

That was the God with whom you and I are dealing. He is our Father.

If Abraham could accept the testimony of an angel, can't we accept the testimony of the new covenant? We have become the very sons and daughters of God Almighty.

By a new creation, we are partakers of His very nature. We have become heirs of God, joint heirs with Jesus Christ. We are the next of kin to the Son of God. How it thrills the heart!

And you understand that in another chapter, I have shown you that Jesus has given us the power of attorney to use His name.

When the Master was ready to leave the earth to go back to the Father, He said:

> *All authority hath been given unto me in heaven and on earth. Go ye therefore, and make disciples of all the nations, baptizing them into the name of the Father and of the Son and of the Holy Spirit: teaching them to observe all things whatsoever I commanded you: and lo, I am with you always, even unto the end of the world.* (Matthew 28:18–20 ASV)

You see what we have now?

We have never taught them to observe or to do all that He commanded.

Didn't He command them with love's commandment to love one another, even as He had loved, to bear one another's burdens as He bore ours, to lay hands on the sick, and to cast out demons in His name?

Can't you see what it meant when He said, *"Lo, I am with you always, even unto the end of the world"* (Matthew 28:20)?

If we would use that name with the authority invested in it, we could break the power of Satan over our loved ones; we could heal the sick. Instead of there being just one George Müller caring for thousands of little orphans by faith, there would be thousands of men and women whose prayers would feed and clothe the needy and the hungry.

We have never taken the Word seriously. We have never acted as though it were true.

If someone wrote a letter to you and told you that he had deposited five thousand dollars in your bank account to take care of your bills, and if you knew that he was financially able to do it, you would not hesitate a moment. You could hardly wait to get to the bank. You would hand the letter to the cashier with confidence. You know the man who wrote the letter; you know the promise he made; you know the money is there waiting for you.

Is the Word of your Father, the Word of the Master, to be depended upon as the word of a friend?

What a background this is for faith! What a prayer life can grow out of truth like this!

You can see what He is to us and what we are to Him.

Nothing is impossible to Him, and all His ability is ours.

What an opportunity to bless and help by our prayers!

GOD'S WORD

When the angel visited Mary to tell her the glad tidings of the Father's will for her to be the mother of the incarnate One, she said a remarkable thing: *"Behold the handmaid of the Lord; be it unto me according to thy word"* (Luke 1:38).

How that grips the heart! Hear her say, "Behold, here am I, your slave of love. Be it unto me, oh Lord, according to thy Word."

What sublime confidence that Jewish maid had in the word of that angel when she said this.

Previously she had spoken, "How can it be? I am not a married woman." (See Luke 1:34.)

> *The angel answered her, "The holy Spirit will come upon you, the power of the Most High will overshadow you; hence what is born will be called holy, Son of God."* (Luke 1:35 MOFF)

And then the angel said, *"For with God nothing shall be impossible"* (Luke 1:37). This has also been translated as, *"For no word from God shall be void of power"* (ASV), and *"For with God nothing is ever impossible"* (MOFF).

This is creative ability. This is God's Word.

How it thrills our hearts when we realize that God and His Word are one. Mary recognized that God and His Word were one. God's Word is God's faith expressed. It is God's confession about Himself. His Word is invested with God's authority and God's ability.

You remember that He said, *"By the word of the LORD were the heavens made"* (Psalm 33:6).

> *By faith we understand that the worlds have been framed by the word of God, so that what is seen hath not been made out of things which appear.* (Hebrews 11:3 ASV)

That is faith's creative ability through words.

You remember that practically all of Jesus's miracles were performed with words. He said this significant thing: *"What you hear me say is not my word but the word of the Father who sent me"* (John 14:24 MOFF).

In John 12:49 (MOFF), we read, *"I have not spoken of my own accord—the Father who sent me, he it was who ordered me what to say and what to speak."*

So, Jesus was not using His own words, but the Father's words. The words that have come down to us spoken by the Master were the words of the Father. They were creative words; they were healing words; they were demon-dominating words, words filled with God and His faith.

I have been thrilled lately by noticing the faith of Jesus. He believed that He could redeem men if He became sin and suffered in their stead. He believed that if He conquered Satan, men would accept that victory as their own.

He believed that if He arose from the dead, men would believe that He was the very Son of God. He believed in the merits of His finished work, that men could stand in His presence without condemnation.

He believed that He could take these old, broken, wrecked human beings and recreate them and make them the very sons and daughters of God.

He believed that He could take this wreck of a human who had been dominated by sickness and sin through the ages and make him a new creation, make him to dominate the devil and circumstances, and make him master where he had served as a slave.

Jesus believed in Himself and in what He did. He believed that men would respond to it, would accept it, and would receive eternal life, the nature of the Father. They would then become worthy sons and daughters of God Almighty.

The Word can't lie. It is a part of God Himself.

We act on the Word. God will make it good.

What a foundation is this for a prayer life!

We have God's own Word to back us. No Word from God can fail.

We can have real assurance in our prayer. When we pray in Jesus's name, it is as though He prayed. It is answered.

SOME FACTS ABOUT THE BELIEVER

The believer is a child of God, a new creation. His spirit has been recreated. He has come into the family of God. He is in the realm of the supernatural. He is in perfect union with the Master.

The believer and Jesus are one. He is the head and they are the body; so He says, "*All things are possible to him that believeth*" (Mark 9:23).

That means all things are possible to a believing one—one who has come into the family of God, who has become a new creation created in Christ Jesus.

This is not a hyperbole; this is just a statement of fact. Just as all things were possible with Jesus, all things are possible to the believer through the name of Jesus.

You remember that 1 John 4:4 reads, "*Ye are of God, little children, and have overcome them* [demonic forces]: *because greater is he that is in you, than he that is in the world.*"

You grasp it. Your heart knows it. You are of God, born from above.

God Himself recreated you, imparted to your spirit His own nature. Now you stand before Him as though you had never been weak, as though you had never been a failure, as though you had never been under condemnation. Again, He says, "Nothing shall be impossible unto you."

This is to the man of faith.

This is the man created out of righteousness and holiness of truth. He is talking about the one that He came to recreate, this new man.

Of him, He says, "There is now no condemnation to you because you are in Christ Jesus." (See Romans 8:1.)

There is a perfect union of your spirit with His Spirit. You are His representative here on earth.

He says we are ambassadors on behalf of Christ. An ambassador is an empowered representative of a country where his citizenship is located.

You are born of heaven; your citizenship is there. You have received your credentials from heaven.

God is your actual Father. You are His child.

Your Lord and Master has told you that all authority has been given to Him in heaven and on earth. "*Go ye therefore, and make disciples of all the nations*" (Matthew 28:19 ASV). He said, "Don't forget to teach them all that I have commanded you."

That is a mighty ministry.

In John 14:12, we read, *"He that believeth on me, the works that I do shall he do also; and greater works than these shall he do; because I go unto my Father."*

He went unto the Father to become the Mediator, Intercessor, Savior, Advocate, and Lord of the church. He is now at the right hand of the Father. He is going to enable us to take His place and do the same kind of works that He did before He went away.

In the next verse, He gives us the power of attorney to use His name: *"Whatsoever ye shall ask in my name, that will I do"* (verse 13).

This is not prayer to the Father.

This is dealing with demonic forces as illustrated in Acts 3, where we see the man lying at the Beautiful gate of the temple, evidently with infantile paralysis. *"And Peter, fastening his eyes upon him with John, said, Look on us"* (verse 4). Then, *"In the name of Jesus Christ of Nazareth rise up and walk"* (verse 6).

In that name, Peter broke the dominion of Satan over the man.

That man had believed in sickness and weakness, believed he was helpless.

The name of Jesus broke the dominion of faith in disease and weakness; in its place came perfect healing and a new faith in health.

Notice again, *"Whatsoever ye shall ask in my name"* (John 14:13). In the Greek, that word *ask* is "demand." Jesus is saying, "Whatsoever you shall demand in my name, I shall make good."

We are coming into the realm of the supernatural, where we see ourselves as representatives of omnipotence and where we have an opportunity to draw on omnipotence to meet Satan in open combat.

John 15:7 says, *"If ye abide in me, and my words abide in you, ye shall ask what ye will, and it shall be done unto you."*

That lets us into the realm of cooperation with the Father.

We are taking Jesus's place here on earth; we are acting in His stead. We are doing the work that He began to do.

He came to destroy the works of the adversary.

We are continuing that work of destruction.

We are His co-laborers, working under His direction, setting man free from the dominion of the prince of darkness.

You see, the believer is united with all authority, all ability.

You remember that just before His ascension, Jesus said, *"Ye shall receive power, when the Holy Spirit is come upon you: and ye shall be my witnesses"* (Acts 1:8 ASV).

The word "power" comes from the Greek word *dunamis,* which means ability.

Jesus is saying, "You have the ability to use My name and cast out demons, heal the sick, and deliver men from the bondage of want into the liberty wherewith I have made you free.

"You have the ability to understand Me and to make Me known.

"You have the ability to understand the revelation that I am going to give through My slave of love, Paul."

Ability means wisdom. Wisdom is ability to use knowledge, handle circumstances, and take advantage of opportunities.

The believer has the very nature of God. God is love.

We are born of love. We are a love creation.

We have the ability to love even as He loved.

We have the ability to know men and be able to meet their need and help them.

You see, the believer has God in him. For it is God who is at work within you, willing and working His own good pleasure. (See Philippians 2:13.)

How limitless becomes our ministry when we realize the integrity of the Word, when we know we have what He says we have, when we know we are what He says we are, and when we know we can do what He says we can do!

We step out of the narrow limits of theology and sense knowledge into the boundless ability of God.

Now we understand what it means when we say, *"I can do all things through Christ which strengtheneth me"* (Philippians 4:13).

With quiet confidence, we face the impossible, knowing that He is Master.

You understand that we never pray for anything we can do or accomplish ourselves.

We are asking God to enable us to do the impossible.

That makes us world conquerors.

We know that greater is He that is in us than any opposition that can confront us.

Our sufficiency is of God, who has made us sufficient as ministers of a new covenant.

What courage it puts into one to know that he has God's sufficiency.

One translator says, "He makes us sufficient for anything." So, with boundless confidence, we swing free in this glorious ministry into which He has called us, the ministry of prayer.

You have seen what you are in Christ; now take your place as a prayer warrior. Make hell fear you. Make heaven glad. Fill hearts of men with joy, witnessing your winning prayer life.

Healing the sick is His will. Saving the lost is His will. Breaking Satan's dominion over men is His will.

Praying for ministers and missionaries is His will. Pray for this literature we are sending out that men will take their places as they know the Word.

Now swing free in your prayer life. Be big! Honor the Word.

Dare to do exploits for Him.

SO SHALL MY WORD BE

We are going to take a trip now amid some of the mighty Scriptures, mostly from the Old Testament. It will be like a trip into the redwoods of California, where you stand in the presence of those mighty trees lifting their proud heads up toward the clouds.

> *God is not a man, that he should lie; neither the son of man, that he should repent: hath he said, and shall he not do it? or hath he spoken, and shall he not make it good?* (Numbers 23:19)

This gets into the blood. This gives us a warrior spirit. This makes you confident of your place in Christ.

This makes you know that you are what He says you are and you can do what He says you can do.

The Word of our God shall stand forever, and you are trusting in that Word.

Your confidence is in that Word that cannot be broken.

We think of the hills and their steadfastness...and yet you know the day will come when they will stop being.

"But the Word that I speak to you," said Jesus, "shall never pass away." (See Matthew 24:35.)

> *So shall my word be that goeth forth out of my mouth: it shall not return unto me void, but it shall accomplish that which I please, and it shall prosper in the thing whereto I sent it.* (Isaiah 55:11)

You feel like David must have felt when he said, *"For by thee I have run through a troop"* (Psalm 18:29)

You become by this study a master of circumstances.

"I have learned, in whatsoever state I am, therewith to be content" (Philippians 4:11).

You see, when you get tied up with God, when you and God become identified as you do in the new creation, you pass out of the realm of "I can't" into the realm of "I can." You are no longer a failure. You know that you can do all things in Him who strengthens you.

Jeremiah 1:12 (ASV) states, *"I watch over my word to perform it."*

How many hard places this has bridged! Impassable gulfs have become level roads to us when we realized that God was watching over His Word.

We take His Word and carry it into His presence. You repeat it and say, "Father, this is what you said."

We would not say that we knew He kept His Word. That is an insult.

We just look up and say, "Father, I thank you."

Did you ever notice Hebrews 6:18? *"That by two immutable things, in which it was impossible for God to lie, we might have a strong consolation"* or *"encouragement"* (ASV).

We see all that Christianity has built in the last three hundred years disintegrating, just melting under the terrific onslaught of satanic forces through dictators with their selfish ambitions, and yet we turn back to the living Word with confidence.

We are dealing with Him who cannot lie.

The dictators are liars; they are the sons of the old liar, the destroyer of the whole inherited earth.

You see, *"He abideth faithful: he cannot deny himself"* (2 Timothy 2:13).

No word from God can ever be defaulted. There never can be any denying of His own Word.

We did not ask Him to write the Word, nor to see that it was preserved for us.

He did that; He has encouraged us to trust Him.

We would never walk by faith if He had not enticed us to walk that pleasant road.

We would never have depended on prayer, nor rested on His Word, unless He had challenged us with love's own challenge.

Isaiah 45:23 says, *"I have sworn by myself."*

God's throne is behind this. This is repeating what He said to Abraham.

I wonder if our hearts can take it.

God is throwing a cable about the throne and dropping the cable over for us to grasp.

He said, "Do you see? I am putting my throne as surety for my Word. My very Self is enwrapped in this." Then we remember Hebrews 7:22, where He said that Jesus was made the surety of the new covenant. Now we have the Father and Jesus and the throne behind every Word. If that Word should fail, it would dethrone God.

It cannot fail.

God cannot be separated from His Word.

Every Word of God abides.

The word of man is as grass, but the Word of God lives on through the ages.

This Word is like God.

Now you can understand John 1:1–3:

> *In the beginning was the Word, and the Word was with God, and the Word was God. The same was in the beginning with God. All things were made by him; and without him was not any thing made that was made.*

That Word is the Creator and the creative element of the universe. You remember that it is with the Word *"we have to do."* (See Hebrews 4:12–13.)

We contact God through the Word. God contacts us through the Word. We act on the Word.

Now arise in your prayer life. Take the place God has given you. Set men free, heal the sick, and save the lost. You can do it.

AS THE FATHER SEES US

What assurance it gives to the heart when we come to know that the Father loves us even as He loved Jesus, that He is vitally interested in us as He was in His Son when He walked the earth.

You know that the four Gospels are Jesus introducing the Father, and the Epistles are the Father introducing Jesus and what He did. They also introduce the sons and daughters of God to the world.

The church and Jesus are one. He is the Head of the body.

> *And he is the head of the body, the church: who is the beginning, the firstborn from the dead; that in all things he might have the preeminence.* (Colossians 1:18)

Jesus was the first person ever born again. He was born twice. He was born of the Virgin Mary; then on the cross, He was made sin with our sin, as our substitute. Then after He had satisfied the claims of justice, He was justified in spirit, made righteous in spirit, and made alive in spirit. This was the new birth.

That is why the Father, speaking of the resurrection of the Lord Jesus, said, *"Thou art my Son, this day have I begotten thee"* (Acts 13:33).

This Scripture wonderfully helped me to understand the substitutionary work of Jesus. He had actually become sin, was forsaken of God, a curse because He had hung upon the tree. After meeting every demand of justice,

He was born again out of death, recreated, and became a partaker of eternal life.

Now He is called the firstborn out of death, the Head of the new creation.

You know that Ephesians 2:10 says, *"For we are his workmanship, created in Christ Jesus unto good works, which God hath before ordained that we should walk in them."*

It was that morning when Jesus was recreated that the whole church by faith came into being. In reality, it began on the day of Pentecost and it has continued until now.

So, I want you to see yourself as the Father sees you in Christ. As He sees us by faith, He is able to make us by grace. As we walk in love, we are being transformed into His image.

One of the most graphic pictures is given in John's gospel. John 1:16 says, *"Of his fulness have all we received, and grace for grace."* His fullness here means His ability, His love, His righteousness, and His utter completeness—and we have received it.

I used to wonder why He said, *"And grace for grace."* Now my heart can understand it.

I shrank back and said, "Lord, it cannot be possible that I have received this fullness."

And just as you would give a fainting one a drink of water, He gave me a drink of grace, and it strengthened me to look again. I saw myself in Christ and I saw myself receiving of His fullness and His grace, His love life and wisdom, His very being and substance.

I could hardly understand it; I said, "Lord, it is too much."

Then He gave me another taste of His grace, as it were.

I arose up and said, "It is true, I am a branch of the vine; I am a partaker of the divine nature."

As we act on the Word, the Word reacts in us; it is built into us and so we grow up in Christ. We are partakers of His nature, of His very substance and being.

In Ephesians 1:3, it says God has *"blessed us with all spiritual blessings in heavenly places in Christ."*

I wondered what He meant—that He had blessed us with every spiritual blessing. Something kept saying, "You are blessed. You are rich; you have His fullness. All that He is, you have."

My spirit seemed to be numb and could not take it in. And then in His great grace, He seemed to enfold me, breathe into my spirit His own life.

I said, "Yes, Lord, I am what you say I am."

And the Father has told me that I am in the beloved.

Why, love marked us out for the position of sons way back before the morning stars sang their first anthem, and we are made unto the praise of His glory. He planned that we should be holy and without blemish before Him. He marked us out for the position of sons through Jesus Christ unto Himself. And you are the marked one.

You remember in Malachi 3:17: "*They shall be mine, saith the* L*ORD of hosts, in that day when I make up my jewels; and I will spare them, as a man spareth his own son that serveth him.*"

The Father sees us as His own righteousness in Christ Jesus.

For a long time, that bothered me.

> *He hath made him to be sin for us, who knew no sin; that we might be made the righteousness of God in him.* (2 Corinthians 5:21)

I said, "I cannot understand, Lord, how You can make me as Your righteousness. But You say You have and because You said it, I accept it."

He says we are complete in Him. (See Colossians 2:10.)

You see, righteousness gives us the ability to stand in His presence without the sense of guilt or inferiority, and this completeness is over and above all that we can ask or think or desire.

It is the measure filled full, shaken down, and running over. (See Luke 6:38.) It is the Father's love for me.

I want you to see one other picture.

Jesus said, "If you love Me, you will keep My word, and the Father and I will love you and come and make Our home with you." (See John 14:23.)

That is a Christian home. That is living with the Father and Jesus. The Father and Jesus make themselves One with us. That is just like His incarnation, where He came and made Himself one with man.

In the new birth, He makes us one with Himself; He comes and lives with us.

Now you know what you are in Christ. You see your vast responsibility.

You can pray, for you know how.

Take your place in Christ.

Dare to act your part.

Dare to let God use you.

Dare to let love reign in your life.

Dare to be in your daily life what He says you are.

Dare to *do* what He says you can do.

Dare to confess that you are what He says you are!

All is yours. Use it.

THE RELATION OF LOVE TO PRAYER

God is love.

We are the sons of love.

Love gave us birth.

Love planned our redemption. Love consummated it in a new creation and then Jesus gave them the new law.

> *A new commandment I give unto you, That ye love one another; as I have loved you, that ye also love one another. By this shall all men know that ye are my disciples, if ye have love one to another.* (John 13:34–35)

This new law is to govern the walk of the church, the sons of God.

Jesus set an example of how we should walk, and then, in the new birth, He gave us the ability to walk even as He walked. He does not ask us to do a thing that cannot be done.

You understand that we have the nature of God, eternal life. The very substance of God has come into our spirits. We have been redeemed out of the hand of the enemy; we have been translated into the kingdom of the Son of His love in whom we have our redemption.

Not only are we new creations, but we have become the very righteousness of God in Christ.

This gives us boldness in the Father's presence, and it gives us fearlessness in the presence of the enemy or any of his works.

Then He gave to us the legal right to the use of His name so that we can rule over the adversary. He has made us masters of demons. How little we have appreciated it.

We are in God's family. God is our Father, we are His very sons and daughters.

We are to walk in love. Love is to govern our conversation, our conduct toward one another.

When we step out of love into selfishness, we break fellowship with love.

No one can walk in selfishness and pray the prayer of faith.

Here is a graphic picture of the relationship of love to answered prayer:

> *Hereby perceive we the love of God, because he laid down his life for us: and we ought to lay down our lives for the brethren. But whoso hath this world's good* [wealth], *and seeth his brother have need, and shutteth up his bowels of compassion from him, how dwelleth the love of God in him? My little children, let us not love in word, neither in tongue; but in deed and in truth. And hereby we know that we are of the truth, and shall assure our hearts before him. For if our heart condemn us, God is greater than our heart, and knoweth all things. Beloved, if our heart condemn us not, then have we confidence toward God.* (1 John 3:16–21)

Just before this, John wrote:

> *We know that we have passed from death unto life, because we love the brethren. He that loveth not his brother abideth in death. Whosoever hateth his brother is a murderer: and ye know that no murderer hath eternal life abiding in him.* (1 John 3:14–15)

This is putting the case very clearly.

We have passed out of the realm of satanic union, spiritual death, into the union of eternal life and love.

Jesus laid down His life for us.

Now Love says that we ought to live for fellow Christians, and then He asks that remarkable question, "If someone has the world's goods and sees his brother in need and has no compassion for him, how can the love of God abide in him?" (See 1 John 3:17.)

The world's goods are the things that we prize most highly: land, houses, bonds, stocks, money, and beautiful things. We have taken Satan's appraisal of their value.

These worldly things have made us selfish.

This new kind of love is to break the monopoly of selfishness and establish a new order of life.

This new man is no longer to live unto himself, but is to give his life for others.

If he shuts up his compassion from his brother and refuses to bear his burdens and pay his bills, he at once sins against love and God says, "How does the new kind of love abide in him?"

Unless we walk in love and have yielded to the lordship of love, God cannot manifest Himself through us.

The ability of God is realized only in love's freedom to act.

Selfishness imprisons love.

"My little children, let us not love in word, neither in tongue; but in deed and in truth" or reality (1 John 3:18).

He wants us to be the Lord's truth-doers.

You remember that Jesus said:

> *Every one therefore that heareth these words of mine, and doeth them, shall be likened unto a wise man, who built his house upon the rock: and the rain descended, and the floods came, and the winds blew, and beat upon that house; and it fell not: for it was founded upon the rock.*
>
> (Matthew 7:24–25 ASV)

You remember that James said, *"But be ye doers of the word, and not hearers only, deceiving your own selves"* (James 1:22).

This lover is a doer of love. He lives in the love realm. It is not the old *phileo* love, but the new kind of love that Jesus brought, *agape,* and so we love in deed and in reality.

Hereby shall we know that we are of the truth and persuade our hearts when we stand before Him in prayer.

If you walk in love, you can walk into the Father's presence just as Jesus did, and know that your prayers will be answered.

There is no problem of faith to confront us; you are walking in love; you are doing the word; and you are letting Jesus live His life in you.

The Father can see Jesus in us, feeling Jesus in our petitions for others.

"For if our heart condemn us, God is greater than our heart, and knoweth all things" (1 John 3:20).

Your heart is your spirit.

Your heart knows whether you are practicing love towards men. If they need clothes and you are able to give them, and they cannot get them, then it is up to you to meet that need. You are to treat them as Jesus has treated you. He died for you; you live for them. Hear this: "Beloved, if our heart does not condemn us, we have boldness toward God, and whatsoever we ask, we receive of Him because we are walking in love." (See 1 John 3:21–22.) We will do the things that are pleasing in His sight.

It makes no difference how many promises you plead. If you are not walking in love, your prayer life will be a failure.

Many people have come to me for prayer when they were sick, and I have prayed for them and obtained no results. When I asked them why my prayers were not answered, they confessed that they had bitterness in their heart toward someone. The moment that bitterness was taken away, they were perfectly well.

This verse is worthy of much meditation:

> *This is his commandment, That we should believe on the name of his Son Jesus Christ, and love one another.* (1 John 3:23)

If you have not understood what it means to believe in the name of Jesus, another chapter will explain it to you fully.

It is enough to know that He has given us the legal right to the use of His name, and then He tells us, *"All authority hath been given unto me in heaven and on earth"* (Matthew 28:18 ASV). He gives us a legal right to use this *"all authority."*

Do you remember 1 John 5:14? *"And this is the confidence that we have in him, that, if we ask any thing according to his will, he heareth us."*

If we walk in love, we never pray out of His will, and if we know that He hears us, whatever we ask, we know that we have the petitions we ask of Him.

This leads us right into the heart of the Father. Now we can understand Hebrews 4:16, *"Let us therefore come boldly unto the throne of grace, that we may obtain mercy, and find grace to help in time of need."*

This love life permits us to walk into the very presence of the Father. You may go into the throne room and stand in His presence and make your petitions known in the name of Jesus, and, as sure as you do, that petition is heard.

We were doers of selfishness, but we have become doers of love. We have consented to the dethroning of sense knowledge that has reigned in us. These five senses of hearing, seeing, tasting, smelling, and feeling have ruled us. In other words, our physical bodies have sat upon the throne of our lives. Now we are crowning our spirits, or to put it more clearly, we are recognizing the lordship of Jesus Christ and crowning Him as Lord of our whole being.

It was a wonderful day when love dethroned greed and love was crowned in the hearts of the new creation.

Here are three love scenes in the book of Acts. Few of us have realized what it must have meant to the Father to have love take over a group of men and women as it did in that upper room on the Day of Pentecost.

> *And fear came upon every soul: and many wonders and signs were done through the apostles. And all that believed were together, and had all things common; and they sold their possessions and goods, and parted them to all, according as any man had need. And day by day, continuing stedfastly with one accord in the temple, and breaking bread at home, they took their food with gladness and singleness of heart, praising God, and having favor with all the people. And the Lord added to them day by day those that were saved.* (Acts 2:43–47 ASV)

Here is a picture of outpoured love in the recreated men and women; all who believed were together and had all things in common.

In a single instant, those selfish Jews who had lived to make money have dethroned greed and crowned love as the Lord of their lives. It is a record of love at work, salvaging wrecked humanity.

Satan is dethroned; selfishness and greed meet their death stroke. The Father's love nature is taking control of men in Jerusalem. They have yielded to the lordship of love.

You remember that Jesus said, *"But tarry ye in the city* [Jerusalem], *until ye be clothed with power from on high"* (Luke 24:49 ASV), and, *"Ye shall receive power, when the Holy Spirit is come upon you"* (Acts 1:8 ASV).

The Greek word translated "power" means ability. See how it reads: tarry in Jerusalem until you receive ability from on High. These disciples had received God's own ability.

Already, they had performed many wonders and signs, but the mightiest of them all was when they had all things in common and no man said that what he possessed was his own. That was the miracle of miracles; they sold their possessions and shared with one another, according to each other's needs. Here is love gaining the mastery.

> *And the multitude of them that believed were of one heart and of one soul: neither said any of them that ought of the things which he possessed was his own; but they had all things common. And with great power gave the apostles witness of the resurrection of the Lord Jesus: and great grace was upon them all. Neither was there any among them that lacked: for as many as were possessors of lands or houses sold them, and brought the prices of the things that were sold, and laid them down at the apostles' feet: and distribution was made unto every man according as he had need.*
> (Acts 4:32–35)

We have another thrilling picture: *"And the multitude of them that believed were of one heart and of one soul."* Not one of them said that any of the things that he possessed was his own, but they had all things in common.

You have wanted to see God really work, haven't you? Well, if you can get a group of men and women together who will love like this, you will see the power of God because the next verse says, *"And with great power gave the apostles witness of the resurrection of the Lord Jesus: and great grace was upon them all."*

Of all the miracles from the incarnation of Jesus to His being seated on the throne, there is no miracle greater than this. This is a real recreation. This is a picture of the sons of God letting love loose in them.

Remember, it is God who is at work within you, willing and working His own good pleasure. (See Philippians 2:13.)

God is love.

This could read, "For it is love which is at work within you."

When love is really let loose, given freedom, then miracles follow.

First John 4:4 says, "*Ye are of God, my little children.*" Or one could say, "You are of love, for God is love, and you have overcome the forces of evil." Why? "Because greater is love in you than the selfishness, hatred, and jealousy around you."

If you would say it over: I am in love. Love reigns in me. God and I have become one in love. Now His love life is pouring through me, blessing and helping men.

What a wonderful outburst of love it was following the day of Pentecost. But then comes a flash of destruction and everyone is hurt:

> *But a certain man named Ananias, with Sapphira his wife, sold a possession, and kept back part of the price, his wife also being privy to it, and brought a certain part, and laid it at the apostles' feet. But Peter said, Ananias, why hath Satan filled thine heart to lie to the Holy Ghost, and to keep back part of the price of the land? Whiles it remained, was it not thine own? and after it was sold, was it not in thine own power? why hast thou conceived this thing in thine heart? thou hast not lied unto men, but unto God. And Ananias hearing these words fell down, and gave up the ghost: and great fear came on all them that heard these things. And the young men arose, wound him up, and carried him out, and buried him. And it was about the space of three hours after, when his wife, not knowing what was done, came in. And Peter answered unto her, Tell me whether ye sold the land for so much? And she said, Yea, for so much. Then Peter said unto her, How is it that ye have agreed together to tempt the Spirit of the Lord? behold, the feet of them which have buried thy husband are at the door, and shall carry thee out. Then fell she down straightway at his feet, and yielded up the ghost: and the young men came in, and found her dead, and, carrying her forth, buried her by her husband. And great fear came upon all the church, and upon as many as heard these things.*
>
> (Acts 5:1–11)

Men and women had been selling their goods, bringing in the money they made, and laying it at the apostles' feet. No one had asked them to do it. They did it of their own free will. Love had gained the ascendancy and they were practicing what Jesus began to teach.

I wonder if you have seen, in these chapters, the relation of giving to answered prayer. I wonder if you have seen the relation of giving to love. No other sins are mentioned in this connection. Just one: Ananias and Sapphira had lied about their giving. They pretended to give more than they gave and judgment came upon them.

It is a very solemn warning to every one of us. We say, "Lord, I have given my all" and yet we have kept back a part of the price.

When you recognize the lordship of love, it takes in all that you are, all that you are able to do, and all that you are able to be. It takes in your ability, plus God's ability. It takes in your ability to bless and help humanity.

We have never given love its place in the ministry of the Word. We have never made men see what it would mean to transgress the love law and step out of love into selfishness.

19

WHAT PRODUCES THE HIGHEST TYPE OF FAITH?

One who read part of this manuscript asked, "What is the object of this book?"

I answered by asking him a question: "What do you think the object is?"

He said, "To produce faith."

Here are a few things that have been covered in other parts of this book, but I want to bring them together so that you may intelligently check your own life and settle some great issues for yourself.

First, it is necessary to know the integrity of the Word, to know that this Word is actually what it declares itself to be: a revelation from God to us.

We should know that it is God speaking to us. It is not only a Book of the past and future, but it is a Book of now, that it is a God-breathed, a God-indwelt, and a God-inspired message.

Second, it is necessary for us to know the actual reality of our redemption in Christ—not as a doctrine, not as a philosophy, but as an actual redemption out of the authority of Satan—and that by the new birth, we have been translated into the kingdom of the Son of His love, or, in other words, into the very family of God.

Satan's dominion over us as a new creation is ended. Jesus is the Lord and head of this new body.

Satan is a defeated foe over whom we reign through the name of Jesus.

Satan has lost his dominion over our bodies, over our minds, over our finances, and over the circumstances of life.

When we know this, as we know that four plus four equals eight, the problem of faith will never bother us.

Third, it is necessary for us to know the reality of the new creation, to know the legal side of it, that in the mind of justice, we were created in Christ Jesus when He was recreated after He had been made sin as our substitute.

We should know that vitally, the moment we accepted Jesus Christ as our Savior and confessed Him as our Lord, God recreated us and made the legal thing a reality. We have today in our spirits the very nature and life of God.

It is not an experience.

It is not a religion.

It is not joining a church.

But it is an actual birth of our spirits. We are the very sons and daughters of God Almighty.

We know this thing just as we know hunger and its satisfaction, as we know heat and cold.

We know that we have passed out of Satan's dominion, spiritual death, into the realm of life through Jesus Christ.

We know it!

What will be the effect of this knowledge?

Why, God is your very Father and you are His very child.

You have as much freedom in His fellowship as Jesus had in His earth walk, and the Father loves you even as He loved Jesus.

Fourth, we must know the reality of our righteousness in Christ.

There is no *theory* about this.

We know that Romans 3:26 (ASV) is a reality: "*That he might himself be just* [righteous], *and the justifier of him that hath faith in Jesus.*"

God the Father became our righteousness when He imparted to us His own nature, eternal life, in the new creation.

Jesus became our righteousness the moment we took Him as our Savior and confessed Him as our Lord.

He then became our sponsor, our Lord, our Head, our very life.

But in that great revelation, the Holy Spirit, through Paul, says, *"Him who knew no sin he made to be sin on our behalf; that we might become the righteousness of God in him"* (2 Corinthians 5:21 ASV).

Not only is Jesus our righteousness, and the Father our righteousness, but we have become *"the righteousness of God"* in Him.

This means that our standing before the throne is a standing sponsored by God Himself, and by His Son, by His own works wrought in us, and by the Holy Spirit, through the Word.

We are what He says we are.

This means we can stand in His presence without any sense of guilt, condemnation, or inferiority.

This means that the prayer problem is settled. We are no longer going into His presence tongue-tied because of condemnation or fear-filled because of ignorance.

We know what we are in Christ.

We know that He made us what we are.

It is not a problem of feeling or a problem of faith.

This does not require faith any more than Jesus required faith to go into the presence of His Father.

Jesus was, and we are.

Fifth, it is necessary for us to know the reality of indwelling.

Of all the mighty truths connected with redemption, this is the climax: that God Himself, after He has recreated us, made us His own, and is actually making our bodies His home.

No longer does He dwell in an earth-made holy of holies. Our bodies have become His temples.

> *Know ye not that your body is a temple of the Holy Spirit which is in you, which ye have from God? and ye are not your own; for ye were bought with a price: glorify God therefore in your body.*
>
> (1 Corinthians 6:19–20 ASV)

That didn't seem possible to me. What a vision I caught of what we are in Christ!

When one becomes God-inside minded, when he takes for granted that "greater is He that is in him than he that is in the world" (see 1 John 4:4), he goes out and faces life's problems with the sense of a conqueror.

This is almost an unknown practice in the church for men and women to say in every crisis of their life, "I am a conqueror; I am more than a victor because the Creator dwells in me. He can put me over. He can make me a success. I can't fail."

What effect will this knowledge, put into practice daily, have upon the prayer life?

Romans 8:26, then, can be a reality: "*Likewise the Spirit also helpeth our infirmities: for we know not what we should pray for as we ought: but the Spirit itself maketh intercession for us with groanings which cannot be uttered.*"

Really, that will solve the prayer problem.

If the Holy Spirit is voicing the desires of the Father through your lips, those desires will be met and granted.

Sixth, it is necessary for us to know the reality of our fellowship with the Father.

This is the very heart reason for redemption.

> *God is faithful, by whom ye were called unto the fellowship of his Son Jesus Christ our Lord.* (1 Corinthians 1:9)

Fellowship means sharing, equally bearing the burden, sharing in the victories; and He has called us to share with His Son.

John tells us, "*Truly our fellowship is with the Father, and with his Son Jesus Christ*" (1 John 1:3) and "*We have fellowship one with another*" (verse 7). We have the joy of walking in the light as He is in the light.

The highest honor the Father has ever conferred upon us is to fellowship with Himself, with His Son, and with the Holy Spirit in carrying out His dream for redemption of the human race.

Relationship without fellowship is an insipid, tasteless thing.

It is like marriage without love.

Fellowship is the very mother of faith, the parent of joy, and the source of victory; He has called us individually into fellowship with His Son.

If you have fellowship with Him and if you are walking in the light, as He is in the light, prayer becomes one of the sweetest privileges, one of the greatest assets that we have fallen heir to in Christ.

Again, it is necessary for us to know the authority of the name of Jesus, not as a part of a creed or a doctrine, but to know it as an actual reality, just as though some wealthy man should give to you a limitless power of attorney to use his name.

What would it mean to you? And what effect would it have if he said to you in that legal document, "Supply every one of your needs and act as though this fortune were your own?"

The Father has given to us the power of attorney to use the name of Jesus, and that name has all authority in heaven and on earth.

That makes us absolute masters of satanic forces.

Jesus said, "*In my name shall they cast out demons...They shall lay hands on the sick, and they shall recover*" (Mark 16:17–18 ASV).

He said, "*Whatsoever ye shall ask the Father in my name, he will give it you*" (John 16:23).

That is limitless.

It is the limitlessness of the prayer life, and it belongs to every child of God.

It is not a problem of faith, but a problem of knowing your legal rights in Christ, and then taking your place as a son and daughter and actually playing the game with Him.

LAST WORDS

You have read the book. Your honest heart has been deeply affected. You have discovered treasures that you never knew existed. You have found your rights and privileges in a prayer life.

Now what are you going to do with this knowledge?

You remember that knowledge brings responsibility; and if we do not assume the responsibility, it brings judgment. You know too much now not to act upon this knowledge. Begin a prayer life of your own; then bring together little groups and teach them this prayer life. You can do it.

You see, prayer is a most vital and necessary thing to know about as a believer. Pray while the glow is upon you.

NEW CREATION REALITIES

CONTENTS

FIRST WORDS

A series of heart messages on the *New Creation Realities*. Little studies on great themes. Investigations about the "hidden man of the heart."

We have found the secret that the psychologists long have sought.

It is "the inward man," it is the recreated spirit; it is the part of man with which God deals.

A delving into the love life of the sons of love, where the "hidden man of the heart" rules.

You will find some suggestions about the combat of the recreated spirit with the senses which govern this outer man.

It is really an unveiling of what we are in Christ today; of what He says we are; what He has made us to be in His great redemptive work.

These messages are largely from the Epistles.

They are not complete, but are suggestions to provoke you to study more deeply in these hidden riches.

We have come to know that one cannot know the incarnate One as we have seen Him in the four Gospels, unless we have had an opportunity to become acquainted with Him in the Epistles.

In the Gospels, He is the lone man of Galilee, the humble Unknown, who ends His earth walk on Calvary.

In the Epistles, He is the risen, triumphant One, the conqueror of death, sin, and Satan.

He is humanity's risen Redeemer, who has met the demands of justice and satisfied every claim against humanity. He made possible the new creation, a new race of men, who can stand in God's presence without the sense of guilt, condemnation or inferiority.

THE REASON WHY

The Pauline Epistles must ever stand as the work of a super genius or a divine revelation.

They reveal what happened on the cross and what followed during the three days and three nights until the Man was raised from the dead.

One cannot grasp the great substitutionary fact in the four Gospels.

Neither can we find the new creation revelation, nor can we discover the ministry of Jesus at the right hand of the Father.

The four Gospels give us a sense knowledge view of the Man. The people stood in the presence of His miracles, overwhelmed with a consciousness that they were in the presence of God.

They call Him the Son of God.

They see Him conquer Satan and demons, but there is no intimation that He is going to make them conquerors of demons, of death and of disease.

What He says to them in regard to it is veiled because they are spiritually unable to grasp spiritual realities.

They have not yet experienced the strange phenomena of the new birth.

So the Pauline revelation is a master stroke of divine grace.

It lets us into the inner secret of God's mighty purpose in the incarnation.

In the Gospels, Jesus acts like deity, talks like deity, dies like deity, and conquers death like God.

He was God manifest in the flesh in His earth walk and He was God in the Spirit in His substitutionary sacrifice.

At God's right hand, He has a glorified body and is Head of the new creation.

You will find that He did a perfect work for us and the Spirit through the Word does a perfect work in us as Jesus is today at the right hand of the Father doing a perfect work for us.

1

THE LIVING WORD

Our attitude toward the Word determines the place that God holds in our daily life.

The Word should always be the Father speaking to us. It should never be like the message from an ordinary book.

It should be as real to you as though the Master stood in the room and spoke to you personally.

This Word was designed by the Father to take Jesus's place in His absence.

When He says, "*The Father himself loveth you*" (John 16:27), it is a personal message to your heart.

When the Master said again, "*If a man love me, he will keep my words: and my Father will love him, and we will come unto him, and make our abode with him*" (John 14:23), that should be as personal as though you were the only one in the world.

It is as though you were sitting at the feet of Jesus, and He looked down into your face and said, "The Father and I will come and make our home with you.

"Be not dismayed, for I am your God.

"I am going to be your strength; I am going to lend to you my own ability.

"When weakness comes, remember that I am the strength of your life.

"When you need finances, remember that I said, '*Your Father knoweth what things ye have need of*' (Matthew 6:8)."

You can whisper to your own heart, "My Father will supply every need of mine. He knows my needs and loves me. He and I are one."

Man's word is usually dead before the printer has finished his work. Few words of man live after a generation, but God's Word is different. It is impregnated with the very life of God, it is eternal.

Hebrews 4:12–13 gives us an illustration: *"For the Logos of God is a living thing, active and more cutting than any sword with double edge, penetrating to the very division of soul and spirit, joints and marrow—scrutinizing the very thoughts and conceptions of the heart. And no created thing is hidden from him; all things lie open and exposed before the eyes of him with whom we have to reckon"* (MOFF).

This is one of the strangest statements about the Word in Paul's epistles.

Notice this thirteenth verse: *"No created thing is hidden from him."*

Of whom is he speaking? The living Word, the *Logos*.

"All things lie open and exposed before the eyes of him with whom we have to reckon."

The Word takes on personality; it becomes Christ Himself. Our contact with the Master, then, is through His Word.

And did you notice, *"the eyes of him."* The Word then has eyes. It sees our conduct, our attitude toward it. It is a Living thing. How deeply that should impress us.

I hold in my hands a book with the very life of God in it, a book that scrutinizes my conduct, that judges me. A book that feeds this inner man—my spirit. It imparts faith to my Spirit, builds love into it. God's only means of reaching me is through His Word. So the Word becomes a vital thing.

It has been rather difficult for some of us to grasp the fact that during the first century, the church did not have our New Testament.

The first epistle that Paul wrote to the Thessalonians was the beginning of the New Testament. It was written seventeen years after his conversion.

> *For this cause also thank we God without ceasing, because, when ye received the word of God which ye heard of us, ye received it not as the word of men, but as it is in truth, the word of God, which effectually worketh also in you that believe.* (1 Thessalonians 2:13)

This Word of God was all they had, whether Paul gave it, or Peter, or John, or any of the apostles. It was God speaking through human lips. It had not yet been put into writing.

Now you can better understand Acts 19:20 telling of that great revival at Ephesus. Luke used this expression: *"So mightily grew the word of God and prevailed."*

It was the spoken Word. The Pauline revelation was only known to those who had heard him. The other apostles did not have it. They had what the Spirit gave them to meet the emergency of the hour.

It is a fact that Christianity is what the Word says about redemption, about the body of Christ, or the new creation.

We become Christ-like in the measure that the Word prevails in us.

The Word is Christ revealed.

The Word is God present with us, speaking the living message of the loving Father God. The Word is always *now*. It is His Word to me today. It is His voice, His last message. It becomes a living thing in my heart as I lovingly act upon it. It becomes a living thing on the lips of love. It has no power on the lips of those whose lives are out of fellowship with Him, who live in the reason realm.

His Word makes our ministry limitless.

His Word is what He is.

It is the mind of the Father.

It is the will of the Father.

It shows the way to the Father.

The Word is the Father speaking.

You notice that it is always in the present tense.

The Word is the bread of heaven, food for our spirits.

> *Man shall not live by bread alone, but by every word that proceedeth out of the mouth of God.* (Matthew 4:4)

> *Thy words were found, and I did eat them; and thy word was unto me the joy and rejoicing of mine heart.* (Jeremiah 15:16)

Job tells us how precious the Word is to him: *"Neither have I gone back from the commandment of his lips; I have esteemed the words of his mouth more than my necessary food"* (Job 23:12).

When a child of God looks upon the Word as Job did, then it becomes a reality in his daily life. Job had no written Word; he had the Word spoken by angels.

We have the written Word. We have it printed in many forms so we may carry it in our pocket. How little we have appreciated the value of His message.

"He sent his word, and healed them" (Psalm 107:20).

That living Word He sent was Jesus.

> *So then after the Lord had spoken unto them, he was received up into heaven, and sat down on the right hand of God. And they went forth, and preached every where, the Lord working with them, and confirming the word with signs following.* (Mark 16:19–20)

Notice that the Lord worked with them. I believe that a revival would break out almost anywhere if the Lord worked with those who preach, and if the Word was as real to them as the spoken Word was real to the early church.

But the word of man has gained the ascendancy and has more authority than His Word has today. He confirms the Word today everywhere that it is preached. I want you to notice how the Father makes the Word good in the lives of men and women as they dare to act upon it.

In the closing sentence of the gospel of Matthew, *"Lo, I am with you always, even unto the end of the world"* (Matthew 28:20), the believer can be sure that though he be forsaken by all others, there is One who will stand by him. But the thing that has most deeply impressed my heart is the reality of God in the Word.

He is not only in the Word, but He breathes His very life through it as it is unfolded.

He said, *"Where two or three are gathered together in my name, there am I in the midst of them"* (Matthew 18:20).

He is in the midst of them in the Word.

Jesus said, *"If a man love me, he will keep my words: and my Father will love him, and we will come unto him, and make our abode with him"* (John 14:23).

If we could only realize that when we open the Word, it is a living thing we are implanting in the hearts of men.

The Word is God present with us speaking the living message of the living Father God.

It is the *now* Word from Him to me. It is His voice.

It becomes a living thing in the heart of faith.

In Romans 10:8, it is called *"the word of faith."*

It is His Word that gives birth to faith in the believer. It is God's faith expressed.

You see, He is a Faith God and He always uses words to do things.

> *Through faith we understand that the worlds were framed by the word of God.* (Hebrews 11:3)

Hear Him whisper, *"By myself have I sworn"* (Genesis 22:16).

He was in the Word. The Word was a part of Him. You can't separate a man from his words; neither can you separate the Father from His Words.

How it thrilled me when I read in Hebrews 7:22 that Jesus is the surety of the new covenant. The new covenant is the Word, and He is the surety of the Word. The Word was a living fact when Jesus spoke it. It is still a living fact.

Jesus was a part of all He said; He and His Word were one.

Jesus is just as real now as He was the day He arose from the dead.

His Word is just as real now as when He inspired John or Peter or Paul to write it. What He said was a part of Himself. Reality throbs in it, flows through it, lives in it. The Word was; the Word is now what it was then.

Here are some other assurances:

> *The Lord is my shepherd.* (Psalm 23:1)

In John 10:14, Jesus said, "I am the good shepherd."

> *Fear thou not; for I am with thee: be not dismayed; for I am thy God.* (Isaiah 41:10)

> *If God be for us, who can be against us?* (Romans 8:31)

> *I can do all things through Christ which strengtheneth me.* (Philippians 4:13)

> *The Lord is the strength of my life; of whom shall I be afraid?* (Psalm 27:1)

My God shall supply all your need according to his riches in glory by Christ Jesus. (Philippians 4:19)

My help cometh from the Lord. (Psalm 121:2)

Blessed is the man whose strength is in thee. (Psalm 84:5)

My refuge, is in God. (Psalm 62:7)

These are living words, and as you feed on them, they build you up. The knowledge of what Christ is and has done for you personally, builds faith in you.

When I turn to the Word and read it as His message to me, He confirms that message in my life. He confirmed the covenant made with Abraham. He confirmed the Word that Jesus spoke through the apostles. (See Mark 16:20.)

Jesus said in John 14:15, *"If ye love me, keep my commandments."*

What was His commandment? That we love one another.

He that hath my commandments, and keepeth them, he it is that loveth me: and he that loveth me shall be loved of my Father, and I will love him. (John 14:21)

Here are some other facts that we ought to remember.

And when he [the Spirit] *is come, he will reprove the world of sin, and of righteousness, and of judgment: of sin, because they believe not on me; of righteousness, because I go to my Father, and ye see me no more; of judgment, because the prince of this world is judged.* (John 16:8–11)

What is going to convince the world? Words in the lips of faith. Only that living word in the lips of faith can take the place of an absent Christ.

The Word talks to us. It takes the place of Jesus.

The Word is the Father speaking to us now. It has the same authority that it would have if the Master stood in the room and spoke it. Faith in the Father is faith in His Word. The Word takes on all that our faith demands.

Jesus said, *"According to your faith be it unto you"* (Matthew 9:29).

As you consider the Word and act upon it, it will become real to you.

This book, the living Word, has God in it. The Word takes the place of the unseen Jesus. Meditation in the Word is like a visit with Jesus.

In Joshua 1:8, God told Joshua to meditate in the Word, day and night; in other words, to live in it.

Jesus said, "*Continue in my word*" (John 8:31).

The Word gets into your blood, into your system, and becomes a part of you.

The Word is inspired. Holy men spoke as they were moved by the Holy Spirit, as they were borne along in their spirit life.

God spoke by the mouth of the holy prophets.

> *The words that I speak unto you, they are spirit, and they are life.*
> (John 6:63)

Every word that God speaks has life in it.

Remember Hebrews 4:12: "*The word of God is quick* [alive]." It is not like man's words which die after a generation; God's Word lives.

I love to think of it as the "prevailing Word," as it was in Ephesus. How it ruled over that wicked city!

Today, the Logos of God is ruling in the hearts of those who yield to its sway. The Word has the authority of God in it now. It has the righteousness of God in it. It has recreating power for the unsaved. It has healing power for the sick. It is the very bread of heaven to the hungry in spirit.

I wish that it could be like this: that when you pick up the Word, it will mean that God is present with you and that the Word is His attitude toward you now.

It is His attitude toward sin, toward redemption, toward righteousness, toward eternal life, toward the sons and daughters of God.

That is the Father's attitude toward all the issues of life.

The Word is the will of the Father.

God watches over His Word.

What God says, becomes.

God is truth, so I will be true.

God is light, so I will walk in the light.

You see, we learn to act on the Word, as we act on the word of a banker or a lawyer in some crisis in our life.

I wonder if you ever realized that the Father is jealous over His Word.

He never set a low estimate upon it. He holds it in the highest regard.

If He said it, that ends it.

To His enemies, it is but paper and ink; but to the lovers, it is life and health; it is joy unspeakable.

The preaching that produces little conviction is caused by the Word not having been in the heart of the teacher.

We are to be sowers of the Word. Jesus gave us, in Matthew 13, a marvelous picture of the art of preaching. It is sowing the Word. It falls upon all kinds of hearts, but the irrigation of the soil is dependent upon the sower. If we irrigate it with prayer and sometimes with tears, it is bound to bring forth a harvest.

Some of us forget the Word in hard places. Unconsciously we walk by sight. The senses take the reality away from the Word, but as the spirit gains the ascendancy over the senses, the Word once more has its place.

Remember, your word is you. You must learn to say, "I gave my word; I must keep it, no matter what it costs." If your word is of no value, you will reason that the Word of God is of no value.

I have found that unbelief in the Word of God is largely because of people's lack of faith in their own word. If you want to build the highest type of faith, be a faithful person yourself. Believe in your own word. Establish a reputation for truth; then the Word will be that to you in your life.

Here are some little facts that may mean much to your life. The Word is on my hands. What am I going to do with it? Am I going to act upon it, let it govern my life, or will I just study it? Will I sit in the Bible class and study it and then go back to my room and study it but not live it? Not let it become a part of my life, but just an intellectual exercise?

The Word is taking the Master's place in my life.

What I do with the Word will determine what the Word will do to me one of these days.

The Word will work in me, building Jesus's life in me, building life, faith, love, grace, and strength into me, or else it will judge me in the last day.

What will it do for me? It will work for me.

If I preach it and live it, it will work for me. It will reveal the very riches of my inheritance to me.

It will give me courage to enter into and enjoy my inheritance. It will build the Master's steadfastness into me.

The very character of Christ will be built into me, and only He knows what it will do through me.

It has saved the lost; it has healed the sick; it has built faith and love in multitudes.

Let the word of Christ dwell in you richly. (Colossians 3:16)

You can so soak in the Word and the Word so soak in you, that your word and God's Word become blended into one. It will be your language and your words, but it will be His Word. His Word in you becomes a part of you. It has made you what you are; it will make others like you. You are lost in the Word, but the Word is found in you.

The Word became flesh once. It is becoming spirit in your spirit. The Word dwells richly in your practice, in your conversation, in your prayer, in your convictions. You are using the Word to cast out diseases, to bring money to people, to save lost souls. This Word and you have become one.

You remember that for more than fifty years after Christ's death, the written word was known only in a very limited way. The New Testament wasn't brought together until the middle of the second century. The words that Jesus spoke were not yet written. It was the "spoken Word," but He was in it. They were a part of Christ and they breathed Christ's nature.

Remember, *"the word of God…liveth and abideth"* (1 Peter 1:23). All right, speak the Word and it will live in the lives of men who hear you.

God said, *"I will hasten my word"* (Jeremiah 1:12). He will watch over the Word you preach and teach.

Jesus said, "If my words are living in you and you are speaking them, I will live in them as they pass from your lips." The Word of Christ becomes a living thing in your lips.

Speak the Word fearlessly.

Let the Word live in you gloriously and richly.

2

TREATING THE WORD AS THOUGH IT WERE A COMMON BOOK

This title bears the heart reason for spiritual failure.

It is the reason why in daily life, the believer breaks down, why the adversary has no trouble in overthrowing him in a crisis; the reason why he is a spiritual hitchhiker, always depending upon someone else's prayers, someone else's wisdom, someone else's interpretation of the Word.

He has no life of his own independent of others.

In the family of God, he is a "yes man," but it is always, "yes" in the wrong place.

Paul describes him in Hebrews 5. I shrink from giving you this Scripture; it is so personal in so many lives.

> *For when for the time ye ought to be teachers, ye have need that one teach you again which be the first principles of the oracles of God.*
>
> (Hebrews 5:12)

It is a pity you seem to have forgotten the first steps in this divine life. Instead of walking out into the fullness and liberty and riches of His grace, you have halted. There has been no growth, no development in your life. The Word doesn't mean much to you. Oh, there are certain Scriptures you know that condemn you and make you feel miserable, but there is no life in the Word for you.

"Thy word is a lamp unto my feet, and a light unto my path" (Psalm 119:105), but it isn't that to you.

The Word hurts and cuts and bruises and makes you feel unhappy when you read it, when it should be manna and food for you. Notice how tenderly Paul said, *"One teach you again which be the first principles,"* the very beginning of the faith life. Why? Because instead of living it, acting it, and taking your place in the Word, you have remained a babe, an undeveloped spirit. Your mind has never been renewed by the Word. You see it can't be renewed until you begin to practice it.

Jesus hit the taproot of it in Matthew 7:24–26:

> *Therefore whosoever heareth these sayings of mine, and doeth them, I will liken him unto a wise man, which built his house upon a rock: and the rain descended, and the floods came, and the winds blew, and beat upon that house; and it fell not: for it was founded upon a rock. And every one that heareth these sayings of mine, and doeth them not, shall be likened unto a foolish man, which built his house upon the sand.*

The first high tide swept him out into the sea.

I am sorry for such folks. They have to be fed with milk all the time. You will find them in the nursery. They always have a bottle. Some of them have the wrong bottle. It is not filled with the sincere milk of the Word.

They are babes in all their conduct.

Paul in 1 Corinthians 3:3, *"Are ye not carnal…?"*

That means they live in the senses; they are ruled by the senses; they are guided by the senses. All their diseases are sense made. He says they are walking after the manner of men, or as "mere men" of the world. Just world folks. There has been no change, no growth, no development in their life whatsoever. They are treating the Word as though it is a common book. They can't get their healing. Others have to pray for them and they are a burden upon the church. They are a spiritual liability.

If they happen to be men and women of ability and of standing in the community, and the church gives them office or a place of responsibility, they become a deadly burden to the church.

They are never in the Bible class.

They do not have family prayer, and seldom ask the blessing at the table.

They belong to a class of hitchhikers.

Their faith is always weak.

You will see them going to the altar but they never get anything. The altar is a place for babes to get an impulse to go to the Word and feed on it. It is not a means to an end. It is just a beginning.

But if you see them going to the altar year after year, you know they have become habitual, spiritual cripples. Satan rules them through the senses. They are afraid of death. They are afraid to meet the Lord. They have thrown away life's privileges because they lightly esteemed the Word of God.

SOME FACTS WE OUGHT TO STUDY IN THIS CONNECTION

When I ask another to pray for my healing or to pray for any of my chronic needs, I reject the gift of my healing, and I doubt the word of the Giver.

I repudiate my own righteousness in Christ, and I refuse to take my place in Christ as a son.

I know that no one has a better standing than I have. No one has a better place in the vine than I have.

No one can draw life from the vine more readily than I can. I am what He made me in Christ.

My righteousness was given to me in Christ.

My right to the use of Jesus's name is a gift, but I have repudiated the whole thing.

I have neglected to develop my gift. I have ignored the admonition of my Lord. I do not study the Word to live it!

I know that my sickness is because of a spiritual condition.

I know that I have walked according to the senses rather than according to the Spirit.

I know that healing cannot be permanent in my body until my spirit is adjusted to the Word.

If sickness is not spiritual, He couldn't have made Christ's spirit sick with my diseases, and if my body is filled with disease, it is because my spirit is not in harmony with the Word.

I am rebelling against the sickness and fighting against the pain, but I don't fight the cause of my sickness. I fight the effect of it. You see, until I take my place in Christ and begin to act the Word and become a doer of the Word instead of a talker, I remain a failure. Sickness is threefold: spiritual, mental, and physical.

All are sick in spirit before they are sick in body!

You see, here is where the trouble is. James 1:22 tells us, *"But be ye doers of the word, and not hearers only, deceiving your own selves."*

One can stay in that condition, until after a while, they begin to believe they are right and God is wrong, and you will hear them whining, "Why does God put these things on me?" and some unwise teacher will say, "He is trying to discipline you."

I tell you, He never uses the devil to discipline His children. Disease is of the devil.

You are suffering the results of refusing to take your place in Christ.

You refuse to study to show yourself approved unto Him.

You have refused to feed on the Word.

You had opportunity to study but you didn't take it.

You would rather read the literature of the hour than to read the Word from heaven.

The great heart of the Master is yearning over you.

His intercession has been ineffectual so far. It can't be effectual until the Word works effectively in your spirit.

You must study to show yourself approved of God.

3

THE FOUR GOSPELS IN CONTRAST WITH THE PAULINE EPISTLES

In the early days of my ministry, German philosophy had gained the ascendency in many of our theological institutions, and there came a strange new slogan.

You've heard it continuously: "Back to Jesus."

It captured my imagination, but I didn't know what it meant.

Then I heard one of our leaders declare that Paul had altogether too much influence over the church, and that we are to give up the Pauline revelation and go "back to Jesus."

That was really the beginning of my study of the Pauline revelation. The four Gospels, you remember, were written years after Christ's resurrection.

Luke's gospel was written from 63 to 80 AD.

The gospel of John was written from 80 to 110 AD.

That meant two generations after the resurrection of Jesus before John wrote.

From my study, I notice this strange fact, that Paul quoted Jesus only twice, and in John's Gospel, there were only two traces of the Pauline revelation.

One is John 1:16–17: *"And of his fulness have all we received, and grace for grace. For the law was given by Moses, but grace and truth came by Jesus Christ."*

I began to wonder why the four Gospels did not have any of the Pauline revelation in them.

Then I discovered that they recorded only events up to the resurrection and ascension.

They knew what had taken place on the day of Pentecost and the tremendous upheaval that followed the preaching of the apostles in Jerusalem, Samaria, and in the Roman Empire, yet they never made mention of it.

I wondered how John could have written his gospel as he did, knowing that he had passed through the great revival in Jerusalem; that he had been a part of all those mighty miracles until the destruction of Jerusalem, when he himself was banished from the holy land; and knowing of the miracles that had attended his ministry before he was banished to the Isle of Patmos, and yet, he did not tell us any of those wonderful things that had taken place.

You remember, in John 20:30–31, he declared,

> *And many other signs truly did Jesus in the presence of his disciples, which are not written in this book: but these are written, that ye might believe that Jesus is the Christ, the Son of God; and that believing ye might have life through his name.*

You see, the object of his writing was that we might have faith in Christ.

Then I said to John, in my imagination, "Brother, why haven't you told us more about the miracles that occurred under your ministry through the name of Jesus?"

And then it seemed to me as though John answered, "I wrote only what the Holy Spirit gave me."

Then I saw one of the greatest literary miracles of all ages.

The four men who had written these Gospels had been shut in, as it were, by the Holy Spirit. They had been unable to give their interpretation of the miracles or what the miracles meant. They wrote only what He had permitted, or rather, had inspired them to write.

You can't conceive of anyone writing a book like Luke or Matthew, or John or Mark, who had the experiences they had, without those experiences intruding themselves into the biography of the man of whom they were written.

Here are some facts:

John didn't write for more than seventy years after the ascension of our Lord.

He must have known of the Pauline revelation.

Paul's letters had some circulation during those two generations, and John had met Paul and had visited with him.

He had learned from the lips of Paul what Christ had done for him in His great substitutionary sacrifice, and yet there is no intimation of it in his gospel.

Luke, a convert of Paul, traveled with him about eighteen years.

He had been Paul's helper and had taken care of him when he was in prison, and yet I challenge you to go through his gospel and find one sentence that indicates that he knew anything about the Pauline revelation.

The same thing is true of the book of Acts.

That is another literary miracle.

Luke loved Paul. He lived in the consciousness of the finished work of Christ.

Christ's ministry at the right hand of the Father was one of the dearest facts of his life without doubt, and yet he never mentions it.

Mark was Paul's companion for years, yet you can see no intimation of the substitutionary sacrifice of Christ in his gospel.

Let us notice some of the things that they knew but utterly ignored.

None of them mention Christ as a substitute, the sin-bearer, the one who would put sin away by the sacrifice of Himself.

The new creation was not developed.

John gives us the little talk that Jesus had with Nicodemus, but the ruler of Israel did not understand it.

John had a great opportunity there to have put in what he had come to know about the new creation.

Not a word is mentioned about Christ becoming our righteousness, or how He was delivered up on account of our trespasses and raised when we were justified.

Not a word is mentioned about the body of Christ. The nearest is John 15:5, where Jesus said, *"I am the vine, ye are the branches."*

What an opportunity John had then to develop the theme and how glad we would have been if he had done it. No, God shut him in and enabled him to say exactly what He wanted him to say and nothing more.

There is nothing about the great ministry of our Master at the right hand of the Father, of His being a Mediator, Intercessor, Advocate, High Priest, and Lord.

All this sums up to one tremendous fact: that when you read the four Gospels, you are standing in the presence of God Himself, unseen, but He is there.

He is the Author of those four matchless documents.

He is there unveiling His Son, and the Son is unveiling Him.

In the Pauline Epistles, we have the Father unveiling the work that He wrought in His Son and through Him. He is also unveiling the family, the body of Christ, the sons of God.

But we are interested in another phase of it—a contrast of the Pauline revelation, and Jesus's teaching. Paul's treatment of faith is an illustration.

Jesus continually urged His hearers, the sons of that first covenant, to believe.

In such Scriptures as Mark 9:23, Jesus said, *"All things are possible to him that believeth."*

Again, He said to His disciples in the midst of that storm on the sea, *"O thou of little faith, wherefore didst thou doubt?"* (Matthew 14:31).

> *Whosoever shall say unto this mountain, Be thou removed, and be thou cast into the sea; and shall not doubt in his heart, but shall believe that those things which he saith shall come to pass; he shall have whatsoever he saith. Therefore I say unto you, What things soever ye desire, when ye pray, believe that ye receive them, and ye shall have them.* (Mark 11:23–24)

Why didn't Paul urge his epistles people to believe?

He urged the unsaved to believe on Christ, but he never urged the church to believe.

That confused me. I wondered why, for I remembered that all of our preachers, evangelists, and teachers have told what we might do as believers if we only had faith.

Then I saw the secret. We are believers. We are the sons of God. Ephesians 1:3 declares, "*Blessed be the God and Father of our Lord Jesus Christ, who hath blessed us with all spiritual blessings.*" We are in the family. All that the Father has and all that He wrought in Christ, and all that Christ is, belongs to us.

We don't need faith for a thing that is already ours.

The thing for which I must have faith is something that I do not possess.

> *Therefore let no man glory in men. For all things are your's.*
> (1 Corinthians 3:21)

Whether Paul gave you the revelation of it or Peter or John, it makes no difference. They unveiled simply what belongs to us.

Now we can understand why our modern preaching in regard to faith has been almost destructive.

Paul's revelation gives us a perfect redemption.

> *In whom we have redemption through his blood, the forgiveness of sins, according to the riches of his grace.* (Ephesians 1:7)

Notice the tense here. Not, we *may* have it if we have faith enough; no, "*In whom we have* [now] *redemption through his blood,*" we have "*the forgiveness of* [our] *sins.*"

The Greek word does not mean *forgiveness,* as it is translated; it is *remission.* That comes always in the new birth. Forgiveness is something we get when we sin as believers. Remission is something that the sinner gets when he comes into the family.

The Greek word *aphesis* is used in Colossians 1:14 and Ephesians 1:7: "*In whom we have redemption...the forgiveness of sins.*"

Not only have we a perfect redemption in the Pauline revelation, but now we can go back and stand by the side of the cross with the disciples, and we can say, "Peter, do you know what Jesus is doing on the cross? He is being made sin now. Watch Him, and when He cries that last bitter cry and yields up His spirit, He is going to the place of suffering as your substitute and mine. He is going to stay there until the demands of justice are met, until Satan is conquered, until the new birth becomes a possibility; until man can be justified, receive the nature and life of deity, and become the very righteousness of God in Christ."

Peter looks mystified. John draws near, and says, "Pardon me, but what are you talking about?"

You see, they knew nothing about what Christ was doing for us. Jesus had broken into the realm of sense knowledge, had been manifest among them as the Son of God for three and a half years, and they didn't know Him. They didn't know what He did on the cross and what He did during the three days and three nights. They didn't know what His resurrection meant, nor what He meant when He said to Mary, *"Touch me not; for I am not yet ascended to my Father"* (John 20:17).

All this was unknown to them.

It is deeply important that we understand the difference between the Pauline revelation and the ministry of Jesus and its teachings as recorded in the four Gospels.

4

PAUL ABOUT PRAYER

Paul teaches us about prayer by his prayers.

True, in Ephesians 6:18, he says, *"With all prayer and supplication in the Spirit, and watching thereunto with all perseverance and supplication for all saints."*

You notice he uses the expression *"with all prayer* [or with all kinds of prayer] *and supplication in the Spirit."*

Whether that be in the Holy Spirit or in his recreated spirit, one can't be sure, but they would actually mean the same thing.

It suggests in 1 Thessalonians 5:17, *"Pray without ceasing."*

Your life becomes a continual intercession.

It is not by words, the spirit in you is doing what Paul mentions in Romans 8:26:

> *Likewise the Spirit also helpeth our infirmities: for we know not what we should pray for as we ought: but the Spirit itself maketh intercession for us with groanings which cannot be uttered.*

I have noticed at times when I have been depressed, and I could think of no reason for the depression, that afterward I discovered it was the Spirit in me making intercession, the silent agony of the Spirit reaching out after someone. It was my spirit blending with the Holy Spirit in supplication for some person who was in need at that hour.

When I was in evangelistic work, the day before I gave the invitation to the unsaved, I would often be overwhelmed with a feeling that is indescribable.

Sometimes I have cried out in agony for relief. It was my spirit and the Holy Spirit in intercession for that unsaved congregation that I would meet at the evening hour. After a while, I learned what these depression periods meant.

But I wish to call your attention especially to Paul's prayers for the church:

> *Wherefore I also, after I heard of your faith in the Lord Jesus, and love unto all the saints, cease not to give thanks for you, making mention of you in my prayers.* (Ephesians 1:15–16)

And here is a remarkable intercession for you and me:

> *That the God of our Lord Jesus Christ, the Father of glory, may give unto you the spirit of wisdom and revelation in the knowledge of him: the eyes of your understanding being enlightened; that ye may know what is the hope of his calling, and what the riches of the glory of his inheritance in the saints.* (Ephesians 1:17–18)

Notice carefully now. He is praying that we may have a spirit of wisdom.

I don't know whether you have noticed it or not, but wisdom and knowledge are different.

Wisdom is the ability to use knowledge.

Wisdom doesn't come from the reasoning faculties; it comes from the human spirit. Whether it is natural wisdom of man outside of Christ, or whether it is God's wisdom, which is given to the new creation. He is praying now that our spirits may have wisdom to grasp the riches of the work that God wrought in Christ Jesus for us. It is revelation knowledge that was given to Paul.

Now we are to have wisdom to understand our share of redemption's unveiling in that knowledge.

He says, in effect, "Having the eyes of our hearts illumined, that we may know the hope of His calling and the riches of the glory of the Father's inheritance in the saints," that is, in you and me.

If our hearts could grasp this, it would transform us.

If we could only realize what an inheritance the Father has in us, how priceless we are to Him.

We have our property insured in case of fire or theft.

We have our bodies insured in case of accident.

I wonder if the Father has His inheritance in us insured.

I wonder if He is as jealous over us as we are over our jewelry and our precious property.

I am sure He is.

Someday, we will make a discovery of how He has insured us. Notice farther in the prayer. He wants us to know "*the exceeding greatness of his power to us-ward who believe*" (Ephesians 1:19).

He said, it is "*according to the working of his mighty power, which he wrought in Christ, when he raised him from the dead*" (verses 19–20). My heart has been slow to grasp this.

When I knew in reality that the same ability that wrought in the dead body of Christ was at work within me, in my spirit, in my soul, in my body, then I knew that I was fortified.

I couldn't fail because I had become the instrument through which that Mighty One was working.

Then Romans 8:11 cleared it up:

> *But if the Spirit of him that raised up Jesus from the dead dwell in you, he that raised up Christ from the dead shall also quicken your mortal bodies by his Spirit that dwelleth in you.*

The same power that wrought in Christ is in you and me.

That resurrection ability is in our bodies.

That means healing and strength and vitality for our present necessities in our daily walk.

But notice another thing, he said:

> *And set him at his own right hand in the heavenly places, far above all principality, and power, and might, and dominion, and every name that is named, not only in this world, but also in that which is to come.*
>
> (Ephesians 1:20–21)

In Ephesians 2:6, he says, "*And hath raised us up together, and made us sit together in heavenly places in Christ Jesus,*" and we are sitting now far above all rule and authority.

That was Paul's prayer for us, or rather, it was the Spirit's prayer through Paul.

And now the Spirit goes farther and says, "He put all things in subjection under our feet."

We are the earthly part of the body of Christ.

The Executive is in the heavens.

The office force is here on the earth; we are a part of that.

We must know that the ability God wrought in Christ when He raised Him from the dead is ours.

Here is another tremendous fact that we have almost utterly forgotten:

> *And hath put all things under his feet, and gave him to be the head over all things to the church.* (Ephesians 1:22)

We must not forget that Satan is defeated; that we were with Christ in that great substitution of which we became a part; that we conquered the adversary with Him; when He arose from the dead, we were raised together with Him; and when He was enthroned at the right hand of the Father, we were enthroned with Him.

He is praying that we may know this, that we may enter into the fullness of it.

That prayer must be answered.

I am asking now that this prayer should be answered for each one of you who read this book.

He has given Jesus "*to be the head over all things to the church.*"

Then the "*over all things*" includes everything that can touch your life and mine. They are all subject to the Head—Christ; and they are subject to us—the body of Christ.

For in that next verse, he says, "*Which is his body, the fulness of him that filleth all in all*" (verse 23).

The body is the fullness of Him. The body is the completeness of Him, and the ability of the body should dominate all things around it.

Our feeble intellects can't grasp this, but our spirits can revel in it.

For our spirits are filled with His fullness, the fullness of His love, the fullness of His grace, the fullness of His wisdom, the fullness of His ability to bless and help men.

His next prayer is in Ephesians 3:14–15: "*For this cause I bow my knees unto the Father of our Lord Jesus Christ, of whom the whole family in heaven and earth is named.*"

Now notice the prayer: "*That he would grant you, according to the riches of his glory, to be strengthened with might by his Spirit in the inner man*" (verse 16).

Strengthened with God's ability.

It doesn't seem to me that we can ever be weak or failures again.

I don't know what all that means, nor do I know the limits of it, but I do know that it makes us more than conquerors in the midst of every perplexing condition.

It puts our heel upon the neck of our enemies, whether they be spiritual enemies or material; it makes us masters.

It strips us of our weakness and inability and clothes us with the ability from on high.

He says, "*That Christ may dwell in your hearts* [in my heart and in yours] *by faith; that ye, being rooted and grounded in love*" (verse 17).

That is the Jesus kind of love—*agape*.

We are not only to be influenced by it, but we are to be rooted and grounded in it; established in love.

> *And we have known and believed the love that God hath to us. God is love; and he that dwelleth in love dwelleth in God, and God in him.*
>
> (1 John 4:16)

I think a better rendering is this: "We have come to believe in the love that God has in our case."

I have come to believe that love, this Jesus-kind-of-love, is better than reason, better than force, better than philosophy of man, better than anything that man can devise.

Man's knowledge can't equal it.

I have come to believe that love's way is the best way, and that the way of love is the way to walk.

When I know that God is love, then the way of God is best.

If I believe in love, I believe in the Author of love.

I do believe in love.

I believe that His love way is best for me, is best for you.

It is the end of strife for ourselves, the end of bitterness and hatred and jealousy.

It is the beginning of Christ dominating our lives in our earth walk. To be rooted and grounded in love is the choicest experience that can ever come to the human heart.

And then we *"may be able to comprehend with all saints what is the breadth, and length, and depth, and height; and to know the love of Christ"* (Ephesians 3:18–19).

We will come to know the love of Christ personally, so we will say, as Paul did, He *"loved me, and gave himself for me"* (Galatians 2:20).

His redemption will be a personal thing.

He did it for me.

It will be as though no other person lived; that I was the one for whom He died.

But you know the next sentence says, *"And to know the love of Christ, which passeth knowledge, that ye might be filled with all the fulness of God"* (Ephesians 3:19).

That was his prayer for me.

That was his prayer for you.

That prayer can't go unanswered.

You remember how he groaned in Colossians 1:28, *"that we may present every man perfect in Christ Jesus."*

That was the Spirit's passion in Paul.

God help me to have the same passion.

That eliminates selfishness utterly, doesn't it?

That is a new self, a self born of God, a self that has no dream but God's dream, no ambition but His ambition.

But hear the closing of that prayer: "*Now unto him that is able to do exceeding abundantly above all that we ask or think*" (Ephesians 3:20).

You see, we swing out of the orbit of sense knowledge, out of the limitations of sense reason, into the realm of the supernatural.

We are living now in the realm of grace, the realm of God.

He says that it is "*above all that we can ask or think, according to the power that worketh in us*" (verse 20).

We have been slow to grasp this, but this is a picture of His grace. This is an illustration of the Father's dream for us.

This illustrates the prayer life of Paul.

It is better than any rules or regulations that man can make in regard to a prayer life.

When you and I realize this prayer was for us, we become anxious that it be answered in us.

That lets Him loose in us to work His own will and His own pleasure in and through us for His glory.

5

CHRIST IN THE LIGHT OF THE PAULINE REVELATION

This is an unveiling of what we are before the Father, and how the Father looks upon us in Christ.

> *I came forth from the Father, and am come into the world: again, I leave the world, and go to the Father.* (John 16:28)

You remember Jesus said in John 3:3, "*Except a man be born again, he cannot see the kingdom of God.*"

The believer is born of God. He comes out of the very womb of God.

> *Whatsoever is born of God overcometh the world.* (1 John 5:4)

> *For by one Spirit are we all baptized into one body…and have been all made to drink into one Spirit.* (1 Corinthians 12:13)

Just as truly as Jesus came out from the Father, so we have come out from God through the energy of the Spirit. We are born of God. In 1 John 4:4, we read, "*Ye are of God, little children.*"

We are a part of the very life of God.

God's very nature has been poured into our spirits, for we are of God.

Now we can understand Jesus's confession. It staggered the Jews. It startled the disciples.

> *I came forth from the Father, and am come into the world: again, I leave the world, and go to the Father.* (John 16:28)

Just as truly as we came out from the Father in our new birth, when we leave our bodies, we go back to our Father.

In John 8:23, Jesus said, *"Ye are from beneath; I am from above."* Jesus was ever conscious of His heavenly origin and of His heavenly relationship.

Nothing would help us so much as to be aware that we do not belong to the earth. We are on the earth but we are not of it. Our citizenship is in heaven.

We are no longer a part of this Satan-ruled world. We are born from above.

We have the nature and the life of the Father. We are in Christ. Believers are in danger of being attracted to earthly things, such as money and the pleasures of life.

If we could know we are not of the earth, as we know we are men or women, and know that our highest joy is to be found alone in Christ, it would make a great difference in our earth walk.

In Matthew 12:42, Jesus said, *"A greater than Solomon is here."* He dared to confess what He actually was.

He dared to tell that generation that looked on Him with suspicion and jealousy and hatred, who He was. *"A greater than Solomon is here."*

I wonder if we have realized who we are. I wonder if we ever considered that we belong to another race.

> *Therefore if any man be in Christ, he is a new creature* [a new species]: *old things* [that belong to the earth walk] *are passed away; behold, all things are become new. And all things are of God, who hath reconciled us to himself.* (2 Corinthians 5:17–18)

We haven't realized that the least in the kingdom of God is greater than Solomon. He was but a servant. His vast wisdom was given to him.

We are the sons of God and Jesus has been made unto us wisdom.

Solomon was but a natural man who lived in the realm of the senses. He had no conception of this divine life that has been given to us.

But we don't think of that.

We have not yet realized our position in Christ; our position in the family.

We are the very sons and daughters of God Almighty. Solomon was but a son of David.

John 8:12 is perhaps one of the greatest sentences that ever fell from the lips of the Master, if we dared to put one Scripture over against another:

> *I am the light of the world: he that followeth me shall not walk in the darkness, but shall have the light of life.*

Jesus dared to say that He represented a new order, a new type of man, that in Him was the light of life; that is, the wisdom that comes from eternal life.

The people who follow Him, walk in His footsteps, and obey His word, should never be caught in the realm of darkness where they cannot see.

> *Who hath delivered us from the power of darkness, and hath translated us into the kingdom of his dear Son.* (Colossians 1:13)

You see, we have been taken out of the realm of darkness where men walk by the senses.

We have been translated into the kingdom of the Son of His love, or in other words, into the very family of God.

We have become partakers of His divine nature. The same life that was in the Son of God is in us. The same light that He had is in us.

Now we can understand 2 Corinthians 6:14:

> *Be ye not unequally yoked together with unbelievers: for what fellowship hath righteousness with unrighteousness? and what communion hath light with darkness?*

In Philippians 2:15, Paul tells us that we are seen *"as lights in the world."* We are holding forth as a lamp, the Word of life.

We are the light of the world. We have taken Jesus's place. His life in us is the source of light.

Light means wisdom and ability to do things, and the Greater One has not only imparted to us His own nature, but He has actually come into us and lives in us—as a part of us.

So when Jesus said, *"I am the light of the world,"* it placed tremendous responsibility upon those who follow in His steps.

If we are partakers of His life, then we have that light and John 1:4 must ever challenge us: *"In him was life; and the life was the light of men."*

We have that life.

With that life has come the light, and we must walk in the light as He is in the light.

To step out of that light is to step into darkness, which means broken fellowship. It means to step out of the realm of love, for that light is really love shining out through us, in our conduct, in our words.

The new kind of love and the new kind of light which Jesus brought are the very nature of the Father.

When we step out of love we step out of light, out of fellowship with heaven.

If we walk in the light as He is in the light, we have fellowship not only with the Father, but with one another. But when we are drawn aside for a moment by the adversary, we step into darkness.

> *He that saith he is in the light, and hateth his brother, is in darkness even until now. He that loveth his brother abideth in the light, and there is none occasion of stumbling in him. But he that hateth his brother is in darkness, and walketh in darkness, and knoweth not whither he goeth, because that darkness hath blinded his eyes.* (1 John 2:9–11)

His spirit is in darkness. Sense knowledge cannot light the path now.

We have taken the Master's place as lights in the world.

Just as Paul says, *"Be ye followers of me, even as I also am of Christ"* (1 Corinthians 11:1), so every one of us are lights in the world, and we are saying to the world, "Follow me, as I follow Christ."

When we step out of light into darkness, we spread confusion around us and folks know not what to do.

We should always remember what we are in Christ.

We should remember we are the lights of the world, and those who follow us must not be led into darkness.

John 14:6 has not only been a challenge, but has been a thrilling joy. Jesus said, *"I am the way, the truth, and the life: no man cometh unto the Father, but by me."*

What a confession that was!

When the Master said, *"I am the way,"* the Spirit at once began to bring to my mind excerpts from the Acts 9, of Paul going to Damascus to see if he could find any who were in "the way," whether men or women, so he could bring them to Jerusalem.

Christianity was the way.

But some *"were hardened, and believed not, but spake evil of that way"* (Acts 19:9).

What did they mean by calling Christianity *"that way"*?

Back yonder in the garden, Adam lost the way—the way into the Father's presence, the way into the Father's heart.

He left the place of light and glory and went out into the world without light.

All down through human history men have been groping for the lost way, the way back into fellowship with the Father, back into that Edenic condition where condemnation would not rule as a Master over the heart.

When Jesus said, *"I am the way,"* He meant He was the way to the Father's heart—the way of life.

Then I saw that every one of us is a light, a signboard pointing to the way.

Now notice carefully what it means to you. You are taking the Master's place; you are the way, and if your life is not in tune with the Master, and you are not living the Word, you may be pointing the wrong way.

He not only said, *"I am the way,"* but He said, *"I am the truth,"* or, "I am the reality."

Jesus is the answer of the age-old cry of the human spirit for reality.

Romans 1:25 reads, *"Who changed the truth* [reality] *of God into a lie."*

Satan is the god of vanity. The major pleasures of the senses of natural man have no actual reality in them.

There is no reality in the moving pictures, in the dance hall, in gambling, or in drinking.

There is nothing in them that the spirit of man can feed upon. Satan has not given to man one thing that has in it any permanent value.

The pleasures of the senses perish with the using.

When Jesus said, in effect, "I am the way, the reality, and the life," He was pointing to something that is different.

In John 16:13, Jesus said, "*When he, the Spirit of truth* [reality], *is come, he will guide you into all truth* [reality]."

Jesus is the way into the thing that the heart has craved through the ages—reality.

It is a strangely realistic truth that no one who has ever actually found eternal life, has ever turned to any other religion.

The metaphysical religions that are born of the senses have no appeal for the man who has found reality.

The human heart can find no reality outside of the man Jesus. The new creation is real.

Our fellowship with the Father is real.

The Word is a real message to the spirit of the new creation. We walk in the light of reality.

Jesus said: "*I am the way, the truth* [reality], *and the life.*"

The Greek word here for *life* is *zoe*. That is the new kind of life Jesus brought to the world.

"*I am come that they might have life, and that they might have it more abundantly*" (John 10:10). What is life? It is the nature of the Father.

In that nature of the Father is all wisdom, all ability, all love. "*He that believeth on me hath everlasting life*" (John 6:47).

Believing is actual possession, so the believer is a possessor of this, the greatest gift ever given to man—eternal life.

In him was life; and the life was the light of men. (John 1:4)

How little we have appreciated the fact that eternal life in man has given to us all the creative ability manifested in this mechanical age.

No heathen nation ever had any inventors or creators until eternal life came to them.

When we boast of Anglo-Saxon superiority, it is simply the superiority of eternal life over natural life.

There are two words translated life in the New Testament: *zoe*—the nature of the Father that Jesus brought, and gives to man in the new creation; and *psuche*—the natural human life.

Psuche has never produced any great literature, has never given to man anything that was of any real value.

Let this become clear in our minds, that *zoe*, this new kind of life, is the nature of the Father, and the Father is Love.

So when this new kind of life comes into a man, it drives out the old nature and the new nature takes possession.

It is just like Israel moving into the promised land, driving out the inhabitants, and taking over the country for themselves. Eternal life has taken us over.

It has captivated our reasoning faculties, illuminating them, making them the slave of this new order, so that wherever a man who has eternal life goes, you see the marks of it.

He is a new creation man. He belongs to the new order of things. He has a new kind of love—*agape*—and that love makes a home in which it is safe for babies to be born.

The other kind of love is the Greek word *phileo,* the love that springs from the natural human heart.

It has never made a home in a heathen country.

It is the parent of all our divorces and broken homes.

Where a man and woman have *agape*, the new kind of love that springs out of this new kind of life, there is never a divorce. This is the greatest thing in the world.

The believer is the signboard pointing toward Jesus—the way, the truth, and the life, and we must be bold in our confession that we are in the way; that we have the reality and are enjoying the fullness of this marvelous life.

Jesus made another confession. *"I am the good shepherd: the good shepherd giveth his life for the sheep"* (John 10:11).

What a beautiful confession, so full of suggestion—the Shepherd.

It brings before the heart the Psalm 23:1–2: *"The Lord is my shepherd; I shall not want. He maketh me to lie down in green pastures: he leadeth me beside the still waters."* He restores my thinking processes so I can think God's thoughts.

He is the Caretaker, the Bread-provider, the Shield, and the Protector of His people.

His ministry is guiding and leading us into the real pastures where the heart learns to feed.

Can you see what this means to you?

The moment we receive eternal life, that moment we become under-shepherds of the flock: we become leaders and teachers of this new order, this new life.

We are the protectors of the lambs from the adversary that would destroy them.

What a ministry of love that shepherd has! What a life of love caring for them, watching over them, feeding them, pointing the way to the water of life, and leading them into the quiet place under the shadow of the great Rock in this weary land.

We ought to make confession of our shepherd responsibility and our ability to guide men.

I was amazed when I found the Greek word translated *power* meant ability, and that Jesus wanted the disciples to tarry in Jerusalem until they had received ability—the Father's ability that Jesus had been manifesting among men.

Now we, the under-shepherds, have His ability. We are partakers of that ability.

He is made unto us wisdom so we may know where to lead the sheep and what to feed them.

The greatest concern I have ever had regarding my ministry was ability to rightly divide the Word so I could give men the food, the bread of the Almighty.

I have wanted to be a faith builder. I wanted to lead men out of the wilderness of sense knowledge into the highlands of our privileges in Christ, which is a Shepherd's responsibility.

Here is another confession of Jesus that has a Pauline ring to it: "*The words that I speak unto you, they are spirit, and they are life*" (John 6:63).

How few of us have realized the power of words. Jesus knew. Jesus's words healed the sick, fed the multitudes, hushed the sea, and raised the dead.

Not only that, but they stirred such malignity and hatred in the hearts of the leaders of Israel that they finally nailed Him to the cross, just because of the words that He had spoken.

Paul makes us see it with a vividness that thrills. "*Through faith we understand that the worlds were framed by the word of God, so that things which are seen were not made of things which do appear*" (Hebrews 11:3).

God created the universe with words.

You remember those three wonderful words, "*Let there be.*" Eight or nine times, those words are recorded in the first chapter of Genesis.

God brought everything that is in the universe into being with words.

But the Spirit climaxes it in John 1:1–3:

> *In the beginning was the Word, and the Word was with God, and the Word was God. The same was in the beginning with God. All things were made by him; and without him was not any thing made that was made.*

He took man's words and filled them with Himself.

He made man's words creative things.

He filled man's words with the very genius of love.

His words dominated.

He indwelled words and made them work for Him.

He counted the things that were not as though they were, and they leaped into being.

Words create.

Then, in Hebrews 1:3, words dominated the things that words had created:

> *Who being the brightness of his glory, and the express image of his person, and upholding all things by the word of his power, when he had by himself purged our sins, sat down on the right hand of the Majesty on high.*

He had brought the world into being with His Word. Now that vast universe is sustained and governed by His Word.

Oh, my heart craves for the hour to come when we will begin to appreciate what words can accomplish.

All the business the world ever did was with words.

With words we make love.

With words we crush hearts.

With words—God-filled words—we build faith into the lives of men.

With words that are filled with sense knowledge, we destroy the faith of men.

Sense knowledge has no other means but words, and so our universities are filled with words, oftentimes destructive words, demoralizing words.

Our high schools are destroying the faith of our nation with false teaching—all with words.

There is nothing holy any longer.

An ideology borne of sense knowledge is dominating our nation, and unless the Word of God gains the ascendency again, all the ideals of our republic will go, and a new type of despotism that is destructive to Christianity will take its place.

Men without God have used the inventions that God has given to the new creation to destroy all God has wrought through the church since the Lutheran Reformation.

When Jesus said, "*The words that I speak unto you, they are spirit, and they are life*" (John 6:63), He was lifting the curtain and letting us see the realities.

Think of it! "*The words that I speak*" have in them the power and energy and creative ability of God.

"*The words that I speak unto you*" are life-giving words, love-building words, faith-creating words.

Now what is our confession?

Our confession is that we are the products of His words, that His words have given to our spirits the very nature of the Father, and that the law that governs this new life is the law of the new covenant.

> *A new commandment I give unto you, That ye love one another; as I have loved you.* (John 13:34)

This new law that grows out of the love nature of the Father is the law that governs us.

We are walking in the light of this new law, this creative, dominating law, this victorious law of love.

What a confession we have to make. God help us to hold fast to it. In John 14:9, Jesus says, *"He that hath seen me hath seen the Father."*

That almost takes one's breath away.

Jesus said, *"Have I been so long time with you, and yet hast thou not known me...?"* (John 14:9).

He said, in effect, "You have been living and walking with God.

"You have seen Him heal the sick and raise the dead.

"You have seen Him feed the multitudes through Me.

"You have felt His love nature in My voice and in My words, and so I say to you today, '*He that hath seen me hath seen the Father.*'

"You need never say again, 'Show us the Father,' for He is with you."

What a confession that was! How it has lingered in the very atmosphere through the ages!

Then, one day, I caught a glimpse of the revelation of the new creation in the Pauline Epistles, and I saw we were actually taking Jesus's place; that we had the same life in us Jesus had, and the same nature of the Father has been imparted to us.

With that nature have come all the attributes that made Jesus so beautiful to the world and made Him stand out as the most unusual character the ages have ever seen.

Every attribute in Jesus that made Him beautiful is in the new creation.

We have the same life that dominated Him—that love nature. We have the same kind of love He had.

He is made unto us *wisdom* from God.

He is made unto us *redemption* from God.

He is made unto us *sanctification* from God.

He is made unto us *righteousness* from God.

Those four attributes of the very nature of the Father were manifest in Jesus.

Redemption from the hand of the adversary had not yet been accomplished when Jesus walked the earth, but it was manifested in Him. He was the Master of demons.

Sanctification was revealed in Him in His utter separation from the world that surrounded Him.

Righteousness, the ability to stand in the Father's presence without the sense of inferiority, the ability to stand in the presence of Satan as a Master—all those gracious manifestations of the divine life were seen in Him.

As I read John 14:6–10, my whole being seems to open up toward Him and my heart cries, "Lord, make this real by thy grace in my life so men who see me will see you; so I can say, perhaps not in words, '*He that hath seen me hath seen the Father.*'"

What a confession Jesus made to the world, and what a confession we have the privilege of making today.

Jesus said, "*I am the vine, ye are the branches*" (John 15:5).

I would that my heart could understand it; that the heart could grasp the reality of our union with Him, of our unusual ability to feed upon the very nature and life of God in Christ.

You see, no branch can be closer to the vine than another branch. Every branch has the same union with the vine for its individual ministry of fruit bearing.

When He said, "*I am the vine, ye are the branches,*" it brought us into the fullest union with Deity.

We are actually partakers of the divine nature.

The very life and substance of deity pours out of the vine into the branch.

Then He prayed, "*And the glory which thou gavest me I have given them; that they may be one, even as we are one: I in them, and thou in me, that they may be made perfect in one*" (John 17:22–23).

Why? "*That they may be made perfect in one; and that the world may know that thou hast sent me, and hast loved them, as thou hast loved me*" (verse 23).

That is the vine life.

That is where the branch is glorified and the fruitage becomes like the fruitage of Jesus in His earth walk.

We can understand now what He meant when He said, "*Greater works than these shall he do; because I go unto my Father*" (John 14:12).

Jesus was limited to physical things.

He could heal the sick, feed the multitudes, raise the dead, and turn water into wine, but He could not recreate anyone.

He could not give anyone eternal life because it was not available until after He had put sin away, until He had satisfied the claims of justice, conquered Satan, arose from the dead, carried His blood into the heavenly Holy of Holies, and sat down at the right hand of the Majesty on high.

6

WHAT THE RESURRECTION GIVES US

Here are some of the riches of this blessed truth gleaned from the Pauline Epistles.

What does His resurrection mean to the Christian in his daily life?

John 19:31–37 tells us of His death, of the spear-thrust in His side, and of blood and water pouring out of that great gaping wound.

It is told in the plainest language that He died of a ruptured heart.

The blood flowed through the rupture in His heart into the sack that holds the heart, and as the body grew cold, the blood had separated and the white serum had settled to the bottom.

The red corpuscles had risen to the top and coagulated, and when that Roman spear pierced it, the white serum gushed out. Then followed clots of the coagulated blood rolling down His side to the ground. Jesus was dead.

> *And after this Joseph of Arimathaea, being a disciple of Jesus, but secretly for fear of the Jews, besought Pilate that he might take away the body of Jesus: and Pilate gave him leave. He came therefore, and took the body of Jesus. And there came also Nicodemus, which at the first came to Jesus by night, and brought a mixture of myrrh and aloes, about an hundred pound weight. Then took they the body of Jesus, and wound it in linen clothes with the spices, as the manner of the Jews is to bury.*
>
> (John 19:38–40)

Here is a drama worthy of inspiration.

Joseph and Nicodemus showed their friendship openly after His death:

> *Now in the place where he was crucified there was a garden; and in the garden a new sepulchre, wherein was never man yet laid. There laid they Jesus therefore because of the Jews' preparation day; for the* [tomb] *was nigh at hand.* (John 19:41–42)

John 20:1–10 gives us a picture of His resurrection:

> *The first day of the week cometh Mary Magdalene early, when it was yet dark, unto the sepulchre, and seeth the stone taken away from the sepulchre. Then she runneth, and cometh to Simon Peter, and to the other disciple, whom Jesus loved, and saith unto them, They have taken away the* LORD *out of the sepulchre, and we know not where they have laid him. Peter therefore went forth, and that other disciple, and came to the sepulchre. So they ran both together: and the other disciple did outrun Peter, and came first to the sepulchre. And he stooping down, and looking in, saw the linen clothes lying; yet went he not in. Then cometh Simon Peter following him, and went into the sepulchre, and seeth the linen clothes lie, and the napkin, that was about his head, not lying with the linen clothes, but wrapped together in a place by itself. Then went in also that other disciple, which came first to the sepulchre, and he saw, and believed. For as yet they knew not the scripture, that he must rise again from the dead. Then the disciples went away again unto their own home.*

What a shock it must have been to Mary.

She had come to the sepulchre to finish the embalming and saw the stone rolled away.

She never stopped to look in but turned and ran back to the room where Peter and John were stopping.

Bursting in upon them she cried, "*They have taken away the* LORD *out of the sepulchre, and we know not where they have laid him.*"

Who had dared to desecrate the tomb?

No people among all the nations paid such reverence to the dead as the Hebrew nation.

The Romans had stripped Him; they had scourged Him; they had nailed Him to the cross, with a mock crown on His Head. That wasn't enough.

Had they dared to desecrate the grave?

Peter and John would not wait; they both started toward the tomb. John outran Peter and arrived there first.

Stooping down, he looked into the tomb and was staggered at what he saw.

Peter came. He hadn't the fine feelings that actuated John. He just bowed his head and stepped into the sepulchre and John followed him.

Notice the language: *"Seeth the linen clothes lie, and the napkin, that was about his head, not lying with the linen clothes, but wrapped together in a place by itself."*

When Jesus came out of the grave clothes, there was no hurry. He picked up the napkin that had been upon His face, folded it up, and laid it in a niche in the tomb.

There is something about that act of the Master that reaches deep into my spirit-consciousness.

He doesn't act like a man, does He?

Only God would act like that in an hour of such triumph.

"Then went in also that other disciple, which came first to the sepulchre, and he saw, and believed."

What did John see in the sepulchre that made him believe that Jesus was resurrected?

"For as yet they knew not the scripture, that he must rise again from the dead."

You understand, Jesus's body had been embalmed as the custom of the Jews was to bury.

Nearly every rich family had a slave who understood embalming.

They had one hundred pounds of a mixture composed of myrrh and aloes and a bundle of linen cloths.

They cut the linen up into strips, smeared it with this mixture as you would a bandage to wrap around a wounded finger, and then wrapped the body of Jesus.

Every finger was wrapped separately and then the hands and arms, until the whole body was wrapped as an Egyptian mummy. When it was finished, they took the embalmed body and put it into the sepulchre, and it was sealed by Roman authority.

Notice, the body of Jesus likely weighed 180 to 200 pounds in his health. He would shrink about twenty pounds in the crucifixion.

There was a hundred pound weight of myrrh and aloes, besides the linen cloths they used in embalming. Then the body would weigh about 280 pounds.

When they had finished the embalming, His body was completely encased except for His face.

If Jesus had not died of a ruptured heart and the spear thrust, He certainly would have died in the three days and three nights of embalming.

No one could have lived through that.

The embalming cloth had grown hard and stiff in that dry cell in the seventy-two hours He was there.

The cloth had not been rent or torn. He had come out of the grave clothes through the narrow aperture where His face had been. What do you think Peter and John did?

No sooner had they left the sepulchre, than they rushed through the streets crying, "He is risen! He is risen!"

Their hearts were so overcharged with emotion they couldn't resist proclaiming the fact.

The tremendous stir His resurrection made in the city, three thousand men that accepted Christ on the day of Pentecost, all prove the historic fact, the absolute certainty of His resurrection.

The whole Jewish nation knew it. They were shaken to the foundation.

First Corinthians 15:1–8 declares that five hundred people saw Him at His ascension.

The early church did not try to prove that Jesus arose from the dead. It was a self-evident fact.

No one ever questioned it in Jerusalem.

They were there when it happened.

They saw the tomb and the empty grave clothes.

Tens of thousands of Jews went to that empty sepulchre, stood there smiting their breasts and rending their garments.

They knew Jesus had risen.

Now what does it mean to us today?

In Revelation 1:17–18, hear the resurrected Master speaking now:

And when I saw him, I fell at his feet as dead. And he laid his right hand upon me, saying unto me, Fear not; I am the first and the last: I am he that liveth, and was dead; and, behold, I am alive for evermore, Amen; and have the keys of hell and of death.

Satan had been conquered.

What a thrill went through the whole spirit world when Jesus came from the dark regions, a Master, holding aloft in His hand the keys of death and of hell.

He had stripped that foul spirit of his authority.

He had left him defeated before his own cohorts.

There was a spiritual earthquake in the region of the damned.

Hebrews 2:14 tells us:

Forasmuch then as the children are partakers of flesh and blood, he also himself likewise took part of the same; that through death he might destroy him that had the power of death, that is, the devil.

Joseph B. Rotherham translates it as "that he might paralyze the death-dealing authority of the devil." Either translation is clear enough.

Before Jesus arose from the dead, He had conquered Satan and stripped him of the authority of which he had robbed man in the garden.

The story of the triumph of Satan's defeat wouldn't be fully described unless we gave you Colossians 2:15: "*Having spoiled principalities and powers, he made a shew of them openly, triumphing over them in it.*"

The margin reads, "Having put off from himself the principalities and the powers."

You see, Jesus was held down there and only God knows what He suffered until He had satisfied the claims of justice, had been made righteous, and made a new creation.

Then Satan's dominion over Him ended. He hurled back the hosts of hell.

He crushed their death-dealing ability.

He stripped Satan of his authority and left him paralyzed and broken. Then He arose from the dead and shouted, "All hail," for redemption morn had come!

Redemption was a fact. Satan was defeated.

Now we can quote Colossians 1:13–14 once more. I want you to become familiar with this Scripture. I want you to know it as you know two and two are four.

> *Who hath delivered us from the power of darkness, and hath translated us into the kingdom of his dear Son: in whom we have redemption through his blood, even the forgiveness of sins.*

That was the greatest moment in human history

That was a moment that will be remembered through all eternity, when Jesus stood before the wondering disciples and shouted, "All hail!"

Angels must have wept before the throne.

The great Father God—what could it have meant to Him? Humanity, the hope of His love and the reason for all creation, was redeemed; the claims of justice were satisfied.

The throne could never be assailed. God had legally redeemed man.

All the ages of eternity will remember the heroic battle that Jesus wrought in order to prove to humanity that God was just and He could on legal grounds justify the ungodly, because His only begotten Son had redeemed them with His own blood.

Now God can on legal grounds give to man eternal life.

John 5:24 can become a part of human experience: "*He that heareth my word, and believeth on him that sent me, hath everlasting life, and shall not come into condemnation; but is passed from death unto life.*" (See also John 6:47.)

I wonder if your heart takes this in?

There will be no judgment for us like there was for the Master; there will be no cross and no crown of thorns.

There will be no suffering in hell for the man who takes Jesus Christ as his Savior—and it is so easy to take Him.

Hear this Scripture: *"He that believeth on me hath everlasting life"* (John 6:47), or he that acts upon the Word that God has spoken has eternal life the moment that he acts.

The man outside of Christ cannot confess the lordship of Jesus and declare that he knows Christ died for his sins and arose when He was justified, without receiving the nature and life of God.

You ask, what is the greatest miracle of all the miracles connected with redemption?

It is not the resurrection of the Lord Jesus, because the Father and the Son were working together in that.

But the greatest miracle happens when a man receives eternal life, when a child of the devil becomes a child of God.

Notice again: when a man who is spiritually dead passes out of the realm of Satan into the realm of life (into the kingdom of the Son of God's love) that is the miracle of miracles.

To the sense knowledge man, the resurrection is the greatest miracle, because that is something the senses can register.

But the new birth is an unseen miracle. It is in the spirit realm. Man's soul or reasoning faculties cannot be born again. They cannot receive the nature of God independent of his spirit. His spirit is the part of him that is recreated.

Second Corinthians 5:17–21 had become a reality the moment Jesus carried His blood into the Holy of Holies and sat down at the right hand of the Father.

Now a man can accept Christ and know that the moment he does, he becomes a new creation.

The old things of his life have passed away, and behold all are become new; and all these things are of God, who has reconciled that man to Himself through Jesus Christ.

What a miracle the new creation is!

Think of taking a man out of the very dregs of our modern civilization and recreating him in a single moment from a convict to a Son of God.

And not only that, but notice that verse 21. Here God whispers, *"He hath made him to be sin for us, who knew no sin; that we might be made the righteousness of God in him."*

That is the Father speaking, and the moment you accept Christ as your Savior and confess Him as your Lord, that moment you become the righteousness of God in Christ.

We could stop here, for this is enough to thrill the ages, but we haven't reached the climax of redemption yet.

> *God is faithful, by whom ye were called unto the fellowship of his Son Jesus Christ our Lord.* (1 Corinthians 1:9)

It took me a good while before I could adjust my heart to the reality of that statement, that the great eternal Father God, the Creator of the universe, should call me, should call you, to fellowship with His Son, to become identified with that Son, to become one with that Son.

Here are a beautiful father and mother. They have a lovely boy, and oh, how careful they have been in his upbringing. Could you think of them going down into the slums and finding a nondescript child to be his associate, to fellowship with that boy? No.

But here is the miracle.

The Father knows when a man accepts His Son as his Savior, and confesses His lordship, that moment He will give that man something that will make him absolutely a new creation.

He will be in the same class with Jesus.

He will be an actual child of God.

The old spiritual nature that links him with Satan has ceased being, and a new nature, God's own nature, is imparted to him.

Now he is as really the Father's son as was Jesus in His earth walk, and he is as righteous as the first begotten, because that first begotten is his righteousness.

You may talk about miraculous things, but I declare to you, this new creation miracle outstrips everything in all creation.

Taking a child of the devil with his hands wet with the blood of his brother, and changing that man's nature! No sir! Giving that man a new nature, destroying the old nature; giving him the position of a son; giving him the rights and privileges of a son; giving him the very place of a Son in the Father's heart and family here is grace; here is love let loose.

This is a picture of Paul.

This is the climax. Now you are ready to turn to 2 Corinthians 2:14:

> *Now thanks be unto God, which always causeth us to triumph in Christ, and maketh manifest the savour of his knowledge by us in every place.*

Now note this:

> *For we are unto God a sweet savour of Christ, in them that are saved, and in them that perish: to the one we are the savour of death unto death; and to the other the savour of life unto life. And who is sufficient for these things?* (verses 15–16)

And then hear this cry: "For we are not as the many, corrupting the word of God: but we have been made sufficient to fulfill this ministry."

But I want you to notice a little sentence taken from the W. J. Conybeare translation commenting on those verses:

> But thanks be to God, who leads me on from place to place in the train of his triumph, to celebrate his victory over the enemies of Christ; and by me sends forth knowledge of Him, a steam of fragrant incense, throughout the world. For Christ's is the fragrance which I offer up to God.

The metaphor is taken from the triumphal procession of a victorious general. God is celebrating His triumph over His enemies; Paul, who had been so great an opponent of the gospel, is a captive following in the train of the triumphal procession, yet at the same time, by a characteristic change of metaphor, an incense-bearer, scattering incense, which was always done on these occasions, as the procession moves on.

Some of the conquered enemies were put to death when the procession reached the capitol; to them the smell of the incense was an odor *"of death unto death"*; to the rest who were spared, an odor *"of life unto life."*

The heart can hardly grasp the significance of it.

We now reign as masters and kings.

Once more I want to give you Romans 5:17, for it fits here perfectly:

For if by one man's offence death reigned by one; much more they which receive abundance of grace and of the gift of righteousness shall reign in life by one, Jesus Christ.

We are now reigning as kings in the realm of life.

We have become masters. We are conquerors.

What does the resurrection mean to us?

It means that He has taken us from slavery to the throne. We were defeated, conquered, and held in bondage.

We are set free, and in the name of Jesus we become the bondage-breakers for the rest of the human race.

He has made us masters where fear held us in captivity.

7

"IN WHOM WE HAVE"

Many believers are afraid to say that they are in Christ and are afraid to act as though it is true.

The Father has declared in the Word what we are in Christ. We find believers seeking to obtain what love has already given them.

We ought to know what we are and what we have in Him.

First, what we have in Christ. *"Who hath delivered us from the power of darkness, and hath translated us into the kingdom of his dear Son: in whom we have redemption through his blood, even the forgiveness of sins"* (Colossians 1:13–14).

I shall use in this the first person singular, as W. J. Conybeare suggests. Then it would read, "Who delivered me out of the authority of darkness and translated me into the kingdom of the Son of his love; in whom I have my redemption and the remission of my sins." Our redemption is from the dominion of Satan, and when Christ arose from the dead and presented His own blood before the supreme court of the universe, and it was accepted, our redemption was a settled thing.

Then He sat down at the right hand of the Majesty on high. When he sat down, Satan had been defeated. Everything that justice had demanded had been accomplished.

Now God has a legal right to give man eternal life, but He had no right to give man eternal life until there had been a perfect redemption.

So, Romans 3:21–26 is the Holy Spirit's exposition of this blessed reality: *"But now the righteousness of God without the law is manifested, being witnessed by the law and the prophets"* (verse 21).

You understand that man's basic need was righteousness, the ability to stand in the Father's presence without the sense of guilt or inferiority, and so

He declares that God has unveiled a new source of righteousness, and that source of righteousness is witnessed by the law and the prophets, *"even the righteousness of God which is by faith of Jesus Christ"* (verse 22).

And the strange thing is that it is based upon simple faith in Jesus, or in acting upon what God has said in regard to His Son. *"Being justified freely by his grace through the redemption that is in Christ Jesus"* (verse 24).

You understand, He was delivered up on the account of our trespasses, and He was raised when we were justified.

Now we can understand that we were justified freely by His grace, through the redemption God wrought in Christ, whom He has set forth to be a sin substitute on the ground of faith and His blood.

God did this to show His righteousness because He had been passing over the sins of Israel for fifteen hundred years.

Now it is demanded that the penalty be paid.

Jesus met that penalty and paid or redeemed the promises that were made each year by the high priest on the great Day of Atonement.

Jesus cashed all those promissory notes and brought redemption to every man who had been blood-covered under the first covenant.

I think we ought to read Hebrews 9:12: *"Neither by the blood of goats and calves, but by his own blood he entered in once into the holy place, having obtained eternal redemption for us."*

I want you to note that this redemption is an eternal redemption, that when Christ carried His blood into the Holy of Holies, and the supreme court of the universe accepted it, redemption was a completed thing.

> *For if the blood of bulls and of goats, and the ashes of a heifer sprinkling the unclean, sanctifieth to the purifying of the flesh: how much more shall the blood of Christ, who through the eternal Spirit offered himself without spot to God, purge your conscience from dead works to serve the living God?*
> (Hebrews 9:13–14)

Did you notice that the blood of bulls and goats only cleanses the flesh?

The cleansing of the flesh means the senses; it did not cleanse the heart; it did not make man a new creation.

And for this cause he is the mediator of the new testament, that by means of death, for the redemption of the transgressions that were under the first testament, they which are called might receive the promise of eternal inheritance. (Hebrews 9:15)

Now you can understand what he meant in Romans 3. He died for the sins of those living under the first covenant that had been covered by blood from year to year, that they might have their share in the inheritance and in this redemption.

You see, the redemption in Christ not only reached forward to us, but reached backward and redeemed every man under the first covenant who had trusted in the blood of bulls and goats.

Hebrews 9:26 now becomes clear to us: "*But now once in the end of the world hath he appeared to put away sin by the sacrifice of himself.*"

He has dealt with the sin problem.

Now it is a sinner problem.

The sin problem is ended and the sinner has the legal right to eternal life, because God so loved him that He gave him His only begotten Son.

Redemption then is a settled fact, and it is possible now for a man to receive eternal life on legal grounds.

Therefore if any man be in Christ, he is a new creature: old things are passed away; behold, all things are become new. And all things are of God, who hath reconciled us to himself by Jesus Christ.
(2 Corinthians 5:17–18)

Note very carefully that in this new creation, the man who accepts Christ receives eternal life.

Spiritual death, the nature of the adversary, is driven out of him, stops being in him, and a new nature is given to him. His spirit is recreated.

His soul or mind will need to be renewed.

But the mind and spirit must be brought into fellowship with each other, and that can only be as the mind is renewed through the Word.

It is very important that the believer sees this fact.

> *For if we have been planted together in the likeness of his death, we shall be also in the likeness of his resurrection: knowing this, that our old man is crucified with him.* (Romans 6:5–6)

The same truth is brought out in Galatians 2:20: *"I am crucified with Christ."*

Our crucifixion and union with Christ on the cross belong to the legal side of the plan of redemption.

All that He did for us in His redemptive work is based on legal grounds.

He was delivered up on account of our trespasses.

He died for our sins.

He arose for our justification.

Now notice Romans 6:6: *"Knowing this, that our old man is crucified with him, that the body of sin might be destroyed, that henceforth we should not serve sin."*

We died with Christ. We were raised together with Him.

So the old man, the sin nature that was a partaker of spiritual death, died with Christ.

When we accept Jesus Christ as our Savior and confess Him as our Lord, we become a new creation, and experimentally that old man stops being and the new man in Christ takes his place.

This has been a hard problem for many people. They say, "How can that be true in the face of Paul's experience in Romans 7?"

Romans 7:7–24 is Paul's experience as a Jew under the Law. It is not the experience of a new creation. He said, *"For we know that the law is spiritual: but I am carnal, sold under sin"* (Romans 7:14).

The Law was fulfilled in Christ. Nobody is under the Law today. It is true, the Jew didn't know that he died with Christ and that his old Law and the first covenant all ceased to be in Christ. He doesn't know it today, but it is the truth.

The Law was the Jews' schoolmaster until Christ; not as some translators try to make us believe, that the Law is our schoolmaster to lead us to Christ. The Greek text shows conclusively that the Law was until Christ, and when

Christ arose from the dead and sat down on the right hand of the Majesty on high, the Abrahamic covenant and the Mosaic law stopped functioning.

There is no one under the Mosaic law today. They can't get under it.

They may attempt it as many are doing today, but it is only a farce.

We have a new law that belongs to the new covenant, of which Christ is the Head, and that new law is to govern the new creation in Christ Jesus.

So 1 John 5:12–13 becomes a blessed reality:

> *He that hath the Son hath life; and he that hath not the Son of God hath not life. These things have I written unto you that believe on the name of the Son of God; that ye may know that ye have eternal life, and that ye may believe on the name of the Son of God.*

The believer has eternal life.

He has passed out of death into life; out of the realm of Satan into the realm of Christ; out of the realm of spiritual death where Satan reigns, into the realm of eternal life, where Jesus Christ reigns.

Notice the first sentence in 1 John 4:4: "*Ye are of God, little children.*"

We are of God. That fits in perfectly with John 3:6–7, where Jesus said to Nicodemus, "*That which is born of the flesh is flesh; and that which is born of the Spirit is spirit. Marvel not that I said unto thee, Ye must be born again.*"

The new creation is born from above.

They came from God.

This new nature flowed out from the very heart of the Father into their spirits, when they crowned Jesus as Lord of their lives.

> *Blessed be the God and Father of our Lord Jesus Christ, who hath blessed us with all spiritual blessings in heavenly places in Christ.* (Ephesians 1:3)

When we accepted Jesus Christ as our Savior, then Romans 8:31–32 became an actual reality:

> *What shall we then say to these things? If God be for us, who can be against us? He that spared not his own Son, but delivered him up for us all, how shall he not with him also freely give us all things?*

In the prior verse, you will notice that He has blessed us with *"all spiritual blessings."*

Everything that Christ wrought in His redemptive work belongs to the new creation.

You do not need to pray for it or seek for it, nor believe for it; it is yours.

Philippians 4:6–7 gives us just another angle of our inheritance in Christ. *"Be careful for nothing; but in every thing by prayer and supplication with thanksgiving let your requests be made known unto God."* Then a miracle happens: *"The peace of God, which passeth all understanding, shall keep your hearts and minds through Christ Jesus."*

When we know what our redemption means to the Father, and what He intended it should mean to us, then we pass out of the realm of worry and fear and doubt.

> *Not that I speak in respect of want: for I have learned, in whatsoever state I am, therewith to be content [independent of circumstances].*
>
> (Philippians 4:11)

Why can we be independent of circumstances? Because verse 13 says, *"I can do all things through Christ which strengtheneth me."*

You see, this redemption in the mind of the Father means a new creation.

It means sonship with all its privileges. It means we have come into the family and have family rights and privileges now that nothing can interrupt as long as we walk in love with Him.

The second fact is what we are in Christ.

It is necessary for us to review a little.

We are redeemed. Satan's dominion over us is ended. He no longer reigns over us.

Not only are we redeemed, but the moment we came into the family of God, we became Satan's master.

God has given to us a legal right to the use of Jesus's name, and Matthew 28:18–20 declares:

> *All power is given unto me in heaven and in earth. Go ye therefore, and teach all nations...and, lo, I am with you always, even unto the end of the world.*

How is He with us? He is with us, in His name, in His Word, and in the person of the Holy Spirit.

In Mark 16:17–18, He said,

> *And these signs shall follow them that believe; in my name shall they cast out devils; they shall speak with new tongues; they shall take up serpents; and if they drink any deadly thing, it shall not hurt them; they shall lay hands on the sick, and they shall recover.*

And verse 20: *"And they went forth, and preached every where, the Lord working with them, and confirming the word with signs following."*

You see, He has not left us at the mercy of an enemy.

The youngest babe in Christ has a legal right to the name of Jesus.

Not only that, but he has a legal right to the indwelling presence of the Holy Spirit.

I can never tell you what that means to my heart.

> *Greater is he that is in you, than he that is in the world.* (1 John 4:4)

What will He do when He comes in? He will guide us into all truth or reality. (See John 16:13.)

He will take the things of Jesus and unveil them to our hearts. He will impart to us the very ability of God.

If you remember, before Jesus went away, He told His disciples to tarry in Jerusalem until they be endued with power from on high.

That word power means ability.

The Holy Spirit was going to come into them with divine ability and make them masters of circumstances, masters of situations, masters of nations.

> *Fear thou not; for I am with thee: be not dismayed; for I am thy God: I will strengthen thee; yea, I will help thee; yea, I will uphold thee with the right hand of my righteousness.* (Isaiah 41:10)

That belongs to us today. That is a picture of the new creation.

Not only did He give us eternal life and the great mighty Holy Spirit to live in our bodies, but He has made us the righteousness of God in Christ.

Jesus's life during His earth walk was amazing to men of sense knowledge.

Righteousness made Jesus absolute master of every situation, a master of all men because all men were sin-conscious. Jesus was not.

Shakespeare said, "The conscience [sin] makes cowards of us all." He struck the taproot of the sin problem.

When a man becomes a new creation, he receives the same righteousness that Jesus had.

Jesus becomes his righteousness. (See 1 Corinthians 1:30.)

That righteousness makes him a master of demons; makes him a master of circumstances.

He is not afraid of Satan, or anything Satan can do or has done. The early church lived the new creation in reality. They were the righteousness of God in actual demonstration.

Not only did the early Christians have righteousness given to them but they were made the righteousness of God in Christ. When they received the righteous nature of the Father, that nature made them righteous.

When they received the love nature of the Father, it made them sons of love.

That is the reason they could suffer any kind of persecution and yet love the persecutor.

Jesus loved Judas and the man who drove the nails into His hands and feet.

Paul loved the men who beat him and stoned him.

Stephen, when he was dying, said, "*Lord, lay not this sin to their charge*" (Acts 7:60).

That was a new kind of love the world had never known.

God is love.

The new creation has the love nature of the Father.

There is another outstanding feature that we must not overlook. We have known God as a loving God, a just God, a holy God, but we have never thought of Him as a faith God.

That is an outstanding characteristic of God.

He created the universe by faith.

Everything that came into being at creation, came into being by faith. All He did was to say, *"Let there be..."* and things became. God is a faith God.

No doubt everyone reading this will look back at his early Christian life.

When he was first born again, he was filled with love; he was filled with zeal that was born of faith.

Could he have had the right teaching, he would have walked into a life of faith that would have shaken the community.

You see, we become partakers of the faith and nature of God. That explains that passage in Romans 12:3: *"According as God hath dealt to every man the measure of faith."*

Every man at the new birth has a measure of faith. That measure can be increased as he uses it. But under the modern teaching, what faith was given to him in the new birth is usually destroyed by sense knowledge teaching.

We must not omit Ephesians 2:10: *"For we are his workmanship, created in Christ Jesus unto good works, which God hath before ordained that we should walk in them."*

If we could continually remember that we are God's new creations, that He was the Author and Finisher of these new creations, just as He is the Author and Finisher of faith, then life would be victorious.

He gave birth to us in the birth throes of agony in His substitutionary work. We are the product of that birth.

You see, we have become the sons and daughters of God. We remember that Jesus is our example.

Jesus never tried to believe. He acted on the Word of His Father. He never sought faith.

He said He did what His Father told Him to do.

We urge the unsaved to get something. We should urge them to act on the Word.

Jesus belongs to them. All they need to do is to confess His lordship, and the moment they do, they receive eternal life.

Believing is acting on the Word.

The believer is one who has acted on the Word.

The unbeliever is one who has not yet acted.

The one is a *possesser*; the other may be merely a *seeker* after something that he has not claimed as his own.

I want you to know in your heart that you are what He says you are.

He wants you to act it, to confess what He has done in you; what He has made you to be.

This will glorify Him and strengthen your faith.

To deny what we are, and to tell what Satan is doing in our bodies or minds, is denying what we are in Christ.

All things are possible now, for we are the children of God. We are united with Him.

8

THE LEGAL AND VITAL ASPECTS OF REDEMPTION

Until one becomes conscious of these two phases of revelation, there will be haziness in his teaching and a lack of solidity in his thinking and living.

The legal side of redemption is what God did for us in Christ. It is in the past.

Romans 4:25 is a good illustration: "*Who was delivered for our offences, and was raised again for our justification.*"

Here is another:

> *For I delivered unto you first of all that which I also received, how that Christ died for our sins according to the scriptures; and that he was buried, and that he rose again the third day according to the scriptures.*
> (1 Corinthians 15:3–4)

These two Scriptures perfectly illustrate what God did for us in His redemptive work.

The vital can be illustrated.

> *There is therefore now no condemnation to them which are in Christ Jesus.* (Romans 8:1)

> *In whom we have redemption through his blood, even the forgiveness of sins.* (Colossians 1:14)

The vital is what we really have now; what the Holy Spirit is doing in us today.

If one only had the legal side of the plan of redemption, it would lead him into cold, dead formalism.

It would make doctrines out of reality and sense knowledge would rule.

The vital teachings alone will lead into fanaticism, magnifying experiences above the Word.

When the vital aspect is understood, we know what belongs to us in Christ.

We know a son's rights. We learn to take our place. We enjoy our privileges, and the vital side then becomes a reality.

All that is legally ours may become vitally ours by the ministry of the Spirit through the Word in us.

A little study of the legal side may help us.

> *For he hath made him to be sin for us, who knew no sin; that we might be made the righteousness of God in him.* (2 Corinthians 5:21)

That is what God wrought in Christ.

He laid our sins upon Christ.

He was stricken, smitten of God and afflicted.

> *He was wounded for our transgressions, he was bruised for our iniquities: the chastisement of our peace was upon him; and with his stripes we are healed. All we like sheep have gone astray; we have turned every one to his own way; and the Lord hath laid on him the iniquity of us all.* (Isaiah 53:5–6)

He not only laid our sins on Jesus, but He made Jesus sin.

Romans 3:21–26 is perhaps the great master sentence illustrating this legal side of the plan of redemption.

> *But now the righteousness of God without the law is manifested* [unveiled, or as one translator puts it, "brought to light"], *being witnessed by the law and the prophets; even the righteousness of God which is by faith of Jesus Christ unto all and upon all them that believe: for there is no difference: for all have sinned, and come short of the glory of God.* (verses 21–23)

Here is a little touch of the vital in verse 24: *"Being justified freely by his grace through the redemption that is in Christ Jesus."*

In verses 25–26, we swing back again to the legal:

> *Whom God hath set forth to be a propitiation* [or a mercy seat where the blood was sprinkled by the high priest] *through faith in his blood, to declare his righteousness for the remission of sins that are past, through the forbearance of God; to declare, I say, at this time his righteousness.*

Here we catch a glimpse of the vital: *"that he might be just, and the justifier of him which believeth in Jesus"* (verse 26).

You see, the Spirit has based our present righteousness upon the work that had been accomplished in His great substitutionary work.

Titus 2:14 is another Scripture showing the legal side: *"Who gave himself for us, that he might redeem us from all iniquity, and purify unto himself a peculiar people, zealous of good works."*

SOME VITAL FACTS

One of the most priceless vital Scriptures is 2 Corinthians 5:17–18:

> *Therefore if any man be in Christ, he is a new creature: old things are passed away; behold, all things are become new. And all things are of God, who hath reconciled us to himself by Jesus Christ, and hath given to us the ministry of reconciliation.*

It is very important that we recognize this fact, that all that has been wrought for us by Christ in His substitutionary sacrifice, belongs to the individual believer.

Ephesians 1:17–23 is a part of the great charter of our redemption, and this is both legal and vital.

He reveals what He did for us.

He reveals His process of building the very nature and life of the Father into our spirits.

He said, "I want you to know what is the exceeding greatness of His ability on our behalf who believe."

> *According to the working of his mighty power, which he wrought in Christ, when he raised him from the dead, and set him at his own right hand in the heavenly places, far above all principality, and power, and might, and dominion, and every name that is named, not only in this world, but also in that which is to come: and hath put all things under his feet, and gave him to be the head over all things to the church, which is his body, the fulness of him that filleth all in all.* (verses 19–23)

Here we have the legal background of His great substitutionary work, of His absolutely conquering the forces of darkness before He arose from the dead.

Colossians 2:15 says, "*Having spoiled principalities and powers, he made a shew of them openly, triumphing over them in it.*"

We have failed to recognize this blessed fact, that in the substitutionary work of Christ, it was as though we ourselves were with Him.

He not only was crucified, but in Romans 6:8, it says, "*Now if we be dead with Christ, we believe that we shall also live with him.*"

Not only were we crucified with Him, but we died with Him.

In Colossians 2:12, we were buried with Him.

In 1 Timothy 3:15, we were justified with Him.

In Colossians 2:13, we were made alive with Him: "*And you...hath he quickened together with him.*"

Then, in Ephesians 2:6, He raised us up with Him and made us to sit with Him in the heavenlies.

In these Scriptures, we get a living picture of the entire substitutionary work of Christ, in which we have a perfect identification. It was done for us.

It is the legal background of our redemption.

You can say, "Yes, I was crucified with Him. I was identified with Him in His shame and His deep agonies on the cross.

"More than that, God not only put my sin upon Him and made Him sin with my sin, but He put me upon Him.

"He was taking my place. He was acting in my stead.

"It was my sin that stripped Him naked.

"It was my sin that caused the crown of thorns to be put upon His brow.

"It was my sin that drove the nails into His hands and feet.

"It was love that was taking my place and suffering in my stead that I might be ransomed out of the authority of darkness and the power of sin and spiritual death.

"I can say I died with Him; that when He died on the cross, He partook of my spiritual death, and I was identified with Him in that spiritual death.

"It was as though I had been there in person and we had left His body together.

"When He died on the cross, He and I went to the place where I should have gone alone, but He went with me as my substitute. He went with me to suffer in my stead.

"He was bearing my sin with me, that old spiritually dead self. He suffered there until the claims of justice against me had been satisfied and there was no longer any charge against me.

"My spiritual death and union with Satan were wiped out. And then He was justified in Spirit.

"His justification was for me, for you see, He went there for me.

"He didn't go there on His own account. He went on my account, and as soon as He was justified, He was recreated—made alive in spirit, and that wonderful Scripture in Acts 13:33, '*Thou art my Son, this day have I begotten thee,*' was made real.

"Right there in those awful surroundings He was born again. He had become the very righteousness of God right there.

"And now I can understand Ephesians 2:10: '*We are his workmanship, created in Christ Jesus.*'

"That is the legal side of the new birth. In the mind of justice, we were recreated down there at the time Christ was, because He is the Head of the body, the firstborn from among the dead.

"He was the first person ever born again. In His birth, the whole body of Christ had the legal work accomplished for them.

"Then, He conquered the adversary, but in the mind of justice I was with Him.

"When He stripped Satan of his authority and dominion, it was your victory and mine.

"We were there in the mind of justice.

"We put our heels upon the neck of the enemy; we stripped him of his authority; we left him defeated and broken, and then we were raised together with Christ.

"Satan is conquered.

"The new birth has been accomplished."

The new creation, in the mind of justice, has become effective, and now we are not only raised together with Christ, but we are seated with Him.

In the mind of justice, every member of the body of Christ is seated at the right hand of the Majesty on high.

In the mind of justice, we are utterly one with Him. We are complete in Him.

All what He did, He did for us.

He is the Head of the body, and as the Head of the body, He cannot be exalted so high but what the body is there with Him sharing in His glory, sharing in all of His victories.

Ephesians 1:4–6 gives us a preview of our redemption:

> *According as he hath chosen us in him before the foundation of the world, that we should be holy and without blame before him in love: having predestinated us unto the adoption of children by Jesus Christ to himself, according to the good pleasure of his will, to the praise of the glory of his grace, wherein he hath made us accepted in the beloved.*

The next verses swing into the vital:

> *In whom we have redemption through his blood, the forgiveness of sins, according to the riches of his grace; wherein he hath abounded toward us in all wisdom and prudence; having made known unto us the mystery of his will.* (verses 7–9)

Now we can see the background of a vital union with Christ.

We can understand what it means to have him say, *"For it is God which worketh in you both to will and to do of his good pleasure"* (Philippians 2:13).

We can understand Colossians 1:28–29: *"That we may present every man perfect in Christ Jesus: whereunto I also labour, striving according to his working, which worketh in me mightily."*

Paul's dream in Christ was to present every believer perfect, *"not having spot, or wrinkle, or any such thing"* (Ephesians 5:27).

What a dream it must have been.

Now we can understand Ephesians 3:16: *"That he would grant you, according to the riches of his glory, to be strengthened with might by his Spirit in the inner man."*

This inner man has become a new creation. He has received the life and nature of the Father, and now the Spirit through the Word is building into this *"hidden man of the heart"* (1 Peter 3:4) the ability to live as Jesus did in His earth walk.

You remember we are to walk in love; we are to follow after love. We remember that love never fails, and it thinks no evil; always good thoughts, beautiful thoughts about everyone. (See 1 Corinthians 13.)

It never holds any enmity.

We treat the one who has lied about us, just as Jesus treated Peter after the resurrection.

Can't you imagine Jesus hunting up the man who drove the nails into His hands and telling him, "I died for you"? Finding the man who made the crown of thorns and pressed it upon His brow, telling him, "I am going to give you a crown of righteousness, a crown of glory, and a crown of life."

Paul said, *"That Christ may dwell in your hearts by faith"* (Ephesians 3:17).

You see, Christ and the Word are one.

When the Word dwells in a believer's heart, gains control of his whole being, that is Christ gaining control. The lordship of Jesus over a life is in reality the lordship of the Word. The Word gains the ascendency in such an absolute way that it dominates his thinking.

The lordship of Jesus and the lordship of the Word are really the lordship of this new kind of love—*agape*.

What beautiful lives that makes.

When this "inner man," this "*hidden man of the heart,*" becomes governed by the love nature of the Father, he unconsciously takes Jesus's place.

You see, we become rooted and grounded in *agape*.

We do not hold it as a doctrine.

It is not a mental concept. It is actual.

The Father has so filled us with His nature that we do love acts unconsciously.

We have received the ability to understand the nature of the love of Christ, which surpasses our sense knowledge apprehension, and now at last the dream of the Father for us is being fulfilled. We are filled with all the fullness of God.

The love nature has swallowed us up, just as in 2 Corinthians 5:4: "*But clothed upon, that mortality might be swallowed up of life.*"

The life is *zoe*—the nature of the Father, and the nature of the Father is love. We are swallowed up, immersed, overwhelmed in love.

Now we can understand Ephesians 3:20: "*Now unto him that is able to do exceeding abundantly above all that we ask or think, according to the power that worketh in us.*"

It is the ability of the Father unveiled.

Not only is it revealed, but it is clasping the hand of omnipotent love; my whole inner being swinging me out of the orbit of sense knowledge into the orbit of revelation knowledge or revelation reality.

Now I know what Jesus meant when He said,

> *Howbeit when he, the Spirit of truth* [or reality], *is come, he will guide you into all truth: for he shall not speak of himself; but whatsoever he shall hear, that shall he speak: and he will shew you things to come.* (John 16:13)

He meant the new creation things, the unveiling of the very nature of the Father, which He declares in Christ. First, "*He shall glorify me: for he shall receive of mine, and shall shew it unto you*" (verse 14).

This is resurrection life in us. This is the Holy Spirit working in us through the Word; all that was purchased for us; all that is legally ours for our daily walk.

You see, the Father had a dream for us.

In that little preview of the new creation that I gave you, He gave us a suggestion of His intense love for us, and how He was going to build us over into Himself.

He was going to take His righteousness and His holiness and His truth or reality and build them into us until we fit into His dream, and He could say, as He did to the wondering disciples, *"This is my beloved Son, in whom I am well pleased"* (Matthew 3:17).

Then He would say, "These are my beloved sons, in whom my heart has found perfect rest and satisfaction."

9

SHARING WITH HIM

In Galatians 2:20, we get one of the richest views of Christ's ministry for us: *"I am crucified with Christ: nevertheless I live; yet not I, but Christ liveth in me."*

The heart can hardly take in the reality that is unveiled to us. We have shared in His crucifixion.

This is the legal side of our identification with Christ.

You see, He shared with us in His incarnation. He became one with us.

He gave us His kingly glory and became one with suffering, lost humanity.

He was one with us in His substitution.

He shares with us; He shares our sins, our infirmities, our diseases. He took them upon Himself.

The sharing was so real that *"he hath made him to be sin for us, who knew no sin"* (2 Corinthians 5:21) in order to become identified with us, to come to our level.

He not only had sin reckoned to Him, sin laid upon Him as the high priest laid the sin of Israel upon the goat, but He actually became sin.

We can hardly grasp the fact that deity could become sin, but He did. He died spiritually. The righteous for the unrighteous, that He might bring us to God.

In the new creation, we shared with Him. He is the Head; we are the body.

He has imparted Himself to us, and when He imparted Himself to us, He gave to us a new self in the place of our old self.

That old, fallen, sin-ruled self was displaced and the new Jesus self, the new creation self, the godlike self, the self that is made in the image of Christ, became our new self.

You see how utterly He shared with us; how much He became one with us.

But in Colossians 3:1–3, Paul says:

> *If ye then be risen with Christ, seek those things which are above, where Christ sitteth on the right hand of God. Set your affection on things above, not on things on the earth. For ye are dead, and your life is hid with Christ in God.*

Here we catch a glimpse of our utter oneness with Him, of the completeness of this union.

What is more real than this: *"I am the vine, ye are the branches."* (John 15:5).

Here He shows us we are the fruit-bearing part of Him.

We are the love-revealing part of Him.

We are the part of Him that blesses and touches humanity. We are the part of Him that brings eternal life to lost man. We are sharing in His resurrection.

The heart is thrilled.

If we share in His resurrection, we share in His victory over Satan: we share in His victory over sin.

We have been raised together with Him.

We are sharing His victory over the adversary.

Then Satan knows that we conquered him in Christ, that we were with the Master when He put him to naught and triumphed over him, and put off from Himself the principalities and the powers, when Jesus made a show of Satan before his own hosts in the dark regions; that we shared with Him and were a part in that great victory.

And did you notice, we are sharing in the things on High where Messiah is enthroned at the right hand of God?

We are seated with Him.

You see, in Ephesians 2:6–8, we were raised together with Him; and then not only were we raised with Him, but we were seated with Him:

> *And hath raised us up together, and made us sit together in heavenly places in Christ Jesus: that in the ages to come he might shew the exceeding riches of his grace in his kindness toward us through Christ Jesus. For by grace are ye saved through faith; and that not of yourselves: it is the gift of God.*

We are seated as one with Him on the throne now.

He is the Head of the body; we are members of the body. Where the Head is, the body is.

The authority that belongs to the Head belongs to the body. Now you can understand Matthew 28:18: *"All power is given unto me in heaven and in earth."* All authority; all dominion.

You understand now why He could have *"spoiled principalities and powers"* (Colossians 2:15).

You can understand how He *"made a shew of them openly"* (verse 15).

He was the Master, with the omnipotence and ability of the Father.

We share in that.

He has given us the legal use of His name. In that name is invested all the authority the Father gave Him after His resurrection. That name is ours, and we have a legal right to use it.

Oh, I wish that our hearts could take it in. The days of our defeat and failure would then be over.

Romans 6 throws much light upon our union with Christ:

> *How shall we, that are dead to sin, live any longer therein? Know ye not, that so many of us as were baptized into Jesus Christ were baptized into his death? Therefore we are buried with him by baptism into death: that like as Christ was raised up from the dead by the glory of the Father, even so we also should walk in newness of life. For if we have been planted together in the likeness of his death, we shall be also in the likeness of his resurrection: knowing this, that our old man is crucified with him, that the body of sin might be destroyed, that henceforth we should not serve sin.* (Romans 6:2–6)

Notice that we shared with Christ in His death, we shared with Him in His resurrection, and we are sharing now with Him at the right hand of the Father.

From another angle, He is sharing with us in our ministry as branches of the vine.

We are His testimony.

We are now His confession.

We are boldly telling the world what we are in Christ.

We have taken our place in Christ.

We are acting as a part of Him.

We share in everything that He did. He is sharing in everything that we are.

This brings a nearness to the reality of that great oneness between the Head and the body.

You see, we suffered with Him; we shared in it.

We shared in His justification.

We shared with Him when He was made alive down in that dark region, and we heard the Father whisper, *"Thou art my Son, this day have I begotten thee"* (Acts 13:33), speaking of His resurrection.

We shared in that resurrection. We shared in the power and authority of it.

When He put all the enemies beneath His feet, they were beneath our feet.

When He triumphed over them, that was our triumph.

And now we are carrying out His precious will in the earth. He is sharing His ability, wisdom, and love with us.

You caught that in Romans 6:6, we shared in His resurrection; and in Ephesians 2:5–6, we share in His life and in His throne. In Romans 6:8, you get it clearly: we shared in His new life, the new resurrection life; the same wonderful life that Jesus had.

> *And you, being dead in your sins and the uncircumcision of your flesh, hath he quickened together with him, having forgiven you all trespasses.*
> (Colossians 2:13)

Can't you see the utter oneness, our absolute union in Christ?

Can't you see that today you are partaking of His divine nature, that as you yield to the inward life of God in your spirit, you will slowly but surely gain the ascendency over your reasoning faculties until your mind becomes renewed through the reading of the Word, which is really the unveiling mind of Christ?

You will have the mind of Christ.

Don't forget for a moment that in the mind of the Father, you are sharing in the throne of grace. You own a share in it.

> *And hath raised us up together, and made us sit together in heavenly places in Christ Jesus.* (Ephesians 2:6)

Why in heavenly places? Because our Head is there. Our Lord is there. Marvelous, isn't it?

I sometimes wonder how Paul and John and the rest of them who are gathered about the Throne feel about us down here.

I imagine Paul is just yearning over us that we might understand the riches of the unveilings that he gave to us of the living Christ in His resurrection.

Can't you see how we reign with Him?

In His substitution, we share with Him from the cross to the throne.

We were crucified with Him; we died with Him; we suffered with Him; we were justified with Him; we were made alive with Him; raised with Him; and are now seated with Him.

> *For if by one man's offence death reigned by one; much more they which receive abundance of grace and of the gift of righteousness shall reign in life by one, Jesus Christ.* (Romans 5:17)

This is the climax of our earth walk.

That overflowing grace is the overflowing of the love nature of the Father that is shed abroad in our hearts by the Holy Spirit.

The gift of righteousness gives us our legal standing before the Father.

The overflowing grace was the incoming of the nature and life, the substance and being of our Father into our spirits. The nature of the Father coming in has made us righteous, made us like the Father, like Jesus; made us utterly one with Him.

Now we reign as kings in the realm of this new life through Jesus Christ our Lord.

You see, we were in slavery and servants of the adversary. We are now the joyful love-slaves of Jesus.

We are heirs of God and joint heirs with Christ, and we are coming into that new knowledge of what we are in Christ.

Sin-consciousness has robbed us in the past of our faith; robbed us of our sense of worthiness; robbed us of our joy of sonship.

We know now that sin-consciousness was just a camouflage of the adversary.

We were standing complete in Christ, but we did not know it. We were the righteousness of God in Christ and we did not know it.

As long as Satan could keep us in ignorance, he kept us in darkness and weakness.

But the veil has been torn away. The light has shone in.

The light that we had before was darkness, but now this is the light of life: *"He that followeth me shall not walk in darkness"* (John 8:12).

We walked in the darkness, but now He is the light of our life. He is our life. He is our light.

We have become like those whose eyes had been blinded but now have received light, and we see things as they really are.

Before, we were groping and hoping. Now we have passed out of the realm of hope into the realm of assurance.

It is the realm of reality.

We know who we are, what we are. We know what grace has been bestowed upon us.

We are walking in the light of this wonderful life Christ brought into the world.

10

THE LAW OF LIFE

The law of the new covenant is a perfect contrast to the law of the old covenant.

The first covenant law is called the "law of sin and death." The law of the new covenant is called the "law of the Spirit of life."

One law put men in bondage; the other law made them free from the law of sin and death.

That was a fearful title that was given to the first law—"of sin and death."

Both sin and death are of the adversary, and so the old covenant law was given to men who were governed by the adversary, who had a satanic nature and lived in Satan's realm.

It was never given for new creation folks.

No man that is born again has any part or lot in the Ten Commandments.

They were all fulfilled in Christ and set aside.

You see, He fulfilled the Abrahamic covenant first, and after that was fulfilled, everything connected with that covenant was set aside and finished and rolled up together in that first document.

Then Jesus inaugurated a new covenant.

The first covenant was sealed with the blood of bulls and goats. The second covenant was sealed with the blood of Jesus.

The new creation that is under the new covenant had a new law given to them. Jesus gave it.

> *A new commandment I give unto you, that ye love one another; as I have loved you, that ye also love one another. By this shall all men know that ye are my disciples, if ye have love one to another.* (John 13:34–35)

The Pauline Epistles are a revelation and an exposition of this new law.

Just as Leviticus, Numbers, and Deuteronomy are an exposition of the law of the first covenant, so these epistles of Paul are given us to explain the new covenant law.

THE LOVE LAW

First Corinthians 13 is a revelation of what this new love law is, what it does, and what it does not do.

In Paul's other epistles, we see this new law being demonstrated in the daily life of the new creation.

It is very important that we understand this fact: the new covenant law is not designed for men outside of Christ.

The natural man cannot obey the new commandment that Jesus gave.

There is only one commandment to rule the new creation, and that is, to love one another even as Jesus loved us.

That new commandment made any other commandment absolutely unnecessary, for the man who walks in love will never do wrong.

As love was the fulfillment of the old covenant, it is also the fulfillment of the new.

Someone asks, "Why is the Mosaic law called the 'law of sin and death?'" Because it was to govern spiritually dead men.

The law of the Spirit of life is to govern recreated men. It is the Spirit of love.

It is the law of the very heart of Christ.

The law that governed the dead in spirit is the law of Moses.

It is impossible for anyone to live under the Mosaic law today because it has been fulfilled and laid aside with the Abrahamic covenant.

You see, the "law of the Spirit of life" in Christ Jesus made the new creation Jew free from the "law of sin and death."

> *For if there had been a law given which could have given life, verily righteousness should have been by the law.* (Galatians 3:21)

This is a striking sentence. If there had been a law given that could give men eternal life, then righteousness would have been of the law.

> *But the scripture hath concluded all under sin, that the promise by faith of Jesus Christ might be given to them that believe.* (verse 22)

Now notice this next Scripture:

> *But before faith came, we* [the Jews] *we were kept under the law, shut up unto the faith which should afterwards be revealed. Wherefore the law was our schoolmaster to bring us unto Christ, that we might be justified by faith.* (Galatians 3:23–24)

The Law never brought anyone to Christ.

The Law was a "law of sin and death."

The Holy Spirit is the only One that can bring a man to Christ.

> *But after that faith is come, we are no longer* [as Jews] *under a schoolmaster. For ye are all the children of God by faith in Christ Jesus.* (verses 25–26)

I want you to notice carefully the next sentence:

> *For as many of you as have been baptized into Christ have put on Christ. There is neither Jew nor Greek, there is neither bond nor free, there is neither male nor female: for ye are all one in Christ Jesus.* (verses 27–28)

Now you can understand 1 Corinthians 9:19–20, where Paul said, speaking of his ministry as a soul-winner:

> *For though I be free from all men, yet have I made myself servant unto all, that I might gain the more. And unto the Jews I became as a Jew [when he became a new creation he had stopped being a Jew], that I might gain the Jews; to them that are under the law, as under the law, that I might gain them that are under the law.*

This was written before the temple and the whole Jewish hierarchy had been destroyed by Titus.

We must understand clearly that the moment a gentile becomes a new creation, he stops being a gentile.

In 1 Corinthians 10:32, we have the three ethnical divisions of the human race: "*Give none offence, neither to the Jews, nor to the Gentiles, nor to the church of God.*"

There are no Jews or gentiles in the church of God. We are all one man in Christ.

The gentile stopped being a gentile and the Jew stopped being a Jew the moment they became new creations.

Here is something very important.

The people who are trying to live under the Mosaic covenant must learn this fact, that according to Galatians 3:21, the Law cannot give eternal life to man.

The Law cannot give righteousness to man.

If the Law could have done that, then Christ need not have died, because all man needed to do was to keep the Mosaic law, the Ten Commandments, and he would be alive and righteous.

But because he was not alive nor righteous, he had to be covered with the blood of bulls and goats every year.

That blood represented life, a type of the life of God that was to be given to the new creation.

The Mosaic covenant was given to a spiritually dead people. It was a law that was to govern natural man.

Did you ever notice that the Father does not command the new creation in Christ to love Him? Why?

He has God's nature of love in him and He can't help but love Him.

He is born of love.

Not one of the laws of the Ten Commandments fit a child of God. There is but one law for the new creation—that we love one another even as Jesus loved us. (See John 13:34.)

Moses's law was given by God to Israel through an angel, because God could not speak to man in any other way.

There is a suggestion in Exodus 33 that God spoke to Moses face to face, but that is the only time in all human history that God spoke to man.

So we can see there is a vast difference between the law of life in Christ and the law of death in the first covenant.

Romans has another suggestion for us, *"For the law of the Spirit of life in Christ Jesus hath made me* [as a Jew] *free from the law of sin and death"* (Romans 8:2).

That Scripture cannot apply to a gentile, because no gentile was ever under the "law of sin and death."

Then, it shows you the importance of the Law:

> *For what the law could not do, in that it was weak through the flesh [or through the senses of spiritually dead men], God sending his own Son in the likeness of sinful flesh, and for sin, condemned sin in the flesh: that the righteousness of the law might be fulfilled in us [the new creation], who walk not after the flesh, but after the Spirit.* (Romans 8:3–4)

The Greek word *sarx,* as translated *flesh,* should be translated "senses" every time. It makes it clearer.

Notice Romans 8:5: *"For they that are after the flesh* [senses] *do mind the things of the flesh* [senses]." Why? Because the senses are the children of the physical body.

They are the offspring of natural human life—seeing, hearing, tasting, smelling, and feeling.

They convey all the knowledge to the brain that we have outside of Christ.

So they that are after the senses are ruled by the senses because they are accustomed to obeying them.

They that are after the spirit are accustomed to obeying the things of the spirit.

The word *"spirit"* here means the spirit of the recreated man. So let me read it like this: "For they that are after the senses are going to do the things that the senses suggest. But they that are after the recreated spirit are going to do the things of the recreated spirit that has the nature and life of God in it."

Now the next verse: *"For to be carnally minded is death; but to be spiritually minded is life and peace"* (Romans 8:6). A more literal translation would be: "For the mind of the senses is under the dominion of spiritual death, but the mind of the recreated spirit is under the dominion of *zoe*, the life of God, and that brings peace and rest and quietness."

"Because the carnal mind is enmity against God: for it is not subject to the law of God, neither indeed can be" (Romans 8:7), whether it be the law of the Ten Commandments or the law of the new covenant.

> *So then they that are in the flesh cannot please God.* (Romans 8:8)

Now notice this verse:

> *But ye are not in the flesh, but in the Spirit [that is, your recreated spirit], if so be that the Spirit of God [that is, the Holy Spirit] dwell in you. Now if any man have not the Spirit of Christ, he is none of his.* (Romans 8:9)

That doesn't refer to the Holy Spirit. A better translation is, "If any man has not a Christ-like spirit (that is, a recreated spirit), he is none of his."

Many of our commentators have given us a wrong conception of that. They have suggested that if any man has not the Holy Spirit, he is not a Christian, but that is not true.

A man can be a child of God, receive eternal life, and yet not have received the Holy Spirit, for you remember Luke 11:13 asks, *"How much more shall your heavenly Father give the Holy Spirit to them that ask him?"*

Only sons will ask for the Spirit.

In Acts 8, under Phillip's preaching, many had turned to the Lord in Samaria and had been baptized.

> *Now when the apostles which were at Jerusalem heard that Samaria had received the word of God, they sent unto them Peter and John: who, when they were come down, prayed for them, that they might receive the Holy Ghost: (for as yet he was fallen upon none of them: only they were baptized in the name of the Lord Jesus.)* (Acts 8:14–16)

They had received eternal life.

Then the disciples laid hands on them and they received the Holy Spirit.

When Paul came to Ephesus (see Acts 19:1–7), he asked them, *"Have ye received the Holy Ghost since ye believed?"* (verse 2).

The implication is simple: that all believers do not have the Holy Spirit. If they did, they would be different kind of believers, for when a man receives the Holy Spirit, he has a Teacher in him that can unfold the Word and build into him a godlike spirituality that will make him a blessing to those around him.

Come back to Romans 8:10: *"And if Christ be in you, the body is dead because of sin; but the Spirit is life because of righteousness."*

Notice now, that after Christ is in you, the senses have lost their dominion over you, because when you are made a new creation, the senses cease to be your master.

Your spirit has received eternal life and has become the righteousness of God.

Sin now can no longer govern your senses.

> *But if the Spirit of him that raised up Jesus from the dead dwell in you* [this is the Holy Spirit of whom He is speaking], *he that raised up Christ from the dead shall also quicken* [give life, *zoe*, the nature of God] *your mortal bodies by his Spirit that dwelleth in you.*
>
> (Romans 8:11)

He has given to that person's spirit eternal life and made him a new creation.

Now the promise that Jesus made, *"I am come that they might have life, and that they might have it more abundantly"* (John 10:10), is being realized.

The Holy Spirit has come into man's body and is pouring an abundance of life into his mortal body, bringing health and strength and vigor into it.

Now notice this fact: the new law cannot rule spiritually dead men any more than the Ten Commandments can rule the spiritually alive man.

The first law belonged to the old creation.

The new law belongs to the new creation.

This new law of love is to rule our daily life, our business, our homes.

It is to rule the church.

It is to rule our social life.

This new law is as impossible for natural man as the Mosaic law is unnatural and abnormal for the new creation.

The Jew under the first covenant could not keep the law of the new covenant.

So we see clearly that the Ten Commandments are for natural man. Jesus's new commandment was for the new creation man.

The love law is to rule a new love creation.

It would be as absurd for citizens of the United States of America to adopt the laws of Japan and try to put themselves under them, as for gentile men today to adopt the Ten Commandments and attempt to get God to own them as He owned the Jews under that first covenant.

Here is a fact: the first covenant with its commandments was never given to any nation but the Israelites.

Israel alone owned it all. For a gentile today to call himself a Christian and attempt to live under the Abrahamic covenant and the Mosaic law is the most absurd effort ever known.

Only a spiritually dead man would ever attempt it.

11

THE RENEWED MIND

There has never been a great deal of teaching in regard to the necessity of a renewed mind.

We have stressed the need of being converted, being born again, but we have left the convert hanging in the wind, as it were.

Great enthusiasm and joy comes at the new birth, but unless that is cared for and fed by the mind being renewed through feeding on the Word and practicing it, that joy will die out.

When you are born again, your spirit is recreated.

It receives the nature and life of the Father, but the mind that has held your spirit in captivity is the same old mind.

It receives a mighty impetus when the spirit receives eternal life, but that is all.

You understand that all the knowledge the mind had comes from the senses and the senses can never be renewed.

They are a part of the physical body.

They can be brought into subjection; they can be controlled, but they can't be renewed.

The spirit is recreated, but the mind, this brain of ours that receives its knowledge from the five senses, can be brought into subjection to the Word.

I have come to believe that it can be purified by meditation in the Word.

I don't mean purified like the blood of Christ has cleansed us, but I mean that it drops off much that is unnecessary and unwise.

In itself it may not be harmful but it is unnecessary. It takes up time.

The mind slowly but surely, as it feeds on the Word, meditates in the Word, practices and lives the Word, comes into the fellowship of the recreated spirit.

In Romans 12:1, we have one of the most important Scriptures in regard to the physical body and its thinking processes:

> *I beseech you therefore, brethren, by the mercies of God, that ye present your bodies a living sacrifice, holy, acceptable unto God, which is your reasonable service.*

Notice it very carefully now. He is asking you to present your body which holds the five senses. They are the most important parts of that body—the seeing part, the hearing part, the feeling part, the tasting and smelling parts.

They are the five channels to the brain over which travel all the impulses that have taught the brain all that it knows.

Now He says, I want you to give this home of your five senses to the Lord. I want you to lay that body of yours, as it were, upon the altar.

As the Jew laid a dead offering upon the altar, you are to lay your living body upon the altar in the sense that you are dedicating it, giving it over to the lordship of the Word.

Then He says:

> *And be not conformed to this world: but be ye transformed [or transfigured] by the renewing of your mind, that ye may prove what is that good, and acceptable, and perfect, will of God.* (Romans 12:2)

Your mind has been fashioned after the things of this world. The world's ideals probably have been yours.

Now your mind must come under the dominion of your recreated spirit through the Word.

Your mind must recognize the threefold lordship through your recreated spirit, the lordship of the Word, the lordship of Jesus, and the lordship of love.

It may be difficult for your mind to assimilate this; to allow love to become a part of yourself: to allow the Word to utterly dominate; to recognize the love lordship of Jesus.

I know how hard that is, but that must come or else the believer is going to live on the borderland between right and wrong, never knowing whether this is wrong, or that is wrong.

He will be asking his friends, "Is it wrong to do this? Should I do that?"

The reason is, his mind has never been renewed and he is living on the borderland in a sort of semi-spiritual darkness.

But as his mind is renewed, he will come to know the will of the Father. He will walk in the light of the Word.

He will get to know that threefold will—the good, and the acceptable, and the perfect will of the Father.

He will be claiming the highest will of the Father.

He will not be satisfied with "the acceptable and the good," but will want the perfect and the well-pleasing will of the Father.

In John 8:29, Jesus said, *"I do always those things that please* [my Father]."

This new creation man craves that kind of a life.

His spirit is reaching out, sometimes really agonizing in him to become well-pleasing to the Father.

In Colossians 3:5–10, He is unveiling the inner workings of the senses and their control of the mind. Read it carefully.

He says, *"For which things' sake the wrath of God cometh on the children of disobedience"* (Colossians 3:6).

He shows the uncleanness of the natural mind as it is dominated by the senses.

In verse 9, He is speaking to you. He said, I don't want you to lie to one another anymore, since you have put off the old man with his doings.

You see, you are a new creation and you put on the new man, that is being renewed in knowledge after the image of Him that created Him.

This is a message to the new convert primarily.

Old believers have already done this thing.

He wants that new man to be brought into perfect harmony with his thinking faculties, and that can't be until his mind is renewed, until it comes to recognize its position in Christ.

You notice it said, *"Put on the new man, which is renewed in knowledge after the image of him that created him"* (verse 10).

That will be revelation knowledge.

You will know your responsibilities and your ability to meet them. You see, the small faith man is almost invariably a man whose mind has not yet been renewed.

If you find a believer who doesn't walk in love, it is because his mind has not yet been renewed.

His mind can't be renewed by simply studying the Bible. He will have to live it. It has to become a part of His mind.

Many of our Bible teachers have never seen this and their senses govern their mind.

That means their senses govern their teaching; that their recreated spirit has a very small place in their lives.

> *For which cause we faint not; but though our outward man perish, yet the inward man is renewed day by day.* (2 Corinthians 4:16)

The inward man is your spirit that is feeding on the Word, that is being renewed continually.

Your mind should feed on the Word, too.

There should be meditation in the Word.

You remember in Joshua 1:8, Jehovah told him that he was to meditate in the Word *"day and night, that thou mayest observe to do according to all that is written therein: for then thou shalt make thy way prosperous, and then thou shalt have good success."* The same rule that God laid down for Joshua should govern the new creation, this new man who has the mind of Christ.

Another Scripture that might help us a bit is Ephesians 2:10: *"For we are his workmanship, created in Christ Jesus unto good works, which God hath before ordained that we should walk in them."*

He has prepared you to walk in His will.

His ability has been given to you.

His strength is at your disposal.

The good deeds that He would have you perform are within the range of your ability, that is, the ability that He has given to you. He expects you to pray for sick folks.

You will teach the Word; witness to the unsaved; walk in love, and you will walk in the light of the Word and be a blessing to those around you, because your mind now is in perfect harmony with the recreated spirit.

The new commandment *"that ye love one another"* (John 13:34) has become the very heart life of your conduct.

12

GOD REPRODUCING HIMSELF IN US

Every real father desires to reproduce himself in his son. The Father's dream is to reproduce Himself in us.

You understand that the new creation has received the nature and life of the Father.

We invite the Holy Spirit, who has imparted to us this nature from the Father, to come into our body and make His home in us, then as we begin to feed on the Word, practice the Word, live the Word, He builds that Word into us.

The very genius of Christianity is the ability of God to build Himself into us through the Word, so that in our daily walk we live like the Master.

> *Be ye therefore followers of God, as dear children; and walk in love, as Christ also hath loved us, and hath given himself for us.*
>
> (Ephesians 5:1–2)

As children of love, we are to walk in love as Christ walked in love toward the world.

The Father so loved the world that He gave His Son.

Jesus so loved the world that He gave Himself.

Now I so love the world that I give myself.

I don't allow my heart to grow bitter toward it, no matter what the criticism or the persecution may be.

Whenever I am inclined to say, "Well, I am wasting my time on them," I remember Paul and Silas at Philippi. They had been arrested. They had been whipped until their backs were a mass of bleeding flesh, then put into a dungeon with their hands and feet in stocks.

In the midst of that agony, that physical distress, they prayed and sang praises.

They so stirred heaven that the Father had to open the jail; and when the earthquake had so frightened the jailer that he cried out in agony of fear, Paul preached to him with that bleeding back, and the jailer found Jesus.

Then he washed the backs of both Paul and Silas, and a church was formed in the home of the jailer.

If Paul had any other spirit, he could never have done it, but he was like his Master.

He gave himself up to the dominion, the lordship of love.

The Father wants to reproduce Himself in us.

> *My little children, of whom I travail in birth again until Christ be formed in you.* (Galatians 4:19)

The process of building Christ into one may be very slow, but it makes Jesus men and women out of us.

We are created in Christ Jesus. We are His creation; and until Christ is formed in us, the world cannot see anything but religion in us.

> *For it is God which worketh in you both to will and to do of his good pleasure.* (Philippians 2:13)

The Father is actually building His love life, His righteousness, His strength, and His wisdom into our spirits.

Years ago, when I was the head of the school back in the East, after an evangelistic campaign, I would invariably ask some of the teachers, "Have I grown any since you last saw me? Can you see any marks of growth in my spiritual life?"

I was so fearful that a month or two would go by that I hadn't grown in Christ and in knowledge of the Word.

> *But grow in grace, and in the knowledge of our Lord and Saviour Jesus Christ.* (2 Peter 3:18)

Grace means Love at work. The Greek word means *love gifts*. The Spirit longs for us to grow in this love life, to have the love nature of Jesus demonstrated in our daily walk.

I am convinced beyond the shadow of a doubt, that only as we yield ourselves to the lordship of love, can He ever build Himself into us.

It is not knowledge of the Scriptures. I may have a vast knowledge of the Word. That isn't it.

It is the Word that is built into me and becomes a part of me that counts.

As you study the Pauline revelation, you become convinced that the ultimate of every one of those epistles is the building of the Jesus life in the individual.

His plan for building Himself into us is striking.

We must take Jesus's place. We must learn to act in His stead. There must be the conscious training of our spirits to be His actual representatives.

Colossians gives us an intimation of the passion of the Father to make Himself known to us in such a real way that we can enter into all the riches of the fullness of His life that belongs to us.

Here is a prayer of the Spirit through the lips of Paul:

> *For this cause we also, since the day we heard it, do not cease to pray for you, and to desire that ye might be filled with the knowledge of his will in all wisdom and spiritual understanding.* (Colossians 1:9)

The word *knowledge* in the Greek is *epignosis*. It means full knowledge, complete knowledge, exact knowledge.

We should have that kind of knowledge, for it is in this revelation.

We have the Holy Spirit who inspired it as our teacher.

He has never left His position as an instructor. He is here in my heart and yours, and He longs to fill us with the exact knowledge of the Father's will in all spiritual wisdom and understanding.

It will be wisdom to use the knowledge of this revelation in our daily walk.

It will be wisdom to know how to use the statements of fact as well as the promises in the Gospels.

It will be wisdom to know how to make this message known in an attractive way.

We are to have "*knowledge of his will in all wisdom and spiritual understanding,*" a deeper insight into the very heart of the Father.

First Corinthians 2:9 may throw some light on this:

> *Eye hath not seen, nor ear heard, neither have entered into the heart of man, the things which God hath prepared for them that love him.*

These are revealed to us today in this revelation through the Spirit, for the Holy Spirit is able to search all things, yea, the deep things of God, and our recreated spirit is enabled to follow the Holy Spirit in this searching of the riches of His grace.

Most of these riches are in the Pauline revelation.

In Ephesians 3:8, we catch a glimpse of where Paul said, "*Unto me, who am less than the least of all saints, is this grace given, that I should preach among the Gentiles the unsearchable riches of Christ.*"

These unsearchable riches belong to us, but, like pearls, we have to search for them.

> *For what man knoweth the things of a man, save the spirit of man which is in him? even so the things of God knoweth no man, but the Spirit of God.* (1 Corinthians 2:11)

Now note carefully the next verse:

> *Now we have received, not the spirit of the world, but the spirit which is of God; that we might know the things that are freely given to us of God.* (verse 12)

We are learning to grasp this exact truth by the aid of the Spirit.

We find that in Colossians 1:9–10, this knowledge of His will in all spiritual wisdom and understanding is to enable us to walk worthy of the Lord unto all pleasing.

Our walk is before the world.

We might say that it is a twofold walk. One phase of it is before the Father, and the other is before the world.

I am to walk worthy of the Lord before men so they will recognize this new life in me.

I am so "Jesus-ized" (if we could coin the word), that they will become Jesus-conscious in my presence.

I knew a woman who found Christ through my ministry over the air. Her husband was a godless man and she had been a fit companion in his worldliness, but now she had found Christ.

It went on for several weeks until finally one morning before he went to work, he said, "Do you know, woman, that I have been living and sleeping and eating with Jesus Christ for the last two weeks."

She was a keen-minded woman, and she said, "How do you enjoy it?"

Tears filled his eyes. He said, "I wish I was like that. I wish I had that something that has come into your life."

You see, Jesus had so lived in her that the man could feel the presence of the Master in her.

Two young men were working in a shop. One of them was studying the Word in our classes. The fellow working on a lathe next to him said to him one morning, "Harry, I would like to ask you something that is personal. What have you in your life that makes you so different from all the other men here in the room?"

The boy answered, "Jesus."

"Oh," he said, "that is religion; I don't believe in that."

And the young boy said, "It is not religion, it is the living Christ."

Christ magnified in my body, said Paul; Christ made large in my daily walk.

In Philippians 1:21, he said, *"For to me to live is Christ."*

Once, those words burned in my heart for months.

The Master was saying to me, "I want to be magnified in you. I want to absorb your personality. I want to take possession of your dreams and ambitions. I want the first place in your life."

I was afraid of Him. I spoke out, "Lord, I don't dare let you have control of me for if I do I will never achieve the things for which I am so ambitious."

And I shall never forget, a voice in my heart said, "I love you more than you love yourself. I am more ambitious for your success than you are. I have the ability to put you over."

I said, "Lord, don't make me preach on the streets. You will send me down into the slums. I don't want to go there, Lord."

I struggled again, but He was tender with me.

His wisdom became so apparent. Often, in my extremities, He had helped me.

When I would get into difficulties, He would lift me out.

One day, I said, "Master, I will go with You. Here I am; take all of my ability. Swallow up my ambition with Your own, but give me love like Your love. Help me to so live that men can see You in me, feel You, that when I speak it will be Your voice. When I lay hands on the sick, it will be Your hands."

And then I heard a Scripture in Galatians 2:20:

> *I am crucified with Christ: nevertheless I live; yet not I, but Christ liveth in me: and the life which I now live in the flesh I live by the faith of the Son of God, who loved me, and gave himself for me.*

Then I said, "Now Master, I trust you and I give myself up to you.

You see, when we come quietly in our heart life to the place where we say "yes" to Him, then He reveals Himself in us.

It is not forced upon us. He doesn't drive us. He doesn't force us with sickness or the loss of property.

The sickness comes because we are not aware that He can shield us.

We have gone the way of our inclinations.

We have gone the way of our own desires and our plans have been worked out, reasoned out with sense knowledge.

How it must hurt His heart when we are so unwise; when we do so many foolish things.

When His wisdom is at our call, His ability awaits us, we are almost limitless.

All that He is, is at our disposal, but sometimes we choose a road that leads to heartaches and disappointments.

You see, it is this forming of Christ within us. That is the secret that is the genius of the new creation. "*Therefore if any man be in Christ, he is a new creature* [creation]" (2 Corinthians 5:17).

It is perfect as far as it has gone, but He wants to build Himself more fully into that new creation, and so He takes the things of Christ that are unveiled to us in the Word, and the Spirit builds them into us.

We admired the strength and courage of Jesus in His earth walk. We were thrilled at the ability that Christ manifested as He met every difficult situation.

His wisdom, gentleness, and forbearance, we admired, and now the Spirit wants to take all of those things that we *have* admired in Jesus and build them into us.

Can't you see what it means? It is the Father's ambition to make us successful and to enable us to enjoy the riches that belong to us.

I don't know whether you have noticed it or not, but in one of the prayer Scriptures in John 16, Jesus said this: "*And in that day ye shall ask me nothing*" (verse 23). Literally, "And in that day ye shall not pray to me."

> *Verily, verily, I say unto you, Whatsoever ye shall ask the Father in my name, he will give it you. Hitherto have ye asked nothing in my name: ask, and ye shall receive, that your joy may be full.* (John 16:23–24)

Joy is something that comes into the recreated human spirit. The natural man doesn't have it.

Hear Jesus speaking again in John 15:11: "*These things have I spoken unto you, that my joy might remain in you, and that your joy might be full.*"

That is a miracle, that Jesus's joy may be made full in me, that not only will I make Him joyful, but He imparts His joy to me.

That something that makes the evangel irresistible, now fills my heart. When I speak, my face will glow, my voice will be filled with the melody of heaven.

You see, when He builds himself into us and we begin to labor together with Him, we have His life, we have His love, yea, we have Himself.

Christ then is being formed in us.

Now it is no longer I, but Christ.

The men who have grown deeply spiritual, are the men in whom the Word has had full control.

John 15:7 may throw a little light on this: *"If ye abide in me, and my words abide in you."*

Every believer is in Christ, but His words are not in every believer. What does it mean to have His words abiding in me, gaining the absolute ascendency, dominating me in every phase of my thinking and my life?

We feed upon the Word of God. Now I am feeding. I am living in that Word. I am practicing it. I am what James calls, "a doer of the Word." (See James 1:22–23.)

Jesus said that the doer of the Word dug deep and built his house upon the rock, and it made his house able to stand against any storm that might beat against it.

He not only said that, but He said, "If you abide in me, and my words have found their place in you, then you can ask what you will and it shall be created by the Father for you"—brought into being. (See John 15:7.)

Oh, I see it now. I cooperate with him.

In John 15:5, He said, *"I am the vine, ye are the branches."* Now I can understand it.

As a branch, I am going to bear His fruit. I am laboring together with Him. He and I are operating together, are identified one with the other.

He is finding a place for His ability to energize and act here on the earth again.

It is like a wealthy man who finds an intelligent young man that he can set up in business, and the young man has ability to use this wealthy man's money.

Now He and I are laboring together and the Father is glorified because I am bearing much fruit, and I prove by my life my discipleship.

I prove that I am growing in grace, and I am growing in that exact knowledge of God, in all spiritual wisdom and understanding, to the end that I may walk worthy of the Lord unto all pleasing.

I am bearing fruit now in every good work, and I am increasing in that exact knowledge, that perfect knowledge of the Father.

You have noticed in Jesus's life that there was always a sense of sureness, a sense of certainty. There was no vacillating.

He never stopped and said, "Now pray that I may have wisdom." He had it.

Into our lives comes that same quiet sureness, a certainty that we know the Father's will. We are walking in it.

And we are made fruitful with His ability that is at work in us. It is according to the might of His glory, and it has given to us steadfastness and long-suffering, with joy.

> *Giving thanks unto the Father, which hath made us meet to be partakers of the inheritance of the saints in light.* (Colossians 1:12)

This is a climax of the heart desire of the Father, that we should so let Him live His life in us, that we begin to enjoy our share of our inheritance in Christ.

We are drawing dividends on what He has done for us and in us. We are coming to enjoy the riches of His grace.

13

LIMITING GOD IN US

The Spirit speaking through Paul in Philippians 2:13 says, *"For it is God which worketh in you both to will and to do of his good pleasure."*

How hard it has been for some of us to become God-inside minded, to daily remind ourselves that we have Him in us, and that He is there to build Christ into us, to build the living Word into us.

Just as a mason builds a house brick by brick, so the Holy Spirit will take one truth after another and build it into us until we become Jesus-minded, love-controlled, Father-pleasers.

You remember in John 8:29, Jesus said, *"For I do always those things that please him."*

For years that was my heart's slogan.

I sought to make Him happy.

You see, He has done a perfect work for us in the great substitution. There is not a thing left undone.

If we accept that work and let God work in us, it makes us stand well pleasing before the Father.

We become beautiful to Him because His nature was not only given to us, but now He has built into us through the Spirit the new habits that belong to the family of God, the new language that belongs to the new creation.

We never talk doubt or fear or sickness or want.

We have almost forgotten that language.

We have the new language of the overcomer, the language of the man who is tied up with Christ.

It is the language of the branches of the vine.

That "vine life" has so developed in us that we become Jesus men and Jesus women.

In our assembly in Seattle, we speak of them as the Jesus men and Jesus women.

We have Jesus men and women who are going out into the world, touching it, blessing it, illuminating it with the life of Christ in them.

Why can't this spread over the land until there arises a new race of men known as the Jesus folks?

They will be love in action.

They will be living in the Word and the Word will be living in them.

They will be doing the works of the Master.

As Jesus did physical healing and ministered largely in the sense realm, these Jesus folks will minister very largely in the spiritual realm.

> *And God is able to make all grace abound toward you; that ye, always having all sufficiency in all things, may abound to every good work.*
> (2 Corinthians 9:8)

How slow we have been to realize that it was God's ability that could make grace abound in and through us, and that we were being so perfectly supplied by Him that we were having all sufficiency in everything.

He is our sufficiency; He is our ability; He is the strength of our lives.

We have ignored sense reasoning and cast it down and have given our recreated spirits the right of way and the Word the first place.

Notice verses 10–11:

> *Now he that ministereth seed to the sower both minister bread for your food, and multiply your seed sown, and increase the fruits of your righteousness; being enriched in every thing to all bountifulness, which causeth through us thanksgiving to God.*

There has been little majoring of the fruit of righteousness.

I have been asked again and again, "What does it mean?" It means that same kind of fruit that we saw in Jesus's public ministry.

You see, righteousness means the ability to stand in the Father's presence without the sense of guilt or condemnation or inferiority. It means the ability to stand in the presence of Satan and his works without timidity or fear, without any sense of inferiority. Really, it means that you have become superior to Satan.

You have a superiority complex rather than an inferiority complex. You have come to reckon on the ability of the God inside of you. You have at last arrived at the place where you reckon on Him. You plan your work with the idea that He is there to enable you to put it over.

We must not omit Ephesians 1:19–20. I want this Scripture to become so familiar to you that it will be a constant source of comfort and strength:

> *And what is the exceeding greatness of his power to us-ward who believe, according to the working of his mighty power, which he wrought in Christ, when he raised him from the dead.*

A more literal translation would be, "I want you to know what the exceeding greatness of the ability of God is on our behalf who believe. That ability is according to the strength of his might, which he wrought in the Christ when he raised him from the dead."

You can't overestimate this.

This is God working within you.

This is the one who raised Jesus from the dead.

This is the one who recreated you.

This is the Spirit who has all the ability of the God-head that is necessary for you to enjoy; so that you are not afraid of the enemy in any field.

You know He put all things in subjection under His feet, and He gave Him to be Head over all things for the benefit of the church.

Remember, this is the One who is at work within you.

Take Ephesians 3:20: "*Now unto him that is able to do exceeding abundantly above all that we ask or think, according to the power that worketh in us.*"

When this Scripture is understood, put into daily practice, you can know that you have arrived.

At last you are a worthy member of the vine. You are actually bearing fruit to His glory.

In my notes, I have written this: becoming God-inside-minded, knowing that the All-wise One is in me now.

That the God of all ability is in me now.

That the God of all love is in me now.

That God and I are linked up together, laboring together with Him.

We are becoming one in our thoughts and in our actions.

He and I are laboring together to carry out the great dream of grace.

The God of all grace lives in me, and so I say it over and over again, "God, my Father, in the person of the Holy Spirit, through the Living Word, is living in me."

Now I can do all things in Him, because He has become my strength and my ability.

The limitless One is in me.

The Love-God lives in me.

At last I become God-inside minded.

First John 4:4 is not only a Scripture, but it is a living reality: "*Ye are of God, little children, and have overcome them: because greater is he that is in you, than he that is in the world.*"

The God of abundant life is in me.

He is no longer with me to convict me, but He is in me to guide me into all the realities of His mighty ministry.

Now I can understand what Paul meant when he said, in 1 Corinthians 3:9: "*For we are labourers together with God: ye are God's husbandry, ye are God's building.*"

I know what it means now to be a fellow-worker.

I know what it means to be God's tilled land (margin).

My heart and my life are the soil where He sows the seeds of love and they are growing now in me.

I am a part of God's dream and plan.

I am coming to appreciate what it means to have real, intimate fellowship with Him.

14

WHAT WE DARE CONFESS ABOUT OURSELVES

Perhaps we have never majored in our own thinking, in our own inner consciousness, what we really are in Christ; what it means to have Jesus as the Lord of our lives. We read in Paul's or John's epistles what they say about it.

John said, *"Beloved, now are we the sons of God"* (1 John 3:2).

Again, *"Whatsoever is born of God overcometh the world"* (1 John 5:4).

We never associated that with ourselves.

We never seriously said, "Well, John is talking about me now," or, "Paul is describing me."

You know this Pauline revelation is like a family album. We pick it up and look at the first picture taken of us when we were but a babe.

I turn again and I see another picture.

Months have passed since that first one was put in the album, and I see that someone has written underneath it, "When by reason of time ye ought to be teachers, ye have need now that someone teach you the first principles of the rudiments of Christ; you still have to be fed on milk and not on the solid food."

And I notice further: He calls my attention to the fact that I have never taken advantage of my righteousness.

I have lived as a *mere man,* when in reality I was a partaker of the divine nature.

I remember how all these months I had been afraid to acknowledge that I was a Christian.

I had not taken my stand.

My confession had been very uncertain, indefinite. Why? Because I had not studied to show myself approved unto God. I had not lived the Word.

I had not practiced the Word, and so I dared not confess that I was what the Word said I was.

The Word says I am redeemed: *"In whom we have redemption"* (Ephesians 1:7).

But I have no sense of redemption. Satan rules over me. I live a great deal like those about me.

I go to the same places they go.

I listen to their stories and talk.

I go to church, and when they preach a real heart-searching message and give an altar call, I usually go to the altar.

I cry a little and feel mighty sorry that I haven't done any better, but I go out and go back into my old life.

Ah yes, I have eternal life, I know that.

I remember back yonder when one night God gave me eternal life and for a few months I lived in heaven. I had wonderful victory and led several people to Christ.

Then something happened and darkness came down over my life and since that time I have never walked in the light. I did not know how to do it.

I wish I did know how to get back into the old joy I once had.

And then someone whispers to me and says, "Haven't you read in 1 John 1:9: *'If we confess our sins, he is faithful and just to forgive us our sins, and to cleanse us from all unrighteousness'*"?

I answer, "Yes, I know that Scripture. I have done it again and again but I get no relief."

But the same voice whispers again, "Read it once more. *'If we confess our sins'*. You did that?"

"Yes."

"What does it say next?"

"He is faithful and just [or righteous] *to forgive us our sins."*

Well, if you have asked His forgiveness, don't you think He is faithful and righteous enough to make His Word good in your case?

I wait a moment and I look into that Word again and read it once more: "*faithful and just to forgive us our sins.*" My heart leaps for joy.

Why, He has forgiven me! That lost fellowship is restored.

I see it now. I have lived in darkness all these months, when I could have walked in the light as He is in the light. I could have had fellowship with the brethren, and fellowship with heaven and I didn't know it.

But I know it now, and before the world I confess that I am walking in the light.

I confess that God is my Father and I am His child; that I am in His family.

Satan's dominion over me has been broken, and I have in me now the very nature and life of the Son of God. He *gave* it to me.

I am a partaker of the divine nature.

I have passed out of death into life.

I know I am a son of God, and if I am a son, then I am an heir and a joint heir with Jesus Christ.

If that is true, then I have a standing with the Father just like the Master had, because He has become my sponsor. He is my Savior and my Lord.

I see it now. He has made me His righteousness, and I can now stand in the Father's presence just as I did in those first glad days after I accepted Him.

I have a right now to ask Him to come into my body and make it His home.

I remember He said, "*If a man love me, he will keep my words: and my Father will love him, and we will come unto him, and make our abode with him*" (John 14:23).

I wonder if that doesn't mean that He will come and live in me? Wouldn't it be wonderful if He would live in my body, so wherever I went He would be with me; He would be in me.

Then Isaiah 41:10 becomes a reality:

> *Fear thou not; for I am with thee: be not dismayed; for I am thy God: I will strengthen thee; yea, I will help thee; yea, I will uphold thee with the right hand of my righteousness.*

This is mine, all *mine*, and I dare confess it before the world. Wonderful thing, isn't it?

Romans 8:11, at last, is real:

> *But if the Spirit of him that raised up Jesus from the dead dwell in you, he that raised up Christ from the dead shall also quicken your mortal bodies by his Spirit that dwelleth in you.*

Yes, quicken your body; heal it if it is sick; make it strong if it is weak; and pour into your spirit the consciousness of a victor, the sense of an overcomer.

Hebrews 13:20–21 then becomes a living reality:

> *Now the God of peace, that brought again from the dead our Lord Jesus, that great shepherd of the sheep, through the blood of the everlasting covenant, make you perfect in every good work to do his will, working in you that which is wellpleasing in his sight.*

How vividly real this can become to the heart, and it all comes when one dares to confess what he is in Christ; and more than that: confess it in the face of everything.

15

WHAT REPENTANCE MEANS

The problem of repentance in the face of modern preaching is a serious one.

Look at the meaning of the word that was used by Peter on the day of Pentecost: "*Repent, and be baptized every one of you in the name of Jesus Christ for the remission of sins, and ye shall receive the gift of the Holy Ghost*" (Acts 2:38).

The Greek word for *repent* means a "change of principle and practice," "a mental change of attitudes," "a change of mind," or "a change of one's mode of thinking or of one's conduct." Hold these definitions clearly in your mind as we study the Word.

It will be necessary for us first to notice the actual condition of natural man.

THE REAL CONDITION OF NATURAL MAN

> *But the natural man receiveth not the things of the Spirit of God: for they are foolishness unto him: neither can he know them, because they are spiritually discerned.* (1 Corinthians 2:14)

Why is it impossible for the natural man to understand the things of God? Ephesians 2:1–3 will give us a suggestion:

> *And you hath he quickened* [make alive], *who were dead in trespasses and sins; wherein in time past ye walked according to the course of this world, according to the prince of the power of the air, the spirit that now worketh in the children of disobedience: among whom also we all had our conversation in times past in the lusts of our flesh, fulfilling the desires of the flesh and of the mind; and were by nature the children of wrath, even as others.*

Now we will notice it more fully as we go on. Here we found first, that the natural man is dead in trespasses and sins. What does it mean?

Perhaps we may get a suggestion from John 5:24: "*Verily, verily, I say unto you, He that heareth my word, and believeth on him that sent me, hath everlasting life, and shall not come into condemnation; but is passed from death unto life.*"

What does Jesus mean by *death?*

There are two kinds of death mentioned in the Word—physical death and spiritual death.

Spiritual death is the nature of Satan, just as spiritual life is the nature of the Father.

First John 3:14–15 will throw more light upon this:

> *We know that we have passed from death unto life, because we love the brethren. He that loveth not his brother abideth in death. Whosoever hateth his brother is a murderer: and ye know that no murderer hath eternal life abiding in him.*

Here we have the contrast of death and life. Life is the nature of the Father; death is the nature of the enemy, for the natural man is spiritually dead.

He is a partaker of satanic nature that was given to him in the garden, and down through the ages, spiritual death has dominated man.

If you wish to see a vivid contrast, turn to Romans 5:17: "*For if by one man's offence death reigned by one; much more they which receive abundance of grace and of the gift of righteousness shall reign in life by one, Jesus Christ.*"

Spiritual death seized the sovereignty over the human race in the garden and man served as a slave under its dominion.

Paul unveils to us, in Romans 5:12–21, the whole drama of spiritual death.

> *Wherefore, as by one man sin entered into the world, and death by sin; and so death passed upon all men, for that all have sinned.* (Romans 5:12)

Then, verse 14: "*Nevertheless death reigned from Adam to Moses, even over them that had not sinned after the similitude of Adam's transgression.*"

What does he mean? That physical death "*passed upon all men*"? No, spiritual death.

It had reigned without interference until Moses came.

What did Moses give? Moses gave us the atonement in the blood of bulls and goats.

Atonement means to cover.

He took a garment of animal life and spread it over spiritually dead Israel. That garment of blood covered the broken law and the priesthood.

Spiritual death lost its complete sovereignty as long as Israel walked in the first covenant, but when Jesus came, the combat was between life and death. Not physical life nor physical death, but the new kind of life that Jesus brought was at war with spiritual death.

In John 10:10, He says, *"I am come that they might have life, and that they might have it more abundantly."*

The Greek word translated as *life* is *zoe,* which means God's nature, God's substance, God's being, just as spiritual death means Satan's substance, Satan's being.

Out of eternal life have sprung all the beautiful graces which adorn a Christian life.

Out of spiritual death, the garden plot of sin, have grown all the sins that have ever been committed.

Man is united to Satan spiritually.

Perhaps the most awful words that Jesus ever uttered to the Jews are recorded in John 8:44–45:

> *Ye are of your father the devil, and the lusts of your father ye will do. He was a murderer from the beginning, and abode not in the truth, because there is no truth in him. When he speaketh a lie, he speaketh of his own: for he is a liar, and the father of it. And because I tell you the truth, ye believe me not.*

This is a heart-searching Scripture.

Satan was a murderer and a liar. He was a murderer by nature. The very substance and being of Satan are the very opposite of what we see in the man Jesus.

Jesus is truth. He is life. He is love.

Satan is spiritual death. He is a hater, a sin-producer. He is everything that is bad.

Jesus was everything that was good.

First John 3:10 carries us a step farther in this unhappy drama: *"In this the children of God are manifest, and the children of the devil."*

Here we have the two families in contrast—the family of God and the family of the devil.

Ephesians 2:11–12 gives us one of the saddest pictures of the natural man. The Spirit, through Paul, is speaking: *"Wherefore remember, that ye being in time past Gentiles in the flesh, who are called Uncircumcision by that which is called the Circumcision in the flesh made by hands,"* that is, the Jews called the gentiles the *"Uncircumcision."* Why? Because the circumcised man was in the first covenant and had covenant rights and covenant privileges, but the gentile man, the uncircumcised, was outside.

The Jew would not eat at the same table with the gentile, as he was considered unclean. The next verse explains it: *"That at that time ye were without Christ, being aliens from the commonwealth of Israel, and strangers from the covenants of promise, having no hope, and without God in the world."*

All of God's blessings are wrapped up in Christ.

The gentile is separated from Christ.

Second fact: he is alienated even from the commonwealth of Israel, the covenant people who have covenant claims on God, and he is a stranger from any covenant relationship with God or contract with God.

He has no hope; he is without God, and he is in the world. Notice his condition now: he is spiritually dead, united with Satan.

Jesus calls him a child of the devil.

John the Baptist, you remember, called them "vipers." (See Matthew 3:7.) By that, he meant, children of Satan.

He has no covenant claims on God. He is without hope, hopeless; without God, godless, and he is here in the world.

Second Corinthians 4:3–4 reveals more fully his desperate condition:

> *But if our gospel be hid, it is hid to them that are lost: in whom the god of this world hath blinded the minds of them which believe not, lest the light*

of the glorious gospel of Christ, who is the image of God, should shine unto them.

This Scripture hurts. Here the curtain is lifted.

This spiritually dead man is mentally blinded, spiritually blinded.

I do not know how clearly you understand it, but all the knowledge that this spiritually dead man has, comes through the five senses: seeing, hearing, tasting, smelling, and feeling.

There is no other way for natural man to get knowledge. His body has been his laboratory.

I sometimes think of it as just physical body knowledge.

That is all the natural man has.

Is it any wonder that Darwin gave us the hypothesis of evolution?

Sense knowledge can never find God.

Sense knowledge cannot understand spiritual things, and this sense knowledge man ruled by the senses, governed by the senses, is spiritually blinded.

If you want to know more fully about him, turn to Ephesians 4:17–18:

This I say therefore, and testify in the Lord, that ye henceforth walk not as other Gentiles walk, in the vanity of their mind, having the understanding darkened, being alienated from the life of God through the ignorance that is in them, because of the blindness of their heart.

A man may be the head of a university, but he is lost, without God and without hope.

This is a series of Love's photographs of natural man.

Now let us go back and look at repentance again.

The preacher is demanding that this natural man "change his mind and purpose," or "change his principles and practice," "change his mode of conduct," give up his old habits; give up his rebellion against divine authority.

The question is: can he do it?

Will crying and weeping and praying change his nature? Understand, he is by nature a child of wrath. He can't change his own nature.

He may change his mind for a moment but it will come back again. What he must have is a new nature, and this must come from God. How can he get this new nature?

Turn with me to John 3:16–17:

> *For God so loved the world, that he gave his only begotten Son, that whosoever believeth in him should not perish, but have everlasting life. For God sent not his Son into the world to condemn the world; but that the world through him might be saved.*

What is it that the natural man needs?

It is eternal life, the nature of God, and he can't get this by any effort of his own.

He cannot change his nature.

He may give up some of the habits that he has learned, but that does not save him.

Let us go back and notice it once more.

He in himself has no approach to God.

He is an eternal being, but a hopeless one.

His nature is enmity toward God. Satan has blinded his mind. His senseless heart is darkened. Satan has ruled him through his senses.

Love has given Jesus to him. Love has done more than that.

> *Now to him that worketh is the reward not reckoned of grace, but of debt. But to him that worketh not, but believeth on him that justifieth the ungodly, his faith is counted for righteousness.* (Romans 4:4–5)

What does he mean here?

He means one who does not attempt to make himself better or who tries to give up his old habits and his old life, but accepts the gift God has given to him without money and without price, receives eternal life. His old habits stop being and new habits take their place.

Romans 4:25, speaking of Jesus: "*Who was delivered for our offences, and was raised again for our justification.*"

What does that mean? It means that Jesus actually suffered until every claim of justice was satisfied as far as the sinner was concerned.

And the second thing, when the claims of justice were met, He was raised to prove that He had paid the penalty of our trespasses, and now man has justification, righteousness, and eternal life awaiting him.

Being therefore justified by faith, or being therefore declared righteous on the ground of pure grace, God says to the sinner, take Jesus as your Savior, confess Him as your Lord, and I will give you eternal life and make you a new creation.

You see this is all of grace.

When I tell the unsaved man that he must have godly sorrow and repentance, I don't know what I am talking about.

Paul told that Christian young man who had committed an unwholesome sin, that he needed godly sorrow that would work a repentance in his own life.

That message can be preached to the church today.

The church needs to repent.

The unsaved man needs to take Jesus as his Savior and confess Him as his Lord.

The unsaved man needs eternal life and righteousness.

"For we are his workmanship, created in Christ Jesus" (Ephesians 2:10). When were we created in Christ Jesus?

After He had been made sin on our behalf and was made alive. When the Father justified Him in spirit down there in the place of suffering and made Him alive, the church was justified.

There the church was made alive in spirit with Him, or recreated in the mind of the Father.

Now the unsaved man receives that eternal life and righteousness and comes into the family of God.

They are awaiting him. The thing has all been done. The Father's work in Christ is finished.

When Jesus sat down on the right hand of the Majesty on high, it was because He had finished the work of redemption.

There was no more work to be done. Redemption was a settled and fixed thing.

Now I accept it and come into the benefits of the finished work of my Lord.

You see, Jesus belongs to the unsaved man.

The unsaved man has Jesus on his hands. He died for him.

He put sin away for him.

He has made the new birth a possibility for him, but the unsaved man must accept Him.

Romans 10:9–10 tells us:

> *That if thou shalt confess with thy mouth the Lord Jesus, and shalt believe in thine heart that God hath raised him from the dead, thou shalt be saved. For with the heart man believeth unto righteousness; and with the mouth confession is made unto salvation.*

With his lips, he makes confession of his salvation.

Now notice it carefully. Jesus belongs to him but He is of no value to him until he confesses His lordship over his life.

Eternal life belongs to him but he never gets it.

He never has any benefit from it until he accepts Christ as his personal Savior and confesses His Lordship.

Then he becomes a new creation in Christ Jesus.

The old things pass away just at the moment eternal life comes into his spirit.

D. L. Moody used to declare that repentance meant "right about-face." That is true.

The moment that the sinner accepts Jesus Christ, he does a right about-face.

But he can't do it unless he accepts what God has wrought for him in Christ.

The unsaved man has the ability to confess Jesus as Lord over his life with his lips.

He has the ability to make the decision, to take Christ as his Savior.

God's hands are tied until he does make that confession.

He doesn't ask a sinner to confess his sins.

That is a self-evident fact.

He is a sinner, but God demands that he confess the lordship of Jesus, and when he does that, he confesses his faith in the substitutionary work that Christ wrought on his behalf.

Now you can understand Ephesians 2:4–10:

> *But God, who is rich in mercy, for his great love wherewith he loved us, even when we were dead in sins, hath quickened us together with Christ, (by grace ye are saved;) hath raised us up together, and made us sit together in heavenly places in Christ Jesus: that in the ages to come he might shew the exceeding riches of his grace in his kindness toward us through Christ Jesus. For by grace are ye saved through faith; and that not of yourselves: it is the gift of God: not of works, lest any man should boast. For we are his workmanship, created in Christ Jesus.*

We should make the message so clear and simple that the unsaved man can see Jesus as his Savior and Lord.

We should make the message so easy to grasp that he can see that all he needs to do is to act upon the Word.

Do not tell him he needs to believe.

Do not tell him he needs to repent for that will confuse him.

If he accepts Christ as his Savior and confesses Him as his Lord, that is repentance. That is all God requires.

16

HAVING YOUR OWN FAITH LIFE

It is an unhappy thing to be dependent upon another's faith. In a measure, we are all dependent upon others, but in this vital issue of life, no believer should be dependent upon another's ability to approach the throne.

We cannot afford to trust others with vital issues that we ourselves should be able to face.

Faith is measured by our appreciation of our position in the Father's family.

When we know our place as a child, know our rights, know our righteousness, our ability to stand in the Father's presence without the sense of guilt or inferiority, when we know that we have as good a standing before the Father as Jesus had in His earth walk, then the problem of faith is settled.

First Corinthians 1:30 should be a prominent Scripture in our daily walk: *"But of him are ye in Christ Jesus, who of God is made unto us wisdom, and righteousness, and sanctification, and redemption."*

We need a consciousness of both righteousness and wisdom.

We need to know He is now our righteousness, and that 2 Corinthians 5:21—*"For he hath made him to be sin for us, who knew no sin; that we might be made the righteousness of God in him"*—has become a reality.

You see, we have absolutely become, by the new birth, by our being partakers of the divine nature, the very righteousness of God in Christ.

That is not philosophy nor theology; it is a fact.

Just as hunger and thirst are facts, our righteousness and our standing before the Father is a definite, clear-cut reality.

Jesus was made unto us wisdom at the same time He was made unto us righteousness.

We desperately need wisdom to use our righteousness and to use the ability that has been given to us in Christ.

Ephesians 4:7 states a fact that has been ignored by the average believer: *"But unto every one of us is given grace according to the measure of the gift of Christ."*

Grace means ability. Grace means everything that we need in this earth walk.

But we have lacked the wisdom to utilize our abilities, to take advantage of our position in Christ.

Now Jesus is made unto us wisdom.

Every believer ought to know that, just as they know they have an umbrella or a raincoat during the rainy season, and before they start out, they put on their rubber galoshes, don their raincoats, and take their umbrella and go to the office.

When you go out in the morning to face life's hard problems, you should remember these facts:

You have His wisdom now to meet every need of today.

You have to meet a number of people. Some of them are going to be very difficult, but you have His wisdom and His ability to make the contacts and go through the business successfully.

You have wisdom superior to theirs. They have nothing but material, human wisdom. You have His wisdom.

He has been made unto you wisdom.

Not only that, but you are His righteousness.

That gives you access to the throne at any time.

You can stand in His presence just as Jesus did in His earth walk, because Jesus is your righteousness.

There can be no event so great but what His wisdom and His righteousness will enable you to meet it successfully.

You see, when you become the righteousness of God, that really makes you a master of circumstances.

That lets you into the inner circle.

That gives you the advantage of the Father's wisdom and ability to put you over.

Satan cannot cope with the man who knows he is the righteousness of God in Christ, who knows that Jesus has been made unto him wisdom.

That man is a Master man.

You see, that leads you into the superman realm.

Take account of stock for a moment.

You have God's very nature in you.

The old life that kept you in bondage has stopped being.

The old self that was dominated by circumstances and by Satan has stopped being, and a new self, a dominant self, a righteous self, a God-filled self, has taken its place.

You now have a legal right to the use of Jesus's name.

Before the Master ascended, you remember He said in Matthew 28:18: *"All power is given unto me in heaven and in earth."*

That authority is for the members of the body.

Jesus doesn't need it.

He and the Father are one, so all that the Father is, Jesus is. This authority was given to the church.

The ability to use that authority is given to us in the Holy Spirit.

We not only have this authority; but we have the great mighty Spirit who raised Jesus from the dead dwelling in us, and when He came into us, He brought all His ability, the ability that He exercised in the resurrection of the Master, the ability that He exercised in Christ. It is all in Him.

No wonder John said by the Spirit, in 1 John 4:4, *"Greater is he that is in you, than he that is in the world."*

You see, we are dominant people. We have the creative ability of God in us. There is no limit to where we can go.

It is not only these abilities, but there are other abilities that are ours.

Of his fulness have all we received. (John 1:16)

Perhaps among the most important assets that we have is the new kind of love.

Jesus brought it into the world.

When we are recreated, that new kind of love becomes our nature.

We become partakers of the divine nature, for the Father is love. When that love nature comes in, it brings an element into a man that makes him a master.

When a man loses his temper, the person who caused him to lose his temper is superior to him in some way.

He wouldn't lose his temper if that person hadn't outwitted him, "out-generaled" him in some way.

Love makes us impervious to these influences, makes us a master of them.

We rise up in God, that is, we rise up in love; we walk in love; we live in love, and that makes us masters of every person that does not walk in love.

The unpleasant things that he does or says, we know are said by an inferior.

Love never becomes irritated.

Love never loses its poise; never loses its temper.

It is master of itself, and that makes it master of every person outside of love.

This Jesus nature makes you a dominant personality, a master personality.

They can't conquer you any more than they could conquer Christ. They may stone you; they may beat you; they may, because of numbers, take you captive, but you become their master the moment you become their captive. It is a strange fact, but it is true. His love nature makes you a master.

I want you to learn to believe in love.

I want you to learn to rest in it, to depend on it, to expect great things from it. You will not be disappointed.

You remember that passage, "*Ye are of God, little children*" (1 John 4:4). Then, in John 3:5–6, Jesus said, "*Except a man be born of water and of the Spirit, he cannot enter into the kingdom of God. That which is born of the flesh is flesh.*"

Then, He says another startling thing: *"That which is born of the Spirit is spirit."*

Well, then you do not belong to the old order of things. You belong to this new family, this new condition.

You are a partaker of the divine nature.

You are in the realm of life with God, and you reign as a king in this realm of life.

You are a master. What makes you a master? The very nature of the Father that has come into you.

This love gift has made you superior to everything surrounding you.

The forces that surround you emanate from the selfishness of natural man.

You now have the love nature of God. That makes you superior. You must learn to trust this. Think about what you are in Christ. Never think of your lack; think of the vast inheritance that is yours, for you know that He has given you the ability to enjoy all that belongs to you.

Let me give you Colossians 1:12:

> *Giving thanks unto the Father, which hath made us meet to be partakers of the inheritance of the saints in light.*

You have the ability to enter into all the fullness of Christ.

John 1:16 means nothing unless you take advantage of it: *"Of his fulness have all we received, and grace for grace."*

That was not said for angels nor for men during the millennium; that is for us now.

You have His fullness. It may be an undeveloped property in you. You may never have taken advantage of the riches of the glory of your inheritance in Christ.

You may have stayed in the babyhood realm where you are always struggling and trying to get something and to be something. You have passed that; you are something.

He has made you to be what you are in Christ.

You see, you were created in Christ.

Ephesians 2:10 ought to solve every problem of our spiritual conflict:

For we are his workmanship, created in Christ Jesus unto good works, which God hath before ordained that we should walk in them.

There is no limit to your walk and to your ability.

The only limit is the limit you set, and just as soon as you take your hands off of this new creation and let it function and develop in Christ, you become at once an outstanding blessing to the world.

You have an unconscious fellowship with the Father and with Christ.

That fellowship is threefold: it is with the brethren who walk in the light, and oh, what a heavenly thing that is; walking in fellowship with those whom you love and who love you and love our Lord.

Second, it is with Christ as Lord. First Corinthians 1:9: "*Ye were called unto the fellowship of his Son Jesus Christ our Lord.*"

Third, you have fellowship with the Word. The Word becomes to us the very voice of the Master.

It speaks to you; it strengthens you; it comforts you.

You read a passage like this in Colossians 1:27:

To whom God would make known what is the riches of the glory of this mystery among the Gentiles; which is Christ in you, the hope of glory.

You have the riches of His very ability in you.

Or take this one in Colossians 2:6–7:

As ye have therefore received Christ Jesus the Lord, so walk ye in him: rooted and built up in him, and stablished in the faith, as ye have been taught, abounding therein with thanksgiving.

You are in it; you are a part of it. It is yours.

You are not struggling for anything.

You have entered into your rest.

He has become your ability for every emergency.

There was a time when you struggled and prayed and groaned to be something.

But Colossians 3:1–2 is a photograph of yourself:

> *If ye then be risen with Christ, seek those things which are above, where Christ sitteth on the right hand of God. Set your affection on things above, not on things on the earth.*

And then He tells us Christ is our life.

We are absolutely one with Him.

He has become a part of us and we have become a part of Him.

We have learned what John 8:12 means: *"I am the light of the world: he that followeth me shall not walk in darkness, but shall have the light of life."*

Light means wisdom. It is the wisdom of this new kind of life. You have that new kind of life. You have His wisdom, and that wisdom gives you the ability to make the right choices, to do the right thing at the right time. Not only that, but it gives you the ability to enter into all the fullness and all the blessings, and all the riches of His redemptive work. You are outstanding immediately. You are not common.

Now you are reveling in 1 Corinthians 3:21, *"for all things are your's,"* whether the revelation of them came to Paul or to Peter or to John, it doesn't make any difference; they are all yours.

And then another strangely beautiful thing is, *"And ye are Christ's"* (verse 23). You see, you belong to Him. He is yours and you are His.

Just as a husband owns the bride, He owns you and it is an ownership of love.

But that isn't all. Second Corinthians 9:8 ought to thrill our hearts:

> *And God is able to make all grace abound toward you; that ye, always having all sufficiency in all things, may abound to every good work.*

You see, there is nothing narrow or lacking in the Father's blessings. There is a wholesome fullness in His blessings.

He has blessed you with every spiritual blessing in Christ. There isn't a need of yours that hasn't been met.

The ability of the Father is at your disposal in every crisis of your life, and in your daily life, His love so enriches you that there is no wear and tear.

You just pass along on a smooth, easy road, carried by His grace, upheld by His love, but His very fullness of love and grace overshadow you.

You are rich. You are God's cared for.

The reason I am writing this is to give you a photograph of what you are in Christ, so that you will rise up and take your place and enjoy the riches that belong to you, and that you will learn to give place to His ability in you.

You will learn to have confidence in the God who is in you.

You will learn to talk about Him as you talk about a strong man who is working for you, or you brag about a car that laughs at hills and mountains.

Why, greater is He that is in you than any mountain, any difficulty, and any combination of circumstances.

You are tied up with God.

God is on your side. He is fighting your battles.

All you have to do is just to act on His Word; walk in His Word. That is His will for you, and you will be amazed how sweet and beautiful life becomes.

You will learn another thing: the authority and power of the living Word in your lips.

You can say to sickness and disease, "In the name of Jesus, leave this body," and that living Word in your lips will be obeyed by the author of sickness and disease.

His Word in your lips puts Him to work at once; gives Him an opportunity to demonstrate His ability to help man.

His Word in your lips will lead men and women to Christ; will break the power of Satan over the weak.

You will not need another man's faith.

You have passed into the realm of the ones who are not begging for a free ride, but you are able to give a free ride to another.

You have become a dominant spirit rather than a hectored, broken, helpless one.

You have passed out of the realm of liability into God's assets. You are becoming strong, and you are taking over the weaknesses of others.

You see that brother's overload and you get under it.

You will have a joy that is unspeakable now and full of His glory.

17

THE LIMITATIONS OF JESUS

During Jesus's earth walk, He was dealing exclusively with the Jews—the first covenant people.

He was surrounded by men who had never been born again.

No person with whom He dealt had yet received eternal life.

They were all spiritually dead.

John 8:44 is Jesus's description of them: *"Ye are of your father the devil, and the lusts of your father ye will do."*

How hard it must have been for the Master, whose great heart of love yearned over the people, to tell them that unhappy truth.

He never conformed Himself to His surroundings or to the opinions of people.

He always spoke out from His Father.

It has been an unhappy thing that so many of our teachers have spoken of those who walked with Jesus, as though they were already Christians, as though they had received eternal life.

If anyone could have received eternal life before Jesus died and arose again, then He would not have had to suffer, because everyone could have received it.

It is not what a man has done; it is what he is by nature that separates him from God. They were all spiritually dead.

Jesus was limited very largely to the physical realm with them.

He healed their diseases; He raised their dead; He fed the multitudes, but He did not recreate anyone.

He gave no one eternal life.

Man was not yet redeemed; the penalty of sin had not been paid.

Men were by nature children of wrath.

They were all in one class.

The only difference between the Israelite and the gentile was that the former was under the first covenant.

He was circumcised; he was of the family of Abraham.

He had a priesthood that made a yearly atonement for him and laid his sins once a year upon the head of a scapegoat to be borne away into the wilderness.

But that did not make him a new creation.

It gave him a right to the new creation.

You remember Romans 3:25 declares:

> *Whom God hath set forth to be a propitiation through faith in his blood, to declare his righteousness for the remission of sins that are past, through the forbearance of God.*

Then, Hebrews 9:15 explains the thing more fully:

> *For this cause he is the mediator of the new testament, that by means of death, for the redemption of the transgressions that were under the first testament, they which are called might receive the promise of eternal inheritance.*

Christ died for the sins of those under the first covenant.

It was as though a promissory note had been given each year when the high priest entered the Holy of Holies to make the yearly atonement.

Those promissory notes were all cashed when Jesus carried His blood into the heavenly Holy of Holies. So, all the sins under the first covenant were put away, wiped out as though they had never been.

You will understand this more fully in Hebrews 10:1–3:

> *For the law having a shadow of good things to come, and not the very image of the things, can never with those sacrifices which they offered year by year continually make the comers thereunto perfect. For then would they not have ceased to be offered? because that the worshippers once*

> *purged should have had no more conscience of sins. But in those sacrifices there is a remembrance again made of sins every year.*

Why? *"For it is not possible that the blood of bulls and of goats should take away sins"* (verse 4).

"But this man, after he had offered one sacrifice for sins for ever, sat down on the right hand of God" (verse 12).

"For by one offering he hath perfected for ever them that are sanctified" (verse 14).

You get a perfect picture here of the man under the first covenant whose sin was covered, whose sins were typically borne away.

Then Jesus comes and puts away all the sin that had been covered and He remits all the sins that have been borne away typically, so that the Jews who trusted in the atoning blood of animals were saved by His sacrifice.

Notice again that no one could receive eternal life and have his sins remitted until sin was put away, until the claims of justice had been fully met.

Hebrews 2:17 perfectly illustrates that:

> *Wherefore in all things it behoved him to be made like unto his brethren, that he might be a merciful and faithful high priest in things pertaining to God, to make reconciliation for the sins of the people.*

As our High Priest, you remember, He had first to meet the demands of justice, to satisfy the claims of justice against the Jew and gentile.

When He was down in hell, and Satan had been conquered, then man's redemption was a completed thing. That is when God accepted His blood, and He sat down at the right hand of God.

But it was not yet complete while Christ was living, so it was of no value to anybody.

The new creation was not available.

There was no high priest at the right hand of the Father with the blood to show that He had dealt with the sin problem.

There was no mediator at the right hand of God, and until there was a mediator, no human being could approach God.

> *I am the way, the truth, and the life: no man cometh unto the Father, but by me.* (John 14:6)

> *Neither is there salvation in any other: for there is none other name under heaven given among men, whereby we must be saved.* (Acts 4:12)

Jesus's name was not yet available as a Savior.

His mediatorial work was not yet available.

Jesus was a prophet now. He had not yet become a sin substitute; there was no Savior.

He dealt only in the sense realm with men.

He dealt with demons.

He cast them out of individuals.

He broke their power over men, which was all in the sense realm.

It is such a bitter thing for our hearts to realize that Jesus, during His earth walk, didn't have one single spiritually-minded companion.

Good folks loved Him, but their love was the love of natural man.

It was a selfish thing. It was so selfish that when He arose from the dead they said, "Master, are you going to restore the kingdom at this time?" (See Acts 1:6.)

He could not help men spiritually because they were dead in spirit.

I think you can understand this Scripture now: "*Greater works than these shall he do; because I go unto my Father*" (John 14:12).

We are doing greater works than the Master did in His earth walk, because we help men spiritually.

We bring to them the Word of life and they are recreated; they come into the family of God.

We help them to pass out of death unto life.

We teach them through the Word how God has made them His righteousness.

Now they can stand in His presence as though sin had never been.

We are God's agents giving men eternal life, making them masters of demons and of circumstances.

We, through His living Word, have been able to lead men into fellowship and communion with the Father through the new birth.

Our ministry is almost an unlimited ministry.

His Ministry was a limited one.

Jesus healed men's bodies.

We, through the grace of God, heal men's spirits.

He raised men from the dead to die again.

We show them that they were raised together with Christ.

He fed the hungry with loaves of bread and fishes.

We feed the spiritually hungry with His own wonderful words.

We have the Spirit in us who raised Jesus from the dead.

We have a legal right to the use of Jesus's name.

With that name, we do the works that Jesus wrought in His earth walk.

But come back again to the thought of the limitations of Jesus's friendships.

His own mother could not understand Him. His own brothers looked upon Him with suspicion.

To those nearest Him, He was a stranger. He knew them but they didn't know Him.

There can be no deep spiritual friendship unless we know each other.

Jesus's limitations in His earth walk explain much of His teaching.

It might be all right for us to contrast Jesus's and Paul's teachings on the subject of faith.

Jesus demanded that men have faith in Him. He said, *"If ye have faith as a grain of mustard seed, ye shall say unto this mountain, Remove hence to yonder place; and it shall remove"* (Matthew 17:20).

In Mark 11:22, Jesus said, *"Have faith in God."*

The disciples couldn't do that.

No one can have the faith of God until after they have been recreated.

You see, Jesus is the author and finisher of faith, and when we become new creations, we receive a measure of God's faith. (See Romans 12:3.)

We have His nature, His life, and with it comes His faith.

As we grow in grace and in knowledge, we understand the finished work of Christ. As our faith grows, it is really the faith of God.

> *For verily I say unto you, that whosoever shall say unto this mountain, Be thou removed, and be thou cast into the sea; and shall not doubt in his heart, but shall believe that those things which he saith shall come to pass; he shall have whatsoever he saith. Therefore I say unto you, What things soever ye desire, when ye pray, believe that ye receive them, and ye shall have them.* (Mark 11:23–24)

That was a keynote of the ministry of Jesus.

Jesus said to the father who asked for the healing of his child, *"All things are possible to him that believeth"* (Mark 9:23).

> *And all things, whatsoever ye shall ask in prayer, believing, ye shall receive.* (Matthew 21:22)

Paul never tells a believer to believe.

He never urges us to have faith.

That bothered me when I first noticed it; then I saw the truth. We *are* believers.

We had to have faith to get into the family, but when once we come into the family, all things that God wrought in Christ for us are ours.

You notice Jesus, speaking to the church prophetically, for the church had not yet come into being, said in John 15:16:

> *Ye have not chosen me, but I have chosen you, and ordained you, that ye should go and bring forth fruit, and that your fruit should remain: that whatsoever ye shall ask of the Father in my name, he may give it you.*

In this Scripture, and John in 14:14, Jesus gives us a legal right to the use of His name.

It is the same as giving the power of attorney to one.

Jesus actually does this to the church.

But here is the strange thing about it. Take John 16:24: *"Hitherto have ye asked nothing in my name: ask, and ye shall receive, that your joy may be full."* (John 15:16 is prophecy.)

Jesus doesn't mention faith. He doesn't say that they must believe.

Why? They already are believers.

Then all of our preaching about faith and the need of faith has been wrong.

We should have told the believer about what he is in Christ; what his rights and privileges are in Christ and his legal right to the use of Jesus's name.

We should have taught him what it meant to receive the nature and life of God in his spirit, that it would make him an actual new creation.

Not only that, but the new creation had become the righteousness of God in Christ, so he who was once a sinner could now stand in the Father's presence without the sense of fear, condemnation or inferiority.

He could stand there as a son in fullest fellowship with his Father.

If we had been taught this, we would not have had the long struggle for faith.

We would have known who we were and what we were in Christ. We would have learned how to take our place in the family; how to enjoy our privileges.

We would have become acquainted with our Father.

The great facts of substitution and the new creation and redemption would have become spiritual realities to us.

But instead of that, they have preached to us the messages Jesus gave to the Jews during His earth walk, and they don't fit in.

They keep us under condemnation. They make us conscious of our lack.

You see, if I do not know what I am, the Word confuses me, but when I know what I am in Christ, know what my rights are and my privileges, then you can bring no confusion to my spirit.

There was no discord between the teachings of Jesus and the apostle Paul because they were all of God.

18

THE DEFEATED SATAN

Few of us have ever recognized the fact that the Scriptures teach that Satan is defeated as far as the believer is concerned.

He was not conquered by the believer; he was conquered by Christ for the believer in His substitutionary work.

The victory Christ wrought belongs to the believer, because we were identified with Christ in His substitutionary work.

We have mentioned this in another chapter, but I wish to go a little farther with you in this.

In Galatians 2:20, Paul cries, *"I am crucified with Christ."* Back yonder, when Christ hung on the cross, in the mind of justice, every one of us hung there.

We were identified with Him because He was our Substitute. He was taking our place in order that He might redeem us out of the hand of our enemy.

We were with Him when He died, for we died with Him.

We were with Him when He left His body.

We were with Him in His great agony, while He suffered the penalty that was due us.

He was in the prison house of death. Satan was its keeper.

The horror of it will never be known.

Jesus stayed there until He satisfied the claims of justice for us. Romans 4:25 says, *"Who was delivered for our offences,"* that is, He was delivered up to death—spiritual death.

He was delivered up to judgment. He was delivered up to pay the penalty that we owed justice, and when the claims of justice were satisfied, we were justified with Christ.

That is the reason every unsaved man has a legal right to eternal life, because he was legally justified with Christ in that great substitutionary work.

Then Jesus was born again. You remember the Scripture in Acts 13:33, *"Thou art my Son, this day have I begotten thee."* That was the day of our redemption.

I want to pause here just a bit and call your attention to a startling fact.

You remember when Jesus entered the Holy of Holies with His blood, He had just come out of hell, and when the Father justified Him, He was so justified that He could stand in the Father's presence without the slightest bit of condemnation.

Like the three Hebrew children, when they came out of the fiery furnace, there was no smell of fire upon their garments. There was no smell on the garments of our Lord.

Do you know what that shows me? If Jesus could go out of there and go into the presence of the Father, you and I can go out of this world ruled by spiritual death.

We who have received eternal life can go into the presence of the Father without the sense or the smell of spiritual death upon us.

As soon as the Master was made alive in spirit, then Colossians 2:15 became a reality: *"Having spoiled principalities and powers, he made a shew of them openly."*

Right there, in the presence of all the hosts of darkness, Jesus conquered the prince of darkness. *"That through death he might destroy him that had the power of death, that is, the devil"* (Hebrews 2:14), or, as Joseph B. Rotherham translates it: "He paralyzed the death-dealing power of Satan." He paralyzed him. He broke him.

Now this is what I want you to notice: This was an eternal victory. Satan was eternally broken, eternally conquered.

Did you notice how Peter puts it? *"Your adversary the devil, as a roaring lion, walketh about, seeking whom he may devour"* (1 Peter 5:8). Then he says,

"Whom resist stedfast in the faith" (verse 9). Our combat has been fought and won.

There isn't any battle for you to fight except the battle of faith. You are to fight the good fight of faith.

What does that mean? You are to win all your victories with words. You are to learn the words of this wonderful Book, and with words you will conquer your enemy.

All that Peter said to the sick man at the Beautiful Gate was, *"In the name of Jesus Christ of Nazareth rise up and walk"* (Acts 3:6), and the man was set free. He didn't lay hands on him. He didn't pray over him. He simply healed that man with words.

That is the way Jesus healed them—with words.

That is the way the Father created the universe—with words.

You conquer the adversary with words.

Today, you comfort the weak and the broken with words. You heal the sick with words.

Why, when I read Isaiah 53:4—*"Surely he hath borne our griefs, and carried our sorrows: yet we did esteem him stricken, smitten of God, and afflicted"*— then I knew that by His stripes I was healed.

What healed me? Words.

Now you can understand Psalm 107:20: *"He sent his word, and healed them."*

It isn't prayer. It isn't laying on of our hands.

That may be necessary among the babes in Christ, but for the man who is grown up into the full stature of the knowledge of his rights and privileges, the Word heals him.

The Word brought that money to me. I had called my Father's attention to Philippians 4:19, *"My God shall supply all your need,"* and He did it, *"according to his riches in glory by Christ Jesus."*

That settled it. His Word brought comfort and assurance to me. Then I simply said, "In the name of Jesus, you ministering spirits, go and cause that money to come," and the money came. Not once, but it has been coming all these years of my public ministry.

You see, our combat is not against flesh and blood, as the Spirit tells us in Ephesians 6:12, but it is against the defeated principalities and powers.

These principalities and powers have all been conquered.

Their defeat is spoken of in Hebrews 9:12 as an eternal redemption from them.

You are eternally set free.

They are eternally defeated, whipped, conquered.

You get your liberty by remembering these words and then acting accordingly.

You simply refuse to stay in bondage.

With joy you read this Scripture: "*In whom we have redemption through his blood, the forgiveness of sins, according to the riches of his grace*" (Ephesians 1:7).

Can't you see what it means? Satan knows he is whipped but he doesn't want you to know it.

He wants to keep you in ignorance of it.

Revelation 12:11 has been a source of great comfort to me: "*And they overcame him by the blood of the Lamb, and by the word of their testimony.*"

That "*word,*" in Greek, is *logos*. In the beginning was the *logos*, and the *logos* was with God, and the *logos* was God.

Can't you see? They overcame him with the Word of Christ. That meant they overcame him with Christ Himself.

That blood is the basis, the ground of our victory.

It proves to all heaven that Satan was defeated, and I act on the ground of that.

Now I shout! If He is for me (and He *is* for me), then who is there in earth or hell that can stand up against me!

I am a conqueror!

As a nation, we are facing one of the gravest periods of our national life, and it is necessary that there arise a company of men and women who know the power of the name of Jesus and how to use that name against our national enemies.

Our worst enemy is not a foreign enemy. It is a local enemy. It is in our midst.

Now you are to rise up and to use His words, these demon-destroying words; these demon-defeating words; these circumstance-defeating words.

When you go into the throne room, you talk to the Father; you are taking into His presence His own Word.

Jesus no more spoke the Word of the Father than you, if you will use His Word now.

The Father shows respect always to His own Word. He says, *"I will hasten my word to perform it"* (Jeremiah 1:12) and *"My word…shall not return unto me void* [or unfulfilled]*"* (Isaiah 55:11).

Go in there then and lay your request upon that Word.

I like to think that I lay them upon the name of Jesus, and I hold that name up before Him with my request upon it. *"Whatsoever ye shall ask of the Father in my name, he may give it you"* (John 15:16).

We are living in this living truth.

We are taking advantage of its mighty possibilities, and we are daring to pray; we are daring to face the hosts of darkness with a consciousness that our prayers will be answered, and that the forces of darkness are beaten and defeated.

We no longer hold them as doctrines; they are a part of us.

We live these words and they live in us.

John 15:7 declares, *"If ye abide in me, and my words abide in you, ye shall ask what ye will, and it shall be done unto you."* The Father will bring those things to pass Himself.

You understand you didn't choose Him, but He chose you, and He told you to go and bear fruit.

That will be Word fruit; prayer fruit.

We have reached the place where we need to change the minds of men and women around us.

There is a spiritual sense of defeat in the hearts of the great masses in the church.

This has been brought about by the liquor traffic, by the open saloons, by the girls sitting at the bar.

Prostitution and delinquency have run riot with it.

The rebellion of the teenage youth against parental instruction and their absence from the church has broken like a running sore in the heart of the nation.

But has God gone out of business? Has He lost His ability?

Look at the heathen world the little church faced.

Look at the educational skepticism in the Jewish nation.

Look at the whole black picture of the Roman Empire.

The church sent out uneducated, untrained men to face that awful condition and carve new nations out of it. They won, and we can win.

We must check off the world's mental influence.

We must take our place and shout aloud, "We are what He says we are."

We can do what He says we can do.

We are linked with God by His nature. There is a human-divine union between the eternal Father and the believer. Our spirits have the creative energy and ability that is in the Father's Spirit.

We are meeting conditions as conquerors.

His Word in our lips can defeat any force or element that comes against us.

By His all-powerful name, we go against these problems and conquer them.

I can hear Him whisper, "Lo, I am with you; go ahead, I will see you through. I will be with you."

Once again, I hear that song of triumph of the ages: *"Fear thou not; for I am with thee: be not dismayed; for I am thy God"* (Isaiah 41:10).

"The God who opened the Red Sea, who destroyed the power of the flames when those three Hebrew boys were thrown into the fiery furnace is with you.

"I am the God of all ages.

"Lo, I am with you: all My forces are for you, and you are a victor in the face of all your enemies."

19

THE END OF CONDEMNATION

The title to this chapter would likely have confused some of us a few years ago, because all we had ever heard was condemnation.

Most of our great evangelists have been preachers of condemnation, preachers of judgment.

Few of them have ever revealed to us what we were in Christ. They have magnified sin above redemption.

Romans 8:1 has been an almost unknown Scripture: "*There is therefore now no condemnation to them which are in Christ Jesus.*"

If we had known that we could stand before the Father just as freely as Adam did in the garden, as Jesus did in His earth walk, it would have made life a great deal different.

This struggle after faith was because of a sense of unworthiness on our part.

We have had the sense of unrighteousness built into us by our teachers. We have not known what redemption means to the believer.

Second Corinthians 5:17–18 contains the story of the new creation and of man's standing before the Father:

> *Therefore if any man be in Christ, he is a new creature* [a new species]: *old things are passed away; behold, all things are become new. And all things are of God, who hath reconciled us to himself by Jesus Christ, and hath given to us the ministry of reconciliation.*

The old things of condemnation, the old things of sin and weakness, of failure, of doubt and fear are passed away, and there has come into us a new creation without condemnation, without fear.

We have become instantaneously a child of God and we are reconciled to Him.

There is no condemnation, there is no fear, there is no sense of sin or of unworthiness.

Like a child in its mother's bosom, we are perfectly restful and contented.

Not only that, but Christ:

> *Hath given to us the ministry of reconciliation; to wit, that God was in Christ, reconciling the world unto himself, not imputing their trespasses unto them; and hath committed unto us the word of reconciliation.*
> (2 Corinthians 5:18–19)

We have followed in the path of our forefathers who had developed in themselves a sense of unworthiness and sin, so that whenever they prayed they had to ask for forgiveness and cry for mercy.

They acted as though they had never been born again, as though sin had never been put away, and that the Father looked upon them with suspicion and doubt.

But did you notice verse 19? He is not even reckoning the sinners their sins, because He laid their sins on Christ.

Why should he reckon unto us, His own sons and daughters in Christ, a sin-consciousness?

He has not.

We have built it into ourselves through our ignorance.

Our sins have been wiped out as though they had never been.

That old wicked self has been put away and a new self has taken its place.

We are new creations.

Then, in 2 Corinthians 5:21, he says these marvelous words: "*For he hath made him to be sin for us, who knew no sin; that we might be made the righteousness of God in him.*"

And the next verse, did you notice it? "*We then, as workers together with him, beseech you also that ye receive not the grace of God in vain*" (2 Corinthians 6:1).

You couldn't work together with Him unless you were righteous, unless you were in fellowship with Him.

He has made you by the new birth, the very righteousness of God in Christ.

The sin problem is settled for the believer.

Now it is the problem of my entering into my inheritance.

You see, I shared with Him in His death.

I shared with Him in His suffering.

I shared with Him when He was made righteous.

I shared with Him when He was made alive.

I shared with Him when He met the adversary in the dark regions and conquered him.

I shared with Him when he arose from the dead.

I shared with Him in the mind of justice when He sat down at the right hand of the Majesty on high.

I am seated there according to His own Word.

I am free from condemnation.

I am free from the guilt of my old conduct and my union with Satan.

I turn to Romans 8:31 and I read what He inspired Paul to write for me: *"What shall we then say to these things? If God be for us, who can be against us?"*

That settles it. I can hear Him whisper, *"He that spared not his own Son, but delivered him up for us all, how shall he not with him also freely give us all things?"* (verse 32).

And then He says these marvelous words:

> *Who shall lay any thing to the charge of God's elect? It is God that justifieth. Who is he that condemneth? It is Christ that died, yea rather, that is risen again, who is even at the right hand of God, who also maketh intercession for us.* (Romans 8:33–34)

Then He asks this burning question: *"Who shall separate us from the love of Christ? shall tribulation, or distress, or persecution, or famine, or nakedness, or peril, or sword?"* (verse 35).

None of these things can bring the believer under condemnation. (See Romans 8:37–39.)

I wonder if you have read Ephesians 1:5–6 carefully:

> *Having predestinated us unto the adoption of children by Jesus Christ to himself, according to the good pleasure of his will, to the praise of the glory of his grace, wherein he hath made us accepted in the beloved.*

Where are you? You are in the beloved.

That means that you are beloved, that you are a part of the beloved.

You are identified with Him; you are one with Him.

In verse 7, it says, "*We have redemption through his blood.*" We received "*redemption through his blood, the forgiveness of sins, according to the riches of his grace; wherein he hath abounded toward us in all wisdom and prudence*" (verses 7–8).

There is no place for condemnation.

The only problem is this: have we learned how to walk in fellowship with Him?

Have we learned how to maintain our fellowship?

This law is laid down in the Pauline revelation and in John's wonderful epistles.

We must walk in love as Jesus walked in love.

But you ask, "How can I do it?"

You have received the love nature of the Father, haven't you? You have become a partaker of the divine nature. That is love. "God is love."

Then learn to let that love nature dominate you.

Paul said he kept his body under. He meant he kept his senses from dominating him.

As far as the believer is concerned, selfishness emanates from the senses.

Then if you keep the senses in subjection, give love the right of way, you will walk in fellowship with Him.

> *That which we have seen and heard declare we unto you, that ye also may have fellowship with us: and truly our fellowship is with the Father, and*

with his Son Jesus Christ. And these things write we unto you, that your joy may be full. This then is the message which we have heard of him, and declare unto you, that God is light, and in him is no darkness at all. If we say that we have fellowship with him, and walk in darkness, we lie, and do not the truth. (1 John 1:3–6)

What does that mean? If I step out of love, I step out of light into darkness. When I step into darkness, I know not where I am going.

First John 2:10–11 tells us:

He that loveth his brother abideth in the light, and there is none occasion of stumbling in him. But he that hateth his brother is in darkness, and walketh in darkness, and knoweth not whither he goeth, because that darkness hath blinded his eyes.

If we break fellowship, 1 John 1:9 tells us how to have it restored: *"If we confess our sins* [things we have done that brought us into darkness], *he is faithful and just to forgive us our sins, and to cleanse us from all unrighteousness."*

Now you can see that as far as you are concerned as a new creation, you have reached the end of condemnation.

It is not necessary to live in it another day.

The Son has made you free.

Now live and walk in that freedom.

20

WALKING AS MERE MEN

One of the saddest facts that we have to face today is that the sons of God, men with God in them, men with the very nature of God, are walking as mere men of the world.

> *And I, brethren, could not speak unto you as unto spiritual, but as unto carnal, even as unto babes in Christ. I have fed you with milk, and not with meat: for hitherto ye were not able to bear it, neither yet now are ye able. For ye are yet carnal: for whereas there is among you envying, and strife, and divisions, are ye not carnal, and walk as men? For while one saith, I am of Paul; and another, I am of Apollos; are ye not carnal?* (1 Corinthians 3:1–4)

Paul found it impossible to write about the deeply spiritual aspect of Christ's substitution.

He found it impossible to write to them about the new creation because they lived in the realm of the senses.

They had never developed their recreated spirit.

You see, the believer, when born into the family, has a measure of faith, has a measure of love; the love of God is shed abroad in his heart by the Holy Spirit.

But unless he grows in grace and in the knowledge of the Lord Jesus Christ, unless he studies to show himself approved unto the Father, he remains unspiritual.

His spirit is never cultivated, never developed.

You can develop your spirit as you can develop your mind, as you can develop your physical muscles.

The average believer has never developed his spirit. Consequently his faith is weak, his love is weak, and his knowledge is often mixed with error.

You must remember that love does not come from the reasoning faculties; neither does faith.

Faith and love are both born in the recreated human spirit. The reason Jesus said, *"Man shall not live by bread alone, but by every word that proceedeth out of the mouth of God"* (Matthew 4:4) was not to cultivate man's intellectual and reasoning faculties, but to cultivate his spirit.

In Ephesians 1:17–18, Paul had prayed that *"the Father of glory, may give unto you the spirit of wisdom and revelation in the knowledge of him: the eyes of your understanding being enlightened."*

The heart is called, in Romans 7:22, *"the inward man."*

In 1 Peter 3:4, it is *"the hidden man of the heart."*

You see, man is a spirit being and the part of him that is spiritually dead is his spirit.

After he is recreated, then his spirit must be educated, trained, and developed.

As the spirit grows strong and vigorous in the Word, faith becomes strong and love becomes like the Master's love.

As long as we walk in the senses and follow the inclinations of the senses, the spirit is not developed and we are walking as mere men.

We walk as though we had never received eternal life.

The believer has limitless possibilities in this divine life.

Ephesians 1:3 gives us a picture of the developed recreated spirit. It says, *"Jesus Christ, who hath blessed us with all spiritual blessings in heavenly places in Christ."*

If we have those blessings, then the unsearchable riches of Christ really belong to us.

In Ephesians 3:8, Paul says he preached unto the gentiles *"the unsearchable riches of Christ."* In verse 12, he says, *"In whom we have boldness and access with confidence by the faith of him."*

There is no limit to this new life.

He says, in Ephesians 4:7, *"Unto every one of us is given grace according to the measure of the gift of Christ."*

And in Ephesians 4:1, he says, *"I therefore, the prisoner of the Lord, beseech you that ye walk worthy of the vocation wherewith ye are called."* We are to walk in love; to walk in the fullness of His fellowship.

We are to grow in grace and in the knowledge of it *"till we all come in the unity of the faith, and of the knowledge of the Son of God, unto a perfect man, unto the measure of the stature of the fulness of Christ: that we henceforth be no more children, tossed to and fro, and carried about with every wind of doctrine"* (verses 13–14).

He wants us to grow up into the full stature of the Jesus life.

It belongs to us.

You can understand that you have become a partaker of the very nature of the Father, and that everything Jesus purchased for you in His redemptive work is available to you.

There is no ground for a man to be weak.

There is no ground for a man to be always talking about his lack of faith and lack of this or that, for *"of his fulness have all we received, and grace for grace"* (John 1:16).

In the mind of the Father, you are complete in Him, who is the Head of all principality and power. You are complete in His completeness.

I shall never forget the thrill that Ephesians 1:22–23 gave to my heart:

> *And hath put all things under his feet, and gave him to be the head over all things to the church, which is his body, the fulness of him that filleth all in all.*

We are the body; we are the feet of Christ.

We are the part of the body that is running errands for the Master, and He has put all the forces of darkness under our feet.

One of us could chase a thousand, and two could put ten thousand to flight.

The ability of God that is within us is utterly limitless.

What are we going to do with a Scripture like this?:

> *And such trust have we through Christ to God-ward: not that we are sufficient of ourselves to think any thing as of ourselves; but our sufficiency is of God; who also hath made us able ministers of the new testament.*
>
> (2 Corinthians 3:4–6)

The sixth verse doesn't mean preachers only; that means every one of us.

We have His sufficiency; we have His ability.

How it staggers one when we get the right translation of Luke 24:49: *"But tarry ye in the city of Jerusalem, until ye be endued with power from on high."*

This was Jesus's message to the disciples before He ascended. He wanted them clothed with power. The correct word for power means "ability."

Now He says, in effect, "I want you clothed with ability from on high—the Father's ability."

You can hear Him say, "Now you will be able to understand the messages that I have given to you.

"You will have ability to know what the new creation means. You will have ability to enter into the fullness of this divine life. You will have ability to be My witness, to heal the sick, to cast out demons, and to use My name against all the forces of darkness."

You will know what Mark 16:17 means when He says, *"In my name shall they cast out devils."*

Also, John 16:23: *"Whatsoever ye shall ask the Father in my name, he will give it you."*

You see, until our hearts take in these truths, we are going to walk "as mere men."

You remember Samson, that mighty covenant man.

There never was a man like him, and yet when he ignored his covenant rights, the Philistines captured him, put out his eyes, and made a slave of him.

The eyes of the heart of most believers are like Samson's eyes. They have lost their ability to enjoy the fullness of their rights in Christ.

John 10:29–30 has never meant anything to many of them. Let me read it to you:

> *My Father, which gave them me, is greater than all; and no man is able to pluck them out of my Father's hand. I and my Father are one.*

They have never learned to say:

> My Father is greater than all;
> My Father is greater than all.

'Mid life's bitter tears,
Temptations and fears,
My Father is greater than all.

They have never realized they had a Father. He has only been God to them.

They have never whispered, "My Father, I love you."

The Father has never been able to make Himself real to their hearts because sense knowledge has so completely governed them. He is a Father God and He loves you.

Hebrews 7:25 has never been in the background of their consciousness as a great living force:

> *Wherefore he is able also to save them to the uttermost that come unto God by him, seeing he ever liveth to make intercession for them.*

The harder circumstances may press upon you, the more fully does He uphold you.

His intercession for you means there isn't power enough in the world to take you captive if you are in fellowship with the Father. He ever lives for your benefit. He loves you.

He gave Himself up for you. He is longing for you to respond to that love.

He is longing for you to look up and whisper, "Jesus, I love you."

REDEMPTION-MINDED

The Father would like you to become redemption-minded. I do not see how you can act as a *mere man* any longer. Don't cause His heart to ache over you because you have become circumstance-minded, sickness-minded, failure-minded.

He never created a failure; He made us for victory. You have the use of Jesus's name. Use it. It gives you access into the Father's very presence. It gives you victory over disease, over circumstances, over the forces of darkness.

You have the same great, mighty Holy Spirit that Jesus and the apostles had in their walk.

Jesus is your wisdom.

He is today the very strength of your life.

You are now blessed with every spiritual blessing.

You don't need to cry for faith, nor pray for strength.

You have it all; it belongs to you.

You have been blessed with everything that redemption could give.

I would that you might become so conscious of the presence of the Master, that *"Lo, I am with you always"* (Matthew 28:20) will become just an unconscious fact, so that no matter what happens, you know He is there.

"Forgetteth what manner of man he was" (James 1:24). Here, James is describing the "doer of the Word." He is more than a teacher of the Word.

He is more than an admirer of the Word.

He is more than a student of the Word.

The Word is living in him.

He is living so that Word is a part of his very being.

He walks in love. His whole conduct is governed by the new law of the new creation.

He doesn't permit his lips to sin against his spirit.

He has learned to weigh carefully the value of words.

So James 1:22–25 has become a very serious section of the Word to him: *"But be ye doers of the word, and not hearers only, deceiving your own selves"* (verse 22).

How many good people have deluded themselves?

They believe in the teachings of their church.

They don't study the Word much.

They are very careful about what man says and often deny themselves much and put themselves under bondage because of man's word.

James is bringing us face to face with the Father Himself. He says, *"Be ye doers of the word,"* and so I study the Word to find out what it says and then I do it.

The love law was given to govern our conduct toward each other, and so I study it diligently.

> *For if any be a hearer of the word, and not a doer, he is like unto a man beholding his natural face in a glass: for he beholdeth himself, and goeth*

> *his way, and straightway forgetteth what manner of man he was.*
> (James 1:23–24)

Let us see what manner of men we are, what the Father says about us.

We should take account of stock and find what we are in the mind of the Father.

"For as many as are led by the Spirit of God, they are the sons of God" (Romans 8:14), or they become sons of God.

If a man is willing to be led by the Spirit, he will be led into sonship.

> *For ye have not received the spirit of bondage again to fear; but ye have received the Spirit of adoption, whereby we cry, Abba, Father. The Spirit itself beareth witness with our spirit, that we are the children of God: and if children, if children, then heirs; heirs of God, and joint-heirs with Christ.* (Romans 8:15–17)

That is what the Father says we are.

We are in His family; a part of the body of Christ.

We are what the Spirit calls the new creation man.

We have passed out of the realm of satanic relationship into the family of the Father God, *"who hath delivered us from the power of darkness, and hath translated us into the kingdom of his dear Son"* (Colossians 1:13).

If that is true (and it *is* true), then we are a new type, a new class of men.

We should study the Word that we might know what the Father expects of us and what the world has a right to expect from us. We are a supernatural people.

We have the ability of God, the wisdom of God. We have the mind of God in His Word.

We should never forget *"what manner of persons"* we are. (See 2 Peter 3:11.)

No matter what the crisis may be; no matter what testings may come to us, we do not forget what manner of men we are.

You see, we belong to a new order. We belong to the class of people that have a legal right to enter the Father's presence anytime, anywhere. Not only have we a right, but we have a standing invitation to come boldly to the throne of grace.

We are the righteous men.

We have been made righteous by the nature of the Father that was imparted to us when we became new creations. That righteousness of God makes us masters of every force outside of God.

We are in league with heaven and have the backing of heaven. We can hear Paul saying, *"If God be for us, who can be against us?"* (Romans 8:31). He *is* for us; He is on our side.

In Romans 8:31–39, Paul goes over all of the forces that may antagonize us, that may come against us, and he shows us that we can be masters of everything that Satan can possibly bring against us. There isn't a weapon that Satan has, but what we are proof against it.

You see, our combat is not with flesh and blood; it is not with sense knowledge things; it is with spiritual forces, and in all these things, we are more than masters.

They cannot separate us from the love of God that is in Christ Jesus. If they could separate us from His love, they could defeat us; but He loves us and it causes Him to succor us, care for us, watch over us, shield us.

We must not forget for one moment that the great mighty Spirit who raised Jesus from the dead, the Person who gave to the world its vegetation, that Mighty One, is living in us, for it is God who is at work within us willing and working His own good pleasure.

If one accustomed themselves to trust in Him as we trust in the money that is in our pocketbook, as we trust in our car when it is filled with oil and gas, what mighty men and women would walk the earth.

The Father would be so real to them; the name would be so real; there would be a consciousness of the fact that Jesus said, *"All power is given unto me in heaven and in earth"* (Matthew 28:18).

He said, in effect, "Go, as my representatives. I will give you a legal right to the use of My name. In My name, you are the master of demons, of diseases, of the laws of nature that would in any wise hinder you from doing My will."

You see, we are empowered representatives of the heavenly kingdom.

We should never forget what manner of men we are.

We send our ambassador to England.

He must never forget that he is not a *mere man* now. He is a representative of our government. Our government is behind him. He is saying the words that our government has instructed him to say. He is not acting on his own initiative. He is not a mere man. He is an ambassador on the behalf of our government.

I must not forget what manner of man *I* am.

I am an ambassador on behalf of Christ. As an ambassador, I have the backing of the supreme court of the universe. I have the backing of my Father God, of Jesus, of the great, mighty Holy Spirit, and all the angels of God.

You see, I can't be a failure unless I forget what manner of man I am.

I don't know whether you ever noticed 1 Corinthians 3:1: *"And I, brethren, could not speak unto you as unto spiritual, but as unto carnal, even as unto babes in Christ."*

It is just as though Paul said, "I wish I could speak to you as to men who realized who they were, what they were, and what they could do, but I cannot because you are living in the sense realm."

You have no confidence in the great spiritual realities to which you are united.

You are living just like babes.

You don't seem to grasp the reality of your unity with deity.

Paul cries, *"I have fed you with milk, and not with meat: for hitherto ye were not able to bear it, neither yet now are ye able"* (1 Corinthians 3:2).

What a pathetic confession.

What a humiliating confession, when by reason of time they ought to take advantage of what they were in Christ but they haven't done it.

They have been content to listen to the voices of men, to read the literature of men, but have ignored the literature of heaven, the voice of Him who raised Jesus from the dead.

The next verse throws light on it:

> *For ye are yet carnal: for whereas there is among you envying, and strife, and divisions, are ye not carnal, and walk as men?* (1 Corinthians 3:3)

Or, as another puts it, "Your conduct is the conduct of mere men when you might walk as the sons of God."

You might be masters instead of slaves.

Every one of you could be a leader. Instead of that, you are being led, but not led by God. You are led by sense knowledge; consequently, your whole life is disfigured.

You have lost the consciousness of being what you are, and when sickness comes, you are in a quandary; you don't know what to do; your heart is filled with fear.

You have never taken your place in Christ.

You have never taken advantage of your rights and privileges in Christ.

You have never asserted your rights as a son in the family.

You have unconsciously relegated yourself to the place of a servant.

You are depending upon other people, and when the problem of faith comes, you talk about your unbelief and your lack.

You are a spiritual hitchhiker. You have the ability of God, but you do not use it.

You have this living Word of God.

You are eligible to take advantage of all the privileges that belong to the sons of God, and yet you are living as a mere man. You have forgotten what manner of man you are.

Hebrews 5:12–14 describes this type of believer:

> *For when for the time ye ought to be teachers, ye have need that one teach you again which be the first principles of the oracles of God; and are become such as have need of milk, and not of strong meat.* (verse 12)

This is plain speaking. It is the heart of the Father reaching out to his careless, thoughtless children, and He says, "You had plenty of time.

"You could have taken courses in the study of the Word.

"It wouldn't be necessary for you to go away to a Bible school; you could have correspondence courses.

"You could attend Bible classes very likely in your own church or in your own community.

"You have even forgotten the teachings, the first principles of the new creation.

"You have forgotten that you have passed out of death unto life. You have forgotten that you are a new creation created in Christ Jesus.

"You have forgotten that you are tied up with God, that you are a partaker of the divine nature.

"You have forgotten that you have within you the very life of God Himself, and you have at your side the great Paraclete, the Comforter, the Holy Spirit."

He is ready to come in and take possession of you and to be your Teacher and your Guide and your Comforter.

It has been easier for you to read about the Bible than it has to become a student of the Bible and to study to show yourself approved unto God in this living Word.

You have reached a place where you have need of milk. You need baby treatment and baby care. That is an unhappy thing.

And then He says, *"For every one that useth milk is unskilful in the word of righteousness: for he is a babe"* (Hebrews 5:13).

You have never exercised yourself to discern between good and evil. That doesn't mean between sin and righteousness, but between the forces of God and the evil forces that may come disguised to you.

You have lived on the borderland between right and wrong.

You have been asking yourself, *Is it wrong to do this? Should I do that?* These are questions of the babe in Christ.

There has been no growth, no development, and if anyone should ask, "Are you a believer?" it is likely you would answer, "Well, I am trying to be."

You see, there isn't any such thing as a believer trying to be a believer, any more than for a boy to try to be a boy. He is a boy. He may decide to be a better boy.

If you say you are trying to be a believer, then you are not a believer. You are outside.

You have never received eternal life.

Your spirit has never been recreated.

So it is vitally important that you study the Word to find what manner of man you are, how the Father looks upon you, and what He expects from you.

21

BELIEVING IN HIS SUBSTITUTION

When we use the fact of His substitution as we use a bridge, or an elevator, then the Word becomes a reality.

We never think of faith when we take an elevator or train. We simply use them.

If we were new creation-conscious, as conscious of the fact that we are a new creation and have the nature and life of the Father in us, as we are of the things of the senses, then we would walk in the realm of victory.

You cannot be God-inside-conscious without being a victor. Then 1 John 4:4 becomes a reality. Notice it now: *"Ye are of God, little children."* Let that soak into your spirit consciousness.

Say over and over again: "I am of God; I am born from above; I am born of God; I am a new creation, created in Christ Jesus. I am a master of everything connected with the old creation. Satan has no dominion over the new creation. He has no dominion over me. That hidden man of the heart, my spirit, the real me, is a new creation. The old things have passed away."

The old man with its weaknesses, its failings, its doubts, its fears, and its sense of servitude to circumstances is all gone, and the new spirit, the new man in Christ, is now a master where the other was a slave.

This new creation is redeemed out of the hands of its enemies. I can hear Paul whisper, "In whom I have my redemption." (See Ephesians 1:7.)

You see that truth is becoming a reality.

Now I can understand the next sentence in 1 John 4:4: *"Because greater is he that is in you, than he that is in the world."*

I have the life and nature of God in me. That makes me a new creation.

I have invited the One whom raised Jesus from the dead, to make His home in me, and He is there.

When I start to study the Word, I always call His attention to it.

When I am to dictate or to preach, I say, "Holy Spirit, here is Your opportunity. Now speak through me; think through me; live big in me. Unveil Jesus through these lips."

You see, that great substitution is ours. He is ours. His ability is ours.

All that He did is ours, just as our hands and feet are ours.

We look at ourselves now as a new creation. We have been taken out of the realm of death as truly as Jesus was when He was raised from the dead. His body was taken out of the realm of physical death; our spirits have been taken out of the realm of spiritual death.

In the mind of justice, we were raised together with Him. In reality, when we became new creations, we passed out of death into life. We left the realm of spiritual death. We left the dominion of death, the family of Satan.

John 5:24 has become a reality:

> *He that heareth my word, and believeth on him that sent me, hath everlasting life, and shall not come into condemnation; but is passed from death unto life.*

You see, we were born out of spiritual death into the realm of spiritual life. We passed out from Satan's authority and dominion, and have been translated into the kingdom of the Son of His love, in whom we have our redemption, the remission of our trespasses. It is a redemption that is according to the riches of His grace, His love, His ability.

We have actually passed into the very family of God. God is now our Father. We are His very children. When that thing happened, we were looked upon as the sons of God in liberty. For Christ had made us free. Jesus had become our righteousness. By the new birth, we became partakers of the divine nature; we became the righteousness of God in Christ.

That means that we can stand in the Father's presence with the same liberty and freedom that Jesus had. Before that time, we had a sin-consciousness developed in us by spiritual death. Now we have eternal life-consciousness.

We are the sons and daughters of God. We have been growing in righteousness-consciousness and we are beginning to take our place and act the part of sons and daughters. As we act on the Word, we have experience in righteousness.

How vitally necessary it is that we become experienced in the Word which has taught us about righteousness and taking our place in righteousness.

I wonder if you understand what I mean?

You see, when Jesus began His public ministry, He was really the righteousness of God unveiled.

Jesus had no sense of sin, no sense of inferiority.

He was a super-man. He was a Master of demons.

He was a Master of disease and sickness.

He was a Master of want and of hunger.

Well, when you and I came to Christ, He became our righteousness, and then, by the new creation, we became the righteousness of God in Him.

We were not taught about our righteousness.

We were not taught about our freedom in Christ.

We didn't know we were the masters of demons in the name of Jesus.

We didn't know we had authority over all the authority of the enemy.

We didn't know that we could stand in the Father's presence just as freely as Jesus did, with no sense of inferiority, no sense of unworthiness, that we were the very sons and daughters of God.

Jesus wasn't afraid of the adversary.

That is one of the things that startled me in those early days of my study. Jesus could walk into the presence of the devil without any fear. He wasn't afraid when He stood beside the tomb of dead Lazarus, but you know, I was frightened for Him.

In my imagination, I stood there. It was such a vivid scene, and I watched the Master as the crowd gathered, and I heard Him say, with a loud voice, "Roll the stone away!"

Then my heart whispered softly, "Master, you had better go slowly, now; he has been in the tomb four days; he has been dead nearly a week. Martha has told you that *"by this time he stinketh"* (John 11:39)—but He interrupted my thinking and cried again, *"Lazarus, come forth"* (verse 43). Martha tried to intercept but it was too late. Jesus said, *"Loose him, and let him go"* (verse 44), and out of the sepulcher came the man whose body was decaying.

Why was Jesus so fearless? Because He was the righteousness of God. That is all.

He had no sense of sin. He had no sense of condemnation.

If the believer knew that he was the righteousness of God as Jesus knew He was, he would use the name of Jesus with a fearlessness that would startle hell and bless humanity.

Jesus said after He arose from the dead, "All authority has been given unto Me in heaven and in earth; I am the head of the church. (See Matthew 28:18.)

"Now I give you the legal right to use My name, and all this authority is in that name. *'In my name shall they cast out devils'* (Mark 16:17).

"You see, I have given you authority over Satan. I have given you dominion over all the work that he has done.

"I came," said the Master, "to *'destroy the works of the devil'* (1 John 3:8).

"I am leaving it in your hands now."

If a believer becomes righteousness-conscious, Son-conscious, Satan will be afraid of him.

Satan knows that as soon as the church becomes conscious of the reality of redemption, that moment his reign over the earth is interrupted.

Jesus would never have given us the invitation in Hebrews 4:16, to *"come boldly unto the throne of grace,"* unless He had expected us to take our place and to act the part that belonged to us.

You see, we are what He says we are.

We should learn to use that name as we use our own, to use prayer as we use an automobile.

As soon as we think through on these great problems they will become ours.

The trouble is, they have been taught us as doctrines.

They have been a part of a creed that we have believed, and most of us have joined a creedal church.

That creed has locked Jesus up so that He is helpless, and has locked us into a world conformity that makes us useless.

The thing He is trying to do these days is to make us free, to loose us from the bondage that has held us these years.

The Pauline revelation is not a set of doctrines. It is just the Father speaking to us through Paul, unveiling what belongs to us in Christ.

22

THE REST OF REDEMPTION

Few of us know the reality of the rest mentioned in Hebrews 4:1: "*Let us therefore fear, lest, a promise being left us of entering into his rest, any of you should seem to come short of it.*"

When Jesus had finished His work, He sat down at "*the right hand of the Majesty on high*" (Hebrews 1:3).

> *Now of the things which we have spoken this is the sum: We have such an high priest, who is set on the right hand of the throne of the Majesty in the heavens.* (Hebrews 8:1)

> *But this man, after he had offered one sacrifice for sins for ever, sat down on the right hand of God.* (Hebrews 10:12)

He had finished His work.

His work was wrought for us, not for Himself.

He entered into His rest.

And in Hebrews 4:3: "*For we which have believed do enter into rest.*"

And in Hebrews 4:11, "*Let us labour therefore to enter into that rest, lest any man fall after the same example of unbelief* [or 'unpersuadableness']."

That is the rest of faith. It is the end of worry and struggle.

You no longer seek for faith or power.

You have become one with Him.

You have come to appreciate the work that He did for you, and the work that the Holy Spirit, through the Word, has done in you.

You have come to know that you are what He says you are in Him.

You know that you are a new creation.

You know that you have passed from death unto life.

You know that you have the very life and nature of the Father in you.

You know that, as He is now at the right hand of the Father, you are down here on earth.

You know that you are a part of the body, a member of it.

You know that you were raised together with Him.

You know that no matter what may come to your life, you are more than a conqueror.

These are facts that you know.

You now enter into His rest, the rest that He purchased for you.

You have reached the end of the worry route.

You are now so completely identified with Him, so utterly one with Him, that the Father looks upon you as He looks upon His first begotten, and because of that, peace that *"passeth all understanding"* fills your very being.

You remember Philippians 4:6–7. We ought to become thorough masters of that Scripture, and that Scripture should become our master. Notice what it says: *"Be careful* [anxious] *for nothing."* You see, you are in a place of rest. *"But in every thing by prayer and supplication with thanksgiving let your requests be made known unto God."*

Why are you full of thanksgiving? Why is your heart filled with peace and rest? Why are you so joyful? Because you know that whatsoever you ask the Father in Jesus's name He will give it you. Even to Israel, He said, *"Call unto me, and I will answer thee, and show thee great and mighty things, which thou knowest not"* (Jeremiah 33:3).

You are not under the law; you are a Son. You are an heir; you are a member of the body, and He has invited you to come boldly to the throne of grace, and you have accustomed yourself to standing in His presence.

So now you are not anxious; you have believed.

I know the child is sick. The doctors have given him up to die, but you prayed for him.

Your heart is filled with thanksgiving and you are praising the Father.

Your relatives and loved ones can't understand you.

They whisper that mother is beside herself.

You are not; you are beside the Master. The *"Lo, I am with you always"* (Matthew 28:20) is a reality to you.

You have entered into your rest.

You know that no word from God is void of fulfillment, and that in every word there is ability to make good.

You have prayed and you thank Him for the answer. The answer is just as sure as the sun is to shine in the morning. You have made your requests known unto the Father and now the miracle happens. The peace of God which passeth all understanding has taken possession of your heart and your thoughts in Christ Jesus. You haven't a thought of worry or care. You haven't a burden.

First Peter 5:7 illustrates this perfectly: *"Casting all your care upon him; for he careth for you."*

You are not interested in the roaring of the adversary nor the questioning of your friends or the doubts of other people. You know that your expectation is from Him. You rest on His Word. You have entered into His rest.

When Jesus prayed, that settled it. There was no more talk about it. The answer had to come.

"Whatsoever ye shall ask the Father in my name, he will give it you" (John 16:23).

That settles it.

You asked, didn't you? Well, the answer is on the way. You are careful for nothing now.

You know that you and the Father are working together. They can't fence you in with circumstances.

> *Not that I speak in respect of want: for I have learned, in whatsoever state I am, therewith to be content. I know both how to be abased, and I know how to abound: every where and in all things I am instructed both to be full and to be hungry, both to abound and to suffer need. I can do all things through Christ which strengtheneth me.* (Philippians 4:11–13)

You see, you have come into the place where circumstances no longer terrify, where the word of man is but the word of man to you.

The word of a doctor is only the word based on sense evidence.

The Word of God liveth and abideth.

The Word of God is speaking to you.

To you, the Word and God are one.

You haven't learned to separate Jesus from His words.

"The words that I speak unto you, they are spirit, and they are life" (John 6:63). That is, they deal with your spirit nature and they give life and victory and peace and rest to your soul.

You are resting in the Word.

Once you rested in the word of man, but you found that there was no rest for you.

Now you are resting in His rest.

You see, it is the end of the fear of Satan for he has been defeated.

It is the end of the fear of sickness, for by His stripes you are healed.

It is the end of lack; you fear it no longer. *"Your heavenly Father knoweth that ye have need of all these things"* (Matthew 6:32).

Want and fear have stopped being as far as you are concerned. You never think of your weakness, for Jesus has become your ability.

The greater One is living in you.

It is the end of ignorance. You have studied the Pauline revelation until it has become a part of your knowledge, of your very life.

Colossians 1:9 should be a part of your life. It says:

> *We also, since the day we heard it, do not cease to pray for you, and to desire that ye might be filled with the knowledge of his will in all wisdom and spiritual understanding.*

Can you see the breadth of that?

You know His will. You are filled with exact *"knowledge"* of the Father's will in all your life.

You are filled with wisdom to use the knowledge that you have gained in your study of the Word. That wisdom has enabled you to walk worthy unto the Lord in all pleasing.

You have reached the place where you are bearing fruit in every good work.

It is the fruit of righteousness. You have become skilled in the Word of righteousness.

You know your rights and privileges before the throne, and you have faith's fearlessness to enter the Father's presence—anytime, anywhere—and make your requests known.

You lounge around in the throne room visiting with the Father and Jesus.

You are more familiar with your Father and Jesus than you are with those with whom you have associated for years.

I hear your heart whisper, "I know Him in whom I have believed." Now you walk worthy of the Lord and you are pleasing Him. You have become a Father-pleaser, as Jesus was. *"I do always those things that please* [the Father]," saith the Master (John 8:29).

You are increasing, as you study the Word, in that exact knowledge of the Father.

It is a wonderful life you are living because the Wonder One is in you.

The Wonder One is your Teacher.

But hear Colossians 1:11: *"Strengthened with all might, according to his glorious power."*

This has given you steadfastness.

Where other people are breaking down and going to pieces, you are steadfast; you are immovable. You are always abounding in the work of the Lord.

You are strengthened for long-suffering.

People can't understand how you put up with things.

You whisper to them, "All things work together for good to me, because I am in His will (see Romans 8:28), and the very circumstances that rob you of your rest, increase my rest. The very opposition that destroyed your faith, builds mine; and you can't understand why I am filled with joy unspeakable and full of glory. He and I are laboring together. I am a partaker of His faith. I breathe in His very life."

There was a steadfastness and a quietness about Jesus that has stopped being a wonder to me.

It has become my very joy for I have entered into it, and I am increasing continually in this exact knowledge of my rights and privileges in Christ.

This is the reason that I am *"giving thanks unto the Father,"* who has given me the ability to enjoy my share of *"the inheritance of the saints in light."* (See Colossians 1:12.)

You see, I not only enjoy it but I am able to tell others and give them a hunger after it, and then I am able to show them the secret of entering into it.

You remember Colossians 2:2, don't you? *"That their hearts might be comforted, being knit together in love, and unto all riches of the full assurance of understanding."*

"The full assurance"—that is wonderful, isn't it?

That makes you think of verses 9–10: *"For in him dwelleth all the fulness of the Godhead bodily. And ye are complete in him."*

He made me that way. I couldn't do it.

He took me over and He built His fullness, His completeness into me.

Now I am rejoicing in *"the full assurance of understanding, to the acknowledgement of the mystery of God, and of the Father, and of Christ"* (verse 2).

Now hear this third verse: *"In whom are hid all the treasures of wisdom and knowledge."*

Now I am going to take you back to Proverbs 20:27: *"The spirit of man is the candle of the LORD, searching all the inward parts of the belly."*

All the treasures of wisdom and knowledge and love and grace are hidden treasure chambers of Christ. He lighted up my spirit as a lamp and I went down into the hidden treasure chambers of Christ, and I found the riches of His grace.

I became an explorer of the hidden things in Christ, and His light lighted the way into them.

Now I become a possessor of these riches. They are mine and I live in the fullness of my riches in Christ.

See, they belong to us. There is no place for poverty in Him.

The Father never made a weak Christian. He has no pleasure in our weakness.

Some of us have thought that all the trials that come to us are God-sent. They are not.

The Father doesn't need the devil to purify and beautify His own.

No, these trials and difficulties are all Satan-inspired, and God has given us ability to know this now, and so we are taking our place and rebuking the author of our troubles and commanding him to leave us alone.

We have found a strange, sweet quietness in the heart of love. You see, we have entered into our rest.

There is no "unpersuadableness" in our hearts.

No matter how big the thing, how difficult to human reasoning, how many times sense knowledge rejects it, I am persuaded by the very living Word that He is able to lead me into all the riches of the finished work of Christ, and because I know this, I have yielded my spirit to the lordship of love.

I have allowed the Word to dwell in me richly, and I have come to know the reality of these mighty truths of redemption.

23

"IT IS FINISHED"

Perhaps no one sentence from the lips of the Master has been more misunderstood than the one that He uttered on the cross: *"It is finished"* (John 19:30).

Most of us have believed that He meant He had finished His redemptive work, but that is not true.

His work as a substitute was just beginning and it was not consummated until His blood was accepted in the supreme court of the universe, and He had sat down at the right hand of the Majesty on high.

But you ask, *What did He mean then by "It is finished"?*

It meant that He had fulfilled the Abrahamic covenant, of which He, you remember, was a part.

He was born of Abraham's stock.

He was circumcised as a child and came into the Abrahamic covenant.

He had grown up under the laws that governed the Israelite people, who were children of the covenant.

There are only two real covenants in the Word—the old covenant and the new, the Abrahamic covenant and the new covenant in Christ.

God cut that first covenant with Abraham.

Why do we use the phrase "cut a covenant"? Because the Hebrew word means "to cut a covenant."

Nearly all covenants made between men as recorded in the Scripture and as observed among primitive peoples, were solemnized by blood-letting.

Henry Morton Stanley gives us graphic pictures of covenants that he cut with chieftains in the heart of Africa. When preliminaries had been finished,

Stanley's companion offered his wrist to the priest, who made an incision. The son of the chief that was to be his representative, offered his wrist and blood was let. Then the two wrists were rubbed together and each one tasted the blood of the other. Now these two men became blood brothers. Stanley and that chieftain had become blood brothers by substitution.

In Africa, Stanley and David Livingstone both confessed that they had never known of a covenant solemnized like this to be broken. For a man to break it, sealed his own death warrant, for the tribe would not permit him to live and curse them.

So, the Abrahamic covenant was the most sacred covenant known to primitive peoples. Circumcision permitted them to come into the covenant, for when a child was circumcised, the priest would touch that blood to his tongue and that child became a child of the Abrahamic covenant.

When Israel had crossed the Red Sea and gone into the wilderness, God gave them a law—the Ten Commandments. It was the law of the covenant. He gave them a priesthood, because the law was broken and it meant death to them. So, with the priesthood came atonement—a covering for that broken law, for the Hebrew word translated atonement means "to cover." Really, it has no other significance.

Theologians have read all kinds of things into atonement, but it stands simply as a covering for Israel because they were spiritually dead. They have broken the law and it meant death to them if it were not covered.

So, when Jesus came, His first work was to fulfill that Abrahamic covenant and set it aside.

Next, the priesthood and the sacrifice and the law were fulfilled and set aside.

The book of Hebrews covers this ground very clearly.

Romans and Galatians also prove, beyond the shadow of a doubt, that Jesus fulfilled that first covenant, the law—the priesthood and the sacrifices—so that when He hung on the cross, He could say, *"It is finished."*

The work that was not finished until He sat down at the right hand of the Father, was His work as a substitute. He had to die for the sins under the first covenant, and He had to die for our sins, so His substitution points both ways—back to the inception of the Abrahamic covenant, on to the great white throne judgment.

In other chapters in this book, we have shown you how we were identified with Christ in His substitution, because He died as our substitute.

He suffered as our substitute.

Our iniquities and our diseases were laid upon Him.

He was made sin with our sin.

Theologians tell us that they were "reckoned to Him."

If they were only reckoned to Him, then redemption is only reckoned to us and we are not redeemed. If righteousness is only reckoned to us, then eternal life and the new creation are only reckoned to us.

In 1 Corinthians 15:3, it says He died for our sins:

> *For I delivered unto you first of all that which I also received, how that Christ died for our sins according to the scriptures.*

> *He hath made him to be sin for us, who knew no sin; that we might be made the righteousness of God in him.* (2 Corinthians 5:21)

> *But now the righteousness of God without the law is manifested, being witnessed by the law and the prophets; even the righteousness of God which is by faith of Jesus Christ unto all and upon all them that believe: for there is no difference: for all have sinned, and come short of the glory of God; being justified freely by his grace through the redemption that is in Christ Jesus: whom God hath set forth to be a propitiation through faith in his blood, to declare his righteousness for the remission of sins that are past, through the forbearance of God; to declare, I say, at this time his righteousness: that he might be just, and the justifier of him which believeth in Jesus.*
> (Romans 3:21–26)

This shows beyond the shadow of a doubt that Christ was actually our substitute, that He took our place, paid the penalty of the sins under the first covenant, and met the demands of justice for us so that the new birth could become a legal fact.

He not only had made our redemption and our righteousness a legal fact, but He made it possible for God to recreate us, take us into His family, honor us as sons and daughters on legal grounds.

When on the cross, Jesus said, *"It is finished,"* we begin to understand that He had no reference whatever of dealing with the sin problem, the redemption problem, and the putting to naught of Satan, as Paul tells us in Hebrews 2:14.

I want you to understand clearly that there are three phases of Christ's work connected with our redemption.

First, was His work that He wrought in His earth walk, dealing with the first covenant and everything that pertained to it.

Second, His substitutionary work that began when He was made sin on the cross and was consummated when He carried His blood into the heavenly Holy of Holies and it was accepted there for us.

And third, His ministry today at the right hand of the Majesty on high.

That ministry has to deal with the preservation and care of the church.

He is there as our great High Priest, as the surety of the covenant, as our Savior, as our Mediator, our Advocate, and our Lord.

24

JESUS AT THE RIGHT HAND OF THE FATHER

Several times, the Word tells us that Jesus sat down at the right hand of the Majesty on high.

Hebrews 1:3 is a good illustration:

> *Who being the brightness of his glory, and the express image of his person, and upholding all things by the word of his power, when he had by himself purged our sins, sat down on the right hand of the Majesty on high.*

Again, in Hebrews 8:1–2:

> *Now of the things which we have spoken this is the sum: We have such an high priest, who is set on the right hand of the throne of the Majesty in the heavens; a minister of the sanctuary, and of the true tabernacle, which the Lord pitched, and not man.*

There is another expression connected with His heavenly ministry that we ought to notice—this clause: "*He entered in once into the holy place, having obtained eternal redemption for us*" (Hebrews 9:12).

It was a "once and for all" ministry.

Hebrews 7:27 gives us the same thought: "*For this he did once, when he offered up himself.*"

These two expressions are connected with His heavenly ministry.

You remember there are two phases of Christ's ministry.

One is His substitutionary work from the cross until He arose from the dead.

In those three days and three nights, He settled the sin problem, conquered the adversary, made the new birth a possibility, and made righteousness available to every person who receives eternal life.

His work at the right hand of the Father is what we might call a manifold work.

We must learn to appreciate the value of His ministry now at the right hand of the Father on our behalf.

He unveiled it to me very clearly, that had Jesus stopped His work after He had done this great substitutionary ministry from the cross to His resurrection, had it ended there, no one could ever have been saved.

The next step in the drama had to be the carrying of His blood into the heavenly Holy of Holies and making the eternal redemption for us.

You remember in John 20:17, when Mary saw Him, she fell down at His feet and tried to grasp them. Jesus said to her, tenderly, "*Touch me not; for I am not yet ascended to my Father.*"

What did He mean? He arose as the Lord High Priest.

You remember in Matthew 28:5–6, the angel said to the women who came to the sepulcher, "*Fear not ye: for I know that ye seek Jesus, which was crucified. He is not here: for he is risen, as he said. Come, see the place where the Lord lay.*"

He died a Lamb, but He arose as the Lord. Lordship means absolute mastery and dominion.

Jesus died in weakness; He arose with all the authority and power and majesty of deity.

He had conquered the dark forces of Satan.

He had dealt with the sin problem and redeemed humanity.

He made eternal life a possibility and sonship a glory.

Now He says to Mary, "*Touch me not.*"

Why? He had not carried His blood into heaven yet and sealed the document of our redemption. The claims of justice had not been met.

JESUS, OUR HIGH PRIEST

Wherefore in all things it behoved him to be made like unto his brethren, that he might be a merciful and faithful high priest in things pertaining to God, to make reconciliation for the sins of the people. (Hebrews 2:17)

The claims of justice had to be met first.

God had to be vindicated before the supreme court of the universe.

He had given His Son to redeem the human race.

That Son had died as a substitute.

He had risen as the Lord High Priest of a new covenant.

You understand, He had fulfilled the old covenant and there had been the annulling of the priesthood and the law of the sacrifices with the old covenant.

Now a new covenant has come into being and there must be a new priesthood.

There must be a new law.

The old priesthood was to deal with servants.

The new priesthood is to deal with sons.

The old priesthood had the Ten Commandments called "the law of death."

The new covenant has but one commandment, "the law of life."

A new commandment I give unto you, That ye love one another; as I have loved you, that ye also love one another. (John 13:34)

JESUS, OUR MEDIATOR

The first ministry that Jesus took after He had carried His blood into the heavenly Holy of Holies, was that of a mediator.

Neither by the blood of goats and calves, but by his own blood he entered in once into the holy place, having obtained eternal redemption for us. (Hebrews 9:12)

He went in with His own blood and that blood is the seal upon the document of our redemption.

Hebrews 9:24 says that Christ entered *"into heaven itself, now to appear in the presence of God for us."*

His high priestly ministry is over, as far as our redemption is concerned. His work is finished. He said, *"It is finished"* on the cross, but that didn't have reference to His substitutionary work. That had reference to His finishing His work of fulfilling the first covenant and everything that pertained to it.

The priesthood, the sacrifices, the atonement, and the law—all that was finished.

They no longer were operative.

Now the temple can be destroyed: the priesthood can cease to function, because their covenant on which everything was founded has been fulfilled and set aside.

JESUS, OUR SAVIOR

The next office that Jesus fills is that of a Savior.

> *Not purloining, but shewing all good fidelity; that they may adorn the doctrine of God our Saviour in all things. For the grace of God that bringeth salvation hath appeared to all men.* (Titus 2:10–11)

Jesus is God's Savior.

> *For there is none other name under heaven given among men, whereby we must be saved.* (Acts 4:12)

No man can save himself.

No man can make himself righteous or give to himself eternal life. There is but one Savior—the man Christ Jesus, who gave Himself a ransom for us all.

He might be a Savior; He might be God's own Savior, but His work of salvation would be limited and of no real value unless there was a mediator between God and man.

How often we hear in evangelistic meetings, an invitation to come to Jesus and get sins pardoned. If the one who invites the unsaved understood the glad tidings, he would never speak like that. It is not coming to Jesus but it is going to God through Jesus.

> *For there is one God, and one mediator between God and men, the man Christ Jesus; who gave himself a ransom for all.* (1 Timothy 2:5–6)

Until we recognize the mediatorial ministry of Jesus, our ministry will be cramped.

No man can reach the Father but through Him.

> *I am the way, the truth, and the life: no man cometh unto the Father, but by me.* (John 14:6)

Jesus there is magnifying His position as Mediator.

What the sinner needs is eternal life and remission of his trespasses. He must be made a new creation, but he cannot approach God. He has no standing with God.

When Adam sinned in the garden, he forfeited his legal right of approach to God.

Jesus, by His great substitutionary work, purchased the right to be the Mediator between the unapproachable God and the sin-ruled sinner.

When the unsaved man makes his approach today, he wants to reach God.

He wants eternal life.

He wants the wiping out of all his old sins.

Jesus sits there as the Mediator between God and man.

He can be touched with the feeling of the infirmities of that lost world for which He died.

JESUS, OUR INTERCESSOR

He is not only the Mediator between God and man, but the moment that the unsaved man accepts Him as his Savior, He also becomes his Intercessor.

How happy my heart was when I first knew this.

I had someone to pray for me that I knew the Father would hear.

I remember what Jesus said as He stood before the tomb of Lazarus:

> *And Jesus lifted up his eyes, and said, Father, I thank thee that thou hast heard me. And I knew that thou hearest me always.* (John 11:41–42)

I have someone now to vouch for me, someone who never forgets me.

Wherefore he is able also to save them to the uttermost that come unto God by him, seeing he ever liveth to make intercession for them.
(Hebrews 7:25)

Here is a precious fact: the Greek word that is used as *save* here is *sozo,* which can be translated as "heal," and it is rightly used because sin is sickness.

Disease is sickness, and Jesus came to *sozo* us out of the hand of the enemy.

Isn't it wonderful that He ever lives to make intercession for us; to heal us of physical and spiritual diseases; to restore our broken spirits; and to hold us in the hour of temptation and trial?

Not only is Jesus our great Intercessor, I love to think of Him as a high priestly Intercessor. But He is more than that.

JESUS, OUR ADVOCATE

First John 2:1 says, *"My little children, these things write I unto you, that ye sin not. And if any man sin, we have an advocate with the Father, Jesus Christ the righteous."*

That is a remarkable expression and it is a wonderful ministry.

There He sits at the right hand of the Father, as the sinner's Savior, as the believer's Mediator, but now the believer is out of fellowship.

The adversary has gained dominion over him. He is under condemnation.

It seems as though his heart would break, and then he remembers in the midst of his sorrow and grief that Jesus is his Advocate, his lawyer, who ever lives, not only to make intercession for him, but He is there to appear before the Father on his behalf.

So the believer lifts up his voice and cries, "Father, in Jesus's name, forgive me," and his great Advocate whispers, "Father, lay that to My charge."

So everything is wiped out and once more he can stand before the Father without condemnation.

You see, He is called the righteous Advocate, because the believer that has sinned has lost the sense of righteousness and his righteousness is of no avail to him as long as his heart is under condemnation.

Then he needs his righteous Advocate, who can go into the Father's presence and make an appeal for him and restore that lost joy and the sense of righteousness again.

You see, the present ministry of Jesus is of infinite value to the believer.

JESUS, OUR LORD

Not only is He Savior, Intercessor, and Advocate, but He also is our Lord and Head.

> *As ye have therefore received Christ Jesus the Lord, so walk ye in him: rooted and built up in him, and stablished in the faith, as ye have been taught, abounding therein with thanksgiving.* (Colossians 2:6–7)

I read that over and over many times.

That Scripture was like a storehouse filled with priceless treasure, but I couldn't seem to get a key to it.

Then I saw what it meant.

He wanted me to be rooted and established in the reality of the lordship of Jesus over me.

When I first began to study about His lordship, I was afraid of Him. I had a feeling that it meant slavery to me, but it didn't.

It meant just what the Psalm 23:1 says: "*The Lord is my shepherd; I shall not want.*"

Why? He has me lie down in green pastures where food is abundant, where water is near me, where I am fully protected from the elements and from my enemies. (See verses 2–3.)

He is my present Shepherd-Lord.

The word "*Lord*" means "bread provider, shield, and protector."

He is all that a husband can mean to his wife.

He is all that a lover can mean to his beloved.

The Father wants me to be rooted and grounded and built up in this blessed truth.

He wants my faith to rest upon absolute certainty of the lordship of Jesus over me.

Then my heart will be full of abounding joy and thanksgiving.

You see, until we know about the Lordship of Jesus at the right hand of the Father, there will never be that quiet restfulness in our spirit.

You can find that practically all the believers who are living beneath their privileges, are having a hard time in their spiritual life.

They have never been instructed in the ministry of Jesus at the right hand of the Father.

Years ago, I held a blessed campaign in Moncton, New Brunswick, Canada. Months afterward, I returned for another campaign, and I asked the congregation, "What truth helped you the most?"

Many voices answered back, "Your teaching about Jesus's ministry at the right hand of the Father."

JESUS, OUR SURETY OF THE NEW COVENANT

He is not only our High Priest, Savior, Intercessor, Advocate, and Lord, but there is another priceless ministry of my seated Lord. He is the "Surety of the New Covenant."

> *For there is verily a disannulling of the commandment going before for the weakness and unprofitableness thereof. For the law made nothing perfect, but the bringing in of a better hope did; by the which we draw nigh unto God.* (Hebrews 7:18–19)

By a single stroke, He has cleared up the issue of that first covenant and the law.

Because of their weakness, they could not make men righteous; they could not make men holy; they could not give eternal life.

Hebrews 10:1–4 will throw much light on this:

> *For the law having a shadow of good things to come, and not the very image of the things, can never with those sacrifices which they offered year by year continually make the comers thereunto perfect. For then would they not have ceased to be offered? because that the worshippers once purged should have had no more conscience of sins. But in those sacrifices there is a remembrance again made of sins every year. For it is not possible that the blood of bulls and of goats should take away sins.*

But there has come a new covenant, and on the basis of that new covenant, we may be born again, born of heaven, born of God. We receive the nature and life of the Father God.

We may become the very righteousness of God in Him.

Can anyone overestimate the value of such a covenant?

This is a covenant of love, a covenant of life, a covenant of the new creation.

> *And inasmuch as not without an oath he was made priest: (For those priests were made without an oath; but this with an oath by him that said unto him, The Lord sware and will not repent, Thou art a priest for ever...).* (Hebrews 7:20–21)

You see, Jesus was outside of the priestly family.

They became priests by being born into the priesthood naturally. The oldest son was always the high priest.

But Jesus was a Priest by an oath of Jehovah: "*The Lord sware and will not repent, Thou art a priest for ever.*"

Now notice this great sentence:

> *By so much was Jesus made a surety of a better testament. And they truly were many priests, because they were not suffered to continue by reason of death: but this man, because he continueth ever, hath an unchangeable priesthood.* (Hebrews 7:22–24)

There is a priest who abideth forever as the surety of this new covenant.

Back of this new covenant then, what we call the New Testament, we have Jesus as its surety.

From Matthew 1 to Revelation 22, Jesus and His throne are back of every word.

Now you can quote Jeremiah 1:12: "*I will hasten my word to perform it.*" Jesus can say, "*Heaven and earth shall pass away, but my words shall not pass away*" (Matthew 24:35).

That is the Word of the new covenant.

His blood is the red seal upon the document of this covenant. On the ground of the integrity of that indissoluble covenant, you and I can build a faith that cannot be shaken.

"HE...SAT DOWN"

Now you can understand what this beautiful expression means that is used in Hebrews—*"He...sat down."*

We go back to Hebrews 1:3 and feast our spirits upon it: *"Who being the brightness of his glory* [the very outshining of His glory], *and the express image of his person, and upholding all things by the word of his power."*

The word translated *"power"* means "ability." All the ability of deity is back of that covenant.

Now, notice carefully: *"...when he had by himself purged* [or substituted for] *our sins, sat down on the right hand of the Majesty on high."*

He is in the highest seat in the universe and holds the highest office in the universe, and He is my Lord.

He is the Head of the body, and *"of his fulness have all we received, and grace for grace"* (John 1:16).

How rich we are. We can never again talk of our lack of our weakness, of our unworthiness, because that great substitutionary sacrifice that He wrought for us has guaranteed to us eternal life, and a standing with the Father, victory over our enemies, peace that passeth all understanding, joy beyond words.

All are ours because of what He is for us now at the right hand of the Majesty on high.

25

WHY NATURAL MAN CANNOT KNOW HIMSELF

Man in the garden lived in the realm of the spirit. He had perfect fellowship with God. His spirit dominated him. Then sin came and he was driven from the presence of God. From that moment, he lived under the domination of his senses. These five senses became his master. His spirit lost dominion the moment that he became spiritually dead, a partaker of Satan's nature. This, you understand, happened when he sinned.

The real man is a spirit being, but the moment that spiritual death took possession of his spirit, his senses dominated.

He lost his approach to God the moment that he sinned. The nature that he received made him antagonistic to God.

> *Because the carnal mind is enmity against God: for it is not subject to the law of God, neither indeed can be. So then they that are [governed by the senses] cannot please God.* (Romans 8:7–8)

This translation of the Greek word *sant* as *senses* instead of "flesh" gives us the true intent of the word.

First Corinthians 2:14 declares:

> *But the natural man [the man of the senses] receiveth not the things of the Spirit of God: for they are foolishness unto him: neither can he know them, because they are spiritually discerned.*

So when man fell and his spirit received the nature of the adversary, he really became a stranger to himself.

He is a spirit being and is no longer dominated by himself but by his body in which he lives.

It made him a slave to his body instead of a master over it.

You understand that when this thing happened in the garden, he lost contact with God, lost his ability to approach Him, and he went out into the world to live by his senses.

We have a modern saying that "man lives by his wits." That is another way of expressing the same fact.

We know that man cannot contact God through his reasoning faculties; that his only contact with Him is with his spirit. Having died spiritually, he is unable to make this contact.

It is very difficult for man's language to convey God's thought.

The Hebrew language is a dead language and it is a limited language.

We have many words for which the Hebrew language has no equivalent.

For instance, the word *ruach*, translated as "spirit," can mean air, anger, blast, breath, cool, courage, mind, quarters, side, spirit, tempest, wind, vain, or windy; and in one place, it has been translated as whirlwind.

By this, you can see how limited the Hebrew language was to convey God's thoughts.

That is the reason why the word *ruach*, translated as "spirit," is often misunderstood by the sense knowledge of translators. You remember that man's thoughts are not always God's thoughts. Man was love's product created to be His child and companion. He was created in God's class of being, in His image and in His likeness.

God is eternal. Man is eternal.

God is a spirit. Man is a spirit.

Man was so created that he could partake of God's nature and become God's child.

Now mark this fact: man cannot be spiritual unless he is a spirit. He cannot know spiritual things unless he is a spirit.

He cannot partake of God's nature unless he is in God's class of being.

You can understand now the calamity that befell man when his spirit lost control over his senses.

In that moment, his senses governed his spirit. All the knowledge that natural man has, has come through these five avenues of the body—seeing, hearing, tasting, smelling, and feeling.

The brain has no capacity to think independent of sense evidences.

A child that is born without sight, or hearing, or feeling, would be called an imbecile, though its brain was as perfect as the brain of any child.

That brain had no contact with the world because the senses failed to function.

Now we can understand that man's physical contact is with the physical.

His mental contact is with the mental.

His spirit then can contact only the spiritual.

If man's reasoning faculties cannot contact God, then it is up to his spirit to make that contact.

Man's reasoning faculties are utterly dependent upon the senses.

Sense knowledge is unable to contact his spirit in any intelligent way until after that spirit has been recreated, received the nature of God, and his reasoning faculties have been renewed and brought into harmony with the recreated spirit.

Now we can understand the difficulties of psychologists.

You understand this is a study of the mind of man, and if the psychologist doesn't know about the spirit of man, about what happened to the spirit of man in the garden, he will be unable to approach this subject with any clarity of thought.

Most of our psychologists deny that man is a spirit. He is simply a psychical, or soul-based, man.

He denies the existence of the spirit, and this denial makes it impossible for the spirit to function.

Now you can see why natural man cannot know himself, because he is a spirit.

The senses cannot register anything of the spirit or give him any spirit knowledge.

One who knows anatomy and physiology may not know much about the mind and he may not know man himself. All he knows is connected with the physical.

Natural man is in the same condition.

He cannot know spirit or spiritual things, so he cannot know himself, for he is spirit.

This is the reason that modern psychology is often times misleading.

Modern psychologists are majoring functional psychology or psychology based on the study of the five senses and their reaction upon the mind.

The new creation man finds a new self in Christ, and that new self becomes almost independent of the senses when he comes into closest fellowship with the Father.

"Therefore if any man be in Christ, he is a new creature" (2 Corinthians 5:17), a new creation, a new self.

The real self has been made anew, recreated.

That means his spirit has been recreated.

It is imperative now that the mind, which derives all of its impulses, all of its knowledge from the five senses, should come under the dominion of this new recreated spirit or self.

This can only come as man begins to study the Word and then begins to practice and live it.

It is a fact of great importance that every believer should know that there is no such thing as understanding the Word until the mind is renewed.

The reason for that is that the Word is the work of the Holy Spirit and it is a spiritual thing, and sense knowledge cannot understand spiritual things.

So it is necessary that his mind be renewed and come into fellowship with his spirit.

It is almost imperative that this recreated spirit should gain the dominance over his reasoning faculties.

You know how we often fight our conscience, and how it is often in opposition to our reasoning faculties.

That conscience is the voice of our spirit.

If we should learn to obey our conscience, we could walk continuously in fellowship with the Word and with the Father; but the reason is, we have not learned to give our spirit the place of authority and dominion that belongs to it.

EDUCATING OUR SPIRITS

This brings us to another phase of this study.

Your spirit can be educated just as truly as the mind is educated.

It can be built up in strength just as the body can be built up.

That comes by meditation in the Word, by practicing the Word, by giving the Word the first place, and by instantly obeying the voice of our spirit.

After a while, you can know the will of the Father in all the details of life, because He communicates with your spirit, not with the reasoning faculties.

You know Paul speaks of the mind of the spirit.

> *For to be carnally minded is death; but to be spiritually minded [that is our recreated spirit] is life and peace.* (Romans 8:6)

The life there is *zoe*—eternal life—the nature of God.

The spirit mentioned here is the recreated spirit, not the Holy Spirit.

It is hard for us to accept the fact that the natural man is ruled by the five senses.

His body is the teacher of his mind and he cannot grow in knowledge beyond the reactions of his senses upon his brain.

The new creation man has almost an unlimited opportunity of growth because his spirit has received the nature of God.

He is in perfect fellowship with his Father.

He has an unlimited use of the name of Jesus that the natural man does not have.

He has the wisdom of God, for Jesus is made unto him wisdom. Natural man has nothing but the wisdom that comes to him through his "unrecreated" spirit.

The new creation man has the ability of God at his disposal.

You see, he is lifted out of the natural realm into the spiritual realm, and when he is recreated, he has the privilege of having the Holy Spirit, who raised Jesus from the dead, to come and make His home in his body.

Now you can understand Romans 12:1–2:

> *I beseech you therefore, brethren, by the mercies of God, that ye present your bodies a living sacrifice, holy, acceptable unto God, which is your reasonable service. And be not conformed to this world: but be ye transformed by the renewing of your mind, that ye may prove what is that good, and acceptable, and perfect, will of God.*

This shows us why it is imperative to have the body, the university of the mind, under the control of the recreated spirit.

This new creation man does not walk under the dominion of the senses but is to be governed by the Word of God.

It is going to be hard for us to see that this physical body of ours is not only the home of the five senses, but that these five senses have been the instructors and teachers of the brain.

That makes the body the *university* of the brain. The five senses are the instructors.

This body is the laboratory where the brain receives all of its instructions.

These senses are five avenues to the brain, for we know that the brain cannot function without the senses.

Here are some facts that may be hard to assimilate.

The brain has no creative ability. It has nothing of itself by which it can create. It is dependent upon these five instructors.

The brain, by much training, can advise what action is best after the senses have communicated, but if the senses never function, the brain will never develop.

As long as the natural human spirit is held in bondage by spiritual death, it has no creative ability. This can be seen in heathen countries where they have never received eternal life. Spiritually dead men in those countries have no creative ability. They may be able to follow blueprints; they can imitate; they can experiment as they do in chemistry, but it must end there. Man's creative ability is not in the reasoning faculties.

Reader, can't you see the imperative need of giving to the youth of our nation eternal life?

I have proven to you in another chapter, that the children who have received eternal life in the teen age, seldom sow wild oats; seldom ever become criminals. They are easier to rear and to control, and they are more responsive to the appeal of the Word of God.

Another fact: inventors know this to be true, that after hours of experimenting, their minds are worn and tired. They stop to rest, and suddenly, without any effort, the thing they have been searching for flashes into their mind. They know not from whence it came, but it has arrived.

What did it? Their spirits spoke as soon as the reasoning faculties were silent and it could be heard.

Sometimes it comes in a dream or in the early morning when first awaking.

Psychologists have been puzzled by this. They had no answer for what seemed to them a mystery, so they called that something a subconscious mind.

But we of the new creation know there is no such thing as a subconscious mind; it is the mind of the spirit. It is the spirit struggling to express itself.

You ask, *But can't the natural man cultivate his spirit?*

Yes, but it will be the cultivation of a spirit dominated by spiritual death.

That has given to us spiritualism with all those dangerous cults from India; given to us the strange miracles of the occult that often imitate God.

Here are more facts of vital importance.

The recreated spirit becomes the fountain of all the beautiful things that Christianity has given to us.

But the fruit of the Spirit is love, joy, peace, longsuffering, gentleness, goodness, faith, meekness, temperance: against such there is no law. And they that are Christ's have crucified the flesh with the affections and lusts. If we live in the Spirit, let us also walk in the Spirit. (Galatians 5:22–25)

Notice, it is the fruit of the spirit—not the Holy Spirit. Translators should not have capitalized the word spirit. The Holy Spirit does not bear fruit any more than Jesus bears fruit. Jesus said, *"I am the vine, ye are the branches"* (John 15:5). It is the branch that bears fruit.

The Holy Spirit has imparted eternal life to our spirits.

That life is the nature of the Father as unveiled in Jesus, so the first fruit that is seen in the new creation is love.

We know that we have passed from death unto life, because we love the brethren. (1 John 3:14)

And then a joy that is unspeakable and full of glory fills our whole being.

Next, *"the peace of God, which passeth all understanding"* (Philippians 4:7) becomes ours.

The troubled heart is filled with quietness.

Then as he goes out to contact the world, long-suffering is seen; kindness, goodness, faithfulness, meekness, self-control.

These are the fruits of the recreated spirit.

You see, the recreated have crucified the senses and brought them into subjection to the Word.

"If we live by the Spirit [that is, our recreated spirit], *let us also walk in the Spirit"* (Galatians 5:25).

Now you will notice that this is perfectly in harmony with 1 Corinthians 13, where it tells us about that love-law that is to govern the believer.

Love is very patient, very kind. Love knows no jealousy; love makes no parade, gives itself no airs, is never rude, never selfish, never irritated, never resentful. (1 Corinthians 13:4–5 MOFF)

These are the fruits of the recreated spirit.

It is vitally important that we understand that the recreated human spirit is the fountain out of which faith flows. Natural man has only sense knowledge faith. Natural man believes in the things he sees and hears, and the things that have come to him through the five senses, like F. W. Woolworth, who had faith in a five-and-ten-cent store, and like John D. Rockefeller, who had faith in oil and gasoline.

Love and faith and courage are the fruits of the recreated human spirit.

The conduct that has made Christians outstanding in society, has been the fruit of the recreated human spirit.

You can *see* very clearly how the natural man could not know himself.

We must not forget that the natural human spirit can be cultivated.

We see this among the occult societies, among spiritualists and others that are in close fellowship with demons.

> *Who is a wise man and endued with knowledge among you? let him shew out of a good conversation his works with meekness of wisdom. But if ye have bitter envying and strife in your hearts, glory not, and lie not against the truth. This wisdom descendeth not from above, but is earthly, sensual, devilish.* (James 3:13–15)

Then, verse 17 tells of the wisdom that comes down from above. It is true and peaceable. This contrast is suggestive. Wisdom is not a product of the reasoning faculties, but of the human spirit. The natural human spirit can contact demoniacal forces, just as the recreated human spirit contacts God.

Christian workers should become familiar with this truth. They should be able to discern at once whether a person is dominated by a demon or not.

In my work in praying for the insane, I have seen much of the depths of Satan and how he gains absolute mastery over the reasoning faculties through the natural human spirit.

26

SOME FACTS ABOUT PENTECOST

There is always a danger of reading into the Old Testament and the four Gospels some of the facts that are only revealed in the Epistles.

There is a danger of attributing to the disciples, before the day of Pentecost, much that is not true.

Let me make this statement first and then we will prove it.

No one who walked with Jesus during His three-and-one-half years of public ministry was born again, was a new creation, or had eternal life. No one under the first covenant had eternal life until the day of Pentecost.

But someone might ask, *Didn't the disciples believe in Jesus?*

Yes, but not as their substitute, not as their Savior who was going to die and rise again from the dead.

They believed in Him as the Son of God, as a Great Prophet, as the One who was going to redeem them from the Roman yoke and establish again a Jewish nation.

They knew nothing of His substitutionary work.

In John 11:25–27, we read the story of Martha and Jesus's conversation about the dead Lazarus:

> *Jesus said unto her, I am the resurrection, and the life: he that believeth in me, though he were dead, yet shall he live: and whosoever liveth and believeth in me shall never die. Believest thou this? She saith unto him, Yea, Lord: I believe that thou art the Christ, the Son of God, which should come into the world.*

She did not believe in Him as a Savior.

She did not believe in His redemption.

They knew nothing of His redemptive work.

He could not make it clear to them.

Paul tells us why in 1 Corinthians 2:14:

> *But the natural man receiveth not the things of the Spirit of God: for they are foolishness unto him: neither can he know them, because they are spiritually discerned.*

They did not know that He was going to rise from the dead, and even after He arose, they did not believe it.

In Luke 24:11, it says, *"And their words seemed to them as idle tales, and they believed them not."*

They knew nothing of the new creation.

True, Jesus had told Nicodemus, *"Ye must be born again"* (John 3:7), but he didn't understand it.

Nicodemus replied, *"How can these things be?"* (verse 9).

He knew nothing about receiving eternal life and its effect upon man.

True, Jesus said, *"I am come that they might have life, and that they might have it more abundantly"* (John 10:10) and, *"He that heareth my word, and believeth on him that sent me, hath everlasting life, and shall not come into condemnation; but is passed from death unto life"* (John 5:24).

That was prophecy on the part of Jesus.

The disciples knew nothing about righteousness, of the ability to stand in the Father's presence without condemnation.

They knew nothing of fellowship with the Father and with Jesus Christ.

They had never had fellowship with the Master, any more than an unsaved man today can have fellowship with a child of God. They knew nothing of sonship or of the family of God.

They were Jews under law; servants, nothing more.

They knew nothing of the Father in reality.

He was just God to them.

They knew nothing of the indwelling presence of the Holy Spirit.

They had heard Jesus's teaching but they did not grasp it.

They knew nothing of the new kind of love that Jesus brought. It didn't govern their lives or touch them and it could not until they were recreated.

They didn't understand what John the Baptist meant when he said, *"He that cometh after me is mightier than I, whose shoes I am not worthy to bear: he shall baptize* [immerse] *you with the Holy Ghost, and with fire"* (Matthew 3:11).

If you will compare that with 1 Corinthians 12:13, you will know what being baptized in the Holy Spirit means. The term is used incorrectly by most all believers today: *"For by one Spirit are we all baptized into one body, whether we be Jews or Gentiles, whether we be bond or free; and have been all made to drink into one Spirit."*

This has reference to the new birth, the new creation.

Jesus told them, *"For John truly baptized with water; but ye shall be baptized with the Holy Ghost not many days hence"* (Acts 1:5).

You know that when one is baptized, he is put into the water, he is not filled with the water. When he is baptized in the Holy Spirit, he is not filled with the Holy Spirit.

Now read Acts 2:1–4:

> *When the day of Pentecost was fully come, they were all with one accord in one place. And suddenly there came a sound from heaven as of a rushing mighty wind, and it filled all the house where they were sitting. And there appeared unto them cloven tongues like as of fire, and it sat upon each of them. And they were all filled with the Holy Ghost, and began to speak with other tongues, as the Spirit gave them utterance.*

The Holy Spirit filled that upper room where they were sitting, and they were all immersed in the Holy Spirit. In other words, they were all recreated, received eternal life.

The second thing that happened—*"there appeared unto them cloven tongues like as of fire, and it sat upon each of them."* Those tongues of fire showed that the gospel was going to be preached by men with tongues of fire, a message that could not be withstood.

Stephen was the first man who paid the penalty of having a tongue of fire. They stoned him to death.

The third thing that happened in that upper room—*"They were all filled with the Holy Ghost."* You understand that they could not receive the Holy Spirit until they were recreated.

The third thing that happened on that wonderful day was the Spirit entering their bodies.

Jesus said He would be with the disciples, that He would be in them. They did not understand Him, but now the reality of the thing has come. They have been recreated.

They have received the nature and the life of God.

Now the Spirit is going to take them over.

He is going to use their vocal chords to speak His own message. Then the fourth amazing thing took place. They *"began to speak with other tongues, as the Spirit gave them utterance."*

It is very important that we realize this: the disciples were entering into things of which they had no conception whatsoever.

You can understand now what is meant when Jesus said that they were to be baptized in the Spirit. That immersion had meant their receiving eternal life, their union with deity. It meant that the body of Christ had been brought into being. The thing we call the *ecclesia*, the church, had now become a real thing in the world.

God's sons and daughters were in that upper room where only servants had been a few hours before.

The words *"be baptized with the Holy Ghost"* were never used after the day of Pentecost in any place but in Acts 11:16.

This is the story of the gentiles receiving Christ as Savior. Peter was down in Joppa. There a centurion sent for him to come and tell him about the Master. And while Peter was preaching, the Holy Spirit fell on them who heard the Word. It was almost identical with the thing that happened on the day of Pentecost. Peter returned to Jerusalem and told the apostles what had happened, how the gentiles had had the same experience as they had in the upper room.

> *And as I began to speak, the Holy Ghost fell on them, as on us at the beginning. Then remembered I the word of the Lord, how that he said, John indeed baptized with water; but ye shall be baptized with the Holy*

Ghost. Forasmuch then as God gave them the like gift as he did unto us, who believed on the Lord Jesus Christ; what was I, that I could withstand God? (Acts 11:15–17)

The disciples never believed on Jesus until the day of Pentecost. What faith they had was simply sense knowledge faith. They could only believe in the things they could see and hear and feel.

Now notice this fact: the expression, "Have you received your baptism?" is unscriptural when you are talking about the Holy Spirit, for in Acts 8:14–17 is the story of Samaria receiving Christ, of Philip baptizing them and then of the apostles coming down from Jerusalem and laying hands upon them and they received the Holy Spirit.

And it came to pass, that, while Apollos was at Corinth, Paul having passed through the upper coasts came to Ephesus: and finding certain disciples, he said unto them, Have ye received the Holy Ghost since ye believed? And they said unto him, We have not so much as heard whether there be any Holy Ghost. And he said unto them, Unto what then were ye baptized? And they said, Unto John's baptism. Then said Paul, John verily baptized with the baptism of repentance, saying unto the people, that they should believe on him which should come after him, that is, on Christ Jesus. When they heard this, they were baptized in the name of the Lord Jesus. And when Paul had laid his hands upon them, the Holy Ghost came on them; and they spake with tongues, and prophesied. And all the men were about twelve. (Acts 19:1–7)

Understand this fact: nowhere in the Pauline Epistles is that expression used in the way it is used by Christians today. We should never ask a person, "Have you received your baptism?" or "Have you received your experience according to Acts 2:1–4?"

When we do, we betray our lack of knowledge of the Word.

From the book of Acts, it is clear that a man receives eternal life before he can receive the Holy Spirit as an indwelling presence.

27

WHAT HAVE YOU DONE WITH LOVE?

A new kind of love was brought to the world by Jesus. As we understand this new kind of love, we realize there never was any love before.

The thing we have called love has been sex attraction. In heathen countries, there is no love. It is mere sex attraction hardly higher than that seen in the animal world.

But Jesus brought a new thing. The Greek word has been translated *charity* or *love* in our Bibles. It should never have been translated so. The Greek word should have been anglicized—*agape*—with an explanation.

When we are born again, we are born in love. We have found out that God is love and so the new birth is the impartation of this nature of the Father. We become children of love. It is a love family into which we have been born.

Paul speaking in Romans 5:5 says, "*The love of God is shed abroad in our hearts*"—it has absorbed us, taken us over.

This love nature is the law of the new creation.

> *A new commandment I give unto you, That ye love [agape] one another; as I have loved [agape-ed] you, that ye also love [agape] one another. By this shall all men know that ye are my disciples, if ye have love [agape] one to another.* (John 13:34–35)

It was to be the stamp, the brand, if you please, that should differentiate us from the world folks.

Paul said, "*I bear in my body the marks of the Lord Jesus*" (Galatians 6:17). He meant the scars and wounds that had been given to him in his persecutions.

But the believer bears the marks, the brand of love, upon his spirit.

Romans 12:5–6 says that every man, when he comes into the family, has a measure of faith given to him. He is to cultivate that faith and develop it.

The same thing is true in regard to this new kind of love. When you come into the family, a measure of that love is given you. It comes with a new nature, the love nature.

This love nature must be developed as you develop your faith life.

As you give love freedom to grow and act as it naturally should, it will gain control of your whole being. It must be fed by the Word of God; it must express itself in action. *"Man shall not live by bread alone, but by every word that proceedeth out of the mouth of God"* (Matthew 4:4).

You see, the real man of whom He is speaking is your spirit. Your spirit hunger and your spirit needs are just as great as your mental or your physical needs.

Your spirit must have the privilege of meditation in the Word. You must learn to feed upon it just as Jeremiah did: *"Thy words were found, and I did eat them"* (Jeremiah 15:16).

Now you feed and exercise this new thing that has come into you by practicing love. The exercise makes it strong just as exercise makes your body strong.

Colossians 3:16 says, *"Let the word of Christ dwell in you richly,"* gaining the ascendancy over all your faculties. This love life makes you gentle, Jesus-like. It makes you strong and vigorous like the Master. It makes you absolutely fearless in your walk with the Lord.

Some people have imprisoned love. We read recently of a father who locked his boy up in a garret and kept him a prisoner until the child was nearly dead.

How many have done that same thing to love? Instead of letting love have its perfect sway and control, we have limited it. We have forgotten that love will make a man a success. It will put him over where nothing else would make him a victor. Love never fails. It is the Master-ruler. It will lead a man out of selfishness, out of weakness and failure, and into the very strength and ability of Christ.

There is no force in the world that it cannot dominate.

It makes us wanted.

It makes us a blessing.

It enables us to take Jesus's place.

I have sometimes wondered what would happen if a man dared to go the limit with love.

Some have neglected it, acting as though they did not have it; utterly ignoring its very existence, and yet they want the Father's help in time of need.

Love must be enthroned in the heart.

It must govern the life.

As love takes over the kingdom of our spirit, then that wonderful passage in 2 Corinthians 5:14–15 becomes a living reality:

> *For the love of Christ constraineth us [or, better, has gained control and taken us over]; because we thus judge, that if one died for all, then were all dead: and that he died for all, that they which live should not henceforth live unto themselves, but unto him which died for them, and rose again.*

Paul's friends had challenged him. They said he was beside himself, but the love of Christ had so set him on fire that he was slowly burning up. His very being was saturated with the passion that drove Jesus to the cross.

Now you can understand 1 Corinthians 10:24: "*Let no man seek his own, but every man another's wealth.*"

When love burns at a white heat, selfishness stops reigning. What an unhappy thing it is for selfishness to have any part in the government of this new creation.

Selfishness is as deadly as poison.

It is poison to the spirit.

It is poison to the body of Christ.

It causes practically all the diseases in the body.

It is a strange thing how selfishness has never been feared by man.

He fears it in the other man but not in himself.

It is the cause of all the wars that have come; of all the strikes, the battle between labor and capital, and the strife in politics.

That thing born in the garden has grown so mighty that it governs the nations of the earth, and love is the only thing that can destroy it.

First John 4:16 was one of the most difficult Scriptures I ever encountered. It didn't seem that I could ever enter into it:

> *And we have known and believed the love that God hath to us. God is love; and he that dwelleth in love dwelleth in God, and God in him.*

Here are three great facts: first, I have come to believe in love. I believe it is best to let it govern my life. I have come to believe that it is the best method of ruling a home, a business, or a government. You know only a few folks believe in love. They believe in force; they believe in intrigue; they believe in sense knowledge arguments.

If, in your heart, you believe that the love way is best, then act it. Not only is it best, but it is your way. It is the way you are going to walk regardless of how anyone else walks; you are going to walk the love way, and when you do, you discover you are living in the love realm.

Your home is in love. Whenever you step out of love, you step into darkness and unhappiness, and so you have learned to stay in the love way.

You found that living in love is actually living in the highest, sweetest fellowship with the Father.

It is actually living with Him. He has come into your body to make it His home.

The next verse seemed so difficult to me in those early days, when I first discovered this love law and this love way.

> *Herein is our love made perfect, that we may have boldness in the day of judgment: because as he is, so are we in this world.* (1 John 4:17)

What does he mean by that? Love is perfect in itself, but it must gain perfect control of me. When love becomes the rule of my life, I grow up into it until my life is dominated, ruled, governed by it, and that gives me a quiet fearlessness in His presence.

You see, He is love and I am a love child. Now I am walking in the realm of love.

I am thinking in terms of love.

I am acting according to the rule of love.

My whole life is pitched to the key of love.

Then you can understand that there is no fear in love. There is fear in everything else.

When you are out of love, you say and do things that you would be afraid to face. You think things out of love that you wouldn't want to become public property.

> *But perfect love casteth out fear: because fear hath torment [or punishment]. He that feareth is not made perfect in love.* (1 John 4:18)

Now you can understand that if we walk the love way and the love life controls us, we will say nothing; we will do nothing; we will resolutely refuse to think anything outside of love.

Can't you see what a fearless life that would be?

No matter what happens, you know you are walking in love.

When you speak, you know it is in love.

Ephesians 4:15 illustrates this:

> *But speaking the truth in love, may grow up into him in all things, which is the head, even Christ.*

Speaking out of love is speaking out of tune. It is off-key. It breaks harmony.

It jars on the ears of the men and women who walk in love.

So our whole life swings into the orbit of this new kind of love, this new creation life.

This is the thing that Paul gave us.

> *Even as I please all men in all things, not seeking mine own profit, but the profit of many, that they may be saved.* (1 Corinthians 10:33)

And then he says, "*Be ye followers* [imitators] *of me, even as I also am of Christ*" (1 Corinthians 11:1).

That is heart-searching, isn't it?

Not living to profit from my brethren, but living only to help them. But how 1 Corinthians 9:20–22 challenges us:

> *Unto the Jews I became as a Jew, that I might gain the Jews* [he had stopped being a Jew; he had become a new creation, a Christian]*; to them that are under the law, as under the law, that I might gain them that are under the law; to them that are without law, as without law, (being not without law to God, but under the law to Christ,) that I might gain them that are without law. To the weak became I as weak, that I might gain the weak: I am made all things to all men, that I might by all means save some.*

What Christian workers we would make if love melted us into that cast! What Jesus-believers we would be! What soul-winners! What mighty men and women of God!

You see, the gospel comes first.

The lost must be reached; they must know this new life.

In Romans 15:1, there is another challenge of the believer to his brother believer: *"We then that are strong ought to bear the infirmities of the weak, and not to please ourselves."*

In the third verse, he cries, *"For even Christ pleased not himself."* There is a battle line laid down for us.

That is where we must begin our fight with the reign of selfishness.

This is a love affair and we must not live outside of it.

This is a love realm and to live outside of it is to destroy our usefulness.

The new law that was to take the place of the old Ten Commandments was given by Jesus in John 13:34. You remember, He fulfilled the old covenant and established a new covenant in His blood. And now He said, *"A new commandment I give unto you* [or a new law], *That ye love one another; as I have loved you, that ye also love one another."*

The men who live in this realm, under that new law, will never commit sin.

Hear it again, with verse 35: *"By this shall all men know that ye are my disciples, if ye have love one to another."*

Take with that Romans 13:10: *"Love worketh no ill to his neighbour: therefore love is the fulfilling of the law."*

There is no need of the Ten Commandments now for us who are in Christ.

We are in the love family and walk in love, and as we walk in love, we do ill to no one. That will make the most beautiful type of life. Never any more harsh, bitter, unkind words spoken by us. No cruel insinuations, nor biting sarcasm. All our words would be soaked in love before they were uttered, literally saturated with love. Those words would need no artificial perfume. They would have the sweet fragrance of heaven itself.

What homes it would make!

What assemblies of believers where there would never be another unkind word spoken.

You know, as I studied the life of the Master, I saw that He never had suspicion.

I wondered how He could be above suspicion, surrounded He was with that crowd of godless men, but He was love. Love destroys suspicion.

Jesus never stepped out of the realm of love.

He was living the life.

He was walking in the new way. He built the new way.

You see, this is the new order for the full-grown man in Christ.

It is the measure of the stature of the fullness of Christ.

This would create a revival of the Jesus-life among men, wouldn't it?

It would be good for us to read daily 1 Corinthians 13, at least the first eight verses. We would then suffer long with people and be kind while we suffer.

Love would gain such control of us that there would be no envy. We would thank the Father for the success of others.

We would never be elated over our own success, for it says love *"vaunteth not itself, is not puffed up"* (1 Corinthians 13:4).

Our conduct before the world would be one of restraint, love's restraint, and we would be as kind to the outcast as we would to the wealthy.

We would never behave ourselves unseemly.

No one would ever hear a harsh word from our lips, nor an unkind criticism.

The love life would govern us.

It says love *"seeketh not her own"* (verse 5). It is not trying to gain ascendancy over anyone. And if others need what we have, we share with them.

We would never go to law; we would never quarrel or parley even over what belongs to us.

This new kind of love makes us so big that selfishness is utterly eliminated.

You see, in the new creation we were given a new self, a love self; a self born of God, a self like Jesus's self that He had in His earth walk.

We are not seeking our own.

They cannot provoke us, and we refuse to take any account of evil.

We never rejoice in unrighteousness, we only rejoice in the truth, in the things that are real.

Verse 7 startles us. The text says that love *"beareth all things,"* but Robert Young translates it as "covering closely." Joseph Henry Thayer translates it as love "covers over with silence."

What are they talking about? Oh, it is scandal. It is something that has happened that is unseemly; something that if it were known would injure perhaps a lot of people; might cause a division in the assembly; might break up a family.

What do we do? We cover it closely with silence.

We never mention it, and the thing dies there and no one is injured. Hear this: Love *"believeth all things, hopeth all things, endureth all things"* (verse 7). And then the climax: Love *"never faileth"* (verse 8).

We should remember this.

Agape, this new kind of love, never goes into bankruptcy. The red flag is never seen over its dwelling. Here is where love holds sway and rules, a queen upon her throne.

LOVE HAS MADE ME A VICTOR

I saw this translation in my spirit, of 1 John 4:4: *"Ye are of God, little children, and have overcome them: because greater is he that is in you, than he that is in the world."*

Then my heart entered a spiritual clinic, and I began to take a diagnosis of my heart life. I began to investigate love's realities.

I saw that 1 Corinthians 13:1–4 was a sort of a resume of the failure of sense knowledge religion. It is a summary of the best that sense knowledge could give to the world.

If I speak with the tongue of men and of angels, that is the highest achievement of a linguist, but have not love. *"I am become as sounding brass, or a tinkling cymbal"* (1 Corinthians 13:1). My linguistic ability is but noise, a jangling, unharmonious discord. Then, if I have all knowledge and know all mysteries, and have all faith so as to remove mountains, and my sense knowledge faith has made me a great business master, but have not love, I am nothing.

Or if I have knowledge so great that the universities are honored by giving me degrees, (and He says it softly and tenderly), but have not love, *"I am nothing"* (verse 2).

This is God's clinic. This is the most heart-searching thing that the human ever faced.

Now He takes me into the realm of a philanthropist where I become an Andrew Carnegie or a John D. Rockefeller, and I pour out millions upon millions to aid the needy, and I reach the place where I give my body in service until I wear it out, but He says, "If you haven't love, haven't this new kind of love that I have given to the world, all your efforts are nothing."

I stood amazed in the presence of it. I could see now that scholasticism, culture, everything that modern facilities have given us, travel, music, art—all are of no value unless love, this new kind of love, dominates my life.

When at the end of the list, if that is all I have, I go to my Maker empty-handed, I am a failure.

You see, the new creation is the only solution.

The new creation is created out of love. It is created in Christ Jesus. It is the workmanship of God in Christ.

God made the first man out of the dust of the earth.

The second man He makes out of Himself.

The first man is of the earth, earthy.

This last man that He has made was created out of righteousness and holiness and reality, out of the very nature of the Father Himself.

You see, this is the greatest thing in the world. Why?

Because it is God's nature imparted to us.

It is God working in us.

It is God working through us.

It is God building Himself into our spirits, until our spirits dominate our sense knowledge reasoning faculties and bring them into harmony with His knowledge.

It makes us more than well-pleasing. It gives to us love's creative genius that fills the very heart of the Father with joy. We become so Jesus-like, that the vine and the branches illustrate our union. We become a mirror in which the Father sees Himself.

This new love has given us a new self, a love self, a Jesus-self.

The old religion of fighting self and crucifying self is medieval.

It doesn't belong to Christianity. It belongs to the religions of the East.

We see man through new eyes of love.

It is the new kind of love that has given to us new eyesight.

We can only see the good things.

You remember that translation we mentioned before about love, that love beareth all things. It literally covers closely, or covers over with silence all that is unseemly. There is no scandal. There are no old sores to uncover.

Love can see only God in us, and God can only see Himself in us.

We see men's overloads in order that we may bear them.

We see their infirmities that we may share with them.

We see their weakness in order that we may give our strength.

We see their poverty in order that we may give them our money.

We become Jesus men and women.

As a battery is charged with electricity, we are charged with love.

We stay in His presence feeding on the Word until our whole being is saturated with Him.

Then as we go out and minister to the people, we are lights, little luminaries blazing a path in life where sin has no part and the misery that comes from sin can never enter.

Now we understand what it means to walk in love; what it means to be in Christ.

Somehow, the passage of Scripture in 2 Corinthians 5:4 begins to unveil itself, where He speaks of our mortality being *"swallowed up of life."*

That is the nature of the Father. This mortal cannot now put on immortality, yet it puts on the very life and nature of the Father so our faces shine with the glory of our Christ, and His health and vigor and strength pour through us.

We are simply swallowed up of life.

All that was mortal, that which has been giving messages through the senses to the brain, now is enwrapped, immersed, overwhelmed with the love nature of the Father.

Can you imagine what this could mean, my being swallowed up in love, enwrapped in love, immersed in love, until love not only swallows up my mortality, but it swallows up my spirit?

"I am drowned in a sea of life," as Arthur S. Way's translation puts it.

O love that would not let me go until I caught a glimpse of this fountain!

O love that has followed me all these years in order that it might demonstrate in my spirit, soul, and body the completeness of the redemption that it has wrought in the man Christ Jesus!

THE BLOOD COVENANT

CONTENTS

FROM THE PUBLISHER

It is our great honor to make the treasured teachings of E. W. Kenyon widely available to readers from all walks of life. We pray that these books will reach ardent Kenyon admirers, pastors and ministry leaders, and, hopefully, an entirely new generation of believers who are not familiar with his rich library of teachings.

In *The Blood Covenant,* Kenyon reveals the true meaning behind the Lord's Table, as introduced by Jesus at the Last Supper. Gaining a firm understanding of the importance of this new covenant provides a great source of spiritual power, victory, and miracles in the everyday life of the believer.

We believe this wisdom is essentially practical and morally imperative in these modern times. It is our prayer that the teachings of E. W. Kenyon will experience a renaissance of relevancy within the church and throughout the world.

—*Whitaker House*

FOREWORD

This subject opens an absolutely new field for research and study, for those who are deeply interested in obtaining the best and richest of God's provisions for man.

Those who have had the privilege of listening to Dr. Kenyon's lectures on this subject have long been asking that they might be put into print.

Until now, the way has not been opened whereby this might be done, but the time has at last come when the desire in the hearts of the people is to be granted.

The truth, hidden away in the memorial of the Lord's Table, and forming the foundation of it, is of such a nature that your heart will thrill in response to the possibilities that present themselves, and will stir you to lay hold on the same power and victory and miracles that became a part of the everyday life of the apostles.

It is impossible to describe, in words, what the blood covenant will mean to you, once you learn what it is.

My father, Dr. E. W. Kenyon, the author of this manuscript, went home to be with His Lord, March 19, 1948, but the work which he started is still going on and blessing countless thousands.

This book is being printed as a lasting memorial to him, and has been made possible by the loving gifts of those who have been helped and blessed by his ministry.

—*Ruth A. Kenyon*

1

THE NEW COVENANT IN MY BLOOD

For years, I was convinced that there was something in the Lord's Table that I did not understand.

The silence of the disciples when Jesus introduced it, saying "This is my blood of the new covenant, which is poured out for many unto the remission of sins" (see Matthew 26:28); and then told them to eat the bread that was His body and to drink the wine that He declared was His blood—I say, the very silence of the disciples indicates they understood what he meant.

I did not, and it confused me.

For a long time I asked the question, "What is the underlying principle involved in this strange ordinance?"

The very language of Jesus, when He said, *"Verily, verily, I say unto you, Except ye eat of the flesh of the Son of man, and drink his blood, ye have not life in you"* (John 6:53), added to the confusion.

What did He mean by it?

Then, there was placed in my hands a book by Dr. H. Clay Trumbull, the old editor of the *Sunday School Times,* in which he showed there had been a blood covenant practiced by all primitive peoples from time immemorial.

He proved that this blood covenant was the basis of all primitive religions.

He gave data from all parts of the world showing that even to this day, in Africa, India, China, Borneo, and the Islands of the Seas, men are practicing a blood covenant very similar to our Lord's Table.

It was degenerated, but nevertheless, it had the marks of an original revelation from God.

In Stanley's books of exploration in Africa, he tells us that he cut the covenant more than fifty times with different tribes.

Livingstone calls attention to it, as do other explorers and missionaries in Africa.

Perhaps it might help us to understand if we look at the Hebrew word for *covenant*.

It means "to cut." It has the suggestion of an incision where blood flows.

In practically every place where the word is used in the Scripture, it means "to cut the covenant."

We find that Abraham "cut the covenant" with some of his neighbors before he ever entered into the covenant with Jehovah.

2

THE ORIGIN OF THE BLOOD COVENANT

The blood covenant, or what we call the Lord's Table, is based upon the oldest known covenant in the human family.

It evidently began in the garden of Eden.

It is evident that God cut the covenant or entered into a covenant with Adam at the very beginning.

The reason I believe that, is because there isn't a primitive people in the world, as far as we know, that has not practiced the blood covenant in some form, showing that it had a God given origin and so man has practiced the covenant through all the ages.

Today, hundreds of tribes in equatorial Africa cut the covenant.

Stanley cut the covenant fifty times with different tribes.

Livingstone cut the covenant.

Missionaries have seen it enacted, but didn't understand the significance, thinking it was some heathen rite, and not realizing that the blood covenant practiced in Africa today would open the doors in every tribe for the gospel of the Lord Jesus Christ.

If any missionary who understands the language of any of the tribes would explain to them the Lord's Table and let them see what it meant, out of what it grew, it would at once open the door to the gospel to them.

The whole redemptive plan swings about the two covenants.

You remember, we have an old covenant and a new covenant.

Perhaps I had better illustrate to you what this ancient covenant means, because it is practically the same among all peoples.

REASONS FOR CUTTING THE COVENANT

There are three reasons for men cutting the covenant with each other.

If a strong tribe lives by the side of a weaker tribe, and there is danger of the weaker tribe being destroyed, the weaker tribe will seek to "cut the covenant" with the stronger tribe so that they may be preserved.

Second, two business men entering into a partnership might cut the covenant to insure that neither would take advantage of the other.

Third, if two men loved each other as devotedly as David and Jonathan, or as Damon and Pythias in Greek mythology, they would cut the covenant for that love's sake.

THE METHOD OF CUTTING THE COVENANT

The method of cutting the covenant is practically the same all over the world; although there are differences, of course.

In some places it has degenerated into a very grotesque, almost horrible rite, but nevertheless it is the same blood covenant.

That which is practiced by the native tribes of Africa, by the Arabs, by the Syrians, and by the Balkans is this:

Two men wish to cut the covenant; they come together with their friends and a priest.

First, they exchange gifts. By this exchange of gifts they indicate that all that one of them has the other owns if necessary.

After the exchange of gifts, they bring a cup of wine, the priest makes an incision in the arm of one man, and the blood drips into the wine.

An incision is made in the other man's arm and his blood drips into the same cup.

The wine is stirred and the bloods are mixed. Then the cup is handed to one man and he drinks part of it, then he hands it to the other man and he drinks the rest of it.

When they have drunk it, often, they will put their wrists together so that their bloods mingle, or they will touch their tongues to each other's wounds.

Now, they have become blood brothers.

THE SACREDNESS OF THE BLOOD COVENANT

Sir Henry Morton Stanley said he never knew this covenant to be broken in Africa, no matter what the provocation.

Dr. David Livingstone also bears witness, saying that he never knew it to be broken there either.

In other parts of the world, it is claimed that the blood covenant was never broken.

It is one covenant that is perfectly sacred among all primitive peoples.

In Africa, if one was to break the covenant, his own mother or wife, or his nearest relatives would seek his death, would turn him over to the hands of the avenger for destruction. No man can live in Africa who breaks the covenant; he curses the very ground he walks on.

The vilest enemies become trusted friends as soon as the covenant is cut.

No man takes advantage of the covenant or breaks it.

It is so sacred that the children to the third and fourth generations revere it and keep it.

In other words, it is a perpetual covenant, indissoluble, a covenant that cannot be annulled.

3

THE COVENANT IN AFRICA

One illustration of Stanley's might help us to grasp the significance.

When Stanley was seeking Livingstone, he came in contact with a powerful equatorial tribe. They were very war-like.

Stanley was not in condition to fight them.

Finally, his interpreter asked him why he didn't make a strong covenant with them.

He asked what it meant and was told that it meant drinking each other's blood.

Stanley revolted from such a rite, but conditions kept growing worse, until finally the young colored man asked him again why he did not cut the covenant with the chieftain of the tribe.

Stanley asked what the results of such a covenant would be, and the interpreter answered. "Everything the chieftain has will be yours if you need it."

This appealed to Stanley and he investigated.

After several days of negotiation, they arrived at the covenant.

First, there was a parley in which the chieftain questioned Stanley as to his motives and standing, and his ability to keep the covenant.

The next step was an exchange of gifts.

The old chieftain wanted Stanley's new white goat.

Stanley was in poor health and goat's milk was about all he could take for nourishment, so it was very hard for him to give this up, but the chieftain seemed to want nothing else.

So he finally gave up the goat, and the old chieftain handed him his seven-foot, copper-wound spear.

Stanley thought he had been beaten, but he found that wherever he went in Africa with that spear, everybody bowed to him and submitted to him.

The old chieftain then brought in one of his princes.

Stanley led forth one of his men, from England.

Then the priest came forward with a cup of wine, made an incision in the young black's wrist, and let the blood drip into the cup of wine. He cut a like incision in the wrist of the young Englishman, and let his blood also drip into the cup of wine.

Then the wine was stirred and the bloods were mixed.

The priest handed the cup to the Englishman and he drank part of it and then handed it to the black and he drank the rest of it.

Next, they rubbed their wrists together so that their bloods mingled.

Now, they had become blood brothers.

These two men were only substitutes, but they had bound Stanley and the chieftain, and Stanley's men and the chieftain's soldiers into a blood brotherhood that was indissoluble.

Then gunpowder was rubbed into the wound, so that when it healed there would be a black mark to indicate that they were covenant men.

The next step in this ceremony was the planting of trees, trees that were known for their long life.

After the planting of the trees, the chieftain stepped forward and shouted, "Come, buy and sell with Stanley, for he is our blood brother."

A few hours before, Stanley's men had to stand on guard around their bales of cotton cloth and trinkets, but now he could open the bales and leave them on the street and nothing was disturbed.

For anyone to steal from their blood brother, Stanley, was a death penalty.

The old chieftain couldn't do enough for his newfound brother.

Stanley couldn't understand the sacredness of it, and years later wondered about it.

CURSES AND BLESSINGS

I have left out a very important feature of this ceremony.

As soon as the two young men had drunk each other's blood, a priest stepped out and pronounced the most awful curses that Stanley had ever heard, curses that were to come upon him if he broke the covenant.

Then Stanley's interpreter took his part and pronounced curses upon the old king, his wife, his children, and his tribe if they broke the covenant with Stanley.

You remember, when Moses apportioned the land to the different tribes, he called their attention to the mountain of cursing and the mountain of blessing?

In Deuteronomy 11 and 27, you find both the curses and the blessings of the old covenant.

The curses were pronounced from the mount of cursing each year, and the blessings were pronounced from the mount of blessing each year.

THE MEMORIAL

The ceremony of tree planting was always done, if they were in a country where trees grow.

These are called memorial trees, trees of the covenant.

In a place where trees do not grow, they set up a pile of stones or erect a monument as a memorial to remind them and their descendants that they are partners in an indissoluble covenant.

You remember Abraham gave to Abimelech some ewe lambs, and the lambs were for a memorial.

As the lambs grew and the flocks grew, that flock would be a continual reminder of the covenant that had been cut.

The moment a covenant is solemnized, everything that a blood covenant man owns in the world is at the disposal of his blood brother if he needs it, and yet this brother would never ask for anything unless he were absolutely driven by need to do it.

Some of the most beautiful stories I know in the world are the stories of blood covenant brothers.

Another feature of this is that as soon as they cut the covenant, they are recognized as blood brothers by others, and they are called the blood brothers.

4

JEHOVAH CUTS THE COVENANT WITH ABRAHAM

When God entered into the covenant with Abraham, there were several very striking events that took place.

Among them was the changing of Abram's and Sarai's names to Abraham (a prince of God) and Sarah (princess of God).

In other words, He lifted them into the royal family before He cut the covenant with them.

The Abrahamic covenant, which is the basis of Judaism and Christianity, is the most marvelous document in existence.

It was sealed by circumcision. (See Genesis 17.)

This covenant bound Abraham and his descendants by indissoluble ties to Jehovah, and it bound Jehovah to Abraham and his descendants by the same solemn token.

THE CUTTING OF THE COVENANT

When Abraham was ninety-nine years of age, God appeared to him as "God Almighty" or "El Shaddai."

He said unto Abraham, "*Walk before me, and be thou perfect. And I will make my covenant between me and thee, and will multiply thee exceedingly*" (Genesis 17:1–2).

We see Abraham on his face. God is talking with him. God tells him, "*As for me, behold, my covenant is with thee, and thou shalt be a father of many nations. Neither shall thy name any more be called Abram, but thy name shall be Abraham; for the father of many nations have I made thee*" (Genesis 17:4–5).

In Genesis 15:6, God made a promise to Abraham and it says that *"Abraham believed in the Lord; and* [God] *counted it to* [Abraham] *for righteousness."*

This word *"believed"* means that Abraham made an "unqualified committal" of himself and all he was or ever would be, to God.

The word *"believed"* here in the Hebrew means not only a "loving trust," but it also means "give yourself wholly up," or, "to be a part of Himself," or "go right into him," or "the unqualified committal."

Abraham gave himself to God in utter abandonment of self.

On the ground of that, God said, "Take for me," that is, as God's substitute, "an animal and slay it."

Abraham did it.

Then God said, "My substitute has been slain, and I want you to circumcise yourself," so that his blood would mingle with the blood of God's substitute.

When that was done, God and Abraham had entered the covenant.

It meant that all Abraham had or ever would have was laid on the altar.

It meant that God must sustain and protect Abraham to the very limit.

When God cut the covenant with Abraham, the Israelite nation came into being as a covenant people because of this covenant.

This covenant was limited to Israel, the children of Abraham, and had behind it the promise and the oath of God. (See Genesis 22:16–18.)

SOME COVENANT FACTS

The seal of the covenant was circumcision.

Every male child at eight days of age was circumcised, and the circumcision was the entrance into the Abrahamic covenant.

When that child was circumcised and entered into the covenant, then that child became an inheritor of everything connected with the covenant.

If the child's father and mother should die, another Israelite was under obligation to care for the child, or if the husband should die, to care for the widow. It is the law of the covenant.

All things are laid upon the altar of this covenant.

If keeping the covenant with a blood brother meant the death or loss of his wife, or of his first born, or the destruction of his property, or of his own life, all, everything was laid upon the altar.

THE COVENANT OBLIGATIONS

Genesis 17:13: *"And my covenant shall be in your flesh for an everlasting covenant."*

Every male child at eight days of age was circumcised. This mark on their bodies was the seal of their place in the covenant, and as long as Israel kept this covenant, which was renewed in Moses, there weren't enemies enough in the whole world to conquer one little village.

When God led Israel out of Egypt by Moses they had no law, no priesthood.

Then God gave them the Ten Commandments, the priesthood, the atonement, the sacrifices, the offerings, the laws that govern the sacrifices and the offerings, the scapegoat, and the worship. All these belonged to the covenant.

The covenant did not belong to the Ten Commandments as modernists put it, but the covenant was the reason for the law.

It was called the law of the covenant.

Israel were the people of the covenant.

Read Exodus and Leviticus carefully, noting when the word *"atonement"* first occurs, when the law was given, and when the priesthood was set apart.

Study Leviticus 16 and 17 carefully. Note what the blood meant, and the significance of the word *"atonement."*

5

ABRAHAM'S SACRIFICE

T*ake now thy son, thine only son Isaac, whom thou lovest"* (Genesis 22:2).

You know the rest of that fearful command that came to the man, Abraham, as he stood transfixed in the presence of the angel of the covenant.

There was no wavering on the part of Abraham.

Consider what this meant to him. We know how he had hungered for a son.

We know how he expressed his longings to Jehovah in those years when it seemed that such a possibility was gone forever.

Then Jehovah promised him a son.

> *And God said unto Abraham, As for Sarai, thy wife, thou shalt not call her name Sarai, but Sarah shall her name be. And I will bless her, and give thee a son of her: yea I will bless her, and she shall be a mother of nations; kings of peoples shall be of her. Then Abraham fell upon his face, and laughed, and said in his heart, Shall a child be born unto him that is a hundred years old? and shall Sarah, that is ninety years old, bear?*
> (Genesis 17:15–17)

> *And God said, Sarah thy wife shall bear thee a son indeed; and thou shalt call his name Isaac: and I will establish my covenant with him for an everlasting covenant, and with his seed after him.* (Genesis 17:19)

Abraham and Sarah were old. Abraham was nearly a hundred years old, and Sarah was ninety. In the realm of the senses, for them to become the parents of a child was impossible, for the Scripture tells us in Genesis 18:11: *"Now Abraham and Sarah were old and well stricken in age; and it ceased to be with Sarah after the manner of women."*

But Abraham considered not his own body, which was as good as dead, nor the deadness of Sarah's womb, but looking unto God, he waxed strong.

He counted that God was able to make good anything that He promised. The Scripture tells us that Abraham believed God. (See Genesis 15:6.)

> *And the* L*ORD visited Sarah as he had said, and the* L*ORD did unto Sarah as he had spoken. For Sarah conceived, and bare Abraham a son in his old age.... And Abraham called the name of his son...Isaac."*
>
> (Genesis 21:1–3)

The child grew to be 18 or 20 years of age; then God asked for the boy.

He said, "*Take now thy son, thine only son Isaac, whom thou lovest, and get thee into the land of Moriah; and offer him there as a burnt offering upon one of the mountains which I will tell thee of*" (Genesis 22:2).

Abraham did not hesitate, though it meant giving up all he held dear, but took the young man on that three days and three nights journey.

They arrived at Mt. Moriah and together they built the altar.

Abraham laid the young man on the altar and drew the knife to slay him, when the angel of the Lord shouted to him, saying, "*Lay not thine hand upon the lad*" (Genesis 22:11).

God had found a man that would keep the covenant; He had found a covenant-keeping man.

Now hear what God said: "*By myself have I sworn, saith the* L*ORD, for because thou hast done this thing, and hast not withheld thy son, thine only son: that in blessing I will bless thee, and in multiplying I will multiply thy seed as the stars of the heaven*" (Genesis 22:16–17).

Did you notice, "*By myself have I sworn*"? God's throne became the surety of His promise.

It is the most solemn thing that a man can conceive.

Abraham had proved his worthiness of God's confidence.

THE COVENANT KEEPING GOD

You remember that before this thing happened, when God was going to destroy Sodom and Gomorrah, He said it wasn't best to do it without talking it over with Abraham?

You remember Abraham's great appeal and how he talked with God in a manner that would stagger one?

He said, *"Shall not the Judge* [God] *of all the earth do right?"* (Genesis 18:25).

Then he began to plead for the righteous ones in those cities, and God permitted that man on the ground of his blood covenant relationship to become the intercessor for the wicked cities of Sodom and Gomorrah.

When Abraham entered into the covenant, he gained the right to arbitrate between the wicked men of the earth and the God of the whole earth.

Abraham established a blood-covenant precedent of intercession that has stood through all the ages.

6

THE ABRAHAMIC COVENANT

The Abrahamic covenant was the reason for Israel's being.

There would have been no nation, had God not given them the covenant.

You remember that Isaac was born after Abraham was one hundred-years-old, and Sarah was past ninety-years-old.

Isaac, father of the Israelite nation, was a miracle child.

That nation went down into Egypt, after Isaac's grandchildren had grown to manhood. They were delivered out of Egypt, 400 years later, after having served in bondage for over 300 years.

No nation had ever been delivered like that. It was the rarest, most unique national experience in history.

They were delivered because they were God's blood covenant people.

In Exodus 2, when God heard the groanings of Israel in Egypt, He said that He remembered His covenant that He had made with Abraham, Isaac, and Jacob.

God sent Moses down into Egypt to deliver Abraham's blood covenant descendants.

God couldn't break the covenant. He could not forget it nor ignore it.

He is the covenant-keeping God.

Behind Israel was this solemn covenant that God had sealed on His side, by putting Himself in utter, absolute bondage to that covenant.

God and Israel were bound together.

As long as Israel kept the covenant there were no sick people among the Israelites.

When He said, *"I am the Lord that healeth thee"* (Exodus 15:26), that settled it.

Jehovah was their only physician.

He was not only their physician, but He was their succor, He was their protector.

There was never a barren wife, no babies ever died, no young men and women ever died unless they broke the covenant.

As long as they kept the covenant, there were not allied armies enough in the world to conquer one little village.

In battle, no soldiers were slain.

They were blood-covenant men.

Moses led them out of Egypt into a barren desert, comparable to our own Mojave desert, and on the ground of the covenant, God supplied them with water for themselves and their cattle, and manna for the people.

When they came out of Egypt, it was through signs and wonders that staggered the whole world at the time, and have been the wonder and amazement of the world ever since.

God preserved them as a nation because they were His covenant people.

When they sinned and broke the covenant, they were carried away into captivity and into Babylon.

They had sinned against the covenant. They had brought judgment upon themselves.

But, in the face of that, God remembered the covenant He had made with Abraham years before. They were given a revelation of God.

We call it the old covenant; we call it the law of the prophets and the Psalms.

Israel was given this revelation of God and this law of God because they were God's blood covenant people.

Then, later, God gave them Jesus because they were the blood covenant people.

Jesus became the founder of the new covenant. We have that new covenant because they had the Abrahamic covenant.

We enter into the same blessings that they entered into, and richer, because of the new covenant of which Jesus is the surety.

7

ISRAEL, THE BLOOD COVENANT PEOPLE

I want to call your attention to several miraculous things in connection with Israel, the blood covenant people.

This covenant guaranteed to them physical protection: protection from their enemies, from the pestilence, and from diseases.

They went into Egypt and became a great nation of over three million people. God brought them forth by a series of miracles that absolutely stagger the human reason.

He did this because He was in a blood covenant relationship with Israel, and was under bond to deliver them.

As they stood on the shore of the Red Sea, after they had been delivered from their bondage, God said: *"I am the Lord that healeth thee"* (Exodus 15:26).

Then He promised them that none of the diseases of the Egyptians should come upon them.

He was their blood covenant physician. We can hardly grasp this.

We know that for forty years they wandered in the desert land.

God gave them the cloud for protection from that fierce desert sun, and at night he gave them the pillar of fire for light and heat.

God gave them food and water. He met their every need.

THE LAW AND THE PRIESTHOOD

Then God gave them the blood covenant law. We call it the Mosaic law, because Moses was the instrument through which it came to Israel.

This law was to separate them from all other peoples of the earth. It was to make them a peculiar people on whom God could bestow unusual blessings, and it was on the basis of the blood covenant.

The covenant was the center around which all of Israel's life moved.

After the giving of the Law, the Law was broken. A priesthood was imperative.

There had never been a divinely appointed priesthood in the human race before, but now God appointed the priesthood and the high priest.

With the priesthood was given the atonement offerings. Never before had there been an atonement offering or the great Day of Atonement.

The only offerings they had known had been the peace offerings or the whole burnt offering.

Now God appointed a special sacrifice in which the blood was to cover the broken Law, and cover spiritually dead Israel so that God could dwell in their midst.

The word *atonement* in Hebrew means "to cover," and God gave it because of the life that was in the blood, and because that life in the blood served as a covering for spiritually dead Israel and its broken Law, and Israel's unfitness to stand uncovered in the presence of God.

The blood covenant priesthood headed up in the high priest. He became the surety of the covenant. He stood between the people and God.

Once a year he entered into the holy of holies to make the yearly atonement.

This was the only time the high priest ever functioned, unless some grievous sin broke out among the people.

The high priest's function was peculiar in that once a year he made the covering or atonement for the people, and confessed the sins of the people on the head of the scapegoat, and then sent him out in the wilderness to be destroyed.

His presence was necessary to maintain their fellowship and insure their protection.

With the atonement and the priesthood, came the blood covenant sacrifices.

The five great offerings mentioned in the first seven chapters of Leviticus were the whole burnt offering, the meal offering, the peace offering, the trespass offering, and the sin offering.

These offerings were fellowship offerings and broken fellowship offerings.

They had to do with the daily life of the people.

When an Israelite was in fellowship, he could bring the whole burnt offering, the meal offering, or the peace offering.

When he had sinned against his brother, he could bring the trespass offering.

When he had sinned against the holy things of God, he could bring the sin offering.

In this last offering, the high priest, under certain conditions, officiated.

They were blood covenant people and must be kept in fellowship with the blood covenant obligations and privileges.

BLESSINGS OF THE COVENANT

God was under obligation to shield them from the armies of the nations that surrounded them.

God was under obligation to see that their land brought forth large crops.

God was under obligation by the covenant to see that the herds and flocks multiplied.

The hand of God was upon them in blessing.

They became the head of the nations and of wealth.

Jerusalem became the richest city the world had ever known.

Their hillsides were irrigated, their valleys teemed with wealth.

There was no city like it, no nation like it.

God was their God; they were God's covenant people.

Under the covenant, one man could chase a thousand in war, and two could put ten thousand to flight.

In David's day, when covenant truth became a living force in the nation, David had blood covenant warriors that could individually slay eight hundred men in a single combat.

They could kill a lion without weapons as though it had been a cub.

They had physical strength and prowess. They had divine protection that made them the greatest warriors the world ever knew.

They were God's peculiar people. They were the treasure of the heart of God.

THE JUDGMENT

There isn't a more tragic event in human history than the destruction of the city of Jerusalem, and the carrying away of the people into Babylon because they had sinned against the covenant.

The heavens became brass, the earth as iron, their rain was turned to dust; diseases afflicted them and enemies over-ran them, until their great city, the richest city the world had ever known, was but a heap of ruins. The temple, which cost more money than any other ever built, was completely destroyed and lay in dust and ashes.

They had broken the covenant.

8

THE NEW COVENANT

Now then, we have a background.

We come to the New Testament, and see Jesus and the disciples gathered together that night before the crucifixion.

> *And as they were eating, Jesus took bread, and blessed it, and brake it, and gave it to the disciples, and said, Take, eat; this is my body. And he took the cup, and gave thanks, and gave it to them, saying, Drink ye all of it; for this is my blood of the new* [covenant], *which is shed for many for the remission of sins.* (Matthew 25:26–28)

The old blood covenant was the basis on which the new covenant was founded.

Now you can understand that when Jesus said, "This is my blood of the new covenant," the disciples knew what it meant. They knew that when they cut the covenant with Jesus in that upper room that night, they had entered into the strongest, most sacred covenant known to the human heart.

JESUS, THE SURETY

Jesus brings us a new covenant, having displaced and fulfilled the old covenant. (See Hebrews 10:9.)

With the fulfilling of the old covenant, everything connected with it was set aside.

As the old covenant was sealed with circumcision, the new covenant is sealed with the new birth.

The old covenant had the Levitical priesthood.

The new covenant has Jesus as the High Priest, and we as the royal and holy priesthood. (See 1 Peter 2:1–10.)

The first priesthood had a temple in which God dwelt in the holy of holies with the ark of the covenant. (See Exodus 40.)

In the new covenant our bodies are the temple of God, and the Spirit dwells within them.

Jehovah was the surety of the old covenant.

> *By so much was Jesus made a surety of a better* [covenant].
>
> (Hebrews 7:22)

Jesus stands behind every sentence in the new covenant.

He is the great intercessor of the new covenant. *"He is able also to save them to the uttermost that come unto God by him, seeing He ever liveth to make intercession for them"* (Hebrews 7:25).

God bound Himself with an oath to the old covenant. He was the surety of the old covenant. He said, *"I have sworn by myself"* (Isaiah 45:23).

Just as God stood behind the old covenant and was its surety, so Jesus is the surety of every word in the new covenant.

What strong faith should be built upon a foundation like this.

The resources of heaven are behind Jesus and behind that covenant.

9

CONTRAST OF THE TWO COVENANTS

The Bible is composed of two covenants, contracts, or agreements.

The first covenant was between Abraham and Jehovah. It was sealed by circumcision. (See Genesis 17.)

It is often called the "Law covenant" or the "Mosaic covenant." Both titles are wrong.

It is the Abrahamic covenant, and the Law that was given through Moses belonged to the covenant.

When the Israelites were delivered from Egypt, they had no law, nor government, so Jehovah gave them the law.

We call it the Mosaic law. (See Exodus 20.)

It is the covenant law, with its priesthood, sacrifices, ceremonies, and offerings.

The law had no sooner been given than it was broken. Then God provided the atonement (or covering) for the broken law. (See Exodus 24.)

The word *atonement* means "to cover." It is not a New Testament word; it does not appear in the New Testament Greek.

Why?

Because the blood of Jesus Christ cleanses, instead of merely covering.

The first covenant did not take away sin, it merely covered it.

It did not give eternal life or the new birth. It gave a promise of it.

It did not give fellowship with God. It gave a type of it.

It gave protection to Israel as a nation, it met their physical needs.

God was Israel's healer, provider, and protector.

You cannot separate Moses's law from the covenant, so when the covenant was fulfilled, the Law was fulfilled and set aside.

> *For the law having a shadow of the good things to come, not the very image of the things, can never with those sacrifices which they offered year by year continually make the comers thereunto perfect.* (Hebrews 10:1)

All that the Law and the first covenant was, was a shadow.

The sacrifices could never make perfect the man under the covenant: "*For then would they not have ceased to be offered? because that the worshippers once purged should have no more consciousness of sins*" (Hebrews 10:2).

The blood of bulls and goats did not cleanse the conscience, did not take away sin consciousness from man.

The inference is that there is a sacrifice that takes away the sin consciousness so that man stands uncondemned in God's presence.

> *There is therefore now no condemnation to them which are in Christ Jesus."* (Romans 8:1)

> *Being therefore justified by faith, we have peace with God through our Lord Jesus Christ.* (Romans 5:1)

In Romans 3:26, God becomes our righteousness or our justification, "*that he might be just* [righteous], *and the justifier* [righteousness] *of him that hath faith in Jesus.*"

THE MINISTER OF THE SANCTUARY

The first covenant was sealed by the blood of Abraham, and God sacrificed an animal.

This new covenant is sealed with the blood of Jesus Christ, God's own Son.

> *We have such an high priest, who is set on the right hand of the throne of the Majesty in the heavens.* (Hebrews 8:1)

He is the minister of the true tabernacle, which the Lord prepared instead of Moses.

Everything centered around the high priest under the old covenant. When the high priest failed, the people had no approach to God.

Everything centers around our new High Priest under the new covenant, but our High Priest can never fail His people.

> *But now hath He obtained a more excellent ministry, by how much also He is the mediator of a better covenant, which was established upon better promises.* (Hebrews 8:6)

The high priest was an earthly mediator between Israel and Jehovah. Jesus is the mediator of the new covenant.

10

A STUDY IN HEBREWS

The book of Hebrews has several vital contrasts.

There is the contrast of Moses and Jesus; of Aaron, the high priest, and Jesus the new High Priest; and the contrast of the blood of bulls and goats and the blood of Christ.

It is not only a contrast of the bloods, but of the two tabernacles, the one reared by Moses and the one in heaven. Into this latter one Jesus enters, and sits down there as our High Priest.

His home is the holy of holies.

The priest under the old covenant could only stay long enough to make the atonement.

Hebrews 9:21–23 tells how the tabernacle and all the vessels were cleansed with blood:

> *Moreover he sprinkled with blood both the tabernacle, and all the vessels of the ministry. And almost all things are by the law purged with blood; and without shedding of blood is no remission. It was therefore necessary that the patterns of things in the heavens should be purified with these; but the heavenly things themselves with better sacrifices than these.*

This is a startling thing, but Adam's sin had touched heaven itself.

In verse 24: *"For Christ is not entered into the holy place made with hands, which are in the figures of the true; but into heaven itself, now to appear in the presence of God for us."*

This is the climax of it all.

This lets us see the contrast of God's estimation of the blood of Christ and the blood of bulls and goats.

As we come to value the blood of Christ as God values it, then the problem of our standing and relationship never enters our minds.

THE NEW MEDIATOR

The blood of bulls and goats, under the first covenant, only cleansed or sanctified the flesh, but the blood of Christ is to "cleanse our conscience from dead works," so that we may stand uncondemned in the presence of the living God.

Because God accepted Jesus's blood when He carried it into the heavenly holy of holies, He has become by that act the mediator of the new covenant.

> *There is...one mediator between God and men, the man Christ Jesus"*
> (1 Timothy 2:5)

The reason man needs a mediator is because he has lost his standing with God. He has no ground on which he can approach Him.

Natural man is really an outlaw.

Ephesians 2:12 describes his sad condition as "*having no hope, and without God in the world.*"

Jesus is now to be the mediator between God and fallen man.

The blood of bulls and goats did not take away sin, it merely covered it temporarily.

But when Christ came, He redeemed all of those who had trusted in the blood of bulls and goats.

He died "*for the redemption of the transgressions that were under the first* [covenant]" (Hebrews 9;15).

Those sacrifices, under the old covenant, were like a promissory note that He cashed on Calvary.

God kept His covenant with Israel when He sent His Son to become sin, and He laid upon Him all the sins under the first covenant, that by accepting Him as their Savior, Israel might come into the promised redemption.

HE PUT SIN AWAY

This is the great heart teaching of the book of Hebrews.

Under the first covenant sin was "covered." The best that the Israelites had under the first covenant was a blood covering or atonement.

But under the new covenant our sins are not covered. They are put away. They are remitted.

They are as though they had never been.

> *Nor yet that he should offer himself often, as the high priest entereth into the holy place every year with blood of others; For then must he often have suffered since the foundation of the world; but now once in the end of the world hath he appeared to put away sin by the sacrifice of Himself.*
> (Hebrews 9:25–26)

The expression *"end of the world"* really means where the two worlds met.

The cross was where the old method of counting ended, and it was the place where the new time began.

The thing that stood between man and God was Adam's transgression.

Jesus put that away.

> *For he hath made him to be sin for us, who knew no sin.*
> (2 Corinthians 5:21)

Jesus settled the sin problem, made it possible for God to legally remit all that we have ever done, and gave to us eternal life, making us new creations.

> *Therefore if any man be in Christ, he is a new creature: old things are passed away; behold, they are become new. And all things are of God, who hath reconciled us to Himself by Jesus Christ, and hath given to us the ministry of reconciliation.* (2 Corinthians 5:17–18)

11

THE ONE SACRIFICE

The changing of the covenant and the changing of the priesthood left Israel almost homeless.

To leave the gorgeous temple for street preaching, and preaching in grove and cottage meetings, was an innovation that almost staggers one.

The one sacrifice that Jesus made ended the slaughtering of animals, the carrying of blood into the holy of holies.

It was the end of sin covering.

> *But this man, after he had offered one sacrifice for sins for ever, sat down on the right hand of God.* (Hebrews 10:12)

This *"once for all"* (Hebrews 10:10) offering ended the scapegoats bearing away sin.

You must read Leviticus 16:1–22 carefully in order to get the picture of the great Day of Atonement and the scapegoat.

This was the annual day of humiliation and expiation for the sins of the nation, when the high priest made the atonement for the sanctuary, the priests, and the people.

The high priest, laying aside his official ornaments, first offered a sin-offering for himself and for the priesthood, entering into the holy of holies with the blood.

He afterward took two he-goats for the nation. One was slain for Jehovah. On the head of the other the sins of the people were typically laid; it was made the sin-bearer of the nation, and laden with guilt, it was sent away into the wilderness.

Mark 15:38 tells of the death of Jesus and the rending of the veil between the holy place and the holy of holies where the blood was carried and sprinkled upon the mercy seat.

This was the end of the holy of holies on earth.

It was the beginning of a new covenant in His blood.

Acts 20:28 tells us that this was the blood of God.

He had carried this blood of Deity into the holy of holies in the new tabernacle, not made with hands, in the heavens. (See Hebrews 9:12.)

It was what He called the *"once for all"* sacrifice.

12

THE PRESENT MINISTRY OF CHRIST

The present ministry of Christ has been neglected by most Christians. So many, when they think of His giving His life for us, think only of His death and resurrection.

They do not know that when He sat down on the Father's right hand that He began to live for us in as much reality as He had died for us.

He is no longer the lowly man of Galilee. He is not the Son made sin for us, forsaken of God.

He is the Lord of all. He has conquered Satan, sin, and disease. He has conquered death.

He possesses all authority in heaven and in earth. (See Matthew 28:18.)

We can act fearlessly upon His Word because He stands behind it; He is the surety of it.

He is the surety of this new covenant. (See Hebrews 7:22.)

JESUS, OUR HIGH PRIEST

The high priest of the old covenant was a type of Christ, the High Priest of the new covenant.

Once every year, the high priest under the old covenant had entered into the tabernacle on earth with the blood of bulls and goats to make a yearly atonement for the sins of Israel. (See Hebrews 9:25, 10:1–4.)

The priests stood daily, ministering and offering the same sacrifices for the sins of Israel. (See Hebrews 10:11.)

Christ entered into heaven itself with His own blood, having obtained eternal redemption for us.

When God accepted the blood of Jesus Christ, He signified that the claims of justice had been met, and that man could be legally taken from Satan's authority and restored to fellowship with Himself.

By the sacrifice of Himself, Christ had put sin away.

By the sacrifice of Himself, He had sanctified man.

To sanctify means to "set apart," "to separate." He had separated man from Satan's kingdom and family.

When Christ met Mary after His resurrection, He said to her, *"Touch me not; for I am not yet ascended to my Father"* (John 20:17).

He was then on His way to the Father with His own blood, the token of the penalty He had paid, and He could not be touched by human hands.

Jesus's ministry as High Priest did not end with His carrying His blood into the holy place, but He is still the minister of the sanctuary. (See Hebrews 8:2.)

The word *sanctuary* in the Greek means "holy things."

He is ministering in the "holy things." These "holy things" are our prayers and worship.

We do not always know how to worship Him as we ought, but He takes our oftentimes crude petitions and worship and makes them beautiful to the Father.

Every prayer, every worship is accepted by the Father when it is presented in the name of Jesus.

He is a merciful and faithful High Priest. He can be touched with the feelings of our infirmities. (See Hebrews 4:14–16.)

He is High Priest forever. (See Hebrews 6:20.)

JESUS, THE MEDIATOR

When Christ sat down at the Father's right hand, He had satisfied the claims of justice, and He became the mediator between God and man.

Jesus is man's mediator for two reasons: because of what He is, and because of what He has done.

First, Jesus is man's mediator by virtue of what He is; He is the union of God and man.

He is the One who existed on equality with God, made in the likeness of men. (See Philippians 2:8–9.)

He has bridged the gulf between God and man. He is equal with God, and He is equal with man.

He can represent humanity before God.

This however, was not sufficient ground for a mediation between God and man. Man was an eternal criminal before God. Man was alienated from God, and under the judgment of Satan.

This brings us to our second fact. Jesus is man's mediator because of what He has done.

> *Yet now hath He reconciled in the body of His flesh through death, to present you holy and unblameable and unreprovable in his sight.*
>
> (Colossians 1:21–22)

> *Who hath reconciled us to Himself by Jesus Christ.*
>
> (2 Corinthians 5:18)

There could have been no mediator between God and man if there had not been first a reconciliation made between God and man.

Man was unrighteous in His condition of spiritual death. While he was in that condition, He could not approach God. Neither could any mediator have approached God for him.

Christ has reconciled us unto God through His death on the cross, so that He now presents man holy and without blemish before God. Therefore, man has a right to approach God through Christ, his mediator.

From the fall of man until Jesus sat down at God's right hand, no man had ever approached God except over a bleeding sacrifice, through a divinely appointed priesthood, or by an angelic visitation or dream.

On the ground of His high priestly offering of His own blood, He perfected our redemption, He satisfied the claims of justice and made it possible for God to legally give man eternal life, making him righteous, and giving him a standing as a son.

He is the mediator of the new covenant. (See Hebrews 9:15.)

Jesus is seated. He is the high priestly Mediator that is to introduce lost men to God.

Man has no approach now but through the new mediator.

By one sacrifice He has put sin away, and by one act He carried His blood into the holy of holies.

By that one act, Hebrews 10:19 declares that all can now enter boldly through the veil into the very presence of the Father and stand there without condemnation.

I would that we were able to make the church understand this blessed truth.

There is so much sin-consciousness, and so little consciousness of the finished work of Christ.

We hear Him cry, *"Come boldly unto the throne of grace, that we may obtain mercy, and find grace to help in time of need"* (Hebrews 4:14–16).

It seems to me as though the Master were saying, "Stop your crying, stop your groaning, come with joy to the throne of love gifts and let me fill your basket with blessings."

Hebrews 10:12–13 tells us that one sacrifice of His own blood now in the presence of the Father, on the mercy seat, has made all this available to those who take Christ as Savior and Lord.

His work is finished. In the Father's mind our redemption is complete.

JESUS, THE INTERCESSOR

Jesus, as High Priest, carried His blood into the holy of holies, satisfying the claims of justice that were against natural man.

As Mediator, He introduces the unsaved man to God.

Jesus is the way to God, and no one can approach God except through Him. As soon as man accepts Christ he becomes a child of God. Then Christ begins His intercessory work for him. (See John 14:6.)

Jesus is Mediator for the sinner, but He is Intercessor for the Christian.

The first question that comes to us is: "Why does the child of God need someone to intercede for him?

We can find the answer to that in Romans 12:2.

At the new birth, our spirits receive the life of God. The next need is that our minds be renewed.

Before we came into the family, we walked as natural men, Satan-ruled men. Satan ruled our minds.

Now that our spirits have received the life of God, our minds must be renewed so that we will know our privileges and responsibilities as children of God.

The new birth is instantaneous, but the renewing of our mind is a gradual process. Its growth is determined by our study and meditation on the Word.

During this period we need the intercession of Christ.

Many times we strain our fellowship with the Father, as in our ignorance of His will; many times we say and do things that are not pleasing to Him.

Then again, we need His intercession because of demoniacal persecution against us.

Demons persecute us for righteousness' sake. They hate and fear us because God has declared us righteous.

Because we have not fully learned of our authority, they cause us to stumble many times.

Regardless of this, He is able to save us to the uttermost, because He ever lives to pray for us. (See Hebrews 7:25.)

No one can lay anything to the charge of God's child. God has declared him righteous. There is no one to condemn him. Jesus is living to make intercession for him. (See Romans 8:33–34.)

JESUS, THE ADVOCATE

We came to the Father through Christ, our mediator.

We have felt the sweet influence of His intercession on our behalf. Now we want to know Him as our Advocate before the Father.

Many Christians today, who are living in broken fellowship, would be living victorious lives in Christ if they knew that Jesus was their Advocate.

Because of our unrenewed minds and satanic persecution, we sometimes sin and cause our fellowship with the Father to be broken.

Every child of God who breaks fellowship with the Father is under condemnation. If he had no Advocate to plead his case before the Father, he would be in a sad position.

The Word shows us that if we do sin, we have an Advocate with the Father.

Consider the meaning of the word *advocate*. In *Webster's Dictionary*, we read: "One who pleads the cause of another in a court of law; one who defends, vindicates, or espouses a cause by argument; an upholder; a defender; one summoned to aid."

Christ is our Defender, our Upholder. He is always there, at the right hand of God, ready to come to our aid, to intercede on our behalf.

> *My little children, these things write I unto you, that ye sin not. And if any man sin, we have an advocate with the Father, Jesus Christ the righteous.* (1 John 2:1)

In 1 John 1:3–9 is God's method for maintaining our fellowship with Him. If we sin so that our fellowship is broken, we may renew that fellowship by confessing our sin.

He is unable to act as our Advocate unless we confess our sins. The moment we confess them, He takes up our case before the Father.

The Word declares that when we confess our sins, He is righteous and faithful to forgive us our sins and to cleanse us from all unrighteousness, to wipe them out as though they had never been.

It is absolutely essential that Christians know Jesus as their Advocate. Many who are out of fellowship have confessed their sins many times without receiving a sense of restoration, because they did not know Jesus was their Advocate. They did not take forgiveness when they confessed their sins. They did not act upon the Word, which declared that the Father forgives the moment they confess.

No Christian should ever remain in broken fellowship any longer than it takes to ask forgiveness.

What the Father forgives He forgets. A child of His should never dishonor His Word by ever thinking of his sins again.

JESUS, THE SURETY

Jesus is our personal surety. This is the most vital of all the ministries of Jesus at the Father's right hand.

Under the old covenant, the high priest was the surety. If he failed, it interrupted the relationship between God and Israel. The blood of the atonement lost its efficacy.

Under the new covenant, Jesus is the High Priest and the surety of the new covenant.

Our position before the Father is absolutely secure. We know that throughout our lifetime we have at the right hand of God a Man who is there for us.

He is representing us before the Father.

He always has a standing with the Father.

Always, regardless of our standing, we have one representing us before the Father.

Our position is secure.

13

THREE BIG WORDS

"REMISSION"

This is one of the great words of the new covenant.

It means wiping out as though it had never been. When an army is disbanded, it is remitted; it stops being.

When God remits our sins, they are wiped out as though they had never been.

The word *remission* is never used except in connection with the new birth.

After we become Christians, we have our sins forgiven on the basis of our relationship and the intercession of Christ.

When we come to Him as sinners, take Christ as Savior, and confess Him as our Lord, then all that we have ever done is wiped out.

In the new birth, all that we have ever been stops being and a new creation takes the place of the old.

Six or eight times the word *remission* is translated *"forgiveness"* in the Epistles.

> *In whom we have redemption through His blood, the forgiveness of sins.* (Ephesians 1:7, see also Colossians 1:13–14; Luke 24:47; Acts 2:38; 26:18; 10:43)

The remission of our sins takes the place of the scapegoat under the old covenant.

It bore away their sins once a year, while the blood covered Israel as a nation.

On the basis of the blood of Christ, our sins are remitted and we are recreated.

"FORGIVENESS"

Forgiveness is a relationship word.

I am speaking now from a new covenant point of view.

When the sinner accepts Christ as Savior, his spirit is recreated, his sins are remitted, but being ignorant, he will always be conscious of sin.

On the ground of his relationship as a child of God, and Jesus's ministry at the right hand of the Father, there is ground for forgiveness for any sin that he commits.

First John 1 and 2 deals with this great issue of forgiveness.

When a child of God commits sin, he breaks his fellowship with the Father.

He does not break his relationship. He merely breaks the fellowship, just as a husband and wife do when they say an unkind word. It destroys the fellowship of the home, but that can be restored by asking forgiveness.

We are so constituted that we can forgive.

The same holds true between a Christian and the Father.

The moment that we sin and fellowship with the Father is broken, if we confess our sins He is faithful and righteous to forgive us our sins and to cleanse us from all unrighteousness.

> *My little children, these things write I unto you that ye sin not. And if any man sin, we have an advocate with the Father, Jesus Christ the righteous.* (1 John 2:1–2)

That remarkable expression "*the righteous*" holds wrapped within it marvelous grace.

"ATONEMENT"

The first covenant had law, which we call the Mosaic law, the priesthood, sacrifices, and the ordinances.

When the law was broken (as it had to be because Israel was spiritually dead) the priesthood was ordered to make an atonement, or a covering, for them.

They did not have eternal life. That could not come until Jesus came and redeemed us. He said, *"I am come that they might have life, and that they might have it more abundantly."*

You remember that receiving eternal life is the greatest event in any human being's experience.

On the great Day of Atonement we see two remarkable things that take place.

First, surrounded by great precautions, the high priest carries the blood of an innocent animal into the holy of holies and sprinkles it upon the mercy seat that covers the broken law.

Now Israel is blood covered for one year.

Leviticus 17:11 tells us that the blood is given as a covering, or atonement, by reason of the life that is in it.

It is the life of an innocent animal typically spread over spiritually dead Israel.

The next fact is the scapegoat. Aaron lays the sins of Israel upon the head of the scapegoat which is led away into the wilderness to be devoured by wild beasts.

For a year, they are free, blood covered, and their sins are borne away.

14

THE FOURFOLD BLESSINGS

There are fourfold blessings of the covenant.

The first blessing that comes with the covenant is the righteousness that God imparts to every member of the new covenant.

When you accept Jesus Christ as your Savior, the moment you are born again, that moment God imparts to you righteousness.

That gives you a standing in the presence of the Father, identical with the standing of Jesus.

We have never known it. We shrink from it.

After a little while, it is going to take possession of you; you are going to see it and there will be men and women who will rise up and act like Jesus.

He had no consciousness of inferiority before the Father, for He had no consciousness of sin.

If you actually believe the Bible, and believe that God is your righteousness, and that you are a new creation, created in Christ Jesus, you will have no sense of sin.

He has put sin away by sacrificing Himself, and the only consciousness you will ever have of sin is when you do something that is not right; and then you will take advantage of the blood of Christ and of the advocacy of Jesus.

Ever since the Lutheran proclamation we have done one thing! We have magnified sin, we have preached the devil, we have preached our own wickedness and our own unrighteousness, and we have kept it before the people so continuously that no preacher or layman dares think of himself except in the terms of a poor weak worm of the dust!

You know what the evangelists have done. They have come into a church, they want to get results, so they preach so as to bring the whole congregation under condemnation and get them to the altar in order to get a reputation as an evangelist.

We have absolutely taught unbelief! We have taught everything but the gospel of Christ.

What is the gospel?

The gospel is this: that God, on the ground of the substitutionary sacrifice of Jesus Christ, is able to declare that He is righteous, and that He Himself is our righteousness, the moment we believe on Jesus.

This is the most staggering thing the mind ever grasped, that God Almighty becomes your righteousness the moment you believe on the Lord Jesus Christ.

When you learn to walk as Jesus walked, without any consciousness of inferiority to God or Satan, you will have faith that will absolutely stagger the world!

Do you know what hinders our faith today?

We go before the Lord, *but* we listen to the devil before we go there. We go there with a sense of inferiority, the devil's message ringing in our ears!

Christians as a whole are afraid of Satan, dare not say they are free, and dare not face Satan.

God's righteousness makes you fearless in Satan's presence.

We rob the work of Jesus Christ of its efficacy, and we stand powerless before the adversary because we have doubted the integrity of the Word of God.

God's righteousness has been imparted to you, not as an "experience," but as a legal fact.

This is the most tremendous truth that God has given us in the Pauline revelation, and this is the very heart of the new covenant, that God makes us like Himself.

Weren't you made in His image and likeness?

That image is an image of righteousness.

If God declares that you are righteous, what business have you to condemn yourself?

Another blessing that this covenant brings is your union with God.

When those two men drank each other's blood, they became one, absolutely one.

When Abraham and God cut the covenant, they became one.

"I am the vine and ye are the branches" (John 15:5).

Are you a partner of Christ? Do you dwell in Christ? Does Christ dwell in you?

Paul said, *"Nevertheless I live; yet not I, but Christ liveth in me"* (Galations 2:20).

The incarnation was God becoming one with us.

The blood covenant made Paul disown himself and utterly own Christ as his life. It made Christ leave glory and come here to be one with us.

Now you can stand as fearlessly in the presence of hell, in the presence of the devil, as you would in the presence of some little inferior thing.

Didn't Jesus meet him and conquer him for us? Didn't He strip him of his authority? Didn't He take his armor from him, and didn't He leave him paralyzed?

Greater is He that is in us than the devil.

Why should we be afraid of him?

Why not stand before the world as a conqueror?

You are in blood covenant relationship with God Almighty.

When you were born again you entered the covenant.

Let me give you a picture.

You remember the mighty men of David. They were types of Christians. One of those men slew eight hundred men in personal combat in a single day.

He asked, *"How should one chase a thousand, and two put ten thousand to flight…?"* (Deuteronomy 32:30).

Blood covenant men!

As long as David walked with God in the covenant, not one of his warriors were ever slain.

Are you a partaker of the divine nature? Yes.

Are you a son of God? Yes.

Has God given you His righteousness? Yes.

Is God your righteousness? Certainly.

Then, has He given you a legal right to the use of Jesus's name? Certainly.

Do you see what kind of a man you are?

You are not a weakling. You stand like the Son of God. You are a son of God.

Now the only thing is this: we have to overcome the effect of these false teachings.

For generations they have made us sinners, and they have talked to us as sinners.

Almost every one of the old hymns start beautifully, but before they finish we are just poor weaklings, and we are living in sin, and we are under bondage, and they have kept us there.

Christ is almost unknown to us.

THE OBJECT OF THIS REVELATION

What is the object of this revelation? To let us know what we really are in Jesus Christ.

You say, "That is all right, Dr. Kenyon, but if you only knew how weak I am..."

What does He say?

What is the argument and conclusion of the book of Hebrews?

Looking unto Jesus, the author and finisher of our faith. (Hebrews 12:2)

Just as long as you look at yourself you don't amount to anything; you are just like Peter.

When he started to walk with Jesus on the waves, he didn't sink, but the moment he looked at the boisterous waves, that moment he sank.

You are linked up to God Almighty.

These things have I written unto you that believe on the name of the Son of God; that ye may know that ye have eternal life. (1 John 5:13)

That gives you your legal standing before God and gives you your place in the covenant.

I say it reverently, if I understand the gospel of the Lord Jesus Christ; this is the vision He has given me of it: that all of heaven's ability and heaven's glory and heaven's strength are at the disposal of the believer.

This is the most miraculous thing the world ever saw.

I believe that in the last days there is going to be an unveiling of the power of God, and multitudes will arise and live.

Weymouth's translation of Romans 5:17 tells us that we reign as kings in the realm of life in Christ.

We are to absolutely reign as Christ, and with Christ.

How? By faith.

HIS CHALLENGE TO US

Is God your righteousness?

You say, "I am trying to make Him my righteousness."

Can you make Him your righteousness?

If you believe on Jesus Christ, He *is* your righteousness.

Then go out and act it. Dare to let God loose in you.

15

REDEMPTION IS BY GOD

With the horrible picture in view of Satan's finished work, our hearts cry out: "Who is able, who has the ability to meet man's need in a plight like this?"

Thank God, there is an answer.

When God saw the condition of man, He began immediately to make provision for his redemption.

He knew that man could not redeem himself; He knew that man had no ability to approach Him.

So, God gave first the Abrahamic covenant.

Then, with the Abrahamic covenant, when Abraham's descendants became a nation, He gave to them the law of the covenant, the priesthood of the covenant, the atonement of the covenant, and the sacrifices and offerings of the covenant.

All these were given to prepare a people.

Out of that people was to come the incarnate God-Man, and that incarnate God-Man was to break:

First, the power of Satan and redeem man from his bondage, and restore to man his righteousness so he could stand in the Father's presence on as good a footing, if not better, than Adam had before the fall, thus taking from man all the sense of his guilt and his sin.

Second, Satan's dominion, to redeem man so absolutely, to shatter Satan's dominion so completely that the weakest bondman of the devil could become a participator in this restored righteousness, so that man could live a life of victory over this old age-ruler, Satan.

This God-Man, this Incarnate One, was to make such a complete and perfect sacrifice that God could not only legally restore to man his lost righteousness and give to man his perfect redemption, but could also do the mightiest things that beggar the very imagination of man, such as make man a new creation.

What?

Yes, sir! He absolutely makes man a new creation, imparts His own nature to man, and drives out that cringing fear nature, sin nature, Satan nature.

The big, glorious, wonderful nature of God takes its place until we stand in the presence of God, under the blazing light of His grace and love.

We open up as a rose does to the sun, until the fullness of His love comes flooding into our beings and then flows back again to Him, our own wonderful Father. We are His own beloved children.

Reader, you are standing in the presence of the miracle of miracles, the grace of God that is restoring the lost human race, swinging it back out of the orbit of selfishness and weakness and fear into the realm of faith, love, and life of God.

He will not only legally restore righteousness, legally redeem us, and legally make us a new creation, but He will also legally give the Holy Spirit to every one of the new creation.

That great, mighty Spirit that raised Jesus up from the dead can actually come into these bodies of ours and make them His home, until the heart whispers, then sings, and then breaks into the anthem paraphrased from 1 John 4:4: "Greater is He that is in me, than he that is in the world."

On the wings of that anthem we move up and out of the reason realm and soar by faith into the realm of love where faith rules and where Jesus is Lord.

He not only did this, but He also gave to us the legal right to use His name so that we may cast out Satan, lay hands on the sick so they become well, and defeat the very purposes of Satan.

Oh, we have that name. That name makes us just like Jesus.

When you live in that name and walk in that name, the devil cannot tell you from Jesus.

You look like Him. You are clothed in His righteousness; you are filled with His life.

You have His name stamped upon you.

Ah, but He did more than that.

He gave to us a revelation. We call it the Word, and this Word is the Word of the Spirit.

That great, mighty Spirit that raised Jesus from the dead has come into you.

Now, through human lips, the Holy Spirit wields that Word and conquers the vast armies of hell.

You are the very son of God, called into fellowship with Jesus Christ, with restored righteousness, restored liberty and freedom, a new creation indwelt of the Holy Spirit, with the living Word of God.

You have a fellowship richer than Adam ever dreamed of.

When Jesus comes, this body that Satan made mortal will receive immortality and never die again.

Death can never threaten us or fill us with fear.

We stand complete in all the fullness of His completeness now.

What will it be when the pearly gates unfold, and we, His love-subjects, His love-slaves, and His redeemed forever, behold our Lord seated upon the throne of the ages.

16

BENEATH HIS FEET

This is the climax of the redemptive work of Christ.

We have seen Jesus after the resurrection exalted to the highest seat in the universe, with all dominion, all authority, all power beneath His feet. (See Ephesians 1:19–23.)

We know in Colossians 1:18 that we are His feet, His body.

All that is beneath His feet is beneath ours.

His victory is our victory.

There is no reason for Christ's coming and entering the tremendous contest for our redemption unless it was for us.

He did not do it for Himself. What He did for us is ours.

What is ours requires nothing but the taking.

God did not do this work, then lock it up and keep it away from us and dole it out to a few.

In His redemption there is a perfect righteousness given us. (See 2 Corinthians 5:21.)

That righteousness permits us to come boldly to the throne of grace.

That righteousness permits us to enjoy the fullness of our rights in Christ.

That righteousness is based on Romans 4:25 and Romans 5:1: *"Therefore being justified by faith, we have peace with God through our Lord Jesus Christ."*

Through His work on the cross and His death and resurrection, He made peace.

He arose, because He had conquered our enemies.

He had put to naught those who had held us in bondage.

> *Having spoiled principalities and powers, he made a shew of them openly, triumphing over them in it.* (Colossians 2:15)

We know that the Father planned our redemption. (See John 3:16.)

Jesus carried out that plan. (See Ephesians 1:7; 1 Peter 2:24.)

> *Verily, verily, I say unto you, He that believeth on me hath everlasting life.* (John 6:47)

I believe that the plan was carried out, and that I have eternal life; that by *"His stripes* [I am] *healed"* (Isaiah 53:5); by His grace I am more than a conqueror.

First John 5:13 declares that I have eternal life.

If I have eternal life, I have my healing.

(For a complete exposition of healing in the plan of redemption, send for our book, *Jesus the Healer.* Thousands have been healed while reading this book.)

I have every need supplied so that I can do all things in Christ who strengthens me.

There is no struggle, no long agonizing prayer, and no need of fasting to get it.

It is mine!

Ephesians 1:3 says He has blessed me with every spiritual blessing.

How do I get it?

I just thank Him for it.

Thanksgiving throws the door open wide, praise keeps it open.

For years we have been taught that we had to groan and struggle and cry and pray and "hold on" to get the answer.

All that is the work of unbelief, and grows out of our ignorance of the Word and of our rights in Christ.

If 1 Corinthians 3:21 is true, that *"All things are* [ours]"; and Colossians 2:10: "[We] *are complete in Him"*; and Ephesians 1:22: *"All things under his feet"*; and Satan has been conquered; and we are more than victors through Him who loved us; where is the place for begging and crying?

It dishonors the Father.

17

"IN MY NAME"

We are entering into the era of dominion linked with omnipotence, filled with Him who is greater than he that is in the world, with the wisdom of Him who spoke a universe into being, and with a legal right to use His name in every crisis of our lives.

> *And whatsoever ye shall ask in my name, that will I do, that the Father may be glorified in the Son.* (John 14:13–14)

This is not prayer. The promise of the use of His name in prayer is given in chapters 15 and 16.

It is what Peter used at the beautiful gate of the temple as recorded in Acts 3.

He used the name. He said, *"In the name of Jesus Christ of Nazareth rise up and walk"* (Acts 3:6)

That man who had been lame from birth leaped to his feet, perfectly well and strong.

Jesus said, "Whatsoever ye shall demand in my name"—for the word ask means demand—"that will I do." (See John 14:13.)

A woman once came to me with a cancer of the breast. It had been a running sore for a year and a half. She had suffered constant excruciating pain.

In the name of Jesus, I commanded that cancer to stop being. The next day she came back and said the cancer was gone. There was no more pain.

Another with a fibroid tumor that was cancerous in its nature came. The name of Jesus healed it.

Cases of tuberculosis, arthritis, and cancer are defeated by the use of the name. No disease or infirmity can stand against the name.

"In my name shall they cast out devils" (Mark 16:17).

There is no prayer about that, when we come to this bound and afflicted man or woman and say, "In the name of Jesus, Satan we charge you to leave this body, take every demon with you and go back to hell where you belong!"

Satan knows he is defeated, and when we use the name he must leave.

> *That whatsoever ye shall ask of the Father in my name, He may give it you.* (John 15:16)

This is prayer.

You remember the word *"ask"* in the Greek means "demand."

You are not demanding it of God. You are demanding that forces that are injurious shall be broken, that diseases shall be healed, that circumstances shall be changed, that money shall come.

Jesus is going to look after this thing that you demand in His name.

Read carefully John 16:24–27 and you will catch a glimpse of your legal right to use the name of Jesus:

> *Hitherto have ye asked nothing in my name: ask, and ye shall receive, that your joy may be full.*

You have noticed the absence of the word *believe* or the word *faith.*

In all three of these wonderful chapters with these great promises, the words *faith* or *believe* do not occur.

We are in the family, and because we are in the family we have a legal right to these things.

Ephesians 1:3 illustrates it: *"Blessed be the God and Father of our Lord Jesus Christ, who hath blessed us with all spiritual blessings in heavenly places in Christ."*

What Jesus did was for us.

HOW TO USE THE NAME

This is the most vital truth to every one of us. How I have studied this problem.

The name of Jesus is used in two major ways. First, in prayer to the Father.

> *That whatsoever ye shall ask of the Father in my name, He may give it you.* (John 15:16)

> *Whatsoever ye shall ask the Father in my name, He will give it to you.* (John 16:23)

Prayer is to be made to the Father, in Jesus's name, not to the Holy Spirit or Jesus. This is divine order.

Your judgment or my judgment or any other man's opinion is of no value.

"When you pray, say our Father." Jesus stands between us and the Father in His mediatorial, high priestly ministry to make it good.

He declares that whatsoever we ask in that name the Father will give it to us. That is final. That is absolute.

He tells us how to use the name of Jesus in sickness or in adverse circumstances, or any other crisis. (See John 14:13–34.)

This is the way I use the name: Here is a case of T.B. I lay my hands on him and say, "In the name of Jesus Christ, body, obey the Word. The Word declares that 'by His stripes you are healed,' I command you, spirit of T.B. to leave this body now."

The demon of sickness leaves, and the person is healed.

USING THE NAME TODAY

You wonder why the church does not use this name today.

Satan has kept our eyes blinded to its use.

Here in the city of Seattle hardly any of the churches are using this name in their daily life. The sick are taken to the hospital or attended by doctors.

It is a remarkable fact that in our own congregation we have practically no sickness. If there is any, they pray for each other and are immediately healed.

Acts 4:13–22 is the story of the trial of Peter and John for healing that helpless man with the name of Jesus.

> *And beholding the man which was healed standing with them, they could say nothing against it.... But that it spread no further among the people,*

> [they] *straitly threaten*[ed] *them, that they speak henceforth to no man in this name.* (verses 14, 17)

Why?

They did not object to the resurrection being taught, or to the new birth being taught.

But, they objected to teaching in the name because there was the power of healing in that name.

Hebrews 13:8 declares that Jesus Christ is the same yesterday, today, and forever.

There is just as much power in that name as there ever was. It is not a problem of faith, it is a problem of your daring to lay hands upon the sick and see them recover.

It is a problem of your daring to pray to the Father in that name, and miracles will be the result of that prayer.

Stand on your blood covenant rights. Dare to use the name!

18

WHAT THE LORD'S TABLE TEACHES

There are two outstanding characteristics of the Father and Jesus. They are more than characteristics; they are a part of Themselves.

God is love. Not only is He a love God, but He is a Father God. He believed the universe into being. When man went astray, He believed that He could bring him back, that a challenge of love would reach him.

He believes men into new creations, and He believes them into victory. He believes them into the love walk with each other.

God is a Father God; Jesus is like His Father. He was the introducer of love to the world.

Jesus came to introduce His Father, and His Father is love. It was an introduction to a new kind of love to the broken, wrecked human race.

Love is the only universal appeal to man. Love is an appeal to his heart. Faith is an appeal to his imagination, but love is the real appeal.

Jesus so loved that He poured out His life for us.

Jesus believed as the Father believed. Jesus acted His faith. He believed that if He became man's substitute, that man would respond, that if He could prove to the world that He loved men so much that He died for them, that He suffered the torments of the damned for them, there would be a response.

He acted His faith. He has faith in humanity today. He has faith in the church. He has faith in Himself and in His own living Word that it would win out.

He has faith in love.

The Lord's Table is a confession of our faith and our loyalty to love, just as the Father's giving Jesus was a confession of His love. Jesus's coming and giving Himself for us was a confession of His love.

They were both loyal to love.

Jesus said these significant words: "*For as often as ye eat this bread, and drink this cup, ye do shew the Lord's death till he come*" (1 Corinthians 11:26).

It was a covenant. He said, "*This cup is the new testament* [covenant] *in my blood*" (1 Corinthians 11:25). As often as you drink it, you show your faith in His covenant until He comes.

When you eat the bread, and drink the cup, you ratify this covenant. It is a love covenant.

First, it is your loyalty and love to Jesus. Second, it is your loyalty and love for His body, the church.

It is a confession of your love for one another. It is a confession that you have eaten and drunk with them, and now you are going to bear their burdens.

You have identified yourself with each other, just as He identified Himself with you in His incarnation and substitution.

That would be the Master's attitude toward the Lord's Table.

When I break the bread and drink the cup, I not only confess my loyalty to Him, but to every member of the body of Christ who breaks that bread and drinks that cup with me.

If I am strong, I bear the burdens of the weak. I have taken over their weaknesses.

The Lord's Table means that I will never criticize, but I will assume their spiritual responsibilities and weaknesses.

THE NEED OF THE HOUR

Someone is going to rise and understand this.

Some body of people is going to enter into it.

I have a conviction that this is the eleventh hour message, that this is the message for the church today.

In the troubled days that lie ahead, we are going to require all that God can give us and be for us, to stand the tests we are going through and the tests we will go through.

You see, brethren, this blood covenant teaching, this relationship teaching, this ability to use the name of Jesus, this marvelous teaching of our identification and our privileges, is the message for the coming days. It will fit us to meet the very forces of darkness.

Do you know that Jesus, in the Great Commission in the Gospel of Mark, did a peculiar thing?

He said, "*In my name shall they cast out devils*" (Mark 16:17).

I had not seen its significance. I now know what it means. In the last days, demons are going to become very prominent.

Satan, knowing that his days are shortened, is coming to the earth with all his host and we are going to pass into a period of spiritual conflict such as the church has never known.

This will not only be persecution, but it will be demons breaking and crushing the spirit of the church in the individual.

The church must learn the secret of standing against the hosts of darkness in the name of Jesus.

THE BLOOD COVENANT

I've a right to grace, in the hardest place,
    On the ground of the blood covenant;
I've a right to peace that can never cease,
    On the ground of the blood covenant.
I've a right to joy, that can never cloy,
    On the ground of the blood covenant;
I've a right to power, yes, this very hour,
    On the ground of the blood covenant.
I've a right to health, thru my Father's wealth,
    On the ground of the blood covenant;
I my healing take, Satan's hold must break,
    On the ground of the blood covenant.
I've a legal right, now to win this fight,
    On the ground of the blood covenant.
I will take my part with courageous heart,
    On the ground of the blood covenant.
Now my rights I claim, in His mighty name,
    On the ground of the blood covenant;
And my prayers prevail, tho all hell assail,
    On the ground of the blood covenant.
On the ground of the blood,
    On the ground of the blood covenant;
I will claim my rights, tho the enemy fights,
    On the ground of the blood covenant.

—E. W. Kenyon

ABOUT THE AUTHOR

Dr. E. W. Kenyon (1867–1948) was born in Saratoga County, New York. At age nineteen, he preached his first sermon. He pastored several churches in New England and founded the Bethel Bible Institute in Spencer, Massachusetts. This school later became the Providence Bible Institute when it was relocated to Providence, Rhode Island.

Kenyon served as an evangelist for over twenty years. In 1931, he became a pioneer in Christian radio on the Pacific Coast with his show *Kenyon's Church of the Air,* for which he earned the moniker "The Faith Builder." He also began the New Covenant Baptist Church in Seattle.

In addition to his pastoral and radio ministries, Kenyon wrote extensively. Among his books are the Bible courses *The Bible in the Light of Our Redemption: From Genesis Through Revelation* and *Studies in the Deeper Life: A Scriptural Study of Great Christian Truths,* and more than twenty other works, including *The Two Kinds of Knowledge, The New Kind of Love, The Father and His Family, Jesus the Healer, In His Presence: The Secret of Prayer, The Blood Covenant,* and *Two Kinds of Righteousness.*

His words and works live on through Kenyon's Gospel Publishing Society. Please visit www.kenyons.org for more information.

Welcome to Our House!

We Have a Special Gift for You ...

It is our privilege and pleasure to share in your love of Christian classics by publishing books that enrich your life and encourage your faith.

To show our appreciation, we invite you to sign up to receive a specially selected **Reader Appreciation Gift**, with our compliments. Just go to the Web address at the bottom of this page.

God bless you as you seek a deeper walk with Him!

WE HAVE A GIFT FOR YOU

whpub.me/classicthx